BRIDGES TO BETTER WRITING

Luis A. Nazario
Pueblo Community College

Deborah D. Borchers
Pueblo Community College

William F. Lewis
Pueblo Community College

WADSWORTH
CENGAGE Learning

Australia • Brazil • Japan • Korea • Mexico • Singapore • Spain • United Kingdom • United States

WADSWORTH
CENGAGE Learning™

Bridges to Better Writing

Luis A. Nazario, Deborah D. Borchers, William F. Lewis

Publisher: Lyn Uhl

Director of Developmental English: Annie Todd

Development Editor: Marita Sermolins

Assistant Editor: Janine Tangney

Editorial Assistant: Melanie Opacki

Associate Media Editor: Emily Ryan

Marketing Manager: Kirsten Stoller

Marketing Assistant: Ryan Ahern

Senior Content Project Manager: Michael Lepera

Art Director: Marissa Falco

Print Buyer: Betsy Donaghey

Permissions Editor: Timothy Sisler

Text Researcher: Karyn Morrison

Production Service/Compositor: Graphic World Publishing Services

Text Designer: Judith Krimski

Photo Manager: Leitha Etheridge-Sims

Photo Researcher: Catherine Schnurr, Pre-Press PMG

Cover Designer: Beckmeyer Design

Cover Image: © Corbis

For product information and technology assistance, contact us at **Cengage Learning Academic Resource Center, 1-800-423-0563.**

For permission to use material from this text or product, submit all requests online at **www.cengage.com/permissions.** Further permissions questions can be e-mailed to **permissionrequest@cengage.com.**

Library of Congress Control Number: 2008943490

ISBN-13: 978-1-413-03118-8
ISBN-10: 1-413-03118-8

Annotated Instructor's Edition
ISBN-13: 978-1-413-03234-5
ISBN-10: 1-413-03234-6

Wadsworth
20 Channel Center Street
Boston, MA 02210
USA

Cengage Learning products are represented in Canada by Nelson Education, Ltd.

For your course and learning solutions, visit **www.cengage.com.**

Purchase any of our products at your local college store or at our preferred online store **www.ichapters.com.**

Printed in Canada
1 2 3 4 5 6 7 12 11 10 09 08

For my wife, Carmen, and children—Jessica, Louis, and Ryan—for their patience and support; my parents, Irma and Carmelo, for their faith in me; and the faculty and students of Pueblo Community College from whom I'm still learning.

Luis Nazario

To my father, Prof. Edward H. Davidson, for my love of reading and writing; to my husband, Phil, for tutoring me through my first year of teaching; to my son, Nat, who inspires me; and to all of my students who expand my world.

Deborah Borchers

For my wife, Jan, my sons, Owen and John, and my parents, Bill and Louise, with gratitude and love. For my students, whose questions, I hope, are answered in this book.

William Lewis

The overriding goal of *Bridges to Better Writing*

is to give students the tools they need to write clearly and effectively by fully engaging students in the writing process through the following means:

- Demonstrate the value of writing in academic, career, and everyday life
- Provide opportunities for students to practice new concepts as they read about them
- Build continuously on students' previous learning to help them build confidence in their abilities
- Integrate grammar and style into the writing process throughout the book
- Present many samples of effective and ineffective student writing

Too often, textbooks merely present information, leaving teachers to devise ways to use (or not use) textual materials in the classroom. Our many years of experience have taught us that for a text to be effective, it should itself embody the most engaging and effective teaching practices. Our reviewers have told us that *Bridges to Better Writing* is the most classroom-friendly textbook they have seen in years.

"Without being excessive, this promises to be the most complete book of its kind. There really are no other topics to consider for inclusion."
—Jack Macfarlane, San Joaquin Valley College

"The authors communicate with the students on a level they can understand. The explanations are simple, clear, and to the point."
—Roger West, Trident Technical College

"I felt the book would be a good mesh for integrating writing and reading thought process ideas. I also enjoyed the simple straightforward conversational approach to good old-fashion grammar."
—Carol Pizzi, Sandhills Community College

One of the first challenges any teacher faces is to understand students' most prevalent problems. Through our many years of teaching and extensive reviewing, we believe that our students' problems fall into three categories: a lack of motivation, a lack of knowledge, and a lack of skills. The features of *Bridges to Better Writing* were created with these three categories in mind.

How does *Bridges to Better Writing* **help students who lack motivation for the course?**

A constant problem that plagues many courses, motivation is a major struggle for students. Motivation often decreases as the course goes on because students experience the same bumpy ride in college that they suffered in high school; their college writing experience mirrors their earlier struggles. *Bridges to Better Writing* addresses several factors that contribute to student motivation:

PROBLEM

SOLUTION

- **Reading difficulties and associated aversion to reading lengthy passages.** Today's students need to be drawn in immediately to writing assignments rather than inundated by too many instructions and explanations.

The **Previewing Your Writing Task samples** and **Let's Warm Up exercise prompts** at the beginning of the writing chapters offer immediate involvement in writing. Frequent practice activities break up lengthy passages of text, and writing activities provide guided, hands-on application of writing skills. Visuals highlight and clarify major concepts.

PROBLEM

SOLUTION

- **A low sense of self worth in learning situations based on past academic failure.** Students have difficulty with intimidating projects, like essay assignments.

Bridges to Better Writing helps students succeed early on through gradual and recursive introduction of knowledge, then builds on previous success throughout the semester. Students become increasingly confident in their abilities as they work through the text.

PROBLEM

- **A belief that writing is an isolated activity and that success or failure depends entirely on the writer.** Students tend to be social instead of independent learners and feel that writing is lonely and boring.

SOLUTION

The Collaborative Critical Thinking exercises in *Bridges to Better Writing* teach students the social and teamwork aspects of writing and how through peer review their papers can see great improvement.

> Collaborative Critical Thinking
>
> In groups of three or four, develop major and mino
> sentences provided. Rely on facts and details. Answe
>   1. Television promotes violence.

PROBLEM

- **A feeling that writing is not relevant to success in their careers or their lives.** For most students, writing is something they "have to take." They do not see the connections between academic writing and their careers or their own personal uses.

SOLUTION

Bridges to Better Writing integrates **academic, professional, and personal writing in the Previewing Your Task section,** enabling students to develop an appreciation for the range and richness of written expression.

> PREVIEWING YOUR TASK
>
> As you go through college, your instructors will ask you to write often and i
> various subjects—not just in English class! Instructors ask you to write so t
> assess your comprehension of all kinds of subjects: history, psychology, sci
> sometimes even more technical subjects like math or engineering. And onc
> from college and move on to a career, you will be writing more than you mi
> The writing samples that follow demonstrate how you can use description
> fectively in any context.
>
> **Writing for College**
>
> The following selection is an example of descriptive writing about an aesth
> you ever take an art appreciation class, you will be encouraged to describe
> on canvas in such a way that your reader can "see" it as well.
>
> The painting, called *Night in a Forest*, depicts a horrific dream scene
> the subject, a young man, has become lost in a frightening landscape. He
> in dim light in the middle of the canvas, looking up with widened eyes tha

PROBLEM

- **Issues of time management with work, family, and school.** Lack of time outside of class is one of the major hindrances to the success of students.

SOLUTION

Bridges to Better Writing is designed to allow much of the writing process to happen in class. Collaborative brainstorming, sharing of drafts, and peer review allow students to accomplish much of their work under the guidance of instructors and fellow students.

> Collaborative Critical Thinking
>
> **Asking Your Peers**
>
> Once you have completed the writing process and have a poli
> exchange papers with a classmate for peer review. Use the followi
>   1. **Read:** Read the essay through once to understand the ove
>   2. **Track:** On your second reading, do the following:
>   a. Underline the thesis statement.
>   b. Put check marks above the points listed in the essay m

How does *Bridges to Better Writing* **help students who lack knowledge about writing?**

Students coming into this course often lack the basic knowledge needed to create a successful piece of writing. Students who do not know how to pick a topic, create a thesis, choose an audience or tone, or organize details are not going to succeed at writing. *Bridges to Better Writing* addresses several factors that contribute to student knowledge:

PROBLEM   **SOLUTION**

- **Unaware of the advantages of following a writing process.** Too often, students think of their initial effort as a finished product.

In **Part 1: Writing Your Papers,** each chapter follows a consistent pattern that introduces students to a rhetorical pattern and then steps them through writing a paragraph or essay in that pattern. Chapters are designed so that they build upon students' prior knowledge learned in previous chapters and consider what they already bring to the writing task.

PROBLEM   **SOLUTION**

- **Belief that good writing is beyond their creative capacity.** Students struggle to find topics about which they can successfully write. Often a poor choice in topic sabotages the whole essay project.

Not only does each writing chapter demonstrate a different brainstorming technique, but the **Topics to Consider** in each chapter provides diverse topics for academic, career, and personal writing situations.

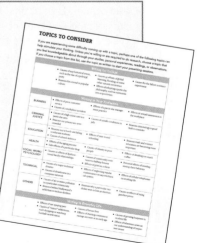

PROBLEM

- **Little knowledge of how the components of good writing—logic, word choice, sentence variety, coherence, and so on—are integrated into effective expression.**

SOLUTION

Bridges to Better Writing takes an **integrated approach** to writing instruction: beginning with the very first writing chapter, the major components of good writing, including grammar, tone, and style are interwoven throughout. Effective use of these concepts is modeled in numerous, **authentic student-authored samples.**

> The painting, called *Night in a Forest*, depicts a horrific dream scene in which the subject, a young man, has become lost in a frightening landscape. He crouches in dim light in the middle of the canvas, looking up with widened eyes that deliberately remind the viewer of Edvard Munch's famous painting, *The Scream*. One arm extends upward to ward away the dark, but the attempt is futile, for surrounding the dimly lit center of the painting, lurid shapes as strange and distorted threaten to close in and destroy the subject. In colors of dark blue-green, black, and deep reds and purples, nightmarish monsters struggle. Some are dragon-like, and others

PROBLEM

- **Unaware that all writers face the same struggles they do.** Students have trouble seeing themselves as writers and relating professional writing samples to their own writing.

SOLUTION

Previewing Your Task provides students with one academic, student-written paper. The **Writing Your Paper** sections in every chapter follow a student's progress from start to finish so students can see the missteps real students make.

PREVIEWING YOUR TASK

As you go through college, your instructors will ask you to write often and in depth about various subjects—not just in English class! Instructors ask you to write so that they can assess your comprehension of all kinds of subjects: history, psychology, science, and sometimes even more technical subjects like the math or engineering. And once you graduate from college and move on to a career, you will be writing more than you might suspect. The writing samples that follow demonstrate how you can use description to write effectively in any context.

Writing for College

The following selection is an example of descriptive writing about an aesthetic subject. If you ever take an art appreciation class, you will be encouraged to describe what you see on canvas in such a way that your reader can "see" it as well.

WRITING YOUR PAPERS

One reassuring quality about writing is that it should be viewed as a process leading to a successful final draft. Instead of being a lightning bolt of inspiration, a good essay usually evolves gradually from brainstorming, to organizing, to drafting, to receiving and digesting feedback, to final editing.

The *writing process* is a way to describe the steps that effective writers follow, from the initial point of coming up with an idea for writing to the final point, the paper that the intended audience reads. To help you understand the process and the many choices and decisions that you as a writer must make, the chapters of *Bridges to Better Writing* guide you from one stage to another of the writing process—from prewriting to the final draft. This is not to say that the writing process is linear, where one stage must

How does *Bridges to Better Writing* **help students who lack the basic skills needed for writing?**

Our incoming students routinely demonstrate a lack of the essential skills needed for writing. Students come to class with a range of problems, such as poor high school preparation, little experience interacting with text, difficulty with grammar, and so on. *Bridges to Better Writing* addresses several factors that contribute to student's lack of basic skills:

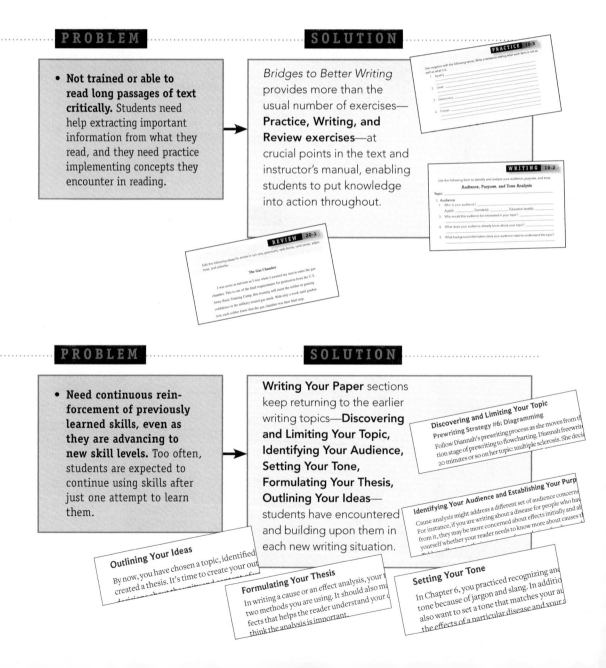

PROBLEM

- **Not trained or able to read long passages of text critically.** Students need help extracting important information from what they read, and they need practice implementing concepts they encounter in reading.

SOLUTION

Bridges to Better Writing provides more than the usual number of exercises—**Practice, Writing, and Review exercises**—at crucial points in the text and instructor's manual, enabling students to put knowledge into action throughout.

PRACTICE 10-5

Use negation with the following terms. Write a sentence stating what each term is not as well as what it is.
1. Apathy
2. Greek
3. Democracy
4. Fitness

WRITING 10-2

Use the following form to identify and analyze your audience, purpose, and tone.

Audience, Purpose, and Tone Analysis

Topic:
1. Audience
   1. Who is your audience?
      Age(s):   Gender(s):   Education level(s):
   3. Why would this audience be interested in your topic?
   4. What does your audience already know about your topic?
   5. What background information does your audience need to understand the topic?

REVIEW 20-1

Edit the following essay for errors in run-ons, pronouns, verb forms, verb tense, adjectives, and adverbs.

The Gas Chamber

I was never as nervous as I was while I awaited my turn to enter the gas chamber. This is one of the final requirements for graduation from the U.S. Army Basic Training Camp, this training will assist the soldier in gaining confidence in the military issued gas mask. With only a week until graduation, each soldier knew that the gas chamber was their final step

PROBLEM

- **Need continuous reinforcement of previously learned skills, even as they are advancing to new skill levels.** Too often, students are expected to continue using skills after just one attempt to learn them.

SOLUTION

Writing Your Paper sections keep returning to the earlier writing topics—**Discovering and Limiting Your Topic, Identifying Your Audience, Setting Your Tone, Formulating Your Thesis, Outlining Your Ideas**— students have encountered and building upon them in each new writing situation.

Discovering and Limiting Your Topic
Prewriting Strategy #6: Diagramming
Follow Diannah's prewriting process as she moves from th tion stage of prewriting to flowcharting. Diannah freewrit 20 minutes or so on her topic: multiple sclerosis. She deci

Identifying Your Audience and Establishing Your Purp
Cause analysis might address a different set of audience concern For instance, if you are writing about a disease for people who have from it, they may be more concerned about effects initially and af yourself whether your reader needs to know more about causes t

Outlining Your Ideas
By now, you have chosen a topic, identified created a thesis. It's time to create your out

Formulating Your Thesis
In writing a cause or an effect analysis, your two methods you are using. It should also ma fects that helps the reader understand your think the analysis is important.

Setting Your Tone
In Chapter 6, you practiced recognizing and tone because of jargon and slang. In additio also want to set a tone that matches your au the effects of a particular disease and your

PROBLEM

- **Tremendous anxiety about and difficulty with grammar.**

SOLUTION

Bridges to Better Writing introduces grammar in manageable chunks seamlessly by way of the **Common Grammar Error, a Grammar Check-up Exercise, and Style Tip** features. Parts 3-6 offer more detailed grammar instruction in a separate section for those students who need further practice.

Common Error #1: Sentence Fragments

A sentence fragment is a group of words that does not form a complete sentence. Since any complete sentence must have a subject and a verb, a fragment is missing a subject, verb, or both, as shown here.

INCORRECT   The lawn mower in the pickup truck. [Missing a verb]
CORRECT   The lawn mower in the pickup truck failed to start.

GRAMMAR CHECKUP   2-1

Mark F for fragment or S for sentence. Repair the fragments by completing each item.

___ 1. An exquisite California Chardonnay from Napa Valley.

Style Tip: Using a Variety of Sentence Lengths

To craft well-written sentences and paragraphs, you need to develop sensitivity to sentence style. Sometimes,

PROBLEM

- **Second language learners find it difficult to make the transition to college level courses.**

SOLUTION

Bridges to Better Writing's simple explanations, constant reinforcement of skills, **effective visuals,** and gradual building on previous knowledge help ESL students, as well as native speakers, make the transition to college level courses.

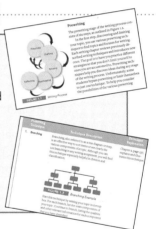

PROBLEM

- **Failure to transfer the writing skills they learned in their English courses to other college level courses.**

SOLUTION

Previewing Your Task's Writing for College gives students the opportunity to see student papers at work in a variety of academic courses and levels of ability. The final **Self-Reflection exercises** encourage students to think beyond their English course and consider how they can apply their new knowledge to their other courses, career, and personal life.

WRITING   3-10

Self-Reflection

Before you hand in your paper, answer the following questions:

1. What do you feel you did best?
2. What part of your paper was most challenging to you?
3. In which areas do you feel you need the most practice?
4. What strategies will you employ to address your challenges or weaknesses and to improve the quality of your essay?

After you have completed this self-reflection, carefully review your own answers to the self-reflection. Make a list of your grammar, punctuation, and spelling errors so that you can follow up

KEY FEATURES

Bridges to Better Writing offers the following features:

- Consistently designed writing chapters, starting with specific goals, an inspiring quotation, a visual, and a writing situation to involve students immediately in the act of writing.

- A variety of student writings to preview the writing tasks so students may draw from prior knowledge, make assumptions about the new writing situation, and have models of the expected outcomes.

- A plethora of writing topics related to students' college courses, their professions, and their everyday lives.

- Many charts and tables that help summarize information as well as help visual learners understand the material.

- Gradual introduction to grammatical concepts through reviews of previous information.

- Collaborative/critical thinking activities to reinforce a sense of a writer's community.

- Sidebars referring students to more information on a certain topic or refresher information.

- Clear visuals ranging from pictures to stimulate thought, to graphics on how body paragraphs support a thesis, to common problem-solution areas to help students during revision to appeal to the different ways students learn.

- Cumulative grammar and punctuation exercises so that students practice previous concepts while they work on new ones.

SUPPLEMENTS

Instructor's Manual and Test Bank

Each chapter of the Instructor's Manual offers suggestions for using visual prompts, provides ideas for incorporating professional and student model paragraphs into the lesson, offers a variety of teaching tips, and presents additional writing assignments and additional collaborative activities for most chapters. To help instructors get all students involved in the learning process, the Instructor's Manual also provides information for teaching to various learning styles and suggests ways to help ESL students make that vital connection in their new culture. The Test Bank, the second half of the Instructor's Manual, provides short quizzes for Chapters 1-14, testing students' understanding of the key concepts presented in each writing chapter in Part 1 of the text, and provides Mastery tests for Chapters 15-27. New teachers will find the Instructor's Manual a valuable resource for helping students get the most out of their learning experience.

WriteSPACE

Cengage Learning WriteSPACE encompasses the interactive online products and services integrated with Wadsworth writing textbook programs. WriteSPACE includes comprehensive grammar diagnostics; practice exercises and writing tutorials; Associated Press Interactives and NewsNow, which draw on current events and emphasize visual literacy; tutoring; an online handbook; a gradebook; and the Plagiarism Prevention Zone.

ACKNOWLEDGMENTS

The authors express their warmest gratitude to the following: our entire Cengage Learning support team, including Development Editor, Marita Sermolins, for her constant encouragement and wise counsel; Director of Developmental English, Annie Todd; Marketing Manager, Kirsten Stoller; Associate Media Editor, Emily Ryan; and Senior Content Project Manager, Michael Lepera. To Ms. Erika Parks, for her careful reading and valuable suggestions; David Hall for suggesting this project; Stephen Dalphin for helping us through the initial stages; and the many authors and authorities in the field of English education that have inspired us.

The authors would also like to thank the many colleagues who reviewed many iterations of manuscript chapters and provided their valuable input on content and design—without their advice this book would not be in its current state: Cathryn Amdahl, Harrisburg Area Community College; Keith Amrine, Genessee Community College; Stephen Black, Southwest Tennessee Community College; Carol Ann Britt, San Antonio College; Cathleen Carosella, Indiana University-Purdue University, Fort Wayne; Gregory Cecere, Palm Beach Community College; Alan Church, University of Texas at Brownsville; J. Andrew Clovis, West Virginia University at Parkersburg; Donna Marie Colonna, Sandhills Community College; Jim Cooney, Montgomery County Community College; Janet Cutshall, Sussex County Community College; Barbara Danley, Sandhills Community College; Magali A. M. Duignan, Augusta State University; Stephanie Dumstorf, Brevard Community College; Margo Eden-Camann, Georgia Perimeter College—Clarkston; Gwen Enright, San Diego City College; Endora Feick, Nashville State Community College; Karen L. Feldman, Seminole Community College; Cathy Gillis, Napa Valley College; Ellen Gilmour, Genessee Community College; José J. González, Jr., South Texas College; Martha Goodwin, Bergen Community College; Robin Griffin, Truckee Meadows Community College; Mary Ellen Haley, Bloomfield College; Nikka Harris, Rochester Community and Technical College; Amy Havel, Southern Maine Community College; Levia DiNardo Hayes, College of Southern Nevada; Linda Houck, Nashville State Community College; Brandon Hudson, McLennen Community College; Marisa Humphrey, Central Washington University; Therese Jones, Lewis University; Jack Macfarlane, San Joaquin Valley College; David Mackinder, Wayne State University; Ami Massengill, Nashville State Community College; Jack Miller, Normandale Community

College; Chris Morelock, Walters State Community College; Betty Palmer Nelson, Volunteer State Community College; Ellen Olmstead, Montgomery College; Roberta Panish, Rockland Community College; Charles E. Porter, Wor-Wic Community College; Jennifer Ratcliff, North Central Texas College; Dana Resente, Montgomery County Community College; Donald Rhyne, San Joaquin Valley College; Edward Roper, Troy University, Montgomery; Jamie Sadler, Richmond Community College; Julie Sanford, Roosevelt University; Anna Schmidt, Cy-Fair College; Deneen Shepherd, Saint Louis Community College at Forest Park; Tamara Shue, Georgia Perimeter College—Dunwoody; Michelle Taylor, Ogeechee Technical College; Michael Tischler, Western Nevada Community College; Lisa Todd, Hudson County Community College; Verne Underwood, Rogue Community College; Mary Beth Van Ness, Terra Community College; Roger West, Trident Technical College; Helena Zacharis, Palm Beach Community College; and William Ziegler, J. Sargeant Reynolds Community College.

The authors would also like to thank the group who carefully reviewed drafts of the Instructor's Manual and Test Bank and provided counsel about and enthusiasm for the project: Phyllis Gowdy, Tidewater Community College—Virginia Beach; Patricia Moseley, Central Carolina Technical College; Linsay Oaken, University of Nevada, Reno; Charles E. Porter, Wor-Wic Community College; and Vicki Sapp, Tarrant County College.

The authors would especially like to thank the following students whose work we present to you in this text:

Leroy Bachicha	Clyde Hazelton	Regina Ritschard
Lora Bailey	Jon-Paul Jared Hunt	Lawrence Rodriguez
Ron Barton	Joshua Janoski	Deborah J. Seaton
Andre Blackwell	JoAnna Johnson	Diannah Sholey
Jamie Bruss	Sheralan Marrott	Chi Yon Sin
Joe Chamberlain	Gabriel Martinez	Kent Spath
Tom Coleman	Jeremy Mathews	Claude Sterner
Loretta Cruz	Lauren Montoya	Angelique Trujillo
Lisa Dosen	Tamra O'Toole	Dustin Wertz
David Farren	Christian Pettie	Dawn Yengich
Marla Grossman	Michael Pino	
Frank Hahn	Theresa Randall	

Luis Nazario

"I saw an opportunity to write a text that engages students visually to create a more dynamic learning experience."

■ Luis Nazario ■

Luis Nazario is Assistant Chair of the English department at Pueblo Community College where he has taught since 1990. Professor Nazario completed his B.A. at Inter American University in Puerto Rico. He pursued his teaching career in both Puerto Rico and the United States where he earned his M.A. in TESOL at New York University.

After joining the English department at Pueblo in 1990, Professor Nazario distinguished himself by developing a set of manuals for part-time faculty that were innovative in their comprehensiveness and use of visual support. With Professor Borchers he presented their work with service learning at conferences and later worked on modules for developmental English to be used in the Department of Corrections. Additionally, he has developed internet courses in both developmental and college level courses and has restructured his course to be taught as a learning community.

Professor Nazario has enjoyed the challenges of creating a textbook with visual appeal. "A whole graphic might spring from a single phrase." He is also energized by offering instructors the power of choice. "Instructors have to be aware of their choices, and in *Bridges to Better Writing*, they can pick and choose chapters to develop their syllabus and create the most effective approach for their students. And we're always including new ways to introduce a composition."

Deborah Borchers

"I always try to perfect the tone, style, and flow to make the chapters as readable as possible."

■ Debbie Borchers ■

Debbie Borchers is Chair of the English department at Pueblo Community College, where she is in her twentieth year as a member of the faculty. Professor Borchers began her teaching career as a student of Near Eastern culture in Cairo. "From Egypt, I went on to teach in Iran, where I eventually had to escape the Iranian Revolution." After she returned to the United States, Prof. Borchers earned her M.A. in TESL from the University of Arizona and eventually moved to Pueblo.

With her Assistant Chair, Luis Nazario, Professor Borchers has implemented innovative service learning programs, student and faculty assessments, and standards for the English curriculum. Additionally, she developed an online Introduction to Literature course and has presented workshops on Writing Across the Curriculum. "Writing is one of the hardest things to teach, and what many people don't realize is that a textbook doesn't have to be just text! There are better ways to teach than to have a student just write a paragraph and do some activities."

William F. Lewis

"My area of concern in the text is—the interrelationship of ideas and the logic of their expression."

■ Bill Lewis ■

Bill Lewis has recently returned to teaching after serving for two years as Director of Planning, Accreditation, and Effectiveness at Pueblo Community College where he is in his fifteenth year as an English teacher. Professor Lewis came to teaching after many years working in the defense industry. He graduated from the University of Colorado and traveled around the country before pursuing his interest in the Russian language at the Defense Language Institute.

He worked in the intelligence community until earning his M.A. in English from George Mason University. He then began his long association with the English department at Pueblo, where he has taught developmental and college level English composition, technical writing, and literature courses. "My recent work on our accreditation has shown me the great strides that Debbie and Luis have made with the English department. Their development of service learning programs and special manuals for adjunct instructors—these are unique and innovative solutions."

BRIEF CONTENTS

DETAILED CONTENTS

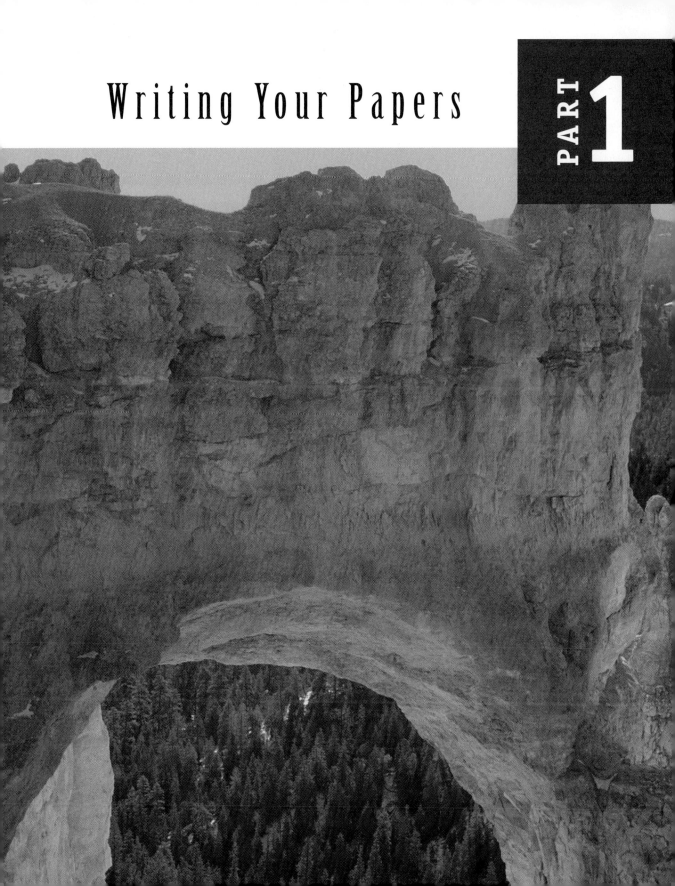

Writing Your Papers

PART 1

CHAPTER 1

Let's Talk about Writing

YOUR GOALS

Understanding That Writing Is Thinking

1. Recognize the connection between writing and critical thinking.

2. Examine realities about writing.

3. Judge your own attitudes about writing.

4. Review and respond to writing myths.

Writing Your Papers

1. Preview prewriting techniques.

2. Discover the value of following a writing process.

"Writing is an exploration.

You start from nothing

and learn as you go."

■ E. L. Doctorow ■

D o you feel dread and anxiety when you are asked to write a report, produce a research paper, or answer essay questions on a U.S. history test? Do you avoid the task as long as possible? And then, when you do sit down to write, do you find yourself blanking out or rambling on just to get something on the empty page?

How should you approach a writing assignment in a confident and systematic way? How can you develop a method for writing that works for a variety of situations, assignments, and readers?

We hope that this text, your writing class, and your writing instructor provide you with an approach and system that works for you and that applies to all three major writing occasions: college, professional, and personal.

In college you will write some or all of the following: science and business reports, academic research papers, answers to essay questions on exams, summaries and critiques of professional articles, and reaction papers to specific theories and proposals.

LET's warm up!

Tetra Images/Jupiter Images

Whether it's our creativity, our ability to use words, our ideas, our style, our ability to spot errors, or our motivation, each of us brings a special skill when we write. Reflect on yourself as a writer. What major strength do you bring to the writing process? Write a short paragraph explaining your strength.

For your professional career, you may have to produce monthly reports of your department's activities or progress on a long-term project, proposals for new marketing plans or patient treatment, summaries of customer satisfaction, or analyses of a patient's progress, and so on.

In your personal life you may write to record a significant event or trip, to explore your family history, to sympathize with a family member over a traumatic event, or to e-mail daily events to family members living at a distance.

If you think of writing as limited to the English classroom, you miss the opportunity to take the skills from your English class and apply them to your other classes, your profession, and your everyday life.

UNDERSTANDING THAT WRITING IS THINKING

Writing is a form of thinking. It certainly isn't the only form of thinking. Our brains process ideas in different ways: mathematically, musically, and visually. But our use of language is the basis of all thinking, and it is what makes us distinctly human. It allows us to share ideas, pass on knowledge, engage in debate, and advance our understanding of the world. In college, writing is the vehicle through which we learn new ideas and share them with one another.

During your college education, you will hear much about *critical thinking*. You may hear many definitions of this term, but basically, *critical thinking* means expressing your ideas in a logical way so that they *make sense*. Learning to write well is the best way to improve your ability to think critically. What are the components of critical thinking? According to the National Council for Excellence in Critical Thinking, the following components are key to the process:

1. **Clarity.** When you express ideas clearly, your audience understands what you are trying to say without difficulty.
2. **Accuracy.** Accurate thinking is true to reality as you understand it.
3. **Precision.** Precise thinking isn't vague; it contains sufficient detail to be informative.
4. **Consistency.** Consistent thinking "holds together"; it doesn't contradict itself.
5. **Relevance.** Relevant writing sticks to the point; it doesn't digress into unrelated subject matter.
6. **Sound evidence.** When you make a statement that needs to be supported, you provide solid evidence that proves your point.
7. **Good reasons.** When you argue for or against an idea, you back up your argument with valid reasoning.
8. **Depth.** Critical thinking is not superficial; it goes beyond the obvious.
9. **Breadth.** Critical thinking incorporates a broad view of the subject matter, showing how it relates to other ideas.
10. **Fairness.** Good writing is fair, both to the subject matter and to other people who may hold different viewpoints.

These components of critical thinking are also components of effective writing. As you work through this course, keep in mind the connection between the quality of your writing and the quality of your thinking. Having good writing skills can be your ticket to better grades in most of your courses in college.

Using and Understanding This Book

This book seeks to guide you through your writing experience, thus contributing to your growth as a professional. Here are some ways to get the most out of this text and this class:

1. **Read and mark your text.** Read actively by underlining useful ideas, writing brief summaries and reactions in the margins, and taking notes main ideas. Remember that effective writing is closely linked to frequent and close reading.

2. **Do every assignment conscientiously.** Your instructor is helping you write a successful final paper by having you complete smaller steps to achieve the final product.
3. **Plan to keep your text for future reference.** You can refresh yourself on the principles of successful writing and use the writing skills for future assignments for school and work.
4. **Use the skills you learn in this course in your other courses.** Whenever you are assigned writing in another class or on the job, try to incorporate the techniques offered in this class.

Take 5 minutes and flip through this book's chapters. Each writing chapter, Chapters 2–12, starts with an activity called Previewing Your Task where you will read academic, professional, and everyday examples of the type of writing you will be drafting in that chapter. The rest of each writing chapter is divided into two main sections:

■ **Understanding.** This section explains the writing task completely. In it, you will examine examples of key concepts and do activities to practice these concepts.

■ **Writing.** This section guides you through the writing process: prewriting, drafting, revising, proofreading, and reflecting. In this section, you will follow a student's writing task from creation to the final draft as you go through the process yourself. This section also provides sufficient explanation and activities to help you understand specific tasks in the writing process.

Being Aware of Writing Realities

Another key to succeeding in your English course is to understand the realities of good writing. Effective writing requires hard work, patience, courage, thought, and honesty.

■ **Hard work.** Few people can produce a polished report, essay, or business plan by just writing "off the top of their heads." Instead, writers often must write several drafts, have others read and comment on them, and then carefully proofread and edit before submitting the final copy.

■ **Patience.** Writers often run into dead ends, finding that a topic isn't working and needing to try a different topic, organization, or focus. Writers have to be patient and willing to experiment with ideas and ways to express them.

■ **Courage.** It takes courage to write because fears of failure, of errors, or of lack of clarity are often lurking in our mind as we compose. We, the writers, fear that the reader may criticize our writing, which we view as almost as an extension of ourselves.

■ **Thought.** Writing can be perfect in grammar, punctuation, organization, and unity but still be a failure because it doesn't say anything of worth. Successful writing and critical thinking are inseparable, requiring us to be able to communicate our ideas.

■ **Honesty.** As writers, we must present ideas honestly to the reader. If the idea comes from an article in a newspaper or from an interview, then we are obligated to give credit to the source. If we are communicating a personal observation or experience, then the information should be as accurate as possible unless the writing is fiction.

Writing is a social, communal activity, involving writers and readers joining together to exchange information, support each other, and work toward a transfer of ideas, experiences, and opinions.

Attitudes and Myths about Writing

PRACTICE   1-1

For the following statements, put a check mark by the ones you agree with and an X by those you do not. Answers will vary.

_____ 1. Good writers have an inborn talent for writing, whereas weak writers are doomed to fail.

_____ 2. Good writers compose effortlessly because they need only to spill what is inside their minds onto the paper.

_____ 3. Once someone has finished the English requirements for a college degree, writing is no longer important or useful.

_____ 4. Since professionals often have administrative assistants to edit their reports, the professionals can depend on their assistants to correct errors in grammar, punctuation, and wording.

_____ 5. Since essay writing is rarely required in most professions, writing essays applies only to English classes.

_____ 6. Writing is like riding a bike: once you learn how, it is an automatic skill.

_____ 7. Copying the writing of others without giving the original authors credit is acceptable since there is so much written material on the Internet that it is difficult to trace writing back to its originator.

_____ 8. It is unnecessary to learn grammar and punctuation since most word processors provide a grammar and spell-check tool.

_____ 9. Writing a research paper is just looking up information and pasting it into a larger document, somewhat like stitching together the pieces of a quilt.

_____ 10. Writing is the mechanical process of typing words into a document, whereas reading and math require deep thinking and problem solving.

Reconsidering Your Attitude about Writing

Having completed the preceding activity, you may realize that most of the statements in Practice 1-1 are false and that by adopting them you are undermining your ability to succeed as a writer. You can adjust your attitudes toward writing as you would tune up a car engine or adjust the thermostat in your home.

- **Motivation.** There is nothing worse than studying a subject or taking a class and thinking that the material and skills won't be useful once the course is over. Nothing could be farther from the truth when it comes to writing. Most employers, when asked what skills are essential for their employees, say effective written and oral communication is vital. On-the-job training can familiarize employees with procedures and policies, but employers do not have the time to teach employees how to write.
- **Self-identity.** See yourself as a writer. Just calling yourself a writer can help you have the confidence to get the writing done.
- **Time and place.** Since writing takes time, work, and concentration, you need to set aside certain writing hours and specific places in which to write.

PRACTICE   1-2

In the spaces that follow, list your best times for writing and places that you feel give you the most peace and quiet (and resources) for the writing process. Answers will vary.

Best times: _____

Possible places (for example, library, home, office, or coffee shop): _____

_____

- **Reader or audience.** If you visualize your English instructor hovering over your paper with red pen in hand to highlight all your errors, then you may lose your desire to communicate. However, if you can imagine an "ignorant" and eager reader, enthusiastically soaking up your ideas, then you will be more committed to writing. And if you adopt a tone of voice in your writing that shows an understanding of and respect for your reader, you should produce an effective piece of writing.
- **Competition.** You might feel that you will never measure up to others in your English class. How do you deal with your sense of inadequacy when you read their successful essays and compare them to yours? But you can benefit from their writing by analyzing their organization and details so that you can improve your own papers.

Finally, view writing as thinking, as the process of examining ideas in depth and of "toning" your mind as you would tone your body in an exercise class. You have really learned and understood a concept, theory, philosophy, or process when you have written about it in such a clear and convincing way that your reader, who may not be familiar with the information, has learned it from you.

WRITING YOUR PAPERS

One reassuring quality about writing is that it should be viewed as a process leading to a successful final draft. Instead of being a lightning bolt of inspiration, a good essay usually evolves gradually from brainstorming, to organizing, to drafting, to receiving and digesting feedback, to final editing.

The *writing process* is a way to describe the steps that effective writers follow, from the initial point of coming up with an idea for writing to the final point, the paper that the intended audience reads. To help you understand the process and the many choices and decisions that you as a writer must make, the chapters of *Bridges to Better Writing* guide you from one stage to another of the writing process—from prewriting to the final draft. This is not to say that the writing process is linear, where one stage must be completed before going on to the next one. Far from it; the writing process is recursive, meaning you repeat specific parts until you're satisfied with the results, like in Figure 1.1.

The Writing Process

The writing process used in *Bridges to Better Writing* consists of five stages.

FIGURE 1.1 *Writing Process*

Prewriting

The prewriting stage of the writing process consists of six steps, as outlined in Figure 1.2.

In the first step, discovering and limiting your topic, you use various prewriting techniques to find topics and focuses for writing. Each writing chapter reviews previously described writing techniques and introduces new ones. The goal is to have you practice different strategies so that you don't limit yourself to ones you are accustomed to. Prewriting techniques help you discover ideas during any stage of the writing process. Unfortunately, some students bypass prewriting or limit themselves to just one technique. To help you consider the possibilities of the various prewriting

PREWRITING

- Discovering and limiting your topic
- Outlining your ideas
- Formulating your thesis
- Setting your tone
- Establishing your purpose
- Identifying your audience

FIGURE 1.2   *Prewriting Stage*

techniques, most writing chapters of *Bridges to Better Writing* ask you to experiment with different types of prewriting techniques. During this exploratory stage, remain open to and consider all ideas that surface through prewriting.

The following list represents the 10 most common prewriting techniques used by students.

Prewriting Technique	Technique Description	Technique Explanation
1. Branching	Branching, also referred to as a tree diagram or map, is an effective way to sort items or see clearly the various components of a topic. Although you can use branching in any writing assignment, you will find this technique especially helpful in division and classification.	Chapter 9, page 237, explains and illustrates this technique.

FIGURE 1.3   *Branching Example*

Start this technique by writing your topic in the top box. For each branch, list the main components of your topic. Continue to branch, listing the qualities and other relevant information for each component that you have identified.

2. **Clustering**

Clustering, also known as mapping or webbing, allows you to see and explore the relationships among ideas visually.

1. Start with a circle in the center of your paper.
2. As you think of ideas related to the topic in the center circle, draw smaller circles and link these ideas with lines.
3. As you think of new ideas related to the smaller circles, draw additional circles and lines to show their relationships.

See Chapter 5, page 103, for a full explanation on and illustration of clustering.

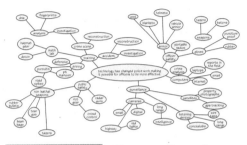

FIGURE 1.4 *Clustering Example*

3. **Cubing**

Cubing helps you look at your topic from six different angles, thus permitting you to explore various approaches to your topic. Imagine or draw a six-sided cube, each side representing a way to examine your topic. In cubing, you respond to the following six prompts, freewriting your answers:

1. Describe it: What does your topic look like?
2. Compare and contrast it: What is your topic similar to or different from?
3. Associate it: What does this topic remind you of?
4. Analyze it: How does your topic work? What is its significance? What does it consist of?
5. Apply it: What are the uses of the topic? What can you do with it?
6. Argue for and against it: What are the benefits or challenges of the topic? What changes should be made?

See Chapter 11, page 297, and examine how cubing was used by a student–writer to gather information for an argumentative essay.

FIGURE 1.5

Cubing Example

Continued

WRITING YOUR PAPERS

| 4. | Flowcharting | Popular in analyzing a process, flowcharting is also a great way to show cause/effect relationships. You visually explore the causes that led to a specific event or result or the effects that resulted from a specific event. | See Chapter 7, page 171, for an example of using flowcharting to gather ideas for cause/effect essays. |

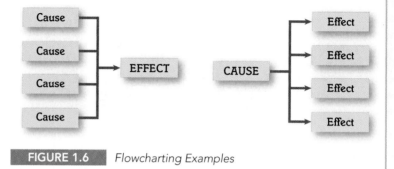

Multiple causes leading to one effect   **One cause leading to multiple effects**

FIGURE 1.6   *Flowcharting Examples*

| 5. | Freewriting | In freewriting, you begin writing nonstop for a certain amount of time, say, 5–10 minutes, jotting down whatever comes to mind. Just keep writing, letting your thoughts flow as they will. If you can't think of something to say, write just that—"I can't think of anything to write"—or keep writing the same word or phrase until something comes to you. When your time is up, review what you have written and choose the ideas that you feel are worth writing about. You can then do a more focused freewriting session on these ideas to generate relevant information on these possible topics. | Chapter 2, page 17, explains and illustrates freewriting and listing. Chapter 4, page 73, combines listing, freewriting, and questioning. |

| 6. | Listing | Listing, also known as brainstorming, is an effective way to get ideas down on paper quickly. Start with an idea—a word or phrase—and jot down every idea you can thing of related to that word or phrase. The goal here is to free associate, so keep your pen, pencil, or word processor moving—writing down one thought after another, whether a word or a phrase. Do this for at least 10 minutes. | See Chapter 2, page 17, Chapter 4, page 73, and Chapter 5, page 103, for how listing, in conjunction with other prewriting techniques, helps students focus and gather information for their topics. |
| | | After your time is up, review all your ideas. See what ideas are related, what ideas stand out in your list, and what ideas you want to explore further. You will end up listing not only good topics to consider for your essays but also details and points that you can use to support your topics. | |

7.	Looping	Looping is excellent for narrowing your topic. After 5–10 minutes of freewriting, pause to choose the best idea and start your next freewriting loop on that idea for another 5- to 10-minute freewriting session. You take the best idea of that loop, and again freewrite on that new idea, repeating the process and making each loop more specific than the previous one.	Chapter 6, page 103, explains and illustrates how a student used looping during the prewriting stage of her essay.
8.	Questioning	The questioning technique asks you to take a journalist's approach in gathering information. Ask yourself the six important questions that most journalists rely on to compile information: Who? What? When? Where? Why? How? This technique is a quick way to gather a lot of information on a specific topic. However, focusing each of these questions so that it applies to your topic may take a little practice.	Examine Chapter 3, page 42, and Chapter 4, page 73, to see how a student employed questioning during the prewriting stage.
9.	Venn diagram	The Venn diagram analyzes similarities and differences on a specific topic. Start this technique by drawing two overlapping circles. In the outer areas, list the differences between your topics, each topic in its own circle. In the area that overlaps, list the similarities that your topics share.	See Chapter 8, page 201, for a full explanation and illustration of a Venn diagram.

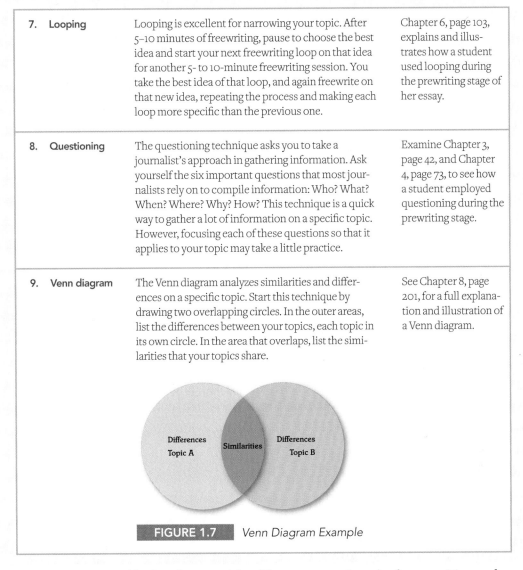

FIGURE 1.7 *Venn Diagram Example*

Be sure to set aside time for prewriting. There are no strict rules for prewriting, and there is no such thing as one technique for a specific essay. Combine and use these techniques for any writing assignment and at any point during the writing process. If necessary, alter the techniques to suit your needs.

Also in the prewriting stage, *Bridges to Better Writing* helps you identify your audience, establish your purpose, set the tone of your essay, formulate your thesis, and outline your ideas. If this isn't enough to break your writer's block, each chapter offers topic ideas to help you start your prewriting activities. As you leave the prewriting stage, always keep in mind that you can return to any step of this stage from any later stage of the writing process. In each chapter, we introduce a student's essay to serve as your model. These student models are far from perfect, so if you're asked to critique any section, it's okay to be brutal. No writing is ever complete.

Drafting

In the drafting stage, you shape your essay. See Figure 1.8 for all the steps involved in drafting.

As we guide you through the introduction, body, and conclusion of the essay, we continue to point out that you don't need to follow this order. It probably makes more sense to write the body of the essay and then determine the most appropriate and effective introduction. But for the purpose of discussion, we follow a linear approach. Each chapter explains and illustrates various strategies you can use and combine to write your introduction. Rather than present in one chapter more than a dozen ways to write your introduction,

FIGURE 1.8   *Drafting Stage*

we spread the various techniques throughout the chapters. We want to encourage you to challenge yourself and try new ways to write your introductions. Too often, we get used to one method and depend on only that method. Start taking risks and experimenting with ways to connect with your reader. In this stage of the writing process, you'll also examine how students draft the body and conclusion of their essays and use transitions and other devices to keep their ideas and paragraphs flowing smoothly.

Revising

In this stage, you try to distance yourself from your essay and attempt to see it as an outsider or a reviewer would so that you can make decisions about improving your draft.

When you revise, you review your draft to see where you can make your writing clearer, more exciting, more meaningful, more informative, or more convincing. Also, you try to examine your paper from different perspectives to determine whether the organization is effective, the tone appropriate, and the information coherent. Each writing chapter includes a style tip to help you write more clearly and accurately and a problem–solution section, addressing basic student concerns.

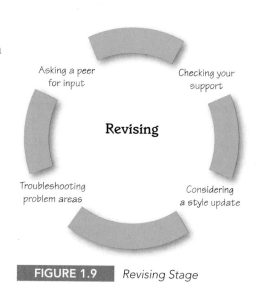

FIGURE 1.9   *Revising Stage*

This stage of the writing process concludes with a peer review activity, in which you share your revised draft with one or more classmates for their comments and suggestions. Your job as the writer is to consider the feedback and incorporate suggestions into your paper that you feel strengthen it. You may even choose to ignore the suggestions; the decision is yours.

Proofreading

In the proofreading stage, you examine your essay for punctuation, spelling, sentence structure, and word usage. Each chapter presents a common grammar error as a starting point for proofreading. If you feel that you need additional practice, a reference to the related chapter in *Bridges to Better Writing* leads you to additional information and practice. To determine the grammatical rule to include in the chapter, we considered two factors: First, we chose grammatical concepts that are the most problematic to most students, and second, we included those concepts that seem to be the most appropriate to the specific writing tasks. Hold yourself accountable for previous errors by eliminating them in your next writing task.

Reflecting

The final stage of the writing process is reflecting. To bring closure to the process, you start by reflecting on your writing experiences in that chapter. You should think of the challenges you encountered as you created your draft and consider how you might address these challenges in your next writing task. You should also comment on your success. What did you do that you initially thought you would be unable to do?

We also want you to consider the broader application of what you learned in the chapter. What connection does this material have to writing in college, for your profession, and in everyday life? Basically, we want you to see yourself as a writer, developing your skills as you grow to become an effective communicator—a crucial characteristic of a first-rate professional.

Collaborative Critical Thinking

In groups of three or four, discuss practical suggestions to resolve the following problems. Share your suggestions with other groups. Answers will vary.

Problem

1. I can't meet the deadline for this assignment.

2. I have no clue as to what I'm going to write about.

3. I'll work on my essay the night before. I always work best under pressure.

4. I can never find my errors until somebody points them out. By then, who cares?

5. It's not fair that I received such a low grade. I worked on this essay for over 12 hours.

6. I don't think my instructor likes me. My friend, who's an English major, told me my paper is great. But look at this grade!

7. I have questions, but I don't want my professor or my classmates to think I'm dumb.

8. Whenever I'm absent, I'm totally lost in class.

9. When I look at other students' writing, they all seem to be getting it and I feel left behind. Am I in the wrong course?

10. I don't like the idea of sharing my writing. Writing is very personal; I hate feeling exposed.

CHAPTER 2

Writing Your Descriptive Paragraph

YOUR GOALS

Understanding Description

1. Use vivid, specific language to convey sensory information.

2. Use figurative language to enhance a description.

3. Select a particular dominant impression and support it using descriptive writing.

Writing Your Descriptive Paragraph

1. Use two brainstorming techniques to discover a topic: listing and freewriting.

2. Outline your ideas to help organize a descriptive paragraph.

3. Write a dominant impression as the controlling idea of your paragraph.

4. Explore the relationship between audience and purpose.

5. Use appropriate transitions.

6. Edit for sentence variety and sentence completeness.

"The key to good description begins with clear seeing and ends with clear writing, the kind of writing that employs fresh images and simple vocabulary."

■ **Stephen King** ■

In an essay question for an art history exam, you are asked to describe Cubism and its geometric forms. You imagine Picasso's Cubist painting *Three Musicians* on page 312 of your art history textbook: its figures, colors, and textures. Your challenge is to find the right language to convey these visual forms to your reader.

As a salesperson for a computer outlet, your job is to describe the features of various computers and other devices so that your customers can make the best choice. Over time, you develop a vocabulary of technical and descriptive terms that seem to speak most directly to customers. You are able to describe not only the operating speeds and storage capacities but also the look and "feel" of different machines.

You have just witnessed a hit-and-run accident at a busy intersection in your hometown. You are interviewed by the police, who ask you to describe the events of the accident. You need to remember such details as color, model, and year of the hit-and-run car; gender and appearance of the driver; speed of the car; details of the impact; and route of escape. You re-create the incident in your mind, searching for the most vivid and concrete language to convey it accurately to the police.

These examples demonstrate the importance of conveying what you mean clearly and accurately, whether in speech or writing. When you describe people, objects, events, or emotions, your task is to find just the right words and arrange them into the clearest possible sentences to allow your reader to understand the subject. But isn't this true of any effective writing? Learning to describe a subject well can give you a firm basis for other kinds of writing because all good writing depends on the qualities of effective description: clarity, concreteness, and vividness.

PREVIEWING YOUR TASK

As you go through college, your instructors will ask you to write often and in depth about various subjects—not just in English class! Instructors ask you to write so that they can assess your comprehension of all kinds of subjects: history, psychology, science, and sometimes even more technical subjects like math or engineering. And once you graduate from college and move on to a career, you will be writing more than you might suspect. The writing samples that follow demonstrate how you can use description to write effectively in any context.

Writing for College

The following selection is an example of descriptive writing about an aesthetic subject. If you ever take an art appreciation class, you will be encouraged to describe what you see on canvas in such a way that your reader can "see" it as well.

> The painting, called *Night in a Forest,* depicts a horrific dream scene in which the subject, a young man, has become lost in a frightening landscape. He crouches in dim light in the middle of the canvas, looking up with widened eyes that deliberately remind the viewer of Edvard Munch's famous painting, *The Scream.* One arm extends upward to ward away the dark, but the attempt is futile, for surrounding the dimly lit center of the painting, lurid shapes as strange and distorted threaten to close in and destroy the subject. In colors of dark blue-green, black, and deep reds and purples, nightmarish monsters struggle. Some are dragon-like, and others fantastical, though they do have recognizable features such as teeth, tongues, and eyes. Viewing the painting is much more than a visual experience: one can almost hear the roaring and snarling of the monsters, and the textures of the painting invite one to touch its rough surface. One figure seems almost human. He stands partially concealed behind the mud-brown trunk of a large tree, and unlike the other monstrous figures, his eyes are directed toward the crouching figure in the middle of the canvas. Clearly, he is meant to represent the controlling figure of the painting, the personification of evil, and the leader of the dark demons of the subconscious.

PRACTICE   2-1

1. What, in your opinion, is the purpose of the paragraph? To illustrate the dramatic power and vividness of the painting and its message.

2. Who is the audience for this paragraph? Who would want or need to read it? The audience could be a student of art or a visitor to an art museum housing the painting.

Writing in Your Profession

The following paragraph about a surge suppressor for a computer illustrates a type of description you might be asked to read or write on the job if your job is technical. Notice that even though the subject is somewhat dry, the paragraph uses many descriptive techniques that make the surge suppressor "visible."

> The Filpi 270 is a compact, lightweight surge suppressor designed to be used during hotel stays while on business travel. It is rectangular, with dimensions of $3'' \times 2'' \times 1''$, and it weighs only ¼ pound. Thus, you can easily store and carry it in a laptop carrying case or handbag. The Filpi 270 is made of durable plastic with a "scaly" texture that allows you to grip it firmly. It requires no power cord because it plugs directly into the wall; the computer cord plugs directly into the Filpi. An interesting feature of the Filpi 270 is its retractable three-prong plug: to pack the device in your luggage, simply retract the plug into the body of the suppressor so that it doesn't interfere with your other items. To use the suppressor, pull the plug out and lock it into place before plugging the device into the wall. When the Filpi is plugged in and working properly, you will see a small green steady light in the display window. If the Filpi is not working properly, a red light flashes and a high-pitched beep sounds every 10 seconds.

PRACTICE 2-2

1. What is the purpose of this paragraph? To promote the Filpi 270, explain its convenient features, and show how it works.

2. Identify three details that help support this paragraph. Its weight of ¼ pound, its retractable plug, and its green and red lights indicating whether or not it is working well.

Writing in Everyday Life

We spend a good deal of energy in our daily lives describing events, places, and objects to other people. The following selection, written by the owner of a home built in 1979, describes her "vision" of how she wants the kitchen to look for the remodeler she has hired.

> Dear Mr. Ward,
>
> After your walkthrough of my kitchen yesterday, I would like to summarize the changes that we discussed to be sure that we are on the same page for this remodeling project.

As you know, I want the kitchen to have a Southwest look instead of its current '70s decor of yellow linoleum, yellow wall tiles, dark brown cabinets, florescent lighting, and butcher-block island. I envision my new kitchen floor as having reddish-brown, smooth tiles in large squares with light pink grout. The old island should be completely ripped out and a new, much larger one installed with a granite countertop with speckles of black, gray, and pink and an overlap for four stools as an informal seating area. The new island should be large enough for a built-in, four-burner glass ceramic cooktop stove and side shelving for my collection of cookbooks. Above the island the ugly rectangular central florescent light should be removed and softer pendant lights hung over it. Instead of tile on the counters, I prefer a laminate that feels like granite to the touch, again in reddish-brown colors to match the floor tiles. Please let me know what other information you need as you plan this remodeling project.

Sincerely,
Ms. Kulik

PRACTICE   **2-3**

1. Write a sentence that captures the purpose of the description. _____
   This description explains to the remodeler the type of upgrades that the customer wants for her kitchen.

2. List four details that help support this purpose. _____
   Reddish-brown, smooth tiles; granite countertop; pendant lights; and double ovens

3. If you were the remodeler, what other details might be included to make your task clearer? Will the old refrigerator stay? Where will the double ovens go? What type of wood is required for the cookbook shelving?

UNDERSTANDING DESCRIPTION

Description—writing about a subject so that the reader can see, taste, smell, hear, or feel it—is a fundamental skill for any writer. In your reading experience, you've probably noticed that writers who can "paint a word picture" of their subjects are more engaging, lively, and memorable in a way that plainer writing is not. Good writers know how to convey to the reader's imagination an abundance of physical, or sensual, detail: words and phrases that appeal to one or more of the five senses.

Using Sensory Details

To communicate clearly and effectively, your writing should contain specific, concrete details to help the reader visualize your ideas. It seems only logical that using sensory details in our writing provides powerful concrete images to help communicate our ideas vividly as well as engage the reader. Examine some uses of sensory details.

EMPHASIS ON SIGHT

Harrow-on-the-Hill, with its <u>pointed spire</u>, <u>rises blue</u> in the <u>distance</u>; and <u>distant</u> ridges, like <u>receding waves</u>, <u>rise into blueness</u>, <u>one after the other</u>, out of the <u>low-lying</u> mist, the <u>last ridge</u> melting into space. (*Peter Ibbetson,* Daphne du Maurier)

EMPHASIS ON SOUND

About half an hour before dawn, Wilbur woke and listened. The barn was still dark. The sheep lay motionless. Even the goose was <u>quiet</u>. Overhead, on the main floor, <u>nothing stirred</u>: the cows were resting, the horses dozed. Templeton had quit work and gone off somewhere on an errand. The only sound was a <u>slight scraping noise</u> from the rooftop, where the weather-vane swung back and forth. (*Charlotte's Web,* E. B. White)

EMPHASIS ON SMELL

All the world knows the <u>poignant</u> smell accompanying a summer shower, when dust is moistened, when parched grass yields a certain <u>acrid scent</u> under the stress of storm. The fresh vigor and brilliancy of roses and of yellow lilies, after rain, is proverbial; but for <u>exquisite beauty of fragrance</u> I know nothing that compares with the <u>aromatic</u>, mystical influence of a <u>blossoming balm of Gilead</u>, <u>rain-swept.</u> (From *Essays and Essay Writing,* William Tanner, editor)

EMPHASIS ON TASTE

In the *mercado* where my mother shopped, we frequently bought *taquitos de nopalitos,* small *tacos* <u>filled with diced cactus, onions, tomatoes, and *jalapeños.*</u> Our friend Don Toribio showed us how to make delicious, crunchy *taquitos* with <u>dried, salted</u> pumpkin seeds. ("Tortillas," José Antonio Burciaga)

EMPHASIS ON TOUCH

The high <u>cold</u> empty gloomy rooms liberated me and I went from room to room singing. From the front window I saw my companions playing below in the street. Their cries reached me weakened and indistinct and, leaving my forehead against the <u>cool</u> glass, I looked at the dark house where she lived. ("Araby," James Joyce)

Notice how the sensory language in these examples helps you imagine the reality being described. Can't you almost see the blue colors of Harrow-on-the-Hill, taste the foods described by Burciaga, and feel the coolness of the glass in Joyce's story? By using these descriptive techniques, the authors have fulfilled every writer's purpose: to fully engage you—mentally and physically—as the reader. As a writer, you can have the same effect on your audience with just a little practice. The following chart gives you a sense of the range of sensual, concrete details you might find in your environment.

Sensory Description Words

1. Sight Words					
Colors	blue	brown	red	green	yellow
	aquamarine	ash	adobe	avocado	butter
	azure	auburn bronze	burgundy	celery	buttercup
	navy	brunette	cardinal	emerald	canary
	ocean	caramel	cherry	forest	gold
	royal	chestnut	crimson	grass	lemon
	sapphire	chocolate	maroon	lime	
	sky	scorched	raspberry	olive	
	turquoise		ruby	teal	
Appearance	bright	dim	freckled	immense	sparkly
	clear	dingy	glassy	light	strange
	cloudy	dismal	glazed	little	translucent
	colorful	dull	glowing	opaque	transparent
	colossal	fancy	hollow	rainbow	ugly
	dark	filthy	homely	shabby	unsightly
	deep	flat	huge	shiny	wrinkled
Shapes	angular	chubby	flared	oval	swollen
	bent	crinkled	flat	rectangular	triangular
	broad	curved	enormous	round	wavy
	broken	fat	lumpy	square	wide
2. Sound Words					
	bang	crackle	loud	scream	stomp
	bark	crunchy	melodious	screech	rattle
	blare	cry	muffled	shout	rustle
	boom	deafening	musical	shriek	tap
	chime	earsplitting	noisy	shrill	thump
	clamor	explode	piercing	slam	thunder
	clap	giggle	quiet	smash	whimper
	clatter	howl	racket	soft	whisper
	commotion	hum	roar	speechless	yell
3. Smell Words					
	acrid	damp	fresh	perfumed	sharp
	aromatic	delicious	medicinal	pungent	spicy
	burning	flowery	musty	rotten	stagnant
	clean	fragrant	odorless	scented	sweet
4. Taste Words					
	bitter	creamy	oily	salty	sugary
	bland	crunchy	raw	sour	sweet
	burnt	hot	revolting	spicy	tangy
	buttery	juicy	ripe	spoiled	tasteless
	cold	mild	rotten	succulent	tasty

Continued

Sensory Description Words—cont'd

5. Touch Words				
bumpy	dry	icy	slimy	sweaty
chilly	dull	loose	slippery	tender
coarse	dusty	mushy	slushy	thick
cold	furry	oily	smooth	thin
cool	greasy	rough	soft	tough
crisp	hairy	sandy	solid	velvety
damp	hard	silky	steamy	warm
dirty	hot	sharp	sticky	wet

This chart is only a starting point for further exploration of descriptive vocabulary. What about vocabulary that describes emotions, thoughts, behaviors, or sensations (such as the feeling in the pit of your stomach when an angry dog growls at you)?

Using Figurative Language

Another way to make your descriptions vivid is to use figurative language, a tool that writers use to help the reader experience writing more directly. Figurative language uses figures of speech to create mental pictures and impressions. The most common figures of speech are simile and metaphor. You use a simile or a metaphor to compare your topic to something familiar and/or vivid to the reader.

A simile compares dissimilar objects by using *like* or *as.*

> **EXAMPLE:**   My car's engine sounds like the rumbling of a distant thunderstorm.

A metaphor sets up an equation of one thing that in some way equals another. It is an implied comparison of two different objects. Unlike a simile, a metaphor does not use *like* and *as* to signal the comparison.

> **EXAMPLE:**   Her life is a fairy tale.

By relying judiciously on simile and metaphor, you can say a great deal economically. Instead of writing extensively about a person's magical life, using the fairy tale metaphor expresses this idea concisely.

PRACTICE   2-4

Write a simile or metaphor to complete each of the following statements. Allow your creative juices to flow! Answers will vary.

Warning: Avoid well-used and tired similes like "I wake up in the morning like a bear emerging from hibernation" or "She works like a dog." Your job as a writer is to invent fresh comparisons that are not familiar yet express your comparison honestly and vividly.

1. I write like an injured bear dragging itself across a mountain pass .
2. I run like a squirrel scampering up a tree .
3. My job is an endless road of construction and roadblocks .
4. I treat my cousin (relative/friend) like a pampered pet .
5. I wake up in the morning like a firecracker exploding .

To make our writing livelier, we can also assign human qualities to nonhuman objects or beings or even to abstract ideas such as love. For example, a reporter describing Hurricane Katrina might write the following:

Katrina blew into New Orleans with all of the might and fury of a lover scorned.

This technique is called *personification,* and it allows the reader to have a concrete, immediate, and living image and a feeling for the subject being described. Personification can be achieved via the verb in the sentence.

- The wind <u>cried</u> pitifully.
- The trees <u>groaned</u>.
- The car engine <u>purred</u> calmly.
- The cat <u>scowled</u>.

Personification can also be expressed by adjectives or adverbs.
- The dandelions <u>saucily</u> dotted my yard.
- As I walked down the darkening alley, the trash cans loomed <u>threateningly</u>.
- The gun hung <u>menacingly</u> above the fireplace.

PRACTICE   **2-5**

1. Use personification to completing the following sentences with a verb or verbs that give the subject human qualities. Answers will vary.

   a. The autumn leaves scratched impatiently on the window .

   b. The lawn mower roars .

   c. The voice message chatters irritatingly .

2. Now experiment with adjectives and adverbs. Answers will vary.

   a. In the spring the lively daffodils bloom.

   b. At the tattoo parlor the machines hummed soothingly .

   c. The domineering SUV swung imposingly around the miniscule Neon.

Deciding on the Dominant Impression

The goal of description is to convey an idea or opinion about a subject. As you describe something, keep in mind that you are doing so to convey an overall idea, or *dominant impression,* of the topic by building up concrete details to support the general point.

For example, in the student paragraph describing *Night in a Forest* (p. 19), what if the author wanted to convey a dominant impression not of terror but of artistic skill? The author would have to describe the use of brushstrokes, perspective, composition, color, and other technical aspects of the painting. As you plan and organize the details of your paragraph, omit any details that are irrelevant to the idea you expressed in your dominant impression; include only those details that help the reader understand the dominant impression.

Your overall idea or dominant impression tells the reader exactly the focus of your description in the entire paragraph; it is the paragraph's main idea. All information in that paragraph should serve to explain this dominant impression.

TOPIC:	The Filpi 270 surge suppressor
DOMINANT IMPRESSION:	Convenient to use
TOPIC:	My kitchen renovation plans
DOMINANT IMPRESSION:	Southwest style

PRACTICE   2-6

For each of the following topics, list three possible dominant impressions. Then compare your ideas with those of your classmates and decide which might make the most interesting paragraph for each topic. Answers will vary.

1. A classic car
    a. Elegant
    b. Timeless
    c. Pristine
2. Computer software for doing taxes
    a. Self-explanatory
    b. Complicated
    c. User friendly
3. A local tattoo parlor
    a. Welcoming
    b. Cluttered
    c. Grungy

Ordering Your Descriptive Details

Once you have a main impression to communicate and sufficient details to support the impression, you must decide on the order in which you will present the details of the description. For instance, in describing a cabin in the mountains, do you start from a wide-angle view and then move in for a close-up? Do you start from the exterior and move to the interior? Clearly, you have many options for ordering any description. It all depends on what you are describing and how you want to develop the description.

WRITING YOUR DESCRIPTIVE PARAGRAPH

Look at this descriptive paragraph written by Leon, a 25-year-old graphic arts student at a local college.

My Aunt's Outfit

The outfit that my aunt wore to my wedding was quite bizarre, attracting the guests' attention. As she entered the church hall, her broad-brimmed hat with purple feathers and pink lace trim bobbed unsteadily above her dangly feather earrings. The earring feathers were a rainbow of turquoise, orange, and green, hanging so low that they rubbed the tops of her shoulders. On her shoulders she had draped a red-fringed shawl so fringy that any slight breeze made the strands leap wildly into the air. The shawl partly covered a white blouse decorated in red roses and enlarged by enormous puff sleeves. The low neck barely covered her cleavage. As if the top half of her body weren't startling enough, the lower half was equally strange as her sheer pink gypsy pants ballooned around her tall legs. The cinched silver belt only added to her bizarre and gypsy-like appearance. The *piece de resistance* was her silver, open-toed sandals dotted with rhinestones and small bells that jingled musically as she walked down the aisle to her seat. The focus of the wedding had obviously shifted away from the bride!

Clearly, this paragraph is full of vivid, descriptive writing. Notice the sensory details devoted to color (purple, pink, turquoise, and so on), movement (bobbed, dangled, and leap), and sound ("jingled musically"). Also notice the use of a simile—"gypsy-like"—to convey the aunt's exotic appearance. All these descriptive details are carefully arranged to support the dominant impression stated in the opening sentence: "bizarre."

Notice the structure of the paragraph. The opening sentence has an important function. In this case, it states the dominant impression that the rest of the paragraph tries to support. Also, notice how the description flows naturally from the aunt's head to her feet; it doesn't skip around illogically. As you develop your own paragraph, think about how best to order the sentences to present a unified picture to your reader.

Now you'll begin writing your own descriptive paragraph. This section guides you through the five major phases of the writing process: prewriting, drafting, revising, proofreading, and reflecting. Keep in mind, however, that writers often find themselves moving back and forth between these stages as their work takes shape. If you get stuck during the drafting stage, for instance, you can always return to some part of the prewriting stage to get your draft moving forward again.

Prewriting

Unless your instructor assigns a topic, you might spend a lot of time staring at a blank page trying to think of something to say. You might even believe you have nothing to say that may interest others. To overcome this sense of frustration, most writers—even professional writers—rely on prewriting techniques. Begin with two prewriting techniques that writers often use to find a topic.

Discovering and Limiting Your Topic

Listing and freewriting techniques should generate plenty of ideas to carry you into the drafting stage. Remember that if you get stuck during the writing process, even as you near the end of your composition, you can always return to prewriting to stimulate further ideas.

Prewriting Strategy #1: Listing

Listing is probably the simplest prewriting strategy and is usually the first method writers use to generate ideas. Listing means exactly what the name implies—listing your ideas and experiences. First set a time limit for this activity; 5–10 minutes is more than enough. Then write down as many ideas as you can without stopping to analyze any of them. Here are Leon's initial listing of ideas about college, his daily routines, and his other activities.

first day of class	relaxing in the backyard	working in teams
rushing to work	the tension of doing my homework	taking my usual shortcut through the park
student orientation		
the bookstore	I get distracted too easy	
visiting my relatives	not being able to think of stuff is a bit scary	walking my dog early mornings
my relatives are happy I'm here—am I?	Can I get out of here early?	I have some strange classmates
rushing to class		going to the gym
working with computers	figuring out my instructor	playing rugby
watching what other students are doing	the first test	
	my art class	

WRITING   2-1

For 5 minutes, in a notebook list all ideas that come to your mind. Don't discard any ideas and don't stop to think: write nonstop.

After you have generated your list of topics, review the list and pick one item that you might like to write about. Now you're ready for the next listing; this time, create a topic-specific list in which you write down as many ideas as you can about the one topic you have selected. This list will help you look for a focus for your descriptive paragraph. Don't stop to analyze any of the ideas. Your goal is to free your mind, so don't worry if you feel you're rambling.

Leon chose "visiting my relatives" to begin his topic-specific list.

Visiting relatives

Uncle is boring

My cousin Alex is cool

My three aunts are weird

Joe plays baseball an awful lot

Dusty field that he thinks is for baseball

Molly and Eric are always on diets

My aunt Kathy is a great cook

Love her spaghetti sauce

Yes, great atmosphere in that Italian restaurant

Can't remember their specialties

Don't like anything too formal

A pain to dress up

Hate ties

Ties get more and more colorful

The more colors, the easier to match

My Uncle is boring but a cool dresser

My Aunt Kathy should take lessons from him

Everyone in church turned to look

Too many colors like ties

Darn, Aunt Kathy sure is a weird dresser

But a darn good cook

Too many secret recipes

Cooking can be kind of fun

That wedding cake was the best I've seen

You can see some ideas emerging, the strongest being food and dress. Leon ends this activity by reviewing his list and circling the idea that catches his interest most.

WRITING 2-2

Choose an idea from your initial listing to start your topic-specific list. For 5 minutes, write down in a notebook all ideas that come to your mind. Don't discard any ideas and don't stop to think: write nonstop.

Prewriting Strategy #2: Freewriting

Freewriting means exactly what the word says, writing freely in sentences and paragraphs without worrying about organization, correctness, and form. Since writing and thinking often happen simultaneously, you can "jump start" your thinking by writing whatever comes into your mind.

Here's what Leon's 5-minute freewriting session yielded about his Aunt Kathy's clothing.

Last week at church we were all decked out in our Sunday best. But like always Aunt Kathy stops the show. She can't continue to embarrass the family, but maybe I'm just exaggerating. We can't all be cool dressers. I'm not sure I'm one either. I like to think I am, but my friend always makes snide remarks when I come in with something new. Funny how people react to the way others dress. I'm guilty of the same thing. I shouldn't be ashamed of my aunt. After all, she's more than just a splash of colors and funny-looking outfits. I wonder how she sees herself. Maybe we're the weird ones. It's not like she's wearing different-colored shoes. Maybe she's just ahead of her time—nah; she's weird. But in a very loving way. I guess. Maybe she's trying to make a statement. Do people really think that strange clothes make statements? They actually do—bad taste. I'm not sure my aunt really has bad taste. Her house is decorated very elegantly. But it sure doesn't reflect her outfit. I worry about her mind. Maybe I should worry about her nerves or about me. Why should I feel ashamed? It's not me. But she does represent the family. I'm in denial.

Since freewriting is spontaneous, a lot of rambling may result. But amid all this digression, possible topics may emerge. The following are some topics in Leon's freewriting activity that may lead to an interesting dominant impression:

- How clothes reflect the person
- Why people react so strongly to style
- Why some people over-react to others' behavior and eccentricities
- How our own personalities develop in the context of family

When you freewrite, keep in mind that your instructor will not critique your freewriting, so don't worry if your ideas are disjointed, sentences are ungrammatical, words are misspelled, and punctuation is lacking. Your goal is to see what ideas surface.

WRITING   2-3

Use an idea from your topic-specific list to start your freewriting experience. For 5 minutes, write in a notebook all ideas that come to your mind in sentence and (if you wish) paragraph form. Don't discard any ideas and don't stop to think: write nonstop.

TOPICS TO CONSIDER

If you're still having problems finding a topic, try using listing and freewriting on one or more of the following topics to get you thinking about things to describe:

Writing for College		
■ A specific painting ■ A type of music	■ The staging of a college play ■ A specific lab class or experiment	■ The sounds of a language ■ An ecological problem

Writing in Your Profession			
BUSINESS	■ The grand opening of a new business	■ An office environment ■ The typical day of a manager	■ A difficult customer
CRIMINAL JUSTICE	■ The scene or victim of a crime ■ A courtroom scene	■ A prison inspection ■ A prison or store surveillance technique	■ The behavior of a suspicious shoplifter
EDUCATION	■ The ideal classroom ■ A parent's attitude in a parent–teacher meeting	■ A specific learning disability	■ The attitude of an ineffective teacher
HEALTH	■ The stage of a certain condition or illness	■ A patient's emotional state upon being admitted to the hospital	■ An MRI machine ■ A busy moment in the emergency room of a hospital
SOCIAL WORK/ PSYCHOLOGY	■ A person experiencing emotional problems	■ A social worker's demeanor when counseling a client	■ A dysfunctional family ■ A women's shelter
TECHNICAL	■ The ideal work area in your field ■ The graphics of a specific video game	■ A multimedia environment ■ A technician performing a specific task for the first time	■ A specific type of video equipment
OTHERS	■ A natural disaster, such as a tornado, hurricane, or snowstorm	■ An archeological dig ■ A specific historical structure, such as a building or statue	■ A specific vacation spa ■ The habitat of a specific animal

Writing in Everyday Life		
■ A recent event, concert, sports event, and so on ■ Your favorite type of music	■ A special heirloom or tool you inherited from your parents or grandparents ■ An object central to your identity or personal history	■ A special room in your house ■ An accomplishment that you are particularly proud of

WRITING YOUR DESCRIPTIVE PARAGRAPH

WRITING   2-4

Based on the prewriting you've done so far, which of your topic ideas seem to be the most interesting or productive? List your three favorite topics here.

Topic #1: _____

Topic #2: _____

Topic #3: _____

Identifying Your Audience

For every piece of writing you do, you should consider your audience, the person or group for whom your writing is intended. In descriptive paragraphs, think about who really would need or want to read your writing and develop the description so that your audience will get the main point. In Chapter 3, we begin looking in more detail at possible audiences for your writing; for now, you might think of your classmates as the primary audience for your descriptive writing.

> **Computer tip**
>
> Don't discard any good ideas that you uncover during freewriting. Copy and paste interesting topics in different files for possible essays in this or other courses.

Establishing Your Purpose

Your main point in a descriptive paragraph or essay is closely related to the dominant impression you hope to convey of the person, place, thing, or event you are describing. Two common writers' purposes in descriptive writing are to inform the reader through careful and accurate description and to entertain the reader with engaging and lively description.

Setting Your Tone

Tone refers to your attitude about your subject. You might think of your subject as serious and weighty, for instance, or lighthearted and humorous. The point here is that you want to help your reader understand your attitude by using the appropriate tone in your writing. If you have a serious subject, you wouldn't want to treat it humorously.

WRITING   2-5

Take a moment to consider your audience and the overall purpose of this paragraph. Who will benefit from reading your description? What will the reader gain? Don't forget that the details you include in your descriptive paragraph should be meaningful to your audience and serve to achieve your purpose.

1. Who will most likely benefit from your descriptive paragraph? _____

_____

2.   How much does your audience already know about your topic? _____
_____

3.   What information will you need to provide? _____
_____

4.   What effects do you want your description to have on your audience? _____
_____

5.   What information will you need to provide to achieve these effects? _____
_____

Stating Your Dominant Impression

At this point, you should have a clear idea of a topic for your descriptive paragraph. Considering your purpose and your intended reader, write in the Writing 2-6 box the topic, audience, purpose, and tentative dominant impression for your descriptive paragraph. This sentence will eventually become the first sentence in your paragraph. You can always go back to your freewriting if you change your mind about your topic or dominant impression.

This is Leon's tentative dominant impression:

Topic:	My aunt
Audience:	My classmates
Purpose:	Entertain the reader with an engaging description of my aunt's way of dressing
Dominant impression:	My aunt's bizarre outfits attract attention.

WRITING   2-6

Fill in the results of your prewriting.

Topic: _____

Audience: _____

Purpose: _____

Dominant impression: _____
_____

Outlining Your Ideas

Now that you have narrowed your topic and have a focus for writing, the next stage of the writing process is to outline your ideas. Outlining serves two main purposes: an outline helps you determine the best way to organize your information, and outlining helps keep you focused on the dominant impression of your paragraph.

Decide on a plan for ordering your details. Will you start at the front of the room and move around the room to the right, back, and left sides? Will you describe your aunt's bizarre outfit by starting with her hat and moving down her body?

Leon's outline of his aunt's strange outfit looks like this:

OUTLINE

Dominant impression: Weird, strange, unique, eye-popping, bizarre, odd
Paragraph detail:

- Big hat
- Dangly feather earrings
- Fringed shawl
- Gypsy clothes
- Silver, open-toed sandals

WRITING   2-7

Create your outline. Don't forget that you can always come back to change your outline. Nothing is final. Follow Leon's example for your topic. Write down as many adjectives as you like for your tentative dominant impression; you can decide which adjective fits best once you have listed the details.

Dominant impression: _____

Paragraph detail:

- _____
- _____
- _____
- _____
- _____

Drafting

You might want to think of writing your paragraph in two major steps:

1. Begin your paragraph by stating your dominant impression. The dominant impression contains the topic (my aunt's outfit) and the focus of the paragraph (bizarre). For instance:

> The outfit that my aunt wore to my wedding was quite bizarre, attracting the guests' attention.

2. After you have written the dominant impression, your next step is to write vivid, concrete sentences to support the dominant impression. Use as many of the five senses as possible to describe your topic to allow the reader to experience it as closely and intimately as possible. Remember that you are your reader's eyes, ears, tongue, fingers, and nose. Sight is the most used sense for description, allowing something unseen to be imagined in the reader's mind. However, don't forget to consider sounds, smells, tastes, and feeling.

Remember, your job is to show, not to tell: you can write that a building is falling apart, but showing by describing the weathered siding, the chipped paint around the door and window frames, the cracked glass, and the rotted beams is more powerful writing.

Look at Leon's first draft:

> My aunt wears such bizarre outfits that I'm embarrassed to claim her as a relative. Her hats are outrageous, her earrings are too fancy and large, and her shawls have so much fringe that ten fringed shawls could be made out of her one. Her shoes are too showy and her outfits belong on a gypsy, not a red-blooded, middle-aged American woman. At a family reunion recently, I had to leave the room to avoid being caught near her and being so distracted by her outfit that I couldn't carry on a conversation with her. My aunt is a character.

Leon's first draft has a strong and clear dominant impression and expresses his own reactions to his aunt firmly. However, this first draft needs some work. The paragraph does not have clear organization. Moreover, Leon could add more specific adjectives to give the reader a better view of his aunt's outfits.

Coherence: Using Transitions

One area in which Leon's first draft is deficient is known as *coherence*. Coherence refers to a characteristic of all effective writing: it "sticks together" logically and flows smoothly from sentence to sentence. You need to think about

> **Computer tip**
>
> Highlight all descriptive words to determine whether they are sufficient and whether you have used words and expressions related to the different senses. Then underline the figures of speech to help decide whether they are appropriate, effective, and not clichéd.

using appropriate words and phrases to connect your ideas so that they flow naturally and make sense. These words and phrases are called *transitions* because they help the reader move from sentence to sentence. Since descriptive details should appear in a certain order, your transitions should support the ordering you choose by making that ordering clear to your reader. Here are some examples of transitions that might be used in descriptive contexts.

To Show Spatial Order or Direction		
above	close	next to
adjacent to	elsewhere	on top of
around	farther on	opposite to
at one end	here	over
below	in front/back of	there
behind	in the background	turning right/left/south
beside	in the distance	to the right/left
beyond	nearby	under

To Show Order of Importance	To Show Time Order
amazingly	concurrently
but the most important	during
equally/increasingly important	finally
even more striking	next
initially	suddenly
strikingly	then
the most/the major/the main	when

WRITING   2-8

Start writing your first draft of your descriptive paragraph.

1. Write your dominant impression of your topic.
2. Write down as many details of sight, sound, smell, taste, and touch as you can think of.
3. Write as many ideas as you can that help explain your dominant impression. If necessary, stop and use listing or freewriting to help you generate more ideas.
4. Work for a particular period (maybe half an hour) and then put your work aside. Return to it later to add or delete details.

Revising

Many students find the revising stage to be the most frustrating and intimidating of all the writing stages. However, revision is probably the most important stage of the writing process. It is in this stage that you really look at your paragraph; you try to distance yourself from your writing as much as possible so that you can look at it objectively.

Consider the purpose of your description. Will the reader be able to "see" what you mean? Does your paragraph have a definite point that you're trying to make—a dominant impression—or does it aimlessly describe a person, place, or object without making a point? Will your reader understand the point you're trying to make? In this stage, don't worry too much about punctuation, spelling, or grammar. You have plenty of time to focus on these problems in the proofreading stage. Review the following common problems students encounter in writing descriptive paragraphs and consider some possible solutions.

Style Tip: Using a Variety of Sentence Lengths

To craft well-written sentences and paragraphs, you need to develop sensitivity to sentence *style*. Sometimes, writing that is perfectly grammatical can be hard for your audience to read or understand. For instance, when a paragraph consists of a string of short sentences, the reader can become bored by the repetition of the same sentence pattern. Conversely, when your sentences are consistently too long, your reader can become confused trying to figure out your meaning. Therefore, try to vary your sentence length: alternate shorter sentences with longer ones. Develop sensitivity to how the length of your sentences affects the "rhythm" of your writing by reading your work aloud to yourself.

> **Computer tip**
>
> Move your cursor through your paragraph, hitting "Enter" after each sentence. Compare the sentences. If you're basically using the same lengths, consider rewriting some of your sentences. If you find ideas that can be combined into one sentence, do so.

> **Bridging Knowledge**
>
> **Go to Chapter** 22 to build your knowledge of sentence variety.

PROBLEM	SOLUTION
DESCRIPTION My description isn't particularly colorful, vivid, or well developed.	1. Have someone else read the paper and suggest details to be added. 2. Add another sense, if appropriate, such as taste or smell. Refer to the chart of sensory details on page 23. 3. Close your eyes and visualize your subject. What do you see that you should have included? 4. If possible, take a picture of your subject. What features do you see in the picture that you should capture in your writing?
WRITING My dominant impression seems too general or vague.	1. Ask yourself, "What does this all mean?" You may have to clarify the dominant impression. 2. Ask someone to read the paragraph and summarize the main idea in one sentence. Then ask yourself, "Is this the point I'm trying to make?" If yes, make sure the point is clearly stated since this is your dominant idea. If not, clarify the dominant idea. 3. Write a few restatements of the dominant idea, and then choose the best or ask others which restatement they find most effective.

COHERENCE

My paragraph seems poorly organized, and the sentences are choppy.

1. Be sure that you have a clear plan of organization—top to bottom, right to left, large to small, least to most exciting, and so on.
2. Pretend you are videotaping your subject. How will you move your camera? On what will you focus your camera longer? Does your paragraph lead your reader through a similar order of details?
3. Add more transitions, and make sure your transitions support your ordering of the description.

Collaborative Critical Thinking

Asking Your Peers

In groups of three or four students, do the following:

- Each student reads his or her paragraph aloud while the others listen and take notes. The writer should read the paragraph twice so that the listeners have time to absorb the details.
- After the first paragraph is read, the listeners should take a few minutes to jot down what they enjoyed about the description and what questions or suggestions they have to offer the writer.
- Each of the listeners comments on the paragraph while the writer takes notes silently. The writer should not speak except to ask questions of the listeners.
- Repeat this activity for each of the paragraphs in the group.
- Each writer should take his or her notes home, consider them, and make revisions in the paragraph.

Proofreading

The proofreading stage of the writing process is probably the one that most students neglect. In this stage, you edit your writing for grammar, punctuation, and sentence structure. Because some students don't know or aren't sure how to approach this task, perhaps overwhelmed by the many rules, they skip this stage and hope that the rest of the paper makes up for this deficiency.

However, proofreading can be done quite efficiently if you just take it one step at a time. Start by looking for the most serious types of errors in most students' writings. In this chapter, we focus on one major type of error, the sentence fragment.

Common Error #1: Sentence Fragments

A sentence fragment is a group of words that does not form a complete sentence. Since any complete sentence must have a subject and a verb, a fragment is missing a subject, a verb, or both, as shown here.

INCORRECT:	The lawn mower in the pickup truck. [Missing a verb]
CORRECT:	The lawn mower in the pickup truck failed to start.
INCORRECT:	Sat on the enormous, colorful, woven Oriental rug. [Missing a subject]
CORRECT:	The cat sat on the enormous, colorful, woven Oriental rug.
INCORRECT:	And the echoes of the loud drum. [Missing both subject and verb]
CORRECT:	The music teacher called for silence in the band room, annoyed by the bleating of the trumpets and the echoes of the loud drum.

GRAMMAR CHECKUP 2-1

Mark F for fragment or S for sentence. Repair the fragments by completing each item.
Answers will vary.

_____F_____ 1. An exquisite California Chardonnay from Napa Valley.

I prefer an exquisite California Chardonnay from Napa Valley.

_____F_____ 2. When you decide to quit.

When you decide to quit, be sure to turn in your tools.

_____F_____ 3. Attempting a difficult calculus problem.

Attempting a difficult calculus problem is a time-consuming task.

_____F_____ 4. Deep in the pine trees on the side of a mountain at an elevation of 13,000 feet.

Deep in the pine trees on the side of a mountain at an elevation of 13,000 feet sits my family cabin.

_____S_____ 5. As she began her descriptive paragraph, her mind filled with sensory details.

Check your answers to this Grammar Checkup on page A-1 in Appendix A. How did you do? If you missed one or more of these items, you may need to review in Chapter 15 how to identify and repair sentence fragments.

Proofread your paragraph. Check for and correct errors in spelling, punctuation, usage, and sentence structure. Personalize this checklist by adding specific errors that continue to occur in your writing.

Final Checklist

1. Does your paragraph begin with a clear topic sentence containing a vivid focus or dominant impression? ☐

2. Does your entire paragraph focus on one specific dominant impression and do all details support that impression? ☐

3. Does your paragraph contain lively and vivid description, using at least two senses to describe the topic? ☐

4. Will your description benefit from using figures of speech? If so, are the figures of speech fresh, unique, or interesting rather than clichéd? ☐

5. Is the organizational structure clear? ☐

6. Does your paragraph contain appropriate and smooth transitions between sentences? ☐

7. Have you used a variety of sentence structures, made sure your sentences are complete (no fragments), and checked carefully for errors in spelling, usage, and punctuation? ☐

Reflecting

Once you have incorporated suggestions from your reader that you feel improve your paragraph, you have completed the writing process. The following activity will help you reflect on what you've accomplished before you hand in your paper, as well as after you get it back with the instructor's comments.

Self-Reflection

Before you hand in your paper, answer the following questions:

1. What do you feel you did best?

2. What part of your paper was most challenging to you?

3. In which areas do you feel you need the most practice?

After you have completed this self-reflection, carefully review your instructor's comments. How are they similar or different from your own answers to the self-reflection? Make a list of your grammar, punctuation, and spelling errors so that you can follow up on the ones that recur. Consider what strategies you will employ to address your challenges or weaknesses and to improve the quality of your paragraph.

How might you use description outside of this English course? Look back at the writing samples in Previewing Your Task in this chapter.

- **College:** _____

- **Your profession:** _____

- **Everyday life:** _____

CHAPTER 3

Writing Your Descriptive Narrative Essay

"If stories come to you, care for them. And learn to give them away where they are needed. Sometimes a person needs a story more than food to stay alive."

■ Barry Lopez ■

YOUR GOALS

Understanding Narrative

1. Use narrative to explore and shape your personal history as well as to generate ideas for future writing.
2. Practice using listing and freewriting to discover a narrative topic.
3. Use an additional prewriting technique, questioning, to refine your topic.
4. Identify and apply a single overall purpose for your narrative.
5. Employ basic storytelling techniques to support your purpose.

Writing Your Descriptive Narrative Essay

1. Write a longer paper by exploring the essay form in the informal context of personal narrative.
2. Use appropriate diction to describe your characters' emotional states.
3. Use verbs to describe actions vividly.
4. Experiment with paragraphing.
5. Incorporate dialogue into your narrative.
6. Use transitions appropriate to narration.
7. Revise your essay for sentence fragments and shifts in verb tense.

One of the requirements listed in your American History syllabus is writing a 3-page personal narrative. The instructor explains that the reason for this assignment is to make you sensitive to the power of history in shaping our present lives. She mentions the slave narratives that helped so many students understand the importance of the civil rights movement in the 1960s.

Upon graduation from college, you apply for a job as an insurance adjustor for a national insurance agency. You are surprised to find that part of the application asks you to write a narrative about the most important event in your life. Although it seems to have little to do with the job, you decide to tell the story of the time you had to rush to the emergency room following your father's heart attack. Your boss tells you later that this narrative essay was the deciding factor in landing you the job.

Standing in line at the supermarket checkout, you spot an old friend you haven't seen since high school. One of the first questions you ask each other is "What have you been up to these last few years?" In response, each of you relates a brief personal history, touching on highlights such as jobs, relationships, children, places you've lived, and so on. Naturally, since the events you are narrating happened chronologically, this is how you relate them. In doing so, you tell a story that begins several years in the past and continues to the present.

These examples only begin to show the range of narrative purposes and contexts. When you tell a story, you could be telling a joke, making up a lie, writing a creative piece of fiction, or explaining to a judge what happened during a crime you witnessed. The list goes on. This chapter introduces you to some basic techniques and purposes of telling a story about yourself. This chapter also lets you experiment with a longer form—the essay—in a nonthreatening and informal context. Narratives can also form the basis of many other kinds of writing.

LET'S warm up!

Take a few moments to think about an event that happened to you recently—an encounter with an old friend, that big fish you caught, a funny episode in your child's development. In your notebook, do some freewriting on this event. Try to tell what happened as if you were speaking to a friend. As you write, think about *why* this event means something to you.

Tim Mueller/AP/Wide World Photos

PREVIEWING YOUR TASK

Why is narrative writing important in a class devoted to learning to write for college? The narrative offers several important benefits:

- It can help you "loosen up" and write naturally. Telling or listening to stories is so enjoyable that learning to write them down is a good way to gain a sense of comfort as a writer.
- You can use narrative as a brainstorming technique to generate ideas for future essays, regardless of the type of essay you are writing.
- You can employ narrative writing, even in expository and argumentative contexts, to introduce your essays and to provide supporting evidence for your body paragraphs.
- Because stories happen in time, you can begin to learn how to pace your writing and provide transitions to enhance the way it "flows." Furthermore, the natural pauses in the flow of most narratives give you the chance to practice describing people, scenery, and emotions.

Narrative writing can benefit you in other settings as well. Look at how narrative can be used in a variety of contexts.

Writing for College

The following essay was written by Jamie, a first-year student in a composition class. Notice the vivid language she uses to describe characters and events.

Just Like Riding a Bike

Shortly after I turned twenty-one, I started dating a Harley-Davidson-Motorcycle-Riding-Hunk, my father's worst nightmare. He brought excitement and danger into my somewhat sheltered life, and I was fascinated by the fact that he was everything that I wasn't. There was no doubt, however, that our differences led to some serious confusion.

At the time, I had my heart set on becoming the next great American poet. One night after spending several days revising and organizing a handful of my poems into a small but proud book, I agreed to take a break and enjoy a warm summer night out with my hunk. As we sat down upon our bar stools, I announced that I had finished my first book. A smile took over his chiseled face. Before that moment he had seemed so disinterested—even oblivious—to my interests in writing, so I was a bit taken aback by his sudden enthusiasm. He looked at me, lovingly, and said, "So which book did you finish reading, anyway?" Perhaps our romance had been doomed from the start. But as I look back now, I see that indeed my biker babe taught me a lot more about writing than either of us would have thought possible.

When he first instructed me to balance on one leg while swinging the other up and over the pile of growling metal, I was horrified. I simply had no idea how intimidating a task it would be just merely to sit on the bike until I stood there beside it. With very little confidence, I took a deep breath and flung my right leg over the seat with clumsy precision. But to my sheer delight, I opened my eyes to find that I hadn't broken any small or large parts on the bike *or myself,* so I then eased into the seat with a satisfied grin.

The very moment we took off for the first time, I instantly became more aware of my own mortality. But after a few miles, I figured out where to keep my hands and where best to prop my feet, and I was somehow able to stop worrying about how long it would take to brush the knots out of my hair. Suddenly, the familiar streets of my hometown started coming to life for me in ways they never had before.

Studying poetry certainly had fueled my desire to write. But my summer romance that year taught me that the more *life* I experienced, the better writer I became. Every stylistic technique I had learned from the great writers was useless to me if I had no stories to tell. And the more things I discovered, the more anxious I was to write. A few days later, my motorcycle man dumped me for some perky blonde. And the poems that I wrote as a result are some of my favorites to this day.

PRACTICE   3-1

1. One of the elements of this style is her use of verbs that convey action and motion to the reader's imagination—verbs such as *balance* and *flung*. Take a few moments to underline five other such verbs throughout the essay.

2. What else do you find engaging and interesting about this essay? _____
   Her vivid description of getting on the motorcycle, the contrast between her interests and her boyfriend's, the humor, and so on.

3. What suggestions would you give the writer to improve this narrative? _____
   More physical description of the boyfriend.

   _____

Writing in Your Profession

Although writing on the job often "looks" different from the other types of writing you encounter—that is, it is more highly formatted and stylistically uniform—it uses the same writing techniques you are learning to employ in this class. The sample that follows is a trip report, a common form of writing in business.

Memorandum

Date: June 15, 2008
From: Giorgio Pizzarelli
To: Dr. Lana Carter
Subject: Trip Report—NCSD Conference, 2008

Dr. Carter:

This is a report on my recent attendance at the 2008 NCSD Conference in Austin, Texas.

Background:

The conference was held at the Austin Convention Center from May 11 to May 13, 2008. The keynote speakers were Dr. Alvin Rollins, head of product development at MicroTech, and Mary Howell, president of that company. Sessions focused on two main topics: research and development on the one hand, and management techniques on the other.

Description:

I attended more sessions on management than on R&D. They were led by national experts on managing change in our industry during this difficult time. One R&D session, however, had particular application to my own project. Several researchers from Colorado State University at Pueblo presented a panel discussion on the latest uses of digital radio frequency devices on the commercial market. Their presentation was eye-opening, to say the least. The other sessions were generally useful in terms of managing new technology integration.

Recommendations:

1. We should invite CSU-P researchers to present at one of our monthly staff meetings.
2. The project management cycle needs more focus on quality improvement.
3. The first day of the conference is not worth our attendance. I recommend that we send representatives only to the second and third days next year.

Let me know if I can provide further information.

PRACTICE   3-2

1. Notice that, like a lot of writing in various professions, this report contains headings for each major section. How do these headings help the reader? _____
   They provide a clear guide to the different types of information and allow
   the reader to skim easily to read the information most relevant to him or her.

2. If this were not a piece of writing about professional concerns, how would you indicate the various sections of the essay—the beginning, the middle, and the end? <u>You might use transitions like "first," "second," and "finally" to</u> <u>guide the reader through the sections of the essay.</u>

Writing in Everyday Life

In our daily lives, we use storytelling techniques to support many kinds of writing: complaint or request letters to companies, letters to friends or family, and letters to the editor of a local newspaper. The author of the following sample is requesting a scholarship to further his college studies.

Because my academic achievements and community service go beyond the standards of the Perkins Presidential Scholarship, I am a deserving candidate for this award to support my studies in the 2008–9 academic year. The story of my personal and intellectual growth will testify to my scholastic promise, leadership potential, and ability to overcome obstacles.

I grew up in a small town in the southwest mountains of Colorado. Neither of my parents graduated from high school, but they worked hard at a variety of service jobs to raise their family. From our earliest school days, my brother and sister and I would pitch in after school and help with household chores, for my parents would not return home until late.

When I reached the age of 16, my father died suddenly. At the time, there was no option except to drop out of school and work to help support the family. Two years later, I watched my friends' high school graduation from the bleachers of our football stadium. That is when I decided on a different course of action.

Even while I continued working to support my family, I began studying, again late at night, to attain my GED. Having accomplished that goal, I enrolled in my local community college and began taking night classes. There I discovered that my early study habits had paved the way for academic success. After two years, I graduated with an associate of arts degree in business management and a GPA of 4.0—straight A's! Fortunately, our area also is home to Ft. Lewis College, where I enrolled as a junior last year. I broadened my extracurricular activities to include volunteering in the migrant community and serving as president of the campus business club. I did all of this while starting my own lawn care business, which now employs 10 part-time employees.

Now, as my senior year approaches, I look forward to continued service to my campus and community. It is my hope to contribute to society by integrating the principles of sound management into businesses and volunteer organizations in my community.

Thank you for considering my application for the Perkins Scholarship. I look forward to continuing the tradition of excellence that it represents.

1. Although this is part of a formal application for a scholarship, it relies on narrative to convince the reader that the application is worth considering. Do you think it succeeds? Why or why not? _____
    Yes, the narrative establishes the student's financial need, motivation, hard work, and excellent academic record.

2. How is the writing style in this letter different from that in "Just Like Riding a Bike" on page 44? Why are they different? _____
    The style is more formal and has a sense of a specific audience—the scholarship committee and a specific request. The two writings have different purposes: one is an entertaining story to illustrate a point; the other is a request for financial assistance based on deserving qualities.

UNDERSTANDING NARRATIVE

A personal narrative is a story—that is, it can use all the techniques that a good short story writer, or a good teller of jokes, employs—but it is based on something that has happened to the author. So it is a "true" story, a nonfiction representation, of a shaping event in your own life.

Using the Elements of Plot

When we think back on important events in our lives, we naturally think about what happened first, what happened next, and so on. But there is more to storytelling than just chronology. For instance, when we tell jokes (which are, after all, very short stories), don't we time the punch line carefully so that it lands with just the right effect? A joke, in other words, is more than just the sequence of events it describes—it leads to a specific and calculated point. Similarly, we tell stories not just to relate events in time but also to demonstrate the meaning of those events.

Any good story is founded on a plot, a sequence of events that enables the characters in the story to learn something, solve a problem, or achieve a new understanding about some issue. This is true of short stories, novels, narrative poems, and even movies and television shows. When you describe what happens in a book or movie in chronological order, you are describing the plot, the events of the story.

Most plots can be broken into three components: *the beginning, the middle,* and *the end.*

The Beginning

The beginning of your personal narrative should "set the scene." It does so by introducing the setting of the narrative (the place and time in which the story occurs), some or all of the main characters who appear in the story, and the general conflict or other situation the story focuses on. The beginning of the story also establishes the tone of the narrative, whether it is humorous, suspenseful, reflective, peaceful, and so on. The beginning of a narrative might occupy one paragraph or several, depending on what you want to say about the setting, characters, and conflict.

The Middle

The middle of the story is where the action takes place. Here, the conflict introduced in the beginning causes the characters to interact with one another in certain ways. The middle is the section of the story that leads to the climax—the high point of the story, the point at which the reader feels the most emotional intensity—through a pattern of rising action or rising intensity. Often, the climax itself occurs at the end of the middle section of the narrative.

There is no right or wrong length for this section of the essay. Some events take longer than others to narrate; just keep in mind that the event you narrate should unfold naturally and without unnecessary detail.

The End

The end of the narrative is where the meaning of the story is revealed or shown. Usually, the end is shorter than the other sections. It might be a paragraph in which you summarize the lesson you learned from the events you've narrated. It could even be a sentence in which you state the "moral" of the story. Sometimes, the climax of the story happens at the end and the meaning of the events is left to the reader to experience alone.

Collaborative Critical Thinking

In groups of four or five, develop a "group story" on any topic. Pick an event that you all have in common, such as registering for classes at your college or attending class for the first day. Make sure your story has a distinct beginning, middle, and end.

Share your story with the other groups and ask them to identify the beginning, middle, end, and climax of the story. Also, ask them to comment on the details of the narrative. What information would improve the narrative?

Supporting Your Narrative

To engage your reader in your story, you must choose your support carefully. Your narrative must provide concrete and descriptive detail to support your main point. What information do you need to give your readers so that they understand your point? What effect or effects do you want your narrative to have on your readers? Choosing the most effective support is essential to addressing those two questions.

Using Descriptive Language

Most narratives use lots of sensory description to help the reader see and hear the characters, scenes, and events of the story.

However, description can often interrupt the flow of a narrative because the observer has actually "stopped" to observe and describe. Although it's fine to stop, observe, and describe some feature of the landscape or some character or emotion, it is important to keep the pace of the narrative moving.

Using Words to Describe Emotions

You can add enormous depth to your writing by showing your reader how your characters feel and what they think about the events you are describing. Although emotions are physical feelings based on chemical changes in the brain, they can't be described fully just by words that appeal to the five senses: *red, rough, sour, grating,* and *stinky,* for instance.

You need a different vocabulary to describe your characters' emotional responses to the events in their lives. Here is a list of words that you can use as a starting point in describing emotional states.

> **Bridging Knowledge**
>
> **See Chapter 2** if you need to review the concepts of description that might help you paint a more vivid word picture for your reader.

Words to Describe Emotions

abandoned	bashful	conflicted	discouraged	enthusiastic	generous
affectionate	beaten	confused	disgusted	envious	giddy
afraid	belligerent	content	displeased	exasperated	glad
aggravated	bewildered	courageous	dissatisfied	excited	grief-stricken
aggressive	bitter	curious	disturbed	exhausted	grumpy
agitated	blissful	defeated	dumb	exuberant	guilty
alarmed	bored	defensive	ecstatic	fearful	happy
angry	bothered	defiant	edgy	foolish	hateful
annoyed	calm	delighted	elated	forgiving	helpless
anxious	cautious	depressed	embarrassed	frail	hesitant
apprehensive	clumsy	desperate	excited	frantic	hilarious
arrogant	comfortable	destroyed	encouraged	frightened	hopeful
ashamed	compassionate	determined	energetic	frustrated	hopeless
awkward	confident	disappointed	enraged	furious	horrified

hostile	jolly	overjoyed	resentful	submissive	uneasy
humble	joyful	overwhelmed	restless	sullen	unglued
humiliated	lively	panicky	sad	surly	unhappy
hurt	lonely	paranoid	safe	surprised	unloved
hysterical	lost	pensive	satisfied	suspicious	unprepared
impatient	mad	perplexed	scared	sympathetic	unsure
impotent	mean	petrified	seething	tearful	upset
indecisive	meek	powerful	shaky	tender	vigorous
indifferent	merry	powerless	shameful	tense	virile
indignant	mischievous	proud	sheepish	terrified	warm
innocent	miserable	puzzled	shocked	thankful	weak
insecure	mistreated	quarrelsome	shy	thoughtful	weepy
inspired	nauseated	reckless	silly	threatened	whiny
insulted	neglected	regretful	smug	timid	wild
interested	nervous	rejected	sorrowful	tired	withdrawn
irresponsible	obstinate	relaxed	sorry	tormented	worried
irritated	offended	relieved	starry-eyed	touchy	worthless
isolated	optimistic	repressed	stubborn	trapped	
jealous	outraged	repulsive	stupid	unappreciated	

UNDERSTANDING NARRATIVE

PRACTICE   3-4

In the sentences that follow, provide appropriate words to describe emotional states. Use the Words to Describe Emotions chart to stimulate your thinking, but feel free to think of other words. Answers will vary.

1. __Nervous__, __determined__, and ___eager___, Beth rushed over to shake the governor's hand.

2. Feeling __relieved__ and __exhausted__, the boy sank to his knees after yanking his puppy from the river.

3. The day I passed that class, I thought I'd never again be more __challenged__.

4. In some cultures, women are taught to act _____timid_____ around men, whether or not they feel __powerless__.

5. The roller coaster caused me, the 50-year-old "kid," to have sensations of __exhilaration__ and ____nausea____.

Using Verbs Effectively

Add another concept to your descriptive arsenal: using verbs effectively. When we think of the word *verb*, we often think of everyone's favorite definition: "action word." But some verbs convey no action, and others convey "actions" that are not dynamic in their effect on the reader. Read the following passage:

> The forest was dark green, and the clouds just above the trees were gray and threatening. From where I sat, on the hill above the cottage, I could see the swans flying just between the clouds and the treetops. They were precise in their unison, almost like a ballet in air.

In these few sentences, you find some of the concrete sensual detail you have come to appreciate in descriptive writing. However, pay attention to the *verbs* in these sentences. Notice that the past tense form of the *be* verb occurs three times, twice in the first sentence (*was, were*) and once in the third sentence (*were*). Does the *be* verb convey action or motion? It does not.

The *be* verb is one of several verbs in English that merely equates two things or a thing and its characteristics—for instance, *Alva is a doctor*, or *She is conscientious*. Notice that the main verb in these sentences just equates the two sides of the sentence, almost like an = sign in a math problem. It lacks the character of action.

Although the other verbs in the preceding passage—*sat* and *could see*—convey actions of a sort, they do not convey vivid, flowing, descriptive action. They are flat in their effect on the reader. There is nothing wrong with these verbs, but as a writer, you should ask yourself this question: What other verbs might convey the same basic meaning but in a more vivid, memorable way?

There are two additional principles of vivid writing that are especially useful in description and narration:

1. **Do not overuse the *be* verb as the main verb of your sentences.** Sometimes you can't avoid it, but you should try to use it sparingly.

2. **Select action verbs that paint mental pictures of dynamic action.** Examine how the passage can be revised so that it takes on a more descriptive verbal style.

> The forest <u>loomed</u> dark and green, and the clouds <u>lowered</u> above the trees, gray and threatening. From where I <u>watched</u>, on the hill above the cottage, <u>I could trace</u> the swans' path as they <u>beat</u> the mist between the clouds and the treetops. They <u>dipped</u> in precise unison, almost like a ballet in air.

PRACTICE   3-5

Propose five vivid verbs to replace the main verbs in the following sentences. Use a dictionary or thesaurus. If you are in a computer classroom, log on to the Internet and search for verbal equivalents. Share your answers with the class. Answers will vary.

1.   Three teenage girls are walking into the mall.   Strolling, ambling, rushing, sauntering, marching

2. The old horse went from the stable to the yard and stopped. ___Plodded,___
   trudged, limped, ambled, crept

3. The water in the stream goes quickly downhill. ___Rushes, pours,___
   tumbles, flows, cascades

4. Philosophy students like to think about the great questions of life. _Ponder,_
   ruminate, consider, deliberate, meditate

5. The racecars drove around the track, barely missing one another. _Streaked,_
   barreled, sped, accelerate, whipped

Using Dialogue

Your narrative doesn't necessarily have to contain dialogue, but many narratives are based on interactions among people: discussions, arguments, questions and answers, and so on. Therefore, you need to be aware of some common conventions of writing dialogue.

Bridging Knowledge

See Chapter 27 for additional review and further practice with punctuating dialogue.

Keep the following rules in mind as you try to report the speech of your characters.

1. **Use quotation marks.** When you are writing down the words uttered by your characters directly, enclose those words in quotation marks.

   > Fred said that he's going to climb Pikes Peak.

   Fred's speech is reported not directly but *indirectly*; the author is merely stating the content—not the exact words—of Fred's utterance.

   > Fred said, "I'm going to climb Pikes Peak."

   The author is stating *directly* the exact words Fred uttered and therefore must use quotation marks.

2. **Use correct capitalization within quotations.** Begin quoted sentences with a capital letter. When quoted sentences are interrupted, continue in lowercase.

   > "I'm going to climb Pikes Peak," Fred said, "even if it kills me."

3. **Use correct punctuation within and between quotations.** If a speaker asks a question, make sure the question ends with a question mark. Use commas correctly, just as you would in writing contexts that contain no dialogue.

   > "Are you going to climb Pikes Peak, Fred?" asked Marita. "Do you think you are ready for that?"
   >
   > Fred answered, "Yes, even if it kills me!"
   >
   > "I don't think it's a wise idea," Marita responded, "when you can't even climb two flights of stairs."
   >
   > "I'm climbing Pikes Peak and that's all there is to it!" Fred shouted angrily.

4. **Start a new paragraph when the speaker changes.** Don't worry about having too many short paragraphs when reporting a conversation. Your reader expects a new paragraph to begin each time the speaker changes. Notice in the preceding conversation that when the speaker changes from Fred to Marita, or vice versa, a new paragraph begins.

5. **Identify speakers.** When needed, indicate to the reader exactly who is speaking by inserting phrases such as "Fred said." Otherwise, if two characters (or more) are engaged in conversation, your reader won't be able to tell who is saying what. However, to avoid constant repetition of conversational tags such as "Fred said" and "he said," experiment with different tags to provide variety and interest to your dialogue, as well as reveal your character's feelings, attitude, behavior, or personality. Try to capture just the right emotional situation of each exchange.

The following list may help you vary the word *said*, as well as help you establish the mood you want when you're writing dialogue.

Alternatives to "Said"

accepted	challenged	exclaimed	mandated	reassured	spoke
accused	chuckled	explained	mimicked	remarked	squealed
acknowledged	coaxed	exploded	moaned	reminded	stammered
added	commanded	giggled	mocked	repeated	stated
admitted	complained	groaned	moralized	replied	stressed
agreed	confessed	grumbled	mumbled	reprimanded	stuttered
announced	confided	hollered	murmured	requested	suggested
appealed	confirmed	implored	muttered	responded	swore
argued	consented	injected	nagged	retorted	taunted
asked	cried out	inquired	objected	ridiculed	teased
babbled	criticized	insinuated	opposed	roared	threatened
bantered	debated	insisted	ordered	scolded	thundered
barked	declared	interrogated	persisted	screamed	urged
began	demanded	interrupted	pleaded	shouted	uttered
bellowed	denied	jeered	praised	shrieked	vented
beseeched	dictated	jested	prayed	slurred	vowed
blared	disagreed	joked	probed	snapped	warned
blasted	disputed	justified	quarreled	sneered	wept
boasted	echoed	lamented	questioned	snickered	whined
bragged	emphasized	lashed out	ranted	sobbed	whispered
cautioned	encouraged	lied	reasoned	spluttered	yelled

　　It's not always necessary to use one of these words or a phrase after each line of dialogue. Many times, the speaker and the mood are obvious, so no such word is needed.

WRITING YOUR DESCRIPTIVE NARRATIVE ESSAY

This section guides you through the writing of your own descriptive narrative essay. Look at a descriptive narrative essay written by Joe, a 28-year-old community college student enrolled in English classes to fulfill the requirements for entry into the Emergency Medical Services program.

A Hot Valentine's Night

　　My parents live in an old two-story house in Ordway, Colorado. It was built at the turn of the century, and because it is so old, it is considered a fire hazard. The wooden structure is a fire's favorite meal because the wood is old and dry. Once, my mom thought about the chances of having a fire and bought a smoke detector, but Dad never installed it.

　　"Who needs a smoke alarm?" he barked. "The only time they work is when there is a fire, and this house hasn't had a fire in it since it was built. Next time, buy something worthwhile—there's never going to be a fire here!"

　　I figured Dad was right and that I didn't need to worry about a fire either. Ten years later, I learned that I was wrong. I wished I'd worried about the possibility of fire, and I wished I had installed the smoke detector myself.

　　In 1997, I was living with my parents to save some cash for my upcoming wedding. It was pleasant living back home with Mom and Pop. Mom would do my laundry and always had supper when I got home from work. Most evenings I'd eat supper and then go see my fiancée, Eva.

　　On the evening of Valentine's Day that year, I came home late after visiting Eva and noticed that my mom had washed some of my work shirts and hung them on a rack close to the floor furnace to dry. As I felt one of the shirts to see if it was dry, I noticed the rack was closer to the hot furnace than usual, but I thought nothing of it. My parents were asleep in their bedroom on the main level. I figured it was time to turn in for the night too and climbed the stairs to my bedroom. I shut the door at the top of the stairs before going to my room.

　　Later that night, I sat straight up in bed from a sound sleep. It was as if something had grabbed me by the neck and pulled me up. Even though I was in a sleepy daze, I realized I was smelling smoke. Somehow I convinced myself it was my waterbed heater and that I could wait until morning to look at it. I was about to doze off again when suddenly, from downstairs, I heard a loud pop.

　　I jumped out of bed and bolted to the door. Instantly, smoke surrounded me, and I saw the fire jumping up one of the living room walls, devouring a curtain. The smoke was so thick that the fire looked like distant headlights in a heavy fog.

"Fire!" I screamed as I raced down the stairs. "Fire!" My adrenalin was pumping as I ran downstairs. I was yelling to my parents. Their bedroom was just down the hall from the living room, and my yelling woke them. My mom and dad came flying down the hall with buckets of water.

The fire had started when one of my work shirts slipped off the rack and landed on the hot furnace grate. The shirt probably smoldered for awhile before finally catching on fire. Obviously, a smoke detector would have sensed the smoke from the smoldering shirt and warned us before the shirt caught on fire.

I still shake when I think about how close we came to losing our lives and our home. If the fire had been any more intense, it would have burned the house to the ground. No house is immune from fire, but it is a much safer place with a smoke detector installed in it.

Joe's essay has all the elements of a good narrative: a well-structured plot containing a vivid climax as well as good descriptions of characters, events, and emotions. Follow his writing process as he develops his essay.

Prewriting

The first stage of the writing process helps you find a topic, limit your topic, focus your ideas, and plan your essay.

Discovering and Limiting Your Topic

In Chapter 2, we introduced you to listing and freewriting, two commonly used prewriting techniques to generate topic ideas and supporting detail for a composition. In the context of narration, both techniques can be extremely productive.

Prewriting Strategies #1 and #2: Listing and Freewriting

As Joe began thinking about a topic for his narrative essay, he decided to try his favorite technique, listing, first. Here is his list:

Catching my first fish as a fly fisherman
The house almost burning down
Realizing Eva was the one for me
That time I threw the computer out the window
Coming back to school after 13 years
Discovering my love of animation
Buying my first car
Watching Ronnie get hit by lightning on the golf course

You'd be surprised at the number of important happenings in your life that you've forgotten, so give listing a chance to work. Try to remember not just things that happened to you but also times when you changed your mind about something or came to realize a new truth.

Joe chose not to do a second listing, and, instead, he moved directly to freewriting because it seemed to him a natural way to begin telling a story. Notice that Joe begins his freewriting by focusing on one of his topics but that he moves to another.

> I thought this was going to be an easy assignment for me because I like to tell stories, but I'm having a hard time getting started. I'm stuck! I'm stuck! Writing a story is a lot different than telling one. . . . Anyway, what about the time I threw the computer out the window? There I was, working on a high school assignment . . . I don't even remember what class! I'd been saving all my work every few lines, making sure I wouldn't lose anything if the power went out, and here it was just . . . dead. It didn't matter how many times I saved my work, I'd never see it again as long as I lived. My bedroom was on the second floor of the house right above the driveway. I lost my temper and hoisted the darned thing (one of those old clunkers that weigh 100 pounds) over to the window and out onto the concrete below. God that felt good. Well, so what? Is that the end of the story? What did I learn from THAT? How good it feels to destroy something. Wait a minute! Speaking of being on the second floor, the time the house almost burned down!!!! Now there's a topic with a lesson attached! What's the lesson? Don't listen to your stubborn dad—buy a smoke alarm. Yeah!

As you can see, you should feel free to roam where your memory and imagination take you.

WRITING 3-1

Use listing and freewriting to explore some of your own ideas. In a notebook, create a prewriting list of potential topics for your personal narrative essay. Try to list as many events as you can in 10 minutes. Choose an event and freewrite for 10 minutes about it. Remember the rules of freewriting: don't stop writing—just let your thoughts flow onto the page—and don't worry about grammar or spelling.

Prewriting Strategy #3: Questioning

After doing some listing and freewriting, you may feel that you are beginning to settle on a topic that you know a great deal about. Or you may still feel a bit lost in selecting a topic.

Questioning as a prewriting technique involves asking yourself, or having a classmate or friend ask you, a series of probing questions about the topic idea you are considering. Usually, the questions are fairly straightforward, but they are designed to make you reflect on what you know about the topic. In the case of narrative, the best questions are the traditional "reporter's" questions: Who? What? When? Where? Why? and How?

- *Who* is involved in your narrative besides yourself?
- *What* event or conflict will you narrate?
- *When* and *where* did the story take place?
- *Why* is this story important? *What* did you learn from it?
- *How* did you change as a result of your involvement? How are things different now?

After Joe decided to explore the story about his house catching fire, he decided to answer the reporter's questions as they pertained to his topic.

Who?	Well, there's me, of course. I'm the main character in the story because I'm the one who wakes up first and discovers the fire. I'm also the one who alerts the rest of the house.
	Then there's Dad. He's the stubborn one who makes fun of Mom for wanting to install a smoke alarm in the house. And since a narrative is better developed when there's conflict between a couple of characters, Mom and Dad certainly had a conflict on this issue.
What?	The house catching fire when one of my shirts slips off the drying rack and falls onto the furnace in the basement.
When?	This happened when I was . . . I could just tell my age or how long ago it was. On the other hand, since I was getting ready to marry. . . . I might just use the impending wedding as a way to give a sense of the time in my own life when this happened. We'll see . . .
Where?	Ordway, Colorado, my hometown. I wonder if I should mention the name of the town. I guess I will. People will know from my setting that it's a rural area with lots of older houses.
Why?	Why did this happen? Well, it would have happened even if we had smoke alarms, but we would have known about the danger a lot sooner if we had them. Anyway, we sure didn't wait very long to install alarms after the fire! And that's the "why" of this essay.
How?	I guess, maybe I should describe how my father reacted. Should I include how he felt knowing that his decision not to invest in a smoke detector could have cost us our lives? The experience made me realize that we don't live forever and that life is precious.

WRITING 3-2

Answer the reporter's questions to probe your knowledge and understanding of your topic.

TOPICS TO CONSIDER

The topic ideas listed here demonstrate the range of narrative contexts and uses. Remember, however, that these ideas are broad. You must still perform some prewriting (listing, freewriting, and questioning) to narrow your topic and make it more concrete and interesting.

Writing for College		
■ The events of your week ■ The events of a historical figure ■ Your reaction to a recent ethical dilemma	■ The need for recycling ■ A meeting with a famous political figure, artist, writer, scientist, or psychologist	■ A specific culture; describing an important value of that culture

Writing in Your Profession			
BUSINESS	■ A conference you attended and the main "lesson" you returned with ■ Your interaction with an irate customer	■ A conflict in the workplace that affected teamwork or productivity	■ Professional or unprofessional behavior and consequences
CRIMINAL JUSTICE	■ An event leading to the arrest of a suspect	■ The way an emergency was handled ■ A hate crime	■ The benefits or dangers of an early-release program
EDUCATION	■ Your accomplishments as a teacher as part of your annual evaluation	■ A lesson plan ■ A conflict between faculty and administrators	■ A school safety issue
HEALTH	■ The progress of disease reported by one of your patients	■ A hospital emergency that tested the staff's ability to work as a team	■ An accident resulting from the mishandling of equipment ■ The way a person neglects his or her health
SOCIAL WORK/ PSYCHOLOGY	■ Healthy family interactions ■ An abusive relationship or situation	■ A defense mechanism ■ A consequence of divorce on either the child or the couple	■ The effect(s) of a specific tragedy on a family, a group, or an individual
TECHNICAL	■ An observation of a person's frustration with technology ■ The misuse of a specific technology	■ Effective or ineffective technical support	■ The effects of a certain technology or method
OTHERS	■ An event that inspired you to pursue a specific career ■ An event that challenged you physically or emotionally	■ The significance of "an act of kindness"	■ An urban legend and the reason for its popularity

Writing in Everyday Life		
■ An event in your family life that will be important in some way to your children ■ The story of your breakup with a boyfriend or girlfriend, written in letter form to your best friend	■ An event that demonstrates a unique quality of your community ■ A trip to a specific place that holds special meaning to you	■ An event that changed a relationship ■ A reason a person would lie, the potential consequence of a lie, or both

What interesting events have you discovered so far? List three possible topics that you feel are worth discussing.

Topic #1: _____

Topic #2: _____

Topic #3: _____

Identifying Your Audience

In Chapter 2, we asked you to begin thinking about your audience by envisioning your classmates as the audience for your descriptive paragraph. At this point, we introduce the notion of *analyzing* your audience. To analyze is to break something into its parts so that you better understand the whole. To analyze the audience of your writing is usually to list some of its characteristics. If you can name some of the most important characteristics of your audience, you can then decide what your audience wants or needs.

Establishing Your Purpose

We have already said that your narrative purpose is usually to demonstrate a sequence of events and a sequence of interactions that have taught you something, resolved a conflict, or caused you to understand something differently. Suppose you want to write a personal narrative about the time your car was wrecked because you let an intoxicated friend drive it after a party. Obviously, you think it is important to tell the story to others. And who are those others? Your audience often is implied by your purpose; in thinking of one, you automatically think of the other.

Setting Your Tone

Whatever event or experience you decide to write about, chances are that you have strong feelings about it. To return to the example of the car wreck, at this point in your life you obviously think of the event with a complex set of emotions: lingering fear, regret, gratitude that no one was injured, and so on. In your essay, you need to ensure that you convey your attitude about the seriousness of an event—as well as the importance of the lesson you learned.

WRITING 3-4

Stop a moment to reflect on your audience, purpose, and tone. Fill in the following form.

Audience, Purpose, and Tone Analysis

I. Audience
1. Who is your audience? _____
2. How old is your audience? _____
3. What is their education level? _____
4. Are they employed? _____
5. What kind of work do they do? _____
6. What is their social life like? _____
7. What are their hobbies? _____
8. What are their values or concerns about contemporary issues? _____
    _____

II. Your Purpose
1. Why are you writing for this particular audience? _____
    _____
2. What effect do you hope to have on your audience? _____
    _____

III. Tone
1. What tone should you adopt in this essay? Nostalgic? Humorous? Grave and serious? Other? _____

Formulating Your Thesis

As you already know, you must have a reason for telling your story. This reason becomes the main point of the narrative. The main point can usually be expressed in a single sentence, and this sentence is called the *thesis*.

When determining your thesis, ask yourself, "What is the point I'm trying to make in this story? What insight did I gain about people, life, my community, or the world in general through this experience that I feel is worth sharing with my reader?" The answer to both questions leads you to a thesis.

Determining and writing your thesis is a simple process. You're more familiar with thesis statements than you believe. Think of the many stories, legends, and myths that you've heard in your lifetime. You can almost hear the narrator saying, "And the moral of this story is—." This is what your thesis does; it gives meaning and purpose to your narrative essay.

Topic: A narrative on a childhood experience
Possible Thesis Statements:
1. Children should be allowed to explore their environment.
2. Childhood is not always the most pleasant time.
3. Childhood is a feeling most people try to recapture later in life, but few ever succeed.
4. The shocking realization that parents lie is a child's first step into adulthood.

Wherever you state it in the essay, your thesis must be clear. Usually, it is stated in the beginning or near the end of the essay; however, it's not unusual for some narratives to leave the main point unstated. Omitting the main point does not mean that the narrative has no thesis. Since the main point is obvious to the reader, the writer feels that it's not necessary to state it; thus the thesis is implied.

As Joe formulated his thesis, he decided to keep it simple and direct. Using the pattern shown earlier, he wrote the following:

Topic: The time our house almost burned down
Audience: People who don't have smoke alarms in their houses
Working Thesis: In telling this story, I hope to show that it's a good idea to install smoke detectors in your house, especially if it's old and susceptible to fire.

WRITING 3-5

Take a minute to write down your topic, audience, and working thesis. It's important that you maintain these ideas throughout the process.

Topic: _____

Audience: _____

Working Thesis: _____

_____

Outlining Your Ideas

You'll be happy to learn that narrative outlines are fairly straightforward. Since they contain an identifiable beginning, middle, and end, they can be easily represented in a three-part outline:

   I. **Beginning**
  II. **Middle**
 III. **End**

Furthermore, because narratives are made of events in time order and of descriptions of people, places, and moods, it's relatively easy to build the outline for your own essay. Here's Joe's rough outline:

ESSAY OUTLINE

I. Beginning: Set the scene
  A. Introduce the family home in Ordway
  B. Old, dry wood
  C. Mom buying a smoke detector; Dad refusing to install it
  D. Living there before I married Eva
  E. Introduce Mom and Dad
  F. Set the scene: Valentine's night, checking the laundry, going to bed

II. Middle: The story of the fire
  A. Waking up in the middle of the night, smelling smoke
  B. Hearing a pop, jumping out of bed, running downstairs
  C. Seeing smoke and fire in the living room
  E. Yelling to wake Mom and Dad
  F. Mom and Dad put the fire out with buckets of water

III. End: What we learned
  A. How the fire started
  B. What could have happened
  C. What would probably have happened with a smoke detector
  D. The lesson I learned: "Make sure you install a smoke detector." That should be obvious to the reader. Leave it out?

As you create your outline, don't hesitate to circle, underline, or italicize places where you need to add description when you draft your paper. Your outline is your plan, so feel free to personalize it.

W R I T I N G   3-6

Use the following outline form as the basis for your own outline.

Narrative Essay Outline

Audience: _____

Thesis: _____

_____

I. Beginning: Set the scene _____

    A. _____

    B. _____

    C. _____

    D. _____

II. Middle: Tell the story _____

    A. _____

    B. _____

    C. _____

    D. _____

III. End: Describe the current situation _____

    A. _____

    B. _____

    C. _____

    D. _____

Drafting

Armed with a good working thesis and a clear preliminary outline, you can approach the drafting stage with confidence. Right now, you don't need to concern yourself with the overall flow of the paper. In this stage, you're going to flesh out your ideas, not correct them. If you get stuck in any one section, jump to another.

Paragraphing

The term *paragraphing* refers to starting and stopping paragraphs. Sometimes it's difficult to decide when to end one paragraph and begin another. We propose some general guidelines for paragraphing in a personal narrative essay (Note: Paragraphing in expository essays has a different and more definite set of rules, as you will discover in Chapter 5.)

    Start a new paragraph in these situations:

1. **When the setting changes.** If your characters move from one place to another or if one bit of action happens in the morning and the next in the afternoon (just two examples from many possibilities), help your reader "see" the change of setting by starting a new paragraph.

2. **When the action takes a major step forward.** Some narratives contain dramatic events; others are subtle and might consist more of changes in thinking than of

actual events. Nonetheless, when you feel that your action is moving from one phase to another, help your reader perceive this change by beginning a new paragraph.

3. **When the dialogue switches from one speaker to another.** This is a convention of writing dialogue that you are probably quite familiar with from your personal reading.

Try applying just these three paragraphing rules to your narrative. Once you have written a draft, go back through it looking for places to insert additional paragraph breaks. Try to achieve a balance between paragraphs that are too long and contain too much detail and paragraphs that are too short, creating a distracting lack of continuity.

Writing Your Beginning

You may have seen the *Peanuts* cartoon featuring Snoopy sitting on his doghouse with a typewriter and typing as the first sentence of his great American novel the following: "It was a dark and stormy night." This sentence is actually part of the famous opening sentence of a novel by the nineteenth-century British author Edward George Bulwer-Litton. It is often taken as a tongue-in-cheek example of bad fiction writing.

> Write your working **Computer tip** thesis (the lesson you learned) at the top of a page or computer screen before you begin drafting on that page. When you move on to another page, write your working thesis again at the top of the page. This keeps your purpose right in front of you during the writing process.

But when you think about it, what's really wrong with "It was a dark and stormy night," apart from the fact that it is unoriginal? Doesn't it meet at least one of the requirements of a story's beginning? Doesn't it begin to set the scene? That is your first priority in the opening of your narrative. You want to describe where you are when the narrative begins, what time of year and day it is (if appropriate), and who will be participating in the story with you.

At the beginning of a narrative, you need to set the scene efficiently and briefly because the real point of the narrative is the story itself. Therefore, try to write the opening of your narrative in just a few paragraphs. You can devote a good bit of the beginning to pure description of place, time, people, mood, and situation. Finally, try not to begin the chronological narration of events until the beginning section is over. Your beginning should leave the reader with a clear visual picture of the important aspects of setting.

Here is the first draft of Joe's beginning section. Notice that, because it is a first draft, it is only the starting point for further work.

A Hot Valentine's Night

My parents live in an old two-story house in Ordway, Colorado. It is very old. It is considered a fire hazard because the wood is old and dry. Once, my mom thought about the chances of having a fire and bought a smoke detector. Dad never installed it.

He would just complain about smoke alarms never working. He would also say to Mom that there would never be fire in our house . . . because there never had been!

During that time, I was living with my parents to save some cash for my upcoming wedding. It was pleasant to be back home with Mom and Pop. Mom would do my laundry. She always had supper. Whenever I got home from work, there it was ready for me. I'd eat quickly and go see my fiancée. Her name is Eva.

Writing Your Middle

This section of your paper is where the main events of your story occur. To state it simply: first this happened, then this happened, and so on. Unfortunately, it's not that simple. The hardest part of telling a story is *pacing* the events so that they lead the reader in just the right way to the high point of the story. To accomplish this goal, keep your audience and purpose in mind. At each step of the way, ask yourself, "Does my audience need to know this, or is it just getting in the way?" and "Does this information support what I'm trying to do, or does it just slow things down?" Here is the first draft of Joe's middle section:

On Valentine's Day that year, I came home after visiting Eva. I noticed that my mom had washed some of my work shirts. This was a pleasant surprise since I prefer to do it myself. She had hung them on a rack close to the floor furnace. Then I noticed the rack was too close to the furnace. But I felt she knew what she was doing. My parents were asleep in their bedroom. Then I figured it was time to turn in for the night. I went to my bedroom and shut the door.

Later, I sat straight up in bed from a sound sleep. Even though I was in a sleepy daze, I realized I was smelling smoke. I was about to doze off again when suddenly I heard a loud pop.

I jumped out of bed. Smoke surrounded me, and I saw the fire burning a curtain. The smoke was so thick!

I ran downstairs yelling that there was a fire. I started yelling to my parents. Their bedroom was just down the hall They woke up. My parents put out the fire with buckets of water.

Writing Your End

By the time you are ready to write the end of your narrative, the action of your story has ended. It is time for you to "wrap it all up," to bring the lesson of the story home to the reader in a more explanatory way. Here, you might bring the story into the present, showing how the events of the story have changed you, made you a better person, or shown you the meaning of some aspect of life. The ending of your narrative can be written in a paragraph or two, or it can be done in a sentence. Here is the first draft of Joe's ending:

I still think about that day, and I probably will all my life. Just the thought of losing the people I love terrorizes me. I shudder when I think about life without them. Why can't we just stop being lazy or stop assuming that nothing will ever happen to us? After all, "an ounce of prevention is worth a pound of cure."

WRITING 3-7

Draft the beginning of your own narrative. Be sure to set the scene so that your reader gets a sense of the setting and characters. Use descriptive writing techniques to enable your reader to visualize important scenes and people.

Then, draft the middle of your own narrative. Keep the narrative moving along; don't get bogged down in too much detail. Remember also to lead your reader to an emotional climax in this section. Tip: Use freewriting not just as a prewriting technique but also as a drafting technique. Once you decide which section you want to work on during a given working session, just sit down and write as freely as you can and not worrying about correctness.

Finally, draft the end of your narrative. In this section, try to summarize the meaning of your story and bring the essay to a satisfying close.

Coherence: Using Transitions

Since a good narrative moves through time, you need to make sure that your own narrative does the same. One way to provide coherence in a narrative is to interject "time transitions" in the appropriate places. This chart gives you some ideas.

Transitions to Show Time Order

after	briefly	in the past	right away
after a few days	by now	later	simultaneously
after a short time	concurrently	meanwhile	soon
after a while	currently	not so long ago	soon after
afterward	during	now	suddenly
all the while	earlier	of late	then
at last	eventually	preceding	today
at present	following	presently	tomorrow
at this moment	for a minute/hour	previously	until
at this time	immediately	prior to	until now
before	in the mean time	recently	yesterday

Don't forget to use transitions to show spatial order and direction when you stop your narrative to describe an object or a static scene.

Revising

When you've completed your rough draft (and remember that it is only the first of several drafts), read your essay aloud to yourself to hear how it sounds. Revise by adding or taking out details, inserting time transitions, or expanding on some of the description so that your reader can experience what you experienced.

Style Tip: Varying Sentence Structure

Varying the rhythm of your sentences involves more than just varying their length. It also involves varying their structure. Sentences can take one of four types of structure: simple, compound, complex, or compound-complex. You don't need to memorize these terms, but you should be able to recognize how sentences differ from one another in terms of structure.

SIMPLE SENTENCE:	The fire roared through the house.
COMPOUND SENTENCE:	The fire roared through the house, but the elderly couple was still asleep.
COMPLEX SENTENCE:	As the fire roared through the house, the elderly couple continued sleeping.
COMPOUND-COMPLEX:	As the fire roared through the house, the elderly couple continued sleeping, but the fireman was on the way up the ladder to wake them.

Notice that sentence length can be related to sentence structure. The point here is that you should try to vary the structures of your sentences to provide a pleasing experience for your reader. Such variation characterizes the mature writing style toward which you are working in this course.

> **Bridging Knowledge**
>
> **Go to Chapter 22** to explore ways to vary your sentence structures.

············ **PROBLEM** ············ **SOLUTION** ············

NARRATIVE	
My narrative fails to convey a sense of setting or of how characters look, feel, or behave.	1. Look for opportunities to employ sensory details to paint "word pictures" for your reader. 2. Insert figurative language (metaphor, simile, or personification), in one or two places if it is appropriate. 3. Replace weak or ineffective verbs with vivid, active ones. 4. Add dialogue and the characters' emotional responses.

········ **PROBLEM** ········   ········ **SOLUTION** ········

NARRATIVE

There doesn't seem to be a climax in my narrative.

→

1. If there is no climax, you might not be telling a story. Read just the middle section of your essay again. Are you relating events that lead to a particular moment of awareness?

WRITING

My essay seems to be long winded; I get bogged down in the details of the story.

→

1. Keep your purpose, the lesson you hope to convey, and your main point in mind. Avoid including details that distract your reader from these elements.
2. When you have not consciously stopped the action to describe a person, place, or emotion, make sure your narrative is moving forward in time.
3. Try using less description during the middle section of the narrative.

COHERENCE

My narrative seems to jump from event to event; it doesn't show how one event leads to another.

→

1. Use time transitions to indicate movement from one major part of the action to another.
2. Make sure you don't overuse transitions; don't begin every sentence with *Then*, *Next*, or something similar.

WRITING   **3-8**

Start your revision. Don't leave any part of your essay untouched.

- Make sure your narrative has a clear beginning, middle, and end.
- Be sure to offer sufficient and relevant description of people, places, events, and emotions.
- Check for coherence. Make sure you offer enough transitions to help guide your reader.
- Use a variety of sentence types.

Asking Your Peers

When you think your essay is as good as it can be, seek some feedback from one of your classmates by doing the following activity. Take a few minutes to review your peer's comments and suggestions. Incorporate any suggestion that you feel helps im-improve your essay.

Criteria	Reviewer's Judgment	Reason or Example
The essay's purpose is clear to the reader. The thesis is clearly stated or clearly implied.	Agree: _____ Disagree: _____	_____ _____ _____
The essay has a clear beginning, middle, and end. Each section accomplishes its purpose. In particular, the middle section leads naturally to the climax of the action.	Agree: _____ Disagree: _____	_____ _____ _____
The essay contains sufficient description and dialogue to allow the reader to "feel" the event. Vivid details make the characters, setting, and action believable.	Agree: _____ Disagree: _____	_____ _____ _____
The essay is coher-ent: the narrative is presented in a logical sequence and includes sufficient and appropri-ate transitions to guide the reader.	Agree: _____ Disagree: _____	_____ _____ _____

Proofreading

In this stage, you edit your writing for grammar, punctuation, and sentence structures. Sometimes overwhelming, proofreading can be done quite efficiently if you just take it one step at a time. In this chapter, we focus on one major type of error, shifts in verb tense.

Common Error #2: Editing for Shifts in Verb Tense

In a narrative essay, you are usually trying to tell a story about something that happened in the past, although it is conceivable that you could tell a story in the present or future tense. Whatever basic tense you use, you should maintain that tense throughout your essay.

INCORRECT: One Thursday, as I walked into the office to meet a client, there they were. The police <u>are</u> standing around waiting for me, and they <u>don't</u> look pleased.

CORRECT: One Thursday, as I walked into the office to meet a client, there they were. The police <u>were</u> standing around waiting for me, and they <u>didn't</u> look pleased.

GRAMMAR CHECKUP   3-1

Revise the following paragraphs for unnecessary shifts in tense.

    Shortly after my husband was injured, I ~~realize~~ (realized) just how drastically things ~~are~~ (were) going to change. Before the pain began, life ~~is~~ (was) life. We really didn't appreciate how fun the smallest outings ~~are~~ (were). If it's the park that we're going to, we ~~had~~ (have) to enjoy every minute because we'll be at home for the next few weeks doing what we call "recovery days." Now, it is no longer how it used to be. Work is no longer an option, so forget about those worry-free days when bills were paid and we actually ~~have~~ (had) a savings account. Now, it's on me to pick up the slack and ~~supported~~ (support) my family. For years, I didn't work outside the home while I was raising my children. When I ~~need~~ (needed) to go back into the workforce, I had little experience under my belt, and I had to work two jobs to bring home almost the amount of income he was earning.

Check your answers to this Grammar Checkup in Appendix A on page A-1. How did you do? If you missed even one or two items in this checkup, review shifts in verb tense in Chapter 19.

WRITING   3-9

Begin proofreading your revised draft. Check for and correct errors in spelling, punctuation, verb tense, usage, and sentence structure. Personalize the checklist by adding specific errors that continue to occur in your writing.

Final Checklist

1. Does your essay contain a clear beginning, middle, and end? ☐
2. Does the beginning section introduce the setting and some main characters? ☐
3. Does your essay contain lively and vivid description of people, places, events, and emotions? ☐
4. Do you use verbs vividly, avoiding overuse of the *be* verb in telling your story? ☐
5. Are the time relationships in your narrative clear to the reader? Do you use appropriate and smooth transitions between events? ☐
6. Have you used a variety of sentence structures, made sure your sentences are complete (no fragments), and checked carefully for errors in spelling, usage, and punctuation? ☐

Reflecting

Now that you have completed your essay, take a few minutes to reflect on your writing by completing the following activity.

WRITING   3-10

Self-Reflection

Before you hand in your paper, answer the following questions:

1. What do you feel you did best?

2. What part of your paper was most challenging to you?

3. In which areas do you feel you need the most practice?

4. What strategies will you employ to address your challenges or weaknesses and to improve the quality of your essays?

After you have completed this self-reflection, carefully review your instructor's comments. How are they similar or different from your own answers to the self-reflection? Make a list of your grammar, punctuation, and spelling errors so that you can follow up on the ones that recur. Consider what strategies you will employ to address your challenges or weaknesses and to improve the quality of your essay.

How might you use narration outside of this English course? Look back at the writing samples in Previewing Your Task in this chapter.

• **College:** _____

• **Your profession:** _____

• **Everyday life:** _____

CHAPTER 4

Writing Your Expository Paragraph

YOUR GOALS

Understanding the Expository Paragraph

1. Define and explain the purpose of the expository paragraph.

2. Distinguish general statements from specific statements.

3. Identify levels of generality.

4. Analyze how topics can be limited.

5. Identify and formulate acceptable controlling ideas.

6. Determine whether a paragraph is unified.

Writing Your Expository Paragraph

1. Write appropriate topic sentences.

2. Provide major and minor supports.

3. Create a well-organized, developed, and unified paragraph.

4. Provide transitions to your paragraph to skillfully guide your reader.

5. Punctuate clauses correctly.

"The paragraph is a mini-essay; it is also a maxi-sentence."

▪ Donald Hall ▪

Amonth into the new semester, your biology instructor asks you to write a paragraph explaining the process of cell division, your history instructor wants you to analyze the effects of the U.S. involvement in Iraq on the U.S. economy, and your psychology instructor wants you to compare and contrast the behavioral theories of B. F. Skinner and John B. Watson. You realize that all these assignments call for a similar thinking process—they ask you to *explain* an academic topic.

In your summer internship with a local engineering firm, your supervisor asks you to write a report explaining the causes of a recent bridge collapse in your community. She gives you the analytical data and outlines the causes; your job is to produce a report that engineers, lawyers, and government officials can rely on to understand the collapse of the bridge. You recognize the explanatory purpose of your writing task but are somewhat intimidated because your report will be read by so many high-level people.

Your sister asks for your help writing a letter to her insurance company, which recently raised her premium significantly because of a minor accident. She asks you to explain the circumstances of the accident and then convince the company that she does not deserve the high premium because of her long record of accident-free driving.

The way you gather, organize, and present information in your writing reflects the quality of your thinking and determines how others perceive you. Learning to write effectively will help you succeed in college and earn scholarships or admission into career programs. Similarly, your chances of obtaining the job or promotion you want are greatly increased if you present yourself well in writing situations. This chapter provides you with a firm basis for organizing your ideas and explaining them effectively to others.

LET's warm up!

Withdrawing from courses is a major reason that students are unable to progress in their education, especially if some of those courses are prerequisites to others. What factors do you feel prevent college students from completing their courses? Identify the one reason you feel is most significant and write a paragraph explaining that reason.

OJO images/PhotoLibrary

PREVIEWING YOUR TASK

Much of the writing you do in college will be in response to assignments in other classes: psychology, sociology, history, and so on. Your instructors want to know that you can organize your thoughts and express them clearly in particular fields of study. Your future employers and colleagues will have the same concern. The following readings demonstrate effective writing not only in college but also in work and everyday life.

Writing for College

In the following selection, a student discusses the sport of hunting for an assignment in a biology class.

Benefits of Hunting

Although often criticized, the sport of hunting offers a number of benefits. First, hunting benefits the economy. For example, in order for wildlife conservation to be regulated, people must be employed to do this job; therefore, hunting creates jobs for people. Also, local businesses profit from hunters buying equipment and supplies, and small mountain communities benefit from the business hunting season brings. In addition to the economy, hunting is beneficial to the wildlife population. Since overpopulation can cause wildlife to become diseased or to starve to death, hunting helps prevent this problem. Furthermore, regulated hunting prevents many species from becoming extinct by controlling their environment and predators. Finally, the sport of hunting is beneficial to the hunter. Many hunters hunt strictly for food to feed their families. Moreover, most hunters feel a sense of reward that comes from knowing they are contributing to the preservation of wildlife.

PRACTICE   4-1

1. What is the purpose of this paragraph? To demonstrate the benefits of hunting. It could be partly intended to persuade opponents of hunting to consider some of those benefits.

2. Does the paragraph seem logical and organized to you? Explain your answer. The paragraph is organized according to the benefits (expressed in major supports) and supporting information for each benefit (minor supports).

Writing in Your Profession

This selection presents part of a written report by an insurance investigator based on an interview with the victim of a crime.

When the injured party was interviewed several days later, she reported several negative effects from the encounter with the suspect. First, she showed me a number of severe contusions on her face and hands; these resulted from the fall at the scene of the crime. She believes the time elapsed between the event and her first medical treatment might have worsened the seriousness of the contusions. The victim also displayed the clothing she was wearing on the day of the crime: a fur coat, a formal gown, a pearl necklace, and Italian leather shoes, all of which she claimed were damaged beyond repair. It did appear to me that the clothing was ripped and scuffed and that the jewelry had been cracked and chipped. The victim estimates the damage to her personal property to be about $7,500. Finally, the victim claimed that since the crime she has been depressed and unable to sleep or eat regularly. In fact, she believes she has suffered more emotionally than physically from the incident. She is currently seeking medical treatment for the emotional effects of the crime.

PRACTICE   4-2

1. What is the purpose of this paragraph? To report the effects of a crime from the point of view of the victim.

2. Does the paragraph fulfill this purpose? Explain your answer. Yes. The author presents three major effects as reported by the victim and gives supporting detail that could back up the victim's story.

Writing in Everyday Life

The following selection is an e-mail from Juanita, a bride-to-be who is planning a mid-December wedding in her hometown, to her aunt. Since Juanita is planning the wedding from another state, she has to do much of the arranging via e-mail.

Greetings, Aunt Bertha!
    I was so happy to hear from you and receive your ideas for the wedding. I agree completely with you on the church flowers and the design of the invitations. Moreover, I understand your desire to have the reception in the church hall since it has sentimental attachments for you because of all the family events held there over the years. However, I prefer the hotel ballroom for several reasons. First, the hotel space is much larger than the church hall, and thus 300–400 guests would be much more comfortable in the hotel. Since the church hall barely fits 250 guests, the crowd would probably spill out into the church entryway or even the rectory.

Another attraction of the hotel is the Christmas decorations. Since the wedding is in mid-December, the hotel lobby will have its floor-to-ceiling Christmas tree, its miniature Christmas village, and all the lights and decorations of the season. I'm sure that our guests will enjoy walking through the lobby on the way to the ball-room, absorbing its festive atmosphere. Finally, although our guests will have to drive from the church to the hotel for the reception, they have the option of staying overnight in the hotel in case they drink too freely! I respect your opinion and input on my special day and hope that you agree with these reasons for keeping the reception at the hotel.

Love,
Juanita

PRACTICE 4-3

1. What is the purpose of this e-mail? To convince the writer's aunt to agree not to change the location of the reception.

2. Do you think Juanita does a good job of convincing her aunt? Explain your answer. Generally, the e-mail is effective because it presents reasons and backs them up with specific evidence.

3. How does Juanita maintain a friendly tone even as she disagrees with her aunt about the reception? Through her use of endearing language and a respectful appreciation of the aunt's attachment to the church setting. Also, she relies on the reasons and evidence she presents, not on heated words.

UNDERSTANDING THE EXPOSITORY PARAGRAPH

In Chapters 2 and 3, you focused on description and narration—expressive types of writing that allow you to plant an image in your reader's mind or relate a meaningful personal experience. Chapters 4–10 focus on another type of writing—exposition. Expository writing analyzes and explains information to inform or educate your reader. As we move to expository writing, your knowledge of description and narration will help you provide the vividness and interest essential to effective expository writing. With its emphasis on logic and organization, expository writing is most likely the type of writing you will be doing in college and throughout your career. When you enter the workforce, you will find that expository writing is necessary in almost any profession and that your ability to write exposition requires the same skills necessary to succeed in many careers: thinking critically, analyzing complex situations, and presenting information clearly to coworkers.

Expository Paragraph Structure

A paragraph may stand by itself as a complete piece of writing or appear in a longer composition such as an essay. When paragraphs stand by themselves, many writers organize them into three parts: the topic sentence, support sentences, and a conclusion.

As illustrated in Figure 4.1, the topic sentence, or the main point of the paragraph, is the most general statement—just like the dominant impression in the descriptive paragraph and the main point in the narrative essay. The body of your paragraph contains supporting sentences that provide the reader with specific evidence or reasoning to support the general idea of your topic sentence. Lastly, the conclusion provides closure to the paragraph.

The Topic Sentence

The topic sentence is a general statement that expresses the main point of a paragraph—your opinion, or claim, about the topic—and thus controls what information goes in the rest of the paragraph. One characteristic of a topic sentence is that it is *the most general* statement in a paragraph, one that causes the reader to ask questions to understand the idea fully.

For example, if a friend tells you that her supervisor can't be trusted, you automatically wonder why and may ask your friend to justify her claim. You might even want her to give specific examples that prove her opinion is valid. In other words, you want her to support her claim with evidence.

However, if your friend states that her supervisor is 42 years old, you probably wouldn't question this statement. It's just a statement of fact, not an opinion, and it does not lead to a discussion.

Can you tell which one of the following statements is the most general?
1. Swimming increases muscle strength.
2. Swimming improves posture.
3. Swimming benefits the whole body.
4. Swimming improves cardiovascular conditioning.
5. Swimming tones and strengthens legs, arms, back, and shoulders.

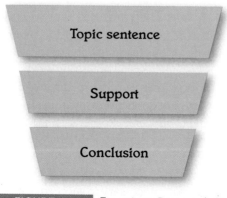

FIGURE 4.1   *Expository Paragraph Structure*

If you chose 3, you are correct. Notice that this statement raises questions if left unsupported. The reader expects to learn *how* swimming benefits the whole body. The other sentences provide more specific answers to this question.

PRACTICE 4-4

Each group of sentences contains a general topic that can be used as the topic sentence for a paragraph. The others are more specific and may serve as evidence. Circle the most general statement. Correct answers are underlined.

1. A. Club members help one another with assignments and projects.

    B. As a club member, a student can form or join study groups.

    C. Being a member of a school club has definite advantages for a college student.

    D. Club members usually share materials, books, and equipment to help save money.

2. A. Dancing is a form of exercise, and most people feel that exercise can improve a person's mood.

    B. Because dancing is a social activity, it can enhance a person's social "presence."

    C. Learning to move and sway on the dance floor, drawing the attention of onlookers, can dramatically increase one's self-esteem.

    D. Learning to dance can have a dramatic effect on a person's personality.

3. A. Intel has a knowledgeable staff.

    B. Most employees of Intel have college degrees.

    C. Intel workers are cross-trained in several disciplines.

    D. Because of low turnover, Intel employees are able to continually add to their expertise.

4. A. People who look at the light side can help improve workplace morale.

    B. A sense of humor is an important asset in the workplace.

    C. Humor keeps the mind sharp and active.

    D. A sense of humor helps a person "slough off" the negativity of workplace doomsayers.

The Topic and the Controlling Idea

The topic sentence consists of two parts: the topic and the controlling idea. The topic is the subject of the paragraph. The controlling idea is what the writer wants to say about the topic—the main point, or focus, of the entire paragraph. Consider the topic sentence of "Benefits of Hunting."

Topic	+	Controlling Idea	=	Topic Sentence
The sport of hunting		offers a number of benefits		The sport of hunting offers a number of benefits.

Here are some other possible topic sentences on the topic "the sport of hunting":

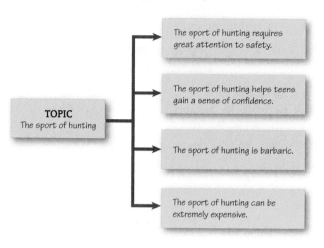

Each of these topic sentences would require a separate paragraph. Notice how each one imposes boundaries on the information inside the paragraph. If you were to write about the first topic sentence (safety), you couldn't include the other controlling ideas in the same paragraph. Under none of these topic sentences could you discuss how hunting is an enjoyable experience, how hunting is regulated, or how deer hunting is different from elk hunting. Although all these additional focuses would make for interesting discussions, the controlling ideas of the example topic sentences do not permit any of these other ideas to be explained in their paragraphs.

PRACTICE   4-5

Examine each of the following topic sentences. Underline the topic once and the controlling idea twice.

Example: <u>Violence in soccer</u> is <u>destroying the quality of the game</u>.

1. A <u>good wine</u> is <u>easily identified by its aroma</u>.
2. <u>Severe winters</u> <u>create a challenge for the conscientious energy consumer</u>.
3. <u>The use of alcohol fuel</u> would <u>clean up much pollution</u>.
4. <u>Negotiation is necessary</u> when adjusting to a roommate.
5. <u>The enrollment procedure at a large university</u> can be <u>stressful</u>.

Limiting Your Topic

Your topic sentence must be limited to a single idea. Therefore, avoid splitting your controlling idea into two parts. The following topic sentence has a split focus: The sport of hunting is rewarding and dangerous.

This sentence makes two statements: one, that hunting is rewarding, and the other, that hunting is dangerous. You should focus your paragraph's main point on one or the other, but don't attempt to do both in one paragraph. By writing both in your controlling idea, you are committed to addressing both ideas. Trying to explain each idea fully can make for a long paragraph, and trying to move from one idea to the next may be confusing for your reader to follow. As a rule, focus each of your paragraphs on just one controlling idea.

BROAD:	Vandalism will continue to escalate.
LIMITED:	Vandalism <u>will continue to escalate in our community for the next 10 years</u>.

Strategies employed:

Topic	+	Effect	+	Place	+	Time
Vandalism		will continue to escalate		in our community		for the next 10 years

Examine how the strategies in the first column of the following table limit (or control) the topic for a more focused topic sentence. Not all sentences use only one strategy.

Limiting Strategy	Topic	Topic Sentence
1. Cause or reason	Loneliness	<u>Loneliness has led international students to make irrational decisions</u>.
2. Difference	Study habits of traditional and nontraditional students	<u>Study habits of traditional and nontraditional students differ considerably</u>.
3. Effect, result, or consequence	Getting my college degree	<u>Getting my college degree has provided me with many job opportunities</u>.
4. Number, list, or process	Setting the date and time in your computer	<u>Setting the date and time in your computer requires three simple steps</u>.
5. Place	West Nile virus	<u>West Nile virus has created a panic in our town</u>.
6. Quality, characteristic, or aspect	Nontraditional students	<u>Nontraditional students are goal oriented</u>.
7. Similarity	Hawaiians and Alaska Natives	<u>Hawaiians and Alaska Natives share cultural similarities</u>.
8. Time	The male's role in the family	<u>The male's role in the family has changed within the last 5 years</u>.

Placement of the Topic Sentence

Since the topic sentence lets the reader know the main point of the paragraph, most writers of exposition place the topic sentence at the beginning of the paragraph. After all, the function of the topic sentence is to introduce the topic and the controlling idea of that paragraph, so what better place could there be? However, there's no rule that the topic sentence must go first. It could go in the middle or at the end, or it might not appear. Sometimes writers leave the formulation of the topic sentence to the attentive reader, skillfully presenting the evidence that leads to an implied controlling idea. The decision is yours, but before you decide, consider the effects that the placement of your topic sentence have on your audience. Does your placement make the paragraph stronger, or does it only confuse your audience?

Examine the supporting details in each of the following paragraphs and then fill in the blank with a topic sentence that captures all the information in the paragraph.

1. Many people claim that reality TV is contributing to antisocial tendencies among young people.

    However, reality TV buffs are completely in touch with pop culture, thus making viewers aware of what is popular; if we know what is popular, we are better equipped to engage in social conversations and social situations. Personally, I thrive in social situations, and if anything, I am overly social. I have no problem conversing with people whom I meet. In fact, reality TV has helped make me even more social.

2. The poaching of tigers in Africa is fueled by the activity of an active underground market.

    Tigers are being killed at alarming rates by well-organized poachers who make large profits due to the underground market's demand. The underground market's success is due in part to certain strong cultural and religious beliefs that medicines made with tiger parts help heal a variety of conditions. Poachers will also take advantage of other cultures' superstitions that a tiger's tooth or claw brings good fortune, so more tigers are sacrificed for the sake of these good luck charms while their skins are used to decorate homes. Tourists will buy illegal tiger products from shops without even a conscious thought of the tiger's plight.

3. The Wizard of Oz is a timeless classic that will live for years to come.

    The Wizard of Oz can be enjoyed by the young and the old. Grandparents can remember watching it when they were children and can relate to their grandchildren's "oohs" and "ahhs" when Dorothy's house falls on the Wicked Witch or when the Munchkins come out to play. The magic that this movie projects to the audience also contributes to its timelessness. Oh, if only a lion could really talk and if only every little girl could go to a magical kingdom and become a heroine. However, the movie's timeless lessons of friendship, faith, family, and love contribute the most to its longevity. Each character contributes to its enduring message that intelligence, feelings, and bravery lie within each of us. This movie will continue to excite many more generations.

The Support: Major and Minor

Once you have expressed your claim, or opinion, in the topic sentence, your next task is to explain the claim so that your reader understands your point clearly and fully. To achieve your goal, your supporting sentences—both major and minor—need to consist of evidence and reasoning that fully explain your topic sentence. These supporting sentences must be organized and presented in a particular way: general sentences must be supported by more specific sentences. Examine the idea of *generality* and how it pertains to expository writing.

Levels of Generality

What's your first impression when you see the following list?

Green beans	Menu items	Chicken
Tea	Coffee	Carrots
Meats	Bread pudding	Lemonade
Banana cream pie	Asparagus	Pork chops
Steak	Drinks	Chocolate cake
Vegetables	Desserts	

Obviously, this list of words has something to do with eating out (the clue here is *menu items*). Beyond that, however, it doesn't seem to have an apparent logical structure—it's just a jumbled and puzzling list of food-related words. A closer look reveals some interesting relationships: Isn't chocolate cake a dessert? And doesn't the word *drinks* include coffee and tea? It begins to appear that the words can be grouped meaningfully, perhaps into menu categories like meats, vegetables, and so on. The problem with the list of words is that it is randomly arranged. If it were a paragraph, the reader would have no idea of its logical structure without doing lots of work.

However, by organizing the list differently, you can make its logical structure clear. If you start with the most general items and then move to the most specific, you might be able to make sense of the list more quickly. In the preceding list, the most general item is *menu items* because it covers or includes all the other words. Therefore, call *menu items* the first level of generality and place it at the top of the list. The next level of generality—*meats, vegetables, desserts,* and *drinks*—explains the first level and limits this level to just four areas. This level of generality is equivalent to the major supports you need to provide to explain your topic sentence (Figure 4.2).

The rest of the items make up the third level of generality. This level is the most concrete level, consisting of specific examples. This level is similar to the

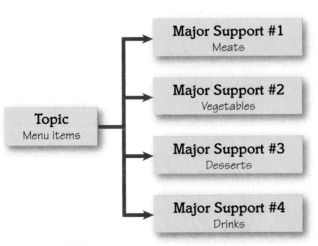

| FIGURE 4.2 | *Levels of Generality and Major Supports* |

minor supports you need to provide in your paragraphs to make your evidence concrete. Rearrange the list by levels of generality.

Topic: Menu Items

1. Meats
   a. Chicken
   b. Pork chops
   c. Steak
2. Vegetables
   a. Asparagus
   b. Carrots
   c. Green beans
3. Desserts
   a. Banana cream pie
   b. Bread pudding
   c. Chocolate cake
4. Drinks
   a. Coffee
   b. Lemonade
   c. Tea

Now the logical structure of the list is clear. Similarly, a good expository paragraph usually has three levels of generality: the topic sentence, the major supports, and the minor supports. Thus, to communicate effectively, your job as a writer is to move your reader from your general claim to the specific information that supports it. Notice that the organized information in the example looks like an outline. This is exactly what outlines do: they help the reader understand the explanation of a topic by giving a visual depiction of the levels of generality.

Developing Your Paragraph with Facts and Details

As you select information to support the main point of your paragraph, don't assume that your audience shares your knowledge of the topic or your experiences with the topic. Your reader wants to know the who, what, when, where, why, and how of your topic, and it is up to you to supply the answers. As you draft your paragraphs, keep in mind that you can use two basic types of support: evidence and reasoning. *Evidence* consists of the facts and details that support your point. *Reasoning* consists of the way you think through a particular topic. For now, let's focus on presenting two types of evidence: facts and details.

■ **Use facts.** Facts are statements that can be verified objectively. For example, we can believe that the Vatican is located in Rome, Italy, even though we have never been there, since we have the words of trustworthy people, have reviewed published information, or can verify this information ourselves by going there. You have a wealth of historical facts, scientific data, and statistics from which to draw support for your points. Some facts that are not common knowledge may require research, but the strength and credibility they give your writing is well worth it.

- **Provide details.** Specific details make the controlling idea not only clearer but also more interesting. Your reader wants to know the details; details hold a reader's interest, and they provide the crucial evidence your reader needs to understand your controlling idea.

Use a combination of methods to support your topic sentences. Through your support, your reader should have a better understanding of your topic.

Collaborative Critical Thinking

In groups of three or four, develop major and minor supports for one of the topic sentences provided. Rely on facts and details. Answers will vary.

1. Television promotes violence.

2. A sense of humor can make difficult times easier to bear.

3. Fairy tales present false values.

Share your supports with the other groups and have each group make suggestions for improvement.

Unity

As you have seen illustrated throughout this chapter, all sentences in the paragraph must be directly related to and explain the topic sentence, which ties the paragraph together. This principle is called *unity*. Anything that does not relate to the controlling idea should not be in the paragraph. Such irrelevant information destroys the unity of your paragraph. If you strongly feel that you must include some specific information in your paragraph, then you'll need to revise your controlling idea to include that aspect.

PRACTICE 4-7

Read the following paragraph outlines and underline the major support that you would not include in the paragraph. If the outline is unified, mark it with *Correct*.

1. **Topic Sentence:** Smoking can affect a person's work environment.

   a. Smoking annoys other workers.

   b. Long or constant breaks decrease productivity.

   c. A smoking ban can lower health insurance premiums.

   d. Smoking increases absenteeism.

2. **Topic Sentence:** Owning a computer has changed my life.

   a. I am able to keep in touch with old and present friends.

   b. Online shopping has saved me time.

   c. I can pay my bills online.

   d. My sister is able to do her homework.

3. **Topic Sentence:** People marry for a variety of reasons.

   a. <u>People need to compromise since marriage is a partnership</u>.

   b. Some people decide to marry for companionship.

   c. People marry because they want children.

   d. Some people marry because they're in love.

The Conclusion

The conclusion of the paragraph is simply a tie-up sentence. You can make a brief restatement of your controlling idea, make a final comment about the main point, or emphasize the insight you have arrived at.

If you decide to use a restatement, make sure you don't repeat the topic sentence; use different ways to state the main point or make the point of the topic sentence.

TOPIC SENTENCE:	We are usually so amazed with the complexity of a language such as Chinese or Arabic that we don't stop to see how English can be just as complex to a non-English speaker.
CONCLUDING SENTENCE:	After all, in how many languages can you add a silent letter to a word and change its meaning and pronunciation, such as *mat* to *mate?*
TOPIC SENTENCE:	Dogs can play important roles in senior citizens' lives.
CONCLUDING SENTENCE:	The problem now is how to keep the dog out of the will.

If you decide to make a final comment about the main point or express an insight about the main point, make sure you go beyond what you have already stated in your topic sentence. Since your reader already knows the point you're trying to make, rather than repeat the point, read your topic sentence and ask, "So what?" Your answer should produce a comment on your main point that is meaningful.

TOPIC SENTENCE:	Some students' classroom habits are distracting to others in the class.
CONCLUDING SENTENCE:	It's time that these students realize that there are serious students in the class who want to learn. [This conclusion highlights the significance of the problem.]
TOPIC SENTENCE:	America's adolescents are becoming less and less active, thus making it harder for them to work off the excess calories.
CONCLUDING SENTENCE:	Unless we deal with this growing problem immediately, we will find the solution costly in a matter of years. [This conclusion emphasizes the urgency of addressing the problem.]

Whatever method you decide to use, make sure that there's a connection between the main point of the paragraph (the topic sentence) and the concluding statement (Figure 4.3).

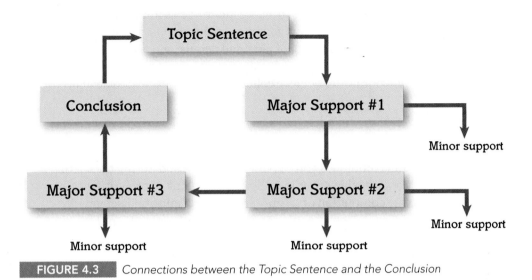

FIGURE 4.3   *Connections between the Topic Sentence and the Conclusion*

WRITING YOUR EXPOSITORY PARAGRAPH

This section provides step-by-step instructions for writing an expository paragraph. Begin by reading an example of such a paragraph. The author is Ron, a college freshman majoring in marketing.

The Annoyance of Television Advertising

Television advertisements can often be annoying. For one thing, too much time is wasted on commercials. Frequently, programming is edited simply to provide more time for ads. A recent study showed that 24% of a 2-hour program consisted of commercials and that 11 minutes of the original movie had been cut to accommodate advertisements. Furthermore, advertisements are also frequently misleading. Some commercials passed off as "specialty programming" are nothing more than half-hour pitches designed to lure the audience into buying products and services. Celebrities also mislead the viewers by promoting products that they, almost surely, have never used. For example, who really believes that Jaclyn Smith buys her clothes at Kmart or that Christina Aguilera drinks Pepsi Cola? Finally, commercials are often so ludicrous to the point of being insulting. Do advertisers really expect people to take the words of a talking dog seriously? On the contrary, most viewers are turned off by such nonsense. In fact, I cringe every time I see the Capital One family on their out-of-season vacation. Can anyone really be that stupid? Clearly, commercials have made television viewing an unpleasant experience.

This paragraph contains the elements we've identified as important components of an expository paragraph: a clear topic sentence, major supporting sentences, minor supporting sentences consisting of facts and details, and a conclusion. It is also unified; that is, none of the sentences stray from the task at hand. Finally, it uses transitional words and phrases to achieve coherence. It is your turn to develop your own paragraph.

Prewriting

Prewriting refers to all techniques you can practice before and during the writing process to generate and organize your ideas. You might think of prewriting as everything leading up to the completion of an outline: brainstorming to discover ideas, connecting related ideas, selecting a topic and narrowing your focus, and creating an outline.

Discovering and Limiting Your Topic: Freewriting and Questioning

Ron began his brainstorming process by listing his hobbies, interests, and pastimes. After creating his list and looking it over, he circled "television" as a potential topic. Then he decided to do 10 minutes of freewriting on that topic to stimulate his creativity.

> Watching TV is a relaxing activity or maybe addictive. Anyway, I like watching TV. I like the comedy shows and the talk shows. I'm really getting into the reality shows. *The Apprentice* is really fun to watch although *American Idol* seems to drag after a few weeks. The real drag are the medical shows. Now everyone I know thinks they're experts and go around diagnosing people. At least I can do some of my math between commercials. Who really watches commercials? Well, some of them are funny, but some I can't even tell what product they're selling. Once I flipped channels and thought I was seeing a really interesting movie but it turned out to be a commercial. Hey, what about the commercial when the guy stops in the desert to eat a burger. Then I have to stop my homework and call for a pizza cause I'm hungry. Is there a rule exactly where in the programs the commercials come? It's a good thing I have classwork to occupy that time because this interruption really gets me mad.

As you can tell, Ron has generated many ideas that would make interesting topics. For example, he can discuss television's relaxing or addictive quality, he can make a claim about reality shows, or he can focus on commercials. Ron chose "commercials," which he circled.

Next, Ron asked himself a series of questions to focus his topic even more. Here are his questions and answers.

Topic: Commercials

1.	What is their nature?	Sales pitch, capitalism, information.
2.	What are the characteristics?	Attention-getter, concise, interrupts, confusing, annoying, dishonest, a con.
3.	How are they done?	Bring in celebrities, pets, cartoons, colors, and people you respect to entice you and make the commercial believable.
4.	How effective are they?	Sales of stupid products keep climbing up until the next "better and improved" one comes up. Sometimes I get good ideas.
5.	Why are they happening?	As consumers, we need to be informed, but the bottom line is money. Keep the economy pumping; keep us spending more and more.
6.	Who is responsible?	Businesses, the governor who won't censor the ones that are in poor taste, the consumer who goes out and gets the product and spends a lot of money rather than take the generic ones.
7.	What are the consequences?	Buy or replace things you don't need, spend more money, go into debt, max credit cards.
8.	How do they make you feel?	Sometimes entertained, interested, sometimes confused, angry, annoyed, irritated.
9.	What kinds or types are there?	Drama, musical, testimonial, cartoons, comedy, mixture, infomercials, hi-tech.
10.	When do they appear?	They seem to pop up when I'm really into the program. It seems that they appear at certain climatic points of the programs. When I flip channels, other stations are also in commercial time. Conspiracy?
11.	Where do most of them occur?	The most popular programs seem to have the most commercials, although each is shorter in duration. These seem to be more costly to produce, but I guess cost is based on the size of the audience. They save the big guns for when they have the most viewers.

Ron could continue asking questions since one question or answer can generate another question. The following questions could also have elicited some interesting information:

■ What do I know about this topic?

■ What is my connection to this topic?

■ What is my attitude about this topic?

■ What do I like most or like least about this topic?

However, Ron stops here since he feels he has enough information to take him to the later parts of the prewriting stage. He can always come back to ask additional questions if necessary.

WRITING   4-1

Start your freewriting session. In a notebook, write nonstop for 10 minutes. Don't stop to think: keep the words pouring out. Once you have completed your freewriting session, review what you've written and circle an aspect of the topic that you feel you can develop further. Take 10 minutes to ask yourself questions about that topic and to write your answers. Focus on informational questions: who, what, when, where, why, and how. As you answer a question, follow it up with another question.

Identifying Your Audience and Establishing Your Purpose

The information that goes in your paragraph is determined by your audience and your purpose. Because expository writing is usually devoted to explaining a topic, you can often assume that your audience wants to be better informed about your topic. Thus, your basic purpose as an expository writer is most often to inform, or educate, your reader.

TOPICS TO CONSIDER

If you're still having trouble finding just the right topic, consider a topic from this list. The following topics are broad. If you choose a topic from this list, use the topic as the basis for your listing, freewriting, and questioning exercise.

Writing for College		
■ A war or a specific battle of a war ■ A biological cell	■ A theory, value, or belief ■ A law, act, or proclamation ■ The term *character* in literature	■ A positive or negative quality of a specific political figure

	Writing in Your Profession		
BUSINESS	■ Advertising ■ Volunteers	■ Customer service ■ Interpersonal skills	
CRIMINAL JUSTICE	■ Rules of conduct ■ Rehabilitation	■ Early parole ■ Juvenile crime	
EDUCATION	■ Peer pressure ■ Classroom discipline	■ Dropouts ■ National testing	
HEALTH	■ Depression ■ Smoking	■ A main cause of depression	■ People's attitudes toward a specific health issue
SOCIAL WORK/ PSYCHOLOGY	■ Racism ■ Teen suicide	■ The importance of family ■ Socializing or fitting in	
TECHNICAL	■ An advantage or disadvantage of a certain software program, such as CAD	■ Synthetic engine oil ■ Saving energy	■ A misuse or overuse of technology
OTHERS	■ The benefits of a certain occupation to society	■ Job-related injuries ■ Stereotyping	■ Sports

Writing in Everyday Life		
■ Living in the city or in a small town ■ Rap, rock, country, or classical music	■ The cost of maintaining a specific type of car ■ Your attitude as a student in high school and your attitude in college	■ The reasons you decided to go to college

Setting Your Tone

The tone of the paragraph reflects the writer's attitude about the topic. Your choice of words and manner of expression help determine your tone. Through your word choice and information, you can express seriousness, humor, sarcasm, or anger. When you decide on the tone of your paragraph, make sure that the tone is appropriate for

WRITING YOUR EXPOSITORY PARAGRAPH

the topic and its controlling idea. Consider the possible tone of the following topic sentences:

| TOPIC SENTENCE: | A diagnosis of cancer affects the entire family, not just the victim. |

Most people agree that a topic on cancer should be handled with sensitivity and thus merits a serious tone.

| TOPIC SENTENCE: | Teachers are experts at seeing through students' excuses. |

This topic may be handled humorously as you give examples of outlandish and ridiculous excuses that your classmates have given, or you can even give your own experience of getting caught exaggerating or lying about why you didn't turn in an assignment or couldn't make it to class. You might even assume a serious tone if you decide to explain the importance to a person's integrity of being honest when submitting late assignments to an instructor.

Here are some common tones that the reader can quickly perceive in your writing.

humorous

serious   angry

Tone = Attitude

sarcastic   pessimistic

lighthearted

Once you have decided on a tone, be consistent. Don't start your first support seriously, then move into humor, and then return to a serious tone again.

WRITING   4-2

Stop a moment to reflect on your audience, purpose, and tone. Fill in the following form.

Audience, Purpose, and Tone Analysis

I. Audience

1. Who is your target audience? _____

2. Why would this audience be interested in your topic? _____

   _____

3. What does your audience already know about your topic? _____

   _____

II. Your Purpose

1. Why did you choose this topic? _____

   _____

2. What is the main point of your paragraph? _____

   _____

3. What effect do you want your paragraph to have on your audience? _____

_____

4. What information must you provide to achieve the desired effect? _____

_____

III. Tone

1. What tone do you hope to establish for this composition? _____

_____

2. How will you achieve this tone? What words or phrases will you use (or avoid) to accurately convey your attitude about the topic? _____

_____

Formulating Your Topic Sentence

Now that you have a clear idea of your audience, purpose, and tone, you can create a topic sentence that takes these factors into account. As you construct your topic sentence, don't forget the formula we discussed:

Topic + Controlling Idea = Topic Sentence

If you feel that your topic sentence is still too broad, apply some of the techniques on page 80 to limit your topic sentence. Here's Ron's topic sentence:

Topic	+	Controlling Idea	=	Topic Sentence
Television advertisements		can often be annoying		Television advertisements can often be annoying.

With this topic and focus, Ron can start to outline his paragraph.

W R I T I N G   4-3

Consider your own topic sentence and write it in the space that follows. Don't forget that everything is tentative at this point and that you can always change your mind.

Topic Sentence: _____

_____

Outlining Your Ideas

An outline is a plan that helps keep your paragraph unified and allows you to make decisions about the organization of your information before you actually start drafting your paragraph. Your outline is not a contract, so always feel free to come back to your outline and add, delete, and modify information. Look at Ron's preliminary outline. Review the major and minor supports and note how they help explain the topic sentence:

PARAGRAPH OUTLINE

Topic Sentence: Television advertisements can often be annoying.

1. Too much time is wasted on commercials.
   a. Edit programs to insert commercials
   b. Statistics: 24% of 2 hours in commercials
2. Advertisements lie to the viewer.
   a. Specialty programs are a con
   b. Celebrities lie
   c. Examples: Jaclyn Smith and Christina Aguilera
3. Advertisements are ridiculous.
   a. Video games
   b. Promise of living like a celebrity

Conclusion: Commercials make us distrust television.

WRITING 4-4

At this time, prepare your own outline using the following form.

Paragraph Outline

Audience: _____

Topic Sentence: _____

_____

1. _____
   a. _____
   b. _____
   c. _____
2. _____
   a. _____
   b. _____
   c. _____
3. _____
   a. _____
   b. _____
   c. _____
4. _____
   a. _____
   b. _____
   c. _____

Conclusion: _____

_____

Drafting

When it comes to the drafting stage of the writing process, many students panic. There's no need for this reaction. You have a good topic, your controlling idea gives you something you want to say, and you have a plan. Keep in mind that this is only a first draft. You're allowed to make mistakes. Don't worry about transitions, diction, grammar, or sentence structure. You'll have time to improve this draft in the revision and proofreading stages. Right now, the important point is to start drafting.

Drafting Your Major and Minor Supports

Because each major support and its related minor supports constitute a logical grouping of sentences that should stick together naturally, a good way to draft a paragraph is to work on one set of major and minor supports until you feel you have adequately developed their point. It doesn't matter which major support you begin with, but once you've begun, try to focus on developing that idea with sufficient facts and details in several minor supporting sentences. If you run out of facts and details, return to the prewriting stage and do some listing and freewriting to stimulate your thinking.

Look at Ron's first draft.

> Television advertisements can often be a pain. I'm sick and tired that so much time is wasted on insulting commercials. They edit programming to simply provide more time for ads. What a waste of time! According to a recent study, 24% of a 2-hour program was made up of commercials. This is just too much time. Imagine, this means that 11 minutes of the original movie had been cut to just to plug in some annoying and boring commercials. And then to top it off, advertisements are always telling us lies. Some commercials, passed off as "specialty programming," are nothing more than half-hour pitches designed to con us into buying products and services that we don't need or care to learn about. Then the phony celebrities mislead us by promoting products that they, almost surely, have never used. Yes, another lie! Who really believes that Jaclyn Smith buys her clothes at Kmart? Britney Spears or Christina Aguilera can't possibly enjoy Pepsi that much. Beer commercials are probably the worst. Are they trying to make us believe that fun is impossible without alcohol? But to top it off, commercials are just plain silly and dumb. Video game manufacturers like Sega and Nintendo seem determined to produce ads that make no sense whatsoever. Do they really think that I'm going to find this appealing? Most viewers are turned off by such stupidity. These commercials have made me distrust TV and turned it into a bad experience.

Ron's draft has a clear topic sentence, and he certainly offers plenty of information. But is this enough? Are his facts and details relevant, sufficient, and appropriate? How about the tone of the paragraph? The tone definitely captures Ron's attitude about his topic, commercials, but do such expressions as "I'm sick and tired," "this is just too much," "phony celebrities," and "such stupidity" help the reader take him seriously? Does Ron alienate the reader? These and more are the questions you'll be asking as you move into the next stage of the writing process, revision.

WRITING   4-5

Draft the major and minor supports of your paragraph. Make sure each major support is sufficiently developed, with minor supporting sentences containing facts and details. Then, draft your concluding sentence. Be sure to return to the idea expressed in the topic sentence, but don't simply repeat the topic sentence in your conclusion.

Coherence: Using Transitions

A coherent paragraph is unified: it is tied together in support of the topic sentence. However, coherence is not only achieved through the unity of major and minor supports. The relationship between the supporting sentences also helps maintain the unity of the paragraph. Each sentence in a coherent paragraph flows smoothly to the next sentence. One way to maintain this type of coherence is through transitional words and phrases. You should employ transitions in your expository paragraphs to establish the relationship between sentences and ideas.

   In an expository paragraph, the logical relationship between ideas determines your choice of transitions. Do you want to introduce an example, make a comparison, show a contrast, give a reason, or signal a consequence? The following chart of transitions, which includes those you encountered in the previous chapters, is organized by the type of transition you might need to make your writing read smoothly and coherently. Although you do not need to include transitional expressions in all sentences, you should use them as necessary and appropriate to help your reader follow your ideas clearly.

Computer tip

As you create your first draft, don't stop to dwell on ideas to support or illustrate a statement you just wrote. You don't want to stifle your flow of ideas. Simply use a symbol such as "XXX" or "????" to remind yourself that you need to return to this spot later.

Purpose	Transitions		
To add another point	along with also as well as finally	first, second, and so on furthermore in addition in fact	moreover next not only . . . but also what is more
To make a comparison (similarity)	also as well at the same time	in comparison in like manner in the same way	likewise similarly to compare

To make a contrast (difference)	although	however	on the contrary
	but	in contrast	on the other hand
	by contrast	instead	whereas
	even though	nonetheless	yet
To give an example	for example	in particular	to illustrate
	for instance	specifically	yet another
	for one	such as	
	in other words	thus	
To give a purpose	as	in order to	to this end
	because	since	
	for this purpose	so that	
To show an effect, consequence, or result	accordingly	consequently	since
	as a consequence	due to	so
	as a result	for this reason	therefore
	because	hence	thus
	because of this	in conclusion	
To show time or chronological sequence	after	finally	recently
	after a few minutes	gradually	shortly
	afterward	immediately	soon
	at present	in the meantime	subsequently
	currently	later	suddenly
	earlier	meanwhile	then
	eventually	presently	
To show space or direction	across	eventually	opposite to
	adjacent to	farther on	there
	behind	here	to the right (left)
	below	in front of	under
	beside	in the distance	within
	beyond	nearby	
	elsewhere	next to	

Writing Your Conclusion

In Ron's early drafts, he struggles with the final or concluding sentence of his paragraph. What more can he say about his topic once he's provided the major and minor supports to develop his main point about advertisements? At first, he writes: "It is obvious that television advertisements are annoying." This statement is just a repetition of his topic sentence, rather than a meaningful final thought for his reader. The reader's reaction is "So what?" Then Ron substitutes the word *painful* for *annoying,* but the paragraph still lacks a forceful ending. Finally, Ron decides to focus on the effects of commercials on the public. He states the following: "Clearly, commercials have made television viewing an unpleasant experience." Now his paragraph has a sense of purpose and impact for the reader.

WRITING YOUR EXPOSITORY PARAGRAPH

Revising

Look at your paragraph as if you're seeing it for the first time. Every paragraph can be improved. Reread your paragraph several times. Are your ideas clear? Do you want to change words or phrases? Do you want to add, delete, or change details or examples? Are you happy with the organization of your paragraph? Does the paragraph flow smoothly? Incorporate whatever changes you feel are necessary to create a more effective paragraph.

As you draft, Computer tip revise, or proofread, keep a journal page open and write down questions and concerns as they occur to you throughout the writing process. At the end of each writing assignment, attempt to answer these questions yourself, ask your peers, or ask your instructor.

Style Tip: Varying Sentence Structure

To avoid using too many short, choppy sentences and to give your style a more pleasing sense of variety, try using subordinating conjunctions to combine shorter sentences into longer ones.

> Mark rode his skateboard to the mall. He was late for his lunch date with Maria.

These two sentences have a logical relationship that is not expressed by writing two separate sentences. In addition, the two sentences are similar in length and structure. Watch what happens when we insert the subordinating conjunction *because*:

> Because Mark rode his skateboard to the mall, he was late for his lunch date with Maria.

> or

> Mark was late for his lunch date with Maria because he rode his skateboard to the mall.

This technique not only makes two short sentences into one longer sentence but also provides the logical connection that was missing in the original (riding his skateboard caused Mark to be late).

Bridging Knowledge

For a full explanation and practice with sentence combining, see Chapter 22.

PROBLEM

SOLUTION

WRITING

My topic sentence seems too broad or not focused enough.

1. Write your topic sentence so that it is a declarative sentence, not a question.
2. Check that your topic sentence is a complete sentence, not a fragment.
3. Focus your controlling idea on a single point, not two or more.
4. Make sure you limit your topic sentence. Use additional strategies to limit the topic sentence if necessary.

.... **PROBLEM** ....   **SOLUTION** ....

WRITING

My sentences don't seem to clearly explain what I mean.

→

1. Present facts that support your point.
2. Provide details by asking what, when, where, why, and how.
3. Return to the brainstorming process to generate additional facts and details.

UNITY

My paragraph seems to digress from the main point.

→

1. Make sure that the major supporting sentences directly support the topic sentence.
2. Check that all minor supporting sentences provide direct support for their major supports.
3. Watch out for sentences that might be related to the topic without actually supporting the controlling idea.

COHERENCE

My paragraph doesn't read smoothly.

→

1. Offer sufficient transitions to keep the sentences and ideas flowing smoothly. Refer to the chart on page 96.
2. Make sure you do not overuse transitions. Your transitions should indicate and establish the relationships within and between sentences.

Collaborative Critical Thinking

Asking Your Peers

Ask one of your classmates to answer the following questions. Review the comments and suggestions, and apply any that you feel would improve your paragraph.

1. Who is the writer of this paragraph? Who is the peer reviewer?
2. What is the purpose of the paragraph?
3. Are all details relevant? If not, what changes would you recommend?
4. What is the major strength of this paragraph?
5. What weaknesses can you identify (support, organization, development, transitions, tone, diction, sentence variety, audience, and so on)?
6. What suggestions can you make to help improve this paper?
7. What major problems in mechanics (spelling, grammar, usage, sentence structure, and so on) should the writer work on?

WRITING YOUR EXPOSITORY PARAGRAPH

Proofreading

In the proofreading stage, you fine-tune your writing. Start by reading your paragraph aloud. Are your sentences complete? Do you detect any missing punctuation? Are the words spelled correctly?

Common Error #3: Punctuating Introductory Elements

Generally, commas are required to separate an introductory phrase or clause from the main part of a sentence. When a sentence begins with a prepositional or verbal phrase, a dependent clause, or another construction longer than a word or two, you need to use a comma after it.

> To get to the bank, go past the hospital and turn right.
> Running along the river, John spotted a sunken canoe.
> On the top of the water tower, two students were found reading Shakespeare.

Punctuating clauses is trickier. Look at two simple rules that can help you decide whether or not to punctuate a subordinate clause.

1. If you start a sentence with a dependent clause, be sure to use a comma at the end of that clause.

   > Although he felt it was wrong, Henry took sick leave to care for his sick collie.

2. If your sentence begins with an independent clause and ends with a dependent clause, no comma is needed between the clauses.

   > Henry took sick leave to care for his sick collie although he felt it was wrong.

GRAMMAR CHECKUP   4-1

Read each item carefully. If the sentence is punctuated correctly, write *Correct*; if not, insert the comma in the correct position.

1. After Paolo turned in his project, he decided that he needed a vacation.
2. Laura wanted to major in education because two of her sisters were teachers. Correct
3. Forced to retire early, Jan decided to return to college to finish her degree. Correct
4. Whether you're talking about hamburgers or pizza, fast food is one of the fastest growing industries.
5. While the audience booed and yelled for a refund, the actors made their getaway through the rear exit.
6. Grazing peacefully on the new grass, the cattle faced in a single direction.
7. If you follow instructions carefully, you will be able to install the new software.
8. Masako failed the test because she studied the wrong chapter. Correct

Check your answers to this Grammar Checkup in Appendix A on page A-2. How did you do? If you missed even one or two of the checkup items, you may need to review the punctuation of clauses in Chapter 26.

WRITING   4-6

Proofread your paragraph. Check for and correct errors in spelling, punctuation, usage, and sentence structure. Personalize the following checklist by adding specific errors that continue to occur in your writing.

Proofreading Checklist

1. Does your topic sentence clearly communicate the topic and focus of the paragraph? ☐
2. Is your topic sentence correctly and effectively placed in the paragraph? ☐
3. Do all supporting details (major and minor) develop the idea of the topic sentence without breaking the rule of unity? ☐
4. Does your paragraph offer sufficient major and minor supporting details to make it complete and convincing? ☐
5. Are the types of support that you offer effective and appropriate? ☐
6. Is the paragraph coherent: is the information presented in a logical sequence and do the sentences include appropriate transitions to guide the reader? ☐
7. Is the paragraph free of sentence fragments? Does it offer a variety of sentence structures? ☐
8. Is the paragraph free of errors in grammar, spelling, and punctuation? ☐

Reflecting

Congratulations! You have completed your first expository paragraph, a task requiring lots of planning, writing, and revising. It is important to stop and reflect on what you've accomplished. Reflection allows you to think about how your writing process went and what you might do differently next time.

WRITING   4-7

Self-Reflection

Before you hand in your paper, write a brief paragraph in which you reflect on your final draft.

1. What do you feel you did best?
2. What part of your paper was most challenging to you?
3. In which areas do you feel you need the most practice?
4. What strategies will you employ to address your challenges or weaknesses and to improve the quality of your paragraphs?

WRITING YOUR EXPOSITORY PARAGRAPH

After you have completed this self-reflection, carefully review your instructor's comments. How are they similar or different from your own answers to the self-reflection? Make a list of your grammar, punctuation, and spelling errors so that you can follow up on the ones that recur. Consider what strategies you will employ to address your challenges or weaknesses and to improve the quality of your paragraph.

How might you use exposition outside of this English course? Look back at the writing samples in Previewing Your Task in this chapter.

- **College:** _____
- **Your profession:** _____
- **Everyday life:** _____

CHAPTER 5

Developing Your Essay through Illustration

YOUR GOALS

Understanding Illustration

1. Support general statements with appropriate examples.

2. Develop examples in sufficient detail to illustrate your point.

3. Employ examples effectively in paragraphs and essays.

Writing Your Illustration Essay

1. Use clustering as a brainstorming technique to discover and limit your topic.

2. Write a clear thesis statement and essay map.

3. Use various strategies to write the lead-in of your introduction.

4. Analyze your audience, purpose, and tone to give focus to your illustration essay.

5. Use transitions that are appropriate for illustration.

6. Write an essay that demonstrates unity, coherence, and completeness.

7. Edit to ensure sentence variety and avoid run-on sentences.

"You don't write because you want to say something: you write because you've got something to say."

■ **F. Scott Fitzgerald** ■

In a philosophy class, you participate in a disturbing discussion about the ethics of the death penalty. Several comments made in class cause you to question your objections to the death penalty. In your notes, you list examples of these comments: what the death penalty means to the victim's family, what it means to the community, and how it can act as a deterrent.

As a pharmacist technician at a local drugstore, you are often asked about side effects of various medications you provide. To help your older customers understand these side effects, you create several handouts, in large font, that list examples of side effects for different classes of drugs. For instance, for cold medications you list dizziness, drowsiness, increased appetite, and irritability.

You have just returned from an interview for a part-time job and are telling a friend about the experience. You say that the interview didn't go well and that you doubt you'll be offered the position. Your friend asks for evidence to support your gloomy conclusion, accusing you of being overly negative. What do you tell her? "The interviewer spent only 10 minutes with me. She took no interest in my previous job experience and didn't give me an opportunity to ask specific questions about the position. She even took several phone calls while I was there."

Why are examples so important for effective thinking and writing? As these scenarios point out, examples help explain, prove, or support positions by providing concrete illustrations of general concepts. Using examples in writing is often called *illustration* because examples help the reader "visualize" concepts that might otherwise seem vague. Whether your goal is to inform or persuade your reader, every time you make a general statement, you should consider illustrating it with convincing examples.

LET's warm up!

How many times have you gone shopping and purchased more than you wanted or even needed? Businesses use many techniques to motivate shoppers to buy. Identify one such technique and write a paragraph describing how effectively this technique worked on you.

Dennis MacDonald/PhotoEdit

PREVIEWING YOUR TASK

When you write papers for any of your courses or respond to an essay question on an exam, your instructors want to know how well you understand the material. They want your papers or answers to be clear and concrete, not vague and uninformative. Illustration helps provide the needed concreteness.

The following readings demonstrate effective illustration in several types of writing you will be doing in college, your workplace, and your daily life. Pay particular attention to the first reading: it is an essay. In this chapter, you are moving from writing paragraphs to writing complete essays.

Writing for College

Read the following essay, written by a student, Lisa, for a psychology class in which she provides four concrete examples to explain her chosen topic.

The Divorce Trap

I have been single parent for almost 15 years. If the divorce and separation weren't hard enough, the life of a divorced woman makes the whole process worse. I feel the hardest part of the whole process was what came after the signing of the divorce papers and the notary stamp. Everything that was normal and accepted by my peers and family changed dramatically. Friendships, finances, social activities, and family were forever changed. It still baffles me that with statistics showing success rates for first marriages at less than 49% people can still be so judgmental.

After I became divorced, friends seemed to be afraid that the divorce was contagious. Women friends became very protective of their husbands. I felt as if they thought I was going to try to steal them away. Some of my friends even believed that I would try to break their marriage up so I would have a "divorce buddy." I was hurt often because I would hear about great parties after they had happened. I was not invited. Since I was now considered outside their "norm," I was no longer welcome. These constant awkward moments were so frustrating that I had to redefine my life and cut my ties to people I had always loved and respected—my friends.

As friendships faded, so did my financial security. Money matters became a true nightmare as a divorcée. Whether a car or a home, there are many hoops to jump through before financing is available. The financial institutions can be daunting for a divorced woman. I soon found out that their guidelines for securing a loan would be more rigid for me. For instance, to prove financial stability, a loan officer might require a married client to provide a couple of months' pay stubs, but a divorcée may be requested to submit a year's worth of stubs and 2 years' worth of bank statements. The whole process is frustrating and demeaning. While purchasing my house last year, I had to have 2 years' worth of bank statements and a printout of every child support payment since August of 1990. Every time the mortgage broker called, the hoops to jump through got smaller and higher. After the papers were signed, I was relieved and glad I had jumped through all of the hoops, but as the excitement subsided, I left the office feeling humiliated and pathetic.

However, participating in social activities was perhaps the most draining and anxiety-raising situation that I had to face. The first few months after my divorce, I noticed that I wasn't invited to many functions, and when I was invited, it was a bad experience: I seemed to attract every loser in the place and ended up leaving because I felt uncomfortable. Even school functions and other activities with my children became very awkward. I no longer looked forward to birthdays, holidays, and special events; I dreaded them. I didn't know where to hold them or whom to invite. Should I hold them at my home? If the in-laws show up, will I have to act as if everything is fine or just be as civil as I can for the sake of the children?

Finally, family gatherings became more of a bother than a fun time after my divorce. In my family, I am the only person who has been divorced. My sisters' disapproving looks blamed me for my broken home. As much as I attempted and needed to maintain my family traditions, I was made to feel a stranger. Although I was invited to most family functions, I knew my family felt uncomfortable. Yes, we were all together, but I was still alone.

Getting a divorce or separating from a partner is often intended to make a person's life better. On the other hand, being divorced makes a woman second-guess her decision to remain single. The couples of the world have a hard time letting us divorcées reside comfortably among them. The divorce rate is climbing, and we are becoming a higher percentage of the population, so with any hope the divorced women of the world might have an easier time when more and more people understand what we are going through.

PRACTICE   5-1

1. What is the writer's purpose in this essay? To educate her audience by giving examples of the difficulties she faced following a divorce.

2. What specific images come to mind as you read about the author's experiences with friends, finances, and family? The imagery of jumping through hoops, being awkwardly alone in social situations, and being looked at rudely by family members.

Writing in Your Profession

In workplace writing, using illustration can help your coworkers and customers understand your message, almost as if you were drawing them a picture. As you read the following memo, notice how the use of examples highlights the urgency of the matter.

Informational Memorandum

August 30, 1999

To: Chief Executive Officer, All Farm Credit System Institutions
From: Roland E. Smith, Director, Office of Examination
Subject: Threats to Information Management Systems

The purpose of this memorandum is to heighten your awareness of the increasing threat to financial institutions, including Farm Credit System (FCS) institutions, from "cyber-terrorism." Cyber-terrorism is generally defined as the use of computing resources against persons or property to intimidate or coerce a government, an entity such as a FCS institution, or persons to disrupt, deny, corrupt, or destroy computer systems or networks. Cyber-terrorists can be individuals, criminal organizations, dissident groups or factions, or another country. Attacks can be generated internally or externally and may be directly against a computer system or focus on the supporting infrastructure (telecommunications, electricity, etc.). Cyber-terrorism includes acts of commercial espionage and employee sabotage and can be one catastrophic attack on your infrastructure or a series of coordinated, seemingly independent attacks. Furthermore, cyber-terrorism does not have to be for the purpose of monetary gain or to obtain information; oftentimes, it is conducted solely to destroy all or part of an information management system.

Financial institutions' vulnerabilities are increasing steadily, and the means to exploit those weaknesses are readily available. Cyber-terrorist attacks can take the following forms:
- Denial or disruptions of computer, cable, satellite, or telecommunications services.
- Monitoring of computer, cable, satellite, or telecommunications systems.
- Disclosure of proprietary, private, or classified information stored within or communicated through computer, cable, and satellite or telecommunications systems.
- Modification or destruction of computer programming codes, computer network databases, stored information, or computer capabilities.
- Manipulation of computer, cable, satellite, or telecommunications services resulting in fraud, financial loss, or other federal criminal violation.

The ultimate threat to computer security remains the insider. Thus, security clearance checks should be required.

(Adapted from the Farm Credit Administration website)

1. In what way is a business memo more direct than most essays about the author's intended audience and purpose? It names the audience in the "To" line and states the purpose and main point in the "Subject" line.

2. Identify five specific details the author uses to illustrate his more general points. (This question should point the reader to the list of forms cyber-terrorism can take.) Denial, monitoring, disclosure, modification, manipulation.

Writing in Everyday Life

Letters of complaint are just one of many types of writing in everyday life that require you to provide specific examples. Without examples, your reader may not take you seriously or know how to fix the problem to avoid future complaints.

G. Raymond
123 First Street
Anytown, ON A1B 2C3

May 16, 2004

Mr. C. Service Manager
Large Hotel Chain
1800 Main Street
Ottawa, ON K2P 2E3

Dear Sir:

I was a patron of your hotel for a three-night stay on April 21–24. I am writing you to express my displeasure with the service I received during the stay.

On the night of April 21, I found my room very hot and uncomfortable. I attempted to adjust the in-room air conditioning but found it insufficient. I called the front desk and was told that the HVAC system was temporarily inoperable because a part was broken and on order. I was told that I could open the window, but it appeared to be stuck with debris. Therefore, I spent three hot and stuffy nights in your hotel.

When I made the reservation, I specifically requested a nonsmoking room; however, upon my arrival I was assigned to a designated smoking room. I requested to be moved to another room, but the front-desk staff indicated that there were no others available. I am allergic to smoke and was unable to get fresh air into the room due to the blocked window. I had to purchase allergy medication and when I returned home, I had to have all my clothes dry-cleaned.

I was very unsatisfied with my stay in your hotel. I mentioned my concerns to your staff on several occasions and found them to be well meaning but unable to address my needs. As a result, I would like to have the $250.00 hotel bill refunded, and I would like to be reimbursed for $85.00 in additional expenses (you will notice receipts included for $15.00 for allergy medication and $60.00 for dry-cleaning). I look forward to meeting with you to discuss this matter. I can be reached at 555-5820.

Sincerely,

G. Raymond

_____

(Adapted from the Fanshawe College website)

PRACTICE   5-3

1. What is the writer's purpose in this letter? To complain about service received during a recent hotel stay and to seek reimbursement.

2. How does the writer illustrate the problems encountered at the hotel? The writer uses descriptive language to convey the heat, stuffiness, and other discomforts of the room he was assigned.

UNDERSTANDING ILLUSTRATION

An example is a particular thing, event, behavior, or idea you select to demonstrate something important about a larger concept. In "The Divorce Trap," Lisa writes about four areas in which her life changed following her divorce—friendships, finances, family, and social life. She then develops each of these ideas with examples she selected from a larger pool of possible instances.

In her fourth paragraph, for instance, she presents a number of specific examples of how her social life deteriorated following her divorce: rarely being invited out, having bad experiences when she was invited out, feeling awkward at school functions, and experiencing confusion at her own holiday gatherings.

PRACTICE   5-4

Reread "The Divorce Trap" to identify examples used in the paragraphs identified here. For each paragraph, list two examples the author uses to support her point. Answers will vary.

Paragraph 2: Friendships

  a. Married women became protective of husbands

  b. No longer invited to parties

Paragraph 3: Finances (requirements for a loan)

    a. Two years' worth of bank receipts

    b. Printouts of child support

Paragraph 5: Family

    a. Sisters' disapproval

    b. Made to feel like a failure

Using Examples for Support

For an example to be effective, your audience needs to be able to "see" or imagine it clearly and vividly. For this reason, you must use vivid, concrete language to describe your examples. Thus, a *concrete example* is one that is vividly presented and described in sufficient detail.

We use examples to provide support for general statements and to help clarify unfamiliar, difficult, or abstract ideas. However, even the best of examples go nowhere if not used effectively. Good illustration requires that you give more than just a random list of examples. For your examples to be effective, they must:

- make a strong connection to something the reader already knows.
- convince the reader that your claim is valid.

In the professional memo on page 107, the examples are presented briefly and in relatively technical language because the author knows his audience can understand and relate to them with ease. If the same examples were presented to a group of retirees who have never owned computers, the writer would fail in his purpose of convincing the audience of the seriousness of the consequences. Remember to use examples that will have the intended effect on your chosen audience.

PRACTICE 5-5

Write three topic sentences about your college. Then list at least three examples to illustrate each topic sentence. Imagine that your audience is a group of high school seniors who are considering attending your college next year. Make sure that your topic sentences express an opinion about some aspect of your college and that your examples are concrete and effective. Answers will vary.

   1. My college offers a number of support services for struggling students.

      a. Tutoring

      b. Mental health counseling for troubled students

      c. Childcare

2. Sometimes it seems students have too much freedom.

    a. The attendance policy is lenient.

    b. There's no punishment for not doing homework.

    c. There's no dress code as in high school.

3. My college is not as expensive as one might believe.

    a. We have ready access to financial aid.

    b. Lots of grants are waiting to be applied for.

    c. In-times of financial emergency, students can ask the college for short-term loans.

How many examples are sufficient? There's no clear answer to this question. Sometimes it's sufficient just to list a number of specific examples without describing them in detail, as in the professional memo shown earlier, and other times, you need to describe just one example in great detail. Three factors help determine the number and types of examples that you should provide:

- The complexity of your topic
- The background of your audience
- Your purpose for writing

A long, well-developed example is known as an *extended example*. The extended example is detailed and stretches over the course of one paragraph or even an entire essay.

Returning to "The Divorce Trap" again, read Lisa's second paragraph carefully (page 105). Notice that she mentions two examples of financial difficulties: securing a loan and getting a mortgage. She devotes cursory attention to the first example, but what about the second? Notice that she goes into greater detail about the mortgage, using narration and description to tell the story of her experience so that you, the reader, can feel her frustration. Lisa is making effective use of extended example in this case.

WRITING YOUR ILLUSTRATION ESSAY

This section provides step-by-step instructions for writing an essay based on examples. If you follow the directions and do the activities, you will produce a well-structured, adequately developed, and interesting essay.

But first, what is an essay, and how is writing an essay different from writing a paragraph? Look at this illustration essay written by a student, Jeremy, a police officer now majoring in social work.

Technology in Police Work

The muscular man waved a knife around and took a step toward me. I ordered him to drop the knife, but he suddenly pressed the knife into his wrist. I had to do something quickly to control this situation. If I didn't do anything, he was going to cut his wrist further and cause serious damage. If I rushed in to get the knife, I could be injured from the knife or be at risk from the blood on his hands. I put my gun back in the holster and pulled out my Taser. With a squeeze of the trigger, two darts hit him in the chest and overpowered his central nervous system. I was then able to secure the knife and gain control of the man without being injured. He had two small marks on his chest, which would heal quickly, but, most importantly, I was able to get him the help he needed. This happy ending was possible with the help of modern technology. This scenario is just one example of how technology has become a vital part of law enforcement, redefining the police officer's role to make the job safer and more efficient. As a result of new technology, police officers have a safer work environment, are able to make their communities safer, and are able to fight crime more efficiently.

One important benefit of technology is the increased safety it gives officers in dangerous situations. For example, officers have always been getting too close to suspects. However, such inventions as the Taser, rubber bullets, bean bags, and pepper spray have given officers the advantage of space. Police realize that a suspect armed with a knife within 21 feet presents a deadly threat. The average person can run 21 feet in about one and a half seconds; that is the time it takes an officer to recognize danger, draw and point his or her weapon, and pull the trigger. Even if the suspect is shot and disabled, the knife is going to be so close to the officer that the suspect's momentum may carry the knife forward, causing injury or death. The Taser can be deployed at a distance of 21 feet, providing the officer with a reasonably safe distance. In addition to Taser, rubber bullets and bean bag rounds, which are shot out of a gun but made to stun rather than penetrate the suspect, can be deployed at a distance, creating a crucial safety barrier. Also, pepper spray, one of the most widely used tools among police, can be sprayed from a distance onto the face of the suspect, causing temporary loss of vision and difficulty breathing. Instead of putting themselves in unnecessary danger, officers use these technologies to disarm suspects quickly, effectively, and humanely, which is an advantage to the officers' security.

Modern technology not only has created a safer work environment for officers but also is making our communities safer. For instance, officers are now better prepared to assist citizens because of computer technology. Having laptop computers in all of the cars lets officers write reports on the streets instead of at the station, giving them more time to patrol the community. Also, some agencies have dispatch screens that officers can watch in the car to see the calls that need to be responded to even before they are put out on the radio. Furthermore, agencies around the country are now set up with e-mail and Internet, allowing officers to communicate and share the latest information in crime and enforcement. Should an officer spot a suspicious car, he or she can run the license plate from the comfort of the police vehicle to check if it is stolen. If the car is stolen, the police officer can then apprehend the suspect before that person commits another crime, thus helping to ensure the safety of the community.

However, the most important benefit of modern technology has been in helping police officers be more efficient. Advances in cameras have resulted in stronger cases in courts and have helped officers in surveillance operations. Also, digital photos of injuries and evidence can be downloaded into a computer and saved for years. Additionally, surveillance conducted with satellites or long-range cameras gives officers a tactical edge by not alerting suspects that they are being watched. Even traffic enforcement is simple with the use of red-light cameras and radar guns. But most impressively, with the help of GPS satellite tracking, suspects and undercover officers can be tracked from a longer distance than ever before. Such tracking systems as Lojack and Onstar make it easier to find stolen vehicles. Also, people can be kept safe with the use of Amber Alerts, which have saved lives and assisted law enforcement in catching dangerous violators. These alerts are broadcast to every officer's computer, as well as on the radio. These and many other technological advances have led to more efficient ways to fight crime than existed even a decade ago.

Crime does not seem to be going away, so it is important that police stay ahead of the criminals. Modern technology provides that head start. Through technology, law enforcement agencies will be better prepared to serve and protect their communities while keeping officers and citizens safe. Taxpayers cannot ask for a better return on their investment. With the right technology, having an officer risking his or her life to apprehend a knife-wielding suspect will be a thing of the past.

Now that you've read two student essays ("The Divorce Trap" and "Technology in Police Work"), you can see that there are two important features of the essay form.

1. **It develops a single idea in greater depth than is possible in a single paragraph.**
2. **It consists of several paragraphs.** There is no definite rule about the number of paragraphs an essay must contain, but most college essays follow a fairly common pattern:
   - One or two paragraphs of introductory material designed to capture the reader's interest and state the topic and main point of the essay, which together are called the *thesis*.
   - Several body paragraphs, each with its own topic sentence, devoted to providing support for the essay's main point.
   - At least one paragraph devoted to concluding the essay.

Figure 5.1 on page 114 demonstrates how the body paragraphs support the thesis, or topic and main point, of the essay.

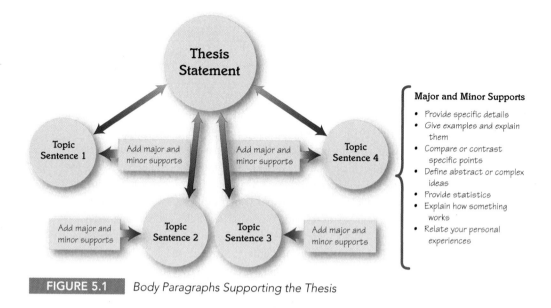

FIGURE 5.1   *Body Paragraphs Supporting the Thesis*

Prewriting

Now that you have a basic understanding of essay structure and development, begin the process of writing your own essay. The first stage of the writing process helps you find a topic, limit your topic, focus your ideas, and plan your essay.

Discovering and Limiting Your Topic

So far you have used listing, freewriting, and questioning as idea-generating strategies. Now, practice clustering as yet another prewriting strategy for discovering information.

Prewriting Strategy #4: Clustering

Before clustering, start by listing ideas or topics that you feel fairly knowledgeable about. Don't stop to think; just list as many ideas, thoughts, and events as you can for at least 5 minutes. After you have completed your listing, review what you have written and circle one idea you would like to explore further. Jeremy chose this item from his list: Technology has changed police work, making it possible for officers to be more effective.

   Jeremy has a good tentative thesis, but he wants to explore more ideas about this topic. So, Jeremy uses clustering to narrow a broad topic to a more focused topic by drawing a diagram. Clustering is an effective prewriting strategy for organizing your thoughts and for generating new ideas and topics, especially for visual learners. Don't concern yourself with spelling or grammar. The procedure for clustering is quite simple:

   1. Write your topic in the center of a sheet of paper and draw a circle around your topic. Then start asking yourself questions about your topic: What is important about this topic? What do I know about this topic? What are some specific examples?

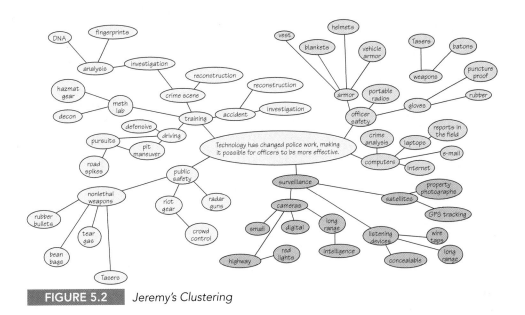

Jeremy's Clustering

2. As words or phrases come to mind about your topic, immediately write them down. Circle ideas and draw lines to connect each idea to the main point in the center of your paper.
3. Continue this process, circling ideas and drawing lines to connect the ones that are associated in some way. As you continue to branch outward from the center, you'll find that your ideas get more specific. Continue this same process repeatedly until you cannot come up with any more new ideas.
4. Review the different groupings of ideas. Don't expect all groups to be useful. Some branches lead to dead ends, while others are filled with interesting and excellent information. Look for those clusters that may serve as the basis of your essay.

Figure 5.2 shows the result of Jeremy's clustering exercise. Notice the many areas and the many possible essays that Jeremy can pursue.

This technique can yield information that you can use to choose a focus (controlling idea) for your essay. It can also offer you information that you can use to support your essay. If you want to focus your topic even more or discover more ideas related to one of the branches of the cluster, you can try making a different circle in the center and then cluster for more specific ideas. You'll be surprised by how quickly you can come up with ideas. Jeremy completed his clustering diagram in less than 15 minutes.

WRITING   5-1

Begin your own brainstorming process. In your notebook, experiment with listing, freewriting, or any other technique to generate some rough topic ideas. Then create a clustering diagram on at least one of your ideas. Give yourself time to allow your ideas to flow, and be sure to draw lines between ideas that seem related.

TOPICS TO CONSIDER

If you're still having problems finding a topic, here are some topics that might interest you. Try using clustering on one or more of the following topics to generate ideas.

Writing for College

■ Freud's concept of the id, ego, and superego	■ The ways in which some politicians can mislead the voters	■ The importance of math in everyday life
■ American's cultural infatuation with violence	■ The Bill of Rights	■ Understanding a scientific concept, such as ozone, minerals, or elements

Writing in Your Profession

BUSINESS	■ Acts of embezzlement ■ Common shoplifting techniques	■ A productive or a nonproductive work environment	■ Qualities of effective negotiation
CRIMINAL JUSTICE	■ Legal or illegal searches ■ Laws that are often abused, misinterpreted, or misapplied	■ Effective or ineffective control of riots or uprising	■ Mishandling of evidence
EDUCATION	■ Students' reading problems ■ Classroom discipline problems	■ Safety issues	■ The lack of or too much accountability
HEALTH	■ The ways that certain patients jeopardize the results of a specific treatment	■ Pain relief without drugs ■ Exercising	■ Dieting
SOCIAL WORK/ PSYCHOLOGY	■ Characteristics of a specific type of abuse	■ Getting involved in families' lives	■ Violence in the home ■ A behavior disorder
TECHNICAL	■ Employees' misuse of computers	■ Burglar alarms ■ Cable TV	■ Bridge design
OTHERS	■ Tabloid journalism ■ Unemployment	■ Sign language	■ IQ tests

Writing in Everyday Life

■ Movies' display of violent acts	■ How people show less (or more) compassion for senior citizens than they used to	■ Children's toys and family values
■ Different ways people celebrate the same holiday	■ Inconsiderate or reckless behavior of a specific group of drivers	■ Qualities of the ideal mate

WRITING   5-2

After doing your own listing and clustering, you should be deciding which one of the many topics that you have discovered you wish to write about. Write your top three topics here.

Topic #1: _____

Topic #2: _____

Topic #3: _____

Identifying Your Audience

In illustration, knowing who your audience is helps you determine what types of examples you should use in your essay. Jeremy decides to write his essay for an audience considering police work as a career. Thus, he chooses examples that demonstrate, in a reassuring way, how the police are better able to protect themselves and their communities as result of new technology.

> **Computer tip**
>
> Use the Internet to look up information about your future career to brainstorm possible topics for your essay.

Establishing Your Purpose

Ask yourself what effect you want your writing to have on your reader—this is your purpose. Jeremy begins his essay with a dramatic scenario of a knife-wielding man threatening a police officer and then turning the knife on himself. Clearly, this opening technique is designed to appeal to the sense of fear Jeremy's audience is likely to feel when the subject of personal threat comes up. And his later examples leave the reader feeling more confident that law enforcement agencies can respond more quickly and safely than in the past. Being aware of your purpose as you draft your essay helps you determine the organization, information, and tone that are appropriate to your audience as you draft your essay.

Setting Your Tone

As you plan and draft your essay, consider your attitude toward your topic and consider how you can enable your audience to perceive that attitude.

How would you describe Jeremy's attitude toward his topic? Remember his audience: people considering police work as a career. Also recall his purpose: to let them know that police work is safer and more efficient than it once was. Clearly, he wants to be reassuring in his presentation of the material. Consider how you want your audience to perceive your attitude. Table 5.1 on page 118 should help you make reasonable choices.

TABLE 5.1	*Tones to Achieve Your Purpose*		
Purpose	**Description of Possible Tone to Achieve Your Purpose**		
TO INFORM	balanced formal impartial	neutral objective tolerant	unbiased
TO ANALYZE	critical consistent logical	open-minded rational serious	straightforward
TO PERSUADE	assertive critical emotional	enthusiastic excited fair	forceful noncondescending respectful
TO ENTERTAIN	casual cheerful humorous	informal joyful optimistic	positive witty

WRITING   5-3

Stop a moment to reflect on your audience, purpose, and tone. Fill in the following form.

Audience, Purpose, and Tone Analysis

Your Topic: _____

I. Audience

1. Who is your target audience? _____

   a. Age(s): _____

   b. Gender(s): _____

   c. Education level(s): _____

2. Why would this audience be interested in your topic? _____
   _____

3. What does your audience already know about your topic? _____
   _____

4. What background information will your audience need to understand the topic?
   _____

II. Your Purpose

1. Why did you choose this topic? _____
   _____

2. What is the controlling idea, or main point, of your essay? _____
   _____

3. What effect do you want your essay to have on your audience? _____

_____

4. What information must you provide to achieve the desired effect? _____

_____

III. Tone

1. What is your personal attitude about this topic? _____

_____

2. What tone do you wish to establish for this essay? _____

_____

3. How will your tone help you relate to your audience and support your purpose?

_____

Formulating Your Thesis

Although the thesis for the illustration essay may seem a bit more complex, it is still a general statement. In an essay, the thesis statement and the topic sentences work together to help break down your ideas so that your reader clearly understands what you're trying to communicate.

The thesis statement is the most general statement in the essay. Its purpose is to let the reader know what the essay is about. A topic sentence is also a general statement, but it is less general than a thesis. Its purpose is to let the reader know what a paragraph is about.

Characteristics of an Effective Thesis

Just like a topic sentence, a thesis statement has two parts: the topic and a main point (controlling idea or focus).

Thesis = Topic + Main Point

The topic is what you plan to discuss in your essay.

TOPIC: Technology in police work

The main point is your claim (or opinion) on your topic. What do you want your reader to believe, accept, or understand about your topic?

CLAIM ON TOPIC OR MAIN POINT: Has made the work safer and more efficient

Topic Main Point

Thesis = Technology + has become a vital part of law enforcement, redefining the police officer's role to make the job safer and more efficient.

Before you try to write your own thesis statement, here are some basic rules.

1. **Make sure that your thesis states an opinion, not a fact.**

AVOID: Today's police carry Tasers and have computers in their cars. [That's fine, but so what? Jeremy wants say something meaningful about how these technologies have changed police work.]

2. **Make sure your thesis expresses your opinion, not someone else's opinion.**

> AVOID: Some people believe that police work is safer now than in the past.
>
> [People think a lot of things, but Jeremy wants to write an essay about what he thinks.]

3. **Write your thesis as a single declarative sentence, not a question.**

> AVOID: Are our communities safer now than in the past because of the new technologies available to law enforcement agencies?
>
> [The reader wants to know what Jeremy thinks about the topic, not be asked a question.]

4. **Make sure that your thesis is a complete sentence, not a fragment.**

> AVOID: Modern technology in law enforcement.
>
> [This is a fragment, not a complete sentence. It might serve as the title of the essay but not as its thesis.]

Notice how each of these rules emphasizes one important characteristic of an effective thesis: it's a statement of what you believe, your opinion.

Look at two distracting habits that some students may have when they phrase their theses.

1. **Avoid making your thesis an announcement of your topic.**

> AVOID: In this essay I'm going to give examples of how technology helps police fight crime.
>
> [Avoid such expressions as "this essay is about . . . ," "I am going to discuss . . . ," "in this essay I will illustrate . . . ," or "the topic of this essay is. . . ." This is an elementary approach that bores the reader. Don't delay your purpose; say exactly what you want to discuss.]

2. **Avoid cluttering your thesis with such useless and empty phrases as "in my opinion," "I think," "I feel," or "I believe."**

> AVOID: I feel that police work is much safer and more efficient now than it was in the past.
>
> [It's obvious you feel this way. After all, you are writing the essay!]

PRACTICE   5-6

Each of the following thesis statements requires revision. Explain the problem by citing the reasons given earlier and then revise the thesis. Answers will vary.

1. Few women are elected to Congress.

Reason: The thesis should state an opinion, not a fact.

Revision: Women still face many obstacles to being elected to Congress.

2. Why did students decide to strike?

Reason: A thesis should not be stated as a question.

Revision: The students decided to strike for three major reasons.

3. Violence in public schools seems to be on the rise.

Reason: Too noncommittal because of *seems*

Revision: Increasing violence in our public schools is causing severe distraction from the learning process.

4. In this essay, I will discuss free day care on campus.

Reason: Announces the topic with "In this essay, I will discuss . . ."

Revision: Our campus needs to implement free day care to help students focus on their studies.

5. The benefits of school uniforms.

Reason: Fragment

Revision: Requiring school uniforms through middle school has many important benefits.

Using an Essay Map with Your Thesis

The essay map, which is a brief listing of the main points of your essay, is a logical extension of the thesis; thus, you can use it in just about any type of writing. Using an essay map has three main benefits:

1. **The essay map helps you limit your thesis.** If you can state the major points you will develop in support of your thesis, you won't be tempted to enter the drafting stage with a thesis that is too vague or general for a short essay.

2. **The essay map provides you, the writer, with a clear sense of direction.** It helps you plan and follow the organization of your paragraphs. Each of your topic sentence's main points will reflect a point of your essay map, and the body paragraphs in your essay will follow the order of your essay map.

3. **The essay map offers that same sense of direction to your reader.** Through your essay map, your reader knows from the start the entire layout of your paper and what specific points you will be discussing and illustrating.

Look at "Technology in Police Work" again to see the relationship of the essay map and topic sentences. Notice how the essay map can be a separate sentence from the thesis.

The essay map helps the writer maintain a focus throughout the essay. It also helps focus the reader on specific areas that the writer discusses in the body of the essay.

For each of the following general statements, provide a reasonable essay map. Answers will vary.

1. The students in this writing class represent a diverse group of people: _____old_____ , _____young_____ , and ___those in between___ .

2. _____River rafting_____ and _____great food_____ are the best qualities that my hometown offers tourists.

3. The qualities that are essential for a successful teacher are ___organization___ , _____enthusiasm_____ , _____fairness_____ , and ___a sense of humor___ .

4. First impressions are crucial to how one initiates relationships with others. Some bases for initial judgments of others are _how they dress_ , _what they say_ , and _how they treat others_ .

5. Participation in such community activities as _____voter drives_____ and _helping the homeless_ can enhance a citizen's life.

Now that you have discovered your topic and established the audience and purpose for your essay, you are ready to write your thesis. Your first attempt will probably be a rough thesis, usually referred to as the *working thesis*, and may not resemble your final thesis. As you go deeper into the writing process, you will find that your thesis may take different shapes. Here's an example of how Jeremy moves from a topic to a working thesis.

TOPIC:	Modern technology in police work
MAIN POINT:	Makes the work safer and easier
WORKING THESIS:	Modern technology in police work makes the work safer and easier.

Keep in mind the three parts you will be using for this essay:

Topic   +   Main Point   +   Essay Map   =   Thesis

Jeremy then refines his working thesis to include the essay map as part of his thesis.

WORKING THESIS:	With modern technology, the police officer is safer, citizens are safer, and law enforcement is easier.

Jeremy continues to inch toward a final thesis, but at this point, his thesis is still a work in progress.

Write out your working thesis here.

Topic   +   Main Point   +   Essay Map   =   Thesis

Working Thesis: _____

_____

Outlining Your Ideas

Your next stage is to create an outline. Your outline helps you organize your ideas before you begin to write; it is your blueprint. A good outline helps you avoid rambling, determine the best sequence of ideas, and break long essays into manageable chunks. Your outline should include all major points that you plan to cover in your essay.

    Your outline consists of three basic areas—an introduction, body paragraphs, and a conclusion. It can help to start by clarifying your audience, purpose, thesis, and essay map. Here's Jeremy's outline. Examine the many details and examples he uses to illustrate his thesis.

> **Computer tip**
>
> Use the outlining feature of your word processor. (You can use the Help function to find out how to use this feature.) Keep yourself focused by writing your audience, purpose, thesis, and essay map at the top of the page before you start your outline.

ESSAY OUTLINE

Audience: People who are considering law enforcement but have yet to decide

Purpose: To convince the reader that modern technology has made police work much safer and more efficient than most people believe

Thesis and Essay Map: With modern technology, the police officer is safer, the citizens are safer, and law enforcement is easier.

I. **Introduction**
   A. Describe a scenario of a life-saving decision.
   B. Show technology at work.
   C. State my thesis and essay map as one sentence.

II. **Body paragraphs**
   A. Topic sentence #1: **Technology has made the job safer.**
      1. Advantages are offered by Taser, rubber bullets, bean bags, and pepper spray.
      2. With technology, the physical distance from the suspect increases.
      3. The use of these tools is simple.
   B. Topic sentence #2: **Technology helps create a safer community for citizens.**
      1. Laptops mean more time in the community.
      2. Technology offers greater response time.
      3. Information crucial for the crime fighter is easily accessible.
      4. Suspects are quickly identified.

C. Topic sentence #3: **Officers can do their job more efficiently.**
   1. Advances in cameras have made strong cases in courts.
   2. Surveillance operations are more efficient.
   3. Tracking can be done from long distances.
   4. Identification of suspects is easier and more reliable.

III. Conclusion
   A. Emphasize that it's crucial that we stay ahead of the criminal.
   B. Restate the thesis.
   C. End with a question or return to the opening scenario.

Once you have completed your outline, you can examine all the parts to make sure that all information is relevant to your thesis, purpose, and audience. You can also check that your examples are relevant and appropriate to their topic sentences. Don't be afraid to add, delete, change, or regroup information. After all, it's your essay, and you want it to show how well and logically you organize your ideas.

WRITING   5-5

Prepare your outline. Examine how each bit of information is related.

Essay Outline

Audience: _____

Purpose: _____

Thesis and Essay Map: _____

_____

I. Introduction: Lead-in strategies
   A. _____
   B. _____
   C. _____

II. Body paragraphs
   A. Topic sentence #1: _____

      1. _____
      2. _____
      3. _____
      4. _____

B. Topic sentence #2: _____

    1. _____

    2. _____

    3. _____

    4. _____

C. Topic sentence #3: _____

    1. _____

    2. _____

    3. _____

    4. _____

D. Topic sentence #4: _____

    1. _____

    2. _____

    3. _____

    4. _____

III. Conclusion

    A. _____

    B. _____

    C. _____

Drafting

Your outline has given you a blueprint or plan for your entire essay. Now, flesh out this plan. In drafting your essay, you explain your ideas by providing examples to illustrate your points. Your draft consists of an introduction, several body paragraphs, and a conclusion.

Writing Your Introduction

Unfortunately, some students feel that the introduction is a mere formality, so they focus all their energy on the body of the essay. However, a hastily written introduction keeps your reader from reading your essay. Why should your reader be interested if you apparently are not? The introduction is not expendable; it is an essential component of your essay that should capture your reader's attention and tell your reader what to expect in the essay.

Lead-in Techniques

Since your introduction presents the initial impression your reader gains of your essay, you must make sure that it captures the reader's interest. The main components of your introduction are your lead-in, your thesis, and your essay map.

Lead-in   +   Thesis   +   Essay Map   =   Introduction

The *lead-in* is an introductory device that uses specific strategies to entice the reader and enable you to indicate the importance of your essay. Here are a few lead-in strategies for you to consider:

1. **Brief description.** By using description as the lead-in, you can paint a vivid picture to make a connection with the reader and introduce the main point of the essay.
2. **Short personal narrative.** Most people enjoy hearing a personal story, so recounting an event that happened to you can pique the reader's interest. Your reader wants to know what happens next.
3. **Anecdote.** Relating a short incident (not necessarily personal and sometimes humorous) not only establishes some background for the reader to understand your topic but also sets the mood of your essay.
4. **Background information.** Sometimes it's necessary to fill your introduction with necessary material or information to help the reader understand the issue you are planning to discuss.

Generally, your lead-in may begin with fairly broad information, but it should become narrower as you approach the thesis. Think of your introductory paragraph as an upside down pyramid, where you start with an attention-getting lead-in and then funnel this information so that it smoothly connects to its topic and main point, the thesis (Figure 5.3).

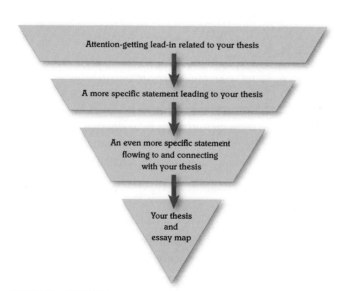

Jeremy decides to use narration as the lead-in to his thesis. His first draft is not quite successful. Note how it limps weakly to his thesis, not making a smooth connection. But at this point of the process, it's a good start. The basic idea that he wants is there, but he needs to work more on his introduction before it's ready for the reader, something Jeremy will do in the revising stage.

Attention-getting lead-in related to your thesis

A more specific statement leading to your thesis

An even more specific statement flowing to and connecting with your thesis

Your thesis and essay map

FIGURE 5.3   *Structure of the Introduction*

> He waved the knife around and took a step toward me. I told him to drop it, and he pressed the knife back into his wrist. So I needed to decide. What should I do? If I didn't do anything, he was going to cut his wrist further and cause serious damage. If I tried to get the knife, I could be injured from the knife or from his blood. I then took out my trusty Taser and squeezed the trigger and two darts hit him. He let go of the knife, and the knife fell on the ground. This shows that modern technology keeps police officers safer, keeps citizens safer, and many tools are at the officer's disposal to do a better, more efficient job.

It is not a rule that you write your introduction first. You already know your thesis, purpose, and audience, so it is acceptable to start by drafting the body paragraphs of your essay. Many writers find that by first drafting the body of the essay they can then write an introduction that is more appropriate and meaningful to the content of the essay.

Writing Your Body Paragraphs

Now that you have a clear thesis and purpose, you are ready to present your evidence in support of the thesis. As you compose this part of your essay, your paragraphs should follow the order of your essay map. If you decide to change the order of your paragraphs, remember to change the order of your map points, too.

Start each paragraph with a clear topic sentence, which is the main point of your paragraph. Your topic sentence corresponds with a point in your essay map. Then explain your topic sentence by providing details and examples to illustrate the idea of the topic sentence or to explain any general statement you made in support of your topic sentence. Again, you're going from the general to the specific. At this point, concern yourself with providing relevant and specific details and examples; you can revise your tone, style, and grammar later.

> **Computer tip**
>
> Start the body of your essay by writing topic sentences in larger, bold font as headings for each page. Then start writing information under each topic sentence. If a detail for another paragraph springs out, scroll to that paragraph and type it immediately. If you wait, chances are you will forget the idea.

Coherence: Using Transitions

When you wrote your descriptive paragraph, you achieved coherence by using spatial order to organize your description. In your narrative you used chronological order, as well as spatial order, to achieve coherence, and in your expository paragraphs you used a variety of transitions, depending on the purpose of the paragraph.

In your illustration essay your paragraphs are coherent when you establish their relationship to one another. Once you have established a logical order, use transitional words and expressions to signal that order. Transitions serve as a bridge between one idea and the next. They help unify your essay and help guide your reader from the first sentence of your essay to the last sentence in your conclusion.

TABLE 5.2	*Transitions for Essay Coherence*	
To Add a Point		
additionally	equally important	moreover
again	finally	next
along with	further	other
also	furthermore	then
and	in addition (to)	too
another	in the first (second, third, . . .) place	what is more
as well	last	
besides	likewise	
To Indicate Illustration or Examples		
an example is	incidentally	specifically
as a case in point	in fact	such as
as an example	in general	that is
as an illustration	in other words	thus
consider as an illustration	in particular	to cite an example
for example	like	to demonstrate
for instance	most important	to illustrate
for one thing	one such	yet another

Use the list of transitions in Table 5.2 to help give your essay coherence. However, make sure that the transitions you select are appropriate, effective, and necessary. Although transitions will help one idea flow smoothly to the next, overusing transitions can be confusing and distracting to the reader.

In addition to using transitional words and expressions, restating key ideas helps keep your essay flowing smoothly. Here are two ways in which you can achieve coherence between paragraphs:

1. **Restate your controlling idea.** Jeremy uses this technique at the beginning of his first body paragraph: One important benefit of technology is the increased safety it gives officers in dangerous situations.
2. **Restate the main point of the previous paragraph.** Jeremy's second body paragraph uses this technique: Modern technology not only has created a safer work environment for officers but also is making our communities safer.

> ### Collaborative Critical Thinking
>
> **In groups of three or four,** review Jeremy's first draft (page 112) and do the following:
> 1. Circle all transitions between paragraphs. Are they effective? Explain your opinion to the other group members. Give suggestions to improve transitions between paragraphs.
> 2. Underline the transitions within each paragraph. Are they effective? Discuss your answer. Explain where you would add, change, or delete transitional words or phrases.

Writing Your Conclusion

Through your conclusion, you bring a sense of closure to your essay. Do more than simply restate your thesis and summarize your key points; give the reader something additional to think about. Your conclusion is your last opportunity to impress your opinion on your reader, so make your conclusion meaningful to the reader. In other words, your conclusion should convey a sense of completeness.

Here's Jeremy's initial conclusion:

> Crime does not seem to be going away, so it is important that police stay ahead of the criminals. As technology continues to advance, law enforcement will be better able to serve and protect their communities while keeping officers and citizens safe. Thus, when officers need to apprehend a suspect or must deal with life-threatening decision when faced with a dangerous person, they will have technology working for them.

Although still in need of revision, Jeremy's conclusion attempts to link the conclusion to his introduction. For example, Jeremy alludes to the scenario he created in the lead-in, thus returning to the introduction. Jeremy feels that this circular technique gives his essay a sense of completeness.

WRITING 5-6

Begin drafting your essay with whichever part you want to start with. Here are some guidelines for each section:

1. Draft your own introduction using one of the lead-in techniques mentioned earlier. You might even draft two or three different introductions, experimenting with several lead-in techniques, just to see which one works best for your essay. Be sure to include a lead-in that captures the reader's attention, sentences that narrow the focus of the paragraph to your particular topic, and your thesis and essay map (if you are using an essay map).

2. Draft your own body paragraphs.

WRITING YOUR ILLUSTRATION ESSAY

3. Start each of your paragraphs with a clear topic sentence. During revision, you may choose to change the position of the topic sentence, but for now it's important that you keep all the information in each paragraph focused only on the idea expressed in the topic sentence.

4. Add as much information as possible to explain each of your topic sentences. If necessary, stop and use any of the prewriting techniques to help you generate ideas for specific topic sentences.

5. Add examples that help your audience understand the points you're making.

6. Add transitions to keep your ideas flowing smoothly and to guide your audience through your information and examples.

7. Write a tentative conclusion for your essay. Review Jeremy's conclusion. Does this approach work for your essay? Whatever you decide, make sure that your conclusion is meaningful and that it effectively wraps up the essay.

Revising

Look at your essay draft as if you're seeing it for the first time. Every essay can be improved. Reread your essay several times. Are your ideas clear? Do you want to change words or phrases? Do you want to add, delete, or change details or examples? Are you happy with the organization of your essay? Does it flow smoothly? Make whatever changes you feel are necessary to create a more effective essay.

WRITING 5-7

Start your revision. Don't leave any part of your essay untouched.

- Make sure your information is organized effectively.
- Be sure to offer sufficient and relevant information.
- Check for coherence. Make sure you offer enough transitions to help guide your reader. Make sure your lead-in moves easily into your thesis and each paragraph flows smoothly to the next.
- Use the chart on page 131 to help you troubleshoot.
- Use a variety of sentence types.

Style Tip: Using Coordination to Combine Sentences

Continue thinking about how to vary your sentences. If your sentences tend to be short and choppy, try combining them by adding coordinating conjunctions to create compound sentences.

Solomon was king of all he surveyed. He wasn't particularly happy.

These two shorter sentences could easily be combined into one longer one by connecting them with the coordinating conjunction *but*.

Solomon was king of all he surveyed, but he wasn't particularly happy.

Not only is the revised sentence longer than either of the originals, but it also shows a logical connection between the two ideas that can help your reader understand your meaning.

Bridging Knowledge

Go to Chapter 22 to get further practice with combining sentences.

PROBLEM .... **SOLUTION** ....

WRITING

My introduction is weak. It just doesn't work.

1. Will it engage or make a connection with your audience? If not, change strategies. You might also be able to combine strategies: description, narrative, anecdote, or background information. For example, use an anecdote and background information.

2. If your thesis sounds as if it just "popped up," add a sentence or two between your lead-in and your thesis that begin to focus the reader's attention on your particular topic.

WRITING

My thesis seems too broad, vague, or unfocused.

1. Try using an essay map.

2. If you have an essay map, look at the points of the essay map. Can you narrow them even more?

3. Take one of the points of the essay map and make that the thesis; then brainstorm for additional support and write an essay map on this new main point.

4. Review your thesis to make sure you didn't commit any of the common errors described on page 120.

5. Look at the restatement of the thesis in your conclusion. If your restatement is better, use it as the thesis. Then write another restatement.

ILLUSTRATION

I can't think of enough information to support my topic sentences.

1. Take a topic sentence or a point in the paragraph you want to develop more and do more prewriting on that particular point. See if this helps generate new ideas.

2. Analyze the examples you have. Did you offer enough examples? Can you provide better, clearer, more interesting, or more relevant examples?

3. Try going on the Internet and doing a little research on your topic. Just don't forget to give credit in your paper to any source you use. Consult your instructor before trying this option.

4. Create a blog post to ask for information on any of your topic sentences or points. You'll be surprised to see how many bloggers come to your rescue.

PROBLEM   **SOLUTION**

COHERENCE

I can't get my
essay to read
smoothly.

1. Circle all your transitions. Did you use enough transitions to guide your reader? If not, see where you can add transitions.

2. Did you overuse transitions? Unnecessary transitions can interrupt the flow of ideas. Eliminate this excess.

3. Make sure that the details in each paragraph are relevant to their topic sentence and that each paragraph is relevant to your thesis statement.

4. Look at your sentence structure. Do you vary the types of sentences you use? If not, combine sentences to form a good balance of compound and complex sentences. See Chapter 22 for explanation and examples of sentence variety.

Collaborative Critical Thinking

Asking Your Peers

Once you have completed the writing process and have a polished final draft, exchange papers with a classmate for peer review. Use the following form:

1. **Read:** Read the essay through once to understand the overall information.

2. **Track:** On your second reading, do the following:

   a. Underline the thesis statement.

   b. Put check marks above the points listed in the essay map.

   c. Go to the body paragraphs and underline each topic sentence.

   d. Underline the sentence in the conclusion that restates the thesis.

3. **Praise:** What works about this essay? Be specific.

4. **Questions:** What would you like to know more about? What don't you understand? List as many concerns as possible.

5. **Suggestions:** What ideas do you have for improving this essay? Be specific.

Return the paper to the writer. Once you receive feedback from your peer, read it carefully. Ask your reviewer for additional questions or clarification if necessary. Consider what changes, if any, to make before submitting your final draft to your instructor.

Proofreading

Numerous or major errors are distracting for the reader and can hurt your credibility as a writer since the reader judges you and your abilities by the way you write. The point of this stage is to check such trouble spots as sentence structure, grammar, usage, and punctuation. In this chapter, focus on looking for fused sentences and comma splices.

Common Error #4: Fused Sentences

A fused sentence—a type of run-on sentence—occurs when two complete sentences appear without any punctuation between them. This type of error is confusing to the reader since the reader must stop to figure out where one idea ends and the next begins and the reader can easily misread what you're trying to say.

INCORRECT:	The 1960s was an important decade in our history the Civil Rights Movement made major gains during that decade.
CORRECT:	The 1960s was an important decade in our history; for one thing, the Civil Rights Movement made major gains during that decade.

Common Error #5: Comma Splice

A comma splice—the other type of run-on sentence—can also cause confusion for the reader, although not at the level of a fused sentence. Basically, a comma splice involves ending a sentence with a comma, rather than a period or a semicolon.

INCORRECT:	Hollywood has made several movies about the CIA, the agency is hardly ever portrayed in a positive light in the movies.
CORRECT:	Hollywood has made several movies about the CIA. The agency is hardly ever portrayed in a positive light in the movies.

GRAMMAR CHECKUP 5-1

Identify each sentence as either a fused sentence (FS) or a comma splice (CS). Then revise the sentence appropriately. Answers will vary for revisions.

CS 1. The speaker on the topic of stem cell research was confusing, he gave too many statistics.

Revision: The speaker on the topic of stem cell research was confusing; he gave too many statistics.

FS 2. The strike created a financial crisis the company was forced to file for bankruptcy.

Revision: The strike created a financial crisis: the company was forced to file for bankruptcy.

FS 3. Ramon is a legal secretary he makes an excellent salary.

Revision: As a legal secretary, Ramon makes an excellent salary.

CS 4. The customer waited impatiently, none of the employees noticed her.

Revision: The customer waited impatiently, but none of the employees noticed her.

FS 5. My *New Yorker* subscription just ran out my husband forgot to renew it.

Revision: My *New Yorker* subscription just ran out because my husband forgot to renew it.

Check your answers to this Grammar Checkup in Appendix A on page A-2. How did you do? If you missed even one of these items, you may need to review the two types of run-on sentences in Chapter 16.

WRITING 5-8

Start proofreading your own essay. Check for and correct errors in sentence structure (fragments, comma splices, and fused sentences). Look for other obvious errors in spelling, punctuation, and so on, as well. Use the following checklist.

Proofreading Checklist

1. Is the lead-in appropriate for the specified audience, is it captivating or attention-getting, and does it lead smoothly to the thesis statement? ☐
2. Does the thesis statement contain the topic of the essay and assert your opinion? Is it clearly stated in the introduction? ☐
3. If you chose to include an essay map, is the essay map appropriate and does it effectively limit the thesis? ☐
4. Does each paragraph have a clearly stated topic sentence? ☐
5. Does each paragraph contain strong, specific, relevant, and sufficient details and examples to illustrate the point made by the topic sentence? ☐
6. Does your essay use a variety of smooth and clear transitions within and between paragraphs? ☐
7. Do you use a variety of sentence structures? ☐
8. Is the language or diction effective and appropriate for the audience and topic? ☐
9. Did you edit carefully for grammar, punctuation, mechanics, and spelling, and is your essay is free of fragments, comma splices, and fused sentences? ☐

Reflecting

Congratulations! You have completed your essay, a major task involving lots of creativity, planning, and, of course, writing and rewriting. After such a major undertaking, it is important to stop and reflect on what you've accomplished. Reflection allows you to think about how your writing process went and what you might do differently next time.

WRITING 5-9

Self-Reflection

Before you hand in your paper, write a brief paragraph in which you reflect on your final draft. Include your feelings on the following questions:

1. What do you feel you did best?

2. What part of your paper was most challenging to you?

3. In which areas do you feel you need the most practice?

4. What strategies will you employ to address your challenges or weaknesses and to improve the quality of your paragraphs?

After you have completed this self-reflection, carefully review your instructor's comments. How are they similar or different from your own answers to the self-reflection? Make a list of your grammar, punctuation, and spelling errors so that you can follow up on the ones that recur. Consider what strategies you will employ to address your challenges or weaknesses and to improve the quality of your essay.

How might you use illustration outside of this English course? Look back at the writing samples in Previewing Your Task in this chapter.

- **College:** _____
- **Your profession:** _____
- **Everyday life:** _____

CHAPTER 6

Developing Your Essay through Process Analysis

YOUR GOALS

Understanding Process Analysis

1. Distinguish between directional and informative processes.

2. Use time order to present steps in a process.

3. Employ warnings and explanations as appropriate in processes.

Writing Your Process Analysis Essay

1. Analyze your target audience(s).

2. Formulate an effective thesis for a process essay.

3. Create an outline for your process essay.

4. Choose appropriate tones for a variety of audiences and purposes.

5. Review your draft for grammar and style.

6. Write an essay that demonstrates unity, coherence, and completeness.

"The best writing is rewriting."

▪ E. B. White ▪

As a student, you follow certain procedures repeatedly: to apply for financial aid, to register for classes, to complete assignments, and to graduate and receive your degree. Your instructors often break learning tasks into steps so that you can gradually acquire important knowledge and skills. In some of your classes, you study the historical or scientific phases leading to certain outcomes or results.

In your daily life, you might need to explain to your insurance agent how an accident occurred or follow instructions for some home improvement task. You might even pick up a self-help book, covering such topics as how to stay healthy and young, how to become an effective leader, or how to improve your love life.

In your career, you may need to give instructions to someone to perform a specific job or task more efficiently, or you may need to follow a process to file a grievance or follow safety procedures to maintain a safe work environment.

All of these activities are processes. Some are designed as instructions that the reader should follow; others describe the way things work. When you write about a process, you want it to have a clear goal, and you want to show how and why the steps in the process lead up to that goal.

LET's warm up!

Whether studying for an exam alone or as part of a group, most of us have one or more methods that have proven successful. Write a paragraph in which you describe an effective method for studying for an exam. What steps should your reader follow to do well on the test?

Tetra Images/Jupiter Images

PREVIEWING YOUR TASK

The following writing samples demonstrate how process analysis can be used in college, work, and everyday life. As you read them, imagine how you could use process writing in each of these settings to strengthen your message.

Writing for College

Because processes occur naturally in a variety of fields—mathematics, science, history, and so on—your college instructors often ask you to write about them. Sometimes, however, you are asked to describe how to accomplish a particular task. In the following student essay, written for a culinary arts class, Tamra describes one way to preserve vegetables.

Freeze Vegetables to Perfection

Have you ever wanted a certain vegetable at the wrong time of the year? Have you ever come home from a long day only to discover that you have no vegetables for your dinner? I've been there. I enjoy having my vegetables with my dinner. Dinner feels incomplete without just the right vegetable on my plate. But it seemed that every time I had an urge for a certain type of vegetable, it was always the wrong time. Well, not anymore! I've begun freezing my own vegetables, and I'm happy to say that now I have my favorite vegetables all year long, not to mention the savings. To most people, freezing vegetables seems like a time-consuming and complex process; however, it's really very simple. You just need to know which kinds of vegetables are freezable, how to prepare them, and how to blanch them.

First, you need to know that not all produce can be successfully frozen. Vegetables such as potatoes, lettuce, cucumbers, and celery tend to turn soft and mushy when they are frozen and then thawed. Other vegetables, such as onions and tomatoes, can be frozen only if they are going to be used in a cooked recipe such as soups or casseroles. They don't taste very good raw after they have been frozen. On the other hand, such vegetables as green beans, peas, asparagus, broccoli, cauliflower, and sweet corn on the cob can be frozen and then removed from the freezer, cooked, and served. They tend to hold their shape and good taste. As an added tip, choose young, tender vegetables that are in good condition, not bruised or soft; and don't use vegetables that are over-ripe since they tend to be tough and flavorless.

After you have decided which vegetables you are going to freeze, you need to prepare them for blanching, the process of boiling food for a very short time. When you prepare vegetables, you convert them from their natural state into edible portions. Green beans need to be stringed, both ends broken off, and then snapped in the middle, for example. Peas need to be removed from their pods, and red beets need the tops and the bottom roots removed; broccoli and Brussels sprouts need to be cut apart. It is important to prepare vegetables for two reasons. One reason is that they won't blanch or freeze properly without preparing them first. Second, it makes it easier for you to wash your vegetables well since they might have pesticides on them or germs from handling on the long journey to the grocery store.

You are now ready for the final main step: blanching your vegetables. Most vegetables need to be blanched before they are frozen. Blanching helps to keep the flavor in frozen vegetables from changing since it stops the action of enzymes that make them mature. There are two methods of blanching. The first method is the boiling water method. For this technique, boil a large pot of water on your stovetop. Then immerse a metal strainer full of washed and prepared vegetables into the water. When the boiling starts again, begin the timing. The second method is the steaming method. For this method, place a vegetable steamer inside a pot. Then put the vegetables in the steamer when the water in the pot below starts to boil. Cover the steamer with its lid and start timing. The blanching time varies depending on the type of vegetable but basically ranges from 1 minute to just a few minutes.

Immediately after the end of each blanching period, you must chill the vegetables in order to stop the cooking process. To do this, simply plunge the vegetables into a sink full of very cold tap water and let the vegetables chill until they are thoroughly cooled on the inside. Test by biting into a piece, just to make sure. When the vegetables are cool, remove them from the water and drain them well. You're ready to place your veggies in the appropriate containers, label them, and then freeze them.

Now, when you make dinner after a long day's work or when you can't get the vegetable you want at the grocery store, you can just go to your freezer and get the vegetable you really desire. The best part is that the vegetables are already cleaned and prepared, so all you need to do is defrost and serve them. *Bon appétit!*

PRACTICE   6-1

1. What is the purpose of this essay? To explain the process of freezing vegetables.
2. After reading the essay, do you believe you could successfully freeze vegetables? Why or why not? Most readers could successfully prepare and blanch vegetables, but the essay does not go into much detail about the freezing process itself. It might have discussed portion size, appropriate containers for freezing, and so on.

Writing in Your Profession

Process analysis is one of the most common kinds of professional writing. Anytime you read a set of instructions for accomplishing a task, you are reading a process analysis.

> **State of California—Health and Human Services Agency**
> **Department of Social Services**
> **Evaluator Manual Transmittal Sheet**
>
> Distribution:
> _X_ All Child Care Evaluator Manual Holders   Transmittal No.
> ___ All Residential Care Evaluator Manual Holders   99RM-03
> ___ All Evaluator Manual Holders   Date Issued
>   July 1999
> Subject: Reporting Requirements
>
> Child Abuse Reporting Procedures
>
> 1. Contact the appropriate Child Protective Agency immediately upon receipt of a complaint alleging child abuse, or as soon as possible thereafter. A "Child Protective Agency" is a police or sheriff's department, a county probation department, or a county welfare department. Experience indicates that most

county probation or welfare departments do not investigate abuse in out-of-home care; therefore, licensing staff could refer to either the police or the sheriff's department.

2. The mandated reporter must provide the following information when making the telephone report:
   - The mandated reporter's name and telephone number
   - Name of the child(ren)
   - Present location of the child(ren)
   - Nature and extent of the injuries
   - Any other relevant information requested by the Child Protective Agency

The following information is not required but should be included if possible:
   - Name of parents and home address(es) and phone number(s) of the child(ren) if known.

1. Within 36 hours of making the telephone report, a written report must be filed with the child Protective Agency. The SS 8572 "Suspected Child Abuse Form" is used for this purpose and is available from the Child Abuse Unit of the U.S. Department of Justice. The back of the SS 8572 lists the instructions for completion of the report and the required distribution.

2. If two or more mandated reporters become aware of a reportable complaint, they may designate one of themselves to make the required telephone and written report. This should be documented by all reporters involved. The LIC 812 should be used for this purpose. If a mandated reporter becomes aware that the designated individual failed to report, he/she must then make the report and document the date and time of the complaint and any other relevant information.

3. Licensing staff must investigate all allegations of corporal punishment in licensed day care facilities. If, during an investigation, it is discovered that an incident not previously reported should have been, it must be reported immediately.

PRACTICE   6-2

1. Notice that in professional writing, the audience is often specified. Who is the audience for this set of instructions? <u>Child care evaluators.</u>

2. If you received this set of instructions at work, would you consider it effective and useful? Why or why not? <u>Yes, in that it clearly lists the information required for the report and the time requirements and punishments if these aren't met.</u>

Writing in Everyday Life

The selection that follows is a personal letter to a friend, but it contains an informal description of a natural process: the change of seasons.

Dear Annie,

You won't believe how beautiful autumn is here in Colorado. It might not be as spectacular as in Virginia, but it has its own kind of vibrancy and freshness. The thing I like about it most is how it arrives very subtly and slowly over several weeks. I've learned to appreciate the slightest changes—in temperature or color—with a renewed sensitivity to my natural surroundings.

The first thing I noticed was just the mildest drop in temperature at night toward the middle of August. During the day, it still got hot—close to 100 by 4 p.m. Over about 3 weeks, that midnight breeze lasted a bit longer each night until one morning I needed a sweater to enjoy my morning coffee on the deck.

Then there were changes in the sounds of the birds. After a couple weeks of cooler nights—as hot as the days continued to be—I stopped hearing some of the gentle summer bird songs that used to wake me and began hearing the more aggressive notes of woodpeckers that were teaming up, surrounding my house in hopes of building nests in the eaves.

The leaves that were the first to change were almost unnoticed on the underside of my tomato plants. Of course, I've known that tomatoes are sensitive to nighttime temperatures, but I've never thought of them as the harbingers of autumn! Then came the yellows and browns of field grasses and elm trees, the pale greens and reds of the maples, and the gold of aspens.

It lasted right through until Thanksgiving, only dropping into the cold browns of winter in December. Now, in January, we are waiting for snow to cover and beautify the dull landscape. You really have to visit me next year during the fall.
Freda

PRACTICE   6-3

1. What writing technique does Freda use to develop her process? Explain.
   <u>Description. Freda describes the weather, the land, the birds, and the trees to</u>
   <u>show the gradual coming of autumn.</u>

2. How is this process different from explaining to someone how to accomplish a particular task, as in the earlier essay on freezing vegetables? <u>It differs in that</u>
   <u>no one is being instructed on steps to achieving a specific goal; rather, this</u>
   <u>essay is an observational essay, painting a picture of nature's changes.</u>

UNDERSTANDING PROCESS ANALYSIS

A process is a series of events leading to an outcome. Here are two examples:

- A set of instructions to prepare a safe campfire
- An explanation of how a forest fire occurred

Both of these examples involve process analysis. However, the first is a *directional* process, intended for the reader to follow. The second is an *informational* process, intended to educate the reader about how something occurred.

The Directional Process

The directional process is the familiar *how-to*. This process offers instructions for the reader to duplicate, like a recipe or driving directions. Your goal when writing a directional process is to supply the reader with clear steps to achieving the desired result. Although this type of process may seem elementary, it can be challenging. Most people are aware of the value and importance of knowing how to perform CPR, but do the following four steps provide the necessary information to effectively perform this lifesaving measure?

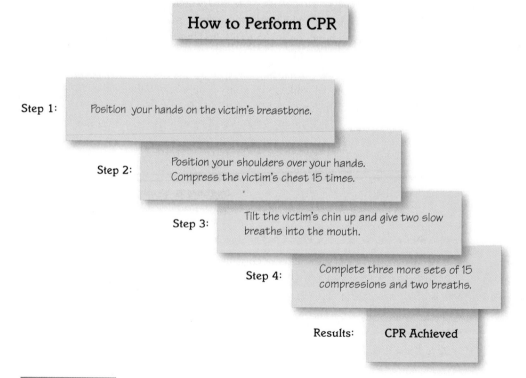

How to Perform CPR

Step 1: Position your hands on the victim's breastbone.

Step 2: Position your shoulders over your hands. Compress the victim's chest 15 times.

Step 3: Tilt the victim's chin up and give two slow breaths into the mouth.

Step 4: Complete three more sets of 15 compressions and two breaths.

Results: **CPR Achieved**

FIGURE 6.1   *Directional Process*

By limiting the information to just these fours steps, the writer makes the following assumptions:

1. The reader possesses some knowledge of CPR, so this is just a reminder.
2. The reader knows where and how to position the hands.
3. The reader understands that the CPR procedure varies by age group—infants, toddlers, and adults—and therefore can apply the steps accordingly.
4. The reader knows that complications can arise in each step and will be able to act appropriately.
5. The reader can react properly to varying situations and surroundings.

If the assumptions are valid, then the four steps of CPR presented here are sufficient. If the assumptions are wrong, however, the four steps would have to be significantly expanded.

Components of a Directional Process

What may be a simple process to the experienced person can be a complex experience to the novice, so don't assume that a process you know well is common sense to your reader. To avoid such assumptions and achieve an effective directional process, you should include the following components:

- A logical, chronological sequence of steps
- Helpful tips to ensure completion of each step
- Definitions of key terms
- Necessary background information to put the steps in context
- Alerts about possible problems
- Warnings that might prevent failure of the process or injury to the reader
- Reasons for following the steps you explain

The Informational Process

The goal of the informational process is to inform, explain, or analyze so that the reader gains an understanding of how something occurred. Your purpose as the writer of an informational process is not to urge the reader to apply or re-create the steps but to explain the process so that the reader understands its results. Thus, the purpose is to educate.

Some of the most common types of informational process are natural/scientific, historical, technical, and personalized:

- **Natural/scientific.** The writer describes processes that occur in the natural world.

  EXAMPLE: How a hurricane forms.

- **Historical.** The writer explains how events in history came to pass.

  EXAMPLE: How George W. Bush became president in 2000.

■ **Technical.** The writer explains how some aspect of technology works to accomplish specific tasks.

> EXAMPLE: How the iPhone works(not how to work the iPhone, but what happens on the screen or inside the machine when the user performs certain actions).

■ **Personalized.** The writer narrates the sequence of events that led to a personal situation.

> EXAMPLE: The steps that made a wedding day a disaster up to the point of the ceremony.

If you choose any of these informative process types, make sure you have the experience and knowledge to divide your topic into its component parts, whether they are called steps, stages, phases, cycles, or some other name (sometimes, these terms are used interchangeably in process writing). Your goal is not to simply list the steps but to explain each one clearly and fully.

PRACTICE   6-4

Next to each process topic, identify it as a directional or informational process ("D" or "I"). If the process is informational, indicate in the second column the type of informative process: natural/scientific, technical, historical, or personalized.

Topic	D/I	Type of Informative Process
1. How Thomas Edison invented the lightbulb	I	Historical
2. How to change the oil in a vehicle	D	
3. How to register for classes	D	
4. How to plan the perfect party	D	
5. How a certain disease evolves	I	Natural/scientific
6. How to work a microwave oven	D	
7. How toothpaste is made	I	Technical
8. How you won an award or competition	I	Personalized
9. How to assemble a bicycle	D	
10. How hurricanes are named	I	Natural/scientific

WRITING YOUR PROCESS ANALYSIS ESSAY

This section provides step-by-step instructions for writing a process essay. The student sample is an informational essay, but we discuss the unique points of writing each type of process essay.

Begin by reading an essay by Elena, a psychology major who is a native of Panama.

Culture Shock: A Roller Coaster Ride

Culture shock is a term used to describe the process a person undergoes when living outside his or her culture for an extended amount of time. Culture shock is a reality to many international students. When moving to a new culture, international students must deal with a language that may be unfamiliar, incomprehensible customs and values, and cultural expectations the students may not be fully aware of. As a result, the students may go through emotional extremes ranging from excitement with the new culture to depression. I, like most foreign students, had to face the harsh reality of culture shock as I pursued my college career. But it wasn't an easy process. There's no magic pill or vaccine. To be successful, international students should become familiar with the process of culture shock, a process that became my roller coaster ride into American culture.

When I first arrived in the United States, I was excited. The delightful aroma of new and different foods seemed to fill the air of the various neighborhoods and the college center. This was a time filled with experimentation—I had to try everything because I was concerned that I would cheat myself of a new and enriching experience. I now realize that I was actually going through what psychologists describe as "the honeymoon period," the first stage of culture shock. This was a time when everything was exciting, exotic, and fascinating. I had no doubt that I made the right decision to come to this country. The people were wonderful. It seemed that everyone I met was more than willing to take time to help me get around the campus and the city. I knew there was a lot I could learn in this country, and I was going to take advantage of each precious moment. This feeling of euphoria lasted close to 3 months, and then things seemed to change.

I'm not sure exactly what happened next, when it began, or how it evolved. As I entered the next phase of culture shock, I found myself withdrawing from the new culture. I felt that I irritated many of the people I met. They seemed bothered by my presence and my questions; they were quick to dismiss me. I started to avoid the new culture more and more. I looked toward other students who shared my culture and feelings. I called home more often and longed for any contact with people, music, or things from Panama. I wanted to do the go back and finish my education there and found myself wishing for a ticket back to my "sensible" country. But what would I tell my family? They had already invested so much.

Every day seemed to get more and more complicated as I continued to feel greater incompetence. Even the language became increasingly confusing as I encountered more idioms and slang than "real" words. I felt English was an exclusive and restricted language, probably created on purpose so that foreigners wouldn't understand. As I lost interest in the language, my grades started to suffer. Slowly, I fell into depression.

Months went by before I found myself gradually adapting to my new culture. I entered a period of adjustment. I started to laugh at myself, and others seemed to enjoy the new me. I made friends with a classmate named Doris, who introduced me to her parents, brothers, and cousins. They were as warm and as caring as my own family. Doris's father spoke some Spanish, and I would laugh when he sometimes rolled his Rs and would pronounce *pero,* meaning "but," as *perro,* meaning "dog." They were a great family, and through them, I met more wonderful people. I was slowly feeling like my old self; I felt I was truly learning the language and developing ways to manage misunderstandings.

Finally, I came to feel at home in America; I reached a level of stability. As I met more people, I became more proficient and confident in the language, and I learned to function in this new culture. My grades improved, and I took pride in this achievement. Gradually, I started to realize and accept both the good and the bad things this culture offered. Now, all my anxieties seem to have left me. At times, I actually feel like a native.

Each stage of culture shock lasts a different time for each individual; it depends on how different the culture is from one's own. Culture shock is the typical reaction to these differences. At first we marvel at the new culture's character, then we perceive it as evil, and finally we learn to appreciate its uniqueness. The difficulties that international students experience as they go through the process of culture shock are very real, but there's hope if they face and learn to understand and accept these differences. I have come to realize that knowing culture shock exists and understanding the nature of culture shock may help reduce its severity.

Although Elena's essay uses elements of narrative and description to convey her personal connection to the topic, it is clearly a process. Notice that the introduction mentions the stages of culture shock and that each body paragraph deals with one of those stages. Follow Elena's writing process as she developed her ideas, drafted her paragraphs, and revised her essay to hand in.

Prewriting

In this chapter, you practice using looping as a prewriting technique. However, don't limit yourself to just this one technique. Feel free to include the previous prewriting techniques before employing looping. The more prewriting techniques you use, the more ideas you're bound to uncover.

Discovering and Limiting Your Topic

Prewriting Strategy #5: Looping

Looping is a useful and effective prewriting tool that helps you uncover ideas you never knew you had and permits you to explore and generate new ideas, narrow down a broad topic, and even come up with a thesis for your essay. Since looping follows naturally from freewriting, you won't find it an unfamiliar process.

Elena starts by writing at the top of her page the topic she wishes to explore.

> Problems a foreign student faces

Loop #1: Elena starts to freewrite on the topic for 5 minutes.

> I've been in this country for three years. I love it here. Sometimes I think of my *patria*, Panama, and wish I could be there. The ocean, the sun, the music. The smell of the foods as I walk my town's plaza. I thought I knew a lot of English when I first came here, but wow, was I surprised how difficult English is. When I started college I learned a lot and found out how very little I actually knew. Of course, it was very hard in the beginning. Learning the slang and learning all the grammar was hard. That's a good topic: How a person can learn a foreign language. I remember all the trouble I had in the beginning and how people would laugh at some of the things I said. I laughed too, but some weren't funny. I would get angry at myself for being quiet and not saying something. But I adjusted. I feel very comfortable living and studying here. But the beaches are not the same.

In this first loop, Elena's reflects on some of her personal struggles and accomplishments when she arrived in the United States. She recalls how difficult it was to learn English. It seems that learning a new language might be her topic, which can be developed as either a directional or an informational process. She circles "But I adjusted" as her center-of-gravity sentence, the one she explores in her next freewriting session. The audience or purpose is not yet evident. See what happens in the next loop.

Loop #2: Elena copies the center-of-gravity sentence she identified in her first loop to start her second loop.

> But I adjusted. But it wasn't easy. At first I felt everybody was interested in me. I went to all places and many states. Everything was different. I never saw so many fast-food places. Yep, I gained 10 pounds in my first year. But then everything started changing, especially when I started school. At first it was wonderful but then everyone started to change. I didn't feel like part of this place. I started to think that people were rude. I think some actually were. Why didn't I see it before. The mall? School cafeteria? Dorms? But wait, me too. I shouldn't point the finger. Now I

know it was me. I was changing as I adapted to this new country, I had to adjust to a new language and culture and not having my family and friends close by. I was away.

As Elena reviews her freewriting, she starts to identify her topic, "adjusting to a new language and culture," which she identifies as the center-of-gravity phrase. However, it is yet not clear whether she will explain how foreign students can best adjust. Her next loop helps make her ideas clearer.

Loop #3: Again, Elena copies her new center-of-gravity phrase to a new page and starts freewriting on that new idea.

Adjust to a new language and culture. This what my teacher says happens to most foreign students. It is called culture shock. In the beginning we like every-thing, then things start to change and we notice things that bother us; we become critical. Yes, it's not the people, it's me. Then I started comparing my country with this country, looking for faults. But it was I who was at fault. I was homesick. Maybe making excuses for myself helped comfort me. I can give many examples of the things that happened to me in all of the stages of culture shock. Some are funny and some are sad. Maybe balance the different examples. Maybe I give too many examples.

Elena's topic is now clear. She will write an informational process analysis on the stages of culture shock. She seems confident that she can offer a lot of information, especially personal examples that would illustrate the various stages of culture shock, but she's still not too certain of the stages of her process since she chose "all the stages of culture shock" as her center-of-gravity phrase. Her final loop helps her define the stages.

Loop #4: Elena copies the new center-of-gravity phrase and starts to freewrite.

All of the stages of culture shock. I need to think of the different stages of culture shock. Give the stages different names. First the marvel stage, where everything seems to be "my *casa* is your *casa*," when everything is great; then the "I miss my *casa*" stage, then the "we can do it better" stage, and then the *"que sera, sera"* stage. Maybe I should use Spanish because I want to show that I did make it through the stages, well maybe a little Spanish to give it a personal touch. But maybe I should do a little research and see what the experts call these stages. Maybe there are stages I don't even know about or don't even know I went through. I know I can explain and give many examples since I lived it. No, I better not use Spanish. People will think I'm showing off. The first step is that everything is great and the last step is that everything is great.

By the end of this loop, Elena feels positive that she has much to contribute on the topic. Her catchy titles for some stages are an indication of the process that she plans to develop, but she also acknowledges that she needs to learn more about the topic. Elena is afraid that she might leave out some important stage, and she's still struggling with her audience and worries how her audience might perceive her use of Spanish. She can address these concerns when she analyzes her audience and determines the tone necessary for that audience.

TOPICS TO CONSIDER

If you are experiencing some difficulty coming up with a topic, perhaps one of the following topics can help stimulate your thinking. If you choose a topic from this list, use the topic as written to start your looping sessions.

Writing for College		
■ How the ozone layer has been damaged ■ How a specific historical event lead to a battle, a movement, or a certain law	■ How the U.S. president is elected ■ How to follow the scientific method to analyze something ■ How a discovery was made, such as electricity, penicillin, or radium	■ How a phenomenon occurs: earthquake, tornado, hurricane, tidal wave, and so on

Writing in Your Profession			
BUSINESS	■ How to build a productive work environment ■ How to handle a specific complaint (sexual harassment, racism, theft, or idleness)	■ How to advertise a specific product effectively	■ How a bank processes a mortgage application
CRIMINAL JUSTICE	■ How a criminal was convicted ■ How a jury is selected	■ How lawyers advise their clients on a specific issue	■ How legal assistants research public records or prepare a witness
EDUCATION	■ How to motivate students to read ■ How to learn a foreign language	■ How to prepare for a parent–teacher conference	■ How to improve student attendance or participation
HEALTH	■ How a hospital emergency room responds to an emergency ■ How to lose weight safely and effectively	■ How ambulance drivers prepare for an emergency or handle an emergency	■ How a dental hygienist performs a specific service
SOCIAL WORK/ PSYCHOLOGY	■ How social workers handle a specific family situation ■ How to help someone deal with a tragedy	■ How a psychologist provides crisis intervention	■ How a social worker, counselor, or psychologist deals with victims of abuse

WRITING YOUR PROCESS ANALYSIS ESSAY

Continued

	Writing in Your Profession—cont'd		
TECHNICAL	■ How to use a specific computer program ■ How to upgrade a computer system	■ How to troubleshoot a specific computer problem	■ How a specific piece of machinery works
OTHERS	■ How to do a specific task at work ■ How air becomes polluted	■ How you perfected your skills in something	■ How to perform a certain dance, wrestling move, or self-defense technique

Writing in Everyday Life		
■ How to prepare a special event, such as a wedding, reunion, graduation, celebration, or birthday party ■ How to choose the ideal roommate, spouse, or job	■ How to overcome a specific addiction, habit, or fear ■ How to perform a specific home improvement project	■ What to do in case of an accident while driving, at home, at work, or in sports ■ How to train a specific pet

In choosing your topic and approach, whether you are writing a directional or an informational process, consider your knowledge and interest in the topic. The tone and development of your essay reflect your attitude.

WRITING 6-1

Perform a looping exercise of four intervals of 5 minutes each. Follow these steps:

1. Pick a topic and write it at the top of your paper.

2. **Loop #1:** Freewrite for 5 minutes. After 5 minutes, stop and review what you've written. Then, select and circle the center-of-gravity sentence.

3. **Loop #2:** Copy the center-of-gravity sentence from loop 1 and freewrite on this key point for 5 minutes. After 5 minutes, stop and review what you've written. Then, select and circle a new center-of-gravity sentence.

4. **Loop #3:** Again, copy the center-of-gravity sentence from loop 2 and freewrite on this key point for 5 minutes. After 5 minutes, stop and review what you've written. Then, select and circle a different center-of-gravity sentence.

5. **Loop #4:** One final time, copy the center-of-gravity sentence from loop 3 and freewrite on this key point for 5 minutes. After 5 minutes, stop and review what you've written. Then, select and circle a final center-of-gravity sentence. (If you need to continue looping through another cycle or two, feel free to do so.)

By now, you should have a fairly clear idea about what you're going to write. Answer these questions to make sure that you are prepared to write on your chosen topic.

1. Do you find your topic interesting? _____Yes _____No

2. Do you know a lot about this process? _____Yes _____No

3. Are you able to supply sufficient information and examples to make the process clear and interesting to your reader? _____Yes _____No

4. Do you need to research any part of your process? _____Yes _____No (If yes, see Chapters 13 and 14 on research methods.)

One final note on topic selection: make sure your topic merits an essay. Your information should be meaningful and sufficient for a full essay. Don't write an essay on something you can say in one paragraph.

Identifying Your Audience and Establishing Your Purpose

A process analysis requires not only a strong sense of purpose but also a logical choice of audience. The audience you choose for the directional process may not be appropriate for the informational process since the purpose of each process differs: one is to direct the reader; the other is to educate. Thus, the topic of your essay and your audience choice are interconnected. Examine the audience and purpose for each goal separately.

Audience and Purpose for a Directional Process

Since the directional process is intended to be reproduced, you need to choose an audience who can perform the type of activity you're describing. Choosing a general audience (anybody) not only is unrealistic but also obscures the purpose of your essay. However, by identifying a specific audience, you can make logical decisions about your style and the content of your essay; thus, your purpose becomes clear throughout your essay.

Table 6.1 illustrates the importance of avoiding a "general" audience by contrasting a poor audience choice with a logical and possible audience choice for specific directional process topics. The reason an audience choice should be revised is given in parentheses.

As you compare both columns, one conclusion is obvious: without a specific and appropriate choice of audience, you are more likely to have problems deciding what information to include and what information to leave out.

TABLE 6.1	*Audience Choices for Directional Processes*	
Topic	**Poor Audience Choice**	**Possible Audience Choice**
How to purchase a car	Drivers (most drivers already know how to purchase a car)	First-time car buyers about to embark on this harrowing venture
How to multiply polynomials	Students in general (the topic doesn't apply to those who aren't taking algebra)	Students having difficulty in algebra
How to apply for a student loan	The public (those who don't need student loans won't care about the topic)	Students and parents of students starting or continuing college

Audience and Purpose for an Informational Process

Unlike the directional process, the audience for the informational process is not applying the information. Nonetheless, your choice of audience is equally important since this is the person or group who benefits from the knowledge you present in your informational process. As with the directional process, you should make your audience choice before you start outlining your topic. See Table 6.2 for examples of logical audience choices for various types of informational processes.

Notice that the audience choices consist of those people most likely to benefit from the knowledge. Some might find the information new, but others' present knowledge might be enriched by what you have to say. Thus, the choice of audience becomes extremely important so that you, the writer, can choose the information that helps sharpen the purpose of the process.

Your decision as to the amount and type of information to include in your essay depends on how well you know your audience. Why do you think advertisers spend considerable time and money researching their market audience before launching an advertisement campaign?

Setting Your Tone

What determines the tone of your essay more than anything else are the words and expressions you use. For instance, would referring to a specific group as "sterile intellects" create a negative tone? Would the reader perceive your writing as angry,

> **Computer tip**
>
> Since your tone may reflect the mood you were in when writing, be careful when writing e-mails without editing for tone. Place the writing aside for a while and then revisit it in a more objective disposition. You'll be surprised at the many changes you make to e-mails after reconsidering their tone.

TABLE 6.2   *Audience Choices for Informational Processes*

Topic	Type of Informational Process	Possible Audience Choice
How cells divide	Natural/scientific	A group of science students interested in more advanced information on the topic or better understanding of the topic
How the United States got involved in Iraq	Historical	History students seeking a better understanding or people trying to justify their position on the topic
How a computer virus spreads	Technical	Students taking a basic computer class or computer users trying to understand how their computer became infected
How you chose your college	Personal	A friend seeking your advice on how to decide on a college

too judgmental, or snobbish? Throughout the writing process, you need to consider the consequences of the tone of your essay on both your reader and your purpose. In writing process essays, you should be especially aware of two types of words and expressions you may be tempted to use: jargon and slang.

Jargon

Jargon is the specialized or technical language of a specific activity, profession, or group. Since jargon is used to communicate and facilitate discussions among the group's members, it may be appropriate and effective when the jargon is part of the culture of your target audience. However, using jargon may be confusing to an outsider of the group. For example, a report targeted to business people may *accommodate concerns* (make room for opinions), discuss the practice of *ambush marketing* (a type of advertising strategy), emphasize the need to *create value* (better products or services), or indicate that someone was *dehired* (fired from a job). Similarly, a construction worker's use of the phrases *200 miles per hour tape* for duct tape, *jitter-bug* for a tool to mix concrete, and *drag-up* to mean resign or quit would be baffling and even comical to someone outside that profession. Unless you want to stop and define the jargon you use in your essay, make sure that the audience you choose understands and shares this specialized language.

Slang

Slang—or informal "street" language associated mostly with young people—has become a functional part of our social culture. It is so ingrained in our everyday life that we are sometimes unaware that many words and expressions we use may be slang. Slang can be effective and appropriate in communicating ideas, but like jargon it limits the types of audience you can choose. First, slang attaches new usage to common words. For example, the words *cool, bad, stupid,* and *dope* can be used to mean *good*. Which audience understands which word? Granted, slang is a creative use of language, but slang can alienate and confuse those outside of that group. If not used appropriately, slang can set the wrong tone in your essay. Don't assume that because you're writing to a group of teenagers, slang helps you set a tone that connects to all teenagers. Also, don't assume that non-native speakers of English understand even the most common slang. If you feel that using slang helps you achieve your purpose, you may need to focus on a more narrow audience.

> **Bridging Knowledge**
>
> **See Chapter 23 for** additional information on slang as well as information on clichés and the use of offensive language. Remember that your word choice affects the tone of your essay.

WRITING 6-2

Fill out the following form to help you analyze your audience, purpose, and tone for your process analysis essay.

Audience, Purpose, and Tone Analysis

Your topic: _____

I. Audience

1. Who is my audience? _____

2. Age: _____; Gender: _____

3. Who would be most interested in my topic? _____
    _____

4. What is my audience's educational background? _____
    _____

5. What does my audience know or assume about my topic? _____
    _____

6. What are my audience's social or cultural interests? _____
    _____

7. Why would my audience be interested in my topic? _____
    _____

8. What connection do I have with this audience? _____
    _____

II. Your Purpose

1. What do I want my audience to understand? _____
    _____

2. Why is this topic important to my audience? _____
    _____

3. What does my audience expect when reading my writing? _____
    _____

4. How do I expect my audience to react?_____
    _____

III. Tone

1. What tone do I hope to establish? _____

2. Are there any special uses of jargon or slang that I should either employ or avoid?
    _____
    _____

Formulating Your Thesis

The thesis for your process analysis should state the process you are analyzing and the main point you want to make about the process.

Process + Main Point

Job hunting can be a frustrating procedure.

All ideas you present in your body paragraphs must flow from that sentence. Avoid such announcements as "In this essay, I will explain . . ." or "I have chosen to write about. . . ." You don't want to sound as if you're making a speech. Also, avoid such expressions as "I think," "I feel," or "In my opinion." Your thesis is your claim, your opinion, so state it. Beginning your ideas with these empty words clutters your style, and your reader might view this as an apology for offering an opinion. Again, words affect tone and create impressions in your readers' minds as they read your essay, so make sure your thesis sets an appropriate tone.

Examine the following thesis statements. Notice how each sets the tone of the essay, whether serious or upbeat, and how each clearly makes the main point (underlined) that a process follows:

- Careful preparation before a tornado is crucial.
- Students who succeed in college courses approach their assignments in four stages.
- The perfect wedding reception is quite an art and requires careful planning.
- To get rid of a jerk, just follow this simple procedure.

You can also use an essay map here, though, in some situations, the essay map is optional. Base your decision on the number of steps your process requires. If you have too many steps, then a long essay map will be awkward and confusing. However, if you're able to group several steps under three or four main steps, stages, or phases, then your essay map might help guide your reader through the essay.

WRITING 6-3

Preparation

Write a tentative thesis statement for your process analysis essay. Include an essay map if you think it is appropriate for your topic.

_____

_____

Discussion

In small groups, share your thesis statements.

1. Discuss the strengths and weaknesses of each thesis statement.

2. Determine whether an essay map would make your thesis more focused and more effective.

3. Offer suggestions that might improve the thesis statement.

Working Thesis

Write your revised working thesis here.

_____

_____

Outlining Your Ideas

By now, you have chosen a topic, identified your audience, established your purpose, and created a thesis. It's time to "draw the picture" of the structure of your essay by preparing your outline. Your outline is vital in helping you make decisions about the unity and content of your essay. The format of your outline is informal and quite simple.

Here is the outline for Elena's essay.

ESSAY OUTLINE

I. Introduction
  A. Definition of culture shock
  B. To whom and why this is important
  C. My connection
  D. My thesis and essay map

II. Body paragraphs
  A. Period of excitement
    1. Exciting arrival
    2. Interesting country and great people
    3. My feelings at this time
    4. This was a dream come true
  B. Period of withdrawal
    1. People seem indifferent
    2. People were unfriendly
    3. Looked for people who felt like me
    4. Some international students left
  C. Time of adjustment
    1. Felt more familiar with my environment
    2. Made friends and met family
    3. Learned to laugh at myself

  D. Stability accomplished
   1. Experience the familiar feeling of joy
   2. Accept differences
   3. Accepted and incorporated the best traits as my own

III. Conclusion
  A. Length of the process
  B. There's still hope
  C. Advice to reader: Overcome challenges and don't give up dreams

WRITING　6-4

Prepare your outline for your topic. Use as many steps as necessary to complete your process. After you have finished your outline, review it carefully. Make sure that you don't leave out a critical step. Since you may know the process so well that you can recite it backward, it's easy to miss a significant element.

Essay Outline

Topic: _____

Audience: _____

Purpose: _____

I.　Introduction

　　A. Lead-in strategies_____

　　　　1. _____

　　　　2. _____

　　B. Working Thesis and map (map is optional). _____

　　　_____

II.　Body paragraphs

　　A. Step #1: _____

　　　　1. _____

　　　　2. _____

　　　　3. _____

　　　　4. _____

　　B. Step #2: _____

　　　　1. _____

　　　　2. _____

　　　　3. _____

　　　　4. _____

C. Step #3: _____

    1. _____

    2. _____

    3. _____

    4. _____

D. Step #4: _____

    1. _____

    2. _____

    3. _____

    4. _____

E. Step #5: _____

    1. _____

    2. _____

    3. _____

    4. _____

F. Step #6: _____

    1. _____

    2. _____

    3. _____

    4. _____

III. Conclusion: Strategies you can use to wrap up your essay

    A. _____

    B. _____

    C. _____

Drafting

As you draft your essay, keep in mind that your major purpose is to lead your reader through a series of steps in time order. These might be major steps in a vast historical process or minor steps in redecorating a room; however, if you depart from the chronology of your process, your essay loses its unity.

Writing Your Introduction

Remember, when drafting your essay, you don't have to start with the introduction. If you wish to plunge right into the body of your essay, feel free to do so. You can even save your introduction for last. The goal is simply to get started.

In Chapter 5, we examined four strategies for writing your introduction: brief description, short personal narrative, anecdote, and background information. These strategies, individually or combined, can also be effective in developing the introduction for your process analysis essay. This chapter introduces three additional strategies: writer's experience with the topic, definition of terms, and humor. As you choose your lead-in strategy, take into account that the introduction sets the tone for your entire essay, grabs the reader's attention, defines your purpose, and declares your thesis.

1. **Explanation of the writer's experience with the topic.** By presenting your connection with and authority on your topic, you establish your creditability as a writer.
2. **Definition of a key term.** By defining a familiar or unfamiliar term, you help the reader prepare for your thesis. Through the definition, you can specify whether you expand, take exception to, or give new meaning to the commonly accepted definition.
3. **Humor.** Using humor to introduce your thesis and grab your reader's interest is a popular and effective strategy. A reader who is entertained most likely wants to read further. However, be cautious when using this strategy. Since your introduction sets the tone of your essay, your use of humor should be relevant to the topic, purpose, and thesis of the essay.

Examine how Elena's initial draft employs the definition of a term as a strategy to develop the introduction. Again, continue to examine how the lead-in flows to the thesis.

> *Culture shock* is a term used to describe the process a person undergoes when living outside his or her culture for an extended amount of time. When moving to a new culture, an international student must deal with a language that may be unfamiliar, customs and values incomprehensible to the visitor, and expectations by the new culture that the visitor may not be fully aware of. As a result, the person may go through such emotional extremes as excitement with the new culture to depression. Most students go through culture shock as they pursue college careers. Unfortunately, some never learn to deal with these feelings and fail to attain their dreams. I, however, learned to deal with culture shock. But it wasn't an easy process. To be able to deal with culture shock, the international student should become familiar with the process of culture shock.

In her introduction, Elena tells the reader what culture shock is before launching into the body of the essay. Elena also uses her own experience with the topic to help move her introduction to her thesis.

Although your introduction may take more than one paragraph, don't ramble without a point. Make sure that the information in your introduction is meaningful. Unnecessarily long introductions only confuse the reader and prompt speculation about whether you actually have a thesis. On the other hand, if your introduction is too short and undeveloped, your reader might feel unprepared to fully understand or appreciate your thesis or purpose. Your choice as to the length of your introduction should be based on your purpose and audience.

The following list may help you decide what to include in your introduction. But remember to keep it to the point; your introduction does not need to answer all of these questions.

- Who uses this process—when, where, and how?
- Why is this process significant?
- Are there other ways to do the process? If so, why is yours different?
- Who or what does the process affect?
- What knowledge (terminology or background) does your audience need to understand your process?
- What special skills, material, equipment, preparation, and/or conditions are necessary to carry out this process?
- How long does the process take?
- How many steps does it take to complete the process?

Whatever information you choose to include in your introduction, don't forget that your lead-in must flow to your thesis, not simply hang there in your introduction, disconnected from your thesis.

WRITING   6-5

Using the thesis you listed on page 156 or another thesis, write two different introductions on separate sheets of paper. Use a combination of two or more of the following strategies: description, personal narrative, anecdote, background information, your experience with the topic, definition of a key term, and humor. When you are finished, select the introduction that seems more interesting, well-developed, and appropriate for your purpose.

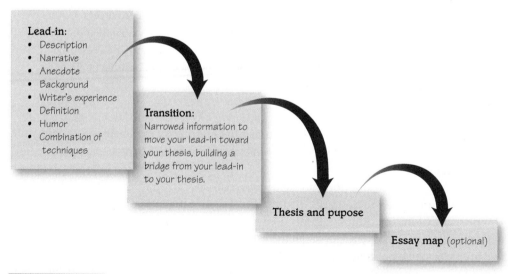

Lead-in:
- Description
- Narrative
- Anecdote
- Background
- Writer's experience
- Definition
- Humor
- Combination of techniques

Transition:
Narrowed information to move your lead-in toward your thesis, building a bridge from your lead-in to your thesis.

Thesis and pupose

Essay map (optional)

FIGURE 6.2   *Flow of Your Introduction*

Writing Your Body Paragraphs

As you draft the body of the essay, refer to your outline. If you feel you need to revise your outline, do so; don't treat your outline as if it were a contract. Always feel free to go back to any earlier part of the writing process. Be sure to include all the steps that you outlined and include any others that you may have forgotten in your outline, but remembered while you were writing. Here's Elena's first two body paragraphs.

> *Culture shock* is a term used to describe the process a person undergoes when living outside his or her culture for an extended amount of time. When moving to a new culture, an international student must deal with a language that may be unfamiliar, customs and values incomprehensible to the visitor, and expectations by the new culture that the visitor may not be fully aware of. As a result, the person may go through such emotional extremes as excitement with the new culture to depression. Most students go through culture shock as they pursue college careers. Unfortunately, some never learn to deal with these feelings and fail to attain their dreams. I, however, learned to deal with culture shock. But it wasn't an easy process. To be able to deal with culture shock, the international student should become familiar with the process of culture shock.
>
> When I first arrived in the United States, I was excited. This was a time filled with experimentation—I had to try everything. I was concerned that I would cheat myself of a new and enriching experience. I now realize that I was actually going through what psychologists describe as the honeymoon period of culture shock, the first stage of culture shock. My excitement wasn't limited to just food and places. The people were wonderful. It seems that everyone I met was more than willing to take time to help me get around the campus and the city. Wow, I was in America! I knew there was a lot I could learn in this country. This feeling seemed to change.

Collaborative Critical Thinking

In small groups, discuss Elena's first two draft body paragraphs. What advice would you give her for the revising stage? Where should she add information, warnings, steps, examples, and further description? Share your answers with other groups.

Coherence: Using Transitions

One danger of writing a process is that the writer organizes and presents the essay as a recipe, thus creating a choppy writing style and making the essay sound incoherent. This problem can be avoided by using effective transitions between and within paragraphs to keep the information flowing smoothly.

Review the following list of transitions that indicate a sequence of events appropriate to process analysis.

Transitions to Show Chronological Sequence		
after	equally important	next
after a few hours	eventually	now
afterward	finally	once you have
all the while	first (second, third, …)	presently
at last	first of all	previously
at present	following	prior to
at the same time	formerly	recently
at this moment	gradually	sequentially
before	in the end	shortly
before this	in the future	simultaneously
briefly	in the meantime	soon
concurrently	in the meanwhile	soon after
currently	lastly	subsequently
during	later	suddenly
earlier	meanwhile	then

The goal in using these transitional words is to connect logically the points that follow one another. Examine in Figure 6.3 how a chain of ideas is held together to make a paragraph coherent.

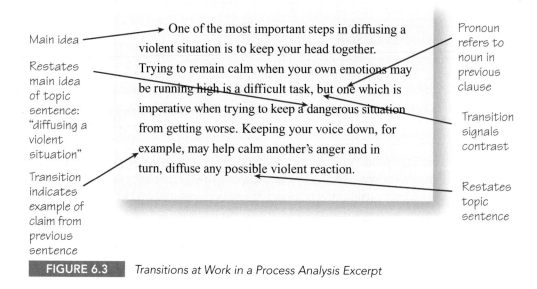

Main idea

Restates main idea of topic sentence: "diffusing a violent situation"

Transition indicates example of claim from previous sentence

Pronoun refers to noun in previous clause

Transition signals contrast

Restates topic sentence

One of the most important steps in diffusing a violent situation is to keep your head together. Trying to remain calm when your own emotions may be running high is a difficult task, but one which is imperative when trying to keep a dangerous situation from getting worse. Keeping your voice down, for example, may help calm another's anger and in turn, diffuse any possible violent reaction.

FIGURE 6.3   *Transitions at Work in a Process Analysis Excerpt*

In addition to transitional words and expressions, repeating key words, referring to previous ideas, and using pronouns that reference specific nouns in the previous sentences help unite all your ideas within each of your paragraphs. Think of the sentences in your paragraphs as links in a chain; if you fail somehow to link one idea to a previous idea, you have broken the chain, causing your paragraph to be choppy and disjointed. By simply adding a word, an expression, or an idea in your sentence that refers to a previous idea, the topic sentence, or the thesis, you can continue to connect the links in the chain as you add fresh ideas.

You can check your paragraphs for coherence by simply examining each sentence and making sure that the idea of each sentence leads smoothly to the next sentence and that each sentence has a word or idea linking that sentence to the previous sentence.

 **=   Poor Coherence**

Transitions between paragraphs should be subtler and require careful handling. You don't want your essay to sound like a list of items by using such transitions as *first, second, third,* and *next.* Permit your transitions to serve a purpose and lead your reader smoothly through the steps of your process. Here are some choices that you might consider:

- **Name the step and its purpose.**
  - EXAMPLE: <u>The final step</u> of DNA replication, joining, involves bonding of complementary nucleotide.

- **Use transitions that link the step of the previous paragraph to the new step by giving a time reference.**
  - EXAMPLE: <u>After you have removed the wheels</u>, start removing the motor.

- **Emphasize that the new step depends on the successful completion of the previous step.**
  - EXAMPLE: <u>Once you have successfully completed the first step</u>, you're ready for the most crucial part of this process, the actual dissection.

- **Establish a union between two actions or events.**
  - EXAMPLE: <u>As you continue</u> to interrogate the suspect, maintain eye contact.

- **Introduce an alternative.**
  - EXAMPLE: <u>If the previous actions prove futile</u>, it's time to take drastic measures.

- **Emphasize the importance of the new step.**
  - EXAMPLE: <u>However, the most difficult and crucial phase</u> of the plan is the actual investigation.

Draft the body of your essay; use the following strategies:

1. Follow your outline. Make any changes to the outline that you feel help your essay.

2. Start each of your body paragraphs by indicating the step you discuss in that paragraph. This is your topic sentence. During revision, you may alter the topic sentence in any or all of your paragraphs, but for now it's important to remain focused on the topic sentence as you write each paragraph.

3. Add the information necessary to help the reader accomplish or understand the step expressed in the topic sentence.

4. Be sure to add necessary warnings, tips, or definitions.

5. Add transitions to keep your ideas flowing smoothly and to guide your audience through your information.

Writing Your Conclusion

The length of your conclusion, just like your introduction, should be appropriate to the length of the whole essay. A 1-page conclusion would definitely be too long for a 2- or 3-page essay. Your conclusion should wrap up the essay by giving it a sense of finality. Don't introduce new information that requires explanation. As you start to plan your conclusion, consider the following approaches:

> **Computer tip**
>
> As you draft, highlight any information you're not sure you want to keep. You can decide later if you need to delete it or rewrite it to make it fit into your essay.

- Close with a brief narrative in which you recount an incident when your skills proved useful or valuable.
- Explain how significant learning the process would be to the reader.
- Emphasize the pleasure or benefits your reader will derive from learning the process.
- Restate the thesis and express a final thought about the topic, such as recommending an action or referring to false assumptions.
- Discuss the results of the process.
- Challenge the reader.
- Refer to some point you made in your introduction to bring your essay full circle. For example, if your started your introduction with a definition, a humorous anecdote, or a brief narration, you might include a reference to this in your conclusion.

As you approach the end of your essay, remember that your thesis controls your conclusion. A good method to determine whether your conclusion is effective is to read your introduction and then jump to the conclusion. Do they connect? Do they flow together? If you feel as if you're reading two different essays, then your conclusion is not coherent. They should be similar in tone and give a sense of unity and completeness to the purpose stated in your introduction. This technique can be applied to the introduction and conclusion of Elena's final draft.

INTRODUCTION

Culture shock is a term used to describe the process a person undergoes when living outside his or her culture for an extended amount of time. Culture shock is a reality to many international students. When moving to a new culture, international students must deal with a language that may be unfamiliar, customs and values incomprehensible to them, and expectations by the new culture that the foreign students may not be fully aware of. As a result, the students may go through such emotional extremes as excitement with the new culture to depression. It's not an easy process. There's no magic pill or vaccine. To be successful, the international student should become familiar with the process of culture shock, a process that became my roller coaster ride into American culture.

CONCLUSION

Each stage of culture shock lasts a different time for each individual. It really depends on how different the culture is from one's own. Culture shock is the typical reaction to these differences. At first we marvel at the new culture's charm, then we perceive it as evil, and finally we learn to appreciate its uniqueness. The difficulties that international students experience as they go through the process of culture shock are very real, but there's hope if they face and learn to understand and accept these differences. This is the magic pill. Unfortunately, some never learn to deal with these feelings and fail to attain their dreams.

WRITING 6-7

Write a tentative conclusion for your essay.

1. Review the different approaches listed on page 164 and combine some of these approaches to create an effective conclusion.

2. Read your introduction and then your conclusion. Is there a smooth connection?

Revising

Start your revising stage by reading your essay out loud. How do you feel about what you have written? Revise your draft to make any changes you feel are necessary.

WRITING 6-8

Start your revision. Don't leave any part of your essay untouched.

- Make sure you didn't omit any necessary step.
- Be sure to offer sufficient, crucial, and relevant information for each step.
- Check for coherence. Make sure you offer enough transitions to help guide your reader.
- Use the chart on page 166 to help you troubleshoot.
- Use a variety of sentence types; if you use the passive voice, make sure it's appropriate.

Style Tip: Choose the Active Voice

Observe the difference between these two sentences:

PASSIVE VOICE:	The next step in the process is accomplished by calling the wedding planner and setting up the date of the reception.
ACTIVE VOICE:	Next, you should call the wedding planner and set up the date for the reception.

The first sentence is in the passive voice; that is, the person doing the action is not the subject of the sentence. The sentence is long and wordy, and you don't get a clear idea of who should make the telephone call. Passive sentences are not incorrect, but they make for an awkward style that can confuse your reader.

> **Bridging Knowledge**
>
> **See Chapter 19** for complete information and practice on choosing the active rather than the passive voice.

The second sentence is in the active voice. The person who does the action ("you") is the subject of the sentence. Notice how much more direct this sentence is. Generally, we encourage you to choose the active voice when you know who is performing the action of the sentence.

PROBLEM

SOLUTION

WRITING

My introduction seems dull, vague, undeveloped, or not engaging.

1. Did you analyze your audience? If not, return to Writing 6-3. Determine and address your audience's interests and needs.

2. Review the various strategies for developing your lead-in and combine a variety of methods that are appropriate to your audience and purpose.

3. Did you identify the process you discuss and its purpose?

4. Make sure that the information in your introduction leads smoothly to your thesis and doesn't just "pop up."

PROCESS ANALYSIS

My process doesn't seem to be developed enough, and I don't know what to add.

1. Include all the crucial steps that your audience needs to know to understand or perform the process.

2. Do you offer sufficient explanation for each step of your process? If not, perhaps several of your steps may benefit from some of the following techniques:

   - Reasons the step is important

   - Description

   - Warnings, cautions, and reminders

   - Definition of important and unfamiliar terms

3. Return to the prewriting stage and do a more focused looping.

PROBLEM   **SOLUTION**

COHERENCE

My essay doesn't
read smoothly.

→

1. Are the steps of your process in strict chronological order?
   If not, rearrange your steps.

2. Do you have a clear thesis statement that drives the
   entire essay? If not, make sure that your thesis names the
   process and the controlling idea (main point).

3. Do your topic sentences clearly identify the major steps
   of your process?

4. Do you have transitional words or phrases to clarify the
   relationship between paragraphs? See the list of transitions on page 162.

5. Does your conclusion effectively wrap up your process? If
   not, see how you can make your conclusion meaningful
   and effective by reviewing the information on page 164.

Collaborative Critical Thinking

Asking Your Peers

Once you have completed the writing process and have a polished final draft,
exchange papers with a classmate for peer review. Use the following form to answer
questions about your peer's paper.

1. Who is the writer? Who is the peer reviewer?

2. What is the purpose of the essay? Is the process directional or informational?

3. Do the first few sentences capture your interest? Explain how. If not, suggest
   a different opening.

4. Is the thesis clearly stated? What can you suggest to improve its overall
   effectiveness?

5. Does the essay include all steps and warnings necessary to understand the
   process? What additional steps, warnings, or both should the writer consider?

6. Does each paragraph contain sufficient information to explain each step
   clearly and fully? Where in the essay should the writer add more details?

7. Does each body paragraph have a topic sentence that clearly lets the reader
   know the step that the paragraph explains? What can you suggest to make
   the topic sentences more effective?

8. Are all steps presented smoothly with appropriate transitions? What can you
   suggest to improve the coherence of the essay?

9. Is the person (first, second, or third) consistent throughout the essay? Circle
   any problem that the writer should address.

10. Is the conclusion effective? What can the writer do to make the conclusion
    more effective?

Proofreading

The focus of the proofreading stage is to check on such trouble spots as grammar, usage, and punctuation. In this chapter, you look for errors in shifts in person.

Common Error #6: Editing for Shifts in Person

One of the most common errors in student writing is shifts in person. All writing appears in one of three "persons": first (*I, we, our, us, myself, ourselves*), second (*you, your, yourself*), or third (*he, she, it, they, them, themselves, everyone*). Problems occur when writers shift unnecessarily between one person and another.

INCORRECT:	If a **person** makes a promise, **you** should make every effort to keep it.
CORRECT:	If a **person** makes a promise, **he or she should** make every effort to keep it.

OR

If **you** make a promise, **you** should make every effort to keep it.

INCORRECT:	**I** enjoy mountain climbing since it brings out the adventurer in **you.**
CORRECT:	**I** enjoy mountain climbing since it brings out the adventurer in **me.**

GRAMMAR CHECKUP 6-1

Examine each sentence carefully. If the sentence contains an unnecessary shift in person, write S for shift in the first line and correct the sentence in the line provided. Write C for correct in the first line if the sentence has no shift in person. Answers will vary.

_S_ 1. In our algebra class, our teacher would give you surprise quizzes.

Revision: In our algebra class, our teacher would give us surprise quizzes.

_____

_S_ 2. We really enjoyed working with her because she always made you feel good about your contribution to the team.

Revision: We really enjoyed working with her because she always made us feel good about our contribution to the team.

_S_ 3. I always felt my parents were unreasonable, but as you get older you realize that they were actually wise.

Revision: I always felt my parents were unreasonable, but as I get older I realize that they were actually wise.

_S_ 4. In our biology class, students are permitted to work individually to complete the lab activities or you can work as a group.

Revision: In our biology class, students are permitted to work individually to complete the lab activities or they can work as a group.

<u>C</u> 5. Students' papers are always more interesting when they write on a topic to which they feel personally connected.

Revision: _____

_____

<u>C</u> 6. It's always a good idea for new students to go to the student orientation so that they can become familiar with the college environment.

Revision: _____

_____

<u>S</u> 1. When we finally arrived, you could sense that no one expected us.

Revision: When we finally arrived, we could sense that no one expected us.

_____

Check your answers to this Grammar Checkup in Appendix A on page A-3. How did you do? If you missed even one of these items, you may need to review shifts in person in Chapter 18.

WRITING 6-9

Start proofreading your own essay. Check for and correct the grammar errors we have studied up through this chapter. Look for other obvious errors in spelling, punctuation, and so on.

Final Checklist

1. Is the nature of the process—what it leads to and what it accomplishes—clearly and creatively stated in the introduction? ☐

2. Is your conclusion appropriate for the essay's purpose? ☐

3. Does your essay have a clear thesis statement and clear essay map (if appropriate) that capture the essay's purpose? ☐

4. Does your essay demonstrate a strong understanding of audience? Do explanation and instruction significantly increase audience understanding and knowledge of the topic? ☐

5. Is each major step or stage of the process expressed as a clear topic sentence? ☐

6. Are the steps or stages in the most logical order possible? ☐

7. Does your process include all necessary steps? ☐

8. Does the essay contain appropriate and varied transitional devices to guide the reader smoothly from one point to the next, both between paragraphs and within paragraphs, and do you include sufficient time markers so that the reader may easily follow the steps to the process? ☐

9. Does the essay demonstrate excellent development of each step or stage of the process; that is, does each paragraph provide substantial, relevant details and examples? ☐
10. Does your essay demonstrate mastery over the basics in sentence completeness (no fragments), structure (no fused sentences and comma splices), sentence variety, and word choice? ☐
11. Did you edit carefully for possible errors in grammar, spelling, and punctuation? ☐

Reflecting

Now that you've completed your process essay, it is important to stop and reflect on what you've accomplished. Reflection allows you to think about how your writing process went and what you might do differently next time.

WRITING **6-10**

Self-Reflection

Before you hand in your paper, write a brief paragraph in which you reflect on your final draft. Include your feelings on the following questions:

1. What do you feel you did best?
2. What part of your paper was most challenging to you?
3. In which areas do you feel you need the most practice?
4. What strategies will you employ to address your challenges or weaknesses and to improve the quality of your essay?

After you have completed this self-reflection, carefully review your instructor's comments. How are they similar or different from your own answers to the self-reflection? Make a list of your grammar, punctuation, and spelling errors so that you can follow up on the ones that recur. Consider what strategies you will employ to address your challenges or weaknesses and to improve the quality of your essay.

How might you use process analysis outside of this English course? Look back at the writing samples in Previewing Your Task in this chapter.

- **College:** _____
- **Your profession:** _____
- **Everyday life:** _____

CHAPTER 7

Developing Your Essay through Cause/Effect Analysis

YOUR GOALS

Understanding Cause/Effect Analysis

1. Distinguish between causes and effects.

2. Identify the basic types of causes and effects.

3. Analyze the organization of the cause/effect essay.

Writing Your Cause/Effect Essay

1. Analyze your target audience.

2. Use diagramming to organize support for your topic.

3. Formulate an effective thesis for a cause/effect essay.

4. Create an outline for your cause/effect essay.

5. Integrate various modes of development as necessary to support your essay.

6. Review your draft for style, grammar, and punctuation.

"Cause and effect, means and ends, seed and fruit cannot be severed; for the effect already blooms in the cause, the end preexists in the means, the fruit in the seed."

■ **Ralph Waldo Emerson** ■

A furious debate erupts one day in your history class over the causes of the American Civil War. Several members of the class insist that slavery was the most important cause, and others argue that the most immediate cause was the secession of the southern states. After a lengthy and emotional discussion, one student says that both sides could be right: slavery could be the most important cause even if southern secession was the most immediate.

In your annual performance review, your boss tells you that you've earned a large raise based on the hard work you've done over the past year. Although you expected a positive review, you did not expect such a generous raise. When you express your disbelief, your boss presents a spreadsheet displaying the results of the new procedures you introduced into your department. "With results like these," he says, "I have no choice but to give you a raise. I can't afford to lose you!"

One of your friends in college is having trouble concentrating in class. You catch him gazing out the window when he should be taking notes, and occasionally he dozes off. In the interest of offering help, you decide to ask him what is wrong. He tells you that his roommates keep him awake all night partying, and now he's fallen so far behind in his studies that he's almost given up.

When you think about how things got to be the way they are, you are considering causes. When you think about the results of a particular situation, you are considering effects. Actually, you can think about almost any condition or situation in both of these ways—the Civil War had many causes, but it also had many effects on American life. This chapter teaches you to analyze the world around you in terms of causes and effects.

LET's warm up!

Global warming is widely recognized as a major factor in world climate change. Even if you haven't studied it formally, you probably have some ideas about what is causing it and how it will affect life in the future. Take a few minutes to freewrite about the causes of global warming. Then write several sentences about the effects of this phenomenon.

Michael Nolan/Peter Arnold

PREVIEWING YOUR TASK

The writing samples that follow show how cause/effect writing can be used in various settings: college, work, and everyday life. As you read them, try to anticipate situations in all three settings for which you can use this type of analysis to strengthen your message.

Writing for College

As a college student, you are often asked to connect your learning to your own life and experience. In the following selection, James, a nursing student, writes about patients' misconceptions about a cold.

The Commonest of Misconceptions

As a nursing student, I've learned that patients' attitudes and beliefs about their health can be an important factor in their treatment. An extreme example is anorexia nervosa, the eating disorder in which patients somehow view themselves as overweight when they might be on the verge of starvation. In my student clinicals, however, I encounter many less extreme cases: patients who refuse certain medications because of religious beliefs, others whose attitude toward their disease—depression, say—makes them more likely to remain ill for a longer period, and so on. Lately, I've become more sensitive to what patients tell me about their illnesses because they often reveal attitudes and beliefs that I can pass on to their physicians. But this sensitivity has also become a kind of hobby; I'm starting to keep track of what patients tell me even in the case of minor illness. One of the most interesting diseases to "investigate" in this way is also the most common: the cold.

People have the strangest beliefs about the common cold. One of my patients believes she'll catch cold if she walks barefoot around the house; another thinks that if he abstains from food during a cold, its symptoms will be lessened. I've even met a patient who firmly believes that if he eats a raw onion, the cold will go away! Clearly, we could do a better job of educating the public about this disease to enable them to avoid it. But it's not easy to overcome such misconceptions; even after learning about the true causes of the cold, I find myself relying on some of the same superstitions as my patients. What does cause a cold? Modern science is providing some reliable answers to this question.

First, being wet and cold does not cause a cold. Nor does walking barefoot around the house, going outside in the night air, or any of the other hundreds of folksy ideas we've all heard about. Therefore, we can quickly rule out such "causes" as contributing factors in catching a cold. Instead, modern science has proven that the one element that must be present is a virus. Other factors might be present, but you won't catch a cold if no virus has been introduced to your body. Fortunately, when you do catch a particular cold virus, your body becomes immune to it in the process of overcoming it. You will never suffer from that same cold virus again. Unfortunately, many cold viruses are in circulation at any given time, and it's possible, although unlikely, to go from one virus to another, experiencing the same cold symptoms even though the main cause is different.

In addition to maintaining a healthy body, one of the most effective ways to attack the main cause of the cold is to wash your hands regularly. Washing your hands can prevent viruses from being introduced into your body (or into other bodies). Conversely, not washing your hands can enable the actual cause, the virus, to do its work.

Clearly, the common cold results from one *main* cause: introduction of a virus into the body. This main cause can be enabled by several *contributing* causes: a weak immune system (which is itself caused by improper eating and so on) and poor sanitary habits. Finally, several *noncauses* tend to obscure the truth about common colds from many patients. When I am a practicing nurse, I hope that I can help educate my patients about their health in the process of treating them.

PRACTICE 7-1

Does the author present the major points of the essay in the best order? Why or why not? Yes, because she discusses the main cause—viruses—first and then the contributing factors, such as a weak immune system and poor sanitary habits.

Writing in Your Profession

The following selection from a longer report written by the U.S. Department of Labor's Occupational Safety and Health Administration (OSHA) is designed to teach accident investigators how to analyze causes. The document is interesting because (1) it talks about different kinds of causes and (2) it provides a diagram showing how those causes can relate to one another.

Accident Investigation

Introduction

Thousands of accidents occur throughout the United States every day. The failure of people, equipment, supplies, or surroundings to behave or react as expected causes most of the accidents. Accident investigations determine how and why these failures occur. By using the information gained through an investigation, a similar or perhaps more disastrous accident may be prevented. Conduct accident investigations with accident prevention in mind. Investigations are NOT to place blame.

An accident is any unplanned event that results in personal injury or in property damage. When the personal injury requires little or no treatment, it is minor. If it results in a fatality or in a permanent total, permanent partial, or temporary total (lost-time) disability, it is serious. Similarly, property damage may be minor or serious. Investigate all accidents regardless of the extent of injury or damage.

Accidents are part of a broad group of events that adversely affect the completion of a task. These events are incidents. For simplicity, the procedures discussed in later sections refer only to accidents. They are, however, also applicable to incidents.

This discussion introduces the reader to basic accident investigation procedures and describes accident analysis techniques.

Accident Prevention

Accidents are usually complex. An accident may have 10 or more events that can be causes. A detailed analysis of an accident normally reveals three cause levels: basic, indirect, and direct. At the lowest level, an accident results only when a person or object receives an amount of energy or hazardous material that cannot be absorbed safely. This energy or hazardous material is the DIRECT CAUSE of the accident. The direct cause is usually the result of one or more unsafe acts, unsafe conditions, or both. Unsafe acts and conditions are the INDIRECT CAUSES or symptoms. In turn, indirect causes are usually traceable to poor management policies and decisions or to personal or environmental factors. These are the BASIC CAUSES.

In spite of their complexity, most accidents are preventable by eliminating one or more causes. Accident investigations determine not only what happened but also how and why. The information gained from these investigations can prevent recurrence of similar or perhaps more disastrous accidents. Accident investigators are interested in each event as well as in the sequence of events that led to an accident. The accident type is also important to the investigator. The recurrence of accidents of a particular type or those with common causes shows areas needing special accident prevention emphasis.

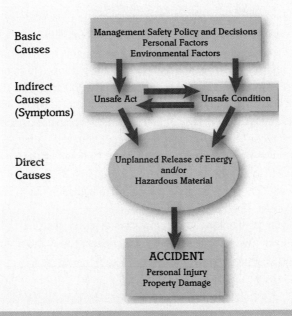

1. Does the visual help you understand the concept? Explain your answer. <u>Yes. The boxes and arrows show the relationships among the causes in a way that is simple and straightforward.</u>

2. Try substituting an accident you are familiar with into the diagram: an accident at work, at home, or on the road. Does your incident fit the given pattern? Explain. <u>A student might remember a childhood accident on a trampoline. On the trampoline, the indirect cause might be the absence of netting to protect the child from falling off the trampoline. The direct causes would be the sudden high jumping of the child. The result would be two broken front teeth from falling off the trampoline.</u>

Writing in Everyday Life

Cause/effect writing is as much a part of our everyday life as it is a part of our work and education. In the following e-mail, the writer tells a relative about a recent drive home through a snowstorm.

Dear Aunt Agnes,

You wouldn't believe what I went through to get home today in the snowstorm. Don't make fun of me. . . . I went to work even though I knew getting home would be dangerous, but I wasn't prepared for this! I was run off the road twice, did a 360 degree spin, and was passed by a dozen or so trucks that splattered snow and ice on my windshield. It was only by luck that I got home safely. If only a few things had been different. . . .

For one thing, my tires are nearly bald. Bill was going to buy new ones last month, but he ended up buying tires for his own car! Naturally, he got home from work just fine this afternoon, but I was slipping and sliding even before the snow got bad on the interstate. Every time I stepped on the gas just a little or tapped the brakes, I'd start to spin out. Then, near exit 83, I did a 360 spin! You'd have been proud of how I just kept on driving after turning completely around on the interstate.

And those stupid drivers! Twice I had to pull over because cars were coming up behind me at record breaking speeds! SUVs, of course . . . they think they own the road. Well, I wasn't going to argue with them; I got out of the way, even driving into snow banks to avoid crashing. Luckily, I was able to back out of them and keep going. But a few miles down the road, two of them had spun out themselves and were stranded on the shoulder. I say that's justice, don't you?

I suppose you are thanking your lucky stars that you missed this storm. I'll be at the airport to get you next week when you get back. Enjoy the rest of your vacation in Florida. Wish I were there!

Love,

Prudence

PRACTICE 7-3

1. Based on your current knowledge, which does this e-mail discuss in greater detail: causes or effects? Explain your answer. <u>Causes. The e-mail focuses not on the results of the accident but on why it happened.</u>

2. If you were to write an essay (not an e-mail) about the same topic, how would the body paragraphs and the style of writing be different? <u>The style would be more formal. I wouldn't start the essay with "You wouldn't believe what. . . ." I would change vocabulary to eliminate informal words, such as *stupid, well, don't you,* and *lucky stars.* I would make sure that the body paragraphs contained a formal topic sentence, introducing each cause for the accident.</u>

UNDERSTANDING CAUSE/EFFECT ANALYSIS

In one way, writing about causes or effects is similar to writing about processes. When you write about a process, you describe the *sequence* of events in a particular procedure. For instance, you might explain what happens first, second, and third when you turn on a computer. However, you are not especially concerned with *how* one step in the process causes another to happen or with *what* happens as a result of a particular step.

In writing about causes and effects, your job is to explain *how* one thing leads to another. "The Commonest of Misconceptions," for instance, shows what causes the common cold and what contributes to that cause. But the author might just as well have developed the symptoms, or *effects,* of the cold. You can write about almost any condition or event in terms of causes *or* effects. Some cause makes it happen; once it happens, it is an effect or a result of that cause; and then, in turn, it may cause other conditions or events.

Cause Analysis

Analyzing causes is not as simple as it may seem at first. Your bias as an author can make you favor certain causes or effects over others. Just skim the editorial page of any major newspaper to encounter conflicting opinions about what has caused a particular social or political situation. Sometimes, we simply do not know what has caused some situation to exist; in these cases, writing about causes becomes a kind of speculation or guesswork. We must avoid errors if we are to explain causes and effects correctly. In this chapter, you begin to develop the critical thinking skills you need to distinguish among various types of causes.

Main and Contributory Causes

Some causes are more important than others because they must be present if the effect is to be produced. We call these *main,* or *necessary, causes.* The virus is the main cause of the common cold. Without the main cause, the effect is not produced.

However, a main cause might not produce the effect by itself. It might need another factor to enable it to do its work. Such is the job of the weakened immune system in the case of the cold. If a cause cannot produce the result by itself but contributes to the main cause, we call it a *contributory cause.*

Collaborative Critical Thinking

1. In small groups of three or four, list as many possible causes as you can think of for one the following effects: Answers will vary.

   a. Low reading scores in K–12 education

   b. The popularity of Starbucks coffee

   c. The high rate of obesity in America

2. Identify the main and contributory causes of the effect you have chosen.

3. Share your answers with the rest of the class.

Immediate and Distant Causes

We can classify causes in another way: in terms of how close in time they occur to the effect. Returning to the common cold, notice that the immune system must be weakened before the virus is introduced; otherwise, the cold virus never takes hold. In most colds, therefore, the main cause (introduction of the virus) is also the most *immediate cause.* The weakening of the immune system is the more *distant cause* (in time) from the introduction of the virus. And the other factors, the ones that can weaken the immune system, most likely begin even earlier (even though they may continue right through the period of the cold itself). We can visualize this time relationship as in Figure 7.1.

Notice an important point here: the fact that these causes must occur in a particular order does not mean that the first one causes the second, the second one causes the third, and so on. The factors on the left contribute to the weakening of the immune system, but the weakened immune system *does not* cause the virus to be introduced.

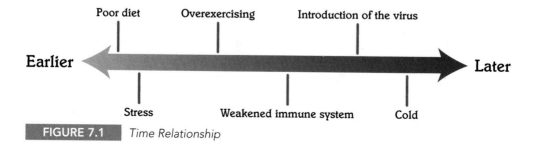

FIGURE 7.1   *Time Relationship*

PRACTICE   7-4

Here is a list of possible causes for two different effects. The steps are not presented in time order. Cross out any noncauses. Identify the main and contributory causes. Then list the main and contributory causes in terms of whether they are immediate or distant.

Effect #1: The collapse of the World Trade Center towers

Causes: Lack of coordination among government agencies Contributory/Distant

Unstable architectural design of the towers Contributory/Distant

Planes striking the towers Main/Immediate

Faulty airport security systems Contributory/Distant

Fire spreading throughout the towers Main/Immediate

Confusion among air traffic controllers Contributory/Immediate

~~The price of oil~~

Effect #2: High rates of divorce in America today

Causes: People get married for the wrong reasons Main/Relatively immediate

Divorce laws have relaxed in the last two decades Main/Distant

The influence of religion has declined since the 1960s Contributory/Distant

~~Men are no longer properly acculturated to be husbands~~

~~Divorce lawyers make a lot of money~~

Since the 1970s, women have more economic independence Contributory/Distant

~~People are not biologically suited for monogamy~~

Chains of Causes

Sometimes, effects are the result of a causal chain. The first cause (the most distant in time) produces an effect, this effect produces another effect, that effect produces the next, and so on. At the end of the chain, you end up with the final and most significant effect, as shown in Figure 7.2.

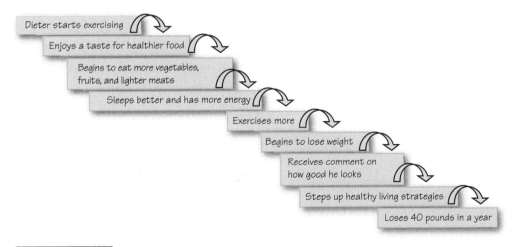

Dieter starts exercising

Enjoys a taste for healthier food

Begins to eat more vegetables, fruits, and lighter meats

Sleeps better and has more energy

Exercises more

Begins to lose weight

Receives comment on how good he looks

Steps up healthy living strategies

Loses 40 pounds in a year

FIGURE 7.2   *Chain of Causes*

Effect Analysis

When you write about the causes of a particular effect, you devote most of your attention to developing those causes in detail and showing how they produced the effect. However, when you write about effects, you want to focus most of your attention on them. In the e-mail on page 176, Prudence mentions causes but devotes most of her e-mail to describing effects—the events that happened to her as result of weather and road conditions. In the case of the common cold, you could write an essay that develops some effects of catching a major cold, as illustrated in Figure 7-3.

When you analyze effects, ask yourself these questions:

1. **How many effects result from the cause?** In your prewriting, make sure to identify all the effects your reader might need to know. If you identify, say, three or four effects about which you can write convincingly, you can be sure you have a suitable topic for a short essay. Sometimes, however, you may discover that a cause has many more effects than you suspected. For instance, what if you chose to write about the effects on American society of the September 11, 2001, attacks? You would quickly discover that the possible supports for your thesis would be overwhelming and that you might have to narrow your topic through further brainstorming. Answering this question helps you organize the body of your essay. For instance, if you discover lots of little effects, you may have to group them into categories so that your body paragraphs contain sufficient detail. If you have just one effect, you may have to break it into three or four parts, brainstorming for sufficient detail about each part so that your essay contains more than one body paragraph.

2. **Which are the major effects, and which are the minor?** Some effects are more serious than others. Depending on the writing situation, you may want to identify effects as major or minor for your reader, group minor effects together into one paragraph, or write about major and minor effects in a particular order.

3. **Which are the short-term effects, and which are the long-term ones?** Another way to think about effects is in terms of how long they last. If the short-term effects of a cold are the sniffling and coughing, longer-term effects may have to do with general physical weakness or interruption of job or school responsibilities. Short- and long-term effects can be ordered in several ways, depending on how many there are and on their severity or importance.

4. **Are the effects related to one another in a chain of effects?** Just as with causes, you can write about effects as occurring in chains. This is similar to writing about

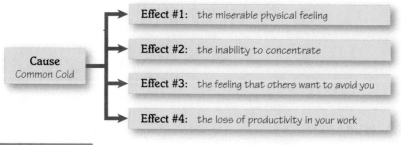

FIGURE 7.3   *One Cause Leading to Multiple Effects*

causal chains, but effect analysis would require that you describe the effects more than the causes.

Problems to Avoid in Cause/Effect Analysis

Analyzing causes and effects can be difficult because it can be easy to make mistakes or let your biases mistakenly identify causes and effects. Therefore, to test whether your own analysis is appropriate, ask yourself these questions:

1. **Have I called something a cause just because it happens earlier than the effect?** For instance, if you go outside in a snowstorm and then, a week later, come down with a cold, you might be tempted to attribute the cold to the snowstorm. These types of illogical cause-effect conclusions based on the time they occur are known as *post hoc, ergo proctor hoc*. Be careful of this error in thinking.

2. **Have I identified only one cause when there might be several?** An example of this type of thinking is the simplification that the Civil War was caused only by slavery when in fact several other major factors were involved.

3. **Have I confused the main cause with contributory causes?** Your job as the writer is to make the relationship between causal factors clear to your reader. Spend some time analyzing that relationship in your prewriting process. For example, if you were to claim that not washing hands causes the common cold, you'd be misleading your reader by implying an incorrect main cause.

4. **Have I failed to distinguish between major and minor, or long-term and short-term, effects?** In writing about effects, you should show they are related to one another to help your reader fully understand your topic. Some effects of the American Civil War are still evident today, more than 150 years after the war ended! Even with less weighty topics, your reader appreciates learning which are the more serious and longer-lasting effects.

If you answer "yes" to any of these questions, you should devote further thought to developing support for your topic.

WRITING YOUR CAUSE/EFFECT ESSAY

This section presents step-by-step instructions for developing an effect analysis essay. Here we follow the writing process of Diannah, a student who has had long personal experience helping her mother cope with a debilitating disease.

Supporting a Parent with MS

Multiple sclerosis is an autoimmune and neurological disorder that affects 2.5 million people worldwide, including 400,000 Americans. In this disease, the nerve insulating myelin of a person's body comes under attack when the body's own defensive immune system no longer recognizes it and takes it for an intruder. The cause is still unknown, but certain environmental triggers and perhaps a virus could be contributing factors.

My mother was diagnosed with multiple sclerosis 13 years ago. My mother unfortunately has a progressive disease course, in which the symptoms worsen as time goes on. She has been through many hospital visits. I was young when her illness began, and my lifestyle has been one of support for my mother ever since. Supporting a parent with MS is a difficult process. MS affects its victims physically, psychologically, and socially, and for each of these types of effects, family members must learn to cope in different ways.

Multiple sclerosis affects a person physically in many ways. Pain, tingling, and numbness in extremities are all things a person with MS may experience. Blurred vision or even blindness can also be symptoms of the disease. To be supportive when these problems occur, a child of someone with MS takes on more responsibility in a daily family routine. Helping around the house more and running errands are only two examples. The parent may no longer be able to walk by herself, so pushing a wheelchair or being a shoulder to lean on becomes natural. Also, with a parent unable to drive, a child might learn to drive at a younger age to help with transportation needs of the family. Driving trips to and from school, doctors' appointments, and the grocery store become necessary parts of daily life. Since my mother was experiencing many physical effects, I learned to drive at age 15 with a hardship license. I drove myself to and from school every day, ran errands for my parents, and took my mom shopping to spend time with her.

While multiple sclerosis causes many well-known physical symptoms, it also produces psychological effects that patients and families have to deal with. Memory loss, anxiety, depression, and stress are all examples of psychological symptoms of this disease. Some symptoms, such as depression and anxiety, can be handled by prescription drugs quite successfully. Other symptoms require occupational and speech therapy. My mother developed slight brain damage, which caused her to have difficulty speaking, moving, and remembering. All of this took quite a toll on me as I was growing up because it was so hard to watch her suffer in these ways. As her mental condition worsened, I developed my own experiences of stress and depression. To overcome some of the psychological difficulties I was having as a child, I attended counseling for more than a year.

Finally, multiple sclerosis leads to serious disturbances in a person's social life. People with MS are physically unable to do as many things as they were able to do before the onset of the disease. Their family and closest friends become their support during these trying times. Children of parents with MS need to customize their lifestyle to accommodate and support their parent. Instead of having an active lifestyle, like playing sports or going for hikes, I found more mellow activities by which to spend treasured moments with my family, such as playing Scrabble and watching movies. The MS Society is also a strong support group that we got interested in. From their website and newsletters, the whole family learned a lot about the disease. We also got together a team and joined in on the annual MS Walk, put on to raise money for research and support of victims of MS. One year, I was the team leader, and we designed a logo for our T-shirts and went around to many businesses and homes to raise money for the cause.

It was a useful thing to do and supported not only my family and mom but also many others with the disease.

Multiple sclerosis is a devastating disease that affects too many people. A cure needs to be found soon, and with the research that is currently happening, I'm sure it will be. Having a mother with this disease made my life different—harder at times than many others, I suspect, but that only made me a stronger person. Learning to be supportive in many different ways helped me grow and even helps me in my life today.

This essay exhibits several interesting features: First, the introduction consists of two paragraphs (although it still follows the pattern of lead-in, transitional material, and thesis and essay map). Second, it uses a mixture of description, narration, and exemplification to develop the effects of multiple sclerosis on Diannah's mother. Finally, the conclusion goes beyond mere repetition to offer a sense of hope to a reader who may have relatives afflicted with MS.

Prewriting

In this chapter, we introduce a more structured prewriting tool that is particularly appropriate to cause/effect writing: *diagramming*, or "drawing a picture" of the relationships between causes and effects. (Clustering is a type of diagramming, but it tends to lack structure because its purpose is more to generate ideas than to organize them.) The most useful form of diagramming for cause/effect writing is called *flowcharting*. Before you begin creating a cause/effect flowchart, however, you should develop your ideas using some methods you already know.

> **Computer tip**
> Try to outline your process by using the flowchart function of your word processor.

Discovering and Limiting Your Topic

Prewriting Strategy #6: Diagramming

Follow Diannah's prewriting process as she moves from the invention stage of prewriting to flowcharting. Diannah freewrites for 20 minutes or so on her topic: multiple sclerosis. She decides to diagram her ideas to allow her to see them more clearly. Here is what she produces.

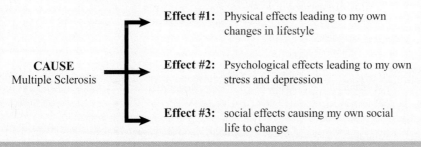

One Cause Leading to Multiple Effects

CAUSE
Multiple Sclerosis

Effect #1: Physical effects leading to my own changes in lifestyle

Effect #2: Psychological effects leading to my own stress and depression

Effect #3: social effects causing my own social life to change

Here we see another variation on the cause/effect theme. Diannah didn't find this pattern in a textbook; rather, it emerged from her mother's experience of a serious disease.

TOPICS TO CONSIDER

If you are experiencing some difficulty coming up with a topic, perhaps one of the following topics can help stimulate your thinking. Unless you're willing or are required to do research, choose a topic that you feel knowledgeable about through your studies, personal experiences, readings, or observations. If you choose a topic from this list, use the topic as written to start your prewriting sessions.

Writing for College		
▪ Causes of any historical event, such as the rise of a political party ▪ Reasons for a trend in popular culture	▪ Causes or effects of global warming, flooding, or some other natural occurrence ▪ Effects of adopting a particular philosophy, such as existentialism or positivism	▪ Causes for the failure a science experiment

	Writing in Your Profession		
BUSINESS	▪ Effects of poor customer service ▪ Causes of a workplace accident	▪ Effects of a particular management practice	▪ Effects of sexual harassment in the workplace
CRIMINAL JUSTICE	▪ Causes of a high crime rate in a particular area ▪ Reasons our prisons are over-crowded	▪ Causes of unsafe conditions in jails	▪ Reasons criminology is good field to consider
EDUCATION	▪ Reasons our schools are failing to educate students ▪ Causes of school violence	▪ Effects of year-round schooling	▪ Reasons math and science education are becoming more important
HEALTH	▪ Effects of the aging process ▪ Side effects of a particular drug	▪ Causes of obesity in poor people	▪ Effects of drinking too much coffee
SOCIAL WORK/ PSYCHOLOGY	▪ Causes or effects of dysfunctional family relationships	▪ Causes of community resistance to halfway houses ▪ Effects of grief on a client	▪ Potential effects of misdiagnosing client behavior
TECHNICAL	▪ Causes of a major technical disaster ▪ Causes of slowdowns in a computer network	▪ Effects of neglecting regular maintenance on any mechanical system	▪ Effects of cellular telephones on working life
OTHERS	▪ Causes of air or water pollution in a particular community ▪ Reasons behind Hollywood's addiction to techno-thrillers	▪ Reasons why a particular candidate won or lost an election	▪ Causes or effects of rising gasoline prices

Writing in Everyday Life		
▪ Effects of not spaying pets ▪ Causes of "minor" addictions, such shopping or watching football on television	▪ Causes of house fires ▪ Effects of starting a retirement savings account at an early age	▪ Causes of growing busyness in modern life ▪ Effects of television news on our understanding of important issues

WRITING 7-1

Do some listing, freewriting, looping, or clustering to begin generating ideas for your cause/effect essay. Once you have plenty of material on paper, select one or two of the best ideas and draw flowcharts to represent the logical connections between causes and effects.

Identifying Your Audience and Establishing Your Purpose

Cause analysis might address a different set of audience concerns than effect analysis. For instance, if you are writing about a disease for people who have just begun to suffer from it, they may be more concerned about effects initially and about causes later. Ask yourself whether your reader needs to know more about causes than effects, or vice versa. Table 7.1 illustrates the importance of your choice of audience when it comes to determining your purpose for writing a cause or an effect analysis.

As you compare the columns in Table 7.1, one conclusion is obvious: without a specific and appropriate choice of audience, you might have problems deciding what information to include and what information to leave out.

Setting Your Tone

In Chapter 6, you practiced recognizing and revising sentences that set an inappropriate tone because of jargon and slang. In addition to avoiding these types of expressions, you also want to set a tone that matches your audience and purpose. If you are writing about the effects of a particular disease and your audience is a patient just diagnosed with the disease, then your tone might be reassuring, sympathetic, and straight-forward. However, if your audience is students in a biology class, then your tone would be more scientific, objective, and analytical. If your audience has some background on the topic, then you want to set a respectful tone by not telling them information that they already know. Finally, be sure to avoid coming across as dogmatic and closed-minded by making statements that assume certain causes or effects in all cases. Instead of declaring that loud

TABLE 7.1 *Importance of Audience When Determining Purpose*

Topic	Audience	Purpose
Effects of global warming on the western states	State legislators	Convince them to vote a certain way, perhaps on a particular bill
Causes of obesity among young people	High school administrators	Cause them to think about changes to school lunch and exercise programs
Causes of heavy traffic in a particular area of town	City council	Make them aware of a problem they can address
Causes of age discrimination in the classroom	Older nontraditional students	Help them understand traditional classroom dynamics

WRITING YOUR CAUSE/EFFECT ESSAY

music causes hearing loss, you should qualify your statement: loud music *can* contribute to hearing loss in some people.

In cause/effect writing, you are usually trying to inform or persuade your reader about the true nature of some cause/effect relationship. At times, your audience knows little or nothing about this relationship; at other times, your audience knows, or believes it knows, quite a lot. Therefore, part of your prewriting task is to determine how much your audience knows (or thinks it knows) about your topic.

Not all of these questions assume equal importance in each writing task; therefore, focus on specific characteristics of your audience that seem to be important in your immediate writing situation.

WRITING   7-2

Record your observations about your audience, purpose, and tone by filling out the following form.

Audience, Purpose, and Tone Analysis

Your topic: _____

I. Audience

1. Who is my audience? _____

2. Age: _____; Gender: _____

3. Who would be the most interested in my topic? _____
   _____

4. What is my audience's educational background? _____
   _____

5. What does my audience know or assume about my topic? _____
   _____

6. What are my audience's social or cultural interests? _____
   _____

7. Why would my audience be interested in my topic? _____
   _____

8. What connection do I have with this audience? _____
   _____

II. Purpose

1. What do I want my audience to understand? _____
   _____

2. Why is this topic important to my audience? _____
   _____

3. What does my audience expect when reading my writing? _____

_____

4. How do I expect my audience to react? _____

_____

III. Tone

1. What tone do I hope to establish? _____

_____

2. Are there any special uses of jargon or slang that I should either employ or avoid? _____

_____

Formulating Your Thesis

In writing a cause or an effect analysis, your thesis should clearly indicate which of the two methods you are using. It should also make an overall claim about the causes or effects that helps the reader understand your connection to the topic and the reason you think the analysis is important.

        Topic   Controlling Idea

{Our move to the country} {resulted in unforeseen, and undesirable, consequences.}

This thesis mentions both cause (moving to the country) and effects (undesirable consequences). This is common in cause/effect writing: even if your essay is devoted to effect analysis, you should mention the cause, and vice versa. This example, although it identifies the cause, clearly serves as the thesis for an effect analysis essay that develops the undesirable consequences of moving to the country. The body of the essay is governed by the controlling idea of the thesis, and the controlling idea is all about effects. Here are some other examples. Notice how the controlling idea (underlined) indicates whether the essay analyzes causes or effects.

CAUSE ANALYSIS	■ In the United States and other developed countries, young people are postponing marriage <u>for several reasons, most of them economic in nature.</u>	■ Hip-hop is so widespread not because it speaks to the deepest concerns of young people but <u>because of brilliant marketing techniques on the part of corporate America.</u>
EFFECT ANALYSIS	■ The scarcity of water resources in the western United States <u>is causing several political conflicts in the region.</u>	■ When my son broke his arm in a football game, our lives <u>suddenly changed dramatically, mostly for the better.</u>

Cause/effect writing is particularly suited to the use of essay maps. Usually, you are trying to show how several causes contribute to an effect or how several effects result from a particular cause. These cases present a natural opportunity to attach an essay map to your thesis, listing the causes or the effects you develop in the essay.

At this point in her writing process, Diannah jots down several versions of her thesis. Her first attempt has no essay map:

> Multiple sclerosis has numerous effects.

However, Diannah soon realizes that an essay map listing the effects makes her thesis clear and definite. Here is her next version of the thesis, this time including an essay map:

> MS affects its victims physically, psychologically, and socially.

She is still not entirely happy with her thesis, but she knows she has plenty of time to continue refining it until it fits within the flow of her introduction.

WRITING 7-3

Write two different thesis statements for your essay that analyzes a cause or an effect.

1. Consider the strengths and weaknesses of each thesis statement.
2. Determine whether an essay map would make your thesis more focused and more effective.
3. Ask others for suggestions that might improve the thesis statement.

Select the best of your draft thesis statements. Then go on to the next part of the pre-writing stage, outlining. You can always come back to rephrase or refocus your thesis.

Outlining Your Ideas

By now, you have chosen a topic, identified your audience, established your purpose, and created a thesis. It's time to create your outline. Your outline is vital in helping you make decisions about the unity and content of your essay. The general format of your outline is informal and quite simple.

Examine Diannah's initial outline for her effect analysis essay.

ESSAY OUTLINE

I. Introduction
   A. Lead-in strategies
      1. Definition of MS
      2. How many people it affects
      3. How I know about it—Mom's diagnosis
   B. My thesis and essay map

II. Body
   A. Physical effects on her and how I help
      1. Pain, tingling, numbness
      2. Blurred vision leading to blindness

    3. I need to help around the house

    4. I started driving at 15 to help out

  B. Psychological effects on her and how I help

    1. Memory loss

    2. Depression and anxiety

    3. Her mental symptoms caused me to have them too

    4. I had to participate in family therapy

  C. Social effects on her and how I help

    1. Her circle of contacts has grown smaller

    2. I limit my activities and stay closer to home

    3. Our involvement in the MS Society

III. Conclusion

  A. Devastating disease

  B. No cure yet

  C. Sense of assurance that family can be supportive

WRITING 7-4

Prepare your outline. In each body paragraph, indicate where you intend to use description, narration, and exemplification to support your point. After you have completed your outline, review it carefully. Compare it to your diagram of the causes or effects, and make sure the outline captures the same relationships you depicted in the diagram.

Essay Outline

Topic: _____

Audience: _____

Purpose: _____

  I. Introduction: Lead-in strategies

    A. Lead-in strategies_____

      1. _____

      2. _____

    B. Thesis and essay map _____

  II. Body paragraphs

    A. Cause/effect #1: _____

      1. _____

      2. _____

      3. _____

       B. Cause/effect #2: _____

          1. _____

          2. _____

          3. _____

       C. Cause/effect #3: _____

          1. _____

          2. _____

          3. _____

       D. Cause/effect #4: _____

          1. _____

          2. _____

          3. _____

  III. Conclusion: Strategies you can use to wrap up your essay

       A. _____

       B. _____

       C. _____

Drafting

As you draft your composition, try to follow a step-by-step thinking process to make sure your draft has the basic components of a good essay.

Writing Your Introduction

As we have indicated before, when drafting your essay, you don't have to start with the introduction. If you wish to plunge right into the body of your essay, feel free to do so. You can even save your introduction for last. The goal is simply to get started with the writing process; sometimes, the introduction is not the easiest place to begin.

Lead-In Techniques

In addition to the techniques introduced previously, you might try to include a startling fact or statistic in your lead-in. For example, in an essay about teen pregnancy, you could open with the striking statistic that 19% of the high school girls in a particular school have had children or are currently pregnant. If you happen to be writing for parents of high school girls, such a figure can immediately grab your audience and keep them interested for the duration of the essay. The fact or statistic you choose should be closely related to your audience's concerns, which you must determine through analysis of your reader.

You can insert a fact from your own experience without basing it on research. However, it might be hard to locate statistics except in published research material. Therefore, at this point in the course, if you wish to use statistics, be sure to ask your instructor for permission to include material derived from sources.

Here is Diannah's introduction. Notice that she uses a statistic that would seem to require a citation. In her case, however, she is probably so immersed in the world of multiple sclerosis that among her acquaintances, her statistics are widely known and quoted.

> Multiple sclerosis is an autoimmune and neurological disorder that affects 2.5 million people worldwide, including 400,000 Americans. In this disease, the nerve insulating myelin of a person's body comes under attack when the body's own defensive immune system no longer recognizes it and takes it for an intruder. The cause is still unknown. MS affects its victims physically, psychologically, and socially, and for each of these types of effect, family members must learn to cope in different ways.

Diannah's introduction is off to a good start. She has used a striking statistic to get the reader's attention, and her thesis and essay map clearly indicate the main point of her essay. However, she has not connected the lead-in with the thesis by providing the connection to her family, and particularly to her mother.

Remember to make sure that the information in your introduction is meaningful and focused. Unnecessarily long introductions only confuse the reader and prompt a search for the hidden thesis. On the other hand, if your introduction is too short and undeveloped, your reader might feel that you are not committed to the writing or not credible as an author. And as we have mentioned before, don't just make your introduction a wordy essay map in which you tell the reader in several sentences what you plan to discuss.

Don't forget that your lead-in must flow naturally to your thesis. Your reader may feel puzzled if you don't provide adequate transition between, say, an opening set of statistics and the thesis.

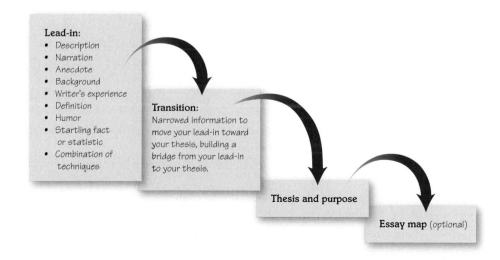

Lead-in:
- Description
- Narration
- Anecdote
- Background
- Writer's experience
- Definition
- Humor
- Startling fact or statistic
- Combination of techniques

Transition:
Narrowed information to move your lead-in toward your thesis, building a bridge from your lead-in to your thesis.

Thesis and purpose

Essay map (optional)

WRITING   7-5

Using the thesis you prepared earlier, write two different introductions. Use a combination of two or more of the following strategies: description, personal narrative, anecdote, background information, your experience with the topic, definition of a key term, humor, or a startling fact or statistic. When you have finished, select the introduction that you believe is most appropriate for your essay.

Writing Your Body Paragraphs

At this point, be aware that you can employ several writing skills that you already know to develop an essay that analyzes a cause or an effect. Specifically, since one of your jobs is to demonstrate the importance or severity of the causes or effects you are writing about, your *descriptive* skills can come in handy. You can also use *narrative* episodes from your own experience to support this type of essay. Also, you might find it useful to give *examples* of effects of a particular set of causes. And since cause/effect relationships happen in time, you may find it necessary to rely on *process* analysis at several points in your essay.

As you draft the body of the essay, refer to your outline. If you need to revise your outline, feel free to do so; don't treat your outline as if it were carved in stone. Always feel free to go back to any earlier part of the writing process. Consider the following points as you write your body paragraphs:

1. Maintain a single focus on one cause *or* one effect in each paragraph, and express that focus as a topic sentence.
2. Make sure that all information in each paragraph relates to and supports its topic sentence.
3. Using transitions, show the kind of causal relationship if appropriate: main or contributory, immediate or distant, and so on.
4. Make sure you are covering the essential and major causes or effects.
5. If a paragraph runs too long, consider breaking it in two, but use transitions to indicate that the new paragraph continues to explain the previous topic.
6. Make sure you present the causes or effects in the best order; if you are writing about a causal chain, the order should be chronological. If you are writing about effects, proceed from least important to most important.
7. Use a variety of techniques to build your body paragraphs. Don't forget that a short description or narration, for example, is an excellent way to provide evidence for many topics.
8. Always remember your audience's needs. Provide the information your audience requires using the appropriate techniques and tone.

Look at Diannah's first draft of the first two body paragraphs of her essay:

Multiple sclerosis affects a person physically in many ways, like pain, tingling, and numbness in extremities. Blurred vision or even blindness, too. Being supportive of these problems that occur, a child of someone with MS will take on more responsibility in a daily family routine. Helping around the household more and running errands are only two examples. Since my mother was experiencing many of these physical effects, I learned to drive at age 15 with a hardship license.

There are also psychological effects for a family to deal with. Some areas, such as depression and anxiety, can be handled by prescription drugs quite successfully. Therapy is also a good idea for the whole family. When I was younger, I had my own experiences of stress and depression. To overcome some of the psychological difficulties I was having as a child, I attended counseling for more than a year. My mother went through a hospital stay where she ended up with slight brain damage. This caused her to have difficulties speaking, moving, and issues with her memory. While still in the hospital recovering, she would go to physical, occupational, and speech therapies daily. They were very difficult for her at first. While this was happening, my mother seemed weak to me, but over the next few weeks, she proved how strong she actually is.

Coherence: Using Transitions

In cause/effect writing, transitions should help the reader properly understand the full relationship between causes and their effects. These relationships have to do with two factors: *time* and the *nature of the relationship* (main or contributory cause, immediate or distant cause, causal chain, and so on). Some of your transitions clarify that causes come before effects in time. In addition, you need to employ other transitions to help the reader see the type of causal relationship you are describing.

Review the following list of transitions that indicate particular features of cause/effect relationships. You have seen some of these transitions in previous chapters because they are common in many writing modes. Notice especially the repetition of some time transitions from the list in Chapter 6. This list is not exhaustive, but you can return to it to generate other ideas for transitions as you need them.

> **Computer tip**
>
> Use your word processor to highlight all your transitions. Have you used sufficient transitions to connect ideas? Where can your essay benefit from additional transitions? Where have you overused transitions?

Transitions to Show Cause/Effect Relationships		
after	cause	for
aftermath	caused by	for these reasons
accordingly	consequently	for this purpose
as a consequence	consequentially	for this reason
as a result (of)	created	further
because (of)	due to	furthermore
because of this	effect	generated
but	end product	gradually
by reason of	end result	hence
by the way	eventually	henceforth
the by-product of	following that	if . . . then

Continued

Transitions to Show Cause/Effect Relationships—cont'd		
impact	on account of	since
induced	on this account	so
incidentally	otherwise	so that
in effect	outcome	started
in fact	outgrowth	subsequently
initiated	owing to	then
in short	produced	thereafter
in view of	ramifications of	therefore
it follows that	reason	thereupon
little by little	result	thus
of course	resulted in	to this end

Remember to employ other coherence devices as well: repeating key words, referring to previous ideas, and using pronouns that reference specific nouns in the previous sentences. Think of the sentences in your paragraphs as links in a chain; if you fail somehow to link one idea to a previous idea, you have broken the chain, causing your paragraph to be choppy and disjointed.

WRITING   7-6

Draft the body of your essay using the following strategies:

1. Follow your outline. Make any changes to the outline that you feel help your essay.

2. Start each of your body paragraphs with a clear topic sentence identifying the cause *or* effect you develop in that paragraph. During revision, you may alter the topic sentence in any or all of your paragraphs, but for now it's important to remain focused on the topic sentence as you write each paragraph.

3. Add transitions to keep your ideas flowing smoothly and to guide your audience through your information.

Writing Your Conclusion

As you start to plan your conclusion, consider the following approaches for cause/effect writing:

- For cause analysis, explain that understanding the true nature of the causes can help the reader in some way.
- For effect analysis, emphasize the seriousness of the effects and the resulting need for further study or action.
- Refer to misconceptions many people have about the causes or the effects, and reiterate your thesis as a way of emphasizing what you believe to be the right interpretation.

- Challenge the reader to do something about the causes or the effects.
- Refer to some point you made in your introduction to bring your essay full circle. For example, if you started your introduction with a definition, a humorous anecdote, or a brief narration, include a reference to this in your conclusion.

Remember that your thesis controls your conclusion as well as the body of the essay. Don't permit your conclusion to go in a separate direction with little or no relationship to your introduction. As mentioned in Chapter 6, a good method to determine whether your conclusion is effective is to read your introduction and then jump to the conclusion. Do they connect? Do they flow together? They should be similar in tone and give a sense of unity and completeness to the purpose stated in your introduction.

WRITING 7-7

Write a tentative conclusion for your essay.

1. Review the different approaches listed on page 194 and combine some of these approaches to create an effective conclusion.

2. Read your introduction and then your conclusion. Is there a smooth connection?

Revising

Start your revising stage by reading your essay aloud. How do you feel about what you have written? Keep these thoughts in mind as you revise your draft as necessary.

Style Tip: Modifying Phrases and Clauses

To avoid confusing your reader, watch your use of modifying phrases and clauses.

INCORRECT:	I was informed that the crash occurred by my office. [Did the crash occur near your office, or did your office inform you about the crash?]
CORRECT:	I was informed by my office that the crash occurred last night.
INCORRECT:	Driving along I-25, the scenery was less than breathtaking. [Who is driving in this sentence? It implies that the scenery was driving.]
CORRECT:	Driving along I-25, I found the scenery less than breathtaking.

PROBLEM   SOLUTION

WRITING

My introduction seems dull, vague, undeveloped, or not engaging.

1. Did you analyze your audience? Determine and address your audience's interests and needs.
2. Have you reviewed the strategies for developing a lead-in? Try combining a variety of methods that are appropriate to your audience and purpose.
3. Make sure that your lead-in flows naturally into your thesis.

CAUSE/EFFECT

My supporting paragraphs don't seem to be developed enough, and I don't know what to add.

1. Have you selected the most relevant and important causes or effects to write about? To check, list all of your causes or your effects and then cross out ones that do not relate to your main idea.
2. Have you experimented with different methods of development in each body paragraph? If not, try combining several of the methods you already know:
   - Description
   - Narration
   - Examples
   - Process analysis
3. Have you tried using looping or any other inventive techniques to discover new information for any of your causes or your effects? Return to the prewriting stage and do a more focused looping.
4. Have you asked someone else's advice? It is not too late to do so now.

COHERENCE

My essay doesn't read smoothly.

1. Have you clarified the time relationships between causes and effects?
2. Do you have a clear thesis statement that drives the entire essay? If not, make sure that your controlling idea says something definite about your causes or your effects.
3. Do your topic sentences clearly identify your causes or your effects? Go to each body paragraph and make sure that you have a topic sentence that lets the reader know the cause *or* effect you discuss in that paragraph.
4. Is all information relevant? Read the supporting details in each paragraph carefully, and then eliminate information that does not relate directly to the topic sentence, or refocus the information to establish its relevancy.
5. Do you have transitional words or phrases to clarify the relationship between paragraphs? Do you vary the types of transitions? See list of transitions on pages 193 and 194.

WRITING 7-8

Start your revision. Don't leave any part of your essay untouched.

- Make sure you discuss all important causes or effects.
- Be sure to use a mixture of description, narration, exemplification, and process analysis to develop your essay. (You don't need to use all four in each body paragraph, but your essay should combine some writing techniques you have practiced before.)
- Check for coherence. Make sure you offer enough transitions to help guide your reader.
- Use the chart on page 196 to help you troubleshoot.
- Use a variety of sentence types and make sure your modifying phrases are not misplaced or dangling.

Collaborative Critical Thinking

Asking Your Peers

Once you have completed the writing process and have a polished final draft, exchange papers with a classmate for peer review. Use the following form to answer questions about your peer's paper.

1. Who is the writer? Who is the peer reviewer?

2. What is the purpose of the essay? Does the paper develop causes or effects?

3. Do the first few sentences capture your interest? Explain how or suggest a better way to make the opening more interesting.

4. Is the thesis clearly stated? What can you suggest to improve its overall effectiveness?

5. If it is a cause essay, does it correctly analyze the major causes? What has the writer missed in terms of the nature of the cause/effect relationships (main or contributory, immediate or distant, causal chain, and so on)?

6. If it is an effect essay, does it adequately discuss the major effects in the best order? What can the author do to better explain how the causes produce the effects?

7. Does each paragraph contain sufficient information to explain each cause or effect clearly and fully? Where in the essay should the writer add more details?

8. Does each body paragraph have a topic sentence that clearly lets the reader know the topic and controlling idea of that paragraph? What can you suggest to make the topic sentences more effective?

9. Does the essay use appropriate transitions? What can you suggest to improve the coherence of the essay?

10. Circle any grammatical problems that you notice and bring them to the attention of the writer.

11. Is the conclusion effective? What can the writer do to make the conclusion more effective?

WRITING YOUR CAUSE/EFFECT ESSAY

Proofreading

Common Error #7: Pronoun–Antecedent Agreement

In the previous chapter, you learned to identify pronouns according to their person and to guard against shifts in person. In this chapter, we focus on a similar problem: making sure your pronouns agree with their antecedents.

Problems in pronoun–antecedent agreement can occur for a variety of reasons. (For more detail about pronoun–antecedent agreement, go to Chapter 18.) Examine the following sentences:

> INCORRECT: **Everyone** should place **their** books on the floor during the test.
> [**Everyone** is singular, and **their** is plural.]

> CORRECT: **Everyone** should place **his or her** books on the floor during the test.
> [The antecedent **everyone** and the pronouns **his or her** are both singular.]
>
> OR
>
> **Students** should place **their** books on the floor during the test.
> [The antecedent **students** and the pronoun **their** are both plural.]

GRAMMAR CHECKUP   7-1

On the line provided, correct the errors in pronoun agreement by replacing the faulty pronoun, changing the antecedent, or rewriting the sentence. Answers will vary.

1. Everybody on the beach lost their towels when the wind whipped up.

   Everybody on the beach lost his or her towel when the wind whipped up.

2. Each of the boys had packed their camping gear correctly.

   Each of the boys had packed his camping gear correctly.

3. Sometimes a law student must forget about their spring break.

   Sometimes law students must forget about their spring break.

4. Not everyone gets their exercise in the same way.

   Not everyone gets his or her exercise in the same way.

5. A new student should never miss their first class.

   New students should never miss their first class.

6. No one has their raincoat!

   No one has his or her raincoat!

7. A person shouldn't tell lies to their boss even when they are at fault.

   People shouldn't tell lies to their boss even when they are at fault.

8. Everyone in the store looked up from their work when the famous actor walked in.

   <u>The staff and customers in the store looked up from their work when the</u>
   <u>famous actor walked in.</u>

9. A teacher shouldn't lose their temper the way you did yesterday.

   <u>You shouldn't lose your temper the way you did yesterday.</u>

10. Somebody left their briefcase on the afternoon train.

   <u>Somebody left his or her briefcase on the afternoon train.</u>

Check your answers to this Grammar Checkup in Appendix A on page A-3. How did you do? If you missed even one of these items, you may need to review errors in pronoun–antecedent agreement in Chapter 18.

WRITING 7-9

Start proofreading your own essay. Check for and correct errors in sentence structure (fragments, comma splices, and fused sentences), use of modifiers, and pronoun agreement; shifts in voice and tense; and passive sentences. Look for other obvious errors in spelling, punctuation, and so on.

Final Checklist

1. Does your introduction have an appropriate and effective lead-in? ☐

2. Is the thesis statement clear and structured appropriately? ☐

3. Have you narrowed the topic so that all parts of the topic are accounted for? ☐

4. Does the essay's body clearly focus on either causes or effects, and is it organized accordingly? ☐

5. Does each paragraph have an appropriate topic sentence that clearly identifies a cause or an effect? ☐

6. Does the essay avoid oversimplification the relationships between causes and effects? ☐

7. Do you provide sufficient and reliable evidence to prove the validity of each cause or effect? ☐

8. Does the essay contain appropriate, varied, and smooth transitions between paragraphs and sentences? ☐

9. Does your essay have varied sentence structures, complete sentences (no fragments, comma splices, or fused sentences), and insignificant errors in spelling, usage, and punctuation? ☐

WRITING YOUR CAUSE/EFFECT ESSAY

Reflecting

As you bring this writing assignment to a close, you naturally want to reflect on what you have accomplished. At the appropriate time, take a moment to respond to the following writing activities.

WRITING   7-10

Self-Reflection

Before you hand in your paper, write a brief paragraph in which you reflect on your final draft. Include your feelings on the following questions:

1. What do you feel you did best?

2. What part of your paper was most challenging to you?

3. In which areas do you feel you need the most practice?

4. What strategies will you employ to address your challenges or weaknesses and to improve the quality of your essay?

After you have completed this self-reflection, carefully review your instructor's comments. How are they similar or different from your own answers to the self-reflection? Make a list of your grammar, punctuation, and spelling errors so that you can follow up on the ones that recur. Consider what strategies you will employ to address your challenges or weaknesses and to improve the quality of your essay.

How might you use cause/effect analysis outside of this English course? Look back at the writing samples in Previewing Your Task in this chapter.

- **College:** _____

- **Your profession:** _____

- **Everyday life:** _____

CHAPTER 8

Developing Your Essay through Comparison or Contrast

YOUR GOALS

Understanding Comparison and Contrast

1. Use similarities (comparison) or differences (contrast) to make a point.

2. Select meaningful bases of comparison or contrast.

3. Provide sufficient evidence to support comparison or contrast analysis.

4. Distinguish between point-by-point and block organizations.

Writing Your Comparison or Contrast Essay

1. Use Venn diagrams as a prewriting technique to discover and limit your topic.

2. Formulate a clear thesis that states a judgment or overall perspective for a comparison or contrast essay.

3. Support each point with details that are convincing and balanced between the two topics.

4. Write to a specific audience for a specific purpose.

5. Use transitions appropriate to comparison or contrast.

6. Identify and avoid offensive language.

7. Use correct pronoun reference and case.

"We are so made, that we can only derive intense enjoyment from a contrast, and only very little from a state of things."

■ **Sigmund Freud** ■

As the owner of a small printing business, you have seen your work orders increase and are struggling to keep up with the demand. You are considering hiring a third employee but must decide whether the added payroll costs will be worth it. Will the revenue from the increase in business make up for the cost, supervisory time, health benefits, and training of the new employee? You jot down the advantages of hiring a third employee and then the advantages of sticking with the two employees whom you currently have.

You are trying to decide between two previously owned cars. The first is more expensive but gets higher gas mileage, so you might make up the price difference in the long run. Its interior is slightly damaged and the radio doesn't work, so you'd want to invest in repairing those features. The second car is significantly cheaper and has a recently installed sound system, but it only gets 18 miles per gallon and would require an immediate investment in new tires and a tune-up. Which one should you purchase?

In your college classes, you are often asked—whether in tests, writing assignments, or oral presentations—to compare or contrast two concepts. In biology, you might have to compare the mating cycles of two organisms; in political science, you may have to contrast two governmental structures. Clearly, you will have greater academic success if you learn to use this method of development.

LET's warm up!

Remember yourself as a high school student, and then compare who you were then to who you are as a college student today. What are the differences in your two selves, past and present? What have you lost and what have you gained as you advanced into college? Do you have any lessons that you would like to pass on to current high school students? Write a paragraph addressing these questions.

Yukmin/Getty Images

PREVIEWING YOUR TASK

The following writing samples demonstrate the use of comparison and contrast in college, work, and everyday life. Keep in mind that, although it is sometimes desirable to use *both* comparison and contrast in the same piece of writing, this chapter focuses on using *either* comparison or contrast in a single assignment.

Writing for College

A common way of teaching literature is to ask students to compare or contrast two works in the same genre. Read the following student essay, written for an introduction to literature class by Sarah, an English major.

"Shall I Compare Thee . . ." and Its Update

According to poet Samuel Taylor Coleridge, poetry can be defined as "the best words in the best order." One way to appreciate poetry and its use of "the best words" is to look at a parody of a well-known masterpiece, such as Howard Moss's 1976 parody of William Shakespeare's "Shall I Compare Thee to a Summer's Day?" Although Moss represents Shakespeare's main ideas in his version of the poem, reading both poems side by side reveals differences in terms of form, diction, and figurative language. Of course, Moss's purpose is to highlight the differences between modern times and that of Shakespeare's time and he succeeds.

The two poems differ most obviously in form. Shakespeare's 115-word poem is a sonnet consisting of 14 lines, rhyming in iambic pentameter. Every other line rhymes (*day* and *May, dimmed* and *untrimmed),* except for the last two lines, which are rhyming couplets (*see* and *thee). Moss's 78-word version, however, is a random collection of rhymes and almost rhymes (*days* and *gray, hot* and *not)* and follows no recognizable pattern of verse with a mix of short and long lines.

Another difference between the two poems is the diction that each uses. Shakespeare's words are rich in imagery. For example, the poem starts with these two lines: "Shall I compare thee to a summer's day? / Thou art more lovely and more temperate." In these first lines, the reader has a vision of summer and of *temperate,* which refers to the weather (mild) but also a moderate and restrained person. On the other hand, Moss's poem starts with these lines: "Who says you're like one of the dog days? / You're nicer. And better." There is no richness in these lines with the mundane words *nicer* and *better.* Moss's poem offers the reader nowhere to go in his or her imagination except to everyday life.

One of the greatest appeals of poetry is its use of figurative language—metaphor, simile, and hyperbole. Shakespeare's poem is rich in these poetic devices. For instance, he uses personification, giving death human qualities as in line 11: "Nor shall death brag thou wand'rest in his shade." The whole poem has a sense of exaggeration or hyperbole as the woman is compared to an "eternal summer" that never fades. In contrast, Moss employs only one figure of speech, the opening line, which is a simile. Otherwise, the rest of the poem is full of mundane, straightforward language, such as the final two lines: "After you're dead and gone, / In this poem you'll live on!"

A reader might say that these two poems express the same idea, that the woman immortalized in the poem will never be forgotten because the poems will be read centuries from now. Also, students struggling with understanding poetry may appreciate Moss's more up-to-date version with its everyday vocabulary and familiar images. However, as Moss intended in his parody, anyone seriously studying poetry and savoring its expressions and creativity will find much more to discuss in Shakespeare's original poem than in the modernized version.

PRACTICE 8-1

1. What is the writer's purpose in this literature paper? <u>To show how a modern poet makes a point about some differences between modern poetry and that of Shakespeare's time.</u>

2. Where in the body paragraphs does the writer discuss the Shakespeare poem? <u>In the first part of each body paragraph.</u>

3. Where does the writer discuss the Moss poem? <u>In the second part of each body paragraph.</u>

Writing in Your Profession

The world of work offers many opportunities to practice comparison/contrast thinking. Depending on your job, you may engage in this form of analysis several times a day to make important decisions about hiring or firing, major expenditures, or explaining products to your customers, as in the following example.

What Are the Differences between a Fixed-Rate and Adjustable-Rate Mortgage?

Two popular mortgage rate plans for residential real estate loans include fixed mortgage rates and adjustable mortgage rates. Depending on the mortgage term and financial circumstances of the borrower, these two mortgages appeal to different types of consumers.

Fixed-Rate Mortgage

In a fixed-rate mortgage the interest rate is set for the entire term of the loan, even if the lender's interest rate fluctuates in the future. A fixed-rate mortgage is an attractive option for a long-term borrower since monthly payments do not fluctuate. Predictable payments allow borrowers to budget and plan their finances for the long term. However, for this convenience, lenders often charge higher fixed interest rates.

Borrowers may be hesitant to "lock into" a fixed mortgage rate if they feel that soon after attaining their mortgage, interest rates will fall significantly. If interest rates do fall, in order to attain a lower rate, they will have to qualify and pay for mortgage refinancing. Another issue with fixed-rate mortgages is that lenders will often have a prepayment penalty to discourage borrowers from paying off their mortgage early or refinancing their loan with a lower interest rate.

Adjustable-Rate Mortgage

The adjustable-rate mortgage (ARM), also commonly known as a variable-rate mortgage, is where the interest rate periodically fluctuates based on a predetermined index. As a result, the borrower's monthly payment may vary. In some respects, adjustable rates can be a gamble since the borrower will benefit if the interest rate falls and suffer if the rate rises. Unlike fixed-rate mortgages, some adjustable-rate mortgages offer borrowers the option to repay the initial principal amount borrowed early without a penalty charge.

Oftentimes, lenders sell adjustable-rate mortgages to inexperienced or uneducated customers with the intent of a foreclosure when the borrower is unable to pay back the loan if the interest rate rises. There are several organizations, such as Consumer Federation of America, that fight against these "predatory" lending practices. However, some adjustable-rate mortgages include provisions that protect the borrower. Usually there is a maximum limit that the interest rate can increase in a year and a maximum limit that the interest rate can increase over the course of the mortgage term. Also, borrowers are often offered an initial period with a fixed rate, before the interest rate begins to fluctuate. Since the risk is transferred from the lender to the borrower, lenders often have a much lower initial interest rate (or teaser rate), making adjustable-rate mortgages more attractive for short-term investors.

(Adapted from the Nextag website)

PRACTICE   8-2

1. What is the author's purpose or main point? <u>To distinguish between two popular mortgage options so that the reader can make an informed choice.</u>

2. How is the organization of the body of this piece different from that of the earlier literary essay? <u>In this selection, the author thoroughly discusses the first topic (fixed-rate mortgages) then switches to the second topic. In the literary essay, the author goes back and forth (in an organized way) between the Shakespeare poem and the Moss poem.</u>

Writing in Everyday Life

Since comparison and contrast is such a basic way to think about the world, especially when we are learning about something new or trying to make a decision, we often use it when communicating with others. The following letter to the editor of a local newspaper uses contrast writing to make a point.

Dear Editors,

I'm responding to last week's letter by Jack Wilson regarding the need to build more prisons in our area and lock up as many offenders as we can. I have some experience in this matter, having served time in prison and, currently, in a state hospital. My stay in prison was a waste of time: a short time after my parole, I reoffended and was sentenced to the state hospital. My hospital treatment is changing my life and making me less likely to reoffend. The difference between the two institutions lies in their purpose, social structure, and environment. We should not build more prisons; rather, we should find ways to rehabilitate offenders through psychiatric care such as that provided in our state hospital.

In both places, I was incarcerated but for two completely different purposes. When I was sentenced to prison, I was sent there as a punishment for a crime I committed. The prison served only as a warehouse to hold me until my time was up. True, I had the option to seek out treatment or to participate in some other program to change the way I was, but I chose to do my time the easiest way possible until my parole date. However, at the state hospital, there is no parole date. I could be here from a single day to the rest of my life. The court can only release me once I have been proven sane and am no longer a danger to myself and others. So the amount of time depends on my own actions and behavior.

Another striking difference between the two institutions has to do with the influence of peer pressure. While I was in prison, I had no motivation to change because I wanted to do easy time, and I did this by using drugs and running cons to make my life more comfortable. Most of my peers, as well as the guards, supported me because they were running their own games. Seeking treatment or a change while in prison was frowned on by many. It was seen as a sign of weakness, and in prison, being seen as weak is a dangerous thing. On the other hand, at the state hospital, the "therapeutic mind" is in charge. Con games, drugs, and manipulations are seen as unacceptable behaviors by both the staff and the clients. Human weakness in the state hospital is not only accepted but also seen as an opportunity to turn weaknesses into strengths.

The environment of both institutions has the greatest impact on how inmates turn out. Living in a cage in prison, I was seen as a number instead of a person with a name. I was dressed the same as everyone else. I had to be mean, vicious, and brave; otherwise, I was prey. However, here at the hospital, I can wear my own clothes, and I am called by my given name. I feel as though I am a person with an identity. I can laugh or cry without being afraid that someone will take advantage of me. But most of all, the environment allows me to make individual choices rather than follow the pack. At the hospital, I've regained my humanity. I'm allowed to grow into becoming a better person. I feel that I am investing my time.

My only regret is the time wasted while in prison; I did not have the courage to change because I was so afraid. If prisons were structured more like the hospital system, where a prisoner had to prove before he was released that he was rehabilitated and that he has stepped away from the criminal mind, repeat crimes would decline dramatically. Until we change the prison system, making it more like the state hospital, we should never build another one.

PRACTICE 8-3

1. Describe the writer of this advice. What is your attitude toward him as a person? Most readers should develop sympathy for the author because of the difficulty of his former life.

2. What is his purpose for writing this advice? Does he succeed in his purpose? Explain. The writer succeeds in bringing his own experience to bear on a topic most of us know little about. His letter convincingly demonstrates that prisons could be more like hospitals and thus more useful components of the justice system.

UNDERSTANDING COMPARISON AND CONTRAST

If you have ever been faced with a choice between two options, you have practiced thinking in terms of comparison (how two topics are alike) or contrast (how two topics are different). We are all faced with such choices constantly: what clothes to wear in the morning, which route to take to work, which assignment to tackle first during our study time. When we have to make a selection, we naturally consider how our options are similar or different.

Often, this selection process happens without much conscious thought: for instance, you might choose to wear a particular pair of slacks based simply on a moment's preference. However, for more important choices—long-term relationships, jobs, classes in college, medical procedures—you may need to write down the similarities and differences between two choices to make the best decision.

In your college classes, you may have noticed that when your instructors want you to learn something new, they try to show how two concepts, historical events, or scientific processes are similar to or different from something you already know. They realize that you acquire new knowledge mainly by comparing and contrasting it with previous knowledge and then placing it in the context of what you already know.

When you compare or contrast two topics, whether or not you are writing an essay, you should integrate the following components into your thinking:

1. The two topics to be compared or contrasted
2. Clear bases, or points, of comparison or contrast
3. Sufficient evidence to fully describe the nature of the similarities or differences
4. The most appropriate organization of your material

Two Topics to Be Compared or Contrasted

There's no reason you couldn't compare or contrast more than two topics, but in practice it's complicated and confusing. In our daily lives and at work, we usually narrow the choices presented to us to just two before we make a final decision. Furthermore, in a short essay you simply don't have the time or space to deal with more than two topics.

But what kinds of topics can you consider? Sometimes it helps to think of possible topics for comparison or contrast according to the following technique. When you think of comparing two topics, pick two topics that are unlike each other. Think of a continuum that represents all possible topics within a broad logical category. The farther apart your topics are on this continuum, the more dissimilar they are.

Suppose Figure 8.1 represents types of cars. Topic A and topic B represent cars that are unlike each other, for example, a Lamborghini and a Toyota Prius. Their contrasting features are so obvious to the reader that writing an essay contrasting these two topics would be uninteresting. Investigating how these two vehicles are similar might be a more creative approach to the topic, and it could serve as the basis for a challenging and meaningful essay: you would get your reader to think differently about two topics never seen as being alike. As a general rule, the more dissimilar (farther apart on the continuum) your topics are, the better it is to compare them.

The opposite applies to your choice of contrasting topics. Revisit the continuum (Figure 8.2).

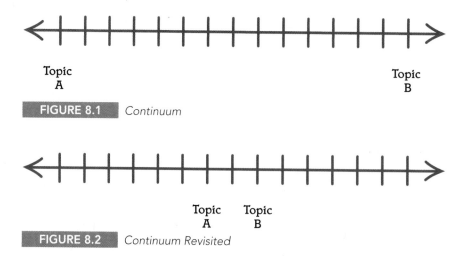

Topic
A

Topic
B

FIGURE 8.1   *Continuum*

Topic   Topic
A   B

FIGURE 8.2   *Continuum Revisited*

In contrasting topics, your challenge lies in showing how two topics that most people accept as being similar are actually quite different. For example, contrasting two economy cars or two luxury cars makes for a more meaningful essay than contrasting a luxury car and an economy car. Thus, as a general rule, the more alike (closer together on the continuum) your topics are, the better it is to contrast them.

PRACTICE 8-4

For each of the following topics, write which would make a more interesting focus, comparison or contrast.

1. Fishing and shopping: _Comparison_____
2. Two over-the-counter sleeping pills: _Contrast_____
3. Growing plants in pots and in gardens: _Contrast_____
4. A college math instructor and a college English instructor: _Comparison or contrast_
5. Manual labor and reading a romance novel: _Comparison_____
6. Ordering textbooks online and buying them in the college bookstore: _Contrast___

> **Collaborative Critical Thinking**
>
> **In small groups of three or four,** choose topics for both comparison and contrast for each of the following topics and place them in a continuum. Each topic should have four topics plotted in the continuum: two for contrast papers and two for comparison.
>
> 1. **Topic:** Types of college students
> 2. **Topic:** Competitive sports
> 3. **Topic:** Television programs
>
> Share your answers with other groups. Answers will vary.

Clear Bases of Comparison or Contrast

When you buy a car, what characteristics do you look for? Some people look for affordability and reliability, others look for comfort and style, and still others look for some combination of these factors. Suppose you are looking for a car. You want something that gets you around town and perhaps, occasionally, handles a longer trip. It should be a small car because of the crowded parking around campus, and above all, it should be inexpensive to purchase and maintain. These characteristics are called *bases* (plural of *basis*), or points, of comparison or contrast. Anytime you think in terms of comparison or contrast, you must have several such points in mind.

Suppose that in your search for a car you settle on two choices: a 2006 Honda Civic and a 2004 Toyota Corolla. In making a choice between these two cars, you must contrast them, so you design a worksheet as in Table 8.1 (you fill in the details as you investigate the differences).

TABLE 8.1	*Contrast Worksheet*	
Bases of Contrast	**2006 Honda Civic**	**2004 Toyota Corolla**
Affordability		
Condition		
Safety		
Roominess		
Appearance		

Your job is to apply the same bases of contrast to both topics. Notice also that your own bases of contrast depend on your particular situation and purpose. Someone else might have a different set of criteria for making the same decision.

If you were deciding which of two history classes to take, what bases of contrast would be important to you? Probably, you would think in terms of some of these points:

- When the classes are offered
- Who teaches them
- How many tests and papers are assigned
- Which textbooks are used
- Whether some of your friends will be in one or the other

PRACTICE   8-5

For each of the topics that follow, develop 3–5 points, or bases, of comparison or contrast that you think are important. Be prepared to share your answers with the rest of your class. Answers will vary.

1. Two action movies: Pace of the action, believability of characters, quality of special effects

2. Two teachers on your campus: Enthusiasm, compassion for students, ability as a lecturer

3. Two restaurants in your community: Authenticity, freshness of food, quality of service

4. Two historical periods (the 1960s and today, for instance): Level of political commitment, sense of opportunity, general "excitement to be alive"

5. Two places to work: Working conditions, salary, fairness of the supervisors

Evidence to Describe Similarities or Differences

Once you have settled on two topics to compare or contrast and generated several bases on which to conduct your analysis, the next step is to apply those bases to each topic in turn, seeking evidence to support your analysis.

Return to the example of buying a car. You've found two cars you are interested in learning more about, the Honda Civic and the Toyota Corolla. The first two rows of your worksheet are devoted to the criteria of affordability and condition, so you start there, asking questions to find out about those aspects of your choice. You discover that the Honda Civic, although initially more expensive (it is, after all, newer than the Corolla by 2 years), has been in an accident at some point during its previous ownership and has a leak. This suggests that you might soon have to pay for a repair. You learn that both cars offer about the same gas mileage, and the general maintenance fees would be about the same. But you discover that the insurance payment for the Corolla is higher by about $300 per year.

After gathering all the evidence you can, you are disappointed to learn that in the category of affordability, anyway, the choice is not straightforward. Both cars present positive and negative evidence in that category. Therefore, your decision probably depends on looking at all of the evidence you collect for all points of contrast between the two cars.

In further analyzing the two vehicles, you develop the set of evidence seen in Table 8.2.

The more thorough and specific your evidence, the better decision you ultimately are able to make. Notice, however, that the evidence in this case doesn't point to a clear choice between the two vehicles. This situation often occurs when the options before us are complex. Your job is to objectively gather and document the evidence so that you, or your reader, can carefully consider it when making judgments later.

TABLE 8.2	*Contrast Worksheet Completed*	
Bases of Contrast	**2002 Honda Civic**	**2000 Toyota Corolla**
Affordability	$9,300. Gas 24 mpg. Insurance $800 per year.	$8,100. Gas 26 mpg. Insurance $1,100 per year.
Condition	Generally good. Leaks red oil; may need to have it fixed; estimate unknown. Needs tune-up.	Right rear fender dented. Interior shabby from transporting dogs.
Safety	When new, high safety rating according to the Internet and *Consumer Reports.*	Same as Honda.
Roominess	About the same, but has less trunk space. May not hold my guitar and amp.	Trunk is slightly bigger.
Appearance	Gray. Color is good. Metallic finish has dulled from sitting in the sun.	Blue. Paint in good condition. Exterior well cared for.

Organization of a Comparison or Contrast Analysis

Comparison or contrast essays can be organized in one of two ways. The first is called the *block method,* also known as the *topic-at-a-time method,* and the second is called the *point-by-point method.* These terms pertain to the way the body of your essay is organized, not the introduction or conclusion.

The Block Method

In a block comparison or contrast, you give all information about topic 1 in the first half of the essay's body and then all information for topic 2 in the second half. The advantage of this type of organization is that the reader learns about each topic separately and compactly. This method may also give you the opportunity to discuss each topic in greater detail. The block method uses the structure seen in Figure 8.3.

A disadvantage of the block method is that the reader must work hard to understand each block to avoid having to look for information in the first block while reading the second. This disadvantage can be solved through the effective use of transitions.

The Point-by-Point Method

Another effective way to organize a comparison or contrast analysis is to base each body paragraph on one of your three or four bases of comparison or contrast. The advantage of this method is that that the reader is able to see instantly the comparison or contrast

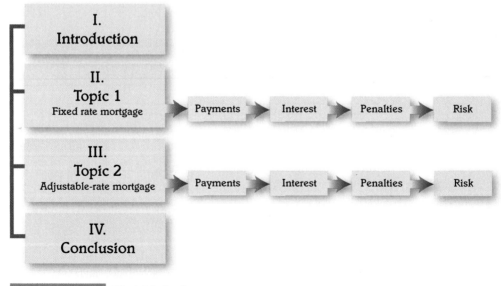

FIGURE 8.3   *Block Method*

without having to go back to earlier sections of the paper. The structure of the point-by-point method would look as shown in Figure 8.4.

With the point-by-point structure, the reader can easily understand how each point differs from the other as the topics are put back to back underneath each main point. One disadvantage of the point-by-point method is falling into a "ping pong" type of writing, in which you jump back and forth between topics, sometimes even in the same sentence, with little or no warning. Again, this disadvantage can be avoided through the careful and consistent use of transitions throughout the body paragraphs.

How do you know which type of organization to choose? This depends on your topics, the amount of information that you have for each one, and the purpose of the essay. For example, if you are contrasting two vacation resorts and plan to describe each one in detail, you might choose the block method so that you can focus on building a unified picture of each resort. On the other hand, if you are comparing writing and home building, dissimilar activities, you might use point-by-point to illustrate the close parallels between the two.

When you have a comparison or contrast assignment, keep the following points in mind:

- The topic of your essay consists of the two topics you choose to compare or contrast.

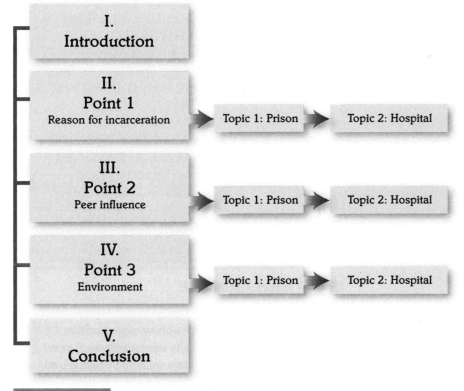

FIGURE 8.4   *Point-by-Point Method*

- The body of your essay is organized according to your bases of comparison or contrast (using either the block or the point-by-point method).
- The supporting sentences of your essay present the evidence you have collected to support each basis of comparison or contrast.

WRITING YOUR COMPARISON OR CONTRAST ESSAY

To illustrate the writing process, we use a contrast essay written by Regina, a 31-year-old mother of two boys who is taking online courses as she prepares to enter the dental hygiene program.

Education 24/7

This time last semester, Brittany was struggling to keep awake in her 8 a.m. sociology class. Her professor, obviously not a morning person himself, let time pass as best he could, asking open-ended questions to which long pauses were the only possible answers. Sunlight streamed in the window. Students dozed at their desks. Occasionally a purse or cell phone would smash to the floor and startle one or two of them awake. The class ended with a collective yawn, moaning, and a dreary shuffling toward the door. Needless to say, sociology wasn't the highlight of Brittany's academic life. This semester, things are different: By 8 a.m., Brittany is asleep in her bed as her body tells her she should be. But 2 a.m. is a different story because that is when Brittany is wide awake and ready to study. In the early hours on a typical morning, she settles into her desk chair, boots up her computer, logs on to her Introduction to Literature class, and begins to read what her classmates have written about William Faulkner's short story "A Rose for Emily." As the sun begins to rise, she is still immersed in the literary discussion, enthusiastically responding to her classmates' ideas. Then she heads to bed, sleeping through the morning and awakening in the afternoon to start her new day.

Brittany has discovered a new way of taking classes, one that better suits her learning style and sleeping habits. Students like Brittany no longer have to be tied to a specific time and place to complete their college classes; they have a multitude of online offerings to choose from. However, they need to be aware of the differences between taking a traditional on-campus course and an online course so that they can decide which is more appropriate for them. Some aspects to consider are the learning environment, the demands, and the expectations.

Of course, the environment differs significantly between traditional and online courses. In the traditional course, one is sitting with other students in a classroom with an instructor in front presenting material, posing questions, offering individual help, and asking for responses. The energy, personalities, temperature, acoustics, furniture, and even time of day make each class period unique. However, the online environment can be a lonely one as the student stares at a screen of information, ponders what the instructor might mean by a question or assignment, and quietly taps on the keyboard to complete the course work. It is just one person, a screen full of information, discussion responses, quizzes and e-mail, the tap of the keyboard, and whatever distractions might be close by.

Not only must students consider the "classroom" environment, but they also should assess the demands of each type of instruction. Having studied in a traditional classroom for 12 years, most students are familiar with its setup and activities: lectures, tests, discussions, and group work. Although online classes include most of these same activities, they are delivered in a more flexible and visual manner. A student can decide when he or she "hops" online and whether to complete a discussion first, review class notes, or watch a PowerPoint; he or she can access the course 1 day a week for 5 hours or every day per week for an hour or less. If the student stops logging on to the course, it may take the instructor longer to notice than when a classroom seat is empty for a week.

Finally, the expectations for each type of course may vary. The student in a traditional class expects the instructor to be there at the scheduled times or provide a substitute or announce a canceled class. Students also expect to get immediate feedback for their questions and timely return of their work. On the other hand, in an online class, because students can access it 24/7, they may expect the instructor to do the same and become upset if they don't receive feedback even though it might be a weekend and the instructor is taking some time off. Similarly, the instructor may expect that students will e-mail if they have questions while the students worry that they will ask a "stupid" question. Sometimes it is more difficult to resolve these problems since the student and instructor don't see each other.

Educationally, we are in an accommodating time. Yet, with these choices comes awareness of the challenges of deciding what type of instruction works for the individual student. For a student who is motivated, disciplined, and willing to endure some feelings of isolation, an online course may be appropriate; in contrast, if the student thrives on the dynamics of a classroom with the give and take of discussion and immediate feedback from the professor, then the traditional classroom is a better choice. So if it's 2 a.m., where are you, in class or sound asleep?

Prewriting

In this chapter, you have the opportunity to experiment with yet another prewriting technique, the Venn diagram. The Venn diagram is a useful visual when analyzing similarities and differences between two topics.

Discovering and Limiting Your Topic

Prewriting Strategy #7: Venn Diagram

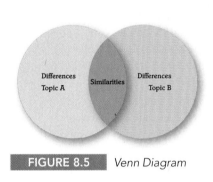

FIGURE 8.5 *Venn Diagram*

Regina first used listing to start her prewriting session. She starts by listing a variety of topics related to college, work, and her personal life and settles on the following: a traditional course and an online course. She then draws a Venn diagram to explore similarities and differences. Start this technique by drawing two overlapping circles. In the outer areas, list the differences between your topics, each topic in its own circle. In the area that overlaps, list the similarities that your topics share.

The Venn diagram permits Regina to conduct a focused listing on the distinctiveness of two topics, as well as their commonalities. It also allows her to step back and visualize the entire topic so that she can determine her approach—comparison, contrast, or both. Here is the result of Regina's 30 minutes of diagramming.

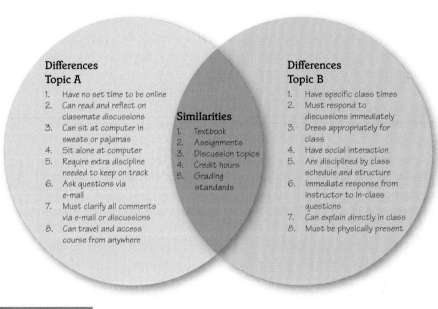

Differences
Topic A

1. Have no set time to be online
2. Can read and reflect on classmate discussions
3. Can sit at computer in sweats or pajamas
4. Sit alone at computer
5. Require extra discipline needed to keep on track
6. Ask questions via e-mail
7. Must clarify all comments via e-mail or discussions
8. Can travel and access course from anywhere

Similarities

1. Textbook
2. Assignments
3. Discussion topics
4. Credit hours
5. Grading standards

Differences
Topic B

1. Have specific class times
2. Must respond to discussions immediately
3. Dress appropriately for class
4. Have social interaction
5. Are disciplined by class schedule and structure
6. Immediate response from instructor to in-class questions
7. Can explain directly in class
8. Must be physically present

FIGURE 8.6 *Regina's Venn Diagram*

Regina has generated lots of ideas. As she reviews these points, she finds that contrasting her topics would be the best approach for two reasons: first, she has generated more material under "differences," and second, the items under "similarities" are obvious and hardly worth writing about. Her next task is to carefully review the information and determine the bases of contrast for her essay.

WRITING 8-1

Start your prewriting sessions to identify your topic, help limit your topic, or both. Use the prewriting techniques you feel are most useful. Try using a Venn diagram as a final technique. Here is a diagram form.

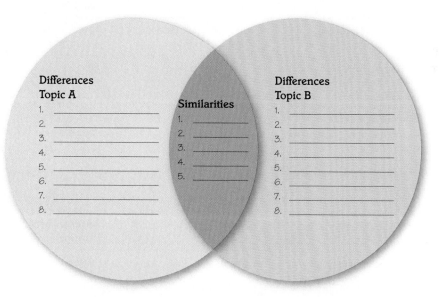

Differences
Topic A
1. _____
2. _____
3. _____
4. _____
5. _____
6. _____
7. _____
8. _____

Similarities
1. _____
2. _____
3. _____
4. _____
5. _____

Differences
Topic B
1. _____
2. _____
3. _____
4. _____
5. _____
6. _____
7. _____
8. _____

Think about the bases of comparison or contrast. What standards should you use to compare or contrast your two topics?

Once you have generated a sufficient number of ideas, don't forget that if you plan to compare, one approach is to use two seemingly unrelated topics, for example bungee jumping and adolescence. However, if you plan to contrast, then choose two closely related topics, such as two hybrid cars. Otherwise, your essay will be too obvious to be worth reading.

WRITING YOUR COMPARISON
OR CONTRAST ESSAY

TOPICS TO CONSIDER

If you're still having problems finding a topic, here are some topics that might interest you. Try using a Venn diagram on one or more of the following topics to generate ideas.

Writing for College		
■ Two theories (economic, political, literary, scientific, philosophical)	■ Two methods of solving a problem ■ Two personality types	■ Two styles of leadership ■ Two scholarships

Writing in Your Profession			
BUSINESS	■ Wholesale and retail ■ Online sales and in-store sales	■ Direct mail advertising and TV ads	■ Flextime and traditional schedules
CRIMINAL JUSTICE	■ Parole and probation ■ Felony and misdemeanor	■ Life in prison and the death penalty	■ Maximum and minimum security prisons
EDUCATION	■ Two early childhood programs ■ Elementary and secondary teaching	■ Two attitudes toward higher education	■ Studying abroad and in the United States
HEALTH	■ Two health fields ■ Two treatments for the same condition	■ Primary care physician and specialist	■ Out-patient and in-patient procedures
SOCIAL WORK/ PSYCHOLOGY	■ Individual and group therapy ■ Two mental illnesses	■ Two treatment plans for depression	■ Two welfare programs
TECHNICAL	■ Two machines used for a similar purpose	■ Two methods of completing a specific task	■ Two software programs for drafting courses ■ Two types of welding
OTHERS	■ Carpeting and wood flooring ■ Urban artist and gallery artist	■ Two airlines	■ Algebra and practical math

Writing in Everyday Life		
■ Two movies or books ■ Two cleaning products	■ Two online dating websites ■ Two child care centers	■ Two automobile magazines ■ Two grocery stores

Identifying Your Audience

As you determine your topic, you should also consider your reader's interest in your topic. If you want to compare your two preschool children, or your previous boyfriend to your current one, you must ask yourself, "Who cares?" You might enjoy exploring these topics yourself, but if your essay is just about your personal life with no larger message or application, then your reader won't have a purpose for reading it. However, if while comparing two boyfriends you can illustrate the dangers of an abusive or unhealthy relationship, or if by comparing your preschool children you can make an important point about child rearing, then you have an essay that appeals to a larger audience with the purpose of warning against certain behaviors in a relationship.

You cannot determine your points of similarity or difference without first deciding to whom you are writing and what topics your chosen audience values most. If you are contrasting two cruises, it matters whether your audience is a retired couple, a family with young children, or a twentysomething single male college student.

Establishing Your Purpose

You can use comparison or contrast to accomplish two major purposes. First, and most commonly, you can give a balanced, objective analysis of two topics so that your reader can form conclusions about the similarities or differences. Second, you can try to persuade your reader to accept or reject one or both topics. Your selection of topic and your audience helps you determine your purpose. For instance, if you are comparing or contrasting two battles during the Civil War, your purpose probably aligns with the first option: a balanced, objective description of each battle. However, if you are contrasting two restaurants, chances are that you want to end your essay by recommending one of the restaurants to your reader.

Setting Your Tone

You mostly want to adhere to an objective, neutral tone whether you are trying to educate or persuade your reader. When you are trying to persuade, there is a danger that your tone can degenerate into sarcasm or become hateful. Even in persuasive contexts, objectivity is preferred. Like all writing techniques, however, comparison or contrast presents unique opportunities for humor—for instance, comparing your mate to an old pair of jeans or your car to a camel. Be open to the humorous potential that exists whenever you bring two topics together and examine them closely.

W R I T I N G   8-2

Use the following form to identify and analyze your audience, purpose, and tone.

Audience, Purpose, and Tone Analysis

Your topic: _____

I. Audience
1. Who is your audience? _____
   Age(s): _____ Gender(s): _____ Education level(s): _____
2. Why would this audience be interested in your topic? _____
   _____
3. What does your audience already know about your topic? _____
   _____
4. What background information does your audience need to understand the topic?
   _____
   _____

II. Your Purpose

1. Why did you choose this topic? _____

   _____

2. What is the controlling, or main, idea of your essay? _____

   _____

3. What effect do you want your essay to have on your audience? _____

   _____

4. What information must you provide to achieve the desired effect? _____

   _____

III. Tone

1. What is your personal attitude about this topic? _____

   _____

2. What tone do you wish to establish for this essay? _____

   _____

3. How does your tone help you relate to your audience and support your purpose?

   _____

   _____

Formulating Your Thesis

The thesis of the comparison or contrast essay, similar to other theses you've written, provides a focus and a sense of direction for your reader. Your thesis should have the following elements:

1. **The two topics to be compared or contrasted.** In comparison or contrast theses, you need to specify both topics so that your reader clearly understands the dual nature of the topic.
2. **A clear sense of audience.** Although you have the option to identify your audience anywhere in your introduction, indicating who benefits from your comparison in the thesis helps focus your discussion.
3. **A purpose.** Do you want your reader to choose one product, place, or person over another? Then, your purpose would be to persuade. Perhaps you want your reader to learn something new or make up his or her own mind; then your purpose would be to explain or inform.
4. **The focus of your essay.** Let the reader know if you are going to focus on similarities, differences, or both.
5. **The points of comparison or contrast.** If you provide an essay map in which you list the bases of comparison or contrast, your reader knows beforehand the scope of your discussion.

You don't have to address each of the elements in this order. You may even place an element or two in other sentences in your introduction or even imply one element. You determine what would be most effective in your essay. Whichever order you choose, you should make your thesis clear so that the reader knows exactly where you're going. Figure 8.8 shows an example of these five elements combined as one sentence.

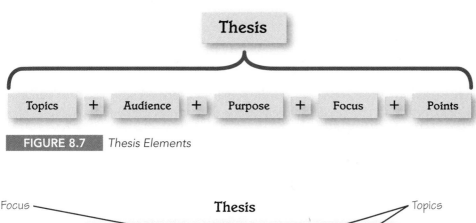

FIGURE 8.7 *Thesis Elements*

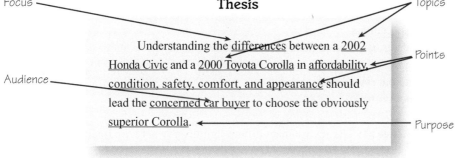

FIGURE 8.8 *Elements within a Thesis*

Once you have selected your two topics, determined your focus, established provisional bases of comparison or contrast, and are fairly sure about your audience and purpose, you have all ingredients necessary to write a working thesis.

Here is Regina's working thesis.

> As students make choices about how they want their education delivered, they need to consider the differences between traditional and online classes: environment, demand, and expectations.

WRITING 8-3

Write your working thesis here.

Working thesis: _____

_____

If you want, write various versions of your thesis and get a classmate's reaction and suggestions.

Outlining Your Ideas

Your outline can take one of two different forms, one for the block method and one for the point-by-point method. It is best to outline your material both ways and then select the best approach depending on your topic, the amount of evidence you have for each point, and your audience's characteristics. Regina chooses the point-by-point method because she wants to highlight for her reader the specific differences that she considers vitally important.

Examine Regina's outline:

ESSAY OUTLINE

Thesis: As students make choices about how they want their education delivered, they need to consider the differences between traditional and online classes: environment, demand, and expectations.

Audience: Students considering taking online classes

Purpose: To show which students would benefit from online courses

Topic A: Traditional course

Topic B: Online course

I. **Topic sentence #1:** The environment differs significantly between traditional and online courses.
   A. Classroom
      1. Sit with other students
      2. All aspects of classroom energizing
   B. Online
      1. Can be lonely
      2. Quiet with few distractions

II. **Topic sentence #2:** The demands of the two types of instructions are not the same.
   A. Classroom
      1. Most students familiar with setting
      2. Students familiar with types of activities
   B. Online
      1. Activities flexible and visual
      2. Students decide order of material
      3. Students decide time

III. **Topic sentence #3:** The expectations vary.
   A. Classroom
      1. Expect instructors to be present
      2. Expect immediate feedback
   B. Online
      1. Instructors may not log on for days
      2. Students may not post questions

WRITING   8-4

Armed with a working thesis and your bases, or points, of comparison or contrast, you are ready to create your outline. Try inserting your topic sentences and supporting evidence in the point-by-point outline form presented here.

Essay Outline: Point-by-Point Method

Thesis: _____

Audience: _____

Purpose: _____

Topic A: _____

Topic B: _____

I. Topic sentence #1: _____
    A. Topic A: _____
       1. _____
       2. _____
       3. _____
    B. Topic B: _____
       1. _____
       2. _____
       3. _____

II. Topic sentence #2: _____
    A. Topic A: _____
       1. _____
       2. _____
       3. _____
    B. Topic B: _____
       1. _____
       2. _____
       3. _____

III. Topic sentence #3: _____
    A. Topic A: _____
       1. _____
       2. _____
       3. _____
    B. Topic B: _____
       1. _____
       2. _____
       3. _____

Create another outline by inserting your topic sentences and supporting evidence in the block outline form presented here. Then compare your outline with the one you completed in Writing 8-4 and select the most appropriate form for your particular essay.

Essay Outline: Block Method

Thesis: _____

Audience: _____

Purpose: _____

  I. Topic A topic sentence: _____

     A. Point #1: _____

     B. Point #2: _____

     C. Point #3: _____

  II. Topic B topic sentence: _____

     A. Point #1: _____

     B. Point #2: _____

     C. Point #3: _____

Drafting

As you begin drafting your essay, keep in mind that one of your goals in writing comparison or contrast is to deal with both topics fairly and objectively. Whether you are using block or point-by-point organization, you should present about the same amount of evidence under each basis of comparison or contrast. This enables your reader to explore fully the similarities and differences between two topics in a balanced and thoughtful way. If you find that you are writing a lot about one topic as you draft your paper, focus your efforts on writing a similar amount of material for the other topic.

Writing Your Introduction

In previous chapters, you have studied several effective ways to introduce your topic, including description, narration, definition, and humor. Two introductory techniques that you may not have tried yet are as follows:

  1. **Quotation.** If you decide to start with a quotation, be sure that you connect it clearly and smoothly to the following statements. No matter how pithy and articulate a quotation is, if it just dangles alone in the beginning of the essay, the reader becomes confused.

  2. **Vivid contrast.** A striking contrast is particularly appropriate and effective for the comparison or contrast essay.

In comparison or contrast, be sure that both topics are introduced before the thesis. This allows the reader to move smoothly into the thesis rather than suddenly being presented with the two topics and wondering how the writer arrived there.

For the introduction of her essay, Regina decides to use a vivid contrast between taking a traditional course and taking an online course the following semester. She feels that drawing a sharp contrast between these two methods of instruction captures her reader's interest. Examine her introduction:

> Last semester, Brittany couldn't keep herself awake in her sociology class. Her professor asked open-ended questions that no one felt motivated to answer. The class ended with a collective yawn, moaning, and a dreary shuffling toward the door. This semester, however, things are different: By 8 a.m. Brittany is asleep in her bed as her body tells her she should be. But 2 a.m. is a different story because that is when Brittany is wide awake and ready to study. She settles into her desk chair, boots up her computer, logs on to her Introduction to Literature class, and begins to read.
>
> Brittany is taking online classes. Students like Brittany no longer have to be tied to a specific time and place to complete their college classes since they now have many online offerings to choose from. But before students make choices about how they want their education delivered, they need to consider the main differences between traditional and online classes: environment, demand, and expectations.

Notice Regina's use of description. Chances are that her reader chuckles in recognition at the description of dozing in class. Anytime you can arouse an emotional or intellectual response in your introduction, you can capture the interest of your reader.

WRITING   8-6

Using the thesis you developed earlier, write two different introductions. Use a combination of two or more of the following strategies: description, personal narrative, anecdote, background information, your experience with the topic, definition of a key term, humor, a startling fact or statistic, a quotation, or a vivid contrast.

Thesis: _____

_____

Audience: _____

Strategies for introduction #1: _____

Strategies for introduction #2: _____

At this point, you don't need to make a final decision about which introduction to use. When you revisit the introductions you've written in Writing 8-6, you might decide to combine the best elements of each to build a strong introduction that's appropriate for your essay.

Writing Your Body Paragraphs

Since you're working with two topics, you need to sharpen your skills in using transitions. In both the point-by-point method and the block method, you use a variety of transitional devices that not only act as bridges to connect your ideas logically but also help unify your paper. Examine how transitions function in both methods of organization.

Coherence: Using Transitions in the Block Method

In the block method, since you first discuss all of topic A, going through one or more paragraphs per point, the essay starts much like most essays you've written. You start each paragraph with a clear topic sentence until you've fully discussed topic A. Up to this point, there is no problem. But a problem with disjointedness usually occurs when you move from topic A to topic B. If you don't transition effectively, it seems as if you're starting a new essay, both joined with no clear cohesiveness.

To maintain your essay's coherence, you can do the following:

1. After you have finished discussing topic A, add a transitional paragraph. A transitional paragraph is a short paragraph, usually consisting of a few sentences, that acts as a conclusion to topic A and an introduction to the next section, topic B. Another advantage of the transitional paragraph is that it reminds your reader of the key points you've made so that your reader can keep these points in mind while approaching topic B.

2. As you present your paragraphs for topic B, use transitions that echo the equivalent points in topic A. For example, you might start with the following transition and topic sentence:

> Unlike the Honda's affordability, the Toyota Corolla can cost more than the customer bargained for.

Coherence: Using Transitions in the Point-by-Point Method

The biggest pitfall in the point-by-point method is to overuse transitions or zigzag from one topic to the next and back again, giving your paragraph a disjointed, ping-pong effect. Since you're working with two topics and the information is parallel (addressing the same ideas for each topic), it's easy to jump back and forth between ideas. To guard against this fault, your transitions must be placed between topics in the same paragraph so that your reader is able to follow your shifts between topics easily. Examine the following paragraph from Regina's essay. Pay close attention to how the transitions guide the reader from one topic to the next.

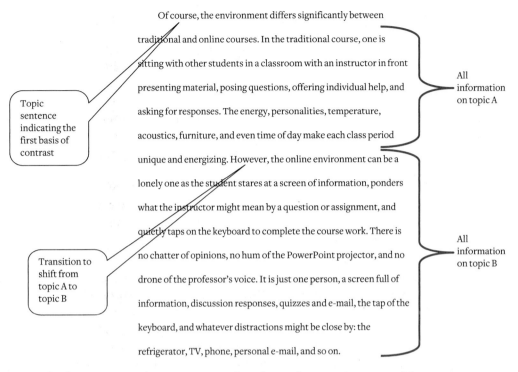

Of course, the environment differs significantly between traditional and online courses. In the traditional course, one is sitting with other students in a classroom with an instructor in front presenting material, posing questions, offering individual help, and asking for responses. The energy, personalities, temperature, acoustics, furniture, and even time of day make each class period unique and energizing. However, the online environment can be a lonely one as the student stares at a screen of information, ponders what the instructor might mean by a question or assignment, and quietly taps on the keyboard to complete the course work. There is no chatter of opinions, no hum of the PowerPoint projector, and no drone of the professor's voice. It is just one person, a screen full of information, discussion responses, quizzes and e-mail, the tap of the keyboard, and whatever distractions might be close by: the refrigerator, TV, phone, personal e-mail, and so on.

Topic sentence indicating the first basis of contrast

Transition to shift from topic A to topic B

All information on topic A

All information on topic B

Whether you organize your comparison by topics or points, transitions are necessary to keep your essay flowing smoothly, to make it clear to the reader when you switch from one topic to the other, and to indicate the logical relationships between ideas within the paragraph The following list of transitions may be helpful in making your essay coherent.

Transitions to Show Comparison		
akin	by the same token	equivalent
also	coincide	exactly
analogous to	comparable	harmonize
another similarity	comparatively	have in common
as	compare (to/with)	homogeneous
as compared with	conform	identical(ly)
as well as	consistent with	in common with
at the same time	correlate	in comparison
balance	equal(ly)	in relation to
both	equally important	in like fashion
by comparison	equate	in like manner

Continued

Transitions to Show Comparison—cont'd

in similar fashion	next likeness	similar aspect
in the same manner	of little difference	similar(ly)
in the same way	of no difference	similar to
just as, like	paralleling	strong resemblance
just the same	parallel (to)	synonymous with
like	relative to	too
likeness	resemblance	to the next extent
likewise	resemble	uniform(ly)
much the same way	resembling	
match(ing)	same as	

Transitions to Show Contrast

a clear difference	even so	regardless
although	even though	striking difference
although this may be true	except for	strong distinction
although true	however	the (next, third, and so on) distinction
another distinction	in another way	the reverse
another striking contrast	in contrast	though
as opposed	in contrast to this	to contradict
at the same time	in sharp contrast	to counter
but	in spite of	to differ (from)
but at the same time	instead (of)	to differentiate
contrarily to	nevertheless	to oppose
contrary to	nonetheless	to the contrary
conversely	notwithstanding	unequal(ly)
counter to	on one hand	unless
despite	on the other hand	unlike
despite this fact	opposing	whereas
different from	opposite	while
dissimilar to	otherwise	while this may be true
distinct difference	otherwise	yet
distinctive	rather	

As you write the body paragraphs of your essay, remember that they are the most important in terms of convincing your reader that you are well informed and purposeful in what you are communicating. Keep in mind the following points for the body paragraphs:

1. Consciously choose one of the methods presented in this chapter—block or point-by-point—to organize your essay. Otherwise, you may end up "flip-flopping" between your two topics.

2. Maintain a single focus for each body paragraph, whether it is organized by the point-by-point or the block method.

3. Follow the order of points as presented in the essay map if you decide to include an essay map. Feel free to change the order of your points if the essay reads more smoothly with a different organization.

4. Keep a logical balance of information for each of the two topics.

5. Check your information and level of formality for appropriateness to your specific audience. If you are comparing two math classes and your audience is future math students, then your style should be more informal than if the audience is the department chair of math or even the college's vice president for instruction.

6. Always keep your purpose in mind. If it is to recommend one product over another, then stick to the points that support your judgment. However, remember that you gain more credibility with your reader if you mention a negative aspect or two about the preferred product since most things have some drawback. Otherwise, if you only praise one product and pan the other, you may sound like an advertiser.

WRITING 8-7

On a separate sheet of paper, start drafting your essay.

1. Make sure you are following either the block or the point-by-point method, not an unclear mixture of the two.

2. Provide examples, description, and relevant information that show the reader how each topic is different or similar.

3. Add transitions to keep your ideas flowing smoothly and to guide your audience through your shifts of topic.

Writing Your Conclusion

By the time you are ready to write the conclusion, you may feel as if you have already said all that you need to say. Still, the reader needs to have the information summed up and the points or purpose reiterated. Remind your audience of the action you recommend, the authority that you have to write about the topic, the perspective that you've gained, the wisdom that you have culled from the comparison or contrast, or a combination of these points. Avoid merely stating that the two topics differ or are alike, which causes the reader to question the usefulness of the essay. Why read an essay if its conclusion is obvious?

Look at Regina's draft conclusion.

> For some students, online courses may work well, but for others, especially those lacking self-discipline and motivation, online courses can be a waste of time and money. Each student must analyze his or her own learning style and consider the three main differences between traditional on-campus courses and online courses: environment, demand, and expectations.

Does Regina's conclusion reflect the importance of her topic? It definitely needs further development if it's to have purpose. Again, these changes occur during the revising stage.

WRITING   8-8

Write a tentative conclusion for your essay. Review Regina's final conclusion earlier in the chapter. Does this approach work for your essay? Whatever you decide, make sure that your conclusion is meaningful and that it effectively wraps up the essay. Then, continue drafting sections of your essay until you feel satisfied with your product. One draft is never enough. Don't forget to keep your audience in mind as you continue to polish your essay.

Revising

Remember to read your draft aloud to yourself or someone else. To avoid reading through errors and missing words, physically run your fingers across the lines to actually touch each word and phrase. When you stumble and have to reread, circle or underline the sentence or phrase so that you can return to it to revise it.

When you start your revision, focus on content. Fill your paragraphs with concrete details and examples that provide the evidence you need. Then turn your attention to other matters.

Style Tip: Avoid Offensive Language

Sometimes, the words and phrases you choose can alienate your reader, even when you believe your language to be harmless. If your audience includes the elderly, for instance, you would probably know not to use the word *geezers* for obvious reasons, but many elderly people these days—living long, healthy, and vibrant lives—would react just as negatively to *old folks*. Be especially careful with unintentionally offensive language in the areas of race, gender, religion, sexual orientation, or age, but also be careful not to violate generally accepted norms of formal speech and writing by using profanity or slang inappropriately. Learn to be sensitive to how other people react to your word choice.

> **Bridging Knowledge**
>
> **See Chapter 23** for additional information and practice in avoiding offensive language.

PROBLEM .... **SOLUTION** ....

WRITING

My introduction is choppy and uninteresting.

→

1. If you employ several lead-in techniques, are they closely related so that you don't seem to be skipping around?

2. Is there a smooth transitional sentence or two between your lead-in and your thesis? Make sure to take your reader from the lead-in to the thesis by "bringing the topic home" to your focus and concern.

3. You probably developed your thesis early in the writing process, so make sure you don't just "drop" it into your introduction. Blend it with the writing style in the rest of the introduction.

WRITING

I need to develop one or more of my body paragraphs because they are too short and abrupt.

→

1. Return to the step of the prewriting stage that you found to be most productive and useful. Focus just on the ideas you are having trouble with.

2. If one of your points doesn't generate enough specifics, do some brainstorming to generate a different point or aspect of the two topics.

3. Sometimes the clue to further development in a comparison or contrast essay can be found in what you've already said about the other topic. If you get lost in developing a contrast, for instance, just return to what you've already written and use that as a starting point for developing the contrast further.

COMPARISON OR CONTRAST

Switching from topic A to topic B seems mechanical, almost like a ping-pong ball going back and forth. How can I make it flow better?

→

1. Did you deliberately choose either the point-by-point or the block method for developing your body paragraphs? If not, you might not be using any particular organizational technique, causing you to switch mechanically from one topic to another.

2. Read through your body paragraphs, looking for places where you might have gone from one topic to another in the same sentence or between two sentences.

3. If you're using the block method, consider using a transitional paragraph to bring closure to topic A and to introduce topic B.

4. Make sure you are providing sufficient evidence to prove the points you are making.

COHERENCE

My essay jumps from topic to topic too abruptly.

→

Review the list of transitions in this chapter and try to vary them as you move between topics.

WRITING YOUR COMPARISON
OR CONTRAST ESSAY

WRITING   8-9

Start your revision. As you revise, address the following questions:

- Does the essay have a clear and meaningful purpose?
- Does it speak to a specific audience?
- Does it interest the reader from the beginning and move smoothly into the thesis?
- Does it follow the essay map in the body paragraphs?
- Are the transitions varied and clear, especially when you switch from one topic to the other?
- Does the conclusion finish with a strong statement of purpose and audience?

Collaborative Critical Thinking

Asking Your Peers

Once you have completed the writing process and have a polished final draft, exchange papers with a classmate for peer review, using these questions to guide your review.

1. Who is the writer? Who is the peer reviewer?

2. What method or methods of introduction did the author use (humor, anecdote, startling fact, rhetorical question, personal narration)? Is this method effective? (Is it interesting? Does it grab your attention?) What can you suggest to improve the introduction?

3. Is the thesis statement clear, and does the introduction lead smoothly to this thesis statement? What suggestions can you offer?

4. Pick two body paragraphs and circle the topic sentence of each. List the basis of comparison stated in each topic sentence (use a word or phrase). If you can't find a basis, write *None*. This may be an indication that the writer has omitted the topic sentence.

5. Read the supporting details of each paragraph. Does the author give you plenty of details, facts, and examples to help make each paragraph clear and concrete? Does the writer dedicate equal time to both topics? Does the writer address similar points for each topic? What suggestions can you offer?

6. Examine each paragraph again. Find the transitional word or expression that the writer uses to shift from topic A to topic B. If you can't find one, write *None*. Are there any problems with transitions that the writer needs to address? Explain.

7. Examine the essay's conclusion. Does it bring the essay to a closure? Is it meaningful? What can you suggest to help improve the conclusion?

Proofreading

Proofread your draft carefully for problems that recurred from past essays. In addition to these problems, focus on two other common errors that deserve your special attention: errors in pronoun reference and errors in pronoun case.

Common Error #8: Pronoun Reference

In the last chapter, you studied errors in pronoun agreement, which happen when a pronoun doesn't match the noun that it is replacing. Another kind of pronoun error is the lack of a clear reference to specific noun. This error occurs when the writer uses a pronoun without providing a clear, single noun to which the pronoun can refer.

> **INCORRECT:** At our local swimming pool, they don't allow running.
> [The pronoun they has no noun to refer to.]

> **CORRECT:** At our local swimming pool, the lifeguards don't allow running.
> [The pronoun is replaced by a noun to clarify the meaning of the sentence.]

> **INCORRECT:** The cruise was a perfect travel experience, from the delicious food, to the onboard activities, to the exotic sea ports that we visited. This made me want to sign up for another cruise the following year.
> [Note the beginning of the second sentence. What does *this* refer to—the cruise, the food, the seaports, or a combination of these?]

> **CORRECT:** The cruise was a perfect travel experience, from the delicious food, to the onboard activities, to the exotic sea ports that we visited. The experience made me want to sign up for another cruise the following year.

GRAMMAR CHECKUP   8-1

Underline the pronoun in each sentence that does not have a clear reference. Then revise the sentence to clarify the reference by rewriting part of the sentence.

1. Online courses require students and instructors to exercise a great deal of discipline and motivation to ensure that <u>they</u> keep up with their responsibilities.

Revision: to ensure that they both keep up

2. Students in on-campus classes have an easier time keeping to an assignment schedule since they get used to a specific class time and place. <u>This</u> is not so easy for online students, who can choose to log on to a course at their convenience.

Revision: Keeping to a schedule is not so easy

3. The student senate president recently announced that <u>their</u> funds cannot be used for parking tickets.

Revision: <u>announced that senate funds cannot be used</u>

4. You can write either a 2-page review of the film or two 1-page research papers on the film's origins. <u>It</u> is due by the end of the month.

Revision: <u>Your assignment is due</u>

Check your answers to this Grammar Checkup in Appendix A on page A-3. How did you do? If you missed even one of these items, you may need to review pronoun reference in Chapter 18.

Common Error #9: Pronoun Case

Errors in pronoun case happen when you use words like *I* or *me, we* or *us, they* or *them,* and *you* or *your* incorrectly.

INCORRECT:	The mother of the bride invited Susan and I to her daughter's bridal shower.
	[The pronoun *I* is in the incorrect case.]
CORRECT:	The mother of the bride invited Susan and me to her daughter's bridal shower.
INCORRECT:	Jean and me have often talked about traveling to Norway together.
	[The pronoun *me* is in the incorrect case.]
CORRECT:	Jean and I have often talked about traveling to Norway together.

To determine whether you need help with pronoun case, do the following activity. One tricky area is the use of pronouns after *than.*

I enjoy my job more than _____ (he or him).

The way to figure out which pronoun to use is to focus on your meaning. If you write, *I enjoy my job more than he* (**does**), you are saying that you like your job more than he likes his. If, however, you write the following: *I enjoy my job more than him,* you are saying that your job is much more fun than hanging out with him. Note in the first example *he* is the subject, whereas in the second example, *him* is the object of the verb *enjoy.*

GRAMMAR CHECKUP   8-2

Circle in the correct pronoun form for the following sentences. If there are two possible answers, be prepared to explain the difference in meaning of each.

1. I have a more challenging job than (<u>he</u>/him) does.

2. Meagan told Mom and (I/<u>me</u>) to pick her up at eight.

3. We were more respectful of our teachers than (<u>they</u>/them) were of us.

4. My instructor and (I/me) get along well.

5. Reading critically is a more difficult skill for me than for (she/<u>her</u>).

Check your answers to this Grammar Checkup in Appendix A on page A-4. How did you do? If you missed even one of these items, you may need to review pronoun case in Chapter 18.

WRITING 8-10

Start proofreading your own essay. Check for and correct any grammatical errors. Look for other obvious errors in spelling, punctuation, and so on.

Final Checklist

1. Does your introduction have an appropriate and effective lead-in? ☐

2. Does the essay establish a clear purpose for comparison or contrast? ☐

3. Does the thesis clearly identify the focus of the essay—similarities or differences—and, if appropriate, contain clear, effective, and appropriate bases of comparison or contrast? ☐

4. Is the pattern of organization—point-by-point or block method—clear and effective? ☐

5. Does the essay contain a sufficient number and variety of transition devices to ensure a smooth flow from one topic to another and from one point to the next? ☐

6. Does each developmental paragraph have a clearly stated topic sentence, treat both topics fairly, choose appropriate characteristics for comparison/contrast, and offer sufficient, relevant, thoughtful, and insightful information or evidence for each topic? ☐

7. Is the diction appropriate to the purpose of the paper and to the intended reader? Is the word choice appropriate and not offensive? ☐

8. Does your essay have varied sentence structures? Is it free of grammatical, spelling, and punctuation errors? ☐

Reflecting

Congratulations! Once again, you have completed a demanding writing task. It is worthwhile at this point to sit back and reflect on what you have accomplished. Do the following activity to help you reflect productively on your writing.

WRITING **8-11**

Self-Reflection

Before you hand in your paper, write a brief paragraph in which you reflect on your final draft. Include your feelings on the following questions:

1. What peer suggestions do you find most useful? What should you change to address the suggestions?

2. What are you most proud of in this essay?

3. What is the weakest aspect of the essay?

4. What types of comments or feedback on this essay do you think would be most helpful to your writing progress?

5. What should you do differently as you write the next essay?

After you have completed this self-reflection, carefully review your instructor's comments. How are they similar or different from your own answers to the self-reflection? Make a list of your grammar, punctuation, and spelling errors so that you can follow up on the ones that recur. Consider what strategies you will employ to address your challenges or weaknesses and to improve the quality of your essay.

How might you use comparison or contrast outside of this English course? Look back at the writing samples in Previewing Your Task in this chapter.

- **College:** _____
- **Your profession:** _____
- **Everyday life:** _____

CHAPTER 9

Developing Your Essay through Division and Classification

YOUR GOALS

Understanding Division and Classification

1. Divide a concept into component parts.

2. Classify multiple items into several categories.

3. Organize classification and division essays.

Writing Your Division or Classification Essay

1. Use diagramming as a prewriting technique to discover and limit your topic.

2. Analyze your audience(s) to determine the purpose of your division or classification.

3. Formulate a thesis appropriate for division or classification.

4. Create an outline for your classification or division essay.

5. Revise your writing to produce a more unified and coherent final draft.

6. Review your draft for style, grammar, and punctuation.

"Crude classifications and false generalizations are the curse of organized life."

■ **George Bernard Shaw** ■

Several of your instructors recommend that you outline your textbook chapters to help you understand the material. They explain that outlining enables you to break down the major idea of each chapter into its component parts. Conversely, when they lecture in class, your instructors often group multiple objects or ideas into types—types of political systems, types of math formulas, or types of essays.

In your work as an intern at a local bank, you learn that loan officers group potential customers into categories to make sound decisions about them—primarily according to two criteria: monthly income and level of debt. Some customers are considered "low risk," some are "medium risk," and some fall into the "high risk" category. Although this grouping may not always seem fair, it is obvious that knowing the type of customer applying for a loan helps the bank make decisions more efficiently and safely.

In a visit to the public library, you know that if you are looking for Ernest Hemingway's *The Old Man and the Sea*, you need to go the section labeled Fiction. Fortunately, grouping books by similarities brings order to chaos, making the task of locating a specific book a simple process. You realize that without such a system, it would take hours to find the book you are looking for.

Think of the many times in your life that you explain tasks, situations, or people's behavior by types. In fact, the phrase "He's the type of person who . . ." is almost cliché. We often rely on division and classification to organize, explain, and understand our world.

LET's **warm up!**

Whether in high school or college, we have probably categorized our classmates into groups. We tend to join groups that have qualities, ideals, behavior, or attitudes similar to our own. If you were to describe the student body of your high school or the students in a class you are taking in college, what three groups stand out the most? Write a paragraph in which you identify each group and describe it briefly. What characteristics make each group unique?

Thinkstock/Jupiter Images

PREVIEWING YOUR TASK

The writing samples presented in this section demonstrate how classification and division work in college, professional, and everyday writing contexts. As you read these samples, consider how you could use classification and division in each of these settings.

Writing for College

You are often called upon to classify ideas or to break them into component parts, whether you are in the traditional liberal arts, the natural sciences, or a career and technical program. The following essay was written by Loretta, a student in an introductory computer information systems course.

Computer Users

Today, computers are no longer a luxury but a necessity in the business world. Everywhere we go, we find some form of computer, and behind each computer we find what is known in the computer world as a *user* (a person). In observing the world of users, what becomes apparent is that no two users are alike in the way they confront computer problems. From my own observations as a computer technician and from the perspective of the computer world, users can be grouped into three categories, which I call Dangerous, Submissive, and Oh, My.

The group specified as Dangerous sends a shiver down the spine of any technical support person who may have the misfortune of assisting them. Dangerous exemplifies a group of users who see all, know all, but worst of all, do all. Dangerous users are firm believers in the browse function, which is their window to the forbidden world. Using browse to remedy a problem, they find files and programs that should never be touched . . . and then touch and delete them anyway. When they are unable to recover the files and have essentially removed all files required to run the operating system, they pick up the phone and call the nearest technical support center. Upon reaching a technician on the phone, Dangerous users announce, "My computer's not working" but leave out the fact that they have been "browsing." Twenty minutes and 20 questions later, the technician, thinking he may have a Dangerous user on the line, asks, "Have you removed any files from the hard drive?" Not wanting to own up to the task, Dangerous replies, "Only files I did not need." The technician, realizing his worst nightmare is on the other end of the phone, surrenders and sends an on-call technician out to rebuild the system.

In contrast to the technician's nightmare is the technician's dream, Submissive users. This type not only answers all questions appropriately and has some idea of what a computer is for but also follows directions word for word, expediting the resolution of the problem. Submissive users call the technical support center when all logical ideas to remedy the problem have been exhausted. When they reach a technician on the phone, they give a step-by-step overview of what the problem is and what they have done to try to resolve the issue. They write down word for word the instructions given by the technician. Once the conversation is over, Submissive users go on to resolve the problem by following instructions carefully.

The final type of computer user is Oh, My. Oh, My users are generally the kindest people a technician encounters, but, on the downside, they are the least informed. Being deathly afraid of computers, they call the technical support center for help powering on the computer. After 10 minutes of explaining where the power button is, the technician achieves, in the eyes of Oh, My users, brilliant status. Having waited by the phone for 20 minutes, the technician receives the second call of the day, questioning what the little foot pedal is for. Another 10 minutes is taken up to explain that it is not a foot pedal but a mouse, and it takes another 20 minutes to explain why it is called a mouse. With the day finally over and after numerous calls, Oh My users profusely thank the technician for all the help, declare him THE computer god.

With users ranging from Dangerous to Oh, My, it is a wonder that more technicians haven't ended up wearing a little white jacket and being carted away. Computer users need to analyze and understand how to resolve their own computer problems, and the next time they need a technician, they need to be kind and, above all, submissive.

PRACTICE   9-1

1. What is the goal of the essay? Did it accomplish this goal? Explain. The goal appears to be to educate the audience in an entertaining way. The fanciful categories and the mildly humorous supporting details accomplish this purpose.

2. Who is the audience? The audience could be fellow technicians who would appreciate the humor or computer users who make frequent use of technical support.

Writing in Your Profession

Classification and division can help you inform your coworkers or clients about large amounts of data so that they can more readily comprehend it. The following writing sample from a project manager to his client was submitted as an e-mail.

To: Pat Owens, Facility Director
From: Louis Toro
Sent: Thursday, March 1, 2008 12:45 PM
Subject: Revised Community Center Expansion Cost

Pat,

As requested, please find attached cost associated with the building expansion of the Alpine Community Center. The following are some clarifications to the attached cost:

  I. Substructure

   • As per the Soils Report dated 1/5/08 by Kumar and Associates, we have figured a deep foundation system made up of drilled caissons 10′ on center drilled to bedrock, which is determined to be 25′ in depth. A 3′ grade beam on 6″ void will span throughout the perimeter of the addition, and intermediate pads will hold interior column loading.

- A reinforced 4″ slab on grade will be placed throughout the building with the exception of the loading bays, which will be 5″. Slab control joints will be at 12′ on center. Second- and third-floor systems will be 3″ slab on deck construction with fiber mesh reinforcement.

II. Superstructure

- Load-bearing steel columns and beams will provide the building's framework, with steel joist and metal decking as floor and roof structure.

- The exterior skin of the building will be structural steel studs with exterior Densglass sheathing and a three-coat synthetic stucco system.

- Window systems will be a combination of structurally glazed curtain wall and storefront with tinted low-E glazing.

- Roofing systems will be an EPDM fully adhered roof system with 4″ polyiso insulation, which provides roughly an R-25 value. Interior roof drains and overflow drains will serve as the roof drainage.

III. Interior Finishes

- We have figured the flooring and wall finishes per the finish schedule, which includes rubber tile flooring in the child watch areas.

- Hollow metal door jambs and solid-core birch doors have been figured at all typical locations. Finish hardware assemblies have been figured at each typical door opening.

IV. Mechanical/Electrical Systems

- Fire sprinkler system has been figured throughout the building.

- HVAC system will be DX rooftop air-handling units and a boiler system with inline pumps.

- Electrical, fire alarm, and lighting systems, per electrical narrative provided, have been included, as well as rough-in for security systems and CATV to be furnished by owner.

V. Sitework

- Due to the lack of information on the drawings, we are still carrying $800,000 for site improvements, asphalt paving, and stripping and landscaping. Upon review of completed drawings, we will price accordingly.

Please review the attached cost summary and don't hesitate to contact me with any questions. As we stated in our previous meeting, with further development in the project documents, we will be able to develop more solid numbers and firm up our price.

Louis A. Toro
Estimator/Project Manager
H. W. Houston Construction Co.

PRACTICE   **9-2**

Given the complexity of a construction project, how does the categorization in this e-mail help you understand the costs? <u>If the details were presented without the categorization, it would be hard to make sense of them.</u>

Writing in Everyday Life

"Classification and division" may sound formal and academic, but we often rely on this form of thinking to convey information to our friends and family. The following e-mail is from a son to his mother, whose 1970s kitchen needs updating.

Mom,

I know how much you have been looking forward to updating your kitchen. Now that you and Dad have put us kids through college and have the financial resources to do this, I'm glad that you are going ahead with the project. You asked me for my ideas since I live in a new condo with an upscale kitchen, so here we go:

Newer kitchens are often designed in three areas referred to as the kitchen workspace or triangle with the purpose of keeping the food preparation area compact and away from traffic through the kitchen. These sections are the sink, the stove or cook area, and the refrigerator.

The sink is in the middle of the triangle so that an equal line can be drawn from its middle to the other two areas of the kitchen. Each side of the triangle should be approximately 4 to 9 feet so that the cook doesn't need to walk long distances between the sink, stove, and refrigerator. For your kitchen, I would suggest that you keep the sink where it is because you have the windows to look out, but consider replacing the aluminum sink with a porcelain one.

For the cook area, currently, you have the stove opposite the sink on the other side of the kitchen. This is too far away, causing more steps and more spilling and mess as you carry washed and diced foods across the floor for cooking. I would suggest installing a stove off one leg of the triangle where you have your island workspace, decreasing its distance from the sink.

Finally, the refrigerator should complete the triangle, opposite the stove and adjacent to the sink. Right now the refrigerator is more than 9 feet from the sink, so I suggest that you create a space closer to the sink and buy a more energy-efficient (and attractive) refrigerator. You might want to consider a side by side to help organize the contents of the refrigerator.

I'm attaching a picture of my kitchen to help you visualize this triangle. I hope that these suggestions help you out. I can't wait for my next visit home to see the new kitchen!

Love,

Nathan

PRACTICE   9-3

If this were an essay rather than an e-mail, what extra descriptive details would you provide in the body paragraphs? _Because the addressee of the e-mail is thoroughly familiar with the setting, the writer can omit some of descriptive detail that would be needed in an essay. If this were an essay, more of the theory of modern kitchen design might also be needed._

UNDERSTANDING DIVISION AND CLASSIFICATION

Classification and division can be more challenging than the other modes you've encountered. Sometimes they are easily confused with each other, even by practiced writers. Therefore, it's crucial that you understand the differences between them.

Division

In *division*, you take a concept and break it into its components or building blocks. For example, a breakdown of the main components of a plant might look like what you see in Figure 9.1.

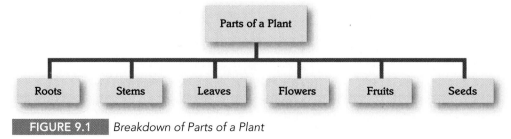

FIGURE 9.1   *Breakdown of Parts of a Plant*

You're more familiar with division than you realize. Every time you prepare an outline for one of your essays, you use division. Through your outline, you break an essay into its various components: introduction, body, and conclusion. Then you divide each component even further: topic sentence, major supports, and minor supports.

As a consumer, you expect stores to organize their wares so that locating specific products is a simple, stress-free process: children's wear, ladies' wear, men's wear, electronics, sports, and so on. Look at some other examples of division in Table 9.1. The Cedar Falls, Iowa, police department divides its organization into three main components: patrol, investigation, and identification. Through division, the police department is able to describe more effectively the layout and elements of this agency.

For an engineering class, you might want to write a paper explaining the parts of a bridge. After selecting a specific type of bridge, you can divide it into manageable parts (as illustrated in Figure 9.2) and then discuss each part fully.

In the e-mail you read about kitchen remodeling on page 242, the son wishes to tell his mother about the arrangement of the modern kitchen. Quickly, division comes to the rescue, as seen in Figure 9.3.

Note that in all these examples the components are part of a single whole. The point of the division is to show how all parts "add up" to the whole. By focusing on each component individually, you are able to understand the topic better and explain it more fully and logically.

TABLE 9.1	*Divisions of a Police Department*	
Cedar Falls Police Department		
Division	**Staff**	**Responsibilities**
Patrol	Uniformed officers	• Making arrests • Responding to calls for service • Initiating reports of incidents • Enforcing traffic laws • Engaging in school talks • Preventing crime
Investigation	Plainclothes officers and civilian secretaries	Conducting follow-up criminal investigations, such as fraud, narcotics, property crimes, crimes against persons, juvenile offenses, and internal investigations
Identification	Uniformed officers	• Collecting and preserving evidence and property • Processing crime scenes • Executing police laboratory work • Performing computer entry of data • Consigning materials to major labs for analysis • Writing reports

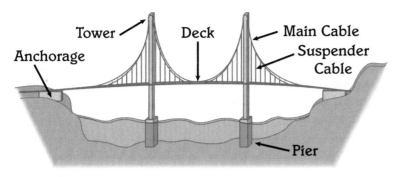

FIGURE 9.2   *Division of a Suspension Bridge*

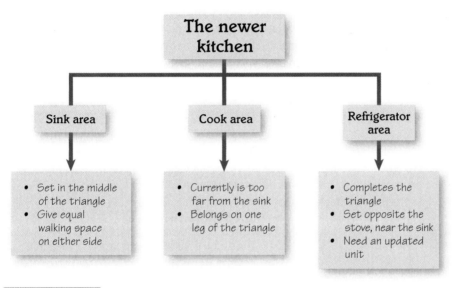

FIGURE 9.3   *Division of Kitchen Remodel*

PRACTICE   9-4

Break each of the given topics given here into the most common components. Answers will vary.

1. Parts of a ballpoint pen — Outer casing, retracting mechanism, ink-containing interior cylinder

2. Parts of a computer — Central processing unit, monitor, keyboard, mouse

3. Parts of an essay — Introduction, body, conclusion

Classification

Unlike division, which breaks a single item into its components, *classification* takes a large number of items and arranges them into different *categories*, often referred to as *types*.

Many of our daily experiences require us to categorize objects, events, or people according to types. For example, when we are trying to decide what restaurant to go to, we might mentally start by thinking of restaurants according to their ethnic type: Italian, Indian, Chinese, or Mexican.

In many of your courses, your instructors, as well as your textbooks, employ classification as a way to organize data. For instance, in a psychology class you look at types of human behaviors, whereas in a business management class you might classify businesses according to the type of product or service they provide.

In the illustration of the bridge in Figure 9.2, you were looking at the parts of one type of bridge, the suspension bridge. But what if you considered all bridges? Think of all the bridges you've seen in your life. Are they all the same? Do any of them share features that others lack? As it happens, bridges can be classified into one or a combination of the four basic types as in Figure 9.4.

Notice how much easier it is to understand the concept of bridges if we break the group of all bridges down into categories, or types, that share similar features. Classification can be tricky, however. When you classify items into types, you must do so on the basis of a guiding principle. Examine this concept in detail.

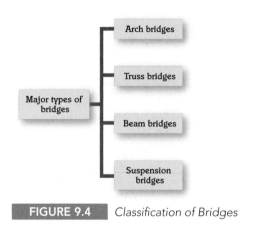

FIGURE 9.4 *Classification of Bridges*

A Guiding Principle

Since the goal of classification is to group several items into categories to distinguish among categories, the items in each category should share a common bond. The *guiding principle* lets your reader know how you are going to relate the various groups to one another. Revisit the introduction of the essay "Computer Users."

Today, computers are no longer a luxury but a necessity in the business world. Everywhere we go, we find some form of computer, and behind each computer we find what is known in the computer world as a *user* (a person). In observing the world of users, what becomes apparent is that no two users are alike in the way they confront computer problems. From my own observations as a computer technician and from the perspective of the computer world, users can be grouped into three categories, which I call Dangerous, Submissive, and Oh, My.

From this introduction, we know two important factors that help us understand this essay:

- By stating that computer users are different "in the way they confront computer problems," Loretta lets us know that she is contrasting computer users on the basis of how each type tries to solve problems.
- Loretta then indicates that she is categorizing (classifying) three types of computer users, whom she humorously names Dangerous, Submissive, and Oh, My. Your first reaction might be that the range of computer users cannot possibly or fairly be placed into just three groups. However, Loretta adds her guiding principle, "in the way they confront computer problems," thus limiting the group. In this manner, she avoids being accused of excluding people from her classification.

When determining categories, adhere to the following four rules:

1. **Don't mix principles.** Make sure that each of your categories results from the same principle. For example, if you're going to rate airlines from best to worst based on quality of service, don't include a category discussing airlines that are the most inexpensive, which is a different guiding principle. The key is to choose only one guiding principle and stick to it.
2. **Make sure your categories don't overlap.** Overlapping occurs when an item in one category could fit just as well into another category. If this happens, then narrow your guiding principle to make each category distinct.
3. **Don't omit an important category.** If your essay doesn't completely classify the topic, your reader cannot trust your analysis. For example, if you pick up a book on great American sports, you expect to find information about most of the sports you enjoy. However, if you find that the book is entirely about football, basketball, and baseball, you may feel that the author misled you, especially if your favorite sports were omitted. Therefore, as a writer, make sure you fulfill your audience's expectations by making your classification complete. In not doing so, you risk annoying your audience and losing credibility as a writer.
4. **Make your categories meaningful.** For instance, if you're going to group parents, some meaningful guiding principles might be the way they discipline their children, their attitude on education, or the level of involvement in their children's life. It would be meaningless for most people to read an essay about parents if you group them by the type of chores they do or the types of interests they have or hobbies they enjoy.

Collaborative Critical Thinking

In small groups, identify categories that fully address the following topic and guiding principle. Answers will vary.

Topic: Cell phones

Guiding principle: Types of cell phone users we're likely to meet in public places.

Share your answers with other groups. What categories did others have that you didn't?

For each of the given topics, write a possible guiding principle in the first column and, in the second column, list categories appropriate for the guiding principle you indicated. Answers will vary.

Topic	Guiding Principle	Categories
1. Types of drinkers (alcohol)	Frequency	• Once a month or less • Several times per week • Daily
2. Types of student excuses	Origin	• From the known stock of excuses • Based on unfamiliar French short stories • Utterly original
3. Types of tourists	Geographic	• The bungling American • The photo-snapping Japanese • The sophisticated European

By grouping people, places, behaviors, phenomena, or events by common features, you can better explain, analyze, understand, or propose solutions to different situations. Through classification you are not too quick to suggest one "cure all" and are on your way to a more insightful paper.

WRITING YOUR DIVISION OR CLASSIFICATION ESSAY

To illustrate the writing process, we use a student's classification essay. Lawrence is a 26-year-old psychology major. Rather than write on one of the many interesting topics in his major, he has chosen to write about one of his greatest passions—football.

Football Fans

What would possess professionals in all fields, or any normal person for that matter, to drop all semblance of respectability and become creatures alien to even themselves? Football, of course! Each week during football season, thousands of enthusiastic fans from all walks of life fill the stadiums to capacity to watch their favorite teams do battle. However, football has a special breed of fans who endure a lengthy wait each week before their favorite team takes the field, 6 days to be exact. So come Sunday afternoon, the fans are so pumped up that they can hardly control themselves.

Arriving in vans, buses, cars, and RVs, the fans fill the parking lot 4 hours before the game begins. By kickoff, the energy has reached such a high level that goose bumps form on the arms and a tingling sensation rushes throughout the body. To the untrained eye, each fan appears the same. However, after years of attending professional games and studying the behavioral patterns and characteristics of each type of fan, I have come to understand that all fans are not created equal. Football fans come to the game with quirks and uniqueness that set them apart from the rest, and it is these characteristics that expose their true level of passion for the game.

The novice, or better known as the rookie, is easy to pick out in a crowd of thousands. He is the one who enters the stadium with mouth agape and eyes wide open, looking everywhere except where he's going. After bumping into numerous people, a rookie may finally find his seat, a major accomplishment that usually takes the better half of the first quarter. By the time he settles in, he has missed 10 minutes of the game. To get caught up, he begins to ask everyone around him, "What did I miss?"

However, the rookie's most exasperating quality is his ignorance of "fan etiquette," which dictates that all fans before getting up and leaving their seats must show respect by considering the other fans in the area. The rookie will either stand up or walk in front of another fan at the precise moment of the most exciting plays, blocking the view of the field and leaving others asking, "What happened?" After other fans and the rookie completely miss a play, the rookie will add insult to injury by uttering the worst imaginable words to most fans: "I should have stayed home. I could have seen it better on TV."

As distracting as the rookie, but definitely unique, is another type of fan who stands out, the partier. This group's primary focus is to have a good time by consuming as much alcohol as is humanly possible without getting sick or passing out. The partier starts his Sunday off with a stop at the bar on this way to the stadium and then continues with the tailgate party in the parking lot of the stadium. (This is where most of the "serious drinking" takes place.) Come game time, the partier doesn't really care who's playing or what the outcome might be. There seems to be only one goal these fans shoot for, to be the most obnoxious group in the section they're in, accomplished by standing up and screaming (actually slurring profanities at the top of their lungs), by stumbling over and falling on the people two rows in front of them, and by arguing continuously with the fans around them. When partiers are asked to be quiet and settle down, they brazenly blare, "I paid good money for these tickets, and I'm gonna get my money's worth!" By the start of the fourth quarter, the partier has slammed so many beers so quickly that he slowly passes out, never getting a chance to see the end of the game—unfortunately for him but fine for everyone seated around him.

Probably the fans who stand out the most are the attention-seeking fans, whose self-absorption gives them almost celebrity status among fans. This type of fan loses complete touch with reality, becomes possessed by his alter ego, and throws caution to the wind. The attention-seeking fan dresses up in brightly colored costumes or arrives shirtless in zero-degree weather. As planned, he sticks out among the sea of 70,000 fans. His goal is not to be quiet or subdued but to wander about the stadium, drawing attention to himself. He is so busy trying to make an impression that he misses the majority of the game. Whether he's leading cheers, throwing candy to children, or taking off his shirt, the attention seeker wants the spotlight.

Fanatical fans make up the final group of fans. Fanatical fans truly love their team and thoroughly enjoy the game. One way they show their devotion and support is by dressing in a distinctive manner. Every Sunday afternoon, they enter the stadium with zubaz pants (usually bearing the same colors of the team they are rooting for), a starter jersey hanging loosely over the torso, a logo athletic hat, and team colors down to their underwear. They're proud to be football fans! With every play, they are up from their seats, offering support to their team or yelling advice to the coach. Fanatical fans know every player's name and every player's position on the field. They are so deeply engrossed in "their" team that they feel they know the players on a first name basis and address them in this manner throughout the game. Fanatical fans never lose faith in their team or ever doubt their team's ability. They are eternal optimists.

At first glance, all fans in a crowded stadium appear the same, but if we take time to look closely, we are able to discern the unique qualities and behaviors that individual fans possess. They have one thing in common: the love of the game. However, with the extreme changes that some undergo, we can't help but wonder if the uninhibited person we are now watching is the true persona, the "Mr. Hyde."

In this essay, Lawrence has classified football fans according to how they behave, and he suggests that these behaviors offer clues about attitudes toward the game. The descriptive detail is vivid and entertaining, and his purpose is to demonstrate an underlying love of the game.

Prewriting

If you don't have a topic yet, start listing ideas as they occur to you. As you think, keep repeating "types of," "parts of," "components of," and "sections in," and write whatever comes to your mind. If after a few minutes you come to a topic, then do a more focused listing, clustering, or looping.

Once you have a topic that is appropriate for division or classification, then try a new prewriting technique, branching.

Discovering and Limiting Your Topic

Prewriting Strategy #8: Branching

Branching is a way of separating and identifying the classification or division of a topic. Imagine your topic being the trunk of a tree and each classification or division representing a separate branch of that tree. If you enjoy drawing, make your diagram in the shape of a tree and label each branch as a part of the topic. However, if drawing isn't for you, a simple diagram made up of circles and lines, much like clustering, works just as well.

Lawrence decided to explore types of football fans, a topic he was familiar with and felt he could develop well. Look at Lawrence's diagram and the branches he identified (Figure 9.5).

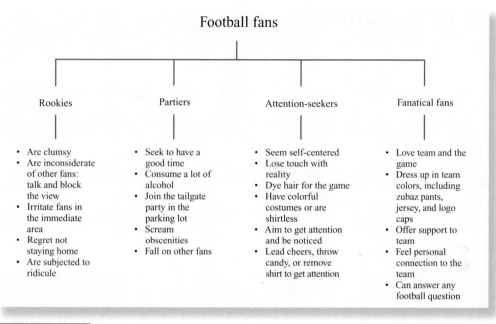

Football fans

Rookies	Partiers	Attention-seekers	Fanatical fans
• Are clumsy • Are inconsiderate of other fans: talk and block the view • Irritate fans in the immediate area • Regret not staying home • Are subjected to ridicule	• Seek to have a good time • Consume a lot of alcohol • Join the tailgate party in the parking lot • Scream obscenities • Fall on other fans	• Seem self-centered • Lose touch with reality • Dye hair for the game • Have colorful costumes or are shirtless • Aim to get attention and be noticed • Lead cheers, throw candy, or remove shirt to get attention	• Love team and the game • Dress up in team colors, including zubaz pants, jersey, and logo caps • Offer support to team • Feel personal connection to the team • Can answer any football question

FIGURE 9.5   *Football Fan Branching*

WRITING 9-1

Start your prewriting sessions to identify your topic, help limit your topic, or both. Use the prewriting techniques you feel are most useful. Try using branching as a final technique. Here is a branching diagram. Add or ignore boxes as necessary to your topic.

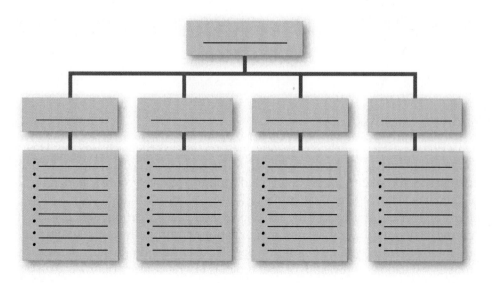

TOPICS TO CONSIDER

If you're still having problems finding a topic, here are some topics that might interest you. Try using branching on one or more of the following topics to generate ideas.

Writing for College		
■ Types of poetry ■ Parts of a novel or short story ■ Types of thunderstorms	■ Types of immigrants to the United States	■ Types of pollution ■ Types of countries

Writing in Your Profession			
BUSINESS	■ Parts of the accounting cycle ■ Types of investments	■ Parts of a business (organizational structure)	■ Types of tax-exempt organizations
CRIMINAL JUSTICE	■ Types of trials ■ Types of acts of violence	■ Sections in a specific law	■ Parts of a trial
EDUCATION	■ Types of class tests ■ Parts of an effective lesson plan	■ Types of student behavior	■ Types of education philosophies
HEALTH	■ Types of patients ■ Types of medication	■ Types of nurses	■ Parts of a hospital, clinic, or ward
SOCIAL WORK/ PSYCHOLOGY	■ Components of effective social care	■ Types of abuses ■ Types of rituals	■ Components of good counseling
TECHNICAL	■ Parts of a computer or a specific software ■ Types of cameras	■ Parts of a specific piece of equipment	■ Types of construction methods
OTHERS	■ Components of good interior design	■ Types of TV programs ■ Types of photography	■ Types of teams

Writing in Everyday Life		
■ Components of productive relaxation ■ Types of jobs	■ Types of waiters ■ Types of shopping centers	■ Types of humor ■ Types of attitudes about money or spending

Identifying Your Audience

When writers consider their audience, one question they ask themselves is this: How will my audience approach this piece of writing? Will my audience read it critically, testing every sentence for validity and accuracy; read it more receptively; or read it merely for entertainment value? When you write a division or classification essay, your audience is often quite serious and critical; the audience is interested in learning about a topic in detail and is checking to see that your categorization of the topic is complete and fully representative of reality. Nonetheless, it is possible to entertain your audience with humorous classifications or divisions of your topic, as Lawrence attempts to do in his essay on football fans.

Establishing Your Purpose

Your purpose is reflected in the method by which you choose to divide or classify a topic. If you are writing about a doctor's office, for instance, you could divide your topic by physical locations (waiting room, reception area, records department, examination rooms, and so on), by the chronology of a patient's experience in the doctor's office (in this case, you probably wouldn't write about the records department), or by functions performed by the doctor's staff (in this case, you might omit the waiting room).

If you are classifying a topic, your purpose is reflected in your guiding principle of classification. Notice that Lawrence's purpose is partially humorous, so he invents his own classification of football fans. A more objective classification would use a different guiding principle—the economic status of fans, for instance.

Setting Your Tone

Lawrence's essay on football is mildly humorous, but it still captures some important truths about the fans he encounters at a football game. If you choose this approach in your own essay, keep in mind that humor can be an effective tool for conveying meaning to your reader; it doesn't always exist just to entertain. And as always, make sure not to offend your reader with unintentional sarcasm or offensive language.

WRITING 9-2

Audience, Purpose, and Tone Analysis

Topic: _____

I. Audience

1. Who is your audience? _____
   Age(s): _____ Gender(s): _____ Education level(s): _____

2. Why would this audience be interested in your topic? _____
   _____

3. What does your audience already know about your topic? _____
   _____

4. What background information does your audience need to understand the topic?
   _____

5. How do you expect your audience to read your essay—critically or for entertainment?
   _____

II. Purpose

1. Why did you choose this topic? _____
   _____

2. What is the controlling, or main, idea of your essay? _____
   _____

3. What effect do you want your essay to have on your audience? _____

_____

4. What information must you provide to achieve the desired effect? _____

_____

III. Tone

1. What is your personal attitude about this topic? _____

_____

2. What tone do you wish to establish for this essay? _____

_____

3. How does your tone help you relate to your audience and support your purpose?

_____

_____

Formulating Your Thesis

When constructing your thesis, avoid oversimplifying it.

> **THESIS:** Athletes can be classified in five ways.

This statement is not only vague but also fails to offer the reader a clear idea of your purpose except that you're going to classify athletes. Instead of such a vague thesis, consider including some information about why you think your classification or division is important. Your thesis can take various forms. Here we illustrate three common structures for your consideration.

1. In its most basic form, your thesis should do two things: state your topic and indicate your controlling idea.

          Topic   Controlling Idea
[To the serious amateur photographer], [starting out with just the right type of camera can make a world of difference.]

2. Some topics may require you to give the main divisions or categories, thus creating an essay map.

          Topic   Controlling Idea   Categories
[America's definition of a family] [has changed to include different situations,] [such as grandparents raising children, single-parent families, same-sex parent families, interracial families, and adoptive families.]

3. Occasionally, stating your purpose as part of your thesis helps unify and strengthen the thesis. It makes the thesis meaningful.

      Topic   Purpose   Controlling Idea
[New students] [will quickly feel part of our campus community] [if they familiarize themselves with four areas crucial to their college success:] [advising, student support services, learning resources, and student activities.]
                                              Categories

WRITING **9-3**

Below, write a tentative thesis for your classification or division essay. Don't forget that nothing is final. You can always come back to rephrase or refocus your thesis.

Tentative thesis: _____

_____

Outlining Your Ideas

Lawrence's outlining process has already begun—a rough version of his outline exists in the branching diagram he created earlier. He established four categories—rookies, partiers, attention seekers, and fanatics—and listed characteristics for each group. He also made each group distinct by providing different characteristics that don't overlap. Such a branching diagram corresponds directly to the visual structure of a formal outline. Here's how Lawrence converted his diagram into an outline:

ESSAY OUTLINE

Topic: Football fans
Audience: People who love football
Purpose: Classify football fans in a humorous way by their behavior at a game
Tentative thesis statement: Although all fans in a stadium appear the same at first, each category of fan possesses a different type of behavior and it's not difficult to tell them apart.

I. **Introduction**
   A. Describe the excitement of the stadium
   B. My experience
   C. My thesis

II. **Body paragraphs**
   A. The rookie
      1. Is astonished by being here
      2. Is clumsy
      3. Talks nonstop
      4. Regrets not watching the game on TV
      5. Is ridiculed by other fans
   B. The partier
      1. Only wants to have a good time
      2. Consumes a lot of alcohol
      3. Joins the tailgate party in the parking lot
      4. Screams obscenities
      5. Stumbles and falls on other fans
      6. Passes out once the beer sales stop

C. The attention seeker
   1. Is self-centered
   2. Loses touch with reality
   3. Wears rainbow-colored hair
   4. Is in colorful costumes or shirtless
   5. Wants to get attention and be noticed
   6. Leads cheers, throws candy, or removes shirt
   7. Is happy once he knows he's on TV
D. The fanatic
   1. Loves his team and the game
   2. Dresses up in team colors, including zubaz pants, jersey, and logo caps
   3. Offers support to his team
   4. Feels a personal connection to the team
   5. Shows undying faith in his team's success

III. Conclusion
  A. Restate thesis
  B. Summarize key points

Notice that the names of the categories become the items in the outline identified by capital letters. The list of characteristics appears after Arabic numerals. This outline is a good plan to get Lawrence started, and your initial outline should serve you in the same way.

WRITING 9-4

Prepare your outline for your topic. After you have completed your outline, review it carefully. Make sure that you haven't left out any important categories, that your categories are meaningful, and that each category is distinct (with no overlap).

Essay Outline

Topic: _____

Audience: _____

Purpose: _____

Tentative thesis statement: _____

_____

I. Introduction

  A. Lead-in strategies

    1. _____

    2. _____

  B. Thesis and map _____

_____

II. Body paragraphs

    A. Category #1: _____

        1. _____

        2. _____

        3. _____

        4. _____

    B. Category #2: _____

        1. _____

        2. _____

        3. _____

        4. _____

    C. Category #3: _____

        1. _____

        2. _____

        3. _____

        4. _____

    D. Category #4: _____

        1. _____

        2. _____

        3. _____

        4. _____

    E. Category #5: _____

        1. _____

        2. _____

        3. _____

        4. _____

III. Conclusion: Strategies you can use to wrap up your essay

    A. _____

    B. _____

    C. _____

Drafting

Writing a first draft is an exciting process. It is here that you begin to see your ideas taking shape in sentences and paragraphs. We focus first on the introduction, but remember that you don't have to start with your introduction. Feel free to start with the paragraph you are most anxious to develop.

Writing Your Introduction

By now, you are well aware of the many strategies, individually or combined, that you can use to effectively introduce your thesis. This chapter focuses on one additional strategy: the rhetorical question.

A *rhetorical question* is a question that has an obvious answer. The question catches the reader's attention. Lawrence uses this strategy with his opening question: "What would possess professionals in all fields, or any normal person for that matter, to drop all semblance of respectability and become creatures alien to even themselves?"

As you write your introduction, try combining two or more strategies. Don't trivialize the importance of your introduction. Whatever strategies you choose, always remember that your introduction sets the tone for your entire essay, grabs the reader's attention, and defines your purpose.

Examine Lawrence's initial introduction.

> What would possess professionals in all fields, or any normal person for that matter, to drop all semblance of respectability and become creatures alien to even themselves? Each week, thousands of enthusiastic fans fill the stadiums to watch their favorite teams do battle for 60 minutes. To the untrained eye, each fan appears the same. However, after years of attending games and watching fans, I have come to understand that all fans are not created equal. There are four unique types of football fans: rookies, partiers, attention seeker fans, and fanatical fans.

Following his rhetorical question, Lawrence wants the reader to "see" and understand the grandeur of a professional football game, so he sets the scene with description, but could do better. Lawrence establishes his connection with the topic by mentioning his years of attending professional games, and his lead-in does flow smoothly to his thesis, but he has yet to instill in the reader the excitement he feels for the sport. He also needs to make his thesis and controlling idea work more effectively. Finally, Lawrence has to decide whether he needs to list the categories.

WRITING   9-5

Using the thesis you developed earlier, write an introduction on a separate sheet of paper. Use a combination of at least two of the strategies you've learned. Make sure your introduction indicates your purpose for dividing or classifying your topic.

Writing Your Body Paragraphs

Follow Lawrence as he develops the draft of two of his body paragraphs, using his outline as a guide.

Category #1

First, rookie fans are easy to pick out in a crowd. They are the ones who enter the stadium with mouths agape and eyes wide open, looking everywhere except where they're going. The rookie is usually so excited being at a professional football game that he talks nonstop about everything, which will irritate everyone around him. Throughout the game, the rookie will stand up or walk in front of another fan, usually at the moment of the most exciting plays. In doing so, he blocks the view of the field and leaves others asking, "What happened?" But worst of all, he ends by saying the worst imaginable words to most fans: "I should have stayed home. I could have seen it better on TV."

Lawrence starts with a topic sentence indicating the first category, rookie fans. He begins by describing the unique behavior that distinguishes this group. Lawrence also indicates how other fans are irritated by members of this group. Lawrence has established a basic plan for explaining a group. A reader most likely expects similar information for the other groups.

Category #2

Next, the partier's main goal is to have a good time. Part of having a good time is to drink as much alcohol as is humanly possible without getting sick. The partier starts with a stop to the bar on his way to the stadium and then continues with the tailgate party in the parking lot of the stadium. The partier doesn't really care who's playing or what the outcome might be. They stand up and scream obscenities, stumble and fall over other people, and argue continuously with the fans around them. When partiers are asked to be quiet and settle down, they yell, "I paid good money for these tickets, and I'm gonna get my money's worth!" When beer sales stop, they settle down and pass out.

Again, Lawrence provides a clear topic sentence, naming the next group of fans. His transition "next" is too mechanical, but as a first draft it acts as a marker he can revise later. Just as Lawrence did in the first category, he starts with the entrance of the fan, his characteristic, and his way of irritating other fans.

Coherence: Using Transitions

As you're already aware, transitional words and expressions not only keep your essay reading smoothly but also help establish relationships between ideas and provide connections for your reader to understand your essay. Table 9.2 shows a list of common transitions used in classification and division. You can combine transitions (on the left) with classification or division indicators (on the right) to produce useful transitional phrases—for instance, "Another category of . . ." and "A second component of. . . ." Try different combinations until you find the right transitional expression for your purpose.

TABLE 9.2   *Transitions for Classification or Division*

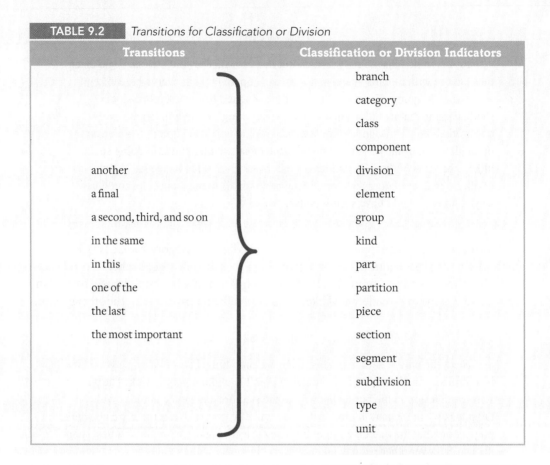

Transitions	Classification or Division Indicators
	branch
	category
	class
	component
another	division
a final	element
a second, third, and so on	group
in the same	kind
in this	part
one of the	partition
the last	piece
the most important	section
	segment
	subdivision
	type
	unit

WRITING   9-6

On a separate sheet of paper, start drafting the body of your essay.

1. Start each body paragraph with a topic sentence that identifies the category you discuss.

2. Provide examples, description, and relevant information that show the reader how each category is unique.

3. Add transitions to keep your ideas flowing smoothly and to guide your audience through your information.

Writing Your Conclusion

Your conclusion should wrap up the essay by giving it a sense of finality; thus, don't introduce new information in your conclusion. Consider the following approaches:

■ Explain how understanding your classification or division can help the reader accomplish certain goals or tasks.

■ In division, show how the parts you describe add up to a meaningful whole.

- In classification, reassure the reader that your classification accounts for all significant types and contributes to a better understanding of the topic.
- Restate the thesis and express a final thought about the topic, such as recommending an action.

For the first draft of his conclusion, Lawrence restates his thesis and summarizes his key points.

> Although at first all fans in a stadium appear the same, if we take time to look closely, we find the unique qualities of the rookie, the partier, the attention seeker, and the fanatical fan. Each possesses a different type of behavior. It's not difficult to tell them apart. The rookie is the one wandering around clueless, the partier is the obnoxious intoxicated fan slurring obscenities, the attention seeker is dressed in a costume and leading cheers, and the fanatical fan is dressed from head to toe in NFL-licensed clothing and giving his team complete control. These are football fans—loud, shocking, but unique.

How effective is this approach? How meaningful is it? Does the reader need to be reminded of what was just read? Lawrence rethinks this technique during the revising stage.

WRITING 9-7

Draft the conclusion of your essay.

1. Avoid trite beginnings such as "All in all, . . ." or "In conclusion, . . ."
2. Don't be tempted just to repeat the main points you've covered in the body of the essay.
3. Go beyond a restatement of the thesis; leave your reader with a sense of the importance of the topic.

Revising

Revision is the most important part of the writing process. Reconsider everything you've written: the thesis, the introduction, your categories, your choice of transitions, your supporting information, and your conclusion.

Style Tip: Avoid Mixed Construction

The phrase *mixed construction* may sound like a building trade term, but in writing it means that parts of a sentence do not fit together. Sometimes as we write quickly we lose track of how we started our sentences and thus mix up their structure.

> **Bridging Knowledge**
>
> **See Chapter 21** for additional information and practice.

INCORRECT:	While completing a research paper for my philosophy class was more demanding than I expected.
CORRECT:	While completing a research paper for my philosophy class, I realized that the project was more demanding than I expected. [The writer started the sentence focused on the research paper but forgot that the verb *was* needed a subject: *the project*.]

INCORRECT:	The reason I feel depressed is because of the long, dark nights.
CORRECT:	I feel depressed because of the long, dark nights.

Note: Do not use expressions such as *is when*, *is because*, and *is where*. After *is*, *was*, and so on, use a noun or adjective.

PROBLEM · SOLUTION

WRITING

My introduction seems lacking in development and "tossed off" thoughtlessly.

1. Have you avoided the temptation to open with a one or two sentence lead-in?

2. Remember that one purpose of the introduction is to establish your credibility as the writer of this essay. It's not always necessary, but if your introduction seems under-developed, consider letting the reader know about your own experience with the topic.

3. "Dropping" a previously written thesis into the introduction can leave the impression of hurrying through the writing task. Ensure that your thesis blends thoughtfully with the preceding sentences.

4. Connect your lead-in to your thesis by explaining why your topic is important.

WRITING

My conclusion is too short and boring; the reader could just skip it and not miss anything important.

1. Try writing a conclusion that doesn't restate your thesis. If you don't restate the thesis, what else can you do? Try some brainstorming to determine another approach.

2. In your body paragraphs, you have shown the reader how each category is different, so for your conclusion consider showing what all have in common.

3. You should use the introduction and conclusion to discuss the purpose of the essay because the body of the essay is devoted to analysis. In your conclusion, develop the reason you thought it was so important for your reader to understand the classification or division.

DIVISION/ CLASSIFICATION

The body of my paper just doesn't seem to be complete or well organized.

1. Are you leaving out any important types or parts of the topic just to make the essay easier to write? Remember that your analysis must closely correspond to your reader's perception of the topic.

2. Are your topic sentences clearly stated? The topic sentence lets the reader know the component you are discussing in a paragraph.

3. Do you support your paragraphs so that your reader understands the component or type you're discussing? Use a combination of examples, description, narration, and other techniques you've learned.

4. If you are having trouble supporting your topic sentences, try the cubing brainstorming method to find other ways of looking at the topic.

5. Are your body paragraphs properly ordered? Make sure you use a clear ordering principle.

6. Is each category distinct? Make sure the information you provide explains the uniqueness of the category or part.

COHERENCE

I use transitions that I learned for other essays. They don't seem appropriate for this one.

Refer to the transitions presented earlier in this chapter and select those that work best in classification or division.

W R I T I N G   9-8

Start your revision. Don't leave any part of your essay untouched.

- Make sure that you didn't omit any necessary categories, that your categories are meaningful, and that each is unique.
- Offer sufficient information to make each category distinct.
- Check for coherence. Make sure you offer enough transitions to help guide your reader and that you vary your choice and style of transition.
- Use a variety of sentence types.

> ## Collaborative Critical Thinking
>
> ### Asking Your Peers
>
> **Get feedback from your peers. Exchange papers with a classmate,** and review the paper by responding on the form presented here.
>
> 1. Who is the writer? Who is the peer reviewer?
> 2. Introduction
>   a. Is the introduction sufficiently developed?
>   b. Does the essay have a clear sense of purpose and audience? What is the purpose?
>   c. Does the introduction have a clearly stated thesis?
>   d. Does the information in the introduction lead smoothly to the thesis?
>   e. If classifying, what is the guiding principle?
>   f. What can you suggest to improve the introduction?
> 3. Body paragraphs
>   a. How many categories has the writer established?
>   b. Is the number sufficient? Explain.
>   c. What other categories or components can you recommend?
>   d. Does the writer provide sufficient information and examples to explain the category fully?
>   e. In which paragraph or paragraphs do you feel the writer should include additional information?
>   f. What questions does the writer need to answer for the reader's full understanding of the category or component?
>   g. Does each paragraph have a clear topic sentence? Indicate which paragraphs' topic sentences need clarification.
>   h. Does the writer use sufficient and appropriate transitions within and between paragraphs to keep the information flowing smoothly?
>   i. Indicate any weakness in coherence.
>   j. What suggestions can you make to help improve this essay?
> 4. Conclusion
>   a. Is the conclusion effective? Is it meaningful?
>   b. What advice can you give to help improve the conclusion?

Proofreading

By now, you are developing a consistent practice of checking your essays for major grammatical errors. In this chapter, we introduce another common error: problems with subject–verb agreement.

Common Error #10: Lack of Agreement between Subjects and Verbs

Every sentence contains a subject and a verb. The following rule applies: *Subjects and verbs must agree with each other.* This means that if a subject is singular, the verb must be singular, and if the subject is plural, the verb must be plural. Problems occur when the writer loses track of whether subjects and verbs are singular or plural.

INCORRECT:	Everyone in the auditorium are standing for the national anthem.
CORRECT:	Everyone in the auditorium is standing for the national anthem. [Here, the subject of the sentence, *everyone*, is singular. Therefore, the verb must be singular: *is standing*.]

INCORRECT:	The papers in the box in the attic is old and moldy.
CORRECT:	The papers in the box in the attic are old and moldy. [Here, because two prepositional phrases come between the subject and the verb (and because each phrase has a singular noun), the writer forgot that the subject, *papers*, is plural.]

GRAMMAR CHECKUP 9-1

Examine each sentence carefully. In the line provided, write a version of the sentence that makes the subject and verb agree.

1. Several cartons of milk is sitting out on the counter.

Revision: Several cartons of milk are sitting out on the counter.

2. None of the students in any of the classes want to go on the field trip.

Revision: None of the students in any of the classes wants to go on the field trip.

3. Every one of the patients have caught pneumonia.

Revision: Every one of the patients has caught pneumonia.

4. In our book club, neither the Johnson girls nor Sondra want to read *War and Peace*.

Revision: In our book club, neither the Johnson girls nor Sondra wants to read *War and Peace*.

5. Each of the runners need water at the halfway point.

Revision: Each of the runners needs water at the halfway point.

Check your answers to this Grammar Checkup in Appendix A on page A-4. How did you do? If you missed even one of these items, you may need to review subject–verb agreement in Chapter 17.

Start proofreading your own essay. Check for and correct grammatical errors you have studied so far. Look for other obvious errors in spelling, punctuation, and so on.

Final Checklist

1. Does your introduction have an appropriate and effective lead-in? ☐

2. Is the thesis statement clear and structured appropriately? ☐

3. Have you narrowed the topic so that all parts of the topic are accounted for? ☐

4. Does each paragraph have an appropriate topic sentence that clearly identifies a category or component? ☐

5. Is the guiding principle clear, logical, interesting, and consistent throughout the essay? ☐

6. Does the support effectively describe or define the general characteristic of the member of the category or component? Does it give interesting and relevant examples to illustrate the characteristics that distinguish a category or component from other (previous) categories or components? ☐

7. Are your categories or parts meaningful and not an oversimplification of a complex topic? ☐

8. Does the essay contain appropriate, varied, and smooth transitions between paragraphs and sentences? ☐

9. Does your essay have varied sentence structures, complete sentences (no fragments, comma splices, or fused sentences), and insignificant errors in spelling, usage, and punctuation? ☐

Reflecting

As you wrap up your essay, take time to reflect on what you've accomplished. Reflection helps you integrate parts of the writing process into your thinking so that you can write more efficiently, clearly, and successfully in your next writing assignment.

WRITING 9-10

Self-Reflection

Before you hand in your paper, write a brief paragraph in which you reflect on your final draft. Include your feelings on the following questions:

1. What peer suggestions do you find most useful? What should you change to address the suggestions?

2. What are you most proud of in this essay?

3. What is the weakest aspect of the essay?

4. What types of comments or feedback on this essay do you think would be most helpful to your writing progress?

5. What should you do differently as you write the next essay?

After you have completed this self-reflection, carefully review your instructor's comments. How are they similar or different from your own answers to the self-reflection? Make a list of your grammar, punctuation, and spelling errors so that you can follow up on the ones that recur. Consider what strategies you will employ to address your challenges or weaknesses and to improve the quality of your essay.

How might you use division or classification outside of this English course? Look back at the writing samples in Previewing Your Task in this chapter.

- **College:** _____

- **Your profession:** _____

- **Everyday life:** _____

CHAPTER 10

Developing Your Essay through Definition

YOUR GOALS

Understanding Definition

1. Distinguish between denotative and connotative meanings.

2. Generate two kinds of definition: formal and extended.

3. Use negation to supplement a definition.

4. Support and clarify definitions using a variety of methods.

Writing Your Definition Essay

1. Use cubing to generate ideas.

2. Define concepts for specific audiences and purposes.

3. Integrate various writing techniques into the body of your essay.

4. Use apostrophes correctly.

5. Edit for parallelism.

"A definition is . . . enclosing a wilderness of an idea within a wall of words."

■ **Samuel Butler** ■

On a take-home essay exam, your biology instructor asks you to define *respiration*. Obviously, her goal is to test your knowledge of biological concepts, but you wonder what information to include beyond the one-sentence scientific definition from your textbook. Should you give examples of how different organisms breathe? Describe the process of respiration? Contrast respiration with other processes? You decide to use a combination of these techniques.

At work, you are required to attend workshops on sexual harassment every 2 years. As a supervisor, you need to know what it is and how to prevent it. Several years ago, a male employee complained to you that a female employee was displaying in her open cubicle a calendar of pictures of men in skimpy bathing suits. Having attended one of the sexual harassment workshops, you knew that the calendar had to be removed to prevent a hostile atmosphere in the workplace. Now, as a supervisor, you need to educate your employees and write a policy defining sexual harassment so that all employees share a common definition.

While you are discussing a new love interest with a close friend, you comment that you think that you might be in love for the first time in your life. Your friend counters with the question, "What do you mean by 'in love'?" You have to think carefully to respond honestly and accurately. How do you distinguish this emotion from others?

Definition plays an important role in our everyday lives. As professionals, students, and citizens, the meanings we attach to words form an important basis of our interactions with others. Therefore, we must learn to define the terms we use so that our meaning is fully understood.

LET's *warm up!*

Think of situations in which you had to work with other people as a team—on a work project, on a sports team, for a fundraiser, for a school project. How would you define *teamwork*? What qualities and beliefs must you have to work well with other people? What were some behaviors and attitudes that interfered with the progress of the team?

Comstock Images/Jupiter Images

PREVIEWING YOUR TASK

We spend much of our waking lives learning to define or explain concepts to ourselves or to others. In college especially, definition is a major learning tool. In the workplace and everyday life, we are often asked to define or explain concepts to our coworkers, customers, friends, and family members. The following writing samples represent a range of writing that defines concepts to clarify and make a point.

Writing for College

In your college classes, you are required to develop definitions—on tests, in writing assignments, for oral presentations, and for in-class discussions—of specialized terms that are at the heart of all academic subjects. Read the following student essay by Lauren, written for a sociology class.

My Generation: "The Millennials"

Albert Einstein once said, "The most important human endeavor is striving for morality in our actions. Our inner balance and even our very existence depend on it. Only morality in action can give beauty and dignity to our selves." This quotation accurately sums up the ethic of my generation. Young people today are striving to become more moral and to better themselves in unique ways. Many believe this is a peculiar characteristic of my generation—the "Millennial Generation." Born between 1980 and 2000, the Millennials have moved beyond the concerns of Generation X to establish our own claims to fame; we are seen as the most social, tech-savvy, and goal-oriented generation, and we hope to use these characteristics to improve the world we live in.

We Millennials are, first and foremost, social and open minded. Growing up in the diverse, rapidly evolving 1990s and 2000s has given us a chance to explore a variety of lifestyle choices. I once had a teacher who said, "You are the generation who most resembles that of the '60s." She may have held this opinion because we are more capable of understanding differences and change than our immediate predecessors could. For example, Millennials are more open to the concept of homosexuality and to the practice of alternative lifestyles and religions than any previous generation. Just drop by the nearest Millennial hangout—the coffee shop on the corner—and you'll see the wildest mix of lifestyle choices, with everyone getting along beautifully.

Ironically—because many older people think technology interferes with social life—we Millennials are highly computer literate and savvy about technology. Today's modern technology ranges from jump drives that hold huge quantities of information to MP3 players that contain 1,000 songs; these devices are specifically targeted to the tech-savvy Millennials. Most Millennials own their own computer and understand the technical aspects of how it works. By the click of a mouse, we are able to browse the Internet to gather information without leaving the house to search the library shelves. With the world at our fingertips, we are helping bring the world closer through our use of technology.

Finally, we Millennials are goal oriented, smart, and able to use a range of resources in our environment to get important jobs done. Unlike the baby boomers who feel that it is necessary to put in long hours at the office to get the job done right, Millennials prefer to work in informal groups to limit the time on the job while accomplishing the same tasks as those who work long hours at the office. For example, in my work as an independent video producer, I was recently hired to create a promotional video for a statewide nonprofit agency, the Women's Bean Project. I chose to do most of the work on a laptop at my local coffee shop, where I could collaborate with friends, get input from passersby, and enjoy a conversation now and then.

In the movie *Bye, Bye Birdie*, an infuriated Mr. McAfee exclaims: "Kids! I don't know what's wrong with these kids today." Interestingly, this line applied to the kids of the 1960s, but I've heard it applied to us as well. The truth is that nothing is wrong that we can't help fix. My generation is growing into its own. We are no longer too young to understand world events; we are now the future leaders of America, and we have the social sensitivity, technology skills, and independence to move world events in more positive directions. You boomers can retire and relax. We'll take it from here.

PRACTICE 10-1

1. What is Lauren's purpose in defining Millennials? To define her generation positively, educating and perhaps even inspiring her audience with confidence about the future.

2. List her three main points in your own words. Millennials are socially adept and broadminded, technologically sophisticated, and independent learners and workers.

Writing in Your Profession

In your profession, you will often be called upon to clarify a term, reference, or idea by providing an in-depth definition. For instance, to implement a new concept or correct a problem in an organization, employees first need a clear definition of it. The following is a definition of sexual harassment from the U.S. Equal Employment Opportunity Commission (EEOC). Read it carefully and then answer the questions that follow.

Sexual Harassment

Sexual harassment is a form of sex discrimination that violates Title VII of the Civil Rights Act of 1964. Title VII applies to employers with 15 or more employees, including state and local governments. It also applies to employment agencies and to labor organizations, as well as to the federal government.

Unwelcome sexual advances, requests for sexual favors, and other verbal or physical conduct of a sexual nature constitute sexual harassment when this conduct explicitly or implicitly affects an individual's employment, unreasonably interferes with an individual's work performance, or creates an intimidating, hostile, or offensive work environment.

Sexual harassment can occur in a variety of circumstances, including but not limited to the following:

- The victim, as well as the harasser, may be a woman or a man. The victim does not have to be of the opposite sex.

- The harasser can be the victim's supervisor, an agent of the employer, a supervisor in another area, a coworker, or a nonemployee.

- The victim does not have to be the person harassed but could be anyone affected by the offensive conduct.

- Unlawful sexual harassment may occur without economic injury to or discharge of the victim.

- The harasser's conduct must be unwelcome.

It is helpful for the victim to inform the harasser directly that the conduct is unwelcome and must stop. The victim should use any employer complaint mechanism or grievance system available.

When investigating allegations of sexual harassment, EEOC looks at the whole record: the circumstances, such as the nature of the sexual advances, and the context in which the alleged incidents occurred. A determination on the allegations is made from the facts on a case-by-case basis.

Prevention is the best tool to eliminate sexual harassment in the workplace. Employers are encouraged to take steps necessary to prevent sexual harassment from occurring. They should clearly communicate to employees that sexual harassment will not be tolerated. They can do so by providing sexual harassment training to their employees and by establishing an effective complaint or grievance process and taking immediate and appropriate action when an employee complains.

It is also unlawful to retaliate against an individual for opposing employment practices that discriminate based on sex or for filing a discrimination charge, testifying, or participating in any way in an investigation, proceeding, or litigation under Title VII.

PRACTICE   10-2

1. Who is the audience for this definition? <u>Men and women in the workplace.</u>

2. What else could be added to further clarify the definition? <u>This kind of defini-</u>
   <u>tion is often aided by adding short case studies or narrations of hypothetical</u>
   <u>events illustrating certain behaviors.</u>

Writing in Everyday Life

The following is an e-mail sent by a son who is caring for his elderly parents while his siblings live out of state. By defining his role as a caregiver, he urges his siblings to help out.

Greetings, Darla and Ron!

I would like to update you on Mom and Dad's situation and get some advice and assistance because I am becoming stressed and overwhelmed by my role as our parents' main caregiver.

First, I would like to describe a typical day for me. I'm up at about 5:30 a.m. so that I can check on Mom and Dad before going to work. I'm at their house by 6 a.m. I bring in their newspaper, brew the coffee, and set out their breakfast. When I'm sure that they are up and dressed, I rush off to work. After work I drop by their house to bring in their mail and check that Meals on Wheels has delivered their dinner. Once I'm assured that their evening routine has started, I head home, calling them once in the evening for a final check before they go to bed.

Not only must I be there for them physically, but I am also in charge of managing their finances and their medical needs. Once a month I pay their bills and balance their checkbook. Furthermore, I make medical appointments for them that fit into my schedule and add these to my calendar.

I have to admit that because of these responsibilities, I'm beginning to lose sleep and suffer frequent headaches. I no longer have time to enjoy outings on the weekends with my friends to rock climb or mountain bike. Without exercise, I am becoming more stressed. Please know that I love helping our parents and repaying them for all of the years that they raised and loved us. However, I can no longer do it alone; I need help. I propose that since you both live so far away we hire a part-time caregiver who could stay with Mom and Dad during the week to relieve me of the weekday duties. I would then take over on weekends. The three of us could share the cost so that it wouldn't be financially too onerous on any one of us. I hope to hear from you soon.

Love,

Leo

PRACTICE 10-3

1. List the methods of development that Leo uses to develop his definition of his role as a caregiver. Division (of the typical day and of the concept of caring for elderly parents), description, narration, illustration, effect analysis.

2. What is Leo's purpose in writing to his siblings? He is pleading for help and using his extended definition of the role of caregiver to build sympathy.

UNDERSTANDING DEFINITION

To define a term is to express its meaning. Sometimes, we can express the meaning of a term in a single phrase or sentence; at other times, we need to provide more information to flesh out a definition.

Denotative and Connotative Meanings of Words

Because words can have a rich range of meanings, we have to be careful to clarify which meanings we are using as we speak and write. Words can have two basic kinds of meaning: denotative and connotative.

The *denotative* meaning of a word is the literal, or primary meaning, the definition that we commonly accept as a community of English speakers: it is the type of definition we are most likely to find listed first in the dictionary. The *connotative* meanings of a word are the secondary, associated meanings that a word evokes. For example, the denotative meaning of *mother* is a female who has given birth to a child. But *mother* also connotes someone who is warm, caring, and generous. The denotative meaning of *girl* is a female child. Connotatively, *girl* could be used to describe someone who is immature. The connotations of words can have powerful uses; when used to refer to a middle-aged administrative assistant in the workplace, *girl* can be a form of disrespect and humiliation, indicating a subservient status. The use of *girl* to address a female employee even may be considered sexual harassment. Notice the power of a word based on its context.

PRACTICE   10-4

For each of the following words or phrases, write down a dictionary definition (denotation) and then associated meanings (connotations). Answers will vary.

Example: Wife

Denotation: A woman who is married to a man

Connotations: A woman who serves and is submissive to a man

1. Patriotic

    Denotation: Loyal to one's country

    Connotations: Unthinkingly supportive of governmental policies

2. Liberal

    Denotation: Favorable to progress or reform

    Connotations: Favorable to more taxation and government spending

3. Blogger

 Denotation: <u>One who posts messages on a blog site</u>

 Connotations: <u>A subject-matter fanatic or egomaniac</u>

4. Creative

 Denotation: <u>Able to devise new forms, ideas, processes</u>

 Connotations: <u>Unstable, troubled</u>

5. Homeland

 Denotation: <u>One's country of residence</u>

 Connotations: <u>A place of security, safety, nurturance</u>

The Formal Definition

When you need to define a term succinctly, you will likely give a *formal definition*. A formal definition has three parts: the *term* to be defined, a *general category* into which the term fits, and the *specific characteristics* that distinguish the term from other terms within the category.

For example, the term *appetite* might fit into the general category "strong urges or desires." However, other words fit into this category, too, such as *greed, passion,* or *anger.* To adequately define *appetite,* we need to list the specific characteristics that set *appetite* apart from the other terms. The way we might distinguish *appetite* from *greed* (the desire for greater wealth) is to include its objects—food, drink, activity, love, friendship. A formal definition can be expressed in a single sentence that contains all three elements.

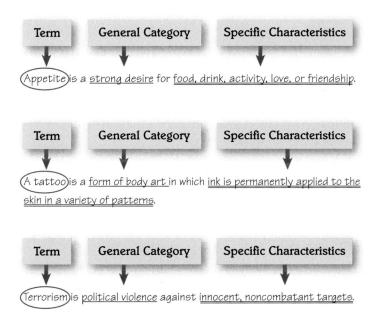

Term	General Category	Specific Characteristics

(Appetite) is a <u>strong desire</u> for <u>food, drink, activity, love, or friendship</u>.

Term	General Category	Specific Characteristics

(A tattoo) is a <u>form of body art</u> in which <u>ink is permanently applied to the skin in a variety of patterns</u>.

Term	General Category	Specific Characteristics

(Terrorism) is <u>political violence</u> against <u>innocent, noncombatant targets</u>.

Once your definition has all three elements, you must check that it makes logical sense. Just listing a few distinguishing characteristics is not enough. Test your definition by applying it to what you know about the world.

A woman is a human who is able to reproduce.

At first, this definition may seem adequate, but you can test it by asking, "Does it distinguish *woman* from the other terms in the category *human?*" The answer is clearly no: men are able to reproduce, too. Actually, since neither can reproduce alone, the definition has two problems. First, it is not specific enough to women, and second, it is incomplete. If not carefully thought out, definitions can be vague and inaccurate.

Collaborative Critical Thinking

In your group, read each definition and circle the term, underline the general category, and double underline the specific characteristic or characteristics. Then explain what makes the definition inadequate. List other words or phrases that fit the same definition. Then rewrite the definition to improve its accuracy.

1. A community college is an institution devoted to instructing students in the local community.
2. A forest fire is nature's way of making room for new plant growth.
3. A date is a formal meeting between a man and a woman for the purpose of getting to know each other better.
4. Travel is a movement from place to place for the purpose of enjoying new locations.
5. Anorexia nervosa is the (medical) condition of not eating enough.

Defining through Negation

Negation is a good way to get rid of any false notions your reader may have about your topic. In negation, you indicate what the term is *not* to separate it from other terms or concepts that might fit the definition. Negation is also a good way to introduce your thesis: first tell the reader what your topic is not, and then tell what it is. Notice how using negation in the following sentences helps focus the extended definition by simply mentioning what something or someone is not.

- Intelligence is not merely a score on an I.Q. test.
- Success is not necessarily material wealth.
- A biker is more than just a figure in leather riding a Harley.

The following example of negation helps focus the qualities of the deaf culture that the writer wants to discuss.

Deaf culture is a community of people bound together not by race, religion, or ethnic background but by a shared history, shared experiences, and a shared means of visual communication.

Use negation with the following terms. Write a sentence stating what each term is not as well as what it is. Answers will vary.

1. Apathy Apathy is not a feeling of antagonism toward authority but simply a lack of any feeling at all.

2. Geek A geek is not quite the traditional type of the serious scholar; rather, a geek is the serious scholar with an important addition: a computer chip where his frontal cerebral lobes used to be.

3. Democracy Many people think of democracy as "one man, one vote," but in America, democracy refers to a more complex system of determining public policy.

4. Fitness Fitness is much more than just exercising; it involves a total lifestyle of good nutrition, stress reduction, productive work, adequate sleep, and healthy relationships.

The Extended Definition

Many concepts, theories, and philosophies are too complex for a one-sentence formal definition. Imagine trying to fully explain sexism in a sentence or two. Think of the various contexts and ways in which sexism can be defined.

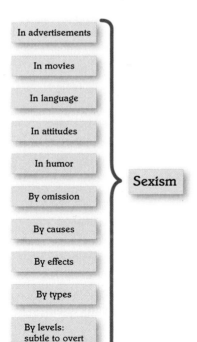

To provide an in-depth understanding of the idea or your opinion, attitude, or judgment about a term, you need to write an *extended definition essay*—or, as it is sometimes called, an *explanation essay*—so that your reader can gain a more complete grasp of the concept.

Developing an Extended Definition

The definition essay offers you the opportunity to draw from the variety of patterns of development that you have mastered in previous chapters—description, narration, process, illustration, cause/effect, comparison or contrast, and classification or division. You would probably not use all of these modes in one essay—just the ones that are most appropriate for explaining your topic. In your brainstorming process, you might try several of these methods of development to generate ideas and decide which are most useful for defining your topic.

For example, examine the topic *road rage*. Here are excerpts from an essay written by a student for her English course, using several patterns of development to explain this concept.

■ Narration and description

The violent incident I witnessed when I was four is a prime example of motorists who fit in the category of violent offenders. My dad and I were in the turning lane, and two men in separate vehicles in front of us were arguing. Both men got out of their vehicles to confront each other. As soon as they reached one another, they started punching each other. The younger man was knocked down, his head slammed into the unyielding concrete. Remarkably, he started to slowly get up, but before he could get to his feet, the older man threw him into the busy street where traffic was quickly moving. My heart stopped when I saw him lying motionless and bleeding in the street. He was unconscious but alive, which is fortunate for incidents involving road rage.

■ Process

Road rage begins with aggressive driving, which can be following too closely, speeding, and making rude comments or gestures to others on the road, and then escalates into a violent retaliation with intent to harm.

■ Classification

It is important to know and recognize all types of aggressive drivers to better understand where road rage originates. I have categorized angry drivers into three groups: quiet steamers, outward aggressors, and violent offenders. The quiet steamers are the drivers who get irritated easily but keep their irritation inside their vehicles. Quiet steamers get aggravated but rarely let the source of their frustration know about it. The outward aggressors are another story. They will honk persistently, yell rude comments out their windows, display rude gestures, and tailgate. They are the type who will drive too close to others, honk needlessly, pass on the shoulder, flip people off, and yell at other drivers and pedestrians. While outward aggressors are seemingly precarious drivers, those who are violent offenders are the most dangerous and the epitome of road rage. They become overly enraged and try to physically harm others. They may start a physical confrontation or use a weapon to reprimand whoever is angering them. This type of driver has extreme road rage. These are the drivers who can cost lives and are consequently the most important type of driver to recognize and avoid.

■ Illustration

Two women were brutally murdered recently in our community by a 23-year-old man in an episode of road rage. He felt he was wronged on the road while riding his bike, so he trailed the vehicle that almost harmed him. Even though the driver did not cause any actual damage to the man or his bike, the man decided to punish the driver for what she nearly did. He stopped the car by riding in front of it with his bike and then attacked them with his bare hands. Another case of road rage occurred last year when a man involved in a car accident shot a police officer after she asked the driver for details.

■ Causes

Congestion, traffic jams, longer commutes, and road construction can all be possible causes for road rage. Delays are annoying to all of us but are not justification for violence. Many people are irritated and aggravated by others several times a day, but rarely do they respond by attempting to destroy the person responsible for their frustrations. So why do so many seemingly normal people react so viciously in their vehicles? I have noticed that many drivers feel their way of driving is the only correct way, and many are enraged easily when they feel someone is not following their "good driving rules." Our stressful lives can also contribute; stress can come from work, home, relationships, and other aspects of life and then be displayed by aggressive driving and road rage.

■ Effects

The effects of road rage are numerous; they could be anything from mere annoyance or fear to serious injuries or even death.

Feel free to use the methods of development and organization that are best suited to your topic and purpose.

The Informal Definition

One type of informal definition occurs when writers invent a definition using humor, extended metaphor, or other techniques—in conjunction with the various methods of development—to entertain and enlighten. For instance, you might define "reading" as "a convenient way to see the world," then support your definition with illustration, narration, and contrast writing.

Another kind of informal definition occurs when writers make up their own words because they have an idea or concept that doesn't fit any current terms. This kind of creativity is the way many new words or phrases enter the language every year. Such words as *yuppie* or *Generation X* entered our language to describe specific types of social groups, whereas words such as *blog* and *googling* resulted from computer use. The growth in computer literacy has also given such common words as *crash, surfing, bug, virus, spam,* and *mouse* a whole new dimension of meaning. For example, what would you call a person who sits in front of a computer just about every day of the week? One website suggests *mouse potato* (similar to a *couch potato*). If you want to be creative and have a little fun, try inventing your own word that captures the gist of the concept you want to define. If your essay is for a class assignment, make sure your instructor approves your topic.

WRITING YOUR DEFINITION ESSAY

To illustrate the writing process, we follow the definition essay of a student, Gabriel. Gabriel has not yet made a career choice. As a student, he's still exploring different areas, but he's sure that his final choice will involve music in some way. He's part of a rock band and feels that this passion provides an interesting topic for a definition essay.

Punk: Oddity or Oracle?

Punk rock is a loud, fast, and deliberately offensive style of rock music, perhaps best exemplified by the California punk band Guttermouth, adored by fans but derided by fans' parents. For decades, punk has been looked upon as the frightening underbelly of Western culture. With spiked hair and colored Mohawks, and clad in leather, chains, and safety pins, punk bands and their fans cut a wide path wherever they go. I remember walking down the street one afternoon with my Mohawk. I was wearing my studded black leather jacket and my 10-hole Doc Martens. A lady with a little girl was walking toward me. About a half a block away, she noticed me, immediately grabbed the girl's hand, and ran across the street to avoid coming closer. Despite my appearance, however, if people only got to know me, they would realize how friendly and unbiased I am. I am hard to the core when it comes to my music, but I am also a loving father and a productive member of society.

Back in the 1980s, the world just didn't get it—"What's wrong with these kids, grinding and pounding idiotically on their instruments, shouting against authority?" At a time when the Cold War was intensifying and shady political deals were being made, punk broke out of the United Kingdom and became a worldwide phenomenon. Few people, however, noticed the connection between the political developments and the ascendance of punk music. Then, along with its popularity, punk gained musical talent and legitimacy. Punk bands now shred leads and rip scales far beyond the simplistic three-chord format that the music evolved from. Yet punk has always been more than just a musical phenomenon; it's a way of life. Although some still associate it with violence and negativity, it actually promotes unity, equality, and world peace.

Punk promotes unity through mixed venues and all-ages shows. Bands from all over the world, with wide varieties of styles and ethnicities such as German thrash, Jamaican ska, Norwegian black metal, British punk, and American hardcore, get together to entertain and educate crowds of all ages and all walks of life. They bring forth a sense of social communion that is otherwise lacking in the world. Blacks, whites, Asians, and Hispanics, men, women, and children can be spotted at the shows, whether in the pit, surfing the crowd, at the merchandise booth, or at the skate ramps. The different styles of artists and entertainment attract many types of people with one common interest—music. In my days as a promoter, I rounded up local bands ranging from female pop music, to thrash, to punk and even grindcore. I also brought bands from Denver, Colorado Springs, and New Mexico, as well as my own, and we had our own outdoor fest at a friend's junkyard.

Racism is sometimes associated with punk because the shaved heads, flight jackets, and Doc Martens were also worn by neo-Nazi groups in the 1980s. However, because society started viewing punks as Nazis and white supremacists, many bands started writing anthems and sing-alongs opposing Hitler, white power, and any Nazi activity. NOFX released a record titled *White Trash, Two Heebs, and a Bean* to display the group's diverse ethnic backgrounds. Murphy's Law, a skinhead band with three black members, did a rendition of Stevie Wonder's "Ebony and Ivory" to pay tribute to equality. Agnostic Front is another band that championed equality with the lyrics, "united strong / blacks and whites, united strong / for everyone." My friends consist of metal heads, skaters, thrashers, jocks, and preps of all races and ages. One reason punk is now so popular is that it promotes the equality of all.

Punk also promotes world peace. Food Not Bombs was started by a West coast punk band to feed the poor and promote world peace. Bands such as Anit'flag, Aus-Rotten, Cryptic Slaughter, Bad Religion, and others dedicate their lyrics to relinquishing arms, freeing humanity, eliminating violence and hatred, stopping political corruption, erasing racism, and emphasizing "No more war / No more."

Punk has become more accepted these days. Everywhere I go, I see people with colored hair, spiked wristbands, and studded belts. I'm willing to bet that most of these people are not punk or don't know what punk is, but the prevalence of punk regalia demonstrates the deep impression the movement has made on society. It also indicates that along with the studs and leather, the positive values of punk are filtering down to every level of our culture, where they will help make the world a better place.

This extended definition of punk culture obviously goes far beyond a mere dictionary definition. The essay offers a nonstandard view of a subculture against which many people react in fear. Notice that an extended definition can be carefully crafted to educate a reader who, in the opinion of the writer, may have based judgments on misinformation.

Prewriting

Sometimes, particular prewriting techniques are well suited to certain methods of development. In the case of definition, however, you should rely on your own favorite techniques to get started. One technique in particular—cubing—can help you move toward a complete and satisfying development of your topic.

Discovering and Limiting Your Topic

Prewriting Strategy #9: Cubing

Determining a topic for definition requires time and thought; you want a topic that you're interested in exploring and about which you have a strong sense of purpose. Cubing is a type of focused listing or freewriting combined with questioning, but it has the advantage of allowing you to look at your topic from different angles or perspectives. In this prewriting technique, you visualize (or draw) a cube and its six sides, each side representing a different dimension of your topic. Each side contains a prompt for you to respond to:

1. **Describe it.** In this prompt you visualize your topic and list as many details, qualities, and characteristics you can think of.
2. **Compare or contrast it.** What is your topic similar to? What is it different from? List as many comparisons as possible.
3. **Associate it.** What does your topic remind you of? What does it make you think of? What other ideas, events, or issues can you associate with your topic?
4. **Analyze it.** What does your topic consist of? What are its parts? How does it work? What types does it consist of? How is your topic meaningful and significant?

5. **Apply it.** What can you do with your topic? How is it meaningful? How is it useful?
6. **Argue for or against it.** What controversies surround your topic? What strengths or weaknesses does it have? What challenges does it face? How can it be improved?

Just as you did in listing, in cubing you move quickly. Dedicate at least 5 minutes to each side. Don't worry if you have more on one side than another. Just keep your pencil moving, jotting down ideas for each side. Continue repeating the prompt, either mentally or out loud, to keep yourself focused. Your cubing activity results in six ways of approaching your topic.

Gabriel is taking a music appreciation course and has studied many styles and types of music. He decides to write a definition of punk rock since he listens to it and wants to explore it in more formal terms to convince his middle-aged instructor that it is a respectable music genre. Choosing to list rather than freewrite, Gabriel spends a half hour jotting down ideas about punk rock, using the cubing method, and comes up with the following information.

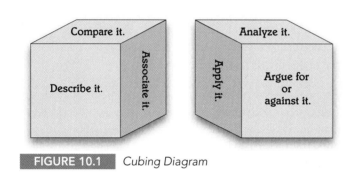

FIGURE 10.1   *Cubing Diagram*

Topic: Punk

Describe It	Compare It	Associate It	Analyze It	Apply It	Argue For or Against It
Fast	Hip-hop	My encounter with woman on street and her avoidance of me because of the way I looked	Stereotypes	Leads to peace	Against Nazis, white power
Harsh	Rap		Types: street punk, crust punk, anarcho punk, Celtic punk	Diversity	For racial diversity,
Mohawks	Heavy metal			Equality	Food not Bombs
Chains	Ska			Unity	Freedom of speech
Spikes	Nazi			Being yourself	No censorship
Blue hair	Skinheads			Standards = rejection of conformity	Don't like politics, don't like ideals, don't want someone's dream—just let me live my life; that's a controversy
Ripping scales	Punk versus poser	Beginnings of punk			
Swastikas	Anarchist	People react with disgust and fear			
Safety pins	Goth				
Body mutilation		NOFX			Antiestablishment
Leather		AAus-Rotten			
Tattoos					
Violence					
Freedom					

Even if you already have your mind set on a topic and feel sure of what your thesis will be, take half an hour and go through this part of the process. You might surprise yourself by finding new angles and new ways to present your information. The more you are aware of all dimensions of your topic, the more in-depth, interesting, and purposeful your essay is to your reader.

WRITING   10-1

Start generating ideas for each "side" of the cube. Dedicate at least 5 minutes of nonstop listing or writing to each dimension of your topic. Once you have completed this activity, review what you've written. Examine the relationship between ideas in different sides of the cube. Do you see any ideas developing? This activity demonstrates the true complexity of your topic. Review the information carefully and determine the points you want to use to define your topic. Don't forget that you can always change your mind.

Topic: _____

Describe It	Compare It	Associate It	Analyze It	Apply It	Argue For or Against It

TOPICS TO CONSIDER

If you're still having problems finding a topic, here are some topics that might interest you. Use cubing with these topics to understand the complexity of these ideas. Then you can determine how best to define your topic and organize your essay.

Writing for College		
■ The definition of poverty in the United States ■ The meaning of existentialism	■ The definition of DNA ■ The meaning of magical realism or minimalism as literary styles	■ The definition of a polynomial

	Writing in Your Profession	
BUSINESS	■ Cost-benefit analysis ■ Bankruptcy	■ Depreciation ■ Embezzlement
CRIMINAL JUSTICE	■ Probation ■ Plea bargain	■ Reasonable doubt ■ Appeals process
EDUCATION	■ Charter school ■ Speech therapy	■ Writing across the curriculum ■ Exit tests
HEALTH	■ A disease ■ Any health profession	■ A health insurance plan ■ Euthanasia
SOCIAL WORK/ PSYCHOLOGY	■ Abnormal behavior ■ Anger management	■ Phobia ■ Peer pressure
TECHNICAL	■ Computer virus ■ Arc welding	■ Machining ■ A hybrid car
OTHERS	■ Self-control ■ Ambition	■ Cult ■ Reggae music

Writing in Everyday Life		
■ Procrastination ■ Long-term goal	■ Ideal career ■ Ideal life partner	■ Faith

Identifying Your Audience and Establishing Your Purpose

As you've discovered previously, audience and purpose are closely related concepts. Examine several definition topics in terms of their audience and purpose.

■ Imagine that you just finished a unit in physics about Einstein's theory of relativity. You are confident that you understand the theory well and could explain it to another student in the class who is struggling with the concept. You decide that the best way to test your own comprehension of the theory and to prepare for the upcoming physics test is to write an essay defining the theory of relativity to a class of eighth graders. Your purpose, then, is twofold:

■ To establish and review your own knowledge of the topic
■ To ensure that eighth-grade students are helped by reading your definition, forcing yourself to be basic, concrete, and visual in your essay

- Imagine that you have a child or relative with attention deficit disorder. You have watched firsthand the symptoms, challenges, and treatment of this condition. Your purpose might be to educate someone else who is in a similar situation to make sure that this person understands the condition and has some ideas for dealing with it.
- If you have been poor at some time and want those who may never have experienced poverty to empathize with those who have, then your definition of poverty might be personal and powerful. You could use the senses so that your reader could feel the poverty—the cold, the hunger, the pain, the rawness.

Warning: If you choose a personal topic, be sure that it has an audience beyond yourself. For example, if you write a definition of your relationship with your girlfriend or boyfriend, be sure that you have something to say to others in a relationship, rather than just recounting your own and leaving the reader to wonder, "Who cares? So what?"

Now that you have a good idea of your topic and some tentative points to start your definition, it's time to think seriously about your audience. As you do Writing 10-2, feel free to go back to any of your prewriting activities to remedy any concern that comes up.

Setting Your Tone

Sensitivity to your audience requires that you pay attention to tone. In definition, you often find yourself arguing with others about the "true" meaning of particular words. Gabriel's essay about punk culture is a good example; it's easy to imagine the parents of teenagers disagreeing strongly with Gabriel, especially if their children have been harmed in any way as a result of involvement with punk culture. Similarly, words that carry political or philosophical "baggage" have to be handled with care. Be careful not to offend a reader who might potentially learn something from your definition by writing from a slanted, or biased, position. Be objective, reasonable, and informative when you are writing about controversial ideas.

WRITING 10-2

Use the following form to identify and analyze your audience, purpose, and tone.

Audience, Purpose, and Tone Analysis

Topic: _____

I. Audience

1. Who is your audience? _____

    Age(s): _____ Gender(s): _____ Education level(s): _____

3. Why would this audience be interested in your topic? _____
    _____

4. What does your audience already know about your topic? _____
    _____

5. What background information does your audience need to understand the topic?
    _____

6. How do you expect your audience read your essay—critically or for entertainment?

_____

II. Purpose

1. Why did you choose this topic? _____

_____

2. What is the controlling, or main, idea of your essay? _____

_____

3. What effect do you want your essay to have on your audience? _____

_____

4. What information must you provide to achieve the desired effect? _____

_____

III. Tone

1. What is your personal attitude about this topic? _____

_____

2. What tone do you wish to establish for this essay? _____

_____

3. How does your tone help you relate to your audience and support your purpose?

_____

Formulating Your Thesis

Once you have a topic that you are enthusiastic about defining, start working on a possible thesis. One approach is to use the formal definition of your topic as the thesis of your essay. Another is to provide a formal definition just before the thesis; in this case, you might state the formal definition as a way of reminding the reader of the commonly accepted understanding of your topic and then present a thesis that introduces a new perspective on that definition. Yet another approach is to leave out the formal definition (for topics whose literal definitions are commonly known) and focus on other aspects of your topic to provide your reader a fuller understanding.

General Category	Specific Characteristics
[An effective manager]	[motivates, inspires, and provides a sense of cohesiveness to employees.]

Especially for personal topics, you may be defining your own perspective on the topic, which another reader may disagree with. Your task is to clarify your outlook on the topic.

FORMAL DEFINITION:	Tattooing is the process of injecting ink into skin to create pictures.
THESIS:	Tattooing is body art meant to express feelings, beliefs, and/or personal history.

Gabriel comes up with the following tentative thesis:

> Punk is more than music; it's a way of life. It promotes unity, equality, and world peace, yet it is associated with violence and negativity.

WRITING 10-3

Write a tentative thesis for your definition essay. Don't forget that nothing is final. You can always come back to rephrase or refocus your thesis.

Tentative thesis: _____

_____

Outlining Your Ideas

As you prepare to outline your essay, consider the most appropriate pattern for organizing your information. Also, consider the patterns that you might use within your paragraphs. Don't limit yourself. As you explore all possibilities, keep your audience and purpose in mind. What information should you present to achieve your purpose? Review the following summary of the tools at your disposal:

- Description (describe your favorite tattoos)
- Narration (tell a story that generated a tattoo)
- Process (explain how tattoos are done)
- Comparison or contrast (contrast tattoos to body piercings or two types of tattoos)
- Classification (group tattoos—romantic, patriotic, group affiliations, and so on)
- Illustration or examples (list different tattoo designs)
- Cause/effect (provide reasons people get tattoos and/or results or effects of showing off tattoos)
- Negation (explain what tattoos are not ugly, scarring disfigurements of the skin)

WRITING 10-4

Prepare your outline for your topic. After you have completed your outline, review it carefully. Is each point of the definition distinct from the others, without overlap? Do you plan to incorporate a variety of patterns to make your essay stronger and interesting? Surely, your essay will include plenty of examples, but what else can you offer your reader? See where you can spice up your essay further.

Essay Outline

Topic: _____

Audience: _____

Purpose: _____

Tentative thesis statement: _____

_____

I. Introduction

   A. Lead-in strategies

      1. _____

      2. _____

   B. Thesis and map _____

II.   Body paragraphs

    A. Point #1: _____

        1. _____

        2. _____

        3. _____

        4. _____

    B. Point #2: _____

        1. _____

        2. _____

        3. _____

        4. _____

    C. Point #3: _____

        1. _____

        2. _____

        3. _____

        4. _____

    D. Point #4: _____

        1. _____

        2. _____

        3. _____

        4. _____

    E. Point #5: _____

        1. _____

        2. _____

        3. _____

        4. _____

III. Conclusion: Strategies you can use to wrap up your essay

    A. _____

    B. _____

    C. _____

Drafting

As you begin writing your essay, keep in mind that you may want to begin with the one-sentence dictionary definition of the term and then experiment with various methods of defining and explaining your topic, based on your audience and viewpoint. If you reach a dead end with writing about causes, for instance, or you don't find that process analysis applies to your topic, then try another method of development, such as examples or effects.

Writing Your Introduction

In previous chapters, you have been given a variety of strategies for beginning your essays, from vivid contrast, anecdote, humor, and rhetorical questions to historical detail and brief description. Especially with definition, you may want to start by exploring several meanings of a word or term before narrowing the topic to the focus of your essay. Be warned, however, to avoid the overused opening, "According to *Webster's*. . . ." Also, avoid the phrases *is where* and *is when,* for example, "*Patriotism* is when. . . ."

Examine Gabriel's first attempt at his introduction.

> Punk rock is a loud, fast, and offensive style of rock music. For decades, punk has been looked upon as a rebellious and delinquent influence on kids. With spiked hair and colored Mohawks, clad with leather, chains, and safety pins, punk rockers look intimidating. If people only got to know these rockers, they would see that Punk is more than music; it's a way of life. It promotes unity, equality, and world peace, yet it is associated with violence and negativity.

Gabriel begins with an unappealing definition of the music to deal with its stereotype before he moves on to his positive, inspiring definition, which sets up the body paragraphs. Through his use of vivid description, he gets his reader's attention. However, his introduction lacks development, and his thesis at the end fails to say anything definite or unique about his topic. His interesting start doesn't seem to connect with his thesis.

WRITING 10-5

On a separate sheet of paper, write a tentative introduction. Combine the different techniques you have practiced throughout the text. This introduction is tentative; you can revise it or change it completely if you wish. Don't forget to include your thesis. Without the thesis, your introduction goes nowhere.

Which techniques did you use? _____

Writing Your Body Paragraphs

As you compose your body paragraphs, be sure to use your outline to guide your writing. Keep the following points in mind:

1. **Try as many types of development as possible, even if some don't seem to apply to your topic.** For example, compare or contrast your topic to events, feelings, people, or ideas with which your reader may be familiar. Remember that you may use more than one type of pattern of development in a body paragraph if appropriate (comparison and narrative, for instance).

2. **Be sure that each topic sentence refers to a quality or characteristic of the topic.** Each topic sentence should further your definition, not discuss what your reader already knows or what you have already covered.

3. **Get rid of false notions by using negation.** You'll be surprised how much clearer your definition becomes when it is free of misunderstandings.

4. **Keep your purpose at the forefront of the essay.** Are you dispelling a misconception or introducing your reader to a new yet important concept? Are you providing your own personal definition of a commonly used word or phrase?

Examine a body paragraph from Gabriel's first draft.

> Punk spreads the message of unity through mixed venues and all-ages shows. Bands from all over the world with varieties of styles and ethnicities get together to entertain and educate crowds of all ages and all walks of life. They bring forth a sense of social communion that is otherwise lacking in the world. The different styles of artists and entertainment attract many types of people with one common interest—music. In my days as a promoter, I rounded up local bands ranging from female pop music, to thrash, to punk, and even grindcore. I also brought bands from Denver, Colorado Springs, and New Mexico as well as my own, and we had our own outdoor fest at a friend's junkyard.

Note that Gabriel has the main points that he wants to make in the paragraph— unity through geography, ethnicity, and age. However, as readers, we want examples of countries represented, ethnic groups, and diverse styles of music to convince us that punk rock is a unifying force. Gabriel also promises in the topic sentence that all ages are involved, yet in the examples, age groups are not mentioned. It's not uncommon that we are so familiar with and so connected to our topic that we forget our audience.

Coherence: Using Transitions

Transitions for definition essays are less obvious and mechanical than those for the process or comparison or contrast essays. You should use the transitions appropriate for the method of development that you choose to help you define your topic.

W R I T I N G   10-6

On a separate piece of paper, start drafting your essay.

1. Start each body paragraph with a quality or type of development or statement of negation.

2. Develop each body paragraph as completely as possible, constantly checking the topic sentence to be sure that you are fulfilling its promise.

3. Add transitions so that the definition isn't jumping from one idea to the next.

Writing Your Conclusion

Your conclusion is your final impression on your audience, and it should bring closure to your definition. Look at Gabriel's conclusion.

> Punk has become more accepted these days. Everywhere I go, I see punk-looking people. I'm willing to bet that most of these people are not punk or don't know what punk is, but it shows the impression that it has left on society.

Does Gabriel's conclusion point out the main qualities of punk rock that make it a positive force in society? Does it leave the reader feeling as if understanding punk rock is worth the effort? Does it dispel some stereotypes of punk rock? In sum, does Gabriel accomplish his purpose? Clearly, Gabriel needs to review his conclusion carefully.

WRITING   10-7

Write a tentative conclusion for your essay. Don't forget that you can use the same techniques in your conclusion that you used for your introduction. Just as your introduction is the first impression your reader has of you, the writer, your conclusion is the final impression. How do you want your reader to remember you?

Revising

As you approach the revising stage of the writing process, don't lose sight of two of the most important elements in writing: your audience and your purpose. Enjoy writing your essay. If you're not enjoying it, why would your reader enjoy it?

Style Tip: Use Parallel Constructions Correctly

In math, if two lines are parallel, they are the exact length and spacing from each other. In other words, they match each other visually. In the same way, in writing, if words, phrases, or sentences are connected in a list of two or more items, then they should look alike or be presented in the same structure.

    INCORRECT: I enjoy a number of outdoor activities, including <u>mountain biking, hiking, fishing, and rollerblading.</u>

Note that the list of activities is all nouns. Problems occur when the writer lists items of different grammatical types.

    CORRECT: I enjoy a number of outdoor activities, including <u>mountain biking, hiking, fishing, and I also like to rollerblade.</u>

> **Bridging Knowledge**
>
> **See Chapter 21** for additional information and practice with parallelism.

In this case, the writer inserts a clause into a list of nouns, creating a problem in parallelism.

WRITING

My essay seems too mechanical.

1. Did you vary the types of support? For example, did you use comparison, contrast, illustration, process, and so on?

2. If you did vary the types of support, are they appropriate and effective? Ask someone to read one or two paragraphs that you feel are weak. Ask your reviewer what is confusing or troublesome; then revise these areas.

WRITING

My essay just doesn't seem engaging.

1. Did you choose a topic that you are interested in? If it's boring to you, it will be boring to your reader. Consider a new topic. If it's not the topic, then consider a new angle. Go back to your cubing exercise and see what other ideas you listed.

2. Review your writing style. Make sure you show variation in your sentence structure.

3. Examine your word choice. Use vivid verbs, an appropriate level of formality, and appropriate diction, especially nonoffensive language.

DEFINITION

My definition seems stale and predictable.

1. Did you choose the best points to define your topic? Review your points. Are they fresh, unique, and important? Tell your readers something they don't already know.

2. Don't get preachy or moralize to your reader. When defining such topics as faith, marriage, and family, it's easy to impose your values on your audience. What does your audience gain from your writing?

3. Avoid turning your essay into a self-help essay. You cannot solve a complex problem in a short essay, nor does your reader expect you to.

COHERENCE

The body of my essay seems to be in "chunks" of information that aren't connected smoothly.

1. When you move from one method of development to another within the body of your essay, make sure your transitions are strong enough to signal the switch from one method to another.

2. As you write your sentences, make sure that each sentence flows smoothly from one idea to the next. Use a combination of transitional words or phrases, repetition of key ideas, and pronouns to tie your sentences together.

WRITING 10-8

Start your revision. Don't leave any part of your essay untouched. As you revise, address the following questions.

- Does the essay have a strong purpose and a clear audience?
- Are the body paragraphs organized for the audience and the flow of the essay?
- Are there sufficient transitions so that the information is easy to follow?
- Does the conclusion sum up the definition and reinforce the essay's purpose?

Collaborative Critical Thinking

Asking Your Peers

Once you have completed the writing process and have a polished final draft, exchange papers with a classmate for peer review, using these questions to guide your review.

1. Who is the writer? Who is the peer reviewer?

2. Read through the essay once and then write a definition of the topic in your own words from what you gleaned from the essay.

3. What was the clearest, easiest-to-understand section of the essay?

4. What section of the essay is more challenging to read? Provide specific suggestions for improvement (add an example, reorder the information, add transitions, change wording in certain sentences, add a topic sentence, and so on)

5. Underline the thesis statement. Suggest any changes to make it fit the essay more effectively.

6. Evaluate the introduction. Does it provide interest, give necessary background information to the topic, and lead smoothly into the thesis?

7. What methods of development did the writer use to expand on the definition? What other methods could be used to clarify the definition?

8. Evaluate the conclusion. Does it sum up the topic well and give the reader a sense of the usefulness of the information in the essay?

9. Provide at least three specific suggestions for improving the essay.

WRITING YOUR DEFINITION ESSAY

Proofreading

During the proofreading stage, you need to look for the major errors we have identified in previous chapters, but you should also learn to spot hard-to-miss errors such as mistakes in the use of punctuation. One of the most common misuses of punctuation has to do with the apostrophe.

Common Error # 11: Missing or Misplaced Apostrophes

One of the most annoying errors, to your teachers if not to you, is the misuse of apostrophes. The apostrophe has two uses:

1. To signal possession with nouns.

    CORRECT: This is John's notebook. [singular]

    CORRECT: The students' notebooks are on the bus. [plural]

Note: Possessive pronouns do not use the apostrophe:

    CORRECT: The book is a beautiful example of the art of binding. Its cover is made of embossed leather.

2. To signal a contraction.

    CORRECT: It's sitting on the desk, so it can't be in the closet.
    [*It's* is a contraction of *It is. Can't* is a contraction of *cannot.*]

Problems occur when the writer omits the apostrophe or puts it in the wrong place.

    INCORRECT: This is Johns notebook.

    OR

    INCORRECT: This is Johns' notebook.

Using "s" without the apostrophe indicates a plural noun, not possession. Placing the apostrophe after the "s" indicates plural possession.

GRAMMAR CHECKUP 10-1

Examine each sentence carefully. Underline words that misuse or omit the apostrophe. On the line provided, write the correct form of the words.

1. The <u>parents</u> objections took the form of a massive sit-in in the school parking lot. __parents'__

2. <u>Its</u> a bird! <u>Its</u> a plane! <u>Its</u> Superman! __It's__

3. The plane took off from <u>it's</u> home base in New Mexico. __its__

4. The <u>cars</u> headlight needs to be replaced before dusk. __car's__

5. They <u>dont</u> have the foggiest idea what to do about <u>Marys'</u> low algebra grade. __don't/Mary's__

Check your answers to this Grammar Checkup in Appendix A on page A-4. How did you do? If you missed even one of these items, you may need to review apostrophes in Chapter 27.

WRITING 10-9

Start proofreading your own essay. Check for and correct any grammatical errors. Look for other obvious errors in spelling, punctuation, and so on.

Final Checklist

1. Does your introduction have an appropriate and effective lead-in? ☐

2. Does the thesis statement provide a brief definition of the topic? ☐

3. Does each paragraph have an appropriate topic sentence that clearly identifies a characteristic or quality of the topic or illustrates what the topic is not? ☐

4. Do the supporting details make use of a range of types of development? ☐

5. Does the essay contain appropriate, varied, and smooth transitions between paragraphs and sentences? ☐

6. Does your essay have varied sentence structures, complete sentences (no fragments, comma splices, or fused sentences), and insignificant errors in spelling, usage, and punctuation? ☐

Reflecting

Once you have received your feedback from either your peers or your instructor, incorporate as many of your reviewers' suggestions as needed to help polish your final draft. Then, as you prepare to hand in your paper, begin reflecting on your writing process.

WRITING 10-10

Self-Reflection

Before you hand in your paper, write a brief paragraph in which you reflect on your final draft. Include your feelings on the following questions:

1. What peer suggestions do you find most useful? What should you change to address the suggestions?

2. What are you most proud of in this essay?

3. What is the weakest aspect of the essay?

4. What types of comments or feedback on this essay do you think would be most helpful to your writing progress?

5. What should you do differently as you write the next essay?

After you have completed this self-reflection, carefully review your instructor's comments. How are they similar or different from your own answers to the self-reflection? Make a list of your grammar, punctuation, and spelling errors so that you can follow up on the ones that recur. Consider what strategies you will employ to address your challenges or weaknesses and to improve the quality of your essay.

How might you use definition outside of this English course? Look back at the writing samples in Previewing Your Task in this chapter.

- **College:** _____

- **Your profession:** _____

- **Everyday life:** _____

CHAPTER 11

Developing Your Essay through Argumentation

YOUR GOALS

Understanding Argument

1. Use effective organizational patterns to support your arguments.

2. Support your position with sufficient evidence.

3. Respond to opposing arguments effectively.

4. Use logic to argue convincingly.

5. Eliminate logical fallacies.

Writing Your Argumentative Essay

1. Write a thesis appropriate for an argument essay

2. Write relevant, logical, and convincing supports to prove your thesis.

3. Use a variety of appeals.

4. Establish common ground with your audience.

5. Use research to support your argument (optional).

"In science the credit goes to the man who convinces the world, not to the man to whom the idea first occurs."

▪ **Charles Darwin** ▪

In your biology class, you are assigned to defend Charles Darwin's theory of evolution, using Darwin's own words and those of other renowned scientists. Having been brought up to believe in the literal truth of the biblical creation story, you are skeptical about being able to do justice to Darwin's theory, but you keep an open mind and present his arguments.

As the director of computer services at a local high school, you must present the reasons the computer usage policy must become more restrictive for faculty, students, and staff. You expect resistance to the new rules, such as no game playing or personal e-mails on state-owned computers, but you must try to convince employees that these restrictions are for the greater good and protection of the school.

You live in a suburban neighborhood that lacks adequate recreational venues for teenagers. You hope to convince your neighborhood association and your city council that it is worth investing in a skate park on a vacant piece of land in your area. As you prepare your list of reasons for both organizations, you try to think of negatives, as well as positives, to be ready to address any objections to the proposal.

Arguments are all around us. They are part of our daily conversation, and they are part of our inner conflicts: Should I invest my money? Should I continue to pursue a specific career? Should I start a family? Whom should I vote for in this election year? To resolve these dilemmas, we weigh both sides of the issue and consider all evidence.

LET's warm up!

How many times have you questioned a requirement to take a certain course as part of your degree program? You want to be a dental assistant or an architect and don't see why you should have to take two semesters of English. With a fellow student, identify your respective majors and career goals and make a brief list of the reasons for and against the English requirement.

ImageSource/Image Source

PREVIEWING YOUR TASK

Many people think of the term *argument* as having to do with out-of-control emotions, shouting matches, and longstanding hard feelings. However, true argument is one of the highest forms of the writer's, or speaker's, craft. Higher education has always focused on teaching students how to persuade others and how to be open minded enough to agree that opponents can be right now and then. But argument is just as important in other areas of life. The following selections demonstrate how argument can be used in college, the workplace, and everyday life.

Writing for College

In the following essay, written for an English class, Anne, a student concerned about the latest fad, tattooing, makes an appeal to her peers to support regulating the tattoo industry.

Tattooing: When the Ink Gets Under Your Skin

Tattooing has become a fashionable way to permanently mark the body. This process involves puncturing small holes in the top layer of the skin and inject-ing pigment through them into the lower dermal skin layer. Because the pigment is injected into the dermal layer rather than the epidermis (the top layer that is constantly being replaced), tattoos are permanent and often last a lifetime with little fading or distortion.

In the last 10 years, tattooing has become popular. Even a casual observation at a public place such as the local mall confirms that tattoos are now as com-mon as certain kinds of jeans or jewelry. Fortunately, most people who get tattoos experience few problems, but tragically, recent news stories indicate that HIV and hepatitis B have been linked to improper tattooing procedures. It is crucial that the government take steps to help prevent such consequences by regulating the tattoo industry. In doing so, we can control the composition of the pigment used in the tattooing process, ensure that tattoo artists are properly trained in the process, and prevent the diseases now associated with tattoos.

First, regulation will control the composition of the pigments used in the tattooing process. The Food and Drug Administration (FDA), which regulates all types of additives, including those in food, cosmetic, and drugs, does not regulate the pigments used for tattooing, according to my informal survey of local tattoo artists. In fact, the FDA has not approved the use of any color additives for tat-tooing. Although tattoo businesses fail to see the need for setting such standards, the possibility exists that harmful chemicals are present in tattoo pigments. For decades, the medical field has publicized the harmful effects of lead, and as a result, many manufacturers have removed it from their products, including paint and gasoline. Yet we hear little mentioned of the role played by the tattoo industry in protecting consumers. Properly regulating these pigments will promote the tat-too business as consumer conscious and may result in an increase in profits.

Regulation will also help set standards for training tattoo artists, thus protect-ing the customer and public. No doubt, most tattoo artists are conscientious and do indeed practice safe tattooing procedures. However, the fact remains that improp-erly trained artists can unknowingly cause the possibility of many different health problems to their customers, which can spread to the public if infectious. Under the current system, we can't be sure that all tattoo artists adhere to safe practices. Customers have observed poorly trained tattoo artists licking the needles, using the same gloves for more than one customer or not using gloves, and even pricking their hands to check the sharpness of the needles. However, a training process would set standards for the proper use and sterilization of equipment, as well as provide guidelines for a clean work area. All doctors and nurses, who are responsible for giving injections, are required to undergo a formal and stringent training period before they are permitted to practice, so why should tattoo artists, who poke the skin multiple times, be any different?

Pointing to the thousands of people who have tattoos, opponents of regulation argue that few customers have any health problems resulting from tattooing and that, therefore, regulation is not necessary. However, recent news reports from around the country indicate something different. They demonstrate that health problems associated with tattooing include the transmission of many communicable diseases, such as HIV, hepatitis C, and tuberculosis. One of my own acquaintances was recently diagnosed with hepatitis C, and her doctors believe the most likely cause was the series of tattoos she had done on her lower back over the last 2 years.

Most likely, tattooing will continue to enjoy its popularity for years to come. Therefore, people who make the decision to get tattoos should feel safe with the procedure. Regulating this industry might at first seem unnecessary, but it will promote better health for everyone: the customer, the artists, and the public. Shouldn't our health be everyone's concern?

PRACTICE 11-1

1. After reading this essay, do you have a different opinion of tattooing than you did before? Why or why not? _Discussion might focus on how the argument contributes to the formation or alteration of opinion._

2. Do the body paragraphs adequately support the topic sentences? Could the author have added any additional information that might have helped her case? _Generally, the argument is well supported, but students might know of vivid personal stories that could add an emotional appeal to this argument._

Writing in Your Profession

Argument is one of the most common modes of discourse in the workplace. This doesn't mean you will always be crafting formal written arguments to address workplace concerns, but it does mean that many of the interactions you have—with coworkers, supervisors, or customers—take the form of having to convince someone that you are right about some debatable topic. Take a look at the following memo, which happens to be presented in terms of formal argument.

From: Matthew Barnes, VP for Support Services
To: Mary McCaffery, President
Date: June 7, 2008

Subject: Expansion into La Veta

Mary,

For the past several months, we've been debating the possibility of expanding into La Veta as part of our southern Colorado growth strategy. As you know, this subject is beginning to drain much of the energy we need to devote to other matters. It is time to recognize that our management team will probably never reach consensus on expansion; nonetheless, we can no longer postpone action. We think that despite a shaky bottom line in the near term, the La Veta expansion is necessary to preserve our long-term fiscal health.

Mark claims that the La Veta population is too small to support more than one building supply store at this time. I grant that only one hardware store has survived the years in La Veta, but it is now too outdated to support the needs of the local construction industry. We find that many custom home builders are ordering from Pueblo or even farther north to get the specialized materials and supplies they need for the niche market growing up around La Veta. A new Holmes Industries store not only would meet the needs of the current population but also would lower custom building costs and thus stimulate further development in the mountain areas surrounding the town.

Second, John and Mark believe the investment is too risky at this time given the regional downturn in the housing industry. Nothing could be further from the truth. We have encountered this same situation before—in the Woodlands community project, for instance, before you came on board. In that case, the regional picture also looked grim, but a number of factors combined to make the Woodlands project blossom— the right clientele, banks that were willing to go the extra mile, and the opening of our store in the right place at the right time. It was a risk, but look how it paid off!

Finally, John claims we are in danger of overextending our internal capacity to support an expansion project. On this point I agree completely. If we try to expand into La Veta without opening an additional warehouse and budgeting office, it will prove too great a burden. That's why I'm proposing that we split the SoCo warehouse between our Pueblo and La Veta operations for now. This will involve extending the footprint of the building by one third, but it avoids the costs of new construction. The La Veta budget staff could work in the west end of the building where Martha has her office now. When the new store is ready to become a hub of further growth, we can talk about new office space.

Mary, now is the time. Let's commit to this expansion and get it done before the end of the year. We might see slow returns for a couple of years, but when the industry takes off again, we will be in a good position to reap the rewards.

PRACTICE 11-2

1. Is the evidence in each paragraph adequate to convince the audience and to support the purpose? Explain your answers. In the third paragraph, the reader might reasonably ask for more evidence that the Woodlands project and the proposed project are similar cases.

2. Since this is an argument, what do you think of the fourth paragraph, in which the author agrees with his opponents? Does this paragraph work for or against the argument? It works for the argument by marking the author as reasonable and objective. Also, he uses the concession as a springboard for a proposal that enables his overall plan.

Writing in Everyday Life

Family members argue all the time. Whether successfully or not, they try to convince one another to change or accept a certain behavior or decision. The following letter from a daughter to her mom makes such an attempt.

Dear Mom,

Thanks for having me over last weekend to continue our discussion. I think we are close to an understanding, but I'm still a bit discouraged by your response. Even though you didn't come right out and say it, you let me know just how you feel. I know how much you want me to be an independent adult, living on my own. I'm working toward this goal but need to move home for a while. It seems that Dad and Sheila welcome the idea, but I have to convince you. So here goes.

First, you still need a lot of help around the house, and you know me: housework is my favorite pastime. Dad and Sheila are such slobs, and you spend a lot of time cleaning up after them that you could be using for something more interesting. What about that drawing class you always talk about? Take it! Let me keep house! I might even be able to teach Dad and Sis to pick up after themselves for a change.

Second, since I got my new job, I can help with the budget. I won't be paying $850 a month to rent an apartment, so I'd be glad to give half that amount to you and Dad as rent. I could also buy my own food or give you a percentage toward your grocery bill. If I do contribute in these ways, I could still save close to $600 every month so that I can start college in the fall of next year. Since your house is close to my job, I could walk to work and save the gas money, which is killing me right now.

Third, I don't have a boyfriend anymore, and furthermore, I don't want one for a long time to come. You won't have to worry about my relationships this year. As I told you this weekend, I need to get serious about my future and get ready to go to school.

Despite these huge advantages, I know you'll say the same old thing: "Lisa, you're 34. When are you going to settle down on your own and stop moving back home? This is the sixth time in 10 years." The point, Mom, is that this time I'm preparing for the future. I think I'm finally growing up and realizing what it takes. This will be the last time—I promise. Just think: When I go off to college, Sheila will be a high school graduate, and we can go to school together. You and Dad will finally be empty nesters. Won't that be fun? Please give it some more thought, Mom. How can you say no?

Love,

Lisa

PRACTICE 11-3

1. What are Lisa's main strategies to convince her mother? The offer of help and the promise of a different future.

2. How effective is her letter? What might she add to successfully convince her mother? As far as it goes, the letter is fairly effective, but in Lisa's writing situation, it may not be convincing because of her mother's past experience with the same issue. It is worth noting that sometimes we can't hope to convince all of our opponents, only those who might be willing to change their minds.

UNDERSTANDING ARGUMENT

For many instructors, the argument essay represents the "peak" of the college writing experience and is the main reason to learn the other writing techniques. Why do we consider the argument so important? Basically, there are two main reasons:

1. In our culture in general, but in academic culture especially, *argument is the way knowledge is created and spread*. In colleges and universities, teachers and students engage one another's ideas by means of oral and written argument, letting their positions be refined by willingly subjecting them to the opposing ideas of others.

2. As citizens of a democracy, we conduct our best conversations—the ones that determine policies on important issues—in the form of argument. The more you learn about the value of argument in the political context, the more you are able to fulfill your role as an educated citizen and contribute meaningfully to your community.

Too often, however, we experience argument in confrontational forms, such as when two people resort to name-calling or when, in a political debate, both sides read prepared statements instead of honestly engaging in mutual discussion. Because of this situation, we've grown squeamish and hypersensitive about participating in genuine argument. One purpose of this chapter is to make you more comfortable and skilled in argumentative contexts so that you can participate in productive dialogue with your peers and coworkers.

The Elements of Argument

Most thorough and effective arguments are based on a small set of common elements:

- **A claim (your thesis) about which reasonable people can disagree.** True argument occurs when people with goodwill, adequate knowledge, and the ability to reason happen to disagree on some issue of importance to them. Reasonable people, for instance, can disagree about the claim that elderly drivers should be relicensed annually; both sides have compelling reasons to support their position.

- **Evidence to support each of your reasons.** Reasons are considered valid partly on the basis of the evidence used to support them. In writing an argument, you are not obligated to present the other side's evidence, but you are obligated to fully support your reasons with valid and sufficient evidence.

- **A logical line of reasoning.** Argument requires careful use of reasoning techniques that lead your reader to your conclusion. At any step along the way, it is easy to get off track—to contradict yourself or to write something that might support the other side of the issue instead of your own.

- **Fair acknowledgment of the other side of the debate, including (sometimes) concession of one or two points.** As a reasonable, open-minded person, you are likely to agree with your opponents about one or more of the reasons they've advanced to support their side of the argument. When this is the case, your argument becomes stronger if you concede that your opponents are right (not about the argument as a whole, just about the element you agree with). It helps you establish common ground with your opponents, and it marks you as fair and reasonable.

- **Refutation of the other side's position.** Even though you will probably concede a point or two to your opponents, you also must show that their major arguments fail to lead to their conclusion. In addition to advancing your arguments, then, you must refute some arguments of your opposition.

Types of Claims

Basically, there are four types of claims you can make in your thesis: claims of fact, claims of cause or effect, claims of value, and claims of policy.

- **Claims of fact.** Facts are not absolute truths. People argue about them all the time. For example, most people believe it is a fact that DNA evidence is conclusive; however, lawyers constantly debate the validity of such evidence. Here are some factual questions that, when converted to claims, can be interesting, thought-provoking thesis statements:
  - Is a certain diet fad really dangerous?
  - Will an expected state budget cut really hurt families?
- **Claims of cause/effect.** Since people commonly disagree about the cause/effect of particular situations, these types of claims make perfect argumentative theses: they're based on disagreement. The reader wants to know

what really causes something or what really happens because of it. The following questions can lead to claims of cause/effect suitable for argumentative theses:

- Do smoking bans in public places reduce the incidence of lung cancer?
- Does the use of cell phones in cars increase car accidents?

■ **Claims of value.** Claims of value attempt to argue that the beliefs, behavior, customs, and traditions that we or society hold are worthwhile or undesirable. Religious, political, and moral issues are quite common in such claims. Examine the types of questions that may lead to claims of value:

- Is assisted suicide morally right?
- At what point should we curb freedom of speech?

■ **Claims of policy.** Claims of policy argue for maintaining or changing existing conditions, usually to solve a particular problem. This type of claim argues what should be done, how something should be done, and who should have the authority to do it. Here are some questions that lead to theses arguing claims of policy:

- Should the drinking age be increased?
- Should we spend less on the prison system?

Using Evidence to Support Your Position

To persuade your reader to accept your position, you need to back up your argument at every step of the way with convincing evidence (facts and details that support your point). Fortunately, you've been practicing this skill in your other writing, so you are ready to apply it to argumentation.

In an argument, you need to make sure the evidence you present meets three standards: it must be relevant, representative, and sufficient.

1. **Your body paragraphs need evidence that is *relevant.*** Suppose you want to convince your reader that your college should start an intramural handball competition. One of your reasons to support this proposal is that your college has several racquetball courts and that they are always busy. Is this relevant to your argument? It might seem to be; after all, handball and racquetball are played on similar courts using the same basic set of rules. However, it also assumes that people who play racquetball are ready and willing to switch to handball. If this assumption turns out to be wrong, your argument is weakened. Keep in mind that you have to *prove* the relevance of your evidence. In this case, you could survey the users of the racquetball court; if they indicate a willingness to participate in handball tournaments, you've made the connection that proves the relevance of your point.

2. **The evidence you present must be *representative.*** That is, it must fairly represent the range of possible opinions and data. Sticking with the handball example, suppose you decide to conduct random interviews with three groups on campus: administrators, students, and faculty. Your results turn out to be disappointing to you: 90% of administrators are opposed, 82% of students are in favor, and 60% of

faculty members indicate they are indifferent. You decide to include the 82% result but not the other two. In this case, you are not presenting a sampling of all of the available evidence. Again, this doesn't mean you can't use the data from your survey, but you need to prove that the relevant part of it is the student response, not the other two.

3. **The evidence you present must be *sufficient* to convince your reader that your reasons are valid.** A single piece of evidence, unless it is utterly convincing in itself, is rarely sufficient to convince a skeptical or hostile audience that you are correct. Therefore, you should try to gather several pieces of evidence to bolster each of your supporting arguments.

A Logical Line of Reasoning

An argument is a line of reasoning leading to a conclusion. The way you present your case to your reader not only helps your reader follow your thinking process but also helps establish your credibility as a writer. When organizing the evidence in your paragraphs, you can use two basic types of reasoning: deductive and inductive.

Deductive reasoning means to argue from general principles, which is usually a claim or proposition, to particular observations, your evidence. For instance, the law of gravity holds that objects of a certain weight dropped from a height fall to the ground. Therefore, if I drop a bowling ball from the top of the Leaning Tower of Pisa, it will fall to the ground.

In contrast, *inductive reasoning* means to argue from specific observations to more general principles. For example, every time I drop a bowling ball from the top of the Leaning Tower of Pisa, it falls to the ground. Therefore, there must be a law by which objects of a certain weight dropped from a height will fall to the ground.

In your own writing, it can be difficult to distinguish between deductive and inductive reasoning, especially since most of the time you probably begin your supporting paragraphs with a general topic sentence. However, *a general topic sentence can be the opening of either a deductive or an inductive paragraph.* Look at a couple of examples of paragraphs in outline form.

> **Thesis:** Voters should be demanding that our national leaders make global warming their number one priority.
>
> A. **Topic sentence A:** The evidence is mounting that global warming is causing radical changes to our coastal ecosystems.
>   1. Areas on the east coast of the United States are losing shoreline at higher rates than ever before.
>   2. Water temperatures in coastal estuaries are rising measurably each year.
>   3. Close-in fishing industries are closing shop as fish begin disappearing from our waters.

Paragraph A is inductive: the writer bases the general topic sentence on the evidence scientists have gathered previously.

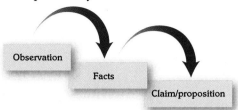

B. **Topic sentence B:** Once our ocean waters reach a certain average temperature, the effects will be drastic and irreversible.
   1. Many of the largest coastal cities will be inundated, causing massive migrations to other parts of the country.
   2. Weather patterns will change in ways we don't yet understand.
   3. New diseases will begin to affect large segments of the population.

Paragraph B is deductive: on the basis of a general principle about rising water temperature, specific effects are predicted. (They haven't happened yet, so they couldn't serve as evidence, could they?)

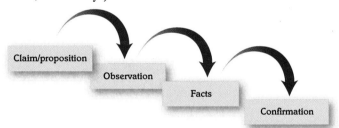

PRACTICE 11-4

Pick one of the following topics. Then show how you would develop two paragraphs to support it, one using deductive and the other using inductive reasoning. You don't need to write the paragraphs; simply outline them and be ready to share your ideas with the rest of the class. Answers will vary.

Topic A: Smoking bans should not include bars and nightclubs. (**Hint:** One paragraph might begin with a statement about the principle of individual rights of business owners. The other might begin, "Evidence is mounting to demonstrate that smoking bans are driving many bars and restaurants out of business." The first paragraph is deductive; what kinds of points would you add to support it? The second is inductive; what kind of evidence could you use to support it?)

Topic B: Graduates of high school should be required to participate in mandatory community service for 1 year before being admitted to college.

Eliminating Common Fallacies in Logic

If an argument is a line of reasoning leading to a conclusion, then the kinds of things that can go wrong in an argument must have to do with the reasoning itself. When your reasons depart from accepted rules of argument, you are committing an error known as a *logical fallacy*. On the positive side, one of the best ways to refute an opposing argument is to show that it fails to support its conclusion.

Most logical fallacies, especially in student writing, are not deliberate. But listen to political ads during election time and you can hear lots of deliberate fallacies designed to mislead you into voting one way or another. Examine a few of the most common fallacies in student arguments.

1. **The red herring.** This phrase comes from the practice of dragging a dead fish across one's trail so that those who are in pursuit, and who have a good sense of smell, will be thrown off track. This fallacy is an attempt to throw your reader off track. Red herrings come in a number of guises; some of them should sound familiar.

   WHY IS THIS STATEMENT A FALLACY?   South High School must adopt an open-campus policy during lunch because all other schools in town have it.

   This is an example of the *bandwagon appeal*, or the "everybody's doing it" argument. Even if South High were the only school in the state with a closed-campus policy, this is no reason to adopt an open one.

   WHY IS THIS STATEMENT A FALLACY?   If South High School doesn't adopt an open-campus policy during lunch, students will stop doing their homework and their performance on the state assessment test will suffer drastically.

   This is called *predicting a false consequence*, or a highly unlikely one, and it's not just because most of the students don't do their homework anyway. Rather, the writer simply has no basis for making this claim.

   WHY IS THIS STATEMENT A FALLACY?   South High School's lunchtime restrictions are reminiscent of Hitler's regime in the 1930s.

   In this case, it is clear that South High's closed-campus policy can in no way be compared with the true horrors of Hitler's reign. This type of comparison is called *false analogy*.

   WHY IS THIS STATEMENT A FALLACY?   Mr. Tompkins apparently believes that even honors students are incapable of taking care of themselves off campus for 45 minutes.

   This is a case of the *straw man* fallacy. In the straw man, the arguer takes the flimsiest, weakest opposition reason just to have something easy to attack. In this case, Mr. Tompkins would probably never make the claim that honors students were incapable of appropriate behavior.

2. **The black or white fallacy.** This is also called the *either/or fallacy*, and it is one of the most common fallacies encountered. It usually takes the form of a statement that "the only alternative to X is Y," except that the statement is false.

   - The only alternative to the death penalty is rampant murder.
   - You've heard the reasons for restricting driving privileges of people over 75.
   - Now is the time to act. If we don't, the alternative is streets and roads overrun by confused baby boomers who don't know which way to turn.

3. **The ad hominem fallacy.** This fallacy occurs when you attack the character of your opponent. Most likely, your attack against the person's character has nothing to do with the issue.

   - Mr. Tompkins has always shown himself to be an uncaring principal—unless the subject is the football team.
   - Those who believe in capital punishment are no better than the murderers they wish to execute.

4. **Hasty generalization.** This common fallacy occurs when you make a large claim on the basis of a small sample, too small a sample to support the claim.

   - My nephew went off to college last year. All he does is skateboard during the day and party at night, yet he has a B average. Clearly, grade inflation is ruining our colleges and universities.
   - Based on a survey I conducted of my classmates in my English class, it is obvious that the requirement to take English should be abolished.

PRACTICE 11-5

Identify the type of logical fallacy illustrated in each of the following statements. Explain your answer. Answers will vary.

1. Legalizing marijuana will result in higher rates of addiction to harder drugs like heroin and cocaine. Predicting a false consequence—there's no evidence.

2. No wonder my opponents want to pass such a vague piece of legislation as Amendment 41—they're all lawyers! Ad hominem attack on the opposition since the term *lawyer* has so many negative connotations.

3. Why shouldn't we authorize casino gambling in the city? Half the towns between here and Nevada have adopted casino gambling. Bandwagon appeal or "everybody's doing it" fallacy.

4. Do we want to allow prayer in schools, or do we want to preserve the freedoms granted to us by the founding fathers? "Either/or" fallacy. The author offers no evidence that allowing prayer in schools will erode our freedoms.

5. In approving the local smoking ban last November, our city council proved itself no better than Hitler. False analogy. Only someone completely unaware of history could make such a claim.

6. Mr. Alvarez's support for the new recreation center is based on his notion that money grows on trees. <u>Straw man fallacy. The author attributes an idea to</u> <u>Mr. Alvarez that Mr. Alvarez may not ascribe to.</u>

7. Based on my "man-on-the-street" survey of 10 students between classes, it is clear that the majority of the student body couldn't care less about whether we have a rap or a metal band at the Spring Fling. <u>Hasty generalization based on</u> <u>incomplete information. A "man-on-the-street" survey is rarely scientific.</u>

Concession of Opposing Arguments

One of the most characteristic features of argument writing is the way it fairly and objectively represents the opposition. When you write an argument, you don't need to fully represent the opposition (that's their job), but you do need to indicate to your reader that you take your opposition seriously and that you have considered its major arguments. If you ignore your opposition or unfairly represent its position, you cause your own argument to fail. Here are the ways you may respond to your opposition:

■ **Acknowledgement.** To acknowledge your opposition is simply to state its main points and its supporting reasons. The following paragraph states the major points of the opposition. Notice that it is the simple statement of these points that gives the needed acknowledgement of the other side.

My opponents believe a parking garage would destroy the architectural unity of our campus. They also claim that it would cost too much and that we should use the money to build further learning center space. Furthermore, they seek to prove that even with a parking garage students will still fight for spaces on the street and in the existing lots simply because these spaces are closer. Finally, they argue that parking garages are inherently unsafe, resulting not only in increased accident rates but also in more assaults and attempted rapes.

■ **Concession (optional).** *Concession,* also known as *accommodation,* means to admit that your opposition has a good point now and then. Concession is realistic, reasonable, and fair in the real world of conflicting ideas. It also has another advantage: it identifies you, the writer of your own argument, as realistic, reasonable, and fair. By acknowledging other opinions beyond your own, you show your reader that you are well informed on the issues and open minded about it. Your reader is more likely to read your essay if you acknowledge other views rather than just insist on your own reasons. Often, the balance of an argument depends on tipping the weight to one side of the scale or the other rather than obvious right and wrong ways of thinking. When your reader sees that you are trying to understand and appreciate the values and ideas of your opposition, your own argument becomes more believable. Here's an example of concession.

I admit that the parking garage will cost a lot of money and that we have long needed a bigger learning center to accommodate our growing enrollment. In this case, my opponents have succeeded in identifying a major project that we must find a way to fund.

Refutation

It might be optional to concede one or more of your opponents' points, but the one thing you must do in an argument is refute your opponents' major arguments; that is, you must show that your opponents' argument is weak in some way. For example, you might point out that the opponents' evidence is incorrect or exaggerated or show how your opponent is not seeing the entire issue. If you do not address and dispel opposing points, your reader is just as likely to accept your opponents' arguments as your own. Notice that in the following selection, the writer refutes the either/or argument of the opposition.

However, the fact is that we need both projects if we are to move forward in serving students. One approach we could take is to divide the available money between the two projects, beginning both of them now, and then use next year's project capital budget to finish both projects. It doesn't have to be one or the other.

Patterns for Organizing an Argument

Although most thorough arguments contain many of the same elements, these elements can be arranged in different ways depending on your topic, your opponent's major reasons, your audience, and other aspects of your writing situation. Look at the three major patterns for organizing an argument.

Pattern A, shown in Figure 11.1, is probably the most commonly used method for organizing an argument. It is sometimes referred to as the *classic pattern*. In this pattern you first present your case and then refute the most valid points of the opposition.

The next pattern is the reverse of pattern A, as shown in Figure 11.2. In this pattern, you first address your opponents' views and then present your side. One advantage of this pattern is that it permits you to deal with your opponents' arguments first so that you can focus on your own defense, leaving the reader with your points as the final impression. Another is that it reassures your opponents that you are familiar with their objections.

The third pattern, shown in Figure 11.3, focuses on opposing views. By refuting the opposition's strongest points, you make your own argument in defense of your thesis at the same time.

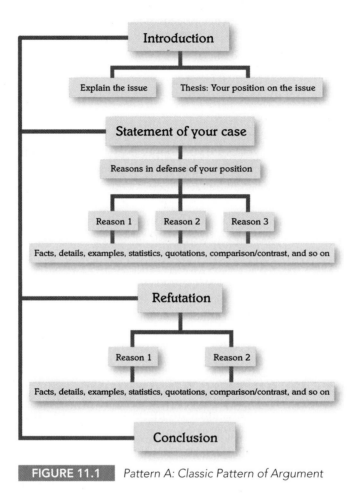

Pattern A: Classic Pattern of Argument

Consider combining the patterns to organize your argument effectively. For example, you can present each pro point followed by a con. It's your essay, so feel free to present your information in the way that best fits your topic and audience.

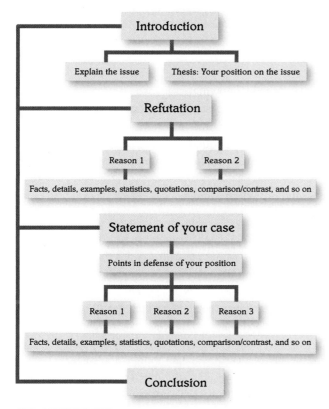

FIGURE 11.2 *Pattern B: Refute-then-Defend Pattern*

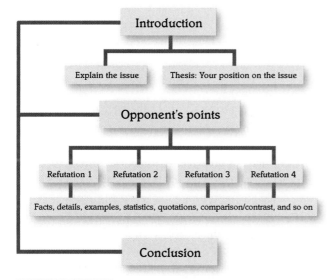

FIGURE 11.3 *Pattern C: Opposing Views Pattern*

WRITING YOUR ARGUMENTATIVE ESSAY

Kent, a student majoring in social work, wrote the following essay for a political science class. This essay contains references to Kent's research sources in Modern Language Association (MLA) style. You will learn about research in Chapter 13 and 14, but we present this essay here to demonstrate that research is often necessary to build an effective argument. Your instructor may or may not ask you to do research for your first argument essay.

The Sound of Falling Money

Cripple Creek, Colorado, was once a quiet mountain town with wooden plank sidewalks, a saddle shop, a couple of bars, and a popular general store where people would stop in on their way through town to someplace else. Today, it's the principle destination of thousands in our state who don't have the time or money to fly to Las Vegas or Reno. The low-key, charming ambience has disappeared, replaced by glitter, neon, and the jingle of falling coins. Some people, for whom gambling is the seed of all evil, lament the passing of the former era; the vast majority, however, for whom gambling is a form of recreation and, at least subconsciously, even the ultimate chance at a better tomorrow, believe we should have more Cripple Creeks around the country—a slot machine within easy reach at all times.

Gambling has long been part of our nation. Our Revolutionary War armies were funded by the original type of gambling—lotteries. As time passed, gambling took different forms, many of them illegal, or completely faded away in some communities. In the 1920s our nation was introduced to legalized horse and dog races, and in 1931 the state of Nevada changed the southwest forever by allowing casinos to open legally. Soon, states across America started reopening lotteries to help fund state projects. In 1987, the Supreme Court allowed Indian tribes to open casinos on their reservations to help combat harsh living conditions. In 1989, America's Mississippi River valley introduced riverboats that gamblers could get on and wager just as if they were in Las Vegas ("Gambling").

One fact is certain: gambling is controversial wherever it is found. Supporters claim that it is harmless and fun and that it brings wealth to communities; opponents claim that it is addictive and ruinous. Although gambling does carry with it some problems, the benefits far outweigh them, and it is time that we recognize those benefits. With its enormous direct impact on state revenues, the new jobs the industry brings, and the draw for tourism, we should no longer be arguing about this issue.

Since the late 1990s, most states in the union have been forced to make drastic budget cuts, and they've been prevented from raising taxes by their poorly performing economies. Everyone realizes why we have taxes, but we all hate it when they are raised. But what if there were an alternative way to generate revenue? Legalized gambling offers a solution: it can generate enormous revenue for individual states. By replacing tax initiatives with legalized gambling, states would allow citizens to keep more of their money in the expectation that they would go out and gamble. If current trends continue, this expectation is completely realistic: gambling has taken over as America's favorite pastime by leaps and bounds ("Gambling"). In fact, 82% of all adult Americans gamble in one form or another (Vatz and Weinberg). Gambling could help fund public schools, pay for road improvement projects, or cover the increasing costs of caring for the elderly. Without gambling revenues, these and other needed projects will go begging as they have in the past decade.

In addition to direct revenues that gambling would produce for each state, we need to consider the creation of jobs in local communities. The gambling industry produces an enormous number of jobs. In 1987, the government ruled that Indian tribes could open casinos on reservations to help combat the poverty and unemployment levels. Today, more than 120 Indian casinos are in operation in 28 states ("Gambling"). Just think about the jobs new gambling facilities would produce. First, the casinos or racetracks would need to be built, thus creating construction jobs. Then the facilities would need to be operated and managed, necessitating upper-level management positions, gaming positions, maintenance positions, and so on. Mandalay Resort Group President Glenn Schaeffer put it best when he said casino jobs "are not fast-food jobs" but "jobs you can grow in and support a family on" (qtd. in Smith).

Another benefit of legalized gambling is an increase in tourism. With states putting their residents to work creating spectacular new gambling industries, people from other states would rush in to spend money, thus expanding tourism. Imagine a Las Vegas or Atlantic City in every state, each with its own character and a special offering for the recreational gambler who likes to travel. With more tourism, everyone benefits, from local communities to the state budget.

Even with all the benefits gambling would bring states, adversaries of gambling complain about the so-called pathological or compulsive gamblers. Opponents of gambling tell stories about how it leads to bankruptcy, which in turn leads individuals into a life of crime to pay for their debts and then eventually to suicide because they just can't handle the pressure anymore ("Gambling"). The federal government was so worried about these issues in 1999 that it formed a group called the National Gambling Impact Study Commission (NGISC) with the mission to investigate whether gambling was having a negative effect on society. The NGISC determined through a telephone survey that only 1.4% of gamblers were compulsive gamblers (Vatz and Weinberg). This number is quite low, much lower than even most gamblers would have predicted. However, recognizing that compulsive gambling concerns many, every gaming plan should offer programs, funded from gambling revenues, to help those who appear to be harming themselves through gambling.

Anytime a proposed idea involves gambling, the word *crime* is not far behind. Gambling opponents are quick to point out that Las Vegas did not get its "Sin City" nickname for gambling alone. In the 1880s, the prevalence of unsound money practices caused all state lotteries to be terminated ("Gambling"). Today, big gambling towns are associated with the mob, "fixed" sporting events, and the sex and drug trades. It should be obvious, however, that these associations are the result of the long history of illegal gambling in our country. When gambling is made legal everywhere, crime will cease to be part of its aura over time. If we legalize gambling, it should be easier for police departments to focus their energies on truly criminal activities.

Free people in a free country should be free to gamble—for the vast majority of gamblers, it is a harmless recreational activity. However, if legalization is haphazard or poorly planned and regulated, we will continue to lose out on the many public benefits gambling offers. It is time for states across the United States to take a coordinated look at legalization: they need the revenues to support important public projects, their communities need the tourism dollars that gambling can bring, and their citizens need the high-paying jobs. Let's take a bold step: legalize gambling so that we can all enjoy the winnings.

Works Cited

"Gambling." <u>Enotes.</u> 2004. 5 July 2004 <http://www.enotes.com/gambling/>.

Smith, Rod. "Casino Proliferation as Key Is Consensus at Global Expo in
    Las Vegas." <u>Las Vegas Review-Journal</u> 18 Sept. 2003. <u>Newspaper Source.</u>
    EBSCOhost. Pueblo Community Coll. Lib., Pueblo, CO. 5 July 2004
    <http://search.epnet.com>.

Vatz, Richard E., and Lee S. Weinberg. "Gambling, Psychology and State Politics."
    <u>USA Today Magazine</u> May 2003. <u>Academic Search Premier.</u> EBSCOhost. Pue-
    blo Community Coll. Lib., Pueblo, CO. 5 July 2004 <http://search.epnet.com>.

This argument demonstrates a number of strengths: it employs a variety of writing techniques—cause/effect analysis (common in arguments), as well as description and illustration; it provides plenty of evidence to back up its more general assertions; and it uses transitional devices expertly to connect part of the argument.

Prewriting

To maximize the effectiveness of your prewriting experience, use as many techniques as you can to give you the best results. Whenever you can't think of additional or interesting information, stop to use another prewriting technique that you feel would be useful.

Discovering and Limiting Your Topic: Combination of Techniques

You may want to start using listing to generate ideas for your claim. To help increase the variety of possible topics, try a more focused listing by dividing your paper into four areas, dedicating each area to a type of claim. Here's how Kent filled out his brainstorming chart.

Claims of Fact	Claims of Cause/Effect
The true state of climate change is . . .	Effects of global warming on the west.
The Iraq war has helped stability in the Middle East.	Causes of obesity among the young.

Women are underpaid.	Causes of workplace stress.
Schools have dumbed down education.	Effects of sleep deprivation over time.
Claims of Value	**Claims of Policy**
Our media culture is a good thing.	Attendance policies should be stricter.
The book is still the best way to learn.	Gambling should be legalized.
Digital literacy is an important skill.	Marijuana should be legalized.
Parenting skills are undervalued.	No speed limits should be set on interstate highways.
Mentoring is the best volunteer activity.	Lottery funds should go to education.

Kent identified the following claims during his initial prewriting activity.

1. Schools have dumbed down education.
2. Parenting skills are undervalued.
3. Gambling should be legalized.

WRITING 11-1

Fill in as many claims as possible, spending 5–10 minutes on each type of claim. If you get stuck, ask friends and family members for ideas.

Claims of Fact

_____

_____

_____

Claims of Cause/Effect

_____

_____

_____

Claims of Value

_____

_____

_____

Claims of Policy

_____

_____

_____

After you have generated a good list of possible issues and claims, circle the three you feel most interested in and most connected to. Don't worry about making the wrong choice; you can always come back to this list should you change your mind.

Now that you have identified possible issues and claims to write about, use freewriting, looping, clustering, branching, diagramming, or a combination of these to generate ideas, recall knowledge you have about your topic, identify arguments for both sides of the issue, and predict what information you may have to research to prove your claim. If you get stuck or lose interest, go on to your next claim and start generating ideas.

TOPICS TO CONSIDER

If you're experiencing writer's block, review the following list of topics. If you choose from this list, be sure to make a claim so that you can create your thesis.

Writing for College		
■ U.S. involvement in another country ■ Censorship of the arts	■ A national DNA databank ■ Immigration reforms	■ Media's effect on elections ■ Racial profiling

Writing in Your Profession			
BUSINESS	■ Mandatory overtime ■ Surveillance of employees	■ Pay based on performance	■ Mandatory drug testing
CRIMINAL JUSTICE	■ Plea bargaining ■ TV in courts	■ Education for prisoners	■ Early-release programs
EDUCATION	■ School uniforms ■ Scholarships based on ethnicity	■ Drug testing in school	■ Metal detectors in public schools
HEALTH	■ National health insurance ■ Smoking banned from all public places	■ Physician-assisted suicide	■ Mandatory immunizations
SOCIAL WORK/ PSYCHOLOGY	■ Mentally handicapped tried for murder	■ Gay marriages or adoptions ■ Use of drugs to treat depression	■ Welfare policies and practices
TECHNICAL	■ Internet regulation, taxation, or censorship ■ V-chip curbing children's viewing of television violence	■ Downloading of intellectual property, music, and videos	■ Outsourcing of computer technician jobs
OTHERS	■ Hate crime laws ■ A helmet law	■ Opening of the borders to immigrants	■ Lowering of the legal age for drinking

Writing in Everyday Life		
■ A letter to your congressman encouraging support of a certain issue	■ A letter to the editor protesting a change in a city ordinance	■ A letter to a family member arguing for more equitable distribution of a relative's legacy

Identifying Your Audience

For the argumentative essay, you might start by classifying the audiences into four general types; each type requires a personal approach, as seen in Figure 11.4. An important aspect of crafting an effective argument is to consider the ways that you can connect with your audience. Of course, evidence combined with reasoning is your main tool for convincing your reader of the strength of your argument, but appeals to character and emotion can also be powerful when used effectively.

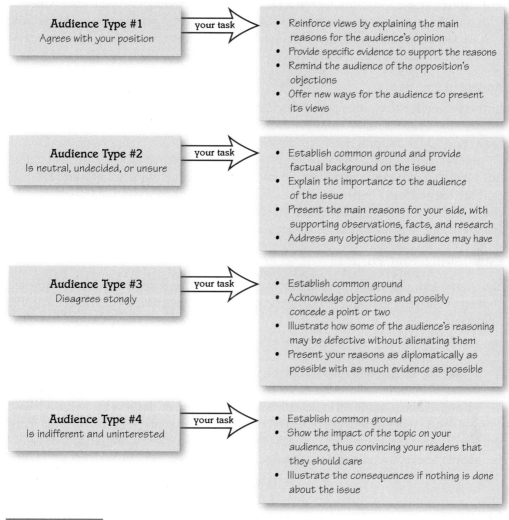

Audience Type #1
Agrees with your position

your task

- Reinforce views by explaining the main reasons for the audience's opinion
- Provide specific evidence to support the reasons
- Remind the audience of the opposition's objections
- Offer new ways for the audience to present its views

Audience Type #2
Is neutral, undecided, or unsure

your task

- Establish common ground and provide factual background on the issue
- Explain the importance to the audience of the issue
- Present the main reasons for your side, with supporting observations, facts, and research
- Address any objections the audience may have

Audience Type #3
Disagrees stongly

your task

- Establish common ground
- Acknowledge objections and possibly concede a point or two
- Illustrate how some of the audience's reasoning may be defective without alienating them
- Present your reasons as diplomatically as possible with as much evidence as possible

Audience Type #4
Is indifferent and uninterested

your task

- Establish common ground
- Show the impact of the topic on your audience, thus convincing your readers that they should care
- Illustrate the consequences if nothing is done about the issue

FIGURE 11.4 *Audience Types in Argumentation*

Appeal to Character

When you appeal to character, you show yourself to be a writer and thinker who is fair minded, objective, thoughtful, and caring about a topic. You establish your credibility with the following:

1. **Language.** Avoid overly emotional or inflammatory language. Don't call the hostile parents *ignorant* and *stupid*. Instead, discuss them as people who need to be made aware of their inappropriate behavior.

2. **Addressing objections to your side.** Avoid just dismissing your opposition's objections—such as the difficulties of policing parents—as unimportant. Instead, take them seriously, concede a point if necessary, and reassure your reader that you have thought carefully about the opposition's concerns.

WRITING YOUR ARGUMENTATIVE ESSAY

3. **Tone.** Tone ties in with your use of language. Be sure to adopt a conciliatory, under-standing tone so that your reader is willing to keep reading and considering your side.
4. **Style.** Tone and style go hand in hand. Use formal diction to maintain an educated tone and use variety in sentence length so that the essay flows smoothly.

Appeal to Emotion

An overly emotional argument alienates an educated, analytical audience and detracts from the logic of your paper. However, some emotion can enhance your argument if you use it sparingly and appropriately.

By dramatizing an idea or situation, especially in the introduction or conclusion, you can move your idea from a mere abstraction to a level of concreteness that your reader can both see and feel. This is one area where your skills for description and narration come in handy. An effective argument should depend primarily on logic (reasoning and evidence), but you may appeal to character and emotion at appropriate times.

Establishing Your Purpose

Your purpose in argument, more so than in other types of writing, depends on the whole context of the writing situation. The elements of the writing context consist mainly of the following:

- The writer's thoughts, beliefs, and concerns
- The reader's thoughts, beliefs, and concerns
- The situation in which the writing is presented
- The content of the argument

All of these factors add up to the purpose of the argument, and it is the writer's job to connect these elements into a coherent whole. As you plan your essay, keep in mind that the more in depth your analysis is of each of these elements, the more confident you will feel about the effectiveness and of the success of your paper.

WRITING 11-2

Look at your writing context and answer the following questions.

Your claim: _____

You the Writer

1. Why is this topic important to you? Why does it interest you? _____

_____

2. On a scale of 1–10, how strongly do you feel about your claim? _____

3. Do you already have assumptions or opinions about the topic you plan to research? _____

_____

4. What is your attitude or opinion about this topic? _____

_____

5. How much do you already know about this topic? _____

_____

6. Do you know your reader personally? _____

7. What do you and your reader have in common? _____

_____

Your Reader

1. What audience (person or group) would benefit most from your writing? _____

_____

2. How agreeable is your audience to your claim? Is your audience against it?

_____

3. What would your reader gain from your essay? _____

_____

4. What previous knowledge does the audience have of your topic? _____

_____

5. What information does your audience need? _____

_____

Your Writing Situation

1. Is this topic related to another class, a particular project, a strongly held personal belief, or something else? _____

_____

2. What format, requirements, or constraints must you observe? _____

_____

Your Content

1. What kind of sources do you need to consult? _____

_____

2. What information do you need first? _____

_____

3. What kind of source is likely to supply it? _____

4. Review your answers and reflect on your writing context. At this point, what
strategies do you feel can help make your essay effective: illustration, process,
classification, cause/effect, comparison/contrast, definition? _____

_____

5. What pattern should you use to organize your essay? _____

Your Purpose

What effect do you want your essay to have on your audience? _____

_____

Setting Your Tone

Once you have chosen an audience, you must keep that audience in mind as you are crafting your sentences so as not to alienate, insult, or offend them. One method of connecting with your audience is to choose your words carefully; a second way is to establish common ground.

- **Use appropriate language.** Although you most likely feel passionate and emotional about your topic, don't let your word choice reflect such emotions as anger, impatience, or intolerance. Don't risk alienating your audience and losing your own credibility as a reasonable thinker. Instead, use tactful, courteous language.
- **Establish common ground.** Most argument topics have reasons with which most people can agree. For example, if you are discussing whether the death penalty should be allowed, you could certainly mention that we all value human life. If the topic is whether a specific class should be a requirement, couldn't we all agree that we value knowledge and education?

Formulating Your Thesis

Your thesis, also known as your claim or proposition, should have the following characteristics:

1. **Your thesis should express your opinion.** Not all opinions make good argumentative topics. For example, the statements "This is the best spaghetti sauce this side of the Mississippi" or "After 50 years of rock n' roll, Elvis is still my favorite performer" are definitely opinions; however, they would not be suitable as an argumentative thesis.

2. **Your thesis should be debatable.** If you can't imagine someone disagreeing with your claim, you have no argument. Which of the following statements would make a good thesis?
   - Building more prisons is the best way to deal with our growing prison population.
   - The prison population continues to increase annually.

   If you chose the first statement, you're correct. A large audience would disagree with this claim. Your opponents may well argue that we should, instead, reduce the penalties for victimless crimes to create prison space for major felony convictions. The point is that such statements create disagreement and can, therefore, engage the reader in a debate. The second example is a simple statement of fact requiring no proof; therefore, there is no issue to debate.

3. **Your thesis should be focused.** As you are deciding on a topic, be careful that you don't take on too broad of a topic, not allowing you to convince your reader of anything. For example, a popular topic for argument is whether or not children should have to wear uniforms to school. To focus the topic, ask yourself the following questions:
   - What age group could I concentrate on?
   - What location or types of schools could be discussed—urban, suburban, rural?
   - To whom should I write this argument?

4. **Your thesis should include three main parts:**
   - The topic
   - The claim (opinion)
   - The reasons to support your opinion

Examine the following thesis statements.

- Children of illegal immigrants should be provided with basic human services such as health care and schooling so that they don't miss out on important aspects of their development.
- The arts should be required as core classes K–12 because they help students develop self-esteem, thinking and listening skills, discipline, and coordination.

Armed with a good claim and a good awareness of the writing context, you can confidently write your thesis. Don't forget the equation:

Thesis = Topic/Issue + Claim/Position + Focus (Reason for Claim)

Here is how Kent phrased his thesis initially.

> Gambling's destructive and addictive side is not sufficient reason to keep gambling illegal; gambling should be legalized in every state in the Union.

As you can see from Kent's working thesis, your thesis doesn't need to be perfect at this stage. If you are bothered by his beginning with the negative "destructive and addictive behavior," you are correct because this phrase actually works against his claim in the minds of some readers. As Kent drafts and revises his essay, he has plenty of opportunities to polish his thesis statement. But for now, he has a debatable issue, a claim that he feels strongly about, and a focus.

WRITING 11-3

Take a few minutes to review your analysis of your own writing context, as well as some ideas you generated from your prewriting activities, and then write your thesis here.

Working thesis: _____

_____

Outlining Your Ideas

Before you start your outline, create a list of arguments on both sides of your topic. Such a list is called a *pro/con list* because it lists arguments in favor of your thesis (pro) and arguments against your thesis (con). Draw arrows from the argument in the Pro column to its matching argument in the Con column. If there's no match, leave it alone.

This can help you determine how you can best organize the information in your outline. For example, you can use the points that match in the refutation section of your paper: you argue against them to prove your claim. If all points match, you might consider using pattern C to organize your essay (see page 313). However, if you have stand-alone points, you may want to handle those separately, in which case, perhaps pattern A or B may be your choice. Examine Kent's pro/con list.

Topic: Legalized gambling
Thesis: Every state should legalize gambling.

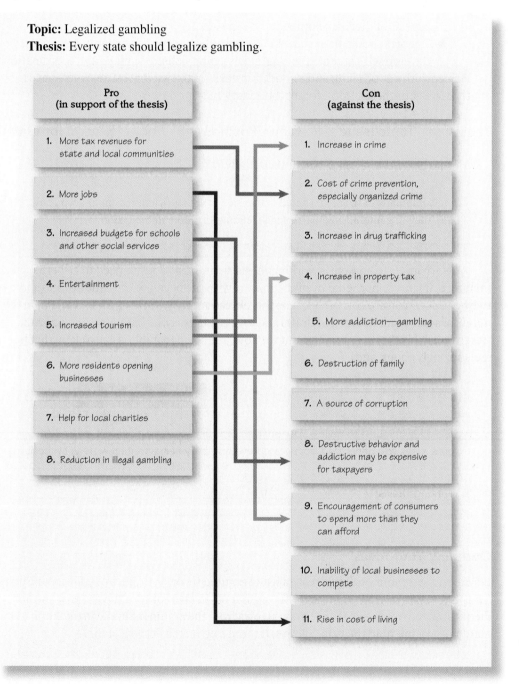

Pro (in support of the thesis)	Con (against the thesis)
1. More tax revenues for state and local communities	1. Increase in crime
2. More jobs	2. Cost of crime prevention, especially organized crime
3. Increased budgets for schools and other social services	3. Increase in drug trafficking
4. Entertainment	4. Increase in property tax
5. Increased tourism	5. More addiction—gambling
6. More residents opening businesses	6. Destruction of family
7. Help for local charities	7. A source of corruption
8. Reduction in illegal gambling	8. Destructive behavior and addiction may be expensive for taxpayers
	9. Encouragement of consumers to spend more than they can afford
	10. Inability of local businesses to compete
	11. Rise in cost of living

Creating a pro/con list is a good way of testing whether you have sufficient evidence to argue your case, at the same time permitting you to anticipate opposing arguments. If during this activity you discover a better focus for your thesis, don't hesitate to change it; it's not uncommon for students to change their position after considering all evidence. There's nothing wrong with this. Such are the rewards of critical thinking.

You should feel ready to create your own pro/con list on your issue. See how many valid points you can come up with on both sides of the issue, not just on your own. Feel free to talk to others who can give you good arguments. First ask them how they feel about the issue, and then ask why. You'll be surprised what you can learn from others.

WRITING 11-4

List as many arguments as you can think of on both sides of your topic. Then use arrows to match the points that can be matched.

Thesis: _____

Pro	Con
1.	1.
2.	2.
3.	3.
4.	4.
5.	5.

WRITING 11-5

What pattern do you feel would work best for your audience, purpose, and writing situation? Refresh your memory of the patterns on pages 312-313. Choose the outline that works best for you and write it down on a separate piece of paper. As you write your outline, don't assume that each point takes only one paragraph to discuss. This may not be the case. If you need to use more than one paragraph to discuss a particular topic sentence, make sure that your transitions establish the relationship between or among those paragraphs. Let your reader know that you're still proving the same point. Also, the number of points you want to include in your argument is up to you. Although it's unlikely that one or two points would be sufficient evidence (unless the evidence is indisputable and convincing), always consider your audience, purpose, and writing situation when determining the content of your paper.

Drafting

As you enter the drafting stage of the writing process, keep in mind the parts of the argumentative essay shown in Figure 11.5.

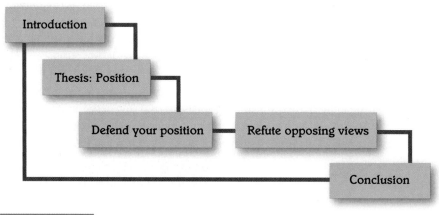

FIGURE 11.5   *Parts of the Argumentative Essay*

Writing Your Introduction

In your introduction, you want to grab the reader's attention, establish your credibility and authority, and provide background information on the issue.

In addition to other lead-in techniques, you should supply some background on the topic so that your reader understands the basics. Don't assume that your reader fully understands the topic or shares your level of knowledge before you start supporting a particular stance. As you define the issue, be as objective as possible. Don't argue in your introduction; save your argument for the body of your paper. Your goal in the introduction is to introduce your thesis, not to defend your position.

Examine Kent's first draft of his introduction and his working thesis.

> Gambling is a practice that dates back to the start of our nation. Our Revolutionary War armies were funded by the original type of gambling, lotteries ("Gambling"). As time passed, gambling evolved and at times faded away. In the '20s our nation was introduced to horse and dog races; then in 1931 the state of Nevada would change the southwest forever by allowing casinos to open. Soon states all across America started reopening lotteries to help fund state projects. In 1987 the Supreme Court allowed Native American tribes to open casinos on their reservations to help combat harsh living conditions. In 1989, America's Mississippi River valley introduced riverboats that gamblers could get on and wager just as if they were in Las Vegas ("Gambling"). Gambling's destructive and addictive side is not sufficient reason to keep gambling illegal; gambling should be legalized in every state in the Union. With the enormous amount of new revenue for states, all the new jobs the industry brings, the draw for tourism, and simply because we live in a free nation and gambling is fun, this shouldn't even be an issue. Every state should legalize and expand its gambling practices.

Kent's introduction is basically a brief history of gambling. This may be important, but Kent fails to establish its importance to the thesis. His working thesis definitely limits and focuses the issue, but there is little connection to the history that Kent offers to introduce the thesis. By limiting his lead-in to just the history, Kent seems to imply that his only argument is that "gambling has always been and will continue to be, so get over it." It is not likely that many readers would be interested in reading further.

Start writing your introduction for your argumentative essay by completing the next activity. Don't forget that you can always come back to it and revise it anytime which is exactly what Kent did with his introduction.

WRITING 11-6

On a separate sheet of paper, start drafting your introduction. As you create the draft, consider the following qualities:

1. Your introduction should engage your reader, making the reader want to read more.

2. Your introduction should establish the tone of your paper and assert your character as a reasonable, critical thinker.

3. If necessary, use your introduction to build common ground.

4. Your introduction should make your topic clear and let the reader know why your topic is important.

5. Through your introduction, you should give your reader all information necessary to understand the issue, the controversy, and your position on the controversy.

6. Your introduction should contain a thesis that lets the reader know the position you are defending, gives the reader an idea of how you organize the information, and helps the reader understand the type of evidence you provide.

Writing Your Body Paragraphs

Examine these two body paragraphs from Kent's essay: the third pro from his first draft that defends his position and one con refuting a point of opposition.

Pro #3

In addition, people from other states would be rushing to gambling states to spend money, thus expanding tourism. Believe it or not, Nevada is hoping for gambling expansion itself. Since many of the slot machines are made in Nevada and since the Nevada market is mostly tapped out, state officials are hoping for some out-of-state customers. Imagine a Las Vegas in every state, each with a special offering for the recreational gambler who likes to travel. Therefore, gambling needs to be leveled across the board so that the high rollers could land anywhere and have a casino or racetrack where they can lay their money down. With more tourism, everyone benefits: local communities and Uncle Sam as well.

In this paragraph, Kent starts with a transition and a topic sentence—not a bad first attempt. He can still come back and improve his topic sentence and opening transition. He can also build on his examples and details and provide stronger evidence. The point is that Kent has the foundation of an essay when he starts to revise it.

Con #1

Even with all the great things that gambling would bring states, opponents of gambling cry out about the so-called pathological or compulsive gamblers. Antigamblers tell stories that gambling may easily lead to bankruptcy, which in turn leads individuals into a life of crime to pay for their debts, eventually ending in suicide because they just can't handle the pressure anymore. The government was so worried about it in 1999 that it put together a group called the National Gambling Impact Study Commission (NGISC). The commission was to investigate whether gambling was having a negative effect on society (Vatz and Weinberg). This is where reality sets in. For something to be addictive, it has to change the composition of your body in some way. Gambling does no such thing (Vatz and Weinberg). Life is full of "adult decisions" and gambling is one of them. If individuals gamble themselves into bankruptcy, they are not addicts; they are choosing to act recklessly (Vatz and Weinberg). But to appease the weak minded, every gaming plan should have programs put in place and money set aside from revenue to finance these programs that council and help these so-called addicts.

Kent draws heavily from his sources in this paragraph refuting the opposition's claim. He may need to rethink the value of some of his information. Does he need to go into more history? What information do you feel is irrelevant? Initially, there's never too much information. Always remember that it's easier to cut information than to add it.

Coherence: Using Transitions

In argument, you use types of transitions that we have covered in the previous writing chapters of this text. The following list of transitions focuses on two areas that help your argument flow smoothly: emphasizing key points and granting points to opposing arguments.

As you consider the most effective and appropriate transitions to connect your ideas, keep in mind that the purpose of this list is not for you to just pick the most logical ones to connect your ideas and plug them in. Your transitions must appear naturally and help your essay read smoothly. First, write your essay; then during revision, read it carefully to see what is holding your ideas together. If you feel that your paper sounds choppy, refer to this and other lists of transitions to help glue your ideas together.

Transitions to Help Emphasize Key Points

above all	in truth	there is no question that
again	main problem, issue, concern	to add to that
as a matter of fact	major point, reason, argument for	to clarify
as noted	more importantly	to emphasize
certainly	most dramatic	to repeat
chiefly	obviously	to stress
definitely	of course	to underscore
in any case	of greater concern	truly
in any event	of greater consequence	unquestionably
indeed	once again	without doubt
in effect	surely	without fail
in fact	that is	without question

Transitions to Help Grant or Concede a Point

after all	naturally	to agree
although	no doubt	to concur
although this may be true	of course	unfortunately
at the same time	to acknowledge	while it is true
granted (that)	to admit	

WRITING 11-7

Start creating the body of your first draft. Your goal is to prove your thesis. Don't forget that you can always change your mind and return to the prewriting stage. Follow these guidelines.

1. Follow your outline. Make any changes to the outline that you feel help your essay.

2. Choose the most effective pattern for organizing your argument. Consider your purpose in light of your writing context. Again, you can always change your mind. The goal now is to start.

3. Start each of your body paragraphs with a clear topic sentence. During the revising stage, you may change the position of your topic sentence, but for now, keeping it as the first sentence may keep you focused on the main point of the paragraph as you provide your supporting evidence.

4. Use appeals to character and emotions effectively.

5. Add transitions to keep your ideas flowing smoothly and to guide your audience through your information.

6. If you run out of ideas in any of your paragraphs, stop and use one or more prewriting techniques to get your creative juices flowing.

Writing Your Conclusion

In his conclusion, Kent attempts to do three things: emphasize his claim, give his essay a sense of closure by summing up his key points, and leave the reader with something to think about. He doesn't want the reader to end the essay wondering, "So what?" He wants to show that his essay is meaningful, leaves a lasting impression, and perhaps incites the reader into action. The question is how strongly and effectively does he achieve this?

> Between the enjoyment of gambling and the chance of hitting it big, free people in a free country should be free to gamble. If you take away the fact that the generated revenue would be a gigantic help to state budgets and the industry would employ countless number of people, and take away that gamers wouldn't be able to wait for their next trip to a new town to try their luck, then gambling simply adds a fun element to life. So before states start cutting money from public schools or nursing home budgets, we need to support legalized gambling.

Kent has made a bold start; you see in his final draft how he builds on his strengths during revision.

WRITING 11-8

Write a conclusion for your argumentative essay. Here are some ideas:

1. Let the reader understand the importance and significance of your topic.

2. If you choose to summarize your key points, don't just repeat the same points mechanically. You can be sure that your reader hasn't forgotten them. Instead, show how these points are vital evidence in proving your thesis.

3. Consider using an emotional appeal. But be careful not to overdo it.

4. Pose a question so that you leave your reader pondering something.

5. Emphasize the urgency of the issue by making a call for action.

6. Build on or refer to a scenario, example, description, or anecdote that may have been in your introduction. This approach not only gives cohesiveness to your essay but also lets the reader know that you have accomplished your goal.

7. Read your introduction and then your conclusion to make sure that there's a smooth connection between both.

Revising

Start the revising stage with this question: Do you feel you have accomplished your goal? Review your first draft; circle the strengths and underline the weaknesses as you perceive them. How can you build on your strengths? How should you address the weaknesses? With these questions in mind, start revising the content of your paper.

Style Tip: Use Levels of Formality

When you communicate with friends, you may rely on slang, clipped words, and even made-up words in conversation. Your use of language in this case is informal. In contrast, when you speak to an instructor, an employer, or a government official, you tend to be more formal. In writing, you also choose levels of formality based on your audience.

As you edit your argumentative essay, pay close attention to your word choice. Since the audience for an argument tends to be precise and critical, using a style that is too informal hurts your credibility as a writer. Avoid slang and colloquial expressions, and beware of words that don't convey precise meaning, such as the following:

> **Bridging Knowledge**
>
> **For more information** about levels of formality, go to Chapter 23.

awesome	great	thing
bad	incredible	well ("Well, the next effect is even more incredible.")
fantastic	nice	
good	terrible	

PROBLEM

SOLUTION

WRITING

My introduction seems dull, vague, undeveloped, and/ or not engaging. →

1. Did you analyze your writing context? Argumentative essays usually address audiences who may not be receptive to your point of view. Try building common ground in your introduction.
2. Is the background information you offered meaningful? You need to show your reader that you understand the issue, so offer background information that is relevant and that leads to the purpose of your argument.
3. Does your introduction grab the reader's attention? Once you have a clear idea of your audience, use a strategy that is most likely to interest that reader. Review the various strategies for developing your lead-in.
4. Did you establish an appropriate tone for your audience and purpose? Your reader needs to see you as a reasonable and credible writer. Don't start with a combative tone or with emotional outbursts that alienates your reader. That first impression is crucial.
5. Is your thesis clearly stated and placed in a logical position? Nothing bothers a reader more than not knowing what to expect.

WRITING

My paragraphs don't seem to be developed enough, nor does my evidence seem too convincing. What should I add?

1. Employ any technique that effectively proves your point:

   a. **Illustration.** What examples can you give to illustrate your points?

   b. **Classification.** In any of your paragraphs, can you explain your points by breaking down your idea into categories?

   c. **Comparison/contrast.** Discuss similarities, differences, or both. Compare an idea, concept, or practice to one with which your audience can easily identify. Offer a simile to connect the familiar with the unfamiliar.

   d. **Definition.** Are there any abstract or technical terms that you should define? Perhaps there's a term that you are using differently from how it's normally used.

   e. **Cause/effect.** Are there reasons, consequences (results), or both that you need to explain or clarify?

   f. **Process.** In any of your paragraphs, would it help explain how something occurred or how a situation developed?

2. Do you offer sufficient, relevant, accurate information? Make sure that you have enough evidence to prove your topic sentences and to help your reader follow your argument. If your instructor approves, conduct research.

WRITING

My conclusion is too brief and abrupt.

1. Does your conclusion effectively wrap up your process? If not, see how you can make your conclusion meaningful by stressing the importance of your thesis, referring to some point or example that you made in your introduction, or both, thus bringing your reader full circle.

2. Does your conclusion attempt to connect with the reader? Try to show how the issue can impact the reader's life, challenge the reader to be part of the solution, or urge action, or leave your reader with a profound question that lingers.

········ **PROBLEM** ·· **SOLUTION** ········

ARGUMENT

My refutation doesn't seem just right. Also, I seem to rely less on evidence and reasoning in some places and more on just stating my feelings and beliefs.

1. If appropriate, use a transitional paragraph to introduce your refutation. Review your main arguments and then end with a sentence or two that indicates you are moving to the refutation, for example, "But these points are not readily accepted. Opponents of this policy offer three main objections: X, Y, and Z."

2. Make sure that when you introduce your opponents' points your transitions and lead-ins make the distinction that these are not your arguments but your counterarguments. Without proper transitions, your reader might start a paragraph believing that you changed your position.

3. Are the points you're refuting important claims made by your opponents or just easy claims to refute? Your opponents want you to address their questions to their satisfaction; don't run away from the hard questions.

4. Do you remain focused on your opponents' issue? Check carefully for logical fallacies, especially red herrings. It's quite easy to stray from points that you don't believe in and go more into emotional appeals than into reason and logic. Get the facts. Facts are what eventually prove your case.

WRITING 11-9

Start your revision. Don't leave any part of your essay untouched.

- Be sure your evidence is relevant, representative, and sufficient.
- Be sure to respond to opposing arguments that are valid.
- Check for coherence. Make sure you offer enough transitions to help guide your reader.
- Be sure that your tone or diction doesn't alienate your reader.
- Review your paper carefully to remove any logical fallacies it may contain.
- Use a variety of sentence types to spice up your paper.

> **Collaborative Critical Thinking**
>
> ## Asking Your Peers
>
> Once you have completed the writing process and have a polished final draft, exchange papers with a classmate for peer review. Use the following form to answer questions about your peer's paper.
>
> 1. Who is the writer? Who is the peer reviewer?
> 2. Briefly describe the method or methods the writer uses to introduce the thesis. Do these methods of introduction grab your interest? Explain.
> 3. Underline the thesis statement in the essay. Is the thesis clear? Does the writer limit the topic? What is the writer's position on the topic?
> 4. Where does the writer give background information on the topic? Is the information clear and relevant?
> 5. What additional information do you feel the writer should supply in the introduction?
> 6. How does the writer support his or her views (examples, statistics, facts, testimony, and so on)? Is the support sufficient?
> 7. Which point has the least support? What might the writer add?
> 8. Is the majority of the support based on research? Is it effective?
> 9. Should the writer include more research? Is the research well integrated?
> 10. Has all information that is not the writer's personal experiences or observations been properly documented?
> 11. Does the writer refute at least two opposing views? How convincing is the refutation? Explain.
> 12. What might the writer add?
> 13. Circle any points that are illogical, confusing, or ambiguous.
> 14. Give examples of how the writer appeals to the reader (reason, ethics, emotions, and character).
> 15. Is the conclusion effective?
> 16. If you were neutral or opposed to this opinion, would you be convinced or at least have an understanding of this opinion after reading this essay? Why or why not?

Proofreading

One of the more difficult grammatical concepts to understand, much less execute correctly, is the use of commas with modifying phrases or clauses. As you continue editing for the major errors covered in this book, add the following to your grammar toolkit.

Common Error #12: Misusing Commas with Restrictive or Nonrestrictive Elements

A *restrictive element* is necessary to the meaning of a sentence. It "restricts" or limits the meaning of the noun it modifies.

> **RESTRICTIVE ELEMENT:**   The woman wearing the blue dress got up to leave.

The phrase "wearing the blue dress" is restrictive because it restricts the meaning of the sentence to one particular woman. The other women present in this case, presumably, did not get up to leave.

Do not use commas to separate restrictive elements from the rest of the sentence:

> **INCORRECT:**   The collie, sitting near the back of the cage, is the one she wants.
> **CORRECT:**   The collie sitting near the back of the cage is the one she wants.

A *nonrestrictive element* may look like a restrictive element, but it does not restrict the meaning of the sentence. It simply adds additional information; if you were to remove a nonrestrictive element, the meaning of the sentence would be the same.

> **NONRESTRICTIVE ELEMENT:**   That gentleman, who graduated with my father, has made a fortune in the car business.

Use commas to separate nonrestrictive elements from the rest of the sentence.

> **INCORRECT:**   Her son's present which had dropped from her hand was run over by a bus.
> **CORRECT:**   Her son's present, which had dropped from her hand, was run over by a bus.

To determine whether you need help with restrictive and nonrestrictive elements, do the following activity.

GRAMMAR CHECKUP 11-1

If the following sentences contain nonrestrictive elements, insert commas to separate those elements from the rest of the sentence. If the sentences only contain restrictive elements, write "No change."

1. The computer with the blue monitor is the one that no longer works. No change

2. That teacher, waving her arms wildly, needs to take a break.

3. The red package, which has been sitting in the corner for days, is too late to worry about.

4. The passenger who fell asleep is the one we need to watch carefully. No change

5. A pack of dogs, yelping and racing up the street, is causing a lot of commotion in the neighborhood.

Check your answers to this Grammar Checkup in Appendix A on page A-5. How did you do? If you missed even one of these items, you may need to review restrictive and nonrestrictive elements in Chapter 26.

WRITING 11-10

Start proofreading your own essay. Check for and correct any grammatical errors. Look for other obvious errors in spelling, punctuation, and so on.

Final Checklist

1. Does your introduction define the issue and offer essential background information? Does it lead smoothly to the thesis? ☐

2. Does the thesis assert a position on an issue that is clear and arguable? ☐

3. Is the organization of your essay effective? ☐

4. Does the essay offer sufficient evidence for each reason? Is the evidence informative and persuasive? ☐

5. Does your essay consider valid opposing arguments and offer logical responses to each counterargument or effectively concede a point? ☐

6. Is the tone, diction, or manner of expression appropriate and effective for your audience? ☐

7. Does your essay provide sufficient and effective transitional devices to guide the reader through the argument, particularly when you shift from your side to the opposition's reasoning? ☐

8. Does your paper demonstrate mastery over the basics in sentence completeness (no fragments), structure (no fused sentences or comma splices), sentence variety, and word choice? ☐

9. Did you edit carefully for possible errors in grammar, spelling, and punctuation? ☐

Reflecting

You are completing one of the most difficult writing assignments in this course: the argument. It has involved all of the skills you learned in previous chapters plus several additional ones. Take some time to reflect on what you have accomplished. Reflection can make the next argument you write a more successful experience.

Self-Reflection

Before you hand in your paper, write a brief paragraph in which you reflect on your final draft. Include your feelings on the following questions:

1. What peer suggestions do you find most useful? What should you change to address the suggestions?

2. What are you most proud of in this essay?

3. What is the weakest aspect of the essay?

4. What type of comments or feedback on this essay do you think would be most helpful to your writing progress?

5. What should you do differently as you write the next essay?

After you have completed this self-reflection, carefully review your instructor's comments. How are they similar or different from your own answers to the self-reflection? Make a list of your grammar, punctuation, and spelling errors so that you can follow up on the ones that recur. Consider what strategies you will employ to address your challenges or weaknesses and to improve the quality of your essay.

How might you use argument outside of this English course? Look back at the writing samples in Previewing Your Task in this chapter.

- **College:** _____
- **Your profession:** _____
- **Everyday life:** _____

CHAPTER 12

Making Choices: Developing an Integrated Essay

"Writing became such a process of discovery that I couldn't wait to get to work in the morning: I wanted to know what I was going to say."

■ **Sharon O'Brien** ■

YOUR GOALS

Understanding the Integrated Essay

1. Demonstrate an understanding of the choices necessary for an effective integrated essay.

2. Analyze the interrelationship among audience, purpose, and writing situation.

Writing Your Integrated Essay

1. Use visual approaches to determine topics and strategies.

2. Mix and match writing techniques creatively.

3. Revise your writing by creating various drafts to produce a more effective and polished final draft.

4. Review your draft for style, grammar, and punctuation.

5. Write an essay that demonstrates unity, coherence, and completeness.

You are assigned different papers to write for different courses, each with different expectations. Some instructors have clear guidelines; for example, your history instructor asks you to write on the consequences of a certain treaty, making your choice of strategy easier since you are given the primary pattern of development—effects. However, some instructors allow you to choose any topic relevant to the course, unit, or period. You've studied the many patterns of organizing your essay. But how do you approach your various writing tasks?

You have some ideas to make your workplace more effective. Your supervisor likes your ideas and asks you to write them up and submit them to management. Should you just list your ideas? Should you explain the events that led to your ideas? Should you recommend how your ideas can be implemented efficiently? Should you compare your plan to what is currently being done?

Your growing appreciation for writing as a way of thinking has prompted you to write regularly at home. Each evening, you sit down at the computer and work on blogs, e-mails, or discussion board posts that you write for your own enjoyment. Your writing takes many forms, combining and recombining all the techniques you have learned in your composition class. Nonetheless, each evening as you sit down to write, your first questions are "How should I begin, what's my topic today, and how will I approach it?"

BananaStock/Jupiter Images

LET's warm up!

You have already gained a lot of experience in writing essays. You are also aware that good writing is the result of careful planning and revision. Nonetheless, there's always a degree of uncertainty and at times apprehension about whether your writing is worth submitting to your instructor. Reflect for a few minutes on the essays you've written in this and other courses. Then write a paragraph in which you discuss the qualities of an effective essay. What makes an essay work?

In this chapter, we focus on the variety of choices you have as a writer and suggest ways you can sharpen your critical thinking skills by applying previous knowledge to new writing situations. This chapter follows a different pattern from previous writing chapters. Its purpose is to challenge your creative side and cause you to think in new ways about your writing.

PREVIEWING YOUR TASK

Whether you're writing for college, writing in your profession, or writing in everyday life, one fact remains: effective writing is the result of careful planning. As you plan your writing, you're faced with many choices. To highlight and illustrate the many choices you make as a writer, we preview one integrated essay whose author makes some interesting choices to achieve his purpose.

Angered and frustrated by his peers' passivity on social issues, Claude, a nontraditional student majoring in computer information systems, writes an essay on political involvement using a variety of tools to explain his thesis. After analyzing his writing context, he establishes the following audience, purpose, and effect:

> **Audience:** People who feel powerless and disenfranchised and those passive critics who don't exercise their right to vote
>
> **Purpose:** To convince my audience that each individual can make a difference
>
> **Effect:** Make my audience feel empowered, show them that they can make a difference, and, hopefully, have them take action
>
> **Approach:** I want my audience to feel that I'm one of them, and like them, I can make a difference. In a sense, I'd like to be their conscience. I also want them to see me as someone who's been there, is knowledgeable, and is now aware of his social responsibilities.

As you read Claude's essay, refer to the explanatory notes provided in the margin. Also, note the use of the following tools that you've been learning about:

- Choice of tone, style, diction, and point of view
- Combination of patterns: illustration, narrative, comparison/contrast, cause/effect, and process
- Use of analogy

$(1+1)^2$

Have you ever felt like a penny? Know what I mean—the common, ordinary everyday penny? You've seen these coins. They are everywhere, easy to find and even easier to overlook. A penny has value, but the value is not all that great. What can you buy with a penny? Not much! Lose a $100 bill and you worry until you find it. But lose a penny—who really cares? It's hardly missed.

So there you are—a common, ordinary, everyday person. You have value, and you know

Introduction
- Claude starts with rhetorical questions.
- He uses second person to engage the reader. Although his instructor prefers third person, Claude sees the benefit of using second person to achieve the desired effect.
- Claude identifies the type of audience he's trying to reach and states the thesis—"You have

it because you hear that from all kinds of speakers and read it in all kinds of books and magazines. But how much do you see yourself being worth? Like a penny, is your value unimportant in the scheme of life? If you die, how much would you be missed? The "hundred dollar" heroes and heroines who died made headlines, evoked millions of tears, and touched continents of people with their passing. But how badly would your own loss impact the world?

Look at your life through the symbol of a penny—the common, ordinary, easily overlooked, and limited-value penny. Pull two pennies out of your pocket and look at them. One of them is you; the other is just another ordinary, everyday person like yourself: it could be anyone in our world of 6 billion pennies. See a difference? One may be a little more polished, be older or younger, or show evidence of greater wear and use than the other. But the fact remains that for all practical intents and purposes, they are both similar and almost identical. Pick the one that best represents you and lay it down. Now, let me tell you about the remaining penny in your hand.

Perhaps the other penny came from a different mint (background) than did the penny representing you. Perhaps it was a common, everyday person from Atlanta, Georgia, back in 1929. Perhaps he was the son of a Baptist minister, and there was nothing to make his penny stand out from the thousands of other pennies born in that city in that year. However, this ordinary penny found himself suddenly making a world of difference in the economics of human dignity because he refused to see himself as only being worth a small amount. This penny dreamed of investing himself in a dream that exceeded the impact of the $100 bill. How do we know? This penny told us so. On August 28, 1963, this penny stood on the steps of the Lincoln Memorial in Washington, D.C., to tell 200,000 other ordinary pennies like

value"—and implies through his questions that we often underestimate our value.

- By posing more questions, Claude gets the reader to start thinking of the value of an individual.
- In both paragraphs, he compares a person to a penny, establishing the extended analogy he uses throughout the essay.

Body

- Claude starts his analogy, one which he carries from one paragraph to the next. Although most analogies when carried too far become logical fallacy—false analogy—an analogy, nonetheless, can be an effective rhetorical strategy:
  1. It grabs the reader's attention.
  2. It adds creativity to your writing.
  3. It helps the reader understand a difficult or abstract topic more easily and eagerly.
- The tone is friendly and the diction is informal. Claude realizes that to be persuasive, connect with the reader, and maintain the reader's attention, he has to make sure that the reader perceives him as a knowledgeable person, one the reader can trust.
- By using Dr. Martin Luther King Jr. as an example in the analogy, Claude has given his analogy concreteness and has strengthened his thesis—we have value; we can make a difference.

himself, "I have a dream." The *Chronicles of America* records that Dr. Martin Luther King Jr.'s speech "turned the tone of the event from a party into a crusade" (800). One ordinary penny, when joined with 200,000 others, is no "chump change."

There are those who would argue that there was nothing ordinary about Dr. King since he was a man of manifest destiny. But Dr. King began life just as we all do, endured obstacles many of us may never face, and succeeded not so much for who he was but for what he accomplished. He found the value in himself to prove that one penny can make a big difference. This fact is true of not only the father of American Civil Rights but of every other individual (penny) in human history who has made an impact on our world. In every such example, the "movers and shakers" were ordinary people with a dream, coupled with the belief that they could make a difference. The difference was not in the person but in the attitude toward personal value. There is nothing wrong with being common and ordinary; it simply proves that we are human like everyone else.

Okay, so much for the concept of being common and ordinary. We can accept that fact cheerfully. Still, it's hard to imagine our own personal value on par with that of Dr. King, Abraham Lincoln, or Bill Gates. Consider then the age-old saying:

> For the loss of a button, a uniform was lost.
> For the loss of a uniform, a soldier was lost.
> For the loss of a soldier, a battle was lost,
> And all for the loss of a button.

This simple but profound statement tells us not only that one person can make a difference but also that the loss of one ordinary soldier makes a difference. We tend to think that the sergeants and generals decide the outcome of major events when it is the effort

- Claude refutes a possible objection to his previous point. In doing so, he shows his understanding for those who hesitate to agree with him and, at the same time, illustrates his point by presenting two additional examples with which his reader may be familiar, thus making his idea vivid and concrete.
- He uses comparison to make his point that we all have a dream.
- He uses contrast to show that one quality alone differentiates his audience from historical giants.

- The use of transition is informal. Again, Claude feels that this technique is necessary to achieve his purpose. Before you attempt a style this informal, check with your instructor.

- The short verse offers the reader time to think about Claude's comparison and acts as transition to the next point.

of the common and ordinary soldier that really matters. Consider one of the $100 bills of human history, Helen Keller. The impact of this ordinary person in demonstrating the value of people with disabilities is beyond question. Stricken with blindness and deafness when she was only 19 months, at the age of 24 Ms. Keller graduated with honors from Radcliffe College. After World War II, she visited wounded veterans in U.S. hospitals to inspire them to live life beyond their own war-inflicted disabilities. During her lifetime, she authored numerous widely acclaimed books, including an autobiography. The story of Ms. Keller has inspired generations and changed our world. Indeed, if we are pennies, she must have been a $1,000 bill.

- Claude uses illustration, narrative, and effect as support.

Ms. Keller changed the world, but Anne Sullivan was the penny who changed the life of Ms. Keller. It was Ms. Sullivan who took the time to teach the young Ms. Keller to read and write. Without Ms. Sullivan, perhaps there would be no "thousand dollar" difference from Ms. Keller. When considering value and personal wealth, we may never fully understand the long-range impact or value of our participation in the process called life.

- Claude starts the paragraph with effect and uses illustration and effects as support.

This might be a stretch when we think of our own importance in the overall scheme. "I'm just one person. What difference does my effort make?" Have you ever heard someone say, "My vote doesn't count; I'm only one person"? Such erroneous thinking is easy to adopt and equally simple to disprove. The *Chronicle of America* points out that John Adams defeated Thomas Jefferson by only a 3-vote margin (71–68 electoral votes) to become our second president. In 1868, the U.S. House of Representatives voted 126 to 47 to impeach President Andrew Johnson, "one vote shy of the required two-thirds majority" (Calabresi and Yoo 757). How much difference does one vote make? It made all the difference in the world.

- Claude adds a transitional paragraph to reinforce his thesis.

- Research helps establish the writer's credibility where personal experience is lacking.

Are you feeling the power of the ordinary, everyday person yet? This is only the beginning. Take a look at the power of a penny. Looking back at the penny as a way to understand our own self-worth and potential impact on our world, we begin to apply the power of exponential value. Start with that one penny and double it tomorrow. When you go to bed tomorrow night, you will have two pennies. This amount won't buy much, but the value has doubled. Double it again the next day. In 4 days, you are now 8 cents rich! Wow!

Now plan to double your pennies every day for 2 weeks. How hard can that be? By the end of 14 days what started as just 1 ordinary cent has multiplied itself into $81.92. Now you have some buying power. See how easy it is for one penny to come close to making the $100 difference in just 2 weeks? Now apply this principle to your own life. Imagine that each day is 1 year and that each penny represents one person in your world. How hard can it be for you to find enough value in your life to touch one other life in a positive way each year? When you apply the principle of exponential value (remember how Anne Sullivan touched one life and the impact that one life had on others), in 14 years, your impact on one person can affect or influence 8,192 other lives. Clearly, you are influential!

- Again, Claude's transition is informal. Most readers may equate this as a motivational piece of writing, but how will Claude's reader react? That's the risk Claude is taking, but it should work if he did a careful analysis of his audience.
- He presents a process, and reestablishes his extended analogy of the penny to further his thesis and to maintain the unity and coherence of the essay.

Day 1	$0.01	Day 8	1.28
Day 2	0.02	Day 9	2.56
Day 3	0.04	Day 10	5.12
Day 4	0.08	Day 11	10.24
Day 5	0.16	Day 12	20.48
Day 6	0.32	Day 13	40.96
Day 7	0.64	Day 14	81.92

At this point, if the average life span lasted only 14 years, I could conclude this analogy, and you could settle for making an impact on just less than 10,000 other lives. Fortunately, our life spans generally exceed 14 years, so the exponential values continue. Go back to that penny and see what happens over another 2 weeks. Simply by starting with one penny and doubling it every day, by the end of 3 weeks, that penny will have translated its value into more than $10,000. At the end of 4 weeks, just 28 days, that one penny will make you a millionaire. Now, just how powerful and influential is that common, ordinary penny?

Day 15	$163.84	Day 22	20,971.52
Day 16	327.68	Day 23	41,943.04
Day 17	655.36	Day 24	83,886.08
Day 18	1,310.72	Day 25	167,772.16
Day 19	2,621.44	Day 26	335,544.32
Day 20	5,242.88	Day 27	671,088.64
Day 21	10,485.76	Day 28	1,342,177.28

But let's get back to real life. If that first penny is your life and each day represents 1 year in your life, imagine your own impact. If you can so influence one life every year in so positive a fashion that the influenced individual in turn passes that on to one person every year, in a 30-year span you directly and indirectly influence more than 134 million people. Now, how much value does your life hold?

- Claude brings his analogy to an end and emphasizes the point of the analogy to the importance to his thesis.

History is made, influenced, and changed for better or worse by ordinary people, people just like you and me. Sometimes the process is long, and often, like Anne Sullivan, we may never realize during our lifetime the full impact of our efforts. However, it is important to remember, regardless of how

Conclusion

- The conclusion starts by emphasizing the meaningfulness and importance of the topic and thesis of the essay.
- Claude brings up previous examples to give the essay closure and reinforce its unity.

ordinary we feel we may be or how small we estimate our personal value and worth, in the long run, each of us makes a difference. If we could carry on our exponential values for only another 4 years, 32 in all, we would find that the number of lives we have in some way touched would exceed 4 billion. That, my friend, means you have changed the whole world.

- He ends with a challenge to the reader and a call for action.

PRACTICE 12-1

1. Do you feel that Claude accomplishes his established goal? Explain. The essay's friendly tone, the use of the extended analogy, the use of examples, and the final challenge convince the readers that they can make a difference (Claude's purpose and his intended effect).

2. What is your impression of Claude's style and diction? The style and diction are informal. Such informal phrases as "so there you are," "let's get back to real life," and "Okay, so much for the concept," as well as the second person and his constant use of questions, help make the connection to his audience.

3. Claude uses a variety of techniques in his essay. What other patterns could he use? For example, how and where would classification work in this essay? Students might suggest that Claude could have explained the causes of his audience's lack of involvement, perhaps even use classification in explaining levels of passivity.

UNDERSTANDING THE INTEGRATED ESSAY

Throughout *Bridges to Better Writing*, you have applied what you've learned in previous chapters to each new situation. Progressively, you've built on each essay pattern by bridging knowledge from previous writing experiences. Your ability to incorporate the variety of writing modes not only reflects your growth as a writer but also reveals your awareness of a basic fact about writing: most writing strategies can be used to the writer's advantage in any particular essay.

Making Choices

Writing requires that you make choices, and making choices requires you to think critically and creatively about your topic. What do you want to say and why? As interesting and as unique as your idea may seem, don't merely go with the first idea that occurs to you. Carefully examine your options and possibilities. If you end up with your initial approach, that's fine, but the point is that the approach you settle on should be based on a careful analysis of your options. Your first step, then, is to explore the most appropriate and effective approach for your essay based on the most important questions you wish to answer. As you develop your topic, you will find that sentences and paragraphs can use different patterns: illustration, comparison/contrast, process, cause/effect, classification/division, and argumentation. You have many choices before you, and choosing among them can be an exciting, creative act, as you can see in Figure 12.1.

Although most short papers may employ one primary pattern with other patterns woven throughout, longer papers may have two or more primary patterns of development. For example, if you are writing a paper on the causes and effects of child abuse in the foster care system, you might, after the causal analysis, shift the primary focus of the essay to prevention, thus continuing the essay with a process analysis of what the state might do to prevent child abuse. Then you might end the essay by addressing the objections from those defending the system, shifting the focus of the essay to argumentation. Your decision to include other primary patterns depends on your purpose and audience. Your thesis makes your purpose clear to your reader. Then as you develop your essay, you may integrate other patterns into your paragraphs.

Figure 12.2 illustrates the writer's options in combining modes. Keep in mind that this is just one of many possibilities.

An essay with the plan outlined in Figure 12.2 would definitely be longer than three or four pages; therefore, if length is important to your audience, whether your instructor, your peers, or a civic or workplace audience—make length a criterion in your choice of structure and content. As you determine your approach, be creative. But above all, be effective; in a shorter essay, you may not have space to develop more than one primary method of development.

Examine the many choices you have. From this point on, to stimulate your

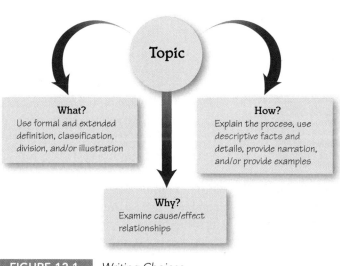

FIGURE 12.1 *Writing Choices*

Topic

What?
Use formal and extended definition, classification, division, and/or illustration

How?
Explain the process, use descriptive facts and details, provide narration, and/or provide examples

Why?
Examine cause/effect relationships

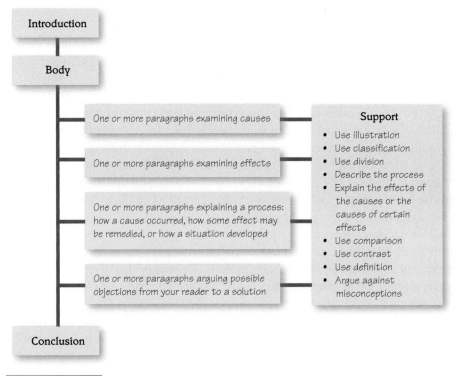

FIGURE 12.2   *Combining Patterns of Development in Writing*

creative thinking processes, we provide visuals to help you create your ideas rather than give you topics from which to select.

Reacting to Your World

First, examine the following photo of a person shoplifting. Look at the details. What's going on? What topics for writing does this photo suggest?

An initial reaction to this photo might be, "Gosh, that's awful. Why would anyone shoplift?" An essay answering this question might prove interesting, but you can expect others

to write essays on basically your same idea and most likely your same points. So how do you make your essay meaningful? Would research help you understand this person's motivation? What other topics does this scene suggest? Start by exploring your options. Notice that Table 12.1 combines several prewriting techniques into one: listing, cubing, and questioning, for instance, are all part of generating ideas in the following categories.

Table 12.1 does not cover all possible approaches. That's the beauty of writing: whether academic or technical, all writing is creative. It is up to you, the writer, to make it work by making meaningful choices. Every day you draw conclusions, make decisions, and respond positively or negatively to what you see, hear, or read. Your everyday activities bring fresh ideas and new questions that translate into exciting and meaningful topics for writing. It's all a matter of looking deeper and questioning what's in front of you. As you consider your topic, think critically and creatively by exploring your many choices.

TABLE 12.1 *Writing Situations for Shoplifting*

Writing Situation	Purpose and Focus	Possible Audience	Intended Effect on Audience	Primary Pattern(s)	Possible Additional Modes
Criminal justice	Explain types of shoplifters	New police officers New security personnel	Educate to increase skills in identifying	Classification	Cause/effect, comparison/contrast, definition, description, illustration, narration, process
	Propose an effective surveillance system	Store managers	Accept suggestion	Persuasive focus: cause/effect, process, argument	Argumentation, cause/effect, comparison/contrast, illustration, narration
	Explain the effects of shoplifting on businesses	Consumers Store personnel Stakeholders	Raise awareness of consumers; urge closer observation; justify or explain loss to stakeholders	Effects	Comparison/contrast, cause, illustration, process
	Propose a way of reorganizing the store to prevent shoplifting	Managers	Consider investing in changes	Persuasive focus: cause/effect, process, argument	Cause/effect, classification, comparison/contrast, definition, description, illustration, narration
Business	Explain why some people resort to shoplifting	Peers Law enforcement	Educate peers; help law enforcement officers understand motives	Causes Narrative	Classification, comparison/contrast, definition, description, effect, illustration, narration, process
	Develop a profile of people most likely to shoplift	Law enforcement Security	Identify possible shoplifters	Description Classification	Cause/effect, classification, comparison/contrast, description, illustration, narration, process

Continued

Writing Situation	Purpose and Focus	Possible Audience	Intended Effect on Audience	Primary Pattern(s)	Possible Additional Modes
Psychology	Explain why consumers fail to report incidences of shoplifting	Consumers	Change attitudes	Causes	Classification, comparison/contrast, description, effect, illustration, narration, process
	Convince the reader that it's everyone's duty to report shoplifters	Consumers	Be more proactive in crime prevention	Argument Narrative	Cause/effect, comparison/contrast, description, illustration, narration

PRACTICE 12-2

Examine the following photos. What connections, issues, or problems do these visuals conjure up?

Frank Micelotta/American Idol/Contributor/ Getty Images

Emmanuel Lattes/Alamy Limited

Using two writing situations based on one of the photos, list possible purposes, audiences, intended effects, primary patterns, and additional modes. Use the chart on page 349 as an example. Feel free to return to your chosen photo repeatedly. The more times you examine it, the more ideas you associate with it. Answers will vary.

> **Collaborative Critical Thinking**
>
> **Form groups according to the photo you chose for Practice 12-2. Then in groups of three or four,** compare the different possibilities that you have for essays about the photo. Answer the following questions. Answers will vary.
>
> 1. How many different focuses (ideas for essays) did the group generate?
>
> 2. Which focuses did you find unique, approaching the topic from a different angle than most people would think of?

WRITING YOUR INTEGRATED ESSAY

3. Which topics would require research?

4. Examine and discuss the intended effect you want each focus to have on the audience. Are the effects reasonable and realistic? Are they appropriate for the focus and the audience? What advice can you give one another?

5. Examine and discuss the primary pattern(s) and additional modes. Are they appropriate? What would you change?

Share your answers with other groups. Apply this activity by discussing any ideas or major changes you would consider in your own writing assignments.

WRITING YOUR INTEGRATED ESSAY

From your previous experiences, you know what makes writing work. You have also seen how the essay can take many unpredictable twists and turns as you embark on your mission to support and prove your thesis. It's all a matter of choice. As you embark on your own essay, start with three basic questions: Who is your audience? What is your purpose? What effect do you want your essay to have on your reader?

To guide you through your integrated essay, we include an essay by Deborah, a social work major taking her first composition course. As you read her essay, note the various techniques and patterns she uses to support her thesis. Also, at various points of this essay, consider other choices Deborah could have made to enhance this essay.

Multicolored Leaves

The crisp autumn leaves had begun to fall, signaling the start of another school year for me and every other school-age child in Southern California. It was 1976, and after a turbulent decade of fighting for equal rights for all, we had finally begun to embrace our differences. But, I knew it wasn't over yet. Even at the tender age of 11, I knew that racism was still alive and well in America. As I trudged to my new school for the first time, absentmindedly crunching leaves of red and gold as I walked, I prepared myself for the inevitable moment when another kid would ask me yet another version of the question I had come to dread—"WHAT! Your brother is a N——R?"

Introduction
- Deborah uses description.
- She gives brief background.
- She presents her topic.
- She uses narrative.

Whatever one's definition, racism is an ugly word. Microsoft *Encarta* defines racism as "making the race of other people a factor in attitudes or actions concerning them. . . . [It] implies a belief in the superiority of one's own race." To me, the word evokes feelings of frustration, hurt, embarrassment, anger, and injustice. Although I'm not biracial, I grew up as a white child in a family where Mama was white and Daddy was black.

- Deborah gives a literal definition.
- She makes a statement of authority.

There has been surprisingly little research conducted on the issue of prejudice toward the biracial, according to Francis Wardle, executive director of the Center for the Study of Biracial Children. However, I know from my own family's experience that it is a bigotry that differs from the traditional view of racism. Many people who don't consider themselves racially biased show a real hostility when asked for their views on interracial marriage and biracial children. This tendency to react with aggression seems to transcend both race and ethnic background (Wardle). I personally have found more acceptance from my stepfather's family than from my mother's or my biological father's family. It's as if the biracial family is an insult and introduces a threat to the ordinary view of the world as it should be.

Body
- Deborah introduces an authority to support her claim.
- Her thesis, or primary focus, is to define.
- She cites an authority to give weight to her own claim.

If facing prejudice is hard for an adult, it's all the more difficult for a child. Adults know that children haven't yet acquired the life skills and sense of self that are necessary to deal with serious issues successfully; however, they subject the biracial child to extreme emotional pain. At such a young age, the child faces hostility at the hands of those who oppose "mixing races." Even more troubling, the pain may be inflicted by people the child looks up to, such as a teacher or a minister. The biracial child must silently work out her feelings of anger, hurt, and injustice that result from being shunned and ridiculed since these are feelings that she can't share, express, or define. Who is there to turn to?

- Deborah uses effect.

Although the majority of children can identify and fit in with one group, biracial children face the problem of not being white or black enough. Biracial children constantly must deal with the taunts from their peer of either race. Such words as *Oreo, half-breed,* and *mutt* become part of their early vocabulary. Kelly Burrello, Diversity Training Group senior associate, points out that the belief in separate but equal rights is so ingrained in some societies that "the homes of interracial families have reportedly been targets of hate crimes by members of their communities who do not accept mixed race households." However, as difficult as these external forces may be, many biracial children do survive. I saw my brother grow up to be a person of great fortitude, resilience, and compassion, and these are priceless character traits. But he is more fortunate than most. He has a strong family to support him.

• Deborah uses illustration.

There's really no secret to raising a happy, healthy biracial child. Some parents wait helplessly to comfort the child. However, parents need to see this situation and climate for what it is: racism, bigotry, and ignorance. My parents found that the most important factor in raising a biracial child is to exemplify the kind of adult they hope their children to be. My parents showed my brother and me what we can be. From my brother's earliest years, they reminded him often how beautiful and unique he is. As he grew older, they let him know that he could come to them to talk about any and all feelings he had about being biracial. In addition, my parents encouraged my brother to explore as much of each parent's culture as he wished. My brother, as well as I, inherited a devotion to family and an appreciation for diversity that embodies a standard of a global society. Yet in a society where we have seen the number of interracial couples quadrupled in the last 35 years (Burrello), it's difficult to explain how such scorn from diverse groups continues to exist.

• Deborah uses process.

The autumn leaves are falling once again. It is now 2007, and the school-age kids, including my young son, have started school. I don't know what sort of struggles my son will be going through for having a black daddy and a white mommy, but I want to hope that we as a society have evolved. Unfortunately, I can't help but sense that we will continue down the wrong path: it's still not over. I still sense the hate in this world for what people can't understand. After all, it wasn't too long ago that the Twin Towers were destroyed in a horrible terrorist act, and in an effort to retaliate against a faceless enemy, some Americans have become terrorists themselves by persecuting and killing our fellow citizens who happen to be Muslims.

As I ponder such events, I occasionally look out of my window to admire the Colorado mountainside now covered in a multitude of colors, shades of gold and brick, and the most vibrant red and orange imaginable. They paint a kind of mosaic with their beautiful colors, colors that would be diminished if not for the colors that contrast and complement them. In our diversity and beauty, humanity has the opportunity to be just as magnificent as the leaves with their collective brilliance. Can we learn from the multicolored leaves?

Conclusion

- Bringing the essay to a close, Deborah goes back to the beginning by describing a similar scene: the season, the leaves, a child going to school, and the feeling that the problem persists.
- She uses comparison to illustrate the senselessness of bigotry, which also echoes the historical events in her introduction.
- She uses description to make a point and as an appeal to emotion. She returns to the leaves as a picture of harmony and unity and then challenges her audience to be receptive.

Prewriting

Choosing the right topic is crucial when writing any essay because it is your topic that shapes the organization and development of your essay. If you have a strong interest or personal connection to the topic, the topic meets the standards set by your instructor or your workplace, or both, you're on your way to an excellent paper. It all starts with your topic.

Discovering and Limiting Your Topic

Prewriting Strategy #10: Responding to Visual Cues

Before we move to your own writing, do the following activity to sharpen the power of the senses and relate your sensual impressions to your thinking. Try to "see the whole picture." This exercise is just a warm-up activity for the rest of the chapter.

PRACTICE 12-3

Examine the following photo and answer the questions that follow. Answers will vary.

Calvin Klein Jeans

L.M.Otero/AP Photo

1. What is your overall impression of this photo? Students may indicate how the photo quickly captured their attention. Some may express admiration for the couple, others may make a personal connection, and some might form judgments, such as about using sex to sell a product.

2. Give a brief description of the photo. Some students may focus their description on the youth and physical attractiveness of the couple; others might make judgments on our changing values or the media's role in setting, imposing, or reinforcing certain values. Either way, a thesis is emerging.

3. Think of ways to develop themes based on this photo.

   a. If you were using classification to develop an essay on an idea based on this photo, what would you classify? Write a possible thesis, and add an essay map to indicate the categories. The types of images advertisers use to grab the public's interest is tied to age, ethnicity, and geographic locations. Some students may choose to classify the types of sexual content in advertisements.

   b. Write a thesis in which you consider effect as your primary pattern of development. Students may focus their thesis on the emotional responses to certain ads or advertising campaigns.

   c. Write a thesis in which you make an argument about an issue that you associate with the photo. Students might mention such issues as freedom of speech, the need to educate the public, or the effects of the media on the family.

Photos capture moments in time and are packed with the emotions and passion of those moments. The following photos are divided into four themes: seeing our changing values, seeking a better world, changing our future, and building bridges. Each theme reflects issues in our society that many of us feel passionate about whether we agree or not. Focus on each theme separately. You are probably familiar with and may have your personal views on most, if not all, of these issues. If you come upon a photo with whose subject you're unfamiliar, attempt it anyway. These photos represent events in our lives as a nation and as global citizens; whether or not we understand the totality of these events, we can still react to them, face global realities, and form our own conclusions. Surprise yourself. Think outside the box.

■ **Theme 1: Seeing our changing values.** Take a moment to examine the following photos. Respond to each photo by raising questions that can result in thesis statements or even research questions for a possible research paper for this or other courses. For each photo, raise two important questions. Don't limit yourself: view each photo from different angles and consider the vast possibilities of what you are observing. Every time you write a question, come back and examine the photo; try to discover something new each time.

1. _____
   _____
   _____
   _____

2. _____
   _____
   _____
   _____

Joe Giblin/AP Photo

3. _____
   _____
   _____
   _____

4. _____
   _____
   _____
   _____

Matt Dunn/Superstock

5. _____
   _____
   _____
   _____

6. _____
   _____
   _____
   _____

Queerstock/Getty Images

W R I T I N G   12-1

Look over your questions. In the space provided, write two questions that you feel would make interesting thesis statements. Make additions, clarifications, or changes as you feel necessary.

1. _____

2. _____

    ■ **Theme 2: Seeking a better world.** When you feel personally connected to your ideas, your essay has a stronger voice. Examine the next set of photos. React to what you're seeing in the same way as you did for theme 1. React also to what you're not seeing but feel should be part of the scene. Omissions of details can generate judgments.

1. _____
   _____
   _____
   _____

2. _____
   _____
   _____
   _____

Eric Feferberg/Getty Images

WRITING YOUR INTEGRATED ESSAY

3. _____

_____

_____

_____

Anna Gowthorpe/PA Wire
URN:546642S/AP/Wide World Photos

4. _____

_____

_____

_____

5. _____

_____

_____

_____

_____

_____

The Paducah Sun/Steve Nagy/AP/Wide
World Photos

6. _____

_____

_____

_____

_____

_____

WRITING   12-2

Again, look over your questions and choose two that you feel you would be interested in writing about. Don't forget to make any additions, clarifications, or changes that you feel are necessary.

1. _____

2. _____

■ **Theme 3: Changing our future.** Are you getting the hang of this? Hopefully, you're becoming excited about some topics you have already written. Look at the next series of photos. Observe carefully; think critically about these true events frozen in time.

1. _____
   _____
   _____
   _____
   _____
   _____

2. _____
   _____
   _____
   _____
   _____
   _____

Mike Derer/AP/Wide World Photos

3. _____
   _____
   _____
   _____

4. _____
   _____
   _____
   _____

Darryl Estrine/PhotoLibrary

5. _____
   _____
   _____
   _____

6. _____
   _____
   _____
   _____

Deborah Cannon, Pool/AP/Wide World Photos

Review your questions and pick two you are interested in writing about. You should make any additions, clarifications, or changes that you feel are necessary.

1. _____

2. _____

■ **Theme 4: Building bridges.** Move on to the final set. Use your power of observation and your critical thinking skills to respond to the following set of events.

1. _____
   _____
   _____
   _____

2. _____
   _____
   _____
   _____

Romeo Ranoco RR/CP/Reuters

3. _____
   _____
   _____
   _____
   _____
   _____

4. _____
   _____
   _____
   _____
   _____
   _____

David McNew/Getty Images

5. _____
   _____
   _____
   _____
   _____

Scott Olson/Getty Images

6. _____
   _____
   _____
   _____
   _____

WRITING 12-4

Pick two of your questions from the final theme that you feel you would be interested in writing about. If necessary, make any additions, clarifications, or changes to the questions.

1. _____

2. _____

You should now have eight exciting questions for possible theses. Review each one. This is the hard part: narrow your list to your top two questions and write them in the space that follows in your order of preference. Again, make any changes you feel help strengthen each one.

1. _____

2. _____

Once you have selected your questions, take the first one and choose any combination of prewriting techniques you feel would generate the most ideas. Your goal at this point is to search for a focus for your thesis and uncover possible supporting details.

Identifying Your Audience, Establishing Your Purpose, and Setting Your Tone

You are already fully aware of the importance of audience, purpose, and tone. Most likely, you have a good idea who your audience is. Nonetheless, it is still helpful to complete a formal analysis because the more you know about your audience, the more effective you can be in making the right choices in developing your essay.

Deborah does an audience analysis to find the most effective approach for her essay. She then establishes the following aims:

Audience: People who don't realize the extent of bigotry and the consequences of their own behavior

Purpose: To convince my audience that we need to embrace differences in spite of our environment

Effect: Appeal to my audience's sense of humanity and have them question the soundness of their personal judgments

Approach: I'd like to establish a compassionate, nonjudgmental tone. To prevent the essay from appearing too emotional (which I am), I'll use some research to support my assertions. I'll use description as a way to appeal to my audience and at the same time make an analogy using nature to reflect the point that what people judge is part of the natural order of life. My own experiences serve as examples to illustrate my points.

WRITING   12-5

Record your observations about your audience, purpose, and tone by filling out the following form.

Audience, Purpose, and Tone Analysis

Topic: _____

I. Audience

1. Who is your reader? _____

   Age: _____ Gender: _____

2. What is your audience's educational background? _____

   _____

3. Who would be the most interested in your topic? _____

   _____

4. What does your reader know or assume about your topic? _____

   _____

5. What are your reader's social or cultural interests? _____

   _____

6. Why would your reader be interested in your topic? _____

   _____

7. What connection do you have with this audience? _____

   _____

II. Purpose

1. What do you want your audience to understand? _____

    _____

2. Why is this topic important to your audience? _____

    _____

3. What does your reader expect when reading your writing? _____

    _____

4. How do you expect your audience to react? _____

    _____

III. Tone

1. What tone do you hope to establish? _____

    _____

2. What can you realistically achieve through this writing? _____

    _____

Renew what you have written and then identify your audience, purpose, effect, and approach.

Audience: _____

Purpose: _____

Effect: _____

Approach: _____

Formulating Your Thesis

Review your question again to formulate your tentative thesis. Whatever form your thesis takes, make sure it clearly states what you intend to prove. Don't forget that your thesis controls your entire essay, so revise it as many times as necessary.

Deborah felt a personal connection to the theme "changing our future" and formulates the following tentative thesis:

> Biracial children struggle silently trying to make sense of the bigotry that surrounds them.

Outlining Your Ideas

Outlining is itself a creative process. As you jot down the elements of your essay, you are still brainstorming, associating ideas, and revising your approach. You can use a rough "scratch outline" to get you started, or you can choose one of the patterns presented in earlier chapters of *Bridges to Better Writing* that offer a close model of the type of essay you might be writing. For example, if you plan to use classification as the primary pattern, go to Chapter 9 for a sample outline. However, if you have no set pattern of development, like Deborah's essay, consider drawing up your own plan for your essay. Don't forget that effective writing is a product of careful planning. Be sure to run your plan by your instructor for feedback. Here's Deborah's outline.

ESSAY OUTLINE

I. **Introduction**
   A. Start with a description to set the scene and establish an analogy to nature using the different colors and shapes of leaves
   B. Give the accepted definition of racism to focus on another type of racism
   C. Support my focus on racism with a statement of authority and mention the limited research of effects of prejudice on biracial children
   D. To set the scene, introduce my topic, and establish credibility, I need three or four paragraphs for my introduction.
   E. Thesis: Biracial children struggle silently trying to make sense of the bigotry that surrounds them.

II. **Body**
   A. Start with the difficulties and emotional effects the biracial child must endure
   B. Explain the feelings of the child and describe how the child deals with these feelings in silence
   C. Show that the biracial child is split between two worlds and does not seem to fit in either world
   D. Show that there is hope; explain how my parents helped my brother appreciate both worlds and helped me understand my role in this new environment
   E. Maintain an upbeat tone throughout the development

III. **Conclusion**
   A. Return to the description and the scenario in the introduction
   B. Continue the analogy of the multicolored leaves
   C. Bring the scenario to the present and show that much hasn't changed, especially with the current world situation
   D. Close with an appeal to emotions

WRITING   12-6

Write your outline. As you determine the information that helps explain your thesis, consider all the choices you have. Design the outline format that is best for your particular essay. However, if you choose to use a specific pattern of development as your primary pattern, go to the appropriate chapter in this book for an outline form.

Drafting

Look at your outline and start drafting any section of your essay: beginning, middle, or end. As you draft sections of your essay, feel free to change your outline. What seemed logical earlier may not be such a good idea now. You can communicate an idea in many ways, so look for the most effective ones.

WRITING 12-7

On a separate sheet of paper, start drafting your essay.

1. Make sure your introduction and conclusion are not merely decorations to fulfill a requirement. Your introduction and conclusion must serve some meaningful purpose.
2. Make sure that each of your paragraphs develops one main idea.
3. Use a variety of patterns and methods to explain, argue, or prove your ideas.
4. Add transitions to keep your ideas flowing smoothly and to guide your audience through your information.
5. Above all, don't lose sight of your audience and purpose.

Revising

Revise! Revise! Revise! Leave nothing untouched. We can't emphasize this stage of the process enough. Rethink every part of your essay. Go back to your audience and purpose analysis and rethink some more. Talk to others about your topic and rethink again.

To solve specific problems in your paper, refer to the troubleshooting sections in chapters of this textbook that pertain to your topic and approach.

WRITING 12-8

Start your revision. Again don't leave any part of your essay untouched. Revise, revise, and revise again.

- Make sure your essay provides specific, purposeful, and creative information (examples, details, observations, combinations of patterns) to explain your topic fully, demonstrating an understanding of the complexity of the topic. Overall, check that your essay has a sense of completeness.
- Check your use of transitions carefully between and within your paragraphs.
- If your essay contains secondary evidence, make sure your sources are integrated smoothly into the text. Your sources should be varied, reliable, and correctly cited using the correct style of documentation. Refer to Chapter 13 for guidance on using sources. Follow your instructor's guidelines.

Asking Your Peers

Get feedback from your peers. Exchange papers with a classmate and review the paper by responding to these questions.

1. Who is the writer? Who is the peer reviewer?
2. What method or methods of introduction did the writer use (humor, anecdote, startling fact, rhetorical question, narration, and so on)?
3. Is the introduction effective? (Is it interesting? Does it grab your attention?)
4. Is the introduction fully developed? What can you suggest to improve the introduction?
5. Is the thesis statement clear, and does the introduction lead smoothly to this thesis statement? What should the writer add?
6. Do the body paragraphs have clear topic sentences? Identify any weaknesses and make suggestions to strengthen these sentences.
7. Read the supporting details of each paragraph. Does the writer give you sufficient details, facts, and/or examples to explain topic sentences or general ideas in the various paragraphs? Where do you feel the essay can use additional support?
8. Does the writer use a combination of patterns to develop the thesis? What suggestions can you make?
9. Make suggestions or comments and circle any unclear or irrelevant information directly on the essay.
10. How does the writer establish credibility: personal experience, research, or both? Is it effective?
11. Is the conclusion meaningful? What can you suggest to improve the conclusion?
12. Give your overall impression of the essay's diction (language). Is it too pompous or elaborate, making the ideas unclear and confusing? Are the sentences too choppy and the word order confusing? Or is it appropriate for the audience?
13. What did you enjoy most about the essay?

Proofreading

Start proofreading your draft by focusing on the most common grammar errors. Table 12.2 can help you locate the writing chapter in which the grammar rules were first introduced and the grammar chapters that provide full explanation and exercises.

TABLE 12.2 *Grammar Rules Covered*

Writing Chapter	Grammar Rule	Grammar Chapter
2	Check for sentence fragments	15
3	Check for shifts in verb tense	19
4	Check for commas after introductory elements	26
5	Edit for fused sentences Check for comma splices	16
6	Check for shifts in person	18
7	Edit for pronoun–antecedent agreement	18
8	Check for pronoun reference and case	18
9	Check for subject–verb agreement	17
10	Check for missing or misplaced apostrophes	27
11	Check for correct punctuation of restrictive and nonrestrictive elements	26

WRITING 12-9

By now, you're probably aware of the grammar, usage, and punctuation rules that you consistently violate.

Final Checklist

1. Does the introduction have a strong and clear purpose statement (suggesting new, broader insights into the topic) that captivates the audience and clearly addresses the complexity of the issue? ☐

2. Does the thesis clearly state the main point of your essay? Does it control the entire essay? Is it smoothly integrated into the introduction? ☐

3. Does each main body paragraph contain a strong, clear topic sentence that supports the thesis? ☐

4. Does your essay provide sufficient information (examples, details, observations, combinations of patterns) to explain your topic fully? ☐

5. Does you essay contain appropriate and smooth transitions between paragraphs and sentences? ☐

6. Does the conclusion bring closure to the essay? Does it emphasize the importance of your topic and give the reader something to think about? ☐

7. Does your essay provide the essential information, tone, and level of formality appropriate to the essay's purpose and audience? ☐

8. Does your essay have varied sentence structures, complete sentences (no fragments, comma splices, or fused sentences) and insignificant errors in spelling, usage, and punctuation? ☐

WRITING YOUR INTEGRATED ESSAY

Reflecting

In this chapter, you have explored a more creative way of making choices about developing your essay. We believe that an open-ended, questioning, yet logical and informed approach can yield the best results, especially as you become more comfortable and fluent as a writer. Remember that an important part of the writing process is reflecting on what you have accomplished. Use the following activity to help you reflect on your writing process in this chapter.

WRITING 12-10

Self-Reflection

Before you hand in your paper, write a brief paragraph in which you reflect on your final draft. Include your feelings on the following questions:

1. What do you feel you did best?

2. What part of your paper was most challenging to you?

3. In which areas do you feel you need the most practice?

4. What strategies could you employ to address your challenges or weaknesses, to improve the quality of your essay, or both?

After you have completed this self-reflection, carefully review your instructor's comments. How are they similar or different from your own answers to the self-reflection? Make a list of your grammar, punctuation, and spelling errors so that you can follow up on the ones that recur. Consider what strategies you will employ to address your challenges or weaknesses and to improve the quality of your essay.

How might you exercise your many choices as a writer outside of this English course?

*   **College:** _____
*   **Your profession:** _____
*   **Everyday life:** _____

Writing with Sources

PART 2

CHAPTER 13

Working with Sources

YOUR GOALS

1. Practice the skills of quoting, paraphrasing, and summarizing from sources.

2. Demonstrate an understanding of plagiarism and identify the various types of plagiarism.

3. Document your sources using an appropriate citation style, such as MLA.

"Plagiarists are always suspicious of being stolen from."

■ Samuel Taylor Coleridge ■

I n a recent assignment, your friend "borrowed" information from an online encyclopedia and simply inserted it word for word into the text of his report, believing that since he included a reference to the source at the end of the paper, he was fulfilling his requirement to document the source. When you try to use this technique in your college history class, your instructor accuses you of plagiarism. Confused, you find that you have no choice but to drop the class. Where did you go wrong?

As a newly hired technical writer for an engineering firm, you are told that "it's okay to swipe information from the Internet" to put in a proposal for city funding to construct portable childproof barriers for parade routes. When you find you need some additional evidence, you copy and paste information from another firm's successful proposal in another city. A city staff person researching your proposal discovers the original source of the information, and your firm loses the bid.

While writing an e-mail to a current romantic interest, you decide to borrow some helpful ideas from Shakespeare's sonnets. In such a personal situation, there can be no legal or practical consequence of this borrowing, so you select freely from Shakespeare's stock of descriptive and figurative ideas—although you are careful not to use his actual language. As it turns out, the object of your desire has been reading the sonnets since an early age and recognizes the fraud in your approach.

The misuse of source material is unacceptable in any context, but especially in college. It violates the rules of academic integrity that most institutions of higher learning adhere to. This chapter shows that using sources means more than just dropping them

LET's warm up!

As a college student, you may feel at times like the image seen here—surrounded by books and needing somehow to use all that valuable source material to create something of your own. How do you go about it? What are the "rules" for extracting ideas and information from your reading so that you can use them in your own research and writing? What does the term *plagiarism* mean, and how can you avoid plagiarizing an author's work?

Take a moment to write a short paragraph that explains your current understanding of the term *plagiarism*. Have you ever known someone who was accused of plagiarism? Have you ever unintentionally plagiarized information only to realize it later? Write about these circumstances.

Todd Davidson/Getty Images

into your paper. Your goal is to show your instructor not that you have found sources related to the topic at hand but rather that you understand your sources—and their relationship to the thesis and purpose of your paper—and that you can skillfully use your sources to support your idea and claims.

UNDERSTANDING SOURCES

Being a college student is all about learning to interact with published materials—it is, in other words, about reading. It is about discussing what you read with others. It is about applying what you read to solve problems or think through important issues. And finally, it is about writing and speaking your own ideas in the context of what you and your classmates have read. This chapter teaches you how to interact with published materials so that you can use them productively throughout your college career. It also provides techniques for avoiding misuse of those materials—in particular, the serious misuse of sources called *plagiarism*.

Reading for College

You've probably noticed that college reading assignments demand a different kind of attention and focus than other types of reading. You might feel challenged by readings that are full of unfamiliar words, complicated sentences, or abstract ideas. Or you may feel overwhelmed by assignments that are longer than anything you have read before.

Why mention this concern at this point? Although this course is concerned mainly with writing, students who read thoughtfully and understand what they read make better writers. To grow as a writer—in terms of the ideas you are able to analyze, as well as your writing style—you must make serious reading a regular part of your life. Your success depends on how accurately and thoroughly you understand what others say about the topics you investigate. Understanding and incorporating source material into your own writing is a high-level skill—one you practice not only in this course but throughout your college education.

In college, you read so that you can give back—contribute your own ideas and reasoning—to the general conversation going on around you. Your ethical obligation, therefore, is to make sure you understand other people's ideas as they were intended to be understood and to report those ideas accurately to your own audiences, giving proper credit where credit is due. Part of this responsibility involves your ability to comprehend what you read, and part of it involves your honesty.

Read the following passage taken from an article by Yvonne Bynoe called "Don't Dismiss Hip-Hop," which appeared in *ColorLines Magazine: Race, Action, Culture* in Spring 2003, and then answer the questions that follow. Answers will vary.

Hip-Hop Culture Left Adrift

Much of the Black Nationalist rhetoric of rap music takes its cues from the Black Power Movement. However, unlike the Black Arts Movement, which was the cultural arm of the Black Power Movement, hip-hop culture never developed as part of any political or economic movement. Although the middle 1980s were populated with politically conscious rap artists such as Public Enemy, X-Clan, Paris, and KRS-One, who highlighted the injustices being experienced by young and poor people of color, they got no love from the civil rights crowd. The civil rights establishment, by failing to critically analyze and distinguish "political" rap from the merely trite and materialistic, missed a significant opportunity to use hip-hop to engage and politicize young people around the reactionary policies of the Reagan/Bush administrations.

Hip-hop culture—abandoned and left to the dictates of multinational corporations—has largely metastasized into apolitical entertainment. Essayist Christopher Tyson states, "Alienated and underestimated, hip-hop became vulnerable to mainstream influence. Since social integrationist philosophy identifies white reality as the default cultural, political, and social norm, hip-hop became in some measure a reflection of the 'American' culture. Therefore, partying and leisure activities were esteemed above the more serious occupations of collective responsibility and organization."

_____

Copyright 2003 *ColorLines Magazine* and Gale Group

1. Does the author admire hip-hop? The author seems to admire hip-hop in its "pure" and politically conscious form but believes it has been manipulated by materialistic forces.

2. How does the quotation from Tyson support the point of the second paragraph? It suggests that the values of the prevailing culture are trivially focused on entertainment, not political responsibility, and that hip-hop has come to reflect the prevailing culture.

3. If you were asked to restate this passage in your own words (in conversation, not writing), what would you say? Hip-hop could have been a powerful political force, but instead it was taken over by the entertainment industry and can no longer serve a more serious cause.

The way you answer such questions depends on how you approach the task of reading. One thing is certain: you probably couldn't give satisfactory answers to these questions after just one quick reading. You had to slow down, reread, and give yourself time to think about what you were reading. At this point, a few strategies for critical reading can enable you to work successfully with sources (and to become a better student generally):

1. **Annotate your reading.** To annotate means to make notes about what you read, usually by writing notes right in the passage itself. Annotation reinforces every response, intellectual or emotional, that you have as you read through a piece of writing. And it's like having a conversation with the author: your brain is stimulated to go beyond just taking in meaning—it begins to create meaning of its own and you begin to understand more about what you have read. Look at how a student has annotated the passage we introduced earlier.

> **Bridging Knowledge**
>
> **See Chapter 28** for additional information on and practice with critical reading.

Hip-Hop Culture Left Adrift

Much of the Black Nationalist rhetoric of rap music <u>takes its cues from the Black Power Movement</u>. However, unlike the Black Arts Movement, which was the cultural arm of the Black Power Movement, hip-hop culture never developed as part of any political or economic movement. Although the middle 1980s were populated with politically conscious rap artists such as Public Enemy, X-Clan, Paris, and KRS-One, who highlighted the injustices being experienced by young and poor people of color, <u>they got no love from the civil rights crowd</u>. The civil rights establishment, by failing to critically analyze and distinguish "political" rap from the merely trite and materialistic, <u>missed a significant opportunity to use hip-hop to engage and politicize young people</u> around the reactionary policies of the Reagan/Bush administrations.

Hip-hop culture—abandoned and left to the dictates of multinational corporations—has largely metastasized into apolitical entertainment. Essayist Christopher Tyson states, "Alienated and underestimated, hip-hop became vulnerable to mainstream influence. Since social integrationist philosophy identifies white reality as the default cultural,

I wasn't aware of this political connection. I thought it was just street slang. How did rap start to separate itself from other movements in the black community?

Don't know if I like the idea of being "used" as a fan of rap. But, I see her point. Wasn't rock used for political purposes by the antiwar movement in the '60s?

Rap is big these days. Is that so bad? Doesn't that mean that its message is spread among a wider audience, with more awareness and sympathy along with it? Or are we all being fooled?

political, and social norm, hip-hop became in some measure a reflection of the 'American' culture. Therefore, partying and leisure activities were esteemed above the more serious occupations of collective responsibility and organization."

2. **Respond in writing, reread the passage, and then respond again.** After you've read a passage and annotated it, write down, briefly but in complete sentences, your overall reaction to the piece. You can respond in many ways:
   ■ state the main point and then write about whether you agree or disagree (and why)
   ■ discuss the author's choice of language or logical development
   ■ put the whole passage in your own words

   The point is to get your thoughts down on paper; once you've done that, reread the original passage again. Has your understanding deepened or changed in some other way? Are there parts of the passage you need to think about more carefully? What words do you need to look up to get at the subtle aspects of the author's meaning? Here's how one student responds in writing to the preceding passage.

I've never thought about rap in this way. I always think of it describing life on the street or in the neighborhood, but it didn't occur to me that rap could be political. The author seems to be saying here that rap's language comes from the radical politics of the civil rights movement but that it has been taken over by the music industry just to make money. We rap fans are being led to believe that listening to rap is an important act that makes a statement when really we are just playing into the hands of the multinational corporations, who are quite happy with the status quo. Anyway, I don't like the idea that whether it's for a good cause or a bad one—politics or big business—there is an assumption that rap fans can be "used" at will by powers that are more conscious than we are about the purposes of the music.

What do you think about this "gut response"? Notice that part of it is devoted to stating the meaning of the passage, another part to evaluating the author's ideas, and yet another part to applying those ideas to the reader's own life. A lot is going on in this brief response, and it all helps the reader understand the author's meaning.

3. **Converse with a partner.** Talking about a reading with someone lets you get your partner's input on the meaning, logic, and expression of the original, and you get to contribute your own reactions to your partner's understanding of the piece.

These are just a few of many possible active reading strategies, but they are sufficient to get you started on a more focused and more useful kind of reading. In this course, learning to read actively has a more practical use: it makes you a better researcher and writer, helping you use others' ideas properly and without misrepresenting those ideas to your own reader.

Why Use Source Material?

Suppose you've been given a short writing assignment in your history class. You are to write a 4-page essay on some aspect of the civil rights movement in the decades following the 1960s. Your instructor's handout says, "Your essay must incorporate two recent sources."

What does it mean to "incorporate sources" into your writing? "Incorporate sources" is a phrase that opens the world to you as a thinker and a writer. Imagine writing a 4-page paper about the civil rights movement based on what you now know. What would you say? Could you give a brief historical summary of the movement? Could you name its major leaders or describe its lasting effects? Could you evaluate the changes it brought to our country? Without exploring source material on your own and reading thoughtfully what you find, chances are you simply don't know enough at this point to write a 4-page paper.

This is true of all of us in our role as learners. Your own understanding is constructed from what you know of others' contributions to that network of knowledge. You might think you are only writing a "history paper and incorporating sources," but what you are really doing is synthesizing the published ideas of other writers to create your own personal contribution to the topic you are writing about.

Types of Source Materials

You can rely on two major types of sources: primary and secondary sources.

Primary Sources

Primary sources are those with which you interact personally, without the intervention of another researcher or scholar. Whether you observe the evidence, speak to people knowledgeable about the issue, or read original documents or files, the evidence is the result of your own interpretation of these experiences, not someone else's. Basically, there are three types of primary evidence:

1. **Personal observation or experience.** Fortunately, you know a lot about this kind of evidence already because you've been using it all semester as you've written your previous essays. It is appropriate to use your own observations and experience to convince your reader that your main point is valid. This kind of evidence might be sufficient; however, you might have to supplement it with other kinds of support.
2. **Interviews or surveys you conduct.** Sometimes you are fortunate to be able to interview someone who knows a lot about your topic. You don't want to interview or survey just anybody, of course, because your interview material must be considered valid by your reader. (Students often want to interview or survey their classmates about certain topics—this might work if the topic concerns a classroom issue, but it won't adequately support a broader topic.)
3. **Original documents.** If you go directly to published historical documents for quotable material—the U.S. Constitution or the Magna Carta, for example, or the text of a speech by Martin Luther King Jr. or Winston Churchill—you are relying on primary documentary evidence.

When you incorporate evidence from primary documents into your writing, you must obey the rules for documenting your sources, which are discussed later in this chapter. Your instructor will tell you if you may use this kind of evidence in your essays.

Secondary Evidence

Secondary evidence is the kind you get from reading the work of other researchers: articles published in newspapers, magazines, journals, encyclopedias, and so on; news broadcasts or documentary films; books written by scholars—the list goes on. This kind of evidence is called *secondary* because it is written or produced by people who have relied on their own observation or experience, their own research into primary historical documents, or their own reading of other secondary material. When you use secondary sources, you are relying on other people's interpretation; therefore, you often must be cautious and check that the evidence is valid.

PRACTICE   13-2

For each of the following sources, write P if the source is primary evidence or S if the source is secondary evidence.

<u>S</u>   1. An article that appears in *Newsweek* magazine

<u>S</u>   2. An article from a medical journal

<u>P</u>   3. A lecture you attended

<u>S</u>   4. An article for a local newspaper

<u>S</u>   5. An article from an international newspaper like the *New York Times*

<u>P</u>   6. Your analysis of a novel by Toni Morrison

<u>P</u>   7. An informal survey you conducted

<u>P</u>   8. A class lecture you refer to

<u>P</u>   9. Information from people's personal letters that you use to form judgments

<u>P</u>   10. A trial transcript you review

How Do I Use Source Material?

Given that you have spent some time in the library or online to locate source material that pertains to your project, you can use one or all of the following methods to incorporate information into your text: quote directly, paraphrase, or summarize.

Bridging Knowledge

See Chapter 14 for instructions on evaluating the reliability of your sources.

Quoting Source Material

When most students think of using source material in their papers, they think of quoting it, or taking it word for word from the original. However, quotation is not the most recommended or commonly used method of incorporating secondary source material. You can easily overuse this technique so that your paper becomes a mass of disconnected quotations. When you do need to quote, however, follow these guidelines:

1. Quote when the material is so well stated that to change it in any way would diminish its power.
2. Limit your use of quotation from secondary sources to a small percentage of the source material you incorporate, say 10–15%.
3. Enclose the quoted information within quotation marks. All information within the quotation marks *must* be exactly as the source states it, including any errors in grammar, spelling, or punctuation.
4. Quote interview sources if you feel it is important to present their exact words. In most interviews you conduct, you are most likely limited to note taking unless the interviewee permits you to tape the discussion. Thus, make sure you distinguish a direct quotation—exactly as the person said it—from your own reconstruction of the conversation from notes. Don't treat your reconstruction as a direct quotation by enclosing the information in quotation marks.
5. In theory, you can quote all you want from primary sources, but you should obey some principle of balance when you do so: if you are writing a 4-page paper, you wouldn't want to quote an entire page or more of a speech of Martin Luther King Jr.
6. Within your paragraphs, make your quotations brief, a phrase or short sentence integrated into your own writing.
7. If you need to include a long quotation, consisting of more than four lines of text, set it off from your text, indenting it 10 spaces from the left margin. But don't build a whole paragraph in your own essay by using a long quotation composed of various paragraphs or several quotations from various sources.
8. When you quote, document the source according to the appropriate citation style.

Look at an example of quotation. The original passage comes from a *New Yorker* article by Jeffrey Goldberg titled "Selling Wal-Mart," published April 2, 2007.

> **ORIGINAL PASSAGE:** "Ethical ambidexterity is not a barrier to success in the public-relations field, particularly in Washington. Many prominent Democrats spend the years between national elections representing corporate clients." (36)

Notice that the first sentence of Goldberg's paragraph is particularly well stated; in this case, you could easily write a paraphrase of the sentence, but you might not catch the same ironic tone as the original. Therefore, quotation is a reasonable choice. Here is how you could do it in the context of your own essay:

> **YOUR QUOTATION:** According to Goldberg, "Ethical ambidexterity is not a barrier to success in the public-relations field, particularly in Washington" (36).

Paraphrasing Source Material

When a passage is too long to quote or not "quote-worthy" in terms of its language or style, you should paraphrase it. To *paraphrase* source material means to put it into your own words in approximately the same length as the original. The purpose of paraphrasing is to capture the main point and supporting ideas of the passage you wish to convey to your reader. Here are some guidelines for paraphrasing:

1. To paraphrase source material, you have to understand it thoroughly in its own context, as well as in the context of your own ideas. Therefore, make sure you read the source critically and actively before you begin trying to paraphrase it.

2. Read the passage with even more attention and focus than you already have. You need to understand the main point and supporting ideas of the passage so well that you can readily put them into your own words.

3. Put the original passage aside or cover it up; then try to state the main point and supporting ideas in your own words. Don't just substitute your own individual words for the original author's. Rethink the sentence structures, as well as the words and phrases, of the original. Note that substituting your own words for the author's is a form of plagiarism in which you "steal" the author's sentence structures. Make sure you completely rewrite the passage.

4. Check your paraphrase against the original. Make sure you have captured the same meaning with the same level of detail and that you have not plagiarized the author's words or sentence structures.

5. Acknowledge the source from which you are paraphrasing. Even though you've put the passage into your own words, you still must indicate to your reader that you are borrowing the ideas from another author.

Warning: Sometimes when you are faced with a particularly challenging text with words or phrases that are unclear, it is tempting to just copy the information. Not only is this outright plagiarism, or stealing, but it's also relatively easy for your instructor to spot. The change in style from your own writing to a more complex, sophisticated wording interrupts the flow of the paper and makes it apparent that the material is copied from the original source.

To get an idea what an effective paraphrase is, look at the following statement, taken from the Goldberg article excerpted earlier:

ORIGINAL PASSAGE: "When Walton retired in 1988 (he died in 1992), the company had revenues of sixteen billion dollars. Today, Wal-Mart is the second-largest company in the world in terms of revenue—only Exxon-Mobil is bigger." (32)

Suppose you rewrite it in your own words and you come up with the following:

YOUR PARAPHRASE: In 1988, when Walton retired, Wal-Mart made $16 billion. Now the company is the second biggest in the world in relation to revenue; only Exxon-Mobil is larger (Goldberg 32).

Does this paraphrase follow all the paraphrase guidelines? Reread point 3 and you realize that you have plagiarized the sentence structure of the original article. So you try again, this time rereading the sentence several times and then covering up the passage. Here is your improved paraphrase:

YOUR PARAPHRASE: Wal-Mart took in $16 billion of revenue in 1988, the year that its founder, Sam Walton, retired. Today, only one company, Exxon-Mobil, is larger than Wal-Mart (Goldberg 32).

Note that in the improved paraphrase, the sentence structure, as well as the phrasing, changed. Also note that you must credit the source of the information. Don't commit the common mistake of believing that just because you used your own words, you do not need to cite the source. Whether you use direct quotation, paraphrase, or summary, you *must* cite your source. Not doing so constitutes plagiarism.

PRACTICE 13-3

Practice paraphrasing with a longer passage from the same article. Before starting your paraphrase, circle the words or phrases that are distinctive to this particular writer so that you remember to either rephrase them or put quotes around them. Compare your choices with those of your fellow students. After reading this passage several times and annotating it, cover it up and write your own paraphrase of the passage. Then check your paraphrase against the original to be sure that you haven't plagiarized any information. Answers will vary.

> The job of the Edelman people—there are about twenty, along with more than three dozen in-house public-relations specialists—is to help Wal-Mart scrub its muddied image. Edelman specializes in helping industries with image problems; another important client is the American Petroleum Institute, a Washington lobbying group that seeks to convince American that oil companies care about the environment and that their profits are reasonable. Edelman does its work by cultivating contacts among the country's opinion elites, with whom it emphasizes the good news, and spins the bad; by such tactics as establishing "Astroturf" groups, seemingly grassroots organizations that are actually fronts for industry; and, as I deduced from my own visit to Bentonville, by advising corporate executives on how to speak like risk-averse politicians. (34)

Your paraphrase: Goldberg describes the work of Edelman as selling to the public a better image of companies whose reputations are suffering. Wal-Mart is just one of Edelman's customers; another is the American Petroleum Institute, which hopes to persuade the public that its members are environmentally friendly and deserving of their profit. According to Goldberg, Edelman contacts the so-called opinion elites to tell its clients' stories and teaches executives how to interact with the public in a low-risk manner (34).

Summarizing Source Material

Summarizing source material is much like paraphrasing except that a summary is significantly shorter than a paraphrase. When you summarize, you capture the main point of a long passage, an article, or even a book in a much shorter expression—even in a single sentence, if it suits your purpose.

With summary you have much less chance of plagiarizing the author's sentence structures, but you still have to be careful not to plagiarize any of the author's substantive words. A summary should be composed of your own words and sentence structures. Here are some guidelines for summarizing:

1. Be sure that you thoroughly understand the original and that your expression of its main point is accurate. Make sure to express the main point of the original—its overall thesis, accomplishment, or contribution to the topic you are researching.

2. In the case of longer pieces, summarize some supporting ideas that back up the main point but be careful not to write too much. A summary should be much shorter than the original and short enough to fit naturally into your paper.

PRACTICE   13-4

Read the following passage from the Wal-Mart article and write a brief (2–3 sentences) summary of the author's main points. Answers will vary.

> More recently, the company experienced a run of bad publicity when it announced new scheduling policies for its store workers (known as "associates"). Under what critics call the "open availability" policy, workers must make themselves available for different shifts from month to month or risk losing hours. Kathleen MacDonald, a cosmetics-counter manager at a Wal-Mart in Aiken, South Carolina, explained to me, "It's simple. They say you have to be there when the computer says the customers will be there. So if you have kids at home you can't show up, but then your hours are being cut."
>
> The company is facing more consequential challenges over its treatment of women. A class-action lawsuit filed in San Francisco in 2001 by six female Wal-Mart employees, alleging that the company has denied promotions and equal pay to women, is proceeding steadily to trial; by some estimates, the suit could cost the company as much as five billion dollars. Wal-Mart has denied that it discriminates against women. Kathleen MacDonald joined the suit after she learned that a male counterpart, who, like her, was stocking shelves, earned more than she did. When she raised the issue, she told me, "My immediate supervisor said, 'Well, God made Adam first, and Eve came from him.' I was, like, what? That's when I decided enough was enough."

Your summary: According to Goldberg, Wal-Mart's image has been tarnished by publicity related to its treatment of employees and, more seriously, a gender discrimination lawsuit filed in 2001 that could cost the company billions of dollars.

Extracting Information from a Source

Look at how a student has extracted information from an article for use in her own paper. In this case, the student is researching the worldwide political response to the global warming crisis and has found an article by Michael Glantz, a senior scientist at the National Center for Atmospheric Research in Boulder, Colorado, which appeared in *Geotimes* in April 2005. She has read the article and annotated it, and she has highlighted the sections she thinks she might use in her paper. Now her job is to extract the material she needs by using paraphrase, summary, quotation, or an appropriate mixture of these.

Global Warming: Whose Problem Is It Anyway?

It no longer seems to make a difference who started the global warming problem, and by "problem," I am referring to the likely enhancement of the naturally occurring greenhouse effect as a result of human activities. Those activities primarily center on the release of carbon dioxide through the burning of fossil fuels such as coal, oil and natural gas. Other heat-trapping greenhouse gases include methane, nitrous oxide and chlorofluorocarbons (CFCs). [. . .]

As we settle into the 21st century, new major greenhouse-gas-producing nations are appearing on the scene, such as India and China. They want to develop their economies, and they have a right, as well as a responsibility, to their citizens to do so. But they are also going to be emitting a larger share of heat-trapping gases, overtaking the industrialized countries that have been the dominant producers of greenhouse gases in the past. Now what? [. . .]

Use this to show that whatever we in the West do, it's the emerging economies of Asia and Latin America that will be hardest to rein in. They say, "You did it—why shouldn't we?"

Since 1985, however, another category has emerged: the ostrich. The ostriches include those who refuse to think about global warming as a problem, who refuse to consider any new scientific research, and who think that someone somewhere will solve this problem before it becomes a crisis. [. . .]

Global warming is not a hoax. It actually happens naturally. Industrialization processes in rich countries and now in developing ones are abetting the naturally occurring greenhouse effect. [. . .]

What will it take to convince naysayers of the seriousness of the problem? This is a task of education.

But although we talk a lot about doing something about global warming, we do not have a whole lot of meaningful action. "Let them eat carbon dioxide" seems to be the current response of various governments, despite words of concern. Is anyone trying to cut back on carbon dioxide emissions?

The business community, at-risk cities and island nations are increasingly calling for action to combat human-induced global warming. What is needed? Only an active government policy around which a coalition can rally will thoroughly address the complex issue.

Alas, the issue demands government leadership from the "bully pulpit" that calls for and wholeheartedly supports an all-out "war on global warming." In my view, it is the only way to address the global warming problem with some sense of optimism. [. . .]

The war on global warming should begin now. With government support (moral and financial) and a search for new ways to keep our industries progressing without adding greenhouse gases to the atmosphere, there is a real chance for the global community to pull together. [. . .]

The Dutch have successfully fought off the floods of the North Sea for centuries, with few breaches in recent times (1953 comes to mind). The Netherlands have even contracted with the U.S. federal government for a few hundred million dollars, to assist in developing levees that can withstand certain intensities of tropical storms around New Orleans.

Despite their levee-making skills, however, the Dutch know their limits. The Netherlands is now working to develop a "Hydropole," a city that can live on the rising waters. They know they need to do something to protect the 70 percent of the country that is below sea level, when a warmer atmosphere leads to rising seas.

Well, if the business community sees the risk, it must be real and it must be bad. I'm not sure how optimistic we can be given that we haven't slowed our production of harmful emissions. How long will it take?

Use this to show that some countries are at least planning to protect their populations.

> Other countries need to follow by accepting the potential changes that lie ahead, and working now to plan for those changes and to curb actions that would otherwise fuel more change. Only with an aggressive war on global warming, supported by the entire international community of nations and with participation of the United States, can we learn to live within the guidelines of nature, respecting her thresholds of change by choosing not to cross them.

Here, the student summarizes a portion of the article:

> In his article, Glantz describes the efforts of the Netherlands to protect its low-lying populations by developing cities that can survive as waters rise around them.

Here are two paraphrases from the article.

PARAPHRASE 1: According to Glantz, the only way we will begin addressing the problem of global warming with any hope for success is for governments to take leadership roles and begin developing policies that lead the way. He notes that the pressure for change is coming from a range of interests, including business, coastal cities, and nations situated on islands.

PARAPHRASE 2 (INCORPORATING QUOTATION): Glantz writes that the newly developing nations of India and China, just to name two, will be increasing contributors to the problem. After all, he claims, "they want to develop their economies, and they have a right, as well as a responsibility, to their citizens to do so." However, this natural desire for economic growth will propel them to overtake Western countries in their production of greenhouse gasses. Glantz wonders how we will approach this difficulty.

And here is a quotation, which the student believes will make a good basis for a hopeful conclusion in her own paper.

> Glantz states, "The war on global warming should begin now. With government support (moral and financial) and a search for new ways to keep our industries progressing without adding greenhouse gases to the atmosphere, there is a real chance for the global community to pull together."

How Do I Integrate Sources?

Now that you've had some practice extracting information from source materials (see Chapter 14 for guidance on recording your paraphrases, summaries, and quotations on note cards), we can discuss the next step: integrating the information into your own writing.

Whenever you use borrowed material in your own work, you must indicate to your reader where the borrowed material begins and ends. Your reader should never be left wondering which words and ideas belong to you and which come from your sources. You also need to integrate borrowed material naturally into your own work so that it reads smoothly as part of your paper. In addition, you must identify the source adequately as part of the integration of the material into your own text, using a *signal phrase*.

A signal phrase is a short phrase you use in your own writing to introduce borrowed material. You've seen several of them already in this chapter: "According to Goldberg, . . .", "Glantz states, . . .", "Glantz writes that . . .", and so on.

> According to Goldberg, "Ethical ambidexterity is not a barrier to success in the public-relations field, particularly in Washington" (36).

In this case, you might think it would be sufficient just to begin the borrowed material with the open quotation mark. After all, wouldn't that be enough to signal to your reader that you are introducing borrowed material? It would, but it wouldn't fulfill the other requirements of integration: the borrowed material must fit smoothly into your paper and you must identify the source adequately as part of the integration. Leaving the signal phrase out results in an error known as *dropped quotation*. Dropped quotations simply appear out of nowhere, and they can confuse your reader and interrupt the flow of your own writing.

DROPPED QUOTATION: Newspapers need to be more innovative in how they deliver news if they hope to capture the youth market. "Younger readers are gleaning their news elsewhere, whether *The Daily Show* or Google's news Web site" (Steinberg). Teens find such methods less time consuming and more entertaining, two important elements of their lifestyles.

SAME QUOTATION INTEGRATED WITH APPROPRIATE SIGNAL PHRASE (LEAD-IN): Newspapers need to be more innovative in how they deliver news if they hope to capture the youth market. According to Brian Steinberg, the new generation of readers "are gleaning their news elsewhere, whether *The Daily Show* or Google's news Web site." Teens find such methods less time consuming and more entertaining, two important elements of their lifestyles.

The following list should help you choose signal phrases to integrate your direct quotations or paraphrased material.

Signal Words to Integrate Quotations or Paraphrased Material into Writing			
according to	comments	explains	refutes
acknowledges	compares	grants	rejects
adds	confirms	illustrates	reports
admits	considers (that)	implies	responds
affirms	contends	insists	states
agrees	declares	in the words of	suggests
alleges	demonstrates	notes	thinks
argues	denies	maintains	underlines
asserts	disputes	observes	writes
believes	emphasizes	points out	
claims	endorses	reasons	

Here are some examples of signal phrases in action:

■ As one critic points out, "…" (Smith 13).
■ Jean-Paul Sartre believed that "…" (87).
■ In the words of St. Thomas Aquinas, "…" (35).
■ According to most critics, the lyrics suggest that "…" (Cooper 34–35).

Besides using signal phrases, you can integrate direct quotations as follows:

1. Make your direct quotation a grammatical component of your sentence.
   ■ One of the most affecting comments from *The Diary of Anne Frank* was that she still believes that "all people are basically good at heart."
   ■ In defense, Mandalay Resort Group President Glenn Schaeffer states that casino jobs are not "fast-food jobs" but jobs "you can grow in and support a family" on (qtd. in Smith 35).
2. Use a form of the word *follow* or a verb (and a colon) to introduce your direct quotation.
   ■ Carrie Russell, a surrogate mother who decided to help others, made the following claim: "I knew I could do it because there were no genetic ties to me" (qtd. in Katz).
   ■ Chad Hills, reporter for *Focus on Social Issues,* writes: "A 73-year-old retired Colorado man gambled away his entire life savings, $63,000, at the nickel slots."

As you incorporate your direct quotations into your paper, remember to integrate each smoothly into your text. You should move the reader from your own thoughts to your sources' ideas and then back again to your discussion. Dropped quotations only disrupt the smooth transition of ideas.

Punctuating Quotations

Some students find that punctuating direct quotations can be confusing. However, by applying six simple rules and editing your writing carefully, you should not have difficulty punctuating direct quotations.

1. When introducing a quotation with a signal phrase, use a comma or a colon to introduce a quotation that can stand alone.

   > According to Glenn Welker, "The Mayan culture was not one unified empire but rather a multitude of separate entities with a common cultural background."

2. If the quotation is a grammatical component of your sentence (a part of your sentence structure), don't use a comma and don't capitalize the first letter of the direct quotation.

   > Recent studies indicate that the Mayan civilization developed an elaborate system of writing "to record the transition of power through the generations" (Welker).

3. Place commas and periods inside quotation marks.

   > "In both the priesthood and the ruling class," reports Glenn Welker, "nepotism was apparently the prevailing system under which new members were chosen."

4. Unlike commas and periods, which go inside the quotation marks, semicolons and colons should be placed outside the quotation marks unless they are part of the quotation.

   > Glenn Welker further reports that after the birth of an heir, a Maya ruler "performed a blood sacrifice": the sacrifice consisted of "drawing blood from his own body and offering to his ancestors"; however, Welker adds that "a human sacrifice was then offered at the time of the new king's installation in office."

5. If the quotation is in the form of a question, then place the question mark inside the quotation mark; however, if you are raising a question and adding a quotation that wasn't originally presented in the source in question form, then place the question mark outside the quotation mark.

   > To encourage reliable research, John Keyser raises the following question: "Why are modern ethnologists and archeologists so confused?" He claims that modern researchers have abandoned their inquiry into the culture of the people to pursue the theory of evolution. However, will these researchers really "lose the tools that would enable them to unravel the mystery of the Maya"?

6. As a general rule, you should quote only as much as you need from a sentence, not necessarily the entire sentence. When you break up your source's sentence, you need to let the reader know that the quotation is not complete and that you have left out part of the passage. Ellipsis points serve this purpose. Ellipsis points are three spaced dots (. . .) signaling to the reader that part of the source's information has been left out. Be careful not to join parts that do not form a complete sentence.

> Michael D. Lemonick further maintains that "four new Maya sites have been uncovered in the jungle-clad mountains of southern Belize . . . that experts assumed the Maya would have shunned."

Paraphrasing

Look again at the student paraphrase from the global warming article.

> Glantz writes that the newly developing nations of India and China, just to name two, will be increasing contributors to the problem. After all, he claims, "they want to develop their economies, and they have a right, as well as a responsibility, to their citizens to do so." However, this natural desire for economic growth will propel them to overtake Western countries in their production of greenhouse gasses. Glantz wonders how we will approach this difficulty.

The difficulty of indicating the beginning and end of paraphrased selections is that paraphrases can be fairly long—a whole paragraph or even longer. When you present a longer paraphrase, you not only need to indicate where it begins but also need occasionally to remind your reader *during* your paraphrase that you are still presenting borrowed material. Notice that the student used a signal phrase to introduce Glantz at the beginning of the paraphrase, then the pronoun *he* to introduce the quotation (otherwise, she would have a dropped quotation), and then Glantz's name at the end to remind the reader that she is still presenting Glantz's ideas in the form of paraphrase. Notice that this is an example of a paraphrase that includes a direct quotation.

Summarizing

In the student's summary of the global warming article, she needs to integrate the source.

> In his article, Glantz describes the efforts of the Netherlands to protect its low-lying populations by developing cities that can survive as waters rise around them.

Because the purpose of summary is to present a short statement about what one of the sources contributes to the paper, it's natural to want to identify that source; doing so usually lends weight and authority to the point the writer is trying to make. Again, you can accomplish this purpose in the signal phrase.

Bringing Borrowed Material to an End

If you use signal phrases to introduce borrowed material, how do you indicate to your reader that the borrowed material has ended? Here are several ways:

1. Use a parenthetical citation as you have seen several times already in this chapter.

> Heiml reports that the Haitian leaders were at first hesitant to act (465). This is just the kind of restraint the country could have used in later years, but there was no such luck.

2. Let the borrowed passage end one of your own paragraphs. When you indent for a new paragraph, your reader understands that you're beginning anew with your own words and ideas.

> Frothermeyer argues that because of their evolutionary past, humans are biologically unable to process large amounts of starchy carbohydrates; furthermore, he claims, almost all diagnosed obesity could be eliminated through dietary changes.
>
> Another inheritance of our biological past is the need for fairly consistent, if not constant, exercise.

3. Start the next sentence with a new signal phrase, indicating the beginning of another borrowed passage or a transition to your own words and ideas.

> MacElwey writes that American education in the 21st century must abandon its traditional way of doing business and adopt models from overseas. According to Galen, the German model of secondary education offers the best hope for our failing system (54).

PRACTICE   13-5

Read the following passages from student research papers. In the space provided, evaluate the integration of source materials and briefly explain your evaluation.

1. Alarmingly, millions of children are being treated for a disease that does not actually exist. Attention deficit/hyperactivity disorder is not a biological disease. "ADHD genetic researchers cannot determine a convincing body of evidence pointing toward genetic factors" (Breggin 126). The list of potential symptoms is rather lengthy and somewhat vague.

   Acceptable _____ **Unacceptable** _X_ **Explanation:** Technically, this is a dropped quotation, appearing in the middle of a passage without a signal phrase to introduce it. Although this practice is relatively common in academic research, it can lead to stylistic clumsiness and lack of coherence.

2. The once-active child becomes less spontaneous and more compliant. How-ever, these children are not learning to become more disciplined; the drugs are merely inhibiting brain function (Breggin 20). Children taking Ritalin certainly become more compliant and passive.

   Acceptable _____ **Unacceptable** __X__ **Explanation:** _This passage fails to_ _identify the source of the obviously paraphrased first and last sentences. Without_ _a signal phrase, the reader doesn't know where the Breggin source begins. The_ _last sentence is not signaled as coming from a source or from the student._

3. A national survey reveals interesting data: "Of 1,261 school administrators, 97% indicated that school violence was increasing across the United States and in their neighboring school districts" (Furlong and Morrison).

   Acceptable __X__ **Unacceptable** _____ **Explanation:** _____

   _____

   _____

   _____

4. Opinion is fairly evenly split across the country. Supporters believe the generous coverage supplied by employers and national health programs causes individu-als to ignore high costs of health care, implying that under the circumstances of paying for health care out of pocket people would shop for cheaper health plans, which in turn would put pressure on suppliers (Bailey).

   Acceptable _____ **Unacceptable** __X__ **Explanation:** _Without a signal phrase,_ _the reader doesn't know if Bailey is the source of the whole passage or just of_ _the second sentence._

   _____

5. In a radio address, President Clinton emphasized the importance of keeping track of sexual predators, thereby reducing crimes against children. He made the following commitment: "Above all, we must move forward to the day when we are no longer numb to acts of violence against children, when their appearance on the evening news is both shocking and rare. Our approach is working. . . . More and more, our children can learn and play and dream without risk of harm. That is an America that is moving in the right direction" (91).

   Acceptable __X__ **Unacceptable** _____ **Explanation:** _____

   _____

   _____

   _____

How Do I Avoid Plagiarism?

If you aren't quoting, paraphrasing, or summarizing your source material correctly, chances are you are plagiarizing it. When you plagiarize, you are stealing someone else's words or ideas and passing them off as your own. Sometimes, students plagiarize unin-tentionally, especially when they are first learning how to work with sources. At other times, students are tempted to plagiarize deliberately. Plagiarism is a serious offense against academic integrity and can result in failure in a course, disciplinary action, or expulsion from a college or university.

It should be clear that you have an important ethical obligation when you work with other people's words and ideas. The rules governing the use of sources have been created over centuries of academic dialogue and debate, and they are the basis of all academic culture. To be sure, the rules are being tested in the age of the Internet, but they still guide the way we integrate the work of other thinkers and writers into our own thinking and writing.

Common Types of Plagiarism

- You plagiarize when you "lift" passages from a source word for word and place them into your own writing without quoting and citing them.
- You plagiarize when you put others' ideas into your own words (even when you do it correctly) but don't cite the source.
- You plagiarize when, in a paraphrase or summary, you use *any* of the author's stylistically characteristic words, phrases, or sentence structures, whether or not you cite the source.

Strategies to Prevent Plagiarism

If you employ the integrating techniques introduced in this chapter, you can avoid plagiarizing from your sources. That is, if you paraphrase correctly, summarize correctly, and quote correctly—and if you cite every source from which you borrow—you won't be guilty of plagiarism. As a summary of this chapter's advice, here are some helpful hints you can use to guide your thinking as you extract words and ideas from your sources.

When paraphrasing, remember the following:

- Read the original actively and critically. Make sure you really understand it before trying to paraphrase it.
- Put the original aside and do your best to capture the main and supporting points without referring back to the original.
- Use short sentences to capture the meaning of the original; then combine your short sentences into longer ones.
- Once you've written a paraphrase, check it against the original to make sure you haven't used any of the author's distinctive words or sentence structures. If you are still too close to the original, try paraphrasing your own paraphrase. Repeat this process several times to gradually move away from the original. Check to make sure that you are retaining the meaning of the original, however.

When summarizing, remember the following:

- Write a sentence that states your own understanding of the source's contribution to the topic you are writing about. Don't take your summary from the introduction of the article or from a book jacket.

- If you are summarizing a longer piece, such as a long research article or a book, your summary may contain additional material. Again, this material must be in your own words and sentence structures.

When quoting, remember the following:

- Extract the material verbatim (word for word) from your source.
- Put quotation marks around all quoted material and punctuate your quotations correctly.

Finally, whether you are paraphrasing, summarizing, or quoting, you *must* document the source of any borrowed material. If you fail to document the source, you could easily be accused of deliberate plagiarism.

How Do I Document My Sources?

Although we use MLA documentation style in this chapter, you are not limited to just this style. Your instructor will let you know the style most appropriate for the course. Different purposes may require different styles. The following are the four most common types of documentation styles:

- Generally, Modern Language Association (MLA) style is used in the humanities in such courses as English, philosophy, and art. It's probably one of the simplest documentation styles to use.
- American Psychological Association (APA) style is often, although not exclusively, used in the social sciences: psychology, sociology, and anthropology. It's not unusual for an instructor in business management, education, or biology to require APA style.
- *The Chicago Manual of Style* (CMS) is often used in the humanities and the social sciences. However, it's more complex than MLA and APA. Again, your instructor or your employer should have the final word.
- Council of Science Editors (CSE) is a scientific style. This system is used to document information in the biological sciences, as well as other scientific classes.

Regardless of the particular citation style they use, all researchers must abide by strict rules to document their use of sources. Documentation consists of two components:

1. In-text citations, which you insert throughout your paper to indicate exactly where you are using source material.
2. A list of all sources, or references, that you use in your paper; in MLA style, this list of references is called *Works Cited*.

These two components work closely together to inform your reader about your use of sources.

Understanding In-Text Citations

Every time you use information or ideas from a source—whether paraphrased, summarized, or quoted—you must acknowledge the source by inserting a reference in your text, crediting that source. You can either mention the source in a signal phrase or indicate the source in parentheses at the end of the information. These in-text citations serve three purposes:

1. They credit your sources for their input to your paper. As you already know, failing to credit your sources is considered plagiarism.
2. They give your reader enough information to locate a complete description of your sources on the Works Cited page.
3. If your source is a print source or a PDF file, the page number lets the reader find in the original text the specific passage your are referencing.

> Recent studies have found that several regions of the brain of a person with autism are different from the norm, but unfortunately, none of these differences alone can account for this condition (Carmichael 53).

Look at some characteristics of this citation:

- Through the parenthetical citation at the end, you immediately know that this information comes from someone other than the student writer.
- Since there are no quotation marks, you can conclude that this passage is a paraphrase, the student's own interpretation of the source.
- The author's last name is Carmichael. To find out more about the Carmichael source, you need only to go to "C" in the Works Cited list, where you can find a full description of the source.
- The page number tells you that the information appears on page 53 in the article.

Here are some basic rules of parenthetical citation:

1. **Place your citation right after the source's information.** Place your own commentaries after the citation to keep your own ideas and knowledge separate from your source's ideas.

    INCORRECT: According to Freud, we go through five stages of development, known as psychosexual stages. In each stage, a person faces a crisis that must be worked out or else become fixated in that stage of development. For example, a Freudian psychologist might explain my brother's smoking and overeating as a result of a fixation in the oral stage (Rivera 102).

    Rivera didn't know your brother; furthermore, Rivera might not have agreed with your example. Place your citations in a manner that distinguishes your interpretations and experiences, although valuable to the paper, from the source's information.

    CORRECT: According to Freud, we go through five stages of development, known as psychosexual stages. In each stage, a person faces a crisis that must be worked out or else become fixated in that stage of development (Rivera 102). For example, a Freudian psychologist might explain my brother's smoking and over eating as a result of a fixation in the oral stage.

2. **Credit all authors.** Don't just credit the first author listed in a source. You must credit all coauthors as well. Also, when crediting coauthors, don't change the order in which the authors are listed in a document. Follow these rules for crediting authors:

> One author: (Smith 13)
> Two authors: (Smith and Jackson 13)
> Three authors: (Smith, Jackson, and Johnson 13)
> Four or more authors: (Smith et al. 13); the abbreviation *et al.* means *et alii*, which is Latin for "and others."

3. **Make your parenthetical citations clear without distracting the reader from the task of reading your paper.** Since the goal is to provide enough information to refer the reader to the Works Cited entry, limit your information to the essentials. Sometimes the page number may not be available. For example, many Internet sources don't supply page numbers unless the document is in a PDF file. If the page number is not available, omit it. When you print your sources from the Internet, your printer numbers your pages, but you should not use these numbers as the source's page numbers.

4. **Permit your reader to locate your source in the Works Cited list without having to search.** Your Works Cited list should be in strict alphabetical order. Therefore, your in-text citation should take the reader directly to the correct entry in the list.

> **CORRECT:** The Small Business Development Center in Maine reports that more than four dollars in state revenue are generated annually for each tax payer dollar that state residents invest in the S.B.D.C. (Turkel).

The reader needs merely to go to "T" in the Works Cited list to find the entire information about the source.

5. **Don't clutter your parenthetical citations.** Keep your citations clear and to the point.

   a. If you name the source in your text, don't repeat it in the parenthetical citation.

> **INCORRECT:** Marie Valdez writes that recent studies indicate that 5 out of every 100 high school students enrolled in October 1999 dropped out of school before October 2000 (Valdez 23).
>
> **CORRECT:** Marie Valdez writes that recent studies indicate that 5 out of every 100 high school students enrolled in October 1999 dropped out of school before October 2000 (23).

OR

> **CORRECT:** Recent studies indicate that 5 out of every 100 high school students enrolled in October 1999 dropped out of school before October 2000 (Valdez 23).

b. Do not break up the parenthetical citation by inserting a comma, *p.*, or *page* between the source and its page number.

> INCORRECT: (Shanstrom, 46) OR (Shanstrom p. 46) OR (Shanstrom page 46)
> CORRECT: (Shanstrom 46)

6. **If the author is unknown, move to the next available unit of information.** Obtaining sources without an author's name is not uncommon. In sources from periodicals or from the Internet, the next unit of information is usually the title of the article or the title of the book.

> ARTICLE: Numerous studies and surveys indicate that occupational pressures are the primary source of stress ("Job Stress" 13).

Note that the quotation marks indicate the title is the name of the article. Don't omit the quotation marks in your citations. The reader can find this source under "J" in the Works Cited list.

> BOOK: The human body has a natural stress reaction that increases "the energy levels to prepare the body for a predicament and then drops the energy level when the situation is over" (<u>Nutrition and You</u> 75).

a. Just as with names of authors, if you name the title of the article or the title of the book in the text, you don't need to repeat it in the citation.

> CORRECT: The *Gazette's* article "Downtown Retailers Hope to Win Holiday Shoppers" points out that most retailers want to attract new customers, and to be successful they realize that they must "combine marketing dollars and promote downtown together" (12).

b. Again, make your parenthetical citations as simple and elegant as possible. It's acceptable to shorten long titles of either books or articles. Just provide enough information so that your reader can locate the source in the Works Cited list.

> INCORRECT: Most retailers want to attract new customers, and to be successful they realize that they must "combine marketing dollars and promote downtown together" ("Downtown Retailers Hope to Win Holiday Shoppers" 12).
> CORRECT: Most retailers want to attract new customers, and to be successful they realize that they must "combine marketing dollars and promote downtown together" ("Downtown" 12).

7. **If you use a quotation that was quoted in another source, indicate this in your parenthetical citation.** For example, suppose that your source is Martha Johnson. As you read the information, you find that Johnson quotes a prominent economist by the name of Benjamin Randall. You want to use Randall's exact quotation for your paper. You have two choices: go to the original source, Randall, or use Johnson

as the source and indicate that Randall is the indirect source. Here's how you would cite this source:

> Economist Benjamin Randall states, "America's current immigration policies . . . fail to recognize the importance of Mexican workers to the national economy" (qtd. in Johnson 18).

By using *qtd. in* (meaning "quoted in"), you're letting the reader know that Randall is not listed in the Works Cited list and that the information appears under Johnson.

8. **If you use two or more sources by the same author, be sure to identify which source you are using.** If you simply give the author's name, the reader looks at the Works Cited list and finds that you have the author listed more than once. Since you do not offer additional clues, your reader does not know where the information comes from. There are several ways you can identify the source:

a. Name the author in the text and the article in the parenthetical citation.

> **CORRECT:** We hesitate to increase our police force because of budget constraints, yet we fail to consider the cost of crime. Raymond Diaz reports that personal crimes alone are "estimated to cost $105 billion annually in medical costs, lost earnings, and public program costs related to victim assistance" ("Rethinking" 61).

b. Name the title of the article in the text and the author in the parenthetical citation.

> **CORRECT:** We hesitate to increase our police force because of budget constraints, yet we fail to consider the cost of crime. The article titled "Rethinking the Cost of Crime in America" states that personal crimes alone are "estimated to cost $105 billion annually in medical costs, lost earnings, and public program costs related to victim assistance" (Diaz 61).

c. Name the author and the title of the article in the text.

> **CORRECT:** We hesitate to increase our police force because of budget constraints, yet we fail to consider the cost of crime. In his article titled "Rethinking the Cost of Crime in America," Raymond Diaz reports that personal crimes alone are "estimated to cost $105 billion annually in medical costs, lost earnings, and public program costs related to victim assistance" (61).

d. Place all information in the parenthetical citation and not in the text.

> **CORRECT:** We hesitate to increase our police force because of budget constraints, yet we fail to consider the cost of crime. Personal crimes alone are "estimated to cost $105 billion annually in medical costs, lost earnings, and public program costs related to victim assistance" (Diaz, "Rethinking" 61).

PRACTICE 13-6

For each set of source information, give a parenthetical citation using the necessary information provided in the bracket. *Do not* edit the text; supply the parenthetical citations only.

1. According to a 2002 article in *The Economist*, "Schools are responsible for instilling in our youths a strong sense of civic responsibilities." [No author is given. The title of the article is "Looking into the Future," which appeared in the September 23, 2002 issue of *The Economist*.] ("Looking").

2. Brian Lawson predicts that the dropout rate would decrease if parents were held more accountable. [This information appeared on page 56 of an article by Brian Lawson titled "The Educational Crisis," published in *Education Outlook* in the April 2007 issue.] (56)

3. Recent surveys indicate that 4 out of 10 high school seniors "in both urban and suburban schools have used illegal drugs." [This was written by Jay Green and Greg Forster. The article, titled "Sex, Drug, and Delinquency in Urban and Suburban Public Schools," was published in January 2004. It appeared on the Manhattan Institute for Policy Research website.] (Green and Forster)

4. The trend continues. Twelve seniors from Willington High School admitted having used prescription drugs they either purchased in Mexico or took from their parent's medicine chests. [The author is unknown; the article, titled "High School Assessment of Drug Use among Seniors," was published on April 25, 2004. It appeared on The Havendale Update, a website at http://www. havendale.com/newaudate/highschool/drugs.html.] ("High School")

5. Leslie Drier, executive director of United for a Drug Free America, states that the use of prescription drugs is "engrained in teen culture and not enough parents are aware of the existing trend." [This information, written by Leonard Rios, appears in an article titled "High School and Drugs." It was published in the October 2005 issue of *Issues in Education*. The information appears on page 73.] (qtd. in Rios 73)

Understanding the Works Cited List

The final page of your research paper is your list of sources. If you're using MLA documentation style, this list is called *Works Cited*. In this section, we discuss the most common sources you are likely to document in most classes. If you use sources other than those listed here, refer to the *MLA Handbook for Writers of Research Papers*.

Your first step is to identify the type of source you're using. For example, is it a book, a periodical (newspaper, magazine, or journal), a website, or an interview? Once you identify the source, you can then focus on the required units of information necessary to document that source. For example, most sources require that you start with the name of the author. A source written by **one author** looks like this:

Carter, Lana.

Note that you invert the name of the author: last name, then a comma, first name, and a period. If you have **two authors,** you must also include the name of the coauthor, but don't invert it.

> Morales, Juan, and Michael Engle.

A source by **three authors** is similar.

> Kingrey, Gail, Nick Alfonso, and Rose H. Santiago.

However, if you have **four or more authors,** list only the first author and use *et al.* (Latin for "and others") to indicate the rest of the coauthors.

> McKinnon, Sara, et al.

If **no author** is listed, jump to the next unit—the title of the book or the title of the article in a periodical, depending on the source you're documenting.

In general, remember the following points:

- Start with the author; if no author is given, jump to the next unit of information.
- Underline titles of books and periodicals.
- Follow punctuation rules carefully. With minor exceptions, as illustrated in the examples throughout this section, place a period after each unit.
- End all entries with a period.
- If one unit of information is missing, jump to the next unit.
- Page numbers are not always required, but if the page numbers for periodicals are available, include the range, for example, 37–42. Your parenthetical citation will give the specific page number.

Documenting Books

Each box represents a unit. Pay close attention to punctuation.

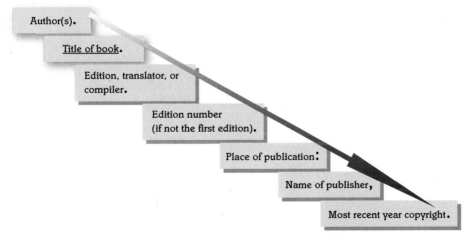

For publisher's names omit articles (*A, An, The*); abbreviations such as *Co., Inc., Ltd.*; and parts of the publisher's name, such as *House, Publishers,* or *Press.* However, if referring to university presses, use UP, e.g. Oxford UP.

1. **Book with one or more authors.**

    Henley, Patricia. <u>The Hummingbird House</u>.
        Denver: MacMurray, 1999.

    > **Sample Parenthetical Citation**
    > (Henley 135)

    Caper, Charles, and Lawrence T. Teamos.
        <u>How to Camp</u>. Philadelphia:
        Doubleday, 1986.

    > **Sample Parenthetical Citation**
    > (Caper and Teamos 105)

    Setmire, Elisa. <u>Studies of Autism</u>. 3rd ed.
        Oxford: Oxford UP, 2007.

    > **Sample Parenthetical Citation**
    > (Setmire 105-106)

    Nichols, James O., and Karen W. Nichols.
        <u>The Departmental Guide and Record
        Book for Student Outcomes and
        Assessment and Institutional
        Effectiveness.</u> New York: Agathon,
        2000.

    > **Sample Parenthetical Citation**
    > (Nichols and Nichols 65)

    Nazario, Luis A., Deborah D. Borchers, and
        William F. Lewis. <u>Bridges to Better
        Writing</u>. Boston: Cengage, 2010.

    > **Sample Parenthetical Citation**
    > (Nazario, Borchers, and Lewis 317)

    Gilman, Sandor, et al. <u>Hysteria Beyond Freud</u>.
        Berkeley: U of California P, 1993.

    > **Sample Parenthetical Citation**
    > (Gilman et al. 370)

2. **Book with no author named.**

    <u>Freedom: A Profile in Courage</u>. New York:
        Macmillan, 2003.

    > **Sample Parenthetical Citation**
    > (<u>Freedom</u> 370)

3. **Book with an editor**

    Chavez, Crystal, ed. <u>Tales of Women
        Entrepreneurs</u>. New York: Bedford/
        St. Martin's, 2007.

    > **Sample Parenthetical Citation**
    > (Chavez 205)

    (Use abbreviation "ed" for "editor" and "eds" for "editors.")

4. **Section from an anthology (a work by many authors or different works by the
    same author)**

    Levy, Steven. "iPOD Nation." <u>Mirror on
        America</u>. Ed. Joan T. Mims, New York:
        Bedford/St. Martins, 2007. 346-59.

    > **Sample Parenthetical Citation**
    > (Levy 349)

Examine the Works Cited page that follows based on the preceding nine books.

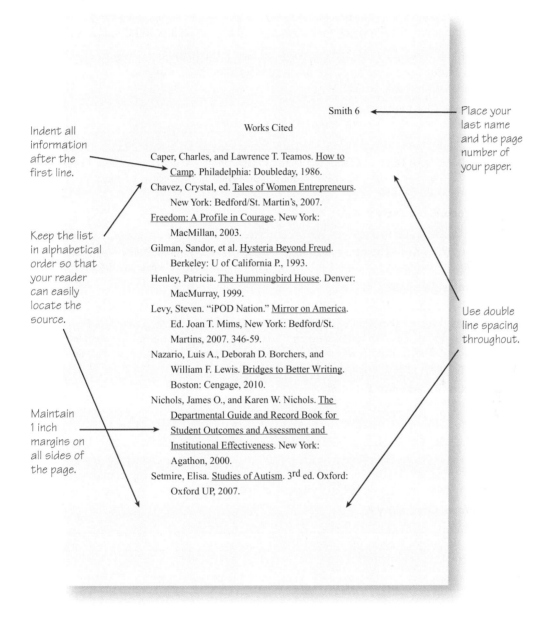

Smith 6

Works Cited

Caper, Charles, and Lawrence T. Teamos. <u>How to Camp</u>. Philadelphia: Doubleday, 1986.

Chavez, Crystal, ed. <u>Tales of Women Entrepreneurs</u>. New York: Bedford/St. Martin's, 2007.

<u>Freedom: A Profile in Courage</u>. New York: MacMillan, 2003.

Gilman, Sandor, et al. <u>Hysteria Beyond Freud</u>. Berkeley: U of California P., 1993.

Henley, Patricia. <u>The Hummingbird House</u>. Denver: MacMurray, 1999.

Levy, Steven. "iPOD Nation." <u>Mirror on America</u>. Ed. Joan T. Mims, New York: Bedford/St. Martins, 2007. 346-59.

Nazario, Luis A., Deborah D. Borchers, and William F. Lewis. <u>Bridges to Better Writing</u>. Boston: Cengage, 2010.

Nichols, James O., and Karen W. Nichols. <u>The Departmental Guide and Record Book for Student Outcomes and Assessment and Institutional Effectiveness</u>. New York: Agathon, 2000.

Setmire, Elisa. <u>Studies of Autism</u>. 3rd ed. Oxford: Oxford UP, 2007.

Indent all information after the first line.

Keep the list in alphabetical order so that your reader can easily locate the source.

Maintain 1 inch margins on all sides of the page.

Place your last name and the page number of your paper.

Use double line spacing throughout.

UNDERSTANDING SOURCES

Write the following books in correct MLA format as they would appear on a Works Cited page. Number the order in which each source would appear on a Works Cited page.

1. A book published by Texas Tech University Press with the title *Children of the Dust: An Okie Family Story*, written in 2006 by Betty Grant Henshaw and published in Lubbock, Texas.

   Works Cited entry #__2__:

   Henshaw, Betty Grant. Children of the Dust: An Okie Family Story. Lubbock:

   ____ Texas Tech UP, 2006.

2. A book titled *House of Tears*, published in Guilford, Connecticut, by Lyons Press in 2005 and edited by Dr. John Hughes, a professor at St. George's School in Vancouver, Canada.

   Works Cited entry #__3__:

   Hughes, John, ed. House of Tears. Guilford, CT: Lyons, 2005.

3. A book by Keith Thomas, a lecturer at Oxford University, titled *Religion and the Decline of Magic*, published in New York in 1999 by Oxford University Press.

   Works Cited entry #__5__:

   Thomas, Keith. Religion and the Decline of Magic. New York: Oxford UP, 1999.

4. A short story titled "Paul's Case" by Willa Cather in an anthology titled *Literature: An Introduction to Reading and Writing* by Edgar V. Roberts and Henry E. Jacobs. The anthology was published in 2004 by Prentice Hall in Upper Saddle River, New Jersey, and the story appears on pages 164–176.

   Works Cited entry #__1__:

   Cather, Willa. "Paul's Case." Literature: An Introduction to Reading and Writing.

   ____ Eds. Edgar V. Roberts and Henry E. Jacobs. Upper Saddle River, NJ:

   ____ Prentice Hall, 2004. 164–76.

5. An essay in *The Best American Essays 2005*, edited by Susan Orlean; the title of the essay is "Old Faithful" by David Sedaris on pages 195–202. The publisher of the book is Houghton Mifflin Company of Boston.

   Works Cited entry #__4__:

   Sedaris, David. "Old Faithful." The Best American Essays 2005. Ed. Susan

   ____ Orlean. Boston: Houghton, 2005. 195–202.

Documenting Periodicals

Periodicals—newspapers, magazines, and journals—can provide current and reliable information if you choose them correctly. The following diagram summarizes the most common types of sources you are most likely to use and document.

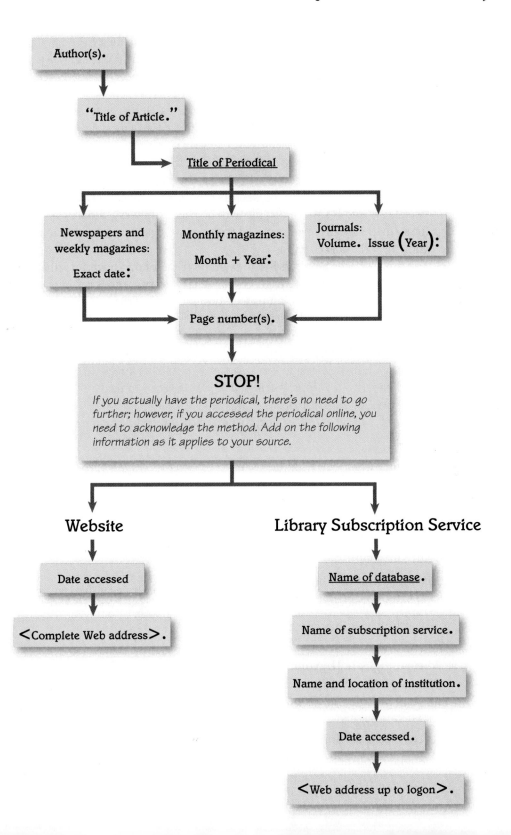

When documenting periodicals, be sure to follow these guidelines.

- Use a colon after the date to indicate the page numbers (Sept. 2007: 45–36.). Articles accessed online often do not have page numbers. In such cases, don't use a colon; use a period.
- Use quotation marks to indicate titles of articles. However, underline titles of periodicals (newspapers, magazines, and journals), names of websites, and names of databases.
- If the online article is provided as a PDF file, which is an actual copy of the article as it was published, you should use the page numbers provided. If a subscription database service, such as EBSCOhost, gives you a choice between PDF and HTML (a text file with no page numbers), choose the PDF file so that you can refer the reader to the exact location of the information in your parenthetical citations.
- The range of page numbers in the examples that follow shows information appearing on consecutive pages. However, if the article does not continue on consecutive pages but jumps to another section of the periodical, let the reader know by giving the starting page and a plus sign (25 Aug. 2006: 17 +.).
- For titles of articles, be sure to capitalize the first letter of the main words (adjectives, adverbs, verbs, nouns, pronouns) even if your source doesn't. Don't capitalize the first letters of articles (*a, an, the*), prepositions, or coordinate conjunctions (*for, and, nor, but, or, yet, so*) unless any of these words start or end the title.

As you review the following examples, go back to the preceding diagram and see how they fit.

1. **Article from a weekly magazine.**

   Carter, Lana. "Educators Advocate Early Intervention." <u>Newsweek</u> 23 June 2007: 36–45.

Sample Parenthetical Citation
(Carter 38)

2. **Article from a monthly magazine.**

   Engle, Michael, and Donna Fitzsimmons. "Gender Violence in Schools." <u>Psychology Issues</u> Feb. 2006: 15–23.

Sample Parenthetical Citation
(Engle and Fitzsimmons 20)

3. **Article from a journal.**
   a. **Journal paginated by volume.** Some journals continue the page numbering throughout the year. For example, the first issue may be from page 1 to 150, the following issue continues from page 151 to 410, and so forth. In this case, you state only the volume number as illustrated here.

   Kingrey, Gail, et al. "Spinal Injuries." <u>New England Journal of Medicine</u> 13 (2006): 413–35.

Sample Parenthetical Citation
(Kingrey et al. 423)

b. **Journal paginated by issue.** If each issue of the journal begins with page 1, then state the number and issue as shown here.

White, Nancy, Martha Augoustinos, and John
Taplin. "Parental Responsibility for the
Illicit Acts of Their Children: Effects of
Age, Type and Severity of Offense."
Journal of Psychology 59.1 (2007): 43–50.

> **Sample Parenthetical Citation**
> (White, Augoustinos, and Taplin 48)

4. **Article from a daily newspaper.**
   a. **Lettered sections.** Some newspapers divide their sections by letters.

Witters, Lani, and Rose Henri Santiago.
"Public Schools in Fairfield under Fire."
The Chieftain 8 Feb. 2006: A2.

> **Sample Parenthetical Citation**
> (Witters and Santiago A2)

   b. **Numbered sections.** Some newspapers mark their sections by numbers.

Alfonso, Nick. "DNA Evidence under
Question." New York Times 31
Nov. 2007, sec. 1: 6.

> **Sample Parenthetical Citation**
> (Alfonso 6)

   c. **Newspaper editorial.** Cite newspaper editorials as you would any newspaper article. Just insert the word *editorial* after the title of the article.

"Let's Send a Message." Editorial. Denver
Post 23 Nov. 2007: A14.

> **Sample Parenthetical Citation**
> ("Let's Send" A14)

5. **Article with no author named.**

"Bilingual Education under Scrutiny:
A Progress Report." The Times
19 Apr. 2007: 25–32.

> **Sample Parenthetical Citation**
> ("Bilingual Education" 27).

6. **Article accessed through a library subscription database service.** Your college library or your public library may provide databases that you can access from your home computer. Through such services as EBSCOhost, Infotrac, Proquest, or Electric Library, you have thousands of periodicals at your disposal. To document such sources, follow the rules for documenting periodicals, and then tag on the service information: name of the database, name of subscription service, name and location of the institution that has the license to give you access, the date you accessed the document, and finally the web address as far as the logon. The entire address is not necessary since your reader cannot use it to access the source. Rather, your reader must go through an institution that has a license. (See the earlier diagram.)

McKinnon, Sara. "Juvenile Overhaul a

Gamble." <u>New Statesman</u> 13 Oct. 2006: 7.

<u>Academic Search Premier</u>. EBSCOhost.

Pueblo Community Coll. Lib., Pueblo,

CO. 12 Nov. 2007 <http://www.epnet.

com.>

> **Sample Parenthetical Citation**
> (McKinnon 7)

7. **Article accessed through a website.** Similar to databases from subscription services, cite the source as you would any periodical. At the end, tag on the date you accessed the document and the complete web address. The entire address is expected since, unlike subscription services, your reader is able to use the address you provide to access the document.

Edwards, David, Nelda Wade, and Cindy

Graham. "Reading, Writing, and

Revolution: A Look at the Artist."

<u>The Literary Review</u> Oct. 2005. 27 Nov.

2007 <http//:www.cds.edu/literary_

review/0800/html.com.>

> **Sample Parenthetical Citation**
> (Edwards, Wade, and Graham)

8. **Two or more articles by the same author.** For both periodicals and books, don't repeat the name of the same author. First, alphabetize the same authors by the next unit: the title of the article or book. Then after the first source, use three hyphens followed by a period to indicate "same as above."

Morales, Juan. "All Facts about

Carbohydrates." <u>Food & Nutrition</u>

12 June 2006: 29–32.

> **Sample Parenthetical Citation**
> (Morales, "All Facts" 32)

---. "Diet Fads and Insanity." <u>Food &</u>

<u>Nutrition</u> 21 Mar. 2006: 7–9.

> **Sample Parenthetical Citation**
> (Morales, "Diet Fads" 8)

Write each of the following periodicals in correct MLA format as it would appear on a Works Cited page. Choose only the information necessary for MLA Works Cited entries. Also, apply the rules for the correct use of capitalization, periods, commas, colons, parentheses, and quotation marks.

1. A monthly magazine article with the title "She Uses Honey, and Pepper, to Get Job Done" by Duane Garrett and Jean Fish-Davis, published in *American Theater* in March 2006 in volume 241, issue 52, on pages 13–21.

   Works Cited entry:
   Garrett, Duane, and Jean Fish-Davis. "She Uses Honey, and Pepper, to Get Job Done." American Theater March 2006: 13–21.

2. In the annals of science section of *The New Yorker*, a magazine article titled "The Denialists: The Dangerous Attacks on the Consensus about H.I.V. and AIDS," published on March 12, 2007, and written by Michael Specter. It appears on pages 32–38.

   Works Cited entry:
   Specter, Michael. "The Denialists: The Dangerous Attacks on the Consensus about H.I.V. and AIDS." The New Yorker 12 Mar. 2007: 32–38.

3. A newspaper article titled "Internet Bullying," written by Denise Borrero and Dina Cerrano. The article, published on July 30, 2008, appears in section B, page 3 of the *San Juan Star*.

   Works Cited entry:
   Borrero, Denise, and Dina Cerrano. "Internet Bullying." San Juan Star 30 July 2008: B3.

4. In the *New York Times*, a newspaper article called "Hard Look at Mission That Ended in Inferno for 3 Women" written by Michael Moss. It appears on page 14 in section 2, dated December 20, 2005.

   Works Cited entry:
   Moss, Michael. "Hard Look at Mission That Ended in Inferno for 3 Women." New York Times 20 Dec. 2005, sec. 2: 14.

5. An article in *Time*, a weekly magazine, published on February 27, 2006, by Tim McGirk and Sally B. Donnelly, with the title "Crossing the Lines." The article appears in volume 167, issue 9, on pages 36–43.

   Works Cited entry:
   McGirk, Tim, and Sally B. Donnelly. "Crossing the Lines." Time 27 Feb. 2006: 36–43.

Documenting Internet Sources

In the preceding section, you cited periodicals from websites and from subscription database services accessed through the Internet. To document such sources, all you needed to do was to tag on at the end of the periodical citation the method you used to retrieve the source. This process also applies to books retrieved through the Internet.

Turn your attention to sources that are not periodicals or books.

1. **Websites.** To document a website, follow the order illustrated here. Skip any unit of information that the website does not provide.

a. **Entire website.**

National Crime Prevention Council. 2006.

    15 Oct. 2007 <http://www.ncpc.org/.>

> **Sample Parenthetical Citation**
> (National)

b. **Article within a website.**

"Racial Profiling: Old and New." American

    Civil Liberties Union. 2007. 23 Jul. 2007

    <http://www.aclu.org/racialjustice/

    racialprofiling/index.html.>

> **Sample Parenthetical Citation**
> ("Racial Profiling")

2. **Online government document.** When documenting government documents, start by indicating the type of government document:

Federal government   =   United States

State government   =   Florida, California, Ohio, and so on

City government   =   Denver, Houston, Portland, and so on

Then name the specific government organization that supplied the information, followed by the title of the document.

United States. Department of Commerce.

    Census Bureau. Income, Poverty, and

    Health Insurance Coverage in the

    United States: 2005. Aug. 2006. 13 Oct.

    2007 <http://www.census.gov/prod/

    2006pubs/p60-231.pdf.>

> **Sample Parenthetical Citation**
> (United States)

Documenting Other Sources

The following types of sources will be common and useful in your courses.

1. **Interview.**

   Milkowski, Melinda. Personal interview.

       6 Oct. 2007.

<table>
<tr><td>**Sample Parenthetical Citation**
(Milkowski)</td></tr>
</table>

2. **CD-ROM.** Document a CD-ROM the same way you would a book. Simply add the word *CD-ROM* after its title.

   "Holocaust." <u>Encarta</u>. CD-ROM. Seattle:

       Microsoft, 2004.

<table>
<tr><td>**Sample Parenthetical Citation**
("Holocaust")</td></tr>
</table>

PRACTICE 13-9

Write the following online sources in correct MLA format as they would appear on a Works Cited page. Use only the information required. Then write the correct parenthetical citation enclosed in parentheses.

1. A short article retrieved from a website, CNN.com, titled "Lack of proper rest poses health, education risks." It was published on September 29, 2000, and accessed by the student on April 6, 2007, at the following web address: http://archives.cnn.com/healtheduction.htm.

   Works Cited entry:

   "Lack of Proper Rest Poses Health, Education Risks." <u>CNN.com</u>. 29 Sep. 2000.
       6 Apr. 2007 <http://archives.cnn.com/healtheduction.htm>.

2. An interview with Esther Huckleberry, director of the Planned Parenthood Center in Paterson, New Jersey, conducted on February 16, 2007.

   Works Cited entry:

   Huckleberry, Esther. Personal interview. 16 Feb. 2007.

3. A CD-ROM written by Sophia Maldonado, titled *Exotic Cuisine*, published in Boston in 2003 by Nutritional Living, Inc.

   Works Cited entry:

   Maldonado, Sophia. <u>Exotic Cuisine</u>. CD-ROM. Boston: Nutritional Living Inc.,
       2003.

4. A short article from the MayoClinic.com website under the Teen's Health section, titled "Teen Sleep: Why Is Your Teen So Tired?" The article was published on August 8, 2005, and accessed by the student on April 6, 2007. The article is a 3-page printout and has the following address: http://www.mayoclinic.com/health/teens-health/CC00019.

   Works Cited entry:

   "Teen Sleep: Why Is Your Teen So Tired?" <u>MayoClinic.com</u>. 8 Aug. 2005. 6 Apr.
       2007 <http://www.mayoclinic.com>.

CHAPTER 14

Writing Your Research Paper

YOUR GOALS

Understanding the Value of Research

1. Understand the importance of research.

2. Use research to tap into a wider academic world.

Writing Your Research Paper

1. Choose a topic for your research paper.

2. Plan your research paper.

3. Use the library and the Internet to gather information.

4. Evaluate the reliability of your sources.

5. Create source cards and note cards as a way to gather and manage information from sources.

6. Prepare a formal outline.

7. Incorporate in-text citations into your draft.

8. Format your draft according to an approved standard.

"Knowledge is of two kinds. We know a subject ourselves, or we know where we can find information on it."

■ Samuel Johnson ■

As a student, you may dread the idea of doing research. You envision yourself spending hours in a quiet library looking for sources and trying to figure out "where this whole thing is going." Yet at some point, we all need to learn how to research topics of interest and importance to us. The ability to conduct research independently is at the heart of what it means to be an educated person.

Professionally, you may have to investigate the marketability of a product; research consumer opinions; talk to different people to assess the benefits of relocating a business; investigate how customers, clients, or employees will react to certain changes or a new policy; or assess the morale in your workplace. All these events require you to seek outside information: they require research.

Research is part of everyday life. When you need to go shopping, you take an inventory of what you have and note what you need; this is research. When you're trying to decide what movie to see, you might go to a website to find out what the critics are saying; and if still not totally convinced, you ask someone who has seen the movie and whose opinion you trust. This is research.

Whether you're trying to figure out a medical condition, learning how to make good investments, determining the causes of a certain behavior in a relative or yourself, or simply checking a TV guide, you're conducting research. So what's all the fuss? This chapter lessens much of the confusion and anxiety surrounding research and shows you how to manage your information, putting you in control of the research process.

LET's warm up!

Study the picture and jot down your reactions to it. Reflect on your experiences researching information in school, for a job, or for personal interest. What activities and challenges do you associate with researching? Make a list of your activities and challenges of researching and then compare it with a classmate's list. How can you deal with some of the challenges of researching a topic?

Tetra Images/Jupiter Images

UNDERSTANDING THE VALUE OF RESEARCH

The word *research* comes from Old French *recherché*—to seek out or search again. As you take on a topic or question to research, you are seeking out information on your topic. The major value of research is that it allows you to learn the truth about something—at least as far as experts in the field know it. For example, if you want to make up your mind about the existence of global warming, then you read a variety of studies by environmental scientists. You try to read enough studies so that you feel comfortable coming to your conclusion about global warming.

Another value of research is that it sharpens your critical thinking skills. You simply cannot accept all information as equally valid and relevant. Instead, you must constantly read with skepticism: Is this study large enough to warrant such a conclusion? Does this writer have the authority to make this claim? Does this researcher cite sufficient sources to verify the information? Is this information relevant to the focus of my research?

Finally, research is the vehicle for transporting you, the student, into a much wider academic world than the one you have access to physically. Through research, you are able to access the best and brightest of minds, and you add your voice and experience to the many experts and scholars who have written on the topic you choose.

Since research can be applied to any essay, this chapter focuses mostly on the skills involved in research, not on particular writing techniques, essay development, coherence, or proofreading.

Nonetheless, we still follow one student's research process as an extended example to illustrate each specific stage of the research process. Joshua, an education major, is a part-time student. He's married, has one child, and holds a part-time job. Therefore, being organized and wasting the least amount of time are crucial to him.

WRITING YOUR RESEARCH PAPER

To ease you through the research process, we have broken it into six main stages that you need to accomplish.

These stages take you from finding a topic to completing the final draft of your research paper. Your goal is not simply to read the information in each stage. If you follow the stages diligently, by the end of this chapter, you should complete your research paper. To begin, review the preceding chart and familiarize yourself with the six stages.

Prewriting and Planning

One pleasure of research is being able to learn new information from experts in the field and not just rely on your experiences and observations. The challenges are organizing your research, finding the information you are looking for, and incorporating it smoothly into your writing style. However, with solid and careful planning, you can make this project a satisfying and manageable one. Just keep in mind that you must break each stage into steps and allot sufficient time to accomplish each one.

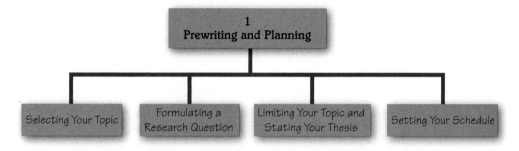

The first stage of this process is prewriting and planning. We take you through four simple steps so that you can complete this stage efficiently.

Selecting Your Topic

Remember that a key point in research is making sure that the topic you choose fits the assignment for the specific course. Your instructor may assign you a topic or give you a choice from several topics. You may also be given general guidelines: for a history paper you may be asked to write about some aspect of the Civil War; for an art history class you may be assigned a Renaissance painter whose style and influence you must explain; for a biology class you may have to describe how a specific organ of the human body functions. Just be sure that you read your instructor's guidelines for the assignment several times and ask questions to ensure that you understand the task.

Here are some basic questions to ask:

- Can you choose your own topic?
- Does the topic have to be approved by your instructor?
- What documentation style is required: MLA, APA, or another style?
- What are the minimum and maximum lengths of the paper?
- Should you write your paper to a specific audience?
- What types of sources are permissible: online, interviews, and so on?
- Will you be able to get your instructor's input on a draft or parts of your paper before you hand it in for a grade?

Brainstorming for a Topic

If your instructor has not assigned a topic, start thinking of the many topics that interest you. Think about your major, the many issues and conflicts in your community, or interesting discussions you have had on topics in other courses. You might start your search for a topic by listing your areas of interest, applying one or more prewriting techniques, and then asking questions to identify a subject so that you can then narrow the subject down to a topic. You have practiced many ways to brainstorm for topics in earlier chapters, and you can use those techniques here.

Formulating a Research Question

Once you have a tentative topic of interest, you need to start asking questions about the topic to guide your research and to lead you to a practical thesis. A useful list of questions with which to start is the traditional who, what, when, where, why, or how questions commonly posed by researchers and journalists. For example, if you choose a topic such as global warming, you might ask *what* evidence exists that global warming is actually occurring.

Before formulating your research questions, try doing some preliminary research. Initially, your research questions should be neither too broad nor too narrow. The number of sources you find during preliminary research helps you determine whether your question is too broad. For instance, if you find so many sources that you're not sure how to even begin a more focused search, the topic of your question may be too broad. In contrast, a topic that is too narrow may be too difficult to research in the time you're given since sources may be scarce or more difficult to locate. However, a question that's sufficiently narrowed may lead to an interesting in-depth discussion.

Practice formulating possible research questions by doing the following activity. Although most of these topics are general and may not require preliminary research, feel free to conduct some research on those with which you are less familiar.

Collaborative Critical Thinking

In small groups, for each of the following topics, put a check mark by the research question that you consider more interesting and relevant for an academic paper. Share your answers with other groups and be prepared to justify your group's choice.

1. Solar power

   _____a. How much does it cost to build a solar home?

   ___✓___b. Should homeowners who live in solar homes receive tax credits?

2. American families and Chinese adoptions

   _____a. How many Chinese orphans are adopted by Americans?

   ___✓___b. What are the advantages and disadvantages for Americans adopting Chinese babies?

3. CEO salaries

   ___✓___a. Why do CEOs of major American companies earn huge salaries even when their companies are losing money?

   _____b. Who are the highest paid CEOs in the United States?

Stop and examine Joshua's process leading to his research questions. Joshua decides to retrieve sources from a subscription database service that helps him locate recently published sources that have a high degree of legitimacy. He can always go to the Internet later, when his knowledge of his topics has grown from other research and he can more easily weed out the useless hits. At the end of this initial plunge into the world of research, Joshua has arrived at a tentative topic:

> Computers in education, and the ways the so-called digital divide is mirrored and propagated in our public school system

Joshua raises the following research questions:

1. What is the status of computerized learning in public schools nationally? In the state?
2. Is there a digital divide in our public schools, and can I find source material to support my answer?
3. If there is such a divide, how are students at each level affected by it?
4. What are some causes of technology gaps in schools?
5. How can those causes be attacked meaningfully?
6. What are schools doing to solve their technology problems?

Choose one topic, conduct preliminary research as necessary, revise your topic if necessary, and write research questions that you may have to consider when you develop your paper. If you find that your first choice of topic is not working out, jump to your second choice. During this stage, everything is tentative. You have plenty of time to focus your topic and, if you choose, to change your topic.

WRITING 14-1

After your preliminary research, write down your topic. Then write as many research questions as you feel you need to answer to fully develop your topic.

Tentative topic: _____

Research questions

1. _____
2. _____
3. _____
4. _____

Limiting Your Topic and Stating Your Thesis

At this point, your topic needs to take on a more narrowed focus and a sense of purpose, which leads you to your thesis. As Joshua continues in his research, he begins to ask questions about the purpose of his paper.

1. Will I explain the digital divide, its origins, and its causes?
2. Will I explore why it took hold so strongly in my community?
3. Will I focus on measures to improve the situation?
4. Will I argue that educational leaders should find ways to reduce the influence that income disparity has on public education?

During this step of prewriting and planning his research, Joshua begins to save the more useful articles to his computer's hard drive so that he can easily find them later. He also prints out sources he feels help him limit and focus his topic. Now he is ready to write a tentative thesis.

Pueblo's digital divide has created a serious problem for the public schools.

Joshua's research questions helped focus his topic, giving his paper some direction. Your own thesis statement results naturally from your questions, providing your paper with a specific and straightforward claim.

WRITING 14-2

Look over your questions, conduct additional research, or review the sources you encountered during your initial research. Then formulate a tentative thesis statement for your topic and write it here.

Tentative thesis: _____

_____

WRITING 14-3

Test your thesis within the writing context by answering the following questions.

You the Writer

1. Why is this topic important to you? Why does it interest you? _____
   _____
   _____

2. On a scale of 1–10, how strongly do you feel about your topic? _____

3. Do you already have assumptions or opinions about the topic you plan to research? _____
   _____

4. What is your attitude or opinion about this topic? _____
   _____

5. How much do you already know about this topic? _____
   _____

6. What do you and your reader have in common? _____
   _____

Your Reader

1. What audience (person or group) would benefit most from your writing? _____
   _____

2. What would your reader gain from your essay? _____
   _____

3. What previous knowledge does the audience have of your topic? _____
   _____

4. What information does your audience need? _____
   _____

5. What is your purpose? _____
   _____

6. What effect do you want your essay to have on your audience? _____
   _____

Your Writing Situation

1. Is this topic related to another class, a particular project, a personal interest, a strongly held belief, or something else? Explain. _____
   _____

2. What format, requirements, or constraints must you observe? _____
   _____

The Content

1. What kind of sources do you need to consult? _____
   _____

2. What information do you need first? _____
   _____

3. What kind of source is likely to supply it? _____
   _____

4. Review your answers and reflect on your writing context. At this point, what strategies can help make your essay effective: illustration, process, classification/division, cause/effect, comparison/contrast, definition? _____
   _____

5. What other information do you need to provide—for example, statistics, cases, or historical background? _____
   _____

Based on your responses here, make any changes to your thesis that you feel are appropriate at this time.

Setting Your Schedule

Divide the task up into weeks and give yourself deadlines. For example, the following schedule might work for you:

Week 1

- Decide on topic
- Find five to seven sources with useful information
- Read the sources and highlight useful information
- Take notes in your own words on note cards or in Word documents

Warning: Be sure that you have enough information for your topic because you don't want to change topics close to the deadline for the paper and thus run out of time to complete the project.

Week 2

- Write a tentative outline of the paper
- Insert your notes into the sections of the paper where they fit
- Look for holes, or areas where more information is needed
- Find more sources to fill gaps in the outline

Warning: Don't become so involved in accumulating sources and finding new information that you get behind in taking notes and deciding on the subtopics of the paper.

Week 3

- Type up a tentative Works Cited page
- Start writing the first draft of the paper, inserting the research (and parenthetical citations) as you go

Warning: Do not put research in the first draft of the paper without crediting the specific source right away. If you try to go back later and remember where your information came from, you may credit the wrong source or forget to credit some information, thus committing plagiarism.

Week 4

- Revise the first draft, omitting information that is irrelevant or extraneous and adding any new and useful information
- Put the paper aside for at least a day and then edit the draft for grammar, punctuation, and transitions
- Polish your Works Cited list

Warning: Proofreading is essential to catching basic and distracting errors. You are checking not just for grammar and punctuation but also for correctness of documentation.

WRITING 14-4

Plan your schedule and make a commitment to stick to it. A research paper is not something you can put together overnight.

Stage and Step of Research Process	Date Due	Date Completed
1. Prewriting and planning		
a. Selecting your topic	_____	_____
b. Formulating a research question	_____	_____
c. Limiting your topic and stating your thesis	_____	_____
d. Setting your schedule	_____	_____
2. Researching your topic		
a. Using the library	_____	_____
b. Using databases	_____	_____
c. Using the Internet	_____	_____
d. Evaluating the reliability of your sources	_____	_____
e. Identifying subtopics	_____	_____
3. Managing your information		
a. Writing bibliography cards	_____	_____
b. Writing note cards or electronic notes	_____	_____
4. Drafting and revising your paper		
a. Preparing your outline	_____	_____
b. Writing your first draft	_____	_____
c. Revising and proofreading your draft	_____	_____
5. Formatting your final paper		
a. Formatting your final outline	_____	_____
b. Formatting your final draft	_____	_____
c. Formatting your final bibliography	_____	_____
6. Reflecting	_____	_____

WRITING YOUR RESEARCH PAPER

Researching Your Topic

You are ready to locate sources that can offer a broad understanding of your topic. During this stage of research, you make a conscientious, careful, thorough attempt to find the most current and informative sources that exist.

This section shows you how to use the library, as well as electronically stored materials, to research your topic.

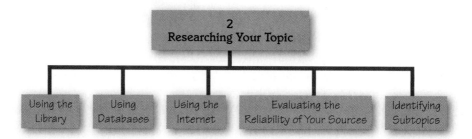

Using the Library

You may wonder why you should bother going to the library when you can go online and find an array of information. Libraries are places where researchers can peruse resources physically. Sometimes new ideas are best stimulated by being surrounded by print sources, which can suggest topics and areas of interest that you might not find online. Also, books are more permanent and stable than online sources: online information can disappear from a website, or the website may change or be deleted. Some databases go back only 5 years; thus, the library contains history that may not be accessible online.

Probably one of the best reasons for visiting a library is to take advantage of the vast knowledge and research skills of a professional reference librarian, who can guide you to many useful and relevant sources. In addition, if the your library doesn't have a promising source, the librarian can order the source from another library through interlibrary loan. Since receiving the source may take time, it's important that you visit the library early in your research process.

You may "visit" your college library online as well. Through the library's website, you can access the databases that the library subscribes to and check what books and journals the library carries through the library catalog and electronic indexes and databases. Through your library catalog, you can locate books, articles in periodicals, and government documents in a short time. You can search for a simple title or author, but if you don't have this information, you can always search by subject.

It's almost impossible for a library to store the thousands of available magazines, journals, and newspapers. Therefore, indexes such as The Reader's Guide to Periodicals, Expanded Academic, and CINAHL provide bibliographical information by author, title, and/or subject so that you can find the article. Although some indexes are available in print form, many are available on CD-ROM or computer databases. Therefore, don't hesitate to consult your librarian, who can guide you through the indexes and through the many databases available to obtain the article you're seeking.

Using Databases

Indexes are databases that reference articles; they don't offer the articles themselves. Such databases are known as *bibliographical databases*. However, some full-text retrieval services, such as the Electric Library, FirstSearch, EBSCOhost, and Ingenta, offer bibliographical information, abstracts, and full-text articles.

Subscription services, such as EBSCOhost, InfoTrac, and ProQuest, offer access to thousands of articles about specific topics. These articles have been "refereed," or evaluated for reliability and credibility by experts before publication. Thus, they are better sources than you can typically find just by surfing the Internet for information. In most cases, by simply going to your library's home page and following the links to electronic resources, you can find these subscription services, which give you access to their many databases.

As you continue to develop your research skills, you continue to discover the types of sources that provide the evidence and support that you need to develop your research paper. With all these sources at your disposal, think twice before telling your instructor that you're unable to locate information on your topic.

Using the Internet

Researching has become simpler in some ways than it used to be with the ease of logging on to the computer and accessing databases or "Googling" a topic. However, the massive amounts of information online can overwhelm you or divert you from your research as you become distracted by e-mail, chat rooms, or downloaded music.

Google is just one popular search engine. There are millions of pages on the Internet; no one engine can search the entire web. Use other search engines such as Yahoo, MSN Search, or Ask.com to broaden your search.

As you gain experience using the Internet to conduct research, you become more proficient and more skillful in narrowing your search to find exactly what you want. Remember, the Internet is huge, and your search may take too much time if you don't enter the right series of words to get the match for the documents you need.

Evaluating the Reliability of Your Sources

You must be critical as a researcher to ensure that the information you use for your papers is worthwhile, accurate, and credible. Anyone can post information to the Internet that may not be true or accurate and make it look as if it is. For example, *Wikipedia*, the online encyclopedia, allows anyone to add entries or edit them. Although there may be a lot of useful information on this site, you should cross-check it with other information sources.

Be especially wary of dot-com sites. Such sites are commercial; thus, one of their goals is to make money. Dot-gov and dot-edu sites have more credibility; however, you still have to be skeptical. For example, a student at a university can put up a personal website, have a dot-edu address, and supply information that is inaccurate. Therefore, it's crucial that you evaluate all sources for credibility and reliability before using them in your research paper.

Criteria for Evaluating Your Sources

Use the following criteria, adapted from "Evaluating Information Found on the Internet," by Elizabeth E. Kirk, to determine the reliability of the sources you find on the Internet:

1. **Authorship.** Most often, you are not familiar with the author of your information. However, it's important that you determine whether the author is one you and your reader can trust. Start by asking the following questions:
   - Who wrote this article and what are their credentials?
   - If the website is related to a particular field, is the writer trained and certified in that field?

■ If the website provides information on a controversial issue, does the author or organization have a political affiliation or a noticeable bias on the topic?

2. **Currency.** How up-to-date is this information? Check the dates of the facts cited, as well as the last update of the article. If you are writing about global warming, what would be the furthest back in history you would go to cite studies about whether or not it is a reality?

3. **Publisher or sponsor.** Study the website carefully to determine who published or sponsored the site. Is it a political organization, a university or college, a nationally known company, an individual, a government agency, a retail store, an organization trying to free political prisoners? Look at the site's home page to find out what the organization's goals are and how it plans to achieve these goals.

4. **Audience.** For whom is the website designed? Whom would it attract or appeal to? If you are doing a paper on global warming and come upon a website designed by Mrs. Smith's fifth-grade class in Helena, Montana, you might decide that the level of research and writing is too basic for your purposes. If the website is sponsored by a group that advocates peaceful demonstrations to protest the proliferation of SUVs, you might be skeptical as well.

5. **Relevancy.** Essential to your research is determining whether or not the information that you've found relates to your topic and thesis. It may be intriguing and you may want to spend time reading it to understand the scope of information on the topic, but it may not fit the focus of your paper. Here are some questions to ask to test relevancy:

   ■ Does this information fit under one of your subtopics?
   ■ Does this information relate to your overall purpose or thesis?
   ■ Can you integrate this information into your paper or does it just seem dropped in?
   ■ Does this information fit what your specific reader needs to know about your topic?

6. **Accuracy of information.** Ask the following questions to determine the quality of the information:

   ■ Do other sources you've read corroborate what this source claims?
   ■ Does this source cite some of the most comprehensive studies on the topic?
   ■ Does any information contradict what you've read in other sources?
   ■ Does the source provide references to verify its information?

7. **Style and format.** When you're reading a professional piece of writing, you have some expectations of the writer's writing and research skills. Ask the following questions:

   ■ How well is the article written? Does it contain grammatical errors, missing words or phrases, misspellings, punctuation errors, or obvious errors of fact?
   ■ What kind of support does the writer offer? Does the writer cite well-respected authorities and provide references so that the reader can verify information?
   ■ What is the tone of the article? Does it contain inflammatory language? Does it try to sell the reader something? Does it ignore other points of view? Does it commit logical fallacies?

(Adapted from the Johns Hopkins University, The Sheridan Libraries, website)

Identifying Subtopics

Before you take off on your research, you need to determine the limits or scope of your research. You can easily become sidetracked and spend hours reading information you may not even need. To maintain your focus on the thesis you have identified, start by specifying the subtopics you need to research to explain or prove your thesis. Can you identify specific causes and effects? What comparisons can you draw? Would your topic benefit from statistics? Where in your paper would you insert these statistics?

As you may recall, Joshua ended his first stage of the research process with the following tentative thesis:

> Pueblo's digital divide has created a serious problem for the public schools.

Now Joshua is ready to do a more focused research for which he has to identify important subtopics to research. He decides to focus his research on explaining the problem by researching the causes and effects of the problem. He identifies the following subtopics:

A. Causes
  1. Hardware deficiencies
  2. Lack of software
  3. Lack of teacher awareness
  4. Lack of expertise
  5. Lack of training

B. Effects
  1. Students don't understand the full potential of computers.
  2. Students don't develop necessary skills.
  3. Graduates have trouble getting jobs.
  4. Community will be affected.

These subtopics need to be more focused, but providing this focus is the purpose of research. For now, Joshua has a plan, as you soon will.

WRITING 14-5

Develop your plan for getting your sources. Start by dividing the idea in your thesis statement into subtopics. Write the subtopics you plan to research in the spaces that follow.

Thesis: _____

_____

Subtopics to research

1. _____

2. _____

3. _____

4. _____

5. _____

Review the subtopics you have identified and make sure that these subtopics indeed explain or prove your thesis statement. If not, revise the subtopics that aren't relevant or refocus your thesis.

Managing Your Information

When you start your preliminary search for materials on your topic, you may become overwhelmed by the amount of information you find. The goal of this stage of the research process is to organize, manage, and think critically about your information.

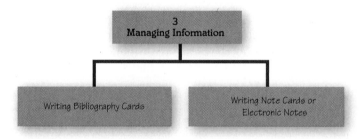

Not being organized makes your research frustrating, and you lose valuable time. Using an index card system to manage your information is a traditional, simple method, but it has proven to be expedient, reliable, and flexible.

Writing Bibliography Cards

You should find bibliography cards helpful. With bibliography cards, you can keep records of all books, periodicals, databases, and websites that you might consider using later.

Basically, bibliography cards serve the following purposes:
1. They keep you organized.
2. They help you record all information needed to locate the source should you decide to use it when you're ready to write your paper.
3. They provide the information you need to prepare your final bibliography—your Works Cited list.

Bibliography cards are usually 3 × 5–inch index cards. Use one card per source. Since at this stage of the research process you are still discovering and gathering information that supports your thesis, it is likely that you will compile more bibliography cards than you ultimately keep and use. In that case, just discard those cards that you're sure you won't use and place the cards you want to use in strict alphabetical order to prepare your bibliography.

Look at the various bibliography cards that Joshua created as a result of the preliminary survey of information on his topic.

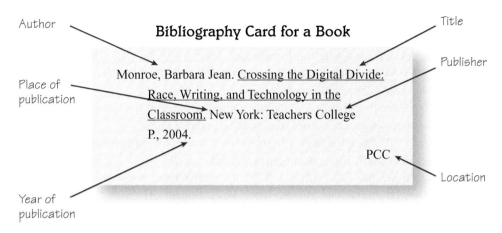

Also, if available, you might include any information about the source that can help you remember and determine the value of this source to your topic. You can write this information either at the end or on the other side of the bibliography card.

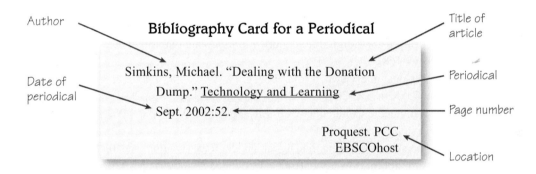

At this point, you can move from bibliography cards to the typed preliminary bibliography, also known as a *working bibliography*. If your instructor wants you to use MLA style, you will later call this page *Works Cited*. It is not unusual to have more sources than you need at this point of your research. When you start drafting your paper, you will most likely discard sources, as well as do additional research to get additional sources or to replace the ones you already have. All you need to do then is delete the sources you didn't use from your preliminary (working) bibliography and add any new sources. By constantly updating your working bibliography, you're on your way toward your final Works Cited or References list, which becomes the last page of your research paper.

Examine Joshua's preliminary bibliography. It should immediately be clear to you that he has entirely too many sources for a 4- to 6-page research paper. At this point, Joshua is still reviewing his sources and is not sure which ones are best for his paper. Also notice that Joshua uses MLA style to document his sources; check with your instructor before you start developing your bibliography cards and bibliography.

Working Bibliography

"Are Teachers Using Computers for Instruction?" Journal of School Health Feb. 2001: 83–84. ProQuest. Pueblo Community Coll. Lib., Pueblo, CO. 20 Mar. 2007 <http://www.proquest.com>.

"Background about the S.E.E.D.S. Program." Operation S.E.E.D.S. 2002. 24 Apr. 2007 <http://www.pcc.cccoes.edu/seeds/background.htm>.

Chideya, Farai. "Bridging the Digital Divide in the Classroom." NPR News & Notes 3 Jan. 2007. Newspaper Source. EBSCOhost. Pueblo Community Coll. Lib., Pueblo, CO. 16 Feb. 2007 <http://search.epnet.com>.

Clements, Douglas H., and Julie Sarama. "The Role of Technology in Early Childhood Learning." Teaching Children Mathematics Feb. 2002: 340–43. ProQuest. Pueblo Community Coll. Lib., Pueblo, CO. 13 Mar. 2007 <http://www.proquest.com>.

Debenham, Jerry, and Gerald R. Smith. "Computers, Schools, and Families: A Radical Vision for Public Education." The Journal 24 (1994): 58. Academic Search Premier. EBSCOhost. Pueblo Community Coll. Lib., Pueblo, CO. 16 Feb. 2007 <http://search.epnet.com>.

"Digital Divide Basics Fact Sheet." Digital Divide Network. 2002. 18 Mar. 2007 <http://www.digitaldividenetwork.org/content/stories/index. cfm?key=168>.

Gill, Keith. Personal interview. 16 Apr. 2007.

Lewis, Anne C. "Kids and Computers." The Education Digest Apr. 2001: 67–69. ProQuest. Pueblo Community Coll. Lib., Pueblo, CO. 13 Mar. 2002 <http://www.proquest.com>.

Monroe, Barbara Jean. Crossing the Digital Divide: Race, Writing, and Technology in the Classroom. New York: Teachers College Press, 2004.

Nielsen, Clark. Personal interview. 20 Apr. 2007.

Simkins, Michael. "Dealing with the Donation Dump." Technology & Learning Sept. 2002: 52. ProQuest. Pueblo Community Coll. Lib., Pueblo, CO. 13 Mar. 2007 <http://www.proquest.com>.

Tucker, Patrick. "A New Ruler for the Digital Divide." The Futurist Mar.–Apr. 2007: 16. Academic Search Premier. EBSCOhost. Pueblo Community Coll. Lib., Pueblo, CO. 15 Feb. 2007 <http://search.epnet.com>.

"What Is the Digital Divide?" Power Up. 2002. 14 Mar. 2007 <http://www.powerup.org/digital_divide.shtml>.

Zucker, Andrew. "Computers in Education: National Policy in the USA." European Journal of Education 17.4 (1982). Academic Search Premier. EBSCOhost. Pueblo Community Coll. Lib., Pueblo, CO. 15 Feb. 2007 <http://search.epnet. com>.

WRITING 14-6

Write bibliography cards for the sources you obtained when you did Writing 14-5. Write one card for each source. Place your bibliography cards in strict alphabetical order, and type an initial Works Cited (MLA) or References (APA) list. Refer to Chapter 13 for explanation and examples of MLA documentation.

Writing Note Cards

From this point on, any additional research is based on the subtopics you've settled on. These subtopics may eventually become the main sections of your paper. Your goal here is to find valid information to support each of the major points of your topic. For each of these subtopics, use several cards from several different sources. As you find interesting and relevant facts in your sources, write them down under the appropriate area.

Look at six types of note cards: quotation, paraphrase, summary, outline, personal, and combination. We use Joshua's sources to illustrate each type of card.

Quotation Note Card

It is crucial that you differentiate your words from your sources' words. Use quotation marks to make this distinction; otherwise, you have committed plagiarism even though you cite your source.

Quotation Note Card

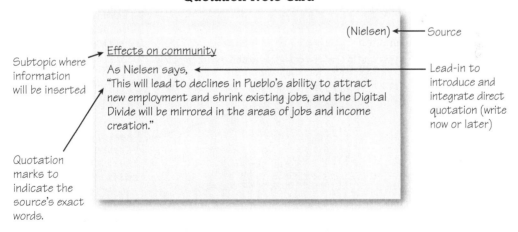

Source

(Nielsen)

Effects on community

Subtopic where information will be inserted

As Nielsen says,
"This will lead to declines in Pueblo's ability to attract new employment and shrink existing jobs, and the Digital Divide will be mirrored in the areas of jobs and income creation."

Lead-in to introduce and integrate direct quotation (write now or later)

Quotation marks to indicate the source's exact words.

Paraphrase Note Card

A paraphrase is simply a restatement of the writer's ideas. When you paraphrase information, you use your own sentence structures, wording, and style. Most information you get from sources will be paraphrased. In fact, every sentence and idea you write down should be in your own words and writing style unless it is directly quoted. If a reader doesn't see quotation marks, the reader assumes that the information is a paraphrase—your own phrasing and style. If this assumption is not correct, you may have committed plagiarism.

Paraphrase Note Card

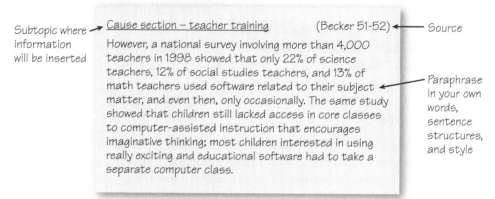

Subtopic where information will be inserted →

Cause section – teacher training   (Becker 51-52) ← Source

However, a national survey involving more than 4,000 teachers in 1998 showed that only 22% of science teachers, 12% of social studies teachers, and 13% of math teachers used software related to their subject matter, and even then, only occasionally. The same study showed that children still lacked access in core classes to computer-assisted instruction that encourages imaginative thinking; most children interested in using really exciting and educational software had to take a separate computer class.

→ Paraphrase in your own words, sentence structures, and style

Bridging Knowledge

See Chapter 13 for information on paraphrasing and quoting information.

Summary Note Card

A summary captures the gist of an author's main idea. It is your condensed version of the main point or points of several paragraphs, an entire essay, a chapter in a book, or the complete book. Since a summary is your analysis and conclusions of a larger text, the wording must be entirely yours.

Summary Note Card

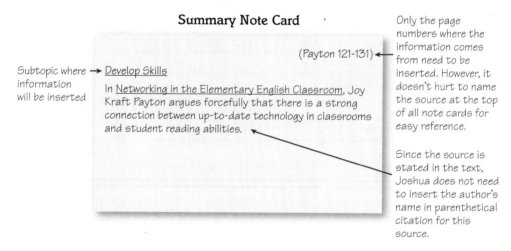

Only the page numbers where the information comes from need to be inserted. However, it doesn't hurt to name the source at the top of all note cards for easy reference.

(Payton 121-131) ←

Subtopic where information will be inserted → *Develop Skills*

In <u>Networking in the Elementary English Classroom</u>, Joy Kraft Payton argues forcefully that there is a strong connection between up-to-date technology in classrooms and student reading abilities.

Since the source is stated in the text, Joshua does not need to insert the author's name in parenthetical citation for this source.

Outline Note Card

Similar to an outline, this type of card notes a series of points made by your source. When you draft your paper, you can then choose to present the information using bullets or numbers, or you can discuss the points in the form of a paragraph. Get your instructor's approval should you decide to use bullets or numbers.

Outline Note Card

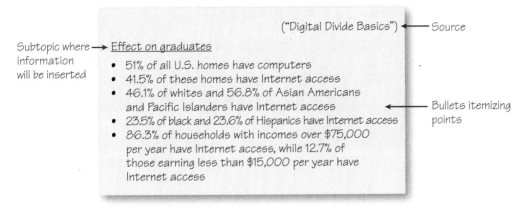

Subtopic where information will be inserted →

Source

Bullets itemizing points

Personal Note Card

As you review your sources, you develop your own ideas about the topic. Write them down immediately on a note card. On a bibliography card, write the word *personal* to indicate that this is your thinking, and indicate the area of your paper where you plan to insert your idea or comment. Then write your comment. There's no need to worry about plagiarism here since you are the author of this idea. Of course, since this information is your thinking, you don't need to cite it in your paper.

Personal Note Card

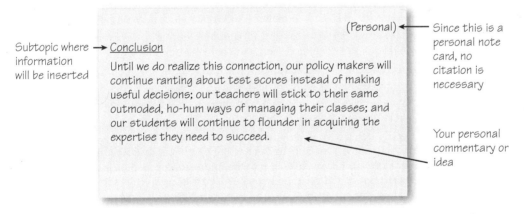

Subtopic where information will be inserted →

Since this is a personal note card, no citation is necessary

Your personal commentary or idea

Combination Note Card

You're allowed to combine any of the preceding types of note cards. However, for obvious reasons, we wouldn't recommend that you combine a personal note with information from a source that you must cite.

Combination Note Card

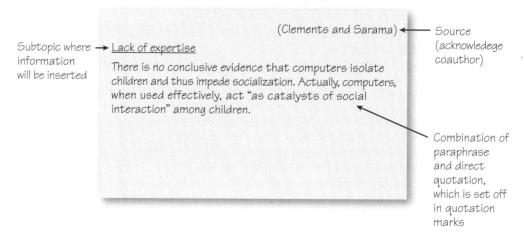

Subtopic where → information will be inserted

Lack of expertise

(Clements and Sarama) ← Source (acknowledege coauthor)

There is no conclusive evidence that computers isolate children and thus impede socialization. Actually, computers, when used effectively, act "as catalysts of social interaction" among children.

Combination of paraphrase and direct quotation, which is set off in quotation marks

WRITING 14-7

Start writing note cards for your topic. When creating note cards, follow these guidelines:

1. Don't combine subtopics in any one card.
2. Make sure you give the source of the information, preferably in the upper-right corner of the card. This notation is how you credit your source in your paper, so make sure that the source you list here matches the first word or words of your bibliography cards, which should match your Works Cited or References page.
3. Indicate whether the card is a paraphrase, summary, quotation, a combination, or your own reflection or thinking about the source's point of view.
4. Write only on the front of the card so that you don't forget any information you may have written on the back of the card.
5. If the information takes more than one card, indicate that the information continues and staple the related cards together.
6. The number of cards per source depends on the amount of information you extract from the source. One source can have one note card; another can easily have over a dozen. Just make sure that the information you choose to use indeed explains one of the subtopics you have identified, which in turn supports the thesis. If this is so, you're on your way to a unified research paper.

Writing Notes Electronically

Just like the bibliography cards, note cards offer the advantage of flexibility—you can group the information in any way you want, sorting it by subtopics. However, regardless of the benefits of using note cards, some students resist them and prefer to gather information using their computers. The important point is that you have a method to manage and document all information you plan on using. You can still use the principles described earlier for organizing information. However, follow these simple guidelines:

1. Do not place all notes from several subtopics on one page. Instead, dedicate one page (or more) to each category.

2. Label each subtopic.

3. As you insert information under the appropriate subtopics, indicate in parentheses either in the upper-right corner or at the end of the information where the information comes from. This point is crucial since this is the citation for this information should you decide to use it. Remember: Not citing your source constitutes plagiarism.

4. Number each piece of information you insert into that subtopic. Whether the information is from the same source or from a different source, you want to remind yourself that each is a separate bit of information. You don't want to make the mistake of blending together information that may not be completely related to a specific point you are making. During the drafting stage, going back to your source and trying to unravel this confusion can cost you precious time.

5. Be sure to place quotation marks around any phrases or sentences you copy directly from your source regardless of how many. The quotation marks remind you that these are not your words and that if you use this source, you should paraphrase the information, integrate it into your text as a direct quotation, or use a combination of paraphrase and direct quotation.

Drafting and Revising Your Paper

Drafting the research paper is essentially a three-step process. You begin by ensuring that your outline is well organized and detailed enough to serve as the basis for your first draft. Then, using your outline and note cards, you create your first draft as quickly and efficiently as possible. Next, you spend considerable time going through your draft, adding to and reorganizing your information and sources, as well as proofreading for grammar and style problems.

Preparing Your Outline

In any research project, you want to work from an outline. You may believe that your writing process is more efficient without an outline; however, for research papers, you should make the formal outline a required part of your process because you have a lot of material to manage. Not only do you have all the source material you collected on note cards, but your own ideas have also been taking shape since the project began. Formal outlines use a standard and common set of visual conventions:

- Write your last name and the page number in the upper-right corner of your outline. The page numbers should be in lowercase Roman numerals, for example, *i, ii, iii, iv, v*. Your actual paper should be in Arabic numbers: 1, 2, 3, 4, and so on.
- Represent higher-level, or more general, ideas to the left of lower-level ideas:
  I. (most general idea)
     A. (less general idea)

- Represent the highest level of ideas with Roman numerals, the next highest with capital letters, the next with Arabic numerals, and the next with lower-case letters. Examine the different levels and note how the position of each level indicates how the information is related to each level:
  I. (most general idea)
     A. (less general idea—supports idea I)
        1. (supports idea A)
        2. (supports idea A)
           a. (supports idea 2)
           b. (supports idea 2)
             (1) (supports idea b)
             (2) (supports idea b)
        3. (supports idea A)
     B. (supports idea I)

- As a reminder to yourself and your reader (sometimes you include an outline with your research paper for evaluation), place your thesis at the beginning of the outline following the title.

Joshua is ready to type his preliminary formal outline. As he types out his outline, he flips through his note cards in order, making sure the outline contains a reference to each source. By doing this, he later knows where to insert each source into the draft. He can eliminate these references from his outline after he's written his draft and is ready to revise his outline. Here is Joshua's typed preliminary outline.

Pueblo's Digital Divide: A Problem for the Public Schools

Thesis: It is unfair to our youth, as well as to the community at large, to let the technology gap continue to grow. Only by understanding it in detail can we begin to solve it.

  I. Introduction
    A. Highlight benefits of computer technology to various types of people
      1. Seniors have new form of enrichment
      2. Families use computers for entertainment and other purposes

    B. Introduce disparities of access to computers
       1. 51% own computers and 41% have access to the Internet ("Digital")
       2. This gap is the digital divide ("What")
       3. Lack of access is related to income levels
    C. Focus on education and narrow the topic to Pueblo
       1. Poorer districts suffer from lack of access
       2. Although Pueblo is technically an urban setting, it shares the lack of technology with poorer rural areas (Nielsen)
    D. Give thesis and three-part map
  II. Causes of the problem
    A. Explore hardware deficiencies
       1. Deficiencies involve many types of hardware: computers, monitors, mouse devices, printers, and so on
       2. Lacking steady funding, schools apply for grants, which are hit or miss (Nielsen)
         a. Relying on grants causes even greater disparities among schools
         b. Minnequa Elementary received the G-Tech grant; test scores went up
       3. Schools try donation programs, such as S.E.E.D.S.
         a. Explain how they work ("Background")
         b. Policies prevent schools from repairing donated items (Gill)
    B. Explain lack of software
       1. Even when schools gain hardware through grants and donations, they have trouble securing licenses for more than a few computers (Nielsen)
       2. Pricing of software licenses can make purchases expensive
    C. Describe lack of teacher awareness, expertise, and training
       1. Curriculum and room design are key features of effective electronic teaching (Clements and Sarama), but few teachers use computers (Becker)
       2. Pueblo teachers seem to lack interest in computerized learning (Nielsen)
 III. Effects of the problem
    A. Today's students can operate computers well enough, but they don't know how to use them to their fullest potential
       1. Research
       2. Communication with experts
       3. Math and science programs
    B. Graduates will have trouble getting good jobs and succeeding in college ("What")
 IV. Conclusion
    A. It is unfair to continue as we have
    B. The technology gap is widening; Pueblo is falling behind

Start preparing your preliminary outline using Joshua's as a model.

Essay Outline

Thesis: _____

I. _____

   A.

      1. _____

      2. _____

   B.

      1. _____

      2. _____

II. _____

   A.

      1. _____

      2. _____

   B.

      1. _____

      2. _____

III. _____

   A.

      1. _____

      2. _____

   B.

      1. _____

      2. _____

Writing Your First Draft

 If you have not completed the stages in this chapter, the best advice we can give you is to stop right here, go back, and do them. If you begin drafting without completing these tasks, you are destined for a confusing and inefficient process.

As you sit down to draft your paper, you should have in front of you only three items: your detailed outline, your note cards, and your computer. Move your sources (the books, articles, printouts of web sources, and so on) to another area where you won't be tempted to look at them as you draft.

As you start drafting, follow the outline you've created. When you reach a point in the draft where you need to incorporate source material, take that source material directly from the card in your stack. Type it into your paper using the same conventions you used in creating the card: if it is a quotation, make sure you are quoting properly; if it is a paraphrase, you should have already paraphrased the information to place it on the note card, so type it into your paper as you put it on the card, with perhaps a few variations as you type. When you are finished with a note card, flip it over so that you see the next one (there should be no writing on the back of any of your note cards). Proceed to the next outline point and continue drafting.

If you find that you are stuck in a particular section, just move to another section, but keep your cards properly organized as you switch between sections. And remember that this is only your first draft. It won't be perfect the first time, nor should you expect it to be.

Writing Your Introduction

In theory, the introduction of a research paper is no different from any other type of introduction you've learned to write. You still must interest the reader in your topic, establish your credibility as a writer, and state your thesis. However, most research papers, in keeping with their serious purpose, adopt an objective and informational tone from the start. Therefore, you probably want to avoid lead-in techniques that are too informal or humorous to play a part in the serious purpose of research. (This is not to say a research paper can *never* be informal or humorous, but it doesn't happen often.)

Instead, keep in mind the two most common purposes of researched writing: to *explain* a topic thoroughly so that the reader understands it in a new way or to *persuade* the reader to adopt a point of view on an issue of importance. Notice that research writing is not its own mode like the others you've learned this semester. All you are doing in this assignment is adding research into the process of developing an explanation or an argument.

WRITING 14-9

Begin drafting your introduction. Don't forget that you can always come back to it and revise it at any time, as many times as you wish. As you create the draft, consider the following issues:

1. Your introduction should be engaging, making your reader want to read more.

2. Your introduction should indicate the serious and objective purpose of your paper, not only in your choice of language but also in the use of source material early in the paper.

3. It is common for the introduction of a research paper to give background information (again, based on source material) as a way of getting the reader into the topic.

4. Your introduction does not have to confine itself to one paragraph; you probably want to use more. However, make sure the introduction has its own unity and coherence leading naturally to the thesis.

5. Your thesis should clearly indicate the focus of your paper: if it is an explanation, which aspects of the topic do you discuss? If it is an argument, what kind of claim are you making and what is your position?

Share your introduction with others. Let them tell you what they enjoy most or least about your introduction. Ask them what they think about the organization of the introduction. Then use their comments as a basis for revision.

Writing Your Body Paragraphs

Examine one body paragraph from Joshua's first draft.

> The first cause is that many schools do not have sufficient hardware to accommodate the number of students. The hardware includes monitors, printers, speakers, mouse devices, and the computer itself. The school districts lack the funds needed to purchase new computer equipment; so instead, they apply for grants given to schools by various computer corporations and organizations, including companies such as Dell and Microsoft. Unfortunately, these grants are only given to a select few schools each year (Nielsen). Essentially, these grants greatly benefit those schools they are given to, but they also increase the inequality among schools because they are not given to every school. Nielsen gives a good example involving three elementary schools within District 60: Minnequa, Columbian, and Bessemer elementary schools. He reports that Minnequa recently received a G-Tech grant that gave the school new state-of-the-art equipment for the classrooms. Minnequa was one of only a handful of lucky schools picked to receive the grant, and Bessemer and Columbian were not among the schools chosen. As a result, Minnequa's state assessment scores were much higher than either of the other two schools. The higher scores may not have been entirely due to the new computer equipment, but the computers are believed to have played a part in the higher scoring, according to Nielsen.

In his first body paragraph, Joshua is off to a good start. He moves quickly to show how technology grants awarded to a small number of schools actually increase the digital divide within school districts. His point makes sense; that is, we can easily see how it might be true. But does he prove that it is true? What is wrong with the quality and representativeness of his evidence in this paragraph? Joshua needs to beef up the evidence and the conclusions he draws from it to thoroughly convince his reader.

WRITING 14-10

Start creating your first draft. Your goal is to fully and completely support your thesis. Don't forget that you can always change your mind and return to the prewriting stage. Follow these guidelines.

1. Try to adhere to your outline. As you draft, however, make any changes to the outline that you feel help your essay.

2. As you encounter the places in your text where you need to use source material, go ahead and make the effort to enter the quotation or paraphrase correctly. Do *not* type borrowed material into your draft without citing it in some way. You are likely to lose track of it and could be guilty of plagiarism in the final product.

3. Make sure your sources are varied in terms of their number and type.

4. Add transitions to keep your ideas flowing smoothly and to guide your audience through your information. Focus especially on signal phrases that should introduce borrowed material smoothly.

5. Try to avoid going back to your printed sources as you draft your paper. This only slows you down and takes you backward in the writing process.

6. If you come across a point that needs support or stronger evidence, make a note that you need to conduct additional research to support that point. But keep drafting.

Writing Your Conclusion

Remember that your conclusion is not a paragraph you can dash off simply by repeating some of the major ideas you've just stated in the paper. You need to devote time and attention to showing the reader the importance of the topic and emphasizing the major point you want to leave the reader with. Even though his paper is an explanation, Joshua hopes to stimulate his reader into thinking about what to do to help solve the problem.

WRITING 14-11

Write a conclusion for your research paper using the skills you have already learned. We repeat some previous advice here:

1. Reiterate the importance and significance of your topic. You can use one of the following techniques to help you do this:

   a. If you choose to summarize your key points, don't just repeat the same points mechanically. You can be sure that your reader hasn't forgotten them. Instead, show how these points are vital evidence in proving your thesis.

   b. Consider using an emotional appeal. But be careful not to overdo it.

   c. Pose a question. Leave your reader pondering the question.

   d. Emphasize the urgency of the issue by making a call for action.

   e. Build on or refer to a scenario, example, description, or anecdote that may have appeared in your introduction. This approach not only gives cohesiveness to your essay but also lets the reader know that you have accomplished your goal.

2. Read your introduction and then your conclusion to make sure that there's a smooth connection between them.

Revising and Proofreading Your Draft

Start the revising stage with this question: "Have I accomplished my goal?" Review your first draft, circling the strengths and underlining the weaknesses as you perceive them. How can you build on your strengths? How should you address the weaknesses? How do you feel about what you have written? With these questions in mind, start revising the content, as well as the integration of sources, in your paper. As you go through your paper, integrate all that you've learned about proofreading to correct errors of grammar and style.

WRITING 14-12

Start your revision. Don't leave any part of your essay untouched. Take a couple of days, if you have them, to read your paper several times, as follows:

1. Read your essay through one time, looking for problems in the organization of your major ideas (usually found in your thesis, topic sentences, and conclusion).

2. Read your essay through again looking for problems with supporting ideas (found in your body paragraphs).

3. Read your essay a third time looking for ways to improve its coherence. Make sure you offer enough transitions, including signal phrases to introduce sources, to help guide your reader.

4. Go through your essay again looking for problems with the use of sources. Make sure your in-text citations lead the reader to the right entry on the Works Cited page. Use the chart on pages 438–439 to help you troubleshoot.

5. Read your essay one more time looking for ways to improve the style: the use of diction, modifying phrases, different types of sentences, active versus passive voice, and so on.

The next section should help you address some of the more confusing problems with sources.

············· **PROBLEM** ·························· **SOLUTION** ··························

RESEARCH

Some of my sources don't seem to add much to my paper.

→

1. Are your sources relatively recent? If you are writing about "hot" contemporary issue, you should be relying on sources published quite recently, perhaps within the last 6 months to a year.

2. Do your sources come primarily from the Internet? Your reader is automatically suspicious of most Internet sources except for government or professional association websites. Make sure you are avoiding general Internet sources.

3. Are your interview sources believable? If you can't find a reliable "expert" to interview, don't use an interview in your paper.

4. Do you rely on multiple sources throughout your paper? If your reader sees the same source repeatedly, that reader will begin to question the thoroughness of your research.

RESEARCH

I just don't know if I'm using my sources correctly, especially when it comes to paraphrasing and quoting.

1. Have you properly understood your sources in their original context? It never hurts to go back and read a source from which you've extracted information just to make sure you've captured the author's intended meaning correctly.

2. Do you use your source appropriately to support a point you are trying to make? Use source material in supporting paragraphs to provide the evidence you need to back up your points.

3. Do your quotations need to be quotations, or would they work better as paraphrases? Remember to use quotation sparingly and only when the phrasing is memorable or unique.

4. Are you overusing research material by inserting source after source (whether paraphrased or quoted) with none of your own thinking and writing included? Remember, a research paper is composed of your own reasoning supported by an appropriate mixture of primary and secondary evidence.

INCORPORATING SOURCES

I don't know if my signal phrases and in-text citations are doing the job they are supposed to do.

1. Do you vary your signal phrases as appropriate throughout the paper? Try to avoid repeating the same signal phrase in the same location ("According to," for instance, at the beginning of every citation).

2. Do you move from source to source, without including your thoughts and ideas about the topic? If so, your essay can sound like a compilation of other people's work, not your own.

Does it all sound confusing? At first, most new things do. Look at the entire canvas and see how it all fits in. Examine how a paragraph of Joshua's revised draft aligns with his bibliography cards, note cards, and Works Cited list.

How does it all fit in?

Note Cards

("Digital")

Working Environment
- 51% of American families own a computer
- 41% are connected to the Internet

Definition ("What")
The digital divide is used to differentiate between the haves and have-nots in terms of technology and its potential.

Family Background (Tucker 16)
Typically, lower-income families are affected, but other factors—family size, location, and ethnic background—determine who is affected. 37% of low-income students have access to home computers; 88% of wealthier children use computers at home.

Bibliography

Janoski 6

Works Cited

"Background About the S.E.E.D.S. Program."
Operation S.E.E.D.S. 2002. 24 Apr. 2004 <http://
wwwpcc.cccoes.edu/seeds/background.htm.>.

Chideya, Farai. "Bridging the Digital Divide in the
Classroom." NPR News & Notes. 3 Jan. 2007.
Newspaper Source. EBSCOhost. Pueblo
Community Coll. Lib., Pueblo, CO.
16 Feb. 2007
<http://search.epnet.com>.

"Digital Divide Basics Fact Sheet." Digital Divide
Network. 2002. 18 Mar. 2007
<http://www.digitaldividenetwork.org/content/
stories/index.cfm?key=168>.

Peyton, Joy Kraft. Networking in the Elementary
Classroom. New York: Burroughs, 2003.

Tucker, Patrick. "A New Ruler for the Digital Divide."
The Futurist Mar.-Apr. 2007: 16. EBSCOhost.
Pueblo Community Coll. Library, Pueblo, CO.
15 Feb. 2007 <http://search.epnet.com>.

"What is the Digital Divide?" Power Up. 2002. 14
Mar. 2002 <http://www.powerup.org/digital_divide.
shtml>.

Research Paper

Janoski 2

However, a disturbing reality casts a shadow over this rosy picture. Overall, only 51% of American families own a computer, and only 41% are connected to the Internet at home, leaving a large population with no immediate access to computer technology ("Digital"). Despite the vast numbers of Americans with computer access, a critical social and economic gap is keeping many from enjoying the benefits of technology. This gap is known as the Digital Divide, a term used to differentiate between those who have access to and understanding of technology and those who do not ("What"). Typically, families with lower incomes are most affected by the divide, but several other factors—including family size, location, and ethnic background—determine who is affected as well. According to Tucker, only 37% of low-income students have access to home computers; 88% of wealthier children use computers at home (16).

Bibliography Cards

"Digital Divide Basics Fact
Sheet." Digital Divide
Network. 2002. 18 Mar.
2007 <http://www.
digitaldividenetwork.org/
content/stories/index.
cfm?key=168>.

"What Is the Digital Divide?"
Power Up. 2002. 14 Mar.
2007<http://www.powerup.
org/digital_divide.shtml>.

Tucker, Patrick. "A New Ruler
for the Digital Divide." The
Futurist. Mar.-Apr. 2007:
16. Academic Search
Premier. EBSCOhost. Pueblo
Community Coll. Lib.,
Pueblo, CO. 15 Feb. 2007
<http://search.epnet.com>.

Collaborative Critical Thinking

Asking Your Peers

Once you have completed the writing process and have a polished final draft, exchange papers with a classmate for peer review. Use the following questions to guide your review of your peer's paper.

1. Who is the writer? Who is the peer reviewer?

2. Go to the essay and underline the thesis statement. Is the thesis clear? Does the introduction lead to the thesis?

3. Where does the writer give background information on the topic? Is the information clear and relevant?

4. What additional background information do you feel the writer should supply?

5. How does the writer support his or her view of the topic (examples, statistics, facts, testimony, and so on)?

6. Is there any weak, unclear, or confusing information? Explain. (Circle any points that are illogical, confusing, or ambiguous.)

7. Evaluate the writer's presentation of the topic. Is it credible? Does it respect the audience? Is it too opinionated? How does the writer come through (negatively or positively)? Explain your view.

8. Does the writer support the topic with sufficient and relevant research materials (for example, examples, statistics, facts, or expert testimony)? Where could the writer strengthen his or her case by adding a reference?

9. Are there any problems in documentation of sources? Explain. (Examine in-text citations and the Works Cited or References page.)

10. List some strengths and weaknesses of the paper.

Formatting Your Final Draft

Welcome to the last stage of the research process. The final goal of this stage is for you to present all parts of your paper—outline, final draft, and bibliography—to your instructor. Your instructor may also want your bibliography cards, note cards, and copies of all your sources. Examine how Joshua prepared his paper. Start with his outline.

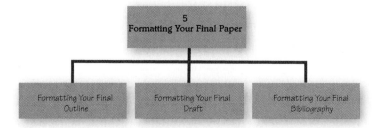

Formatting Your Final Outline

If you recall, Joshua's preliminary outline was rather detailed. Noting lots of details and the sources that support his points helped him draft his paper. In revising his outline, he's moving from his needs as the writer to the needs of the reader. The final outline is concise.

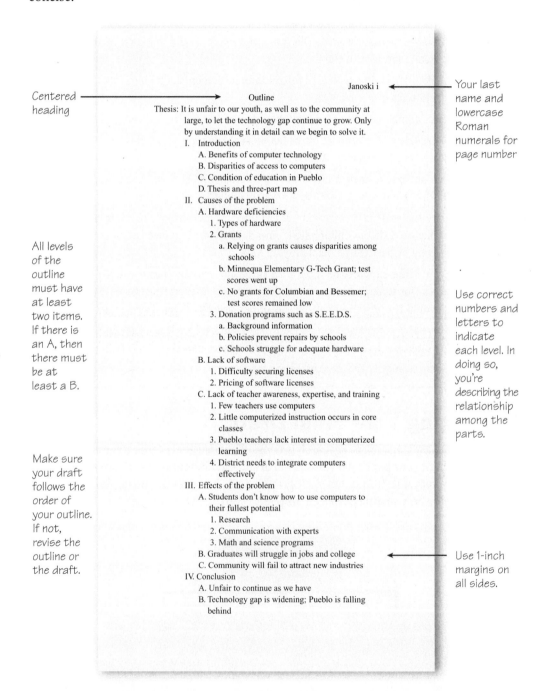

Centered heading

Your last name and lowercase Roman numerals for page number

All levels of the outline must have at least two items. If there is an A, then there must be at least a B.

Use correct numbers and letters to indicate each level. In doing so, you're describing the relationship among the parts.

Make sure your draft follows the order of your outline. If not, revise the outline or the draft.

Use 1-inch margins on all sides.

Janoski i

Outline

Thesis: It is unfair to our youth, as well as to the community at large, to let the technology gap continue to grow. Only by understanding it in detail can we begin to solve it.

I. Introduction
   A. Benefits of computer technology
   B. Disparities of access to computers
   C. Condition of education in Pueblo
   D. Thesis and three-part map
II. Causes of the problem
   A. Hardware deficiencies
     1. Types of hardware
     2. Grants
       a. Relying on grants causes disparities among schools
       b. Minnequa Elementary G-Tech Grant; test scores went up
       c. No grants for Columbian and Bessemer; test scores remained low
     3. Donation programs such as S.E.E.D.S.
       a. Background information
       b. Policies prevent repairs by schools
       c. Schools struggle for adequate hardware
   B. Lack of software
     1. Difficulty securing licenses
     2. Pricing of software licenses
   C. Lack of teacher awareness, expertise, and training
     1. Few teachers use computers
     2. Little computerized instruction occurs in core classes
     3. Pueblo teachers lack interest in computerized learning
     4. District needs to integrate computers effectively
III. Effects of the problem
   A. Students don't know how to use computers to their fullest potential
     1. Research
     2. Communication with experts
     3. Math and science programs
   B. Graduates will struggle in jobs and college
   C. Community will fail to attract new industries
IV. Conclusion
   A. Unfair to continue as we have
   B. Technology gap is widening; Pueblo is falling behind

Formatting Your Final Draft

Just like the outline, your final draft should be presented in the format required by your instructor. Examine Joshua's final draft. Pay close attention to the features pointed out.

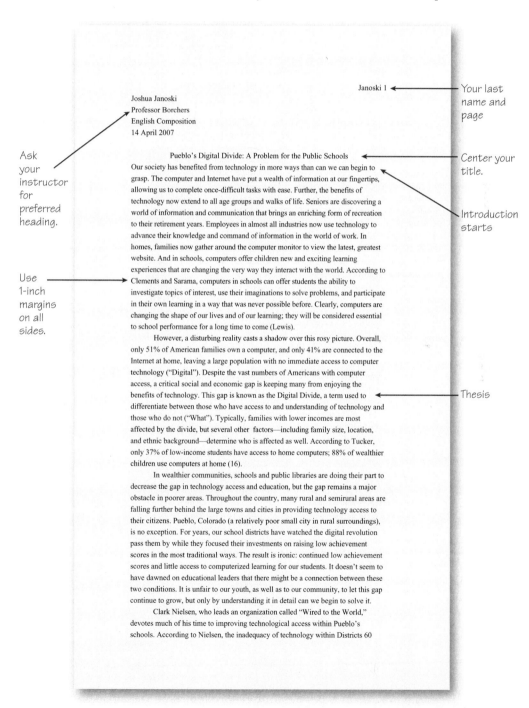

Janoski 1 ← Your last name and page

Joshua Janoski
Professor Borchers
English Composition
14 April 2007

Ask your instructor for preferred heading.

Pueblo's Digital Divide: A Problem for the Public Schools ← Center your title.

Our society has benefited from technology in more ways than can we can begin to grasp. The computer and Internet have put a wealth of information at our fingertips, allowing us to complete once-difficult tasks with ease. Further, the benefits of technology now extend to all age groups and walks of life. Seniors are discovering a world of information and communication that brings an enriching form of recreation to their retirement years. Employees in almost all industries now use technology to advance their knowledge and command of information in the world of work. In homes, families now gather around the computer monitor to view the latest, greatest website. And in schools, computers offer children new and exciting learning experiences that are changing the very way they interact with the world. According to Clements and Sarama, computers in schools can offer students the ability to investigate topics of interest, use their imaginations to solve problems, and participate in their own learning in a way that was never possible before. Clearly, computers are changing the shape of our lives and of our learning; they will be considered essential to school performance for a long time to come (Lewis).

Introduction starts

Use 1-inch margins on all sides.

However, a disturbing reality casts a shadow over this rosy picture. Overall, only 51% of American families own a computer, and only 41% are connected to the Internet at home, leaving a large population with no immediate access to computer technology ("Digital"). Despite the vast numbers of Americans with computer access, a critical social and economic gap is keeping many from enjoying the benefits of technology. This gap is known as the Digital Divide, a term used to differentiate between those who have access to and understanding of technology and those who do not ("What"). Typically, families with lower incomes are most affected by the divide, but several other factors—including family size, location, and ethnic background—determine who is affected as well. According to Tucker, only 37% of low-income students have access to home computers; 88% of wealthier children use computers at home (16).

Thesis

In wealthier communities, schools and public libraries are doing their part to decrease the gap in technology access and education, but the gap remains a major obstacle in poorer areas. Throughout the country, many rural and semirural areas are falling further behind the large towns and cities in providing technology access to their citizens. Pueblo, Colorado (a relatively poor small city in rural surroundings), is no exception. For years, our school districts have watched the digital revolution pass them by while they focused their investments on raising low achievement scores in the most traditional ways. The result is ironic: continued low achievement scores and little access to computerized learning for our students. It doesn't seem to have dawned on educational leaders that there might be a connection between these two conditions. It is unfair to our youth, as well as to our community, to let this gap continue to grow, but only by understanding it in detail can we begin to solve it.

Clark Nielsen, who leads an organization called "Wired to the World," devotes much of his time to improving technological access within Pueblo's schools. According to Nielsen, the inadequacy of technology within Districts 60

Janoski 2

and 70 can be broken into three parts:

    1) Lack of adequate computer hardware in the schools

    2) Lack of the most up-to-date software applications

    3) Lack of teachers who are properly trained to use computers to their
      full potential.

Consider each of these problems separately.

    The first cause is that many schools do not have sufficient hardware to
accommodate the number of students. The needed hardware includes monitors, printers,
speakers, mouse devices, and the computers themselves. Of course, the deeper cause is
that the districts lack the money or the will to apply available funds to technology; instead,
their strategy is to apply for technology grants from various corporations and organizations, including companies such as Dell and Microsoft. Unfortunately, these grants are
awarded only to a select few schools each year, according to Nielsen. While these grants
provide some benefit to a few schools, they have the paradoxical effect of widening the
technology inequities within the districts. Nielsen gives a good example involving three
elementary schools within District 60: Minnequa, Columbian, and Bessemer elementary
schools. He reports that Minnequa recently received a G-Tech grant that gave the school
new state-of-the-art equipment for some classrooms. Bessemer and Columbian were not
among the schools chosen for the grant. When Minnequa later reported higher state
assessment scores than the other two schools, much credit was given to the grant-
supported infusion of computer technology directly into the classroom. It wasn't just the
other two schools but also their students who lost out in this imbalance of resources.
Shanklin reports on another aspect of the hardware problem; she describes an
elementary school in Florida 10 years ago was a "technology showcase" but that has
been unable to fund needed upgrades to its computers. It now is far behind other schools
in the state, writes Shanklin.

    Clearly, technology investment is a long-term process requiring a long-term
commitment. What options are available to schools that don't win the luck of the draw in
the game of technology grants? The answer, unfortunately, is other "patchwork" solutions.
For example, one source of computer technology for public schools is a highly laudable
program begun by Congressman Scott McInnis in 1996 called "Sharing Electronic
Equipment District and Statewide," or S.E.E.D.S. ("Background"). The program receives
computers from businesses and organizations that have upgraded their systems and no
longer need their old equipment. S.E.E.D.S. refurbishes these systems and distributes them
to schools and nonprofit organizations that need them. This is a great way for schools
with small budgets to get computers for their classrooms; however, S.E.E.D.S. can never
provide a comprehensive answer. According to Keith Gill, S.E.E.D.S. coordinator at
Pueblo Community College, the program is limited by district policies that prevent
allocating funds to maintain computers donated by the S.E.E.D.S. program. Instead,
thedistricts insist that donors of used equipment maintain that equipment after it is donated
to the schools. Technology recycling programs have a big enough task collecting,
refurbishing, and delivering computers without having the added cost and burden of
maintaining the systems they donate, so they often refuse to provide the added
maintenance. The result is that many of our schools are left in limbo: they don't receive
grants, and they have no way of supporting used, donated technology. The digital divide
only deepens.

Marginal annotations:

← Map of cause section

← Cause section

Janoski 3

Obtaining the necessary hardware is only part of the problem, however, according to Frank Mortensen, computer engineer and parent of a District 60 elementary student. Schools that manage to jump over the hardware hurdle are faced with another problem: acquiring the appropriate software. Columbian Elementary offers a prime example of this problem. Columbian has some computer hardware but hardly any of the right software to go along with it. As a result, says Mortensen, students are not able to use the equipment to its full potential. Software licenses cost money, and a separate license is required for each computer using a particular brand of software. For example, 20 computers running the Microsoft Windows operating system require 20 licenses to operate legally. For schools trying to run multiple computers, these costs can easily outrun a technology budget, especially because encyclopedias, magazine subscriptions, and other educational software (much of it not to be found in any hardcopy form) are needed to stock a fully functional computerized learning network.

Schools lucky enough to gain grants for hardware and software, meager as those grants often prove to be, must then ensure their teachers, especially teachers of core subjects, can effectively operate the technology and incorporate it into their lesson plans. According to Clements and Sarama, two key components of electronic learning are the way teachers design their curriculum and the layout of their classrooms, and these elements of the teaching situation require significant training before teachers of core subjects can integrate them effectively into their students' daily instruction. However, a national survey involving more than 4,000 teachers in 1998 showed that only 22% of science teachers, 12% of social studies teachers, and 13% of math teachers used software related to their subject matter, and even then, only occasionally. The same study showed that children still lacked access in core classes to computer- assisted instruction that encourages imaginative thinking; most children interested in using exciting and educational software had to take a separate computer class (Becker 51-52).

Although we lack similar data for Pueblo's schools, Mortensen reports that many teachers have no idea of the true power of digitized learning and prefer not to be bothered with "just another initiative of the administration." Somehow, even in cases where we've been able to integrate technology into the classroom, teachers allow their use only for the most basic functions: typing papers, performing routine and uninstructed internet searches, and playing games that come installed on the computers. We could have all the technology in the world, but it will never benefit student learning unless teachers are encouraged to employ it effectively and the districts can train them to do so.

In one sense, the causes are easy enough to understand: it all boils down to money and commitment. But what about the effects? The Digital Divide is increasingly impacting today's generation of students, who may be computer savvy in elementary ways—they know more about operating a computer and fixing its problems than their teachers—but who don't know how to use computers to do research, communicate appropriately with experts in various fields, operate mathematical and scientific software, or present complex concepts to others using combinations of the written word and effective graphics. Without a proper understanding of technology, students will have a hard time obtaining quality jobs in the future and will be deprived of the quality education that all American citizens require to achieve success ("What").

← Effect section

Janoski 4

A lack of motivation among high school graduates to enter higher levels of academics will emerge because almost every college and university now incorporates computer technology into classrooms and lesson plans. In a National Public Radio interview, technology expert Mario Armstrong tells of visiting poor classrooms throughout America and discovering that even in the poorest the existence of technology is a sign to children that "somebody cares" about their education (Chideya). Pueblo's schools are sending the wrong message to students; we should surround them with the tools they need to succeed, but we continue our policies of deprivation.

In addition to the effects on our youth, the Digital Divide will affect our ◄─────── Conclusion
community as a whole. Even some rural schools are now seeing the need to invest in technology and have begun doing so at a faster rate than Pueblo School Districts 60 and 70. If our local districts don't keep pace with technology, our city will maintain its "rural" educational status despite its urban setting and population. As Nielsen says, "This will lead to declines in Pueblo's ability to attract new employment and shrink existing jobs, and the Digital Divide will be mirrored in the areas of jobs and income creation."

It is simply not fair to deprive our youth of educational and employment opportunities that students in other districts are now taking full advantage of because of the foresight of their educational policy makers. We must begin to narrow the gap that is widening faster as the digital revolution picks up speed and momentum. We are falling behind not only in terms of technology but also in terms of student learning, yet nobody seems to realize the connection between the two. The book by Joy Kraft Payton, Networking in the Elementary English Classroom, argues forcefully that there is a strong connection between up-to-date technology in classrooms and student reading abilities. Until we realize this connection, our policy makers will continue to rant about test scores instead of making useful decisions, our teachers will stick to their same outmoded, ho-hum ways of managing their classes, and our students will continue to flounder in acquiring the expertise they need to succeed. The true tragedy will hit later, when our graduates fail to pursue higher education or seek high-paying jobs simply because they are standing on the wrong side of today's Great Divide.

Formatting Your Final Bibliography

You end your research paper with your Works Cited page if you're using MLA or your References page if you're using APA. Examine Joshua's final Works Cited page. Again, pay close attention to the features labeled.

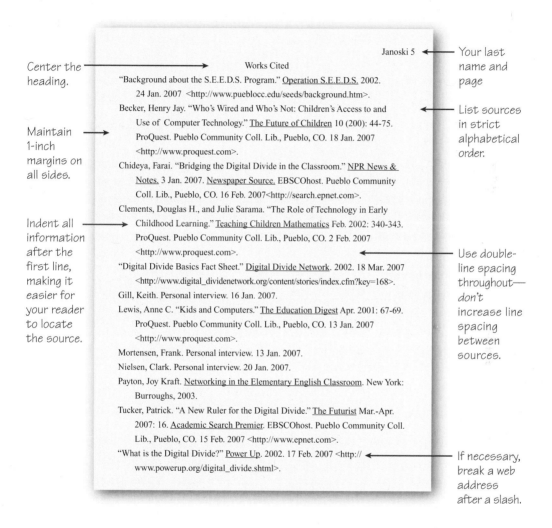

Center the heading.

Maintain 1-inch margins on all sides.

Indent all information after the first line, making it easier for your reader to locate the source.

Janoski 5

Works Cited

"Background about the S.E.E.D.S. Program." Operation S.E.E.D.S. 2002.
    24 Jan. 2007 <http://www.pueblocc.edu/seeds/background.htm>.

Becker, Henry Jay. "Who's Wired and Who's Not: Children's Access to and
    Use of Computer Technology." The Future of Children 10 (200): 44-75.
    ProQuest. Pueblo Community Coll. Lib., Pueblo, CO. 18 Jan. 2007
    <http://www.proquest.com>.

Chideya, Farai. "Bridging the Digital Divide in the Classroom." NPR News &
    Notes. 3 Jan. 2007. Newspaper Source. EBSCOhost. Pueblo Community
    Coll. Lib., Pueblo, CO. 16 Feb. 2007<http://search.epnet.com>.

Clements, Douglas H., and Julie Sarama. "The Role of Technology in Early
    Childhood Learning." Teaching Children Mathematics Feb. 2002: 340-343.
    ProQuest. Pueblo Community Coll. Lib., Pueblo, CO. 2 Feb. 2007
    <http://www.proquest.com>.

"Digital Divide Basics Fact Sheet." Digital Divide Network. 2002. 18 Mar. 2007
    <http://www.digital_dividenetwork.org/content/stories/index.cfm?key=168>.

Gill, Keith. Personal interview. 16 Jan. 2007.

Lewis, Anne C. "Kids and Computers." The Education Digest Apr. 2001: 67-69.
    ProQuest. Pueblo Community Coll. Lib., Pueblo, CO. 13 Jan. 2007
    <http://www.proquest.com>.

Mortensen, Frank. Personal interview. 13 Jan. 2007.

Nielsen, Clark. Personal interview. 20 Jan. 2007.

Payton, Joy Kraft. Networking in the Elementary English Classroom. New York:
    Burroughs, 2003.

Tucker, Patrick. "A New Ruler for the Digital Divide." The Futurist Mar.-Apr.
    2007: 16. Academic Search Premier. EBSCOhost. Pueblo Community Coll.
    Lib., Pueblo, CO. 15 Feb. 2007 <http://www.epnet.com>.

"What is the Digital Divide?" Power Up. 2002. 17 Feb. 2007 <http://
    www.powerup.org/digital_divide.shtml>.

Your last name and page

List sources in strict alphabetical order.

Use double-line spacing throughout—don't increase line spacing between sources.

If necessary, break a web address after a slash.

Reflecting

Any time you complete a research project, spend some time reflecting on how the process went. Research is such a massive undertaking that you are not equally capable in all aspects of it the first time around. Each time you take on a new project, try to improve in your areas of weakness.

WRITING YOUR RESEARCH PAPER

Self-Reflection

Before you hand in your paper, write 1–2 paragraphs in which you reflect on your research process. Referring to specific parts of the research process, include your feelings on the following questions:

1. What do you feel you did best?

2. What part of the process was most challenging to you?

3. In which stages do you feel you need the most practice?

4. How can you address your challenges or weaknesses and improve the quality of future research papers?

After you have completed this self-reflection, carefully review your instructor's comments. Write down your instructor's comments about your use of sources; then write a short response to each one, either acknowledging or questioning its validity. If you don't understand a comment, make sure to visit with your instructor for clarification. How might you use research outside of this English course?

- **College:** _____
- **Your profession:** _____
- **Everyday life:** _____

Editing for Grammar

PART 3

CHAPTER 15

Editing for Fragments

YOUR GOALS

1. Identify the elements of a complete sentence.

2. Identify and revise different types of sentence fragments.

3. Revise paragraphs and essays for sentence fragments.

"Those who write clearly have readers; those who write obscurely have commentators."

■ **Albert Camus** ■

An employee sends the following e-mail to her supervisor:

> Dear Ms. Wasil,
>
> I am very interested in the new position. As Accounts Payable manager. I have been with this company for 7 years. And have worked in various departments. Which has given me an in-depth understanding of what each area does. Having this wide range of experiences. I feel prepared to lead the newly restructured Accounts Payable Department.
>
> As you are aware. I have the interpersonal skills and the communication skills essential to this position. Hope to hear from you and receive your support.
>
> Yours truly,
>
> Gayle Johnson

How competent do you feel Gayle is for the position? Given her vast experience, she is obviously a knowledgeable employee, but her writing reflects a failure to review her work, a lack of knowledge of basic grammar rules, or an inability to see her own writing errors. Her supervisor may even view this e-mail as a reflection of Gayle's character and abilities. Although Ms. Wasil would be incorrect in this opinion, many managers make judgments based on the most immediate evidence.

Gayle could have easily avoided these misconceptions by proofreading her writing for sentence completeness. In her short e-mail, she has written six sentence fragments. If she were to get the promotion, her many letters to vendors would contain the same mistakes and leave the same negative impression. As a manager, would you hire her? Don't permit others to misjudge you through your writing. Learn and apply basic rules.

LET's warm up!

Image Source/Jupiter Images

Why are some writers unable to spot their own mistakes? What is it about proofreading that makes it so difficult to locate errors we consistently repeat? Reflect on this problem for a moment; then write a paragraph in which you discuss one or two important reasons that make finding errors in our own compositions difficult.

UNDERSTANDING SENTENCE FRAGMENTS

Many grammatical errors that occur in student writing result from three common problems in sentence construction:

- Sentence fragments
- Fused sentences
- Comma splices

Each of these errors signals a lack of understanding of sentence boundaries. All three are serious errors because they distract from the clarity of the writing, depict the writer as careless, and raise questions about the writer's credibility—why should the reader trust you if you can't write a simple idea correctly? Keep the following point in mind: Good writing starts with its most basic element, the complete sentence.

A complete sentence expresses a complete idea. Examine the following paragraph for complete sentences.

> [1.]Throughout my career, I have on numerous occasions had to deal with people. [2.]Who have gotten angry enough. [3.]That they become violent. [4.]Whether their behavior stems from the use of alcohol or drugs. [5.]Or simply a lack of emotional control. [6.]These patients can be a threat to others and to themselves. [7.]Dealing with an individual who has become violent. [8.]Isn't an easy task. [9.]How one deals with a violent situation may have serious and unexpected consequences. [10.]Therefore, the procedure that the caregiver employs to defuse violent situations must be carefully calculated.

This paragraph contains many incomplete sentences, known as *fragments*. Notice how the period at the end of each word group breaks the flow of ideas, making some ideas unclear or meaningless. Periods should mark the end of complete ideas. Most fragments are disconnected pieces of a main idea. Examine the word groups in the preceding paragraph to determine which ones represent complete ideas:

> Throughout my career, I have on numerous occasions had to deal with people.

This is a *complete sentence*. If someone were to say this sentence to you, your reaction might be to respond with a question or comment that indicates your understanding of the sentence, such as "What kind of people have you had to deal with?" or "I've dealt with a lot of people, too." The point is that the speaker would have communicated a complete idea, and you are able to grasp the content of that idea.

In contrast, the second sentence is an incomplete idea, a fragment. If someone were to say to you, "Who have gotten angry enough," you probably wouldn't know how to respond. By itself, this group of words is just a bit of information that belongs within a larger idea. This group of words is a *sentence fragment*.

Examine the third string of words. Is this group a complete sentence or a fragment?

> That they become violent.

If you answered *fragment*, you are correct. Again, this string of words is just a piece of information: the idea is incomplete, merely a bit of information detached from its main idea.

Examine the fourth sentence. Is it a fragment or a complete sentence?

Whether their behavior stems from the use of alcohol or drugs.

If you think that this is a fragment, you are correct. Try reading this statement to someone and test that person's reaction. Probably, the person won't know how to respond to this statement with other than a confused "What are you talking about?"

Take a few minutes and carefully examine sentences 5–10 of the example paragraph. Identify each group of words as either a complete sentence or a fragment. Then check your answers in Appendix A.

> **Collaborative Critical Thinking**
>
> **In groups,** rewrite the paragraph on page 453 by attaching the fragments to one another to create complete sentences. After you have completed your revision, compare it to the paragraphs from other groups. Were there any differences? Why? Answers will vary.

Basic Parts of a Sentence

Generally, a *sentence* is a group of words that expresses a complete thought. Unfortunately, as simple as this definition may seem, you can easily read more into a group of words than you have actually written; your string of words may sound like a complete thought to you even if it is a fragment. When you edit your essays for fragments, you are aware of the context of each sentence: you know what you wrote before each sentence and what follows each sentence. This personal knowledge leads you to make sense of your fragments by mentally tying them to the ideas of other sentences and seeing them as complete thoughts. To begin to understand the structure of sentences, consider this example.

Because this example has a subject, *Nat*, and a verb, *left*, we call it a *clause*.

> A **clause** is a group of words containing a subject and a verb.

We return to the idea of clauses later, but first we focus on the heart of a sentence, the verb.

Locating the Verb of a Sentence

Locating the verb of a sentence should not be a problem if you know the characteristics of a verb.

Verbs carry the tense of a sentence; that is, they express when the action took place:

- He is here. [right now]
- He was here. [in the past]
- He will be here. [at any moment in the future]

Some verbs form their past tense when you add *-ed* at the end.

Bridging Knowledge

See Chapter 19, for explanation of verb tense and page 531 for a list of irregular verbs.

Present Tense	Past Tense
want	wanted
decide	decided
walk	walked

However, some verbs are irregular and change form in the past tense. Examine the following examples of irregular verbs. You can most likely think of many more irregular verbs.

Present Tense	Past Tense	Past Participle
speak	spoke	have spoken
give	gave	have given
come	came	have come

Verbs take the *-ing* ending to show continuous action.

Present Continuous	Past Continuous
is speaking	was speaking
is giving	was giving
is coming	was coming

You can show future action by placing the auxiliary (helping) verb *will* in front of the verb.

Present Continuous
will speak
will give
will come

Auxiliary or *helping verbs* help mark the tense of the main verb or give additional meaning to the main verb. Here's a list of the most common helping verbs.

Auxiliary Verbs
am, is, are, was, were, be, been
do, does, did
can, could
may, might, must
shall, should
will, would

If you can change the time expressed by a word by changing its form, adding *-ed* or *-ing*, or putting the word *will* in front of the word, you have most likely identified the verb of the sentence. Once you have located the verb, it's easy to find the subject.

PRACTICE   15-1

Underline the verbs in the following sentences. Include all auxiliary verbs.

1. The trees <u>creaked</u> and <u>shuddered</u> in the powerful wind.
2. Police <u>are investigating</u> the incident.
3. Her dog <u>was acting</u> strangely in front of her house.
4. An ache <u>spread</u> from between her shoulders.
5. The investigator <u>must have noticed</u> the loose wire.
6. The new employee <u>will act</u> quickly on any customer problem.
7. The house manager <u>should have reported</u> the incident to the insurance company.
8. I <u>might resign</u> my job and <u>look</u> for a better one.
9. <u>Does</u> he <u>know</u> the answer to the math problem?
10. You really <u>should take</u> the test over.

Locating the Subject of a Sentence

Read the following sentence:

> The loud child left the room quietly.

First look for the word that gives the time of the action or a word that can take *-ing*, *-ed*, or *will*. If you chose the word *left*, you are correct. *Left* describes past action (for example, "Yesterday, I left."). Although you cannot add *-ed* to *left* because it is an irregular verb, it takes *-ing* (*leav<u>ing</u>*) and the helping verb *will* (*<u>will</u>* leave) to indicate future time.

Now that you have your verb, all you have to do is ask, "Who left?" This leads you to your subject: *child.*

The subject can be in the form of a noun or its pronoun equivalent. The following list gives you a sense of what a noun is and the types of pronouns that can occupy the subject position.

Noun	Examples	Pronoun Substitute
Names of specific people, types of people, and people in general	Michael, Sara, women, soldier, student	I, you, he, she, we, they, anyone, everyone, somebody
Names of places and places in general	New York, Dallas, restaurant, park, house	It, they, anything, something
Names for animals, objects, ideas, and emotions	Dog, tiger, pencil, street, freedom, democracy, hate, depression	It, they, anything, something

If you can make the word plural (book = books), count it (one cake, two cakes), add the article *the* in front of it (the pencil), or make it possessive (the man's wallet), you more than likely have a noun.

However, this does not mean that all nouns are subjects of sentences. The noun that performs the action or idea expressed by the verb is the subject. Examine the underlined nouns in following sentence:

The <u>manager</u> of the <u>restaurant</u> questioned the <u>employees</u> about the <u>accident</u>.

To find the subject, you should locate the main verb (*questioned*) and then determine who (or what) performed the action of the verb by asking "Who questioned the employees?" The answer brings you to the subject: *manager.* Don't be fooled by words that separate the subject from the verb, especially prepositional phrases.

Prepositions are words that give information of time, space, or direction. Here is a list of common prepositions.

about	around	during	of	under
above	at	except	off	until
across	before	for	on	up
after	behind	from	over	with
against	beside	in	through	without
along	between	into	to	
among	by	like	toward	

By eliminating the prepositional phrases, you can quickly see the connection or relationship between the subject and its verb.

The <u>manager</u> ~~of the restaurant~~ <u>questioned</u> the employees ~~about the accident.~~

In the following sentences, cross out all prepositional phrases, underline the subject once, and underline the verb twice.

Example: The large <u>family</u> ~~in the house by the lake~~ <u>moved</u> ~~to the city.~~

1. The <u>female</u> ~~of many animals~~ <u>is</u> larger than the male.
2. <u>Dozens</u> ~~of spectators~~ <u>gathered</u> ~~on the bridge near the site of the accident.~~
3. Many <u>shoppers</u> <u>pulled</u> the fliers ~~from their windshields~~ and angrily <u>threw</u> them ~~on the ground.~~
4. <u>Fruits</u> and <u>vegetables</u> ~~with dangerous sprays~~ <u>should be banned</u> ~~from this country.~~
5. While ~~in Europe,~~ <u>Kevin</u> <u>dieted</u> ~~for a year,~~ <u>took</u> dance lessons, and <u>lost</u> 100 pounds.
6. <u>Everything</u> ~~in the shoe department~~ <u>is</u> on sale ~~at 60 % off.~~
7. The office <u>manager</u> <u>should have been reported</u> ~~for his unprofessional behavior.~~
8. ~~In a fit of anger,~~ <u>Joshua,</u> ~~without consulting his wife,~~ <u>quit</u> his job.
9. ~~Without a doubt,~~ <u>she</u> <u>could have been killed</u> ~~by that falling rock.~~
10. Long <u>lines</u> ~~of southbound geese~~ <u>were flying</u> overhead.

Verb Forms as Subjects

Certain verb forms can act as subjects, which can easily cause fragments if separated from the main verb of the sentence. These verb forms act as nouns. One such verb form, known as a *gerund,* ends in *-ing.*

> <u>Getting up every morning</u> became very difficult.

The main verb of this sentence is *became.* If you ask who or what of the verb, you find that the subject is actually the entire verbal phrase, or gerund: "What became very difficult?" The answer ("Getting up every morning") is the subject.

This does not mean that all verb forms ending in *-ing* are subjects of sentences.

> Getting up every morning to the same routine, Tim became depressed.

If you ask, "Who became depressed," you locate the subject, *Tim,* not the verb form *getting.* This type of verbal phrase is called a *participial phrase* and does not act as a subject.

Another type of verbal phrase that can sometimes act as the subject of the sentence is the *infinitive.* The infinitive consists of the word *to* plus the verb, for example, *to run, to laugh, to exercise.*

> To buy a cabin by a lake became her goal.

If you ask, "What became her goal," you find that the answer and subject is the infinitive, "To buy a cabin by a lake."

PRACTICE 15-3

In the following sentences, underline the subject once and the verb twice. Be careful not to confuse a participial phrase with a gerund phrase.

1. <u>Receiving a bonus</u> <u>was</u> little compensation for all our hard work.
2. <u>To err</u> <u>is</u> human.
3. Removing her jacket, <u>Lorna</u> <u>rushed</u> to pick up the phone.
4. Washing and polishing the car, <u>Ron</u> <u>refused</u> to come in for dinner.
5. <u>Reading a good book on the plane</u> <u>made</u> the trip seem shorter.
6. Trembling with excitement, <u>Michael</u> <u>accepted</u> the award.
7. <u>To succeed in this field</u> <u>takes</u> patience, creativity, and hard work.
8. <u>To tour Australia</u> <u>was</u> Joseph's dream.
9. <u>Megan</u>, watching an old movie, <u>drifted</u> in and out of sleep.
10. <u>Shopping online</u> <u>is</u> Ricardo's favorite pastime.

Independent and Dependent Clauses

Earlier, we defined a clause as a group of words containing a subject and verb. Clauses that can stand alone as sentences are called *independent clauses*. One independent clause can make up a sentence: "Nat left early." A sentence can also be made up of several independent clauses: "Nat left early, and the team was angry."

> An **independent clause** is a group of words containing a subject and a verb that can stand alone as a sentence or be combined with other clauses for longer sentences.

Look at what happens when we add another word in front of "Nat left".

Since Nat left.

It's still a clause, but it's no longer independent; it can't stand alone as a sentence. This group of words is a *dependent clause*. If someone stated "Since Nat left," you wouldn't respond because, most likely, you'd be waiting for the next part of this clause: its main idea, which is an independent clause.

Since Nat left, we decided to break up the team.

Words such as *after, although, because, before, how, if, since, that, unless, when, which,* and *who* introduce dependent clauses.

> A **dependent clause** is a group of words containing a subject and a verb that cannot stand alone as a sentence.

If a dependent clause is separated from the rest of its sentence by a period, it is a fragment even though the clause has a subject and verb.

For the following sentences, underline the independent clause once and the dependent clause twice. Some sentences may have more than one dependent clause.

Example: Raymond was upset that he was not nominated.

1. Our history instructor gave us a test although we did not feel prepared.
2. When I walked into the classroom, I was shocked since I was not expecting a test.
3. I didn't protest because I heard that she held high standards in her courses.
4. Although she noticed our worried expressions, she did not say a word and continued to distribute the test forms.
5. It became clear that this class was going to be demanding.
6. If I wanted to pass this course, I would have to keep up with the work.
7. Before I started the test, I quickly read the questions and gave a sigh of relief.
8. I was surprised when I found myself answering every question on the test.
9. After this experience, I realized the importance of coming to class every day and taking notes if I wanted to understand the material.
10. Most students don't realize how much they learn when they're present for all class activities, lectures, and discussions.

Identifying Fragments

As you have seen, not all sentence fragments are structurally the same. Some fragments may appear to be complete sentences. Here is one method that may help you locate fragments in your compositions.

Start reading your essay sentence by sentence, starting with the last sentence of your essay and working in reverse to the beginning of your essay. This method can help you hear sentences in isolation, apart from the influence of a previous idea. If a sentence doesn't sound right (if it is not a complete idea), it's probably a fragment. To repair it, you may just need to combine it with the sentence before or after it so that the idea is complete. However, if you're still not sure, do one or all of the following tests:

1. Check to see whether the group of words contains a subject and a verb. If one of these elements is missing, add it and make your sentence complete.
2. Add the phrase "Is it true that . . ." or "Is it a fact that . . ." to the beginning of each sentence and read it as if it were a question. If you can answer "yes" or "no," the sentence is complete; if not, you have a fragment.

> We were very busy that day. Because we had to meet our deadline.
> "Is it true that we were busy that day?"
> "Is it true that because we had to meet our deadline?"

The first sentence makes sense, but the second does not. The phrase "Because we had to meet our deadline" is a fragment. You need to restructure such a sentence or attach it to the previous or subsequent sentence. Unfortunately, this test does not work for sentences that are already questions or written in the imperative (commands), but it works for most declarative sentences.

3. Turn the statement into a question by adding a tag question to the end of the sentence.

   ■ She was busy that day, wasn't she? [This is a complete sentence.]
   ■ All people should vote, shouldn't they? [This is a complete sentence.]
   ■ Driving by the park, didn't he? [This question doesn't make sense; it's a fragment.]
   ■ When she decided to leave, didn't she? [This question doesn't make sense; it's a fragment.]

In general, a fragment can be revised by combining it with an independent clause in the paragraph or by turning the fragment into an independent clause. Here are more examples of fragments and some possible revisions.

Fragment	Revision
The student in the white jacket. **Simple test:** Is it true that the student in the white jacket? The question makes no sense, so the statement is a fragment.	The student in the white jacket is my brother. **Simple test:** Is it true that the student in the white jacket is my brother? The question makes sense because the listener can answer "yes" or "no"; thus, this is a complete sentence.
The book that you left under the desk. **Simple test:** Is it true that the book that you left under the desk? The question makes no sense, so the statement is a fragment.	The book that you left under the desk disappeared. **Simple test:** Is it true that the book that you left under the desk disappeared? The question makes sense because the listener can answer "yes" or "no"; thus, this is a complete sentence.
Since you are such a kind, generous person. **Simple test:** Is it true that since you are such a kind, generous person? The question makes no sense, so the statement is a fragment.	Since you are such a kind, generous person, you will have many friends. OR You will have many friends since you are such a kind, generous person. **Simple test:** Is it true that since you are such a kind, generous person, you will have many friends? OR Is it true that you will have many friends since you are such a kind, generous person? Both questions make sense because the listener can answer "yes" or "no"; thus, both are complete sentences.

PRACTICE **15-5**

Try various tests (add "Is it true that . . ." or a tag question) to conclude whether the given sentences are complete or fragments. If the item is a fragment, revise it. Answers will vary.

Example: Taking the exam today.

Test: Taking the exam today, didn't she?

Conclusion: The test question doesn't make sense, so the statement is a fragment.

Revision: Jenny is taking the exam today.

1. Made a phone call after dinner.

Test: Is it true that made a phone call after dinner?

Conclusion: The test question doesn't make sense, so the statement is a fragment.

Revision: Phil made a phone call after dinner.

2. While writing my essay yesterday afternoon.

Test: While writing my essay yesterday afternoon, didn't I?

Conclusion: The test question doesn't make sense, so the statement is a fragment.

Revision: I got writer's block while writing my essay yesterday afternoon.

3. Who stopped me while I was shopping.

Test: Is it true that who stopped me while I was shopping?

Conclusion: The test question doesn't make sense, so the statement is a fragment.

Revision: Damian is the friend who stopped me while I was shopping.

4. The woman delivering the package to the company.

Test: The woman delivering the package to the company, isn't she?

Conclusion: The test question doesn't make sense, so the statement is a fragment.

Revision: The woman delivering the package to the company is running late.

5. As soon as she spoke to me in the corridor.

Test: Is it true that as soon as she spoke to me in the corridor?

Conclusion: The test question doesn't make sense, so the statement is a fragment.

Revision: As soon as she spoke to me in the corridor, I recognized who she was.

Types of Fragments

Examine the six most common types of fragments and see how they may be revised.

■ **Type 1: Subject-only Fragment**

EXAMPLE: The man in the booth.

[This is merely a subject followed by a prepositional phrase. We don't know who or what the man is or what the man did. You need to complete the idea.]

SOLUTION: The man in the booth gave me instructions.
[Complete the idea by adding a predicate (verb + modifiers, if any).]

■ Type 2: Verbal Phrase Fragment

EXAMPLE: I read the list. <u>Hoping to see my name</u>.
[This type of fragment starts with a verb, usually but not always a verb ending in *-ing* or to and a verb. You need to attach the verbal phrase to the sentence in which it belongs.]

SOLUTION: I read the list, <u>hoping to see my name</u>.

OR

I read the list. <u>Hoping to see my name</u>, I searched nervously.
[Attach the fragment to its main idea or complete the idea.]

■ Type 3: Prepositional Phrase Fragment

EXAMPLE: He made many errors. <u>Throughout the report</u>.
[Prepositional phrases (preposition + object) provide bits of information necessary for a full understanding of the idea of the sentence, but prepositional phrases by themselves are not complete ideas.]

SOLUTION: He made many errors throughout the report.
[Attach the prepositional phrase to its main and independent sentence.]

PRACTICE 15-6

Mark the following items as S for complete sentence or F for fragment. If the item is a fragment, revise it. Answers will vary.

__F__ 1. Taking him on a date but forgetting his name.

She enjoyed taking him on a date but kept forgetting his name.

__F__ 2. My hobby being one that most people find boring.

My hobby is one that most people find boring.

__F__ 3. The cabin at the end of the field beyond the bridge.

The cabin at the end of the field beyond the bridge is ours.

__F__ 4. To find that the company was no longer accepting applications.

I went to the job site only to find that the company was no longer accepting applications.

__S__ 5. Preparing herself a snack in the late afternoon, she often dines late.

__F__ 6. My leg broken in the accident.

My leg was broken in the accident.

____F____ 7. My wife thinking of starting her own travel agency.

> My wife is thinking of starting her own travel agency.

____S____ 8. Identity fraud has become a major problem.

____F____ 9. Expecting them to return the merchandise as quickly as possible.

> The company is expecting them to return the merchandise as quickly as possible.

____F___10. All union employees leaving early to protest the new policy.

> All union employees are leaving early to protest the new policy.

■ Type 4: Split Compound Fragment

EXAMPLE: Jessica left early. And took the bus.
[When using a coordinating conjunction (for, and, nor, but, or, yet, so) not followed by a subject, write both parts as one sentence. Do not use a period.]

SOLUTION: Jessica left early and took the bus.

OR

Jessica left early, and she took the bus.
[Attach the fragment to the main sentence. You now have one sentence with a compound verb. Add a subject to the fragment, and change the period of the main sentence to a comma. You now have a compound sentence.]

■ Type 5: Transitional Word Fragment

EXAMPLE: We have been to many exciting cities. For example, Los Angeles.
[When you use transitional words and expressions (thus, especially, for example, for instance, therefore, however, such as) to start a sentence, punctuate the sentence according to your use of the expression. If it is a complete sentence, write it as a separate sentence; if not, connect the expression to an independent clause.]

SOLUTION: We have been to many exciting cities, for example Los Angeles.

OR

We have been to many exciting cities. For example, we have enjoyed Los Angeles.
[Use a comma and attach the fragment to the main sentence, or use a period or semicolon and make the fragment a complete sentence.]

PRACTICE 15-7

The following paragraph contains different types of fragments. First underline the fragments; then revise them. Answers will vary.

<u>With the constant fear of terrorism striking the United States at any moment.</u> Fear and distrust have become growing problems. The increased amount of security within our borders has nearly "handcuffed" this country. <u>For example, personal bags when brought to large public gatherings and events.</u> Are searched before the person is allowed to enter. <u>Causing long lines, frustration, and angry people questioning whether it is even worth the effort to attend.</u> At airports, travelers' personal belongings are checked. <u>And shoes are inspected.</u> <u>Violating every citizen's right to privacy.</u> The long lines of angry citizens being asked to undress themselves in the terminal seem to defy common sense. These precautions may be well intended. <u>And provide a sense of security to some, but they're costing us our dignity.</u>

▪ Type 6: Dependent Clause Fragments

EXAMPLE: When I complete the project.

Notice that the segment "I complete the project" is a complete sentence, but once the writer adds a word such as when in front of the sentence, the reader is expecting another idea to follow. Words such as when create subordinate, less important ideas, converting complete sentences (independent clauses) into dependent clauses. By themselves, dependent clauses are fragments; they need to be attached to an independent clause (complete sentence) for a complete meaning. Here are some common words that create dependent clause fragments:

after	since	where	who
although	that	whereas	whom
as (if)	though	wherever	whose
because	unless	whether	
before	untill	which	
if	when	while	

SOLUTION: <u>When I complete the project</u>, I'll be happy.

OR

I'll be happy <u>when I complete the project</u>.

[Add an independent clause. If you start with a dependent clause, use a comma when introducing this dependent idea.]

Some items that follow contain dependent clause fragments. For each item, underline all fragments and then revise the item in the line provided. If the sentence is correct, write *Correct* on the line.

1. Because Ray was so bossy. Nobody wanted to argue. When he insisted that we leave.

   Because Ray was so bossy, nobody wanted to argue when he insisted that we leave.

2. Although I kept insisting that the answer was wrong. My group ignored my reasoning.

   Although I kept insisting that the answer was wrong, my group ignored my reasoning.

3. He was always in a hurry. Because he was always late. Calling him early didn't seem to help.

   He was always in a hurry because he was always late. Calling him early didn't seem to help.

4. I agreed to pay the cost of the rental although I opposed the entire idea. I hope you consider this before you cash my check. If not, count me out next time.

   Correct

5. I'll have the report ready. Before the end of the month. So that you can implement my suggestions.

   I'll have the report ready before the end of the month so that you can implement my suggestions.

Remember that a sentence fragment is a piece of an idea; it is an incomplete sentence. From the first word to its final period, make sure that your sentence is correctly structured. Be especially carefully with long sentences in which you attempt to give too much information. Your reader may find an excessively long sentence confusing, and in the process of relating so much information, you can easily lose control of its structure and create a fragment.

> The recently elected mayor who was highly praised for his record on human rights but criticized on his position on the U.S. involvement in the Middle East although he tried to clarify and justify his position.

Cross out all dependent clauses and prepositional phrases:

> The recently elected mayor ~~who was highly praised for his record on human rights but criticized on his position on the U.S. involvement in the Middle East although he tried to clarify and justify his position.~~

What's left? Only the subject—a type 1 fragment.

REVIEW 15-1

The following essay consists of different types of fragments. In the answer sheet that follows, label each numbered group of words as follows "S" if it's a complete sentence or "F" is it's a fragment.

My Inheritance

[1]Living in the early 1900s must have been a hard life. [2]Making do with very little. [3]And remaining strong through hard times were necessary skills of pioneers. [4]Although my life is much different from my grandparents' life. [5]The lessons they taught me through the lifestyles they lived were qualities that have helped me survived.

[6]One of these traits is a love and a desire to preserve our family's heritage. [7]We have been ranchers in the mountains of Colorado for four generations. [8]It is with pride that I take my children to the cabin where their great-great-grandparents homesteaded so long ago. [9]This communion with the past not only anchors our lives. [10]But also lets us take pleasure in the simple things that the world seems intent on leaving behind. [11]Simple things like swinging on the creaky rope in a barn that smells of cow and hay, riding horses on a mountain so high that we feel on top of the world, drinking cold spring water. [12]And breathing fresh mountain air. [13]Whenever I begin to feel sorry for myself. [14]Especially when I feel I lack the comfortable lives others have. [15]I try to remember these wonderful gifts. [16]That were preserved through the years. [17]And count my blessings that I have them. [18]It is important to me to pass this love of family roots and values to my children.

[19]Strength of character during hard times. [20]Is another trait of my grandparents that I try to emulate. [21]When I was a child. [22]My grandmother told me a family story that left a strong impression in me. [23]My grandfather had always been a strong and proud person. [24]The type of person who would never humble himself to others. [25]A person who was always in charge. [26]One harsh winter during the Depression. [27]There was little food in the house. [28]And four small children to feed. [29]As a joke, a man in town who was selling 100-pound sacks of potatoes. [30]Told Grandpa that he could have one of the sacks if he took off his shirt and shoes and ran around the town square three times with the sack on his shoulders. [31]My grandmother stared at Grandpa, knowing that he felt insulted and would never agree to such a humiliating act as begging. [32]Especially in front of people who saw him as the epitome of respectability. [33]The winter was frightfully cold, but without a second thought, he took off his shoes and shirt, picked up the sack, and ran.

[34]When I first heard this story. [35]I felt saddened by what I perceived as an embarrassing and degrading situation for a man trying to feed his family.

[36.]Years later I was able to understand the true meaning of this family story. [37.]Because I found myself in a similar situation. [38.]I also had to go through a humiliating experience in order to feed my family. [39.]I had to accept food stamps. [40.]I did not want to do it, but it was necessary. [41.]During that time, I too left my shirt and shoes in the snow, for I learned what Grandpa must've already known on that cold day. [42.]Pride and respectability are not qualities that others can give or take from a person. [43.]Although they may try. [44.]Doing what is right for the good of others only heightens, not diminishes, the worth of a person. [45.]There is dignity in such acts.

[46.]My hardships will never compare with those of my grandparents. [47.]However, I like to think that their ability to cope as well as their wisdom was handed down from their generation to mine. [48.]The values they passed down to me through the examples they set. [49.]Have helped guide me. [50.]And have also given me an appreciation for the life I have.

1. S	11. F	21. F	31. S	41. S
2. F	12. F	22. S	32. F	42. S
3. F	13. F	23. S	33. S	43. F
4. F	14. F	24. F	34. F	44. S
5. S	15. S	25. F	35. S	45. S
6. S	16. F	26. F	36. S	46. S
7. S	17. F	27. S	37. F	47. S
8. S	18. S	28. F	38. S	48. F
9. S	19. F	29. F	39. S	49. F
10. F	20. F	30. F	40. S	50. F

CHAPTER 16

Editing for Run-on Sentences

YOUR GOALS

1. Identify and revise fused sentences.
2. Identify and revise comma splices.
3. Use a variety of methods to revise run-ons.
4. Edit sentences, paragraphs, and essays for run-on sentences.

"I was working on the proof of one of my poems all the morning, and took out a comma. In the afternoon I put it back again."

■ Oscar Wilde ■

A Human Resources director receives the following letter of application:

Dear Mr. Hernandez,

Your company's website indicates that your company has an opening for a youth counselor. I am very interested in this position, I feel that I have the skills and leadership qualities that you described you will find that my employment background is appropriate for the position.

While working toward my college degree, I did volunteer work at the YMCA and at V.P. Youth Homes, these experiences helped to develop further my ability to work and communicate with young men and women with my strong academic background and my experience, I feel I can be effective in this position.

Enclosed is a copy of my resume, it fully details my qualifications for the position. I am eager to learn more about this position and look forward to interviewing with you, I can be reached at 555-0100.

Thank you for your consideration.

James Zorrer

LET's warm up!

Some students fail to edit their writing effectively because they find grammar rules confusing, unimportant, or difficult. Some students even dread this stage of the writing process. They may stare for a while at a draft and finally change a word or two, neglecting to edit for grammar, usage, and punctuation. Write a paragraph in which you explain one reason that students don't edit their drafts properly. Give specific details and examples.

Andersen Ross/Getty Images

Most likely, the preceding letter receives either a rejection letter or no response. Unfortunately, the applicant may never know why he was rejected. Although he might have impressed the interviewer, he'll never have a chance to speak to the interviewer in person.

A first impression is important, and in many job searches, your letter of application may be that first impression. In the preceding case, the potential employer has made assumptions about the applicant's ability and background based on grammar errors in the letter. The assumptions may be inaccurate, but nonetheless, this first impression probably lost the job seeker an opportunity. This is why editing is so important. In this case, the writer needed to edit for two common structural errors, fused sentences and comma splices.

UNDERSTANDING RUN-ON SENTENCES

In Chapter 15, you learned to edit your writing for sentence fragments. In this chapter, you focus on another structural error that is equally distracting and confusing to your reader, the run-on sentence. More specifically, we examine the two types of run-ons, the fused sentence and the comma splice. Although some instructors may refer to the fused sentence as a run-on, separate from the comma splice, we define *run-on* as a general term that includes the comma splice and the fused sentence.

Fused Sentences

Before we define the fused sentence, read the following paragraph.

> The accomplishment I'm most proud of is finishing high school and going straight to college college is very important to my future because I want to be able to help my husband provide for our family without college it won't be possible finishing college is my biggest goal I want to finish college with honors I want to be well prepared for the future.

While you were reading this passage, did you find yourself going back to reread certain parts to try to make sense of it? As you can see, reading a paragraph consisting of sentences with no punctuation is a challenge. It's hard to determine where one idea ends and the next one begins. The paragraph you have just read is made up of fused sentences. Imagine the frustration of a reader trying to make sense of a report or memo with fused sentences.

As you have probably already concluded, a *fused sentence* is an error caused by running (fusing) two complete sentences (independent clauses) together with no separation. The sentences in the preceding sample are hard to read because they lack the punctuation necessary to tell the reader where one idea ends and the next idea begins. Read the same paragraph again; this time, it has been edited to guide you from one idea to the next.

> The accomplishment I'm most proud of is finishing high school and going straight to college. College is very important to my future because I want to be able to help my husband provide for our family; without college it won't be possible. Finishing college is my biggest goal. I want to finish college with honors. I want to be well prepared for the future.

Read each item. If it is correct, write C on the line. If it is a fused sentence, write FS. Then place a period where the first sentence ends and capitalize the first letter of the next word. Carets indicate where sentences should be broken.

FS 1. Sylvia's mother still lives in New Orleans Sylvia moved to Chicago.

FS 2. The clouds are gray and dark it looks as though it could snow.

FS 3. We are going to the festival this weekend last year we missed the medieval dancers.

C 4. My printer is out of ink. It costs too much to replace the cartridge.

FS 5. English has always been my worst subject I could never get along with the picky teachers.

FS 6. The employees are disgruntled managers are wondering what to do.

FS 7. Because Mandy read one book by Hemingway, she wants to become a novelist all she does is sit and stare out the window daydreaming.

FS 8. Ghosts don't exist except in your imagination is something moving over there?

C 9. I came back to school to learn accounting. It was the best decision I ever made.

FS 10. Tom's Harley was stolen from his garage he's in shock he can hardly believe what happened!

Editing for Fused Sentences

As you review your writing and identify a fused sentence, you need to decide how to revise it. In the sections that follow, we examine five common methods of revising a fused sentence and how these methods can help develop your writing style. The same fused sentence is used in each section.

> The conference speaker was famous there was a large audience.

Method #1: Use a Period

Place a period at the end of the first sentence and capitalize the first letter of the second sentence. (If the first sentence is a question, use a question mark instead of a period.)

| The conference speaker was famous | ● | There was a large audience. |

Using this method, the writer maintains two independent clauses or two complete sentences.

Method #2: Use a Semicolon

You can use a semicolon (;) when the ideas are closely related in meaning or intent. Place the semicolon at the end of the first sentence, but *don't* capitalize the first letter of the second sentence.

> The conference speaker was famous **;** there was a large audience.

Using this method, the writer establishes a relationship between the two sentences. In this example, the semicolon highlights a cause/effect relationship. In using this method of combining independent clauses, the writer has created a compound sentence.

PRACTICE 16-2

In the space provided, indicate with a C whether the sentence is correct as written. If the sentence is fused, mark it with an FS and correct it by providing the correct punctuation at the end of the first idea. Carets indicate where sentences should be broken.

__FS__ 1. My son gets little exercise he is totally focused on computers and music.

__FS__ 2. Gradually, the water in the tube freezes the tube will break if it contains too much water.

__FS__ 3. Kremling is a small town in Colorado the walled area in Moscow is spelled "Kremlin."

__FS__ 4. Frank is really moving ahead on the house the walls are up despite all the rain we've had.

__FS__ 5. Guess what I'm now the director of the department.

__C__ 6. I finally figured out the problem with my printer.

__FS__ 7. Sandy was arrested in Las Vegas the police said she caused a riot when her last nickel failed to win the jackpot.

__FS__ 8. Somewhere we'll have to stop for gas the fuel gauge is on "empty" we are about to go into the mountains.

__FS__ 9. Juan is a fan of poetry he's even written a book about poetry that will be published in time for Christmas.

__FS__ 10. This brand of water fountain tends to leak keep an eye on it for a week.

Method #3: Use Coordination

Use a comma (,) with a coordinating conjunction (*for, and, nor, but, or, yet, so*) to separate two fused sentences.

> The conference speaker was famous **,so** there was a large audience.

A popular way to remember these seven coordinating conjunctions is to use the acronym *FANBOYS*:

For   And   Nor   But   Or   Yet   So

Remember that you must use a comma before, not after, the coordinating conjunction. If you use only the comma without the coordinating conjunction, you have created a comma splice, another structural error that we discuss shortly. The main difference between method #2 and this method is that the relationship between the two main ideas is clearly stated by the coordinating conjunction, whereas in method #2 the relationship must be evident for the semicolon to be effective.

Conjunction	Logical Relationship	Example
and	Shows an addition of related ideas to the first idea of the first sentence (meaning "in addition," "also")	Brian is shy, and he usually avoids large crowds.
but, yet	Shows a contrasting idea in the second sentence (meaning "however," "in contrast")	Brian is shy, but he enjoys acting class. Brian is shy, yet he loves to debate.
or	Shows a choice or alternative between ideas in the two sentences (meaning "choice," "otherwise")	Brian is shy, or at least he appears to be.
so	Shows that the second idea is the result or effect of the first (meaning "therefore," "thus")	Brian is shy, so he gets few dates.
nor	Shows a negative alternative between ideas in the two sentences (meaning "neither")	Brian is not sociable, nor is he friendly.
for	Shows that the second idea is the cause or reason of the idea in the first sentence (meaning "because")	Brian is shy, for he has low self-esteem.

PRACTICE 16-3

Revise the following fused sentences using a comma and coordinating conjunction to create compound sentences. Make sure that the coordinating conjunction you choose establishes a logical connection between the two ideas. Answers will vary.

1. Xavier couldn't decide on a new car there were so many attractive models.
   Xavier couldn't decide on a new car, **for** there were so many attractive models.

2. We were grateful for the shelter we stayed there until the blizzard was over.
   We were grateful for the shelter, **so** we stayed there until the blizzard was over.

3. She did not want to sell her car she needed one that was more reliable.
   She did not want to sell her car, **but** she needed one that was more reliable.

4. They can spend the day at the beach they can visit the local art gallery.
   They can spend the day at the beach, **or** they can visit the local art gallery.

5. Because Lydia is afraid of the dark, she is dreading the camping trip she might enjoy it once she realizes there's a night club just across the lake.

   Because Lydia is afraid of the dark, she is dreading the camping trip, **yet** she might enjoy it once she realizes there's a night club just across the lake.

6. It was raining hard all day I borrowed an umbrella.

   It was raining hard all day, **so** I borrowed an umbrella.

7. We stopped at a diner we had not eaten since last night.

   We stopped at a diner, **for** we had not eaten since last night.

8. Gabriella refused to pay for a new computer she agreed to pay the cost for repair.

   Gabriella refused to pay for a new computer, **but** she agreed to pay the cost for repair.

9. We wanted to sit as close as possible to the stage we ordered our tickets early.

   We wanted to sit as close as possible to the stage, **so** we ordered our tickets early.

10. Their house is similar to ours they have an extra room.

    Their house is similar to ours, **but** they have an extra room.

Method #4: Use a Conjunctive Adverb or Transitional Expression

Place a semicolon (;) before a conjunctive adverb or a transitional word, and add a comma after that connector.

The conference speaker was famous **;therefore,** there was a large audience.

Conjunctive adverbs are words that act as transitions between independent clauses, thus establishing a logical, and more complex, relationship between ideas. In various chapters in Part 1, we provided lists of transitional words and expressions. Many of these words are actually conjunctive adverbs, and just like transitional words, these adverbs help you establish the relationship between independent clauses.

Don't forget to insert the semicolon at the end of the first sentence; without it, you still have a fused sentence. Also, notice in the preceding example that, unlike after a period, the first letter of the word following the semicolon is not capitalized. The following are lists of some common conjunctive adverbs and transitional phrases.

Conjunctive Adverbs			
accordingly	further	meanwhile	similarly
also	furthermore	moreover	still
anyway	hence	namely	then
besides	however	nevertheless	thereafter
certainly	incidentally	next	therefore
consequently	indeed	nonetheless	thus
conversely	instead	now	undoubtedly
finally	likewise	otherwise	

Transitional Phrases		
after all	for example	in reality
as a matter of fact	for instance	in the first place
as a result	in addition	in truth
at any rate	in conclusion	on the contrary
at the same time	in fact	on the other hand
even so	in other words	

This sentence-combining technique creates yet another variation of a compound sentence. As you edit your essay for style, consider using different types of compound sentences to spice up your writing style.

PRACTICE 16-4

Revise the following fused sentences by using conjunctive adverbs or transitional words. Vary your choice. Be sure to punctuate correctly. Answers will vary.

1. India has long been a land of mystery, romance, and intrigue many novels, short stories, and movies have used India as their setting.
   India has long been a land of mystery, romance, and intrigue; **consequently,** many novels, short stories, and movies have used India as their setting.

2. India has a variety of languages still used among various groups it has approximately 800 different languages and 2,000 dialects.
   India has a variety of languages still used among various groups; **in fact,** it has approximately 800 different languages and 2,000 dialects.

3. India has 23 official languages Hindi and English are the main languages stipulated by the Constitution of India to be used by the central government.
   India has 23 official languages; **however,** Hindi and English are the main languages stipulated by the Constitution of India to be used by the central government.

4. India is a land of spirituality and philosophy it is the birthplace of Hinduism, Jainism, Sikhism, and Buddhism.
   India is a land of spirituality and philosophy; **for example,** it is the birthplace of Hinduism, Jainism, Sikhism, and Buddhism.

5. Hinduism is the oldest and the third largest existing religion in the world approximately 1 billion followers worldwide, most living in India, adhere to its teachings.
   Hinduism is the oldest and the third largest existing religion in the world; **in fact,** approximately 1 billion followers worldwide, most living in India, adhere to its teachings.

Method #5: Use Subordination

You can use a subordinating conjunction to restructure the sentence so that you no longer have two independent clauses.

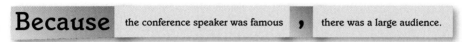

Because the conference speaker was famous **,** there was a large audience.

The word *subordinate* means secondary, lower, or lesser. This is the basic difference between a coordinating and a subordinate conjunction. Coordinating conjunctions establish relationships between two main ideas of equal value and importance, whereas subordinating conjunctions provide additional information of lesser or unequal value to the main idea.

<u>Although no one seemed impressed,</u> I announced that I got the job.

Note the following features in the preceding example:

- You no longer have two complete sentences. The subordinating conjunction, *although*, has changed the first independent clause to a dependent clause. As you may recall from Chapter 15, this simply means that the clause could not stand alone: by itself, it wouldn't make sense. This dependent clause must be attached to a main clause so that it makes sense.
- When you start your sentence with a dependent clause, the comma goes after the clause, not after the subordinating conjunction.
- If by mistake you place a period, question mark, or a semicolon after the dependent clause, you create a sentence fragment.
- The dependent clause provides additional information to supplement and clarify the main clause. Therefore, the meaning of the subordinate clause depends on the main clause.

Here's a list of common subordinating conjunctions.

Common Subordinating Conjunctions			
after	before	so that	where
although	even if	than	whereas
as	even though	though	wherever
as if	if	unless	whether
as long as	in order to	until	while
as though	rather than	when	
because	since	whenever	

By using both a dependent clause and an independent clause in the same sentence, you create a complex sentence, another effective way to vary your sentences when writing.

Bridging Knowledge

For a full explanation of and practice with compound and complex sentences, see Chapter 22.

PRACTICE 16-5

Revise the following fused sentences by using subordinating conjunctions to make one idea less important than the other. If you start the sentence with a subordinate clause, make sure you use a comma after the subordinate clause. Answers will vary, depending on which idea students choose to subordinate.

1. The country of Egypt often brings to mind ancient Egypt with its pharaonic tombs and pyramids, modern Egypt is equally fascinating.

   Although the country of Egypt often brings to mind ancient Egypt **with** its pharaonic tombs and pyramids, modern Egypt is equally fascinating.

2. The Nile River is the life blood of Egypt the majority of Egyptians live along this river for its irrigation and transportation.

   Since the Nile River is the life blood of Egypt, the majority of Egyptians live along this river for its irrigation and transportation.

3. Cairo, the capital city of Egypt, has the most densely populated areas on earth multistoried buildings sometimes collapse under the weight of their residents.

   Because Cairo, the capital city of Egypt, has the most densely populated areas on earth, multistoried buildings sometimes collapse under the weight of their residents.

4. Housing is a challenge to find for many Cairenes some have resorted to camping among the tombs in cemeteries or building shacks on the roofs of apartment buildings.

   Since housing is a challenge to find for many Cairenes, some have resorted to camping among the tombs in cemeteries or building shacks on the roofs of apartment buildings.

5. The pyramids are lit at night they appear much more mysterious and amazing.

   When the pyramids are lit at night, they appear much more mysterious and amazing.

Revising Fused Sentences

To illustrate the many creative choices you have in repairing fused sentences, examine the following revision of a fused sentence. Imagine how your writing can come to life with such variation of sentences.

All the world's a stage all the men and women are merely players.

(Adapted from William Shakespeare, *As You Like It*, II, vii.)

Method #1 (use a period)	All the world's a stage. All the men and women are merely players.
Method #2 (use a semicolon)	All the world's a stage; all the men and women are merely players.
Method #3 (use coordination)	All the world's a stage, **and** all the men and women are merely players.
Method #4 (use a conjunctive adverb or transitional expression)	All the world's a stage; **therefore,** all the men and women are merely players. All the world's a stage; **as a result,** all the men and women are merely players.
Method #5 (use subordination)	**Since** all the world's a stage, all the men and women are merely players.

PRACTICE 16-6

The following paragraph contains fused sentences. Place a period where each sentence ends and capitalize the first letter of the next sentence. Check your answers carefully to be sure that you have not produced fragments. Carets indicate where sentences should be broken.

As the political campaign enters its final months, the negative ads on TV increase in negativism and nastiness, these ads leave viewers weary and disgusted with the whole political process they see attacks from both parties, aimed at scaring the public with harsh sound bites, for example, one candidate is accused of putting politics above the safety of our troops, another will raise our taxes, a third is supposedly in the pockets of the big corporations and lobbyists. A young candidate doesn't have enough leadership experience in contrast, an older candidate is too brainwashed by Washington insiders. One of the worst ploys of these political ads is a visual of the opposition candidate, shown in his or her worst moment of anger or weariness the candidate looks particularly run down or harsh or annoyed or confused, a sinister voice in the background warns viewers that if they vote for so and so, the country will descend into chaos and barbarism. The only relief for the viewer is Election Day when the campaign is done and the negative ads disappear, unfortunately, these types of ads will return to plague us next year.

Comma Splices

Just as the fused sentence is damaging to your credibility as a writer, so is the comma splice. Your reader is your "judge and jury" in assessing your abilities. Don't permit poor editing to create a false impression.

Examine the following sentence:

> The new employee came to work early almost every day, even when the weather was bad, he would march to his office and lock the door.

Upon reading this sentence, the reader might stop to wonder whether the phrase "even when the weather was bad" refers to the employee's coming to work or to his marching to his office. This type of construction is called a *comma splice*. Whereas the fused sentence uses no punctuation, the comma splice misuses a comma to end a sentence. The comma splice is considered a serious error because it reflects not only the writer's failure to recognize a complete thought but also that writer's inability to punctuate correctly.

Editing for Comma Splices

To revise comma splices, you can use the same five methods we described for revising fused sentences. Review these five methods as we revise the following comma splice:

> COMMA SPLICE: Jeff talks too much, nobody seems to mind.

1. Use a period (or question mark) to make two independent clauses:

   > Jeff talks too much. Nobody seems to mind.

2. Use a semicolon to establish the relationship between the two independent clauses. This is a compound sentence:

   > Jeff talks too much; nobody seems to mind.

3. Use a coordinating conjunction (*for, and, nor, but, or, yet, so*) to justify the comma and create a compound sentence:

   > Jeff talks too much, but nobody seems to mind.

4. Use a semicolon and a conjunctive adverb or transitional phrase, followed by a comma. This is also a compound sentence:

   > Jeff talks too much; however, nobody seems to mind.

5. Make one of the sentences a dependent clause by using a subordinating conjunction (*after, although, as if, because, since,* and so on). Don't forget that when you start a sentence with a dependent clause, a comma is necessary at the end of the dependent clause. This is a complex sentence:

   > Although nobody seems to mind, Jeff talks too much.

When choosing a method to revise either a comma splice or a fused sentence, vary your sentence structures so that you may continue to develop your unique writing style.

PRACTICE 16-7

Read each item carefully. Indicate if the item is a complete sentence or if there is a structural error by using one of the following letters: C, Correct sentence; FS, Fused sentence; CS, Comma splice. If there is an error, revise it using two different methods. Vary your methods of revision so that you can practice using all five methods. Make sure your sentences are clear and logical. Answers will vary.

__FS__ 1. Nat's driving makes me nervous everybody's driving makes me nervous.

Revision #1: ___Nat's driving makes me nervous; in fact, everybody's driving makes me___
___nervous.___

Revision #2: ___Nat's driving makes me nervous; everybody's driving makes me nervous.___

__C__ 2. Everyone was surprised to find the teams working so well on their projects.

Revision #1: _____

Revision #2: _____

__C__ 3. The children were frightened by the thunder and foolishly hid under a tree.

Revision #1: _____

Revision #2: _____

__CS__ 4. Last week, we drove to Las Vegas, on the way, we had two flat tires.

Revision #1: ___Last week, we drove to Las Vegas; incidentally, we had two flat tires.___

Revision #2: ___Last week, we drove to Las Vegas, and on the way, we had two flat tires.___

__FS__ 5. Ramon was sifting the flour Lisa built a blazing fire in the fireplace.

Revision #1: ___While Ramon was sifting the flour, Lisa built a blazing fire in the fireplace.___

Revision #2: ___Ramon was sifting the flour; at the same time, Lisa built a blazing fire in the___
___fireplace.___

Strategies for Revising Run-on Sentences

The trickiest part of editing your drafts for fused sentences is that you have to look for independent clauses. Start by applying one of the techniques you used to look for fragments. For example, start reading each sentence by asking the question "Is it true that … ?" Once you locate the end of the sentence, make sure you have a period, semicolon, or a comma with a coordinating conjunction. If not, use one of the five revision methods with which you are now familiar. Although this technique may be time consuming, it helps you develop a sense for sentence completeness, and eventually you will be able to "feel" when a sentence needs to be punctuated.

Editing for comma splices is easier than editing for fused sentences since the commas act as a marker. Start by looking at the clauses on both sides of the comma and follow this chart:

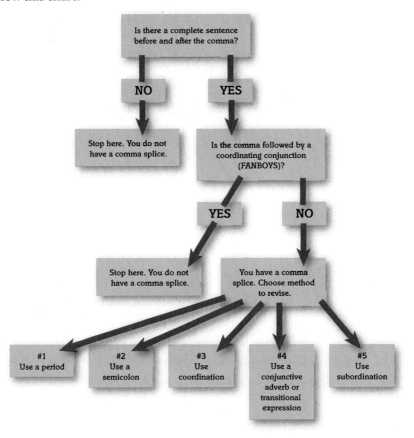

Collaborative Critical Thinking

In groups of two or three, write one or two paragraphs summarizing important information from one of your English class lectures or activities. After you have written the paragraph, edit it carefully for fragments, fused sentences, and comma splices.

Now, rewrite the paragraph and create fragments, comma splices, and fused sentences by eliminating punctuation or punctuating incorrectly. Once you have completed this "quiz draft," exchange papers with another group.

Revise the paragraphs you have just received from the other group. Use the tricks you learned in Chapter 15 and this chapter to locate structural errors, and use various methods to revise these errors.

When you receive your paper back, compare the other group's version with your original draft. Was the other group able to spot all the fragments and run-ons that you purposely created? Did the other group revise your essay effectively? Discuss how that group's version is different from yours. What would your group have done differently? Answers will vary.

REVIEW 16-1

The following essay contains fragments, fused sentences, and comma splices. Correct the errors by providing correct punctuation.

Cleaning Made Easy for Single Men

Are you a slob? Have you ever invited someone special over to your house for dinner? Without thinking of how messy your house is? If the answer to any of these questions is yes. You might be interested in the following advice. I myself have never been married, on more than one occasion between girlfriends I've found myself without anyone to pick up after me. Over the years, I've found some tricks that make a quick cleanup job simple and easy. Little things like dealing with dirty clothes, picking up trash, cleaning windows, dusting, and even vacuuming.

First, I find some music to motivate me. After selecting the right music, I take a look around and try to find a good place to start my cleaning. Dirty clothes always seem to be covering everything behind the couch and under the bed are both good hiding places for my dirty clothes. I've learned I can hide only so much stuff in these two places. So I cram the clothes that don't fit behind the couch or under the bed in the hall closet. When it comes to clothes that smell, like dirty gym socks and work clothes. I hide them directly in the washing machine with a pine-scented air freshener in a day or two the smelly clothes will have the odor of a pine forest.

After clearing away all the dirty clothes. I can see how much trash has accumulated under the clothes, for the trash, I'll need a heavy, strong trash bag and some heavy-duty latex gloves. I never know what I may come across. I seek out the small stuff first. Beer cans, cigarette wrappers, empty potato chip bags, and candy wrappers, then I venture on to the bigger stuff, like pizza boxes and empty 12-pack holders. All that's left now is the stuff I'm not really sure of, like plates with green fury things on them, these get thrown away, plate and all.

Now it's time to move on to the windows and dusting. Doing the windows is the easiest part of house cleaning. I've heard people say that windows are the biggest pain to clean, but what's so hard about closing the drapes? When it comes to dusting, I suppose I should find a clean rag and furniture polish; however, I have found that a little spit on a dirty sock works fine. Except for the television. The television requires a clean, soft cotton towel. I mix 50% rubbing alcohol and 50% water. I spray the solution on my towel, not the television screen. The alcohol solution can cause permanent spots on the screen. I rub the towel gently over the screen. Just hard enough to pick up the dust; it would be heartbreaking if any harm came to the television.

Vacuuming is the final step. Being like most people. I keep my vacuum in the hall closet; however, I have to be careful getting it out of the closet because sometimes I forget about the dirty clothes in there, and they fall out all over the place. Once I have retrieved the vacuum. I check that it's not full. When my Craftsman gets full. It tends to blow the top off, making me have to start cleaning again; in addition, I have to be careful when vacuuming the inch-thick dog fur that covers my carpet. If I mistake my dog's tail for a clump of fur. It's difficult trying to get an angry German shepherd's tail out of a shop vac.

After my vigorous house cleaning. I am ready to entertain guests. As long as they don't snoop around or open the closets. My method of house cleaning doesn't take much time or motivation; in fact, I have only found one other way to clean faster, more simply, and more effectively: get a new girlfriend.

CHAPTER 17

Editing for Subject–Verb Agreement

YOUR GOALS

1. Identify subjects and verbs.

2. Apply basic rules of subject–verb agreement.

3. Revise paragraphs and essays for subject–verb agreement.

"There are just three rules for writing—but nobody knows what they are."

■ **Somerset Maugham** ■

In your work as a customer service representative for a large chain store, you receive the following letter from a disgruntled customer:

Dear Customer Service Manager:

Your store needs to learn something about customer service. Recently, I went there to buy a set of golf clubs. The clubs, a newly manufactured set in an expensive bag, was sitting on a shelf 8 feet off the ground. I called for help, and two of your assistants, Teri and Rona, came to my aid, but only after 15 minutes. This happens every time I need help in your store: the assistant, resting in the back room reading magazines and smoking cigarettes, take forever to respond to calls to help customers. Anyway, Teri and Roni looked at the bag, looked at each other, and walked away. They said they were going to get a ladder, but I never saw them again! Is this the way Top Picks want to run a business? Every one of my friends tell me to stay out of your store, but like an idiot, I keep going back for more.

Please bring this matter to your manager. Every manager who cares about the happiness of customers need to know of these kinds of problems.

Sincerely,

William Owens

LET's **warm up!**

Write a paragraph in which you discuss how you speak in different contexts—in class, for example, versus among friends at work. Give an example or two of the various kinds of language you use in ordinary speech.

I. Rozenbaum & F. Cirou/Jupiter Images

This letter is written in an informal, almost conversational style. You can probably imagine some of these sentences being spoken during a phone conversation. During such a conversation, neither speaker nor listener pays much attention to grammar, for each is focused on "getting the point" in a rapidly passing flow of words. However, because this message is written down, it requires a different kind of attention. A reader is more likely to pay attention to matters of grammar and style in a written message.

As an educated person, when you write in your profession or in college, you're held to a more rigid set of rules. In the previous chapters, you've seen the problem that fragments and run-ons might cause your reader. There's yet another type of error that your audience may react to: errors in subject–verb agreement.

UNDERSTANDING SUBJECT–VERB AGREEMENT

One of the most common errors in spoken language is a lack of agreement between subjects and verbs of sentences. Unfortunately, this conversational usage is the very reason it is so difficult to notice agreement problems in your writing. However, if you can become more conscious of the language you use when writing, you can more easily avoid these and other problems. Over time, you can even "train your ear" to begin hearing grammar problems in spoken language.

Subject–verb agreement boils down to one major rule.

> **The subject and verb of a sentence must agree, or match, in "person" and in "number": singular subjects take singular verbs; plural subjects take plural verbs.**

If all sentences were as simple as these, you might have no difficulty matching subjects and verbs in your own writing. However, sentences appear in many different forms, some more complicated than others, and you need to train yourself to write, edit, and revise such sentences. Begin by reviewing the concepts of grammatical person and number.

The <u>carton is sitting</u> on the counter.

Singular Singular
subject   verb

The <u>cartons are sitting</u> on the counter.

Plural Plural
subject verb

Grammatical Person

As a writer, you use three persons:

1. **First person.** First person is the actual writer. When you use the pronoun *I* or include yourself as part of a group through such pronouns as *we, us,* and *our,* you use first person. The use of first person is common in narratives, personal experiences, and observations. Some instructors discourage the use of first person in academic writing, so it's a good idea to check with your instructor before you use this person.
2. **Second person.** In second person, the writer addresses the reader directly through the use of the pronoun *you.* Second person is common in process writing, where your goal is to give instructions for your reader to follow. Most instructors would prefer that you not use second person for academic writing. Check with your instructor.
3. **Third person.** Third person is usually preferred in academic writing. When you refer to someone or something, you use third person. You can use either nouns (*Felix, Prince Henry, soldier, individual, house, vacation,* and so on) or pronouns (*she, he, it, they, someone, everybody,* and so on).

Fewer errors in subject–verb agreement occur in first and second person. Our ears seem better trained to pick up errors in these cases, such as *I is* or *you is*. However third person presents a unique problem when it comes to subject–verb agreement.

Grammatical Number

The term *number* refers to whether a word is singular or plural. A word is singular when it refers to one person or thing; a word is plural when it refers to two or more persons or things.

Here are some singular nouns:

> **SINGULAR:**   Book, shovel, girlfriend, medium, ox

Here are the same nouns in plural form:

> **PLURAL:**   Books, shovels, girlfriends, media, oxen

Sometimes, it's not so easy to tell whether a word (noun, pronoun, adjective, or verb) is singular or plural. Which of the following words are singular, and which are plural?

couple	fade	most	tries
each	government	philosophy	walks
everybody	mathematics	some	

Notice that this list contains not only nouns (and pronouns) but also several verbs: *walks, fade,* and so on. You might be tempted to think that since you add an -*s* to most nouns to make them plural, you can do the same with verbs. However, just the opposite is true: a verb with -*s* on the end is singular. More specifically, -*s* after a verb means it is third person, present tense, and singular. How can you learn to make this distinction?

An Informal Test for Number

Try this informal method for determining the number of a noun, pronoun, or verb. Given a noun or pronoun whose number you don't know, pair it with a singular and then a plural verb and ask yourself which pairing seems to work best.

Suppose you are working with the pronoun *everyone*. Is it singular or plural? Most people think it's plural. To test whether this is true, pair *everyone* with two verbs, one singular, and one plural.

> Everyone walks.   [*Walks* is singular, as just explained.]
> Everyone walk.   [*Walk* is plural.]

Which of these sentences would you say in a conversation? Hopefully, you would say the first one. Since you know *walks* is singular, this is a clue that *everyone* might be singular.

Use the same test, in reverse, for verbs. Given a verb whose number you don't know, pair it with a singular and then a plural noun or pronoun and ask yourself which pairing seems to work best.

Suppose you are working with the verb *mingle*. Is it singular or plural? Many people think that because it doesn't have an -*s* on the end, it's singular. To test whether this is true, pair *mingle* with two nouns, one singular, and one plural.

> The student mingle.   [*Student,* of course, is singular.]
> The students mingle.   [*Students* is plural.]

Which of these sentences would you say in conversation? Hopefully, you would say the second one. The fact that it "sounds better" is a clue that *mingle* might be the plural form of the verb.

Just as we urged you to develop an ear or sense for identifying fragments and run-ons, so should you train yourself to sense problems with agreement. Fortunately, you won't always have to apply this test. Often, as in the case of the following verbs, you recognize certain forms immediately as singular or plural.

> **SINGULAR:**   am, is, was, has, does, writes (verb + s)
> **PLURAL:**   are, were, have, do, write

PRACTICE 17-1

Train your ear to spot errors in agreement by trying out different pairings of nouns or pronouns and verbs to determine whether the nouns and verbs in the following list are singular or plural. Answers will vary.

1. Milk

   Pairing: Milk is; milk are

   Conclusion: The number of this word is singular.

2. Each

   Pairing: Each does; each do

   Conclusion: The number of this word is singular.

3. Everyone

   Pairing: Everyone wants; everyone want

   Conclusion: The number of this word is singular.

4. Anybody

   Pairing: Anybody knows; anybody know

   Conclusion: The number of this word is singular.

5. Statistics

   Pairing: Statistics is; statistics are

   Conclusion: The number of this word is singular (referring to a class) or plural (referring to different numbers).

The major rule of subject–verb agreement should now make complete sense. Look at this rule one more time: **The subject and verb of a sentence must agree, or match, in "person" and in "number": singular subjects take singular verbs; plural subjects take plural verbs.**

To analyze your sentences for subject–verb agreement, follow this strategy:

- Find the verb and determine its number.
- Find the subject and determine its number.
- Ensure that subject and verb have the same number.

Before you can decide whether a subject and verb agree with each other, you must be able to identify the subject and verb of a sentence.

Revisiting Subjects and Verbs

You need a *strategy* for dissecting sentences that helps you identify the parts of any sentence when you need to. Start by locating the main verb of the sentence. Don't forget the main characteristics of the verb:

1. A verb tells something about time.

> Tom <u>is</u> riding a horse.   [He's doing it in the present.]
> She <u>was</u> in the drugstore.   [She was there at some time in the past.]
> The ghost <u>walks</u> about every night.   [It repeats this action nightly.]
> The king <u>will be slain</u> by his wife.   [She'll kill him in the future.]

2. A verb takes certain recognizable forms. You already intuitively know the difference between past, present, and future verbs when you see them, but remember the following points:

- Regular verbs add -*ed* to form the past tense, as in the following examples.

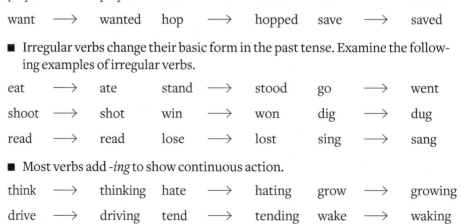

| play | ⟶ | played | hire | ⟶ | hired | ask | ⟶ | asked |
| want | ⟶ | wanted | hop | ⟶ | hopped | save | ⟶ | saved |

- Irregular verbs change their basic form in the past tense. Examine the following examples of irregular verbs.

eat	⟶	ate	stand	⟶	stood	go	⟶	went
shoot	⟶	shot	win	⟶	won	dig	⟶	dug
read	⟶	read	lose	⟶	lost	sing	⟶	sang

- Most verbs add -*ing* to show continuous action.

| think | ⟶ | thinking | hate | ⟶ | hating | grow | ⟶ | growing |
| drive | ⟶ | driving | tend | ⟶ | tending | wake | ⟶ | waking |

■ The auxiliary (helping) verb *will* fits in front of the verb to show future.

will learn   *will* fight   *will* lock

3. If you can change the time of a word by changing its form, adding *-ed*, *-ing*, or *will*, you have most likely identified the verb of the sentence.

Once you can find the verb of a sentence, the subject is easier to locate. Think of it as "the subject of the verb," and ask yourself, "Who or what is this verb talking about?" Look at the following sentence:

Her grandmother runs 5 miles every morning.

Here the verb is *runs.* Ask yourself, "Who runs?" The answer to this question should be the subject of the sentence. Here, the subject is *grandmother.* Here's another example:

The fog caused a 40-car pileup, but everyone walked away unhurt.

How many verbs do you see in this sentence? Notice that this sentence has two complete clauses joined by a comma and the word *but.* Since a clause has a subject and a verb, you should see two verbs and two subjects. Here, the verbs are *caused* and *walked.* Now ask yourself two questions: "What caused the pileup?" and "Who walked away unhurt?" The answers are *fog* and *everyone.* This example demonstrates how careful you must be in analyzing sentences; once you've found one element of a sentence, don't assume your work is finished: analyze the entire sentence!

Don't forget that *a subject can never be inside a prepositional phrase.* If you can identify prepositional phrases and mentally "cross them out," you can find the subject more easily.

Everyone on the boat is leaning to one side.

The verb of this sentence is *is leaning.* When you ask yourself, "Who or what is leaning?" you get two possible answers: *Everyone* and *boat.* How do you decide which one is the subject? First, mentally cross out the prepositional phrase "on the boat"; then look for the subject. Now there are fewer choices, and you can easily see that the subject is *everyone*: Everyone is leaning.

PRACTICE 17-2

In the following sentences, identify the subjects and verbs. Underline the subject once and the verb twice. Make sure that the word or words you choose as the subject are not part of a prepositional phrase.

1. Above the tree line, lightning seeks out the tallest object: the unwary hiker.
2. Two years ago my family visited the Grand Canyon.
3. Over the deck of the ship, the helicopter settles into a landing pattern.
4. Everyone supports the disgraced sheriff.
5. A weekend in the mountains offers you exercise, relaxation, and closeness to nature. [Be careful! In this sentence, is *exercise* a verb or a noun? Why?]

Problems with Subject Number

Once you've located the subject of sentence, you need to figure out if it's singular or plural. This is not always an easy task. Look at some problems that can arise in determining the number of a subject.

Words That Come between the Subject and Verb

Here's another hint to help you with subject–verb agreement:

> **The number of the subject is not changed by words that come between the subject and the verb.**

You already know about one of the types of phrases that can appear between the subject and the verb: prepositional phrases. And you know that by mentally crossing them out, you can focus on the subject. The same basic rule applies to several other kinds of phrases and clauses. Look at other types of intervening phrases and clauses:

> INCORRECT: Henry, not Gracie or George, are prepared for the worst.

Remove the intervening phrase and the subject becomes more obvious:

> CORRECT: Henry, ~~not Gracie or George~~, is prepared for the worst.

Notice that the intervening phrase is easy to spot because it is separated by commas from the rest of the sentence.

> INCORRECT: The book that is lying next to the two ashtrays are hardly ever touched.
>
> CORRECT: The book ~~that is lying next to the two ashtrays~~ is hardly ever touched.
>
> INCORRECT: The rowdy student who causes the problems pass our tests anyway.
>
> CORRECT: The rowdy student ~~who causes the problems~~ passes our tests anyway.

The intervening dependent clauses in these examples are not separated by commas.

> INCORRECT: The dogs running in a pack in the field scares me.

The intervening phrase in this sentence is a verb form known as a *participial phrase*. Be careful not to mistake *running* as the main verb of the sentence. Observe what happens when you eliminate the participial phrase.

> CORRECT: The dogs ~~running in a pack in the field~~ scare me.

Remember: The subject is sometimes obscured by different types of intervening phrases and clauses. Intervening phrases that begin with *accompanied by, as well as, in addition to, including,* and *together with* are easy distracters, so be careful. Learn to find the subject and make the verb agree with it, not with nouns that may appear inside intervening groups of words.

PRACTICE 17-3

Correct the following sentences. In each sentence, locate the phrase or clause that comes between the subject and the verb. Underline it; then cross out the verb and write the correct verb on the line. If the sentence is correct, write *Correct* on the line. Do not change the tense of the verb.

1. The sales reps, <u>who stayed out late last night on the town</u>, ~~seems~~ out of touch with the presentation. seem

2. The fire truck <u>tearing down the street and over Mrs. Sandler's rose bushes</u> ~~are~~ breaking the law. is

3. The cars <u>that I like the best</u> ~~is~~ the Jaguar, the Lamborghini, and the VW Bug. are

4. Slim Pickens, <u>not John Wayne or Clint Eastwood</u>, ~~are~~ my favorite Western actor. is

5. The lady <u>in the red shoes under the pictures of mountain scenes</u> is graceful. Correct

6. The size <u>of the insects</u> ~~are~~ astonishing. is

7. The crate <u>of apples on the loading dock under the windows</u> ~~are~~ ready to be picked up. is

8. Marisa, <u>as well as her two sisters</u>, ~~have~~ a talent for singing. has

9. The various clubs <u>on our campus</u> ~~performs~~ many charitable deeds. perform

10. The building <u>that was considered the most luxurious of all buildings in the area</u> was sold to an out-of-state company. Correct

Indefinite Pronouns as Subjects

If you are like most students, you probably have some trouble with indefinite pronouns: words like *everyone, all, each,* and so on. These words are called *indefinite pronouns* because they don't signal a specific (definite) person or thing. For example, the word *Ralph* is definite, and the pronoun *he* is definite since they both identify a specific person. However, the pronoun *anyone* can fit every person since it doesn't name anyone specifically; it is indefinite. These important words can serve as the subjects of sentences, so you need to learn how to work with them. Here are the "A, B, Cs" of determining the number of indefinite pronouns:

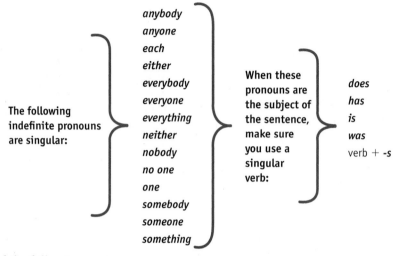

| The following indefinite pronouns are singular: | anybody
anyone
each
either
everybody
everyone
everything
neither
nobody
no one
one
somebody
someone
something | When these pronouns are the subject of the sentence, make sure you use a singular verb: | does
has
is
was
verb + *-s* |

Read the following sentence:

> Each of the dresses are stylish.

How can you tell if the subject and verb agree? First, find the subject. You already know how to do that: find the verb, mentally cross out any prepositional phrases, and then look for the subject.

> Each [~~of the dresses~~] are stylish.

Notice that the subject of this sentence is *each*, not *dresses*. If you look at the preceding chart, you'll find that the pronoun *each* is listed as singular; thus this sentence should have a singular verb.

> Each . . . is stylish.
> <u>Each</u> of the dresses <u>is</u> stylish.

When using indefinite pronouns, students sometimes visualize more than one person and incorrectly choose plural verbs. Some students may even apply the rule and then during revision change the verb because "it doesn't sound right." You're battling a habit that's been with you most of your life, so you need to train your ear. Basically, pronouns ending with *-body* and *-one* are singular. It might also help to substitute another singular, third person pronoun (*she, he, it*) as a test. Any of these techniques can help you train your ear.

However, some indefinite pronouns are always plural. This group rarely presents problems in subject–verb agreement. You won't have trouble remembering this short list.

| The following indefinite pronouns are plural: | both
few
many
several | Make sure you use a plural verb: | are
do
have
were |

Examine two examples:

> <u>Several</u> of the boys <u>are</u> in the room.
> <u>Both</u> of the trucks <u>were</u> in my way.

Finally, one group of indefinite pronouns can go either way, depending on your meaning.

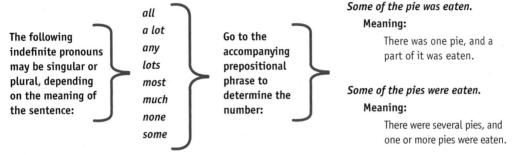

The following indefinite pronouns may be singular or plural, depending on the meaning of the sentence:	all, a lot, any, lots, most, much, none, some	Go to the accompanying prepositional phrase to determine the number:

Some of the pie was eaten.

Meaning:
> There was one pie, and a part of it was eaten.

Some of the pies were eaten.

Meaning:
> There were several pies, and one or more pies were eaten.

This rule may seem a bit complicated, but actually it is quite simple. When one of the preceding indefinite pronouns is the subject of a sentence, you need to look inside the accompanying prepositional phrase for a clue about the subject's number. So you mentally cross out the prepositional phrase to find the subject, but then you mentally reinstate the prepositional phrase to find out if the subject is singular or plural.

> All of the steaks were overcooked.

To find the subject, mentally cross out the prepositional phrase.

> All [of the steak] was overcooked.

Clearly, the subject of the sentence is *all*. But is *all* singular or plural? It depends on what's inside the prepositional phrase! So you have to mentally put the phrase back in its original position.

> All of the steak was overcooked.

Ask yourself whether *steak* is singular or plural. The prepositional phrase defines the number. It tells you that you have one steak and that you overcooked the entire steak. Therefore, *all* is singular in this case, so it needs a singular verb: *was*.

Prepositional phrase with singular object

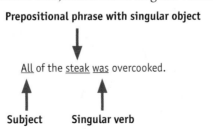

<u>All</u> of the <u>steak</u> <u>was</u> overcooked.

Subject   Singular verb

But what if you had several steaks cooking at the same time and you overcooked all of them?

> All of the steaks were overcooked.

In this case, the prepositional phrase defines the indefinite pronoun as plural. Because *steaks* is plural, *all* is plural, and you need a plural verb.

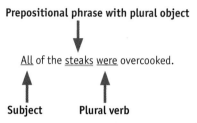

Prepositional phrase with plural object

<u>All</u> of the <u>steaks</u> <u>were</u> overcooked.

Subject   **Plural verb**

PRACTICE   17-4

Read each of the following sentences carefully. If the verb and the subject agree, write *Correct* on the line. If the verb and the subject do not agree, cross out the verb and write the correct form on the line. Do not change the subject of the sentence or the tense of the verb.

1. Each of the dry ingredients is measured first. <u>Correct</u>
2. Neither of the preachers ~~have~~ seen the promised land. <u>has</u>
3. Every one of the sidewalks needs to be washed. <u>Correct</u>
4. Each of them ~~have~~ to submit an application. <u>has</u>
5. Not one of them ~~were~~ hoping for success. <u>was</u>

PRACTICE   17-5

Proofread the following paragraph for subject–verb agreement problems. Change the verb, not the subject. Don't change the tense of the sentences. As you revise, keep in mind the two considerations addressed so far (words that intervene between the subject and its verb and indefinite pronouns as subjects).

Cindy and Marjorie are the best of friends most of the time. Everyone in our class, even the jocks and the nerds, ~~know~~ knows they are inseparable. So we are all surprised to see them feuding over someone like Bill, who is irresponsible and lazy. He, as well as his friends, ~~are~~ is the worst kind of companion for Marjorie, and he's already broken Cindy's heart once before. Why do either one of them care about him? All their friends in the dorm ~~advises~~ advise them to stay away from him, but neither of them ~~listen~~ listens. It must be that devilish grin and "cool" demeanor that ~~makes~~ make him so irresistible. At any rate, they are no longer talking to each other, and anyone without blinders on ~~know~~ knows a beautiful friendship is being threatened because of a low-life jerk.

Compound Subjects

Two or more subjects joined by *and* usually take a plural verb.

> <u>Fanny and Mae</u> are enjoying their ice cream cones.
> <u>She and Gomer</u> run the Boston Marathon every year.

There are times when we consider two nouns a single unit. For example, we consider *macaroni and cheese* to be one dish; therefore, your verb shows this dish as one unit, singular.

> <u>Macaroni and cheese</u> is my favorite dish.

Another exception is when you use *each* or *every* before a compound subject. When you place either of these words in front of a series of nouns, you focus on the items as individual units; therefore, the verb is singular.

PLURAL:	<u>The car and truck</u> <u>are priced</u> below blue book value.
	<u>The player and fan</u> <u>are screaming</u> at the umpire.
SINGULAR:	<u>Each car and truck</u> <u>is priced</u> below blue book value.
	<u>Every player and fan</u> <u>is screaming</u> at the umpire.

However, if you have two or more subjects connected by *or* or *nor* (*either . . . or* or *neither . . . nor*) or by *not only . . . but also,* the noun or pronoun nearer the verb determines the number. Examine the following sentences and note how the verb changes depending on the order of the subjects:

OR:	Appropriate certificates <u>or</u> a signed letter is required.
	A signed letter <u>or</u> appropriate certificates are required.
NEITHER . . . NOR:	<u>Neither</u> the conductor <u>nor</u> the musicians know how to read music.
	<u>Neither</u> the musicians <u>nor</u> the conductor knows how to read music.
EITHER . . . OR:	<u>Either</u> Janet <u>or</u> her parents are delivering the gifts to the hospital.
	<u>Either</u> her parents <u>or</u> Janet is delivering the gifts to the hospital.
NOT ONLY . . . BUT ALSO:	<u>Not only</u> the senators <u>but also</u> the governor is protesting the new federal guidelines.
	<u>Not only</u> the governor <u>but also</u> the senators are protesting the new federal guidelines.

The order of the subject doesn't really matter; both forms are grammatically correct in writing. However, if you feel that the sentence sounds awkward, place the plural subject last.

PRACTICE 17-6

Proofread the following paragraph for subject–verb agreement. Change the verb, not the subject. Don't change the tense of the sentences.

Either Antonia Gaddis' seven children or her husband ~~are~~ [is] inheriting all the land she purchased when she retired from teaching. Each soul and body in Malmar ~~are~~ [is] rooting for the kids, not because we don't like Mr. Gaddis but because we want to watch the kids fight over the land for the next several years. There's not much else to do in our small town. The twins—Harry and Hector (the one who twitches when he gets angry)—~~controls~~ [control] the others most of the time, but we are hoping a big land fight will break their dominance and we'll have a real western on our hands. Several of our crowd ~~thinks~~ [think] the kids might just let Mr. Gaddis have the land, but anyone with any brains ~~know~~ [knows] that when money is at stake even well-raised children can become monsters. Every man, woman, and child in Malmar ~~look~~ [looks] forward to being entertained by the Gaddis family drama. We wish Antonia were alive to enjoy it with us!

Sentences Beginning with *There* and *Here*

Although the words *there* and *here* can occupy the subject position, they are never subjects of sentences. When a sentence begins with *There* or *Here,* the subject is located after the verb.

There <u>are</u> five <u>elephants</u> lounging in the grove.

Note: Generally, try to avoid beginning your sentences with "There is" or "There are," especially if the sentence is an important one, such as a thesis or topic sentence. Using these phrases may weaken the sentence by delaying the subject, and overusing these phrases may be distracting to the reader. Compare the preceding sentence to "Five elephants are lounging in the grove." You can feel which sentence is stronger.

PRACTICE 17-7

Revise the following sentences in two ways: On the first line, revise the sentence by correcting the subject–verb agreement problem. If the sentence is correct, write *Correct* on the line. On the second line, rewrite the sentence without using *there* and *here*. Answers will vary.

1. There on the counter was my wallet and car keys.

Revision: There on the counter were my wallet and car keys.

Rewrite without *there* or *here:* My wallet and car keys were on the counter.

2. There is a briefcase, a laptop, and a calculator in my office.

Revision: There are a briefcase, a laptop, and a calculator in my office.

Rewrite without *there* or *here:* A briefcase, a laptop, and a calculator are in my office.

3. Here are more freeloaders for the open house.

Revision: Correct

Rewrite without *there* or *here:* More freeloaders are present for the open house.

4. Here is two gifts I'd like to receive: a Maltese puppy and an engagement ring.

Revision: Here are two gifts I'd like to receive: a Maltese puppy and an engagement ring.

Rewrite without *there* or *here:* Two gifts I'd like to receive are a Maltese puppy and an engagement ring.

5. There is many opportunities available to students interested in a career in the health field.

Revision: There are many opportunities available to students interested in a career in the health field.

Rewrite without *there* or *here:* Many opportunities are available to students interested in a career in the health field.

Words That Are Plural in Form but Singular in Meaning

The title of a work of art, literature, or music, even when plural in form, takes a singular verb.

- *The Sopranos* <u>has</u> changed television forever.
- *The Three Musketeers* <u>is</u> an exciting novel.
- "<u>Free Radicals</u>" <u>was named</u> by *Rolling Stone* as one of the best songs of 2006.

Words such as *athletics, economics, mathematics, physics, statistics, civics, politics, measles, mumps,* and *news* are usually singular, despite their plural forms.

- <u>Politics</u> <u>is</u> my favorite topic for dinner conversation.
- <u>Economics</u> <u>is</u> almost as interesting as politics.

Names of businesses, words mentioned as names, and verb phrases (gerunds) are singular.

- <u>Two Guys</u> <u>was</u> once a profitable department store.
- *<u>Recommendations</u>* <u>is</u> spelled with two *m*'s.
- <u>Leaving his hometown and friends</u> <u>was</u> not easy for Sandy.

Collective nouns are singular when you refer to them as one unit and plural when you are referring to individual members. Collective nouns represent groups of people or things. The following are common collective nouns:

army	committee	family	orchestra
audience	congress	jury	public
band	couple	majority	staff
class	crowd	minority	troop

When you want to show that the group is acting as a single unit, treat the collective noun as singular and use the singular form of the verb.

SINGULAR (ACTING AS ONE UNIT):	The <u>committee</u> <u>has reached</u> a decision. The <u>group</u> <u>has decided</u> to support the petition. A good <u>audience</u> <u>sets</u> the right atmosphere for the performance.
PLURAL (ACTING SEPARATELY):	The <u>committee</u> <u>have given</u> their opinions. The <u>group</u> <u>have been</u> debating the issue among themselves. The <u>audience</u> <u>have expressed</u> their dissatisfaction with the play.

PRACTICE   17-8

Select five collective nouns from the list above and write two sentences for each, one in which you use the collective noun as singular and the other as plural. Your sentences should clearly show how you are using the noun. Answers will vary.

1. Noun: _staff_

Singular: _The staff is unhappy with the new policy._

Plural: _The staff are divided on whether to protest or not._

2. Noun: _public_

Singular: _The public is in support of the mayor's recommendations._

Plural: _The public have aired their various concerns._

3. Noun: _crowd_

Singular: _The crowd surrounds the beleaguered protester._

Plural: _The crowd stamp their feet in unison._

4. Noun: _class_

Singular: _The class applauds the student's speech._

Plural: _The class compare their grades to figure out who made the top mark._

5. Noun: _jury_

Singular: _The jury announces its verdict._

Plural: _The jury are deeply divided over the crime._

PRACTICE 17-9

Check the following sentences for subject–verb agreement. If the sentence is correct, write *Correct* on the line provided. If incorrect, cross out the verb and write the correct verb.

1. The news of the vaccine ~~are~~ spreading. _is_

2. "Pennies from Heaven" is a famous 1936 American song performed by such greats as Frank Sinatra, Billie Holiday, and Louis Armstrong. _Correct_

3. There are certain mannerisms that may be offensive to your customers. _Correct_

4. Shaking the soda cans ~~cause~~ them to squirt the unsuspecting victims. _causes_

5. My family ~~have~~ never been able to understand my lifestyle. _has_

PRACTICE 17-10

Practice the rules described so far in this chapter by editing the following paragraphs for subject–verb agreement. Cross out each verb that doesn't agree with its subject in number and write the correct verb above it.

My two favorite subjects are politics and economics. Politics ~~are~~ **is** so interesting because I get to study how governments all over the world ~~selects~~ **select** their rulers. There ~~is~~ **are** so many fascinating differences between countries in this area, and studying leadership succession patterns ~~tie~~ **ties** in with another one of my passions—psychology.

Economics ~~are~~ **is** hard for me, but I know politics and economics are related in important ways. Every one of my friends ~~say~~ **says** I'm crazy to study these subjects, but when I mention my goal—a B.A. in political science, an M.A. in political economy, a Ph.D. in psychology, and a law degree—they understand. In case you are interested in this field, Martin Roget's *Political Leaders in Modern Times* ~~paint~~ **paints** a clear picture of how politics ~~interrelate~~ **interrelates** with economics and psychology.

> **Collaborative Critical Thinking**
>
> **In groups of two or three,** write one or two paragraphs summarizing important information about an issue in the news of the day. After you have written the paragraph, edit it carefully for fragments, fused sentences, comma splices, and subject–verb agreement.
>
> Now, rewrite the paragraph and create fragments, comma splices, fused sentences, and subject–verb agreement errors. Once you have completed this "quiz draft," exchange papers with another group.
>
> Revise the paragraph you have just received from the other group. Use the tricks you have learned to locate sentence structure and agreement errors, and use various methods to revise these errors. Return the paper to the writers as soon as you have finished.
>
> When you receive your paper back, compare the other group's version with your original draft. Was the other group able to spot all the errors that you purposely created? Did the other group revise your paragraph effectively? Discuss how that group's version is different from yours. What would your group have done differently?

REVIEW   17-1

Proofread the following paragraphs from a student essay that contains errors in subject–verb agreement. Correct the errors by crossing out the incorrect verbs and writing in the correct verbs. Do not change the subjects or the tense of the verbs.

If a child with parents ~~are~~ *is* well adjusted—mentally and emotionally compatible with peers—then the parents, of whatever sexual orientation, ~~is~~ *are* doing something right. Just because a couple is of the same sex doesn't mean they can't be good parents. Same-sex parents, as long as they are sensitive and caring, ~~raises~~ *raise* children as capably as heterosexual couples. Unless there is sound evidence and consensus among experts, based on valid scientific research, that a couple is not qualified to raise a child, they should be allowed to adopt. There ~~are~~ *is* no good, solid reason to keep a child in need of a permanent home out of the homes of competent, devoted parents who will love them unconditionally.

Conservatives on this issue, who want to ban gay adoption mainly because of a particular religious objection, ~~thinks~~ *think* that gay adoption is simply wrong. These people are putting their personal opinions ahead of their better judgment. If they were truly thinking about what ~~are~~ ^{is} best for the children who need parents, they would see how misguided it is to turn their backs on potential parents because they're gay. The people who offer themselves as parents should be thanked. ^{There are} ~~There's~~ too many children without homes and not enough caring people to take them in.

It's not hard to see that a child is better off with someone who can be a mentor, role model, and companion than being placed with someone he or she will barely get to know before being moved again. So much time has been wasted trying to disprove homosexuals' abilities to raise children. Finding reasons homosexuals, even those with the most stable home life, ^{are} is not a good choice ~~are~~ ^{is} a backward step to finding good parents for parentless children. There are many people in the world, gay and straight, who ^{don't} ~~doesn't~~ make a good choice for adoptive parenting. The best interest of the children ^{demands} ~~demand~~ that we find the people who do.

CHAPTER 18

Editing
for Pronouns

YOUR GOALS

1. Identify and revise pronoun agreement errors.

2. Identify and revise pronoun reference errors.

3. Use correct pronoun case.

4. Maintain consistency in pronoun use.

"The heart of religion lies in its personal pronouns."

■ **Martin Luther** ■

The sports director of a large university decides to send an e-mail to update the campus on various sports accomplishments and activities in the upcoming weeks:

Dear faculty, staff, and students,

As you know, it's been a busy spring term with all of the games, fundraising, and recruitment that the sports department has been involved in. However, they could not have accomplished as much without all of your support and hard work.

Although our basketball team did not make it to the playoffs, they improved their record from the previous year, which is quite an accomplishment considering that they had a new coach and more travel in their game schedule. Coach Bob and his assistant coach Joshua Lane did a magnificent job of training the team; he fostered the kind of teamwork necessary for a winning team. Coach Bob told Coach Lane that he would be recognized for his outstanding coaching this season at the final awards banquet.

Our wrestlers this year faced a rough season due to more injuries than usual and a shortage of players. This contributed to their many losses. On a bright note, however, the Jane Short Foundation has agreed to donate $5,000 for new mats and wrestling gear. We are grateful that they have been so generous.

Thanks for all of your support!

On the surface, the preceding e-mail seems to contain a good overall summary of the sports season for the university. However, a closer look reveals that it is full of pronoun errors (especially the use of *they* and *this*), which can confuse and distract readers and detract from the sports director's credibility. Before sending the e-mail, the director should have edited for pronouns, checking that each pronoun referred clearly and directly to a specific noun in the e-mail.

LET's warm up!

Think of a situation in which someone has received a low evaluation at work. The person feels unfairly treated and believes that some comments in the evaluation are inaccurate. Write a paragraph suggesting how this person should approach the supervisor to protest the evaluation. Do not use "I" or "you" in the paragraph, and be sure to focus on the need for tact and diplomacy.

John Lund/Nevada Wier/Getty Images

UNDERSTANDING PRONOUNS

We use pronouns all the time in our speech and writing. Rather than repeat the same noun, we substitute pronouns to add smoothness, clarity, and conciseness to our sentences. Read the following sentences to get a feeling for what pronouns are and what they do:

NO PRONOUNS:	The manager allowed the manager's employees to use the manager's office for the employees' union meeting.
WITH PRONOUNS:	The manager allowed <u>his</u> employees to use <u>his</u> office for <u>their</u> union meeting.

As you can tell, pronouns are substitutes for nouns. The definition of a *pronoun* is a word that stands for a noun. (Remember that *pro* means "for," as in the *pros* and *cons* of an issue.) Furthermore, pronouns must agree with, or match, the nouns they replace.

The (manager) allowed <u>his</u> (employees) to use <u>his</u> office for <u>their</u> union meeting.

In your writing, you must be aware of the pronouns that you use to replace nouns. Each pronoun must refer clearly to the noun or to the pronoun that it stands for. The object or idea that the pronoun refers to is known as the *antecedent* of the pronoun.

NOUN ANTECEDENT ◄——————► **PRONOUN**

<u>Jean and Jake</u> often study together because <u>they</u> help each other understand difficult biology concepts.

Study the list of personal pronouns in the chart below. You use these pronouns every day without even thinking about them. Nevertheless, you need to familiarize yourself with the various types of pronouns to avoid using them incorrectly in your writing.

Personal Pronouns					
	Person	Subject	Object	Possessive		Reflexive
SINGULAR	First	I	me	my	mine	myself
	Second	you	you	your	yours	yourself
	Third	he	him	his	his	himself
		she	her	her	hers	herself
		it	it	its	its	itself
PLURAL	First	we	us	our	ours	ourselves
	Second	you	you	your	yours	yourselves
	Third	they	them	their	theirs	themselves

Note that the possessive *its*, unlike possessive nouns ending in *-s*, does not add an apostrophe before or after the *-s*. (If you write *it's*, then the meaning is *it is*.)

In the following paragraph, notice how each of the pronouns refers clearly to its antecedent.

> A positive attitude is important in the workplace. Employers value a positive attitude in their employees more than any other quality when doing evaluations. For example, Leonard Garcia, like many of his coworkers, does his work well, but he goes one step further. He makes himself available to coworkers. They appreciate Leonard's help and advice. His interactions help create a positive workplace.

PRACTICE 18-1

Read the following paragraph carefully. Then underline all pronouns, referring to the chart when needed. Finally, from each pronoun, draw an arrow back to its antecedent.

Most colleges and universities offer convenient ways for a student to register and check grades online. Their websites include a Register Now link; it saves students from having to visit a college office or an adviser to sign up for their courses. Once students click the Register Now button, they can log on with a password and pin number, ensuring their privacy. They can then choose the semester for which they plan to register and the courses that they choose to take. If a student lacks the prerequisites for a specific course, the system will not allow him or her to sign up for it. After registering, the student can return to the main menu and print a detailed schedule; it contains the classes, instructors, credit hours, and classrooms of each course. Another convenience that many colleges offer is posting grades online. In the past, students waited a week or two before receiving their grades in the mail. Now, as soon as instructors post them, students know how well they did in their courses. Instead of waiting a week or more, students can check their grades themselves online. Indeed, the computer has given students easy, fast, and convenient access to enrollment and grade checks.

Problems in Pronoun–Antecedent Agreement

In Chapter 17, you learned about the grammatical person and number of pronouns used as subjects in sentences. However, subject pronouns account for only a small percentage of the pronoun problems in student writing. As you're aware from Chapter 17, pronouns have two qualities: they refer to different persons or things (first, second, and third persons), and they are either singular or plural. Many of the pronouns we use have antecedents; that is, they refer to a specific noun or pronoun. In such cases, apply the following two rules:

> **A pronoun agrees in person and number with its antecedent.**

Third person,   Third person,
singular antecedent   singular pronoun
↓   ↓
The <u>high school basketball team</u> had <u>its</u> first winning season.

> **A pronoun should have a clear antecedent.**

ANTECEDENT   PRONOUN
↓   ↓
<u>Students</u> should ask <u>their</u> advisers for help.

ANTECEDENT   PRONOUN
↓   ↓
<u>The student</u> decided to change <u>his</u> major.

We tend to be careless when it comes to pronouns and often encounter this type of construction.

> **INCORRECT:** A reporter usually tells the truth, but I'm sure there's much they choose to cover up.

To the untrained ear, this sentence might sound correct. However, if you examine the sentence closely, you'll find a common writing problem: the pronoun doesn't agree with its antecedent in number.

Third Person   Third Person
SINGULAR   PLURAL
Antecedent   Pronoun

<u>A reporter</u> usually tells the truth, but I'm sure there's much <u>they</u> choose to cover up.

Do you recall this type of error in your writing? Look at another example:

> **INCORRECT:** <u>A person</u> should review all of <u>their</u> options before making a major career decision.

A possible reason for this error is that the writer wants to avoid using "his options" or "her options," thereby excluding one gender.

> **CORRECT:** <u>A person</u> should review all of <u>his or her</u> options before making a major career decision. [Change *their* to *his or her*.]

CORRECT: <u>People</u> should review all of <u>their</u> options before making a major career decision. [Change *a person* to *people* to agree with *their*.]

PRACTICE 18-2

Without looking back at the actual chart, try to fill in the various personal pronouns. Don't worry if you don't recall all of them. The goal is to get you thinking about pronouns: what they are and what forms they take.

Personal Pronouns						
	Person	Subject	Object	Possessive		Reflexive
SINGULAR	First	I	me	my	mine	myself
	Second	you	you	your	yours	yourself
	Third	he	him	his	his	himself
		she	her	her	hers	herself
		it	it	its	its	itself
PLURAL	First	we	us	our	ours	ourselves
	Second	you	you	your	yours	yourselves
	Third	they	them	their	theirs	themselves

PRACTICE 18-3

Edit the following sentences for pronoun–antecedent agreement. If the personal pronoun is incorrect, cross it out and write the correct pronoun on the line provided. Change the number of the verb to agree with the pronoun if necessary, crossing out the original. If the pronoun is correct, write *Correct* on the line.

1. A cell phone is a device of convenience and irritation, depending on how one views ~~them~~. _it_____

2. Cell phones allow users to call from wherever they happen to be. _Correct_____

3. In addition, cell phones have a list of contacts, allowing the phone's owner to store important business and personal phone numbers so that ~~it~~ can be accessed easily. _they_____

4. The text messaging function of cell phones gives the user access to information so that ~~they don't~~ interrupt meetings with annoying chat and ringing. _he or____ _she doesn't_____

5. E-mail, voicemail, Internet service, and a video camera are just a few of the features that a customer can get if ~~they purchase~~ the right phone. _he or she_ _purchases_____

Indefinite Pronouns as Antecedents

Hopefully, you haven't forgotten the indefinite pronouns you used in subject–verb agreement; nonetheless, it's crucial that we remind you that these pronouns are all third person and can be tricky in terms of number. You are again working with these pronouns in this chapter, so review the following chart.

Singular		Plural	Singular or Plural
anybody	neither	both	all
anyone	nobody	few	any
each	no one	many	most
either	one	several	none
every	somebody		some
everybody	someone		
everyone	something		(the number depends on
everything			what the pronoun refers to)

When the antecedent of your pronoun is an indefinite pronoun, make sure that both pronouns agree in person and in number.

Singular Antecedent   **Plural Pronoun**
        ↓   ↓
Each of the employees has taken additional training in their area of expertise.

Solution #1: Make the pronoun singular so that it agrees with its antecedent.

Singular Antecedent   **Singular Pronoun**
        ↓   ↓
Each of the employees has taken additional training in his or her area of expertise.

Solution #2: Make the antecedent plural so that it agrees with the pronoun.

Plural Antecedent   **Plural Pronoun**
        ↓   ↓
Many of the employees have taken additional training in their area of expertise.

OR

Plural Antecedent   **Plural Pronoun**
        ↓   ↓
Some of the employees have taken additional training in their area of expertise.

Using *His or Her* to Avoid Sexist Language

One of your goals as a writer is to be able to connect with your audience. The use of gender-specific pronouns may alienate an audience, so often, especially in speech, people use the plural form of the pronoun.

> **Bridging Knowledge**
>
> **See Chapter 23** for additional information on avoiding offensive use of language.

Everyone in our department spent the entire evening preparing their proposal.

Unfortunately, violating the rule of pronoun–antecedent agreement may not be acceptable in academic writing or in your profession. However, writers have other options:

■ Since the traditional practice of using the masculine pronoun to indicate both genders is now considered sexist, you might alternate the use of masculine and feminine pronouns in your paragraphs. For example, use the feminine pronoun forms in your first paragraph, the masculine form in the second paragraph, and so forth.

■ Another way to avoid the sexist use of pronouns is to use *he or she* or *him or her*.

<u>Everyone</u> in our department spent the entire evening preparing <u>his or her</u> proposal.

Although this method has gained much popularity, when overused, it can be viewed as an awkward and repetitive style.

<u>Everyone</u> in our department spent the entire evening preparing <u>his or her</u> proposal. <u>He or she</u> felt that <u>his or her</u> job would be jeopardized if <u>he or she</u> didn't submit the proposal on time.

One occurrence or two occurrences distant from each other might be fine, but the overuse of this device is wordy, can be distracting, and should be avoided.

■ Probably the most popular option is to make the antecedent plural, thus avoiding gender-specific pronouns.

<u>The executives</u> in our department spent the entire evening preparing <u>their</u> proposal.

■ You might also try replacing the pronoun with an article (*a, an, the*), thus leaving out the pronoun.

<u>Everyone in our department</u> spent the entire evening preparing <u>a</u> proposal.

■ If possible and appropriate, you might change the person from third to first (*I* or *we*) or second (*you*).

<u>We</u> spent the entire evening preparing <u>our</u> proposal.

■ When all else fails, try restructuring your sentence.

ORIGINAL (GENDER SPECIFIC):	If an <u>executive</u> does not submit a proposal, <u>he</u> will be fired.

Here are two of the many ways you might rewrite your sentence:

DEPENDENT CLAUSE:	An <u>executive</u> *who does not submit a proposal* will be fired.
VERB PHRASE:	An <u>executive</u> will be fired for *not submitting a proposal*.

With so many options, there is no reason to violate the rules of pronoun–antecedent agreement. As far as which option is best, the decision is yours; just be fully aware of your audience when you use pronouns.

PRACTICE 18-4

Fill in the correct singular or plural pronoun to agree with its antecedent. Show your awareness of sexist language by alternating your choice of pronouns between masculine and feminine where appropriate. Answers will vary.

1. Every manager did _____her_____ best to promote the product.

2. Each of the siblings had to make _____his_____ own bed.

3. Nobody in the class turned in _____her_____ lab report.

4. If anyone calls, ask _____him_____ to try my cell number.

5. Cynthia, as well as Ruth, had time to complete _____her_____ assignment.

6. Anyone who objects to the new policy should speak to ___his___ immediate supervisor.

7. Neither of the arrested teens would tell the officer _____her_____ name.

8. As each graduate walked across the stage, ___his___ name and major were announced.

9. When a person is drinking and driving, ___she___ may easily cause an accident.

10. Each of the trees around the campus lost most of _____its_____ leaves.

Compound Antecedents

If the pronoun has a compound antecedent connected by *and,* treat it as plural.

- Gary and Melinda vacationed in Mexico, where they first met.
- Mike and Phil went on a road trip, during which they met the most extraordinary people.

However, if you have two or more antecedents connected by *or, nor, either . . . or,* or *neither . . . nor,* make your pronoun agree with the nearer antecedent.

Plural Antecedent   **Plural Pronoun**

Neither the instructor nor the students left their classroom during the fire drill.

Singular Antecedent   **Singular Pronoun**

Neither the students nor the instructor left her classroom during the fire drill.

If you have a singular and a plural antecedent as shown here, you can avoid awkwardness or the wordiness of the *he or she* construction by reversing the order of the antecedents so that the plural antecedent is last. Also, if you have a feminine and a masculine antecedent, don't match your pronoun to the last one since doing so will be distracting.

Neither Phil nor Margaret wanted her palm read.

Instead, rephrase the sentence.

Phil and Margaret didn't want their palms read.

Fill in the correct singular or plural pronoun to agree with its antecedent.

1. Neither Sara nor Tina had mailed _____ her _____ check.
2. Both the manager and the assistant manager did __ their __ best to motivate the employees.
3. Either Leo or Ken will make _____ his _____ presentation first.
4. Jeff and his sister received the bad news when _____ they _____ arrived home.
5. Both Margo and Marie did __ their __ best to complete the project on time.

Collective Nouns as Antecedents

As you may recall, collective nouns indicate a group. Collective nouns such as *audience, family, class, team, jury, troop, committee,* and so on, may be singular or plural, depending on how you are viewing the group. For a collective noun, use the singular pronoun if you are referring to the antecedent as a unit. However, if you are thinking of the antecedent as individual members of the group acting independently, treat it as plural.

The committee has submitted its recommendations.

The singular pronoun *its* refers to the committee as one unit; thus, the entire committee has contributed to and has agreed on a list of recommendations.

The committee have submitted their recommendations.

In the second example, the plural pronoun *their* refers to the committee as individual members; thus, the members of the committee each submitted individual recommendations. Notice how the choice of pronoun can change the idea of the sentence. When you use a collective noun as the antecedent and the sentence sounds awkward to you, simply add a word to clarify your meaning.

The committee members have submitted their recommendations.

Fill in the correct singular or plural pronoun to agree with its antecedent.

1. The committee plans to submit _____ its _____ yearly report next week.
2. The faculty has made __ its __ recommendations for the next academic year.
3. The couple seemed determined to go _____ their _____ separate ways.
4. The jury was unanimous in _____ its _____ verdict.
5. The staff feel that management is using _____ them _____.

Pronoun Reference

When you proofread for pronoun agreement, you are usually checking for problems in number: singular pronouns take singular antecedents and plural pronouns take plural antecedents. (Problems with person agreement are fairly rare.) However, creating shifts in number is not the only problem in pronoun usage that you need to look for in your writing. Another problem with pronouns is that the reader may not be able to identify the antecedents of some of your pronouns. Before you use a pronoun, you need to provide a reference for that pronoun, one that your reader can easily and quickly identify. For example, if all of a sudden your friend states, "I can't stand her!" without pointing at someone, your first reaction is to ask who it is she can't stand. Who is *her*? How often have you stopped someone midsentence to ask, "Who are you talking about?" or "What are you talking about?" You're asking for a reference, an antecedent. This leads us to our second rule:

> **A pronoun requires a clear antecedent—either a noun or another pronoun. The antecedent usually, but not always, appears before the pronoun.**

Examine the following examples of this rule:

- The manager tried to negotiate with the <u>union representatives,</u> but <u>they</u> wouldn't budge.

- <u>Neither</u> of the ladies is in a position to complain about <u>her</u> workload.

- Few realized how awkward <u>I</u> felt walking into a restaurant by <u>myself</u>.

- Before <u>it</u> was disbanded, the <u>Citizens' Network</u> provided many services to the community.

Look at four typical errors of pronoun reference.

Error #1: Two Possible Antecedents

Make sure your pronoun does not refer to two possible antecedents. Your pronoun must clearly refer to one antecedent (even if it's a compound antecedent), not two different antecedents. Examine some examples of this type of error and possible solutions.

INCORRECT: When Juan hung the <u>glass chandelier</u> above the <u>dining room table, it</u> shattered.

[What shattered—the chandelier or the table?]

CORRECT: When Juan hung the glass chandelier above the dining room table, the chandelier shattered.

[Substitute a noun for the unclear pronoun.]

INCORRECT: Mr. Sekii told Mr. Rios that his dog was in his garden.

[Whose dog? Whose garden? Did Mr. Sekii say, "Hey, Mr. Rios, my dog was in your garden"? Or did he say, "Mr. Rios, your dog was in my garden"?]

As you can see, the pronoun cannot refer to two different antecedents. Such unclear references in your writing only confuse the reader. Your job as a writer is to make your writing clear and concrete. Again, the most direct solution is to provide the reader with a clear antecedent to the pronoun.

CORRECT: Mr. Sekii told Mr. Rios that Mr. Rio's dog was in Mr. Sekii's garden.

Although the idea of this sentence is clear, some readers may find this revision too wordy and the repetition of names too distracting. Another solution is to turn this sentence from indirect to direct quotation.

CORRECT: Upon seeing Mr. Rios, Mr. Sekii exclaimed, "Your dog was in my garden."

If this revision is still not acceptable, you might consider dividing the sentence into two sentences.

CORRECT: While in his garden, Mr. Sekii found Mr. Rios' dog. He called Mr. Rios to tell him where his dog was.

The point here is that revision is not limited to one method only. As long as your sentences communicate your ideas clearly, you have achieved your goal.

PRACTICE 18-7

Revise the following sentences so that the pronouns refer clearly to one antecedent. Answers will vary.

1. Before Geraldo gave his dog a stuffed toy, he washed it.

   Before Geraldo gave his dog a stuffed animal, Geraldo washed the dog.

2. After Sara's meeting with her manager, she reported that she wasn't sure if she agreed with her position on the new policy.

   After Sara's meeting with her manager, Sara reported that she wasn't sure if she agreed with her manager's position on the new policy.

3. Carlos told his manager that his watch was wrong.

   Carlos told his manager that the manager's watch was wrong.

4. Lydia told her mother she would have to take the car to the garage.

   Lydia told her mother that her mother would have to take the car to the garage.

5. Ben called his father before he left for work.

   Ben called his father before his father left for work.

Error #2: Pronouns Referencing Broad Ideas

The pronouns *which, this, that,* and *it* should refer to specific antecedents, not to the entire ideas of preceding sentences or clauses. These pronouns are often misused to stand for broad ideas expressed in previous sentences.

> **TOO BROAD:**   The hospital would not tell Mark how bad his uncle's condition was, <u>which</u> upset him.

Was Mark upset because the hospital wouldn't tell him about his uncle's condition or because his uncle was in bad shape?

> **SOLUTION:**   Mark was upset that the hospital wouldn't tell him about his uncle's condition.
>
> OR
>
> Mark was upset at how bad his uncle's condition was.

When you use *which,* place it as close as possible to its antecedent:

> Marked walked to the local <u>hospital, which</u> was next to his house, to see his uncle.

When you proofread your draft and find that the pronouns *which* and *that* are not next to or near their antecedents, you may have used these pronouns too broadly and need to revise your sentence.

Just like the pronoun *which,* the pronoun *this* is often misused to refer to broad ideas in other clauses and sentences.

> **TOO BROAD:**   The couple was impressed by the excellent food, the variety of activities, and the good service on the Caribbean cruise last summer. <u>This</u> made them want to sign up for a second cruise this coming summer.

What does *this* refer to—the food, the activities, the service, the fact that the couple was impressed, or all of these ideas?

The most expedient solution would be to replace the pronoun *this* with the idea that the pronoun is supposed to stand for.

> **SOLUTION:**   The couple was impressed by the excellent food, the variety of activities, and the good service on the Caribbean cruise

last summer. <u>Their positive experience</u> made them want to sign up for a second cruise this coming summer.

TOO BROAD: If a child continues to throw fits in public, it may lead to further problems as the child gets older.

What does *it* refer to? What may lead to further problems?

SOLUTION: Children who throw fits in public may have further problems with anger as they age.

PRACTICE 18-8

Revise the following sentences to avoid broad pronoun references. Answers will vary.

1. Bill didn't know Spanish and had allergies, but this didn't stop him from moving to Puerto Rico.

    Bill didn't know Spanish and had allergies, but these obstacles didn't stop him from moving to Puerto Rico.

2. He was able to finish college after landing a job. We admired him for that.

    We admired him for being able to finish college after landing a job.

3. She now has a college degree and holds an excellent job. This is proof that we were wrong not to trust her.

    She now has a college degree and holds an excellent job, accomplishments that prove we were wrong not to trust her.

4. I was late submitting my research paper, which greatly embarrassed me.

    Being late in submitting my research paper greatly embarrassed me.

5. At the meeting last night, the microphone was too loud and the people were yelling to be heard. That is probably what caused my headache.

    At the meeting last night, I got a headache because the microphone was too loud and because the people were yelling to be heard.

Error #3: Unidentified Antecedents

Don't use a pronoun to refer to an unidentified antecedent. Sometimes we may feel that the antecedent is obvious or that it's unimportant to the meaning of the sentence and, therefore, fail to state it. Again, the rule is that all pronouns must have a clear antecedent; hence, the pronoun you use has to refer to a specific noun or idea rather than an implied one.

IMPLIED: In <u>Dan's</u> essay, <u>he</u> argues that women should not serve on the front lines of battle.

What does *he* refer to? Dan's name is mentioned, but *Dan's* is an adjective (possessive) describing the essay, not a noun meaning the person. Thus, no person has been named to go with the pronoun *he*. Be careful that you don't use a possessive noun as an antecedent.

SOLUTION: In his essay, Dan argues that women should not serve on the front lines of battle.

> **INCORRECT:** I have always been interested in a career in nursing and hope to be <u>one</u> after I finish the nursing program.

What does *one* refer to? The person wants to be a *nursing?* The pronoun *one* has no specific antecedent. The writer probably felt that the occupation was obvious, so stating it would be silly. Regardless of the logic, the antecedent must be clearly stated; it's the rule for clear and correct writing.

> **CORRECT:** I have always been interested in a career in nursing and hope to be <u>a nurse</u> after I finish the nursing program.

Be sure that the pronouns *they, it,* and *you* refer to specific nouns. As you write, you may be thinking of a specific group of people and use *they* to refer to them; however, you must be sure that the group is mentioned and not just implied.

> **INCORRECT:** If you visit Egypt, you'll find that <u>they</u> are friendly, open, and welcoming people.

Who is *they* referring to? The writer is thinking of Egyptians, but there is no plural noun for *they* to refer to.

> **CORRECT:** If you visit Egypt, you'll find that <u>the Egyptians</u> are friendly, open, and welcoming.

Writers who are in doubt or don't stop to think of who or what performed the action of the verb often use a vague *they* to occupy the subject position. Examine a few of these types of errors.

> **INCORRECT:** In England, <u>they</u> call the subway the underground.
> **INCORRECT:** In the company's annual report, <u>they</u> outlined the procedure for a reduction in the workforce.
> **CORRECT:** In England, <u>the British</u> call the subway the underground.
> **CORRECT:** In the company's annual report, <u>the board of directors</u> outlined the procedure for a reduction in the workforce. [Other options are possible.]

Avoid vague use of the pronoun *it.* The sentence structure where this type of error occurs is similar to the preceding sentences illustrating the vague use of *they.* Examine the pattern of the following sentences, and avoid such patterns in your writings.

> **INCORRECT:** In the instruction manual, <u>it</u> gives you the steps for assembling a microwave cart.

What does *it* refer to? You can almost feel the awkwardness and wordiness of these types of sentence.

> **CORRECT:** The instruction manual gives you the steps for assembling a microwave cart.

Avoid using *you* to refer to people in general. *You* is appropriate when addressing someone directly or giving instructions.

| INCORRECT: | In China <u>you</u> should be willing to try many strange and exotic foods. |
| CORRECT: | In China <u>the traveler</u> should be willing to try many strange and exotic foods. |

This type of error uses second person although the meaning is third person: the writer means people in general, not the reader. As a rule, avoid or limit the use of second person unless you are giving instructions for the reader to follow or addressing the reader directly.

PRACTICE   18-9

Revise the following sentences to avoid broad pronoun references. Answers will vary.

1. According to *Newsweek* magazine, it states that the earth's temperature is rising.
   Newsweek magazine states that the earth's temperature is rising.

2. The salsa plate was empty, but we were tired of eating it anyway.
   The salsa plate was empty, but we were tired of eating salsa anyway.

3. They say that the Chinese will soon be the leading consumers of petroleum.
   Economists say that the Chinese will soon be the leading consumers of petroleum.

4. It says in the paper that the president's popularity is increasing.
   The paper states that the president's popularity is increasing.

5. In the contract it states that we will not be entitled to overtime pay.
   The contract states that we will not be entitled to overtime pay.

Collaborative Critical Thinking

In small groups, review the e-mail on page 505 and revise it. Write down your revision and compare your revision with the revisions of the other groups. Answers will vary.

Error #4: Referring to People, Animals, and Things

Use *who, whom,* or *whose* to refer to people; use *which* or *that* to refer to animals or things. One of the most common errors in formal writing is the use of *that* or *which* to refer to people. The pronouns *who, whom, whose, which,* and *that* introduce dependent clauses. By themselves, these clauses are fragments, so they should attach to independent clauses. Since these words are pronouns, known as *relative pronouns,* they should be placed as near as possible to the nouns or pronouns they identify or explain. If the noun is a person, use *who, whom,* and *whose.*

- I know the woman who runs the athletic club.

- I know the woman whom he hired to run the athletic club.

- I know the woman whose son runs the athletic club.

In contrast, the pronouns *which* and *that* should refer to animals and things.

- I was able to sell the house that I inherited.

- I was able to sell my house, which I inherited.

It is incorrect to use *which* and *that* for people; therefore, edit carefully. As you proofread your paper and find one of these pronouns, quickly look at the word in front of it, its antecedent, and make sure that you're using the correct pronoun for that antecedent.

Pronoun Case

Different pronouns perform different functions. Imagine a simple sentence with a subject, verb, and object of the verb.

Subject   **Verb**   **Object**

Jason and Ray will be leaving Wilfred and Marie.

Only certain pronouns can occupy the subject and object positions.

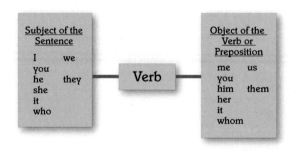

You're already familiar with these pronouns. The only additional pronouns we've added are *who* and *whom.* Notice that *who* is a subject pronoun and *whom* is an object pronoun. When you're trying to determine which pronoun to use, think of the preceding chart. Where does the pronoun fall in the sentence? If it's the subject position, choose from the subject group, but if it's the object of the verb or the object of the preposition, choose from the object group.

Subject   **Verb**   **Object**

He and she will be leaving them here.

The preceding example illustrates a basic sentence. When you choose a pronoun, don't take pronouns from different groups to place in the same position.

INCORRECT:	She and him will be leaving her and I early.
	[Subject and object are mixed.]
CORRECT:	She and he will be leaving her and me early.
	[Pronouns are now from the same groups.]

This seems like a simple rule. However, pronoun case errors are common. For instance, few people would say, "Me left early." However, create a compound subject by adding a noun, and it's not unusual to hear someone say, "John and me left early." It's surprising what an added noun can do if you're not careful.

If you read each pronoun separately, your ear will quickly detect the correct one.

She will be leaving . . .
Him will be leaving . . .   [clashes]
He will be leaving . . .
She will be leaving her.
She will be leaving I.   [clashes]
She will be leaving me.

Unfortunately, one verb that presents a problem to the ear is the verb *be* when it is used as the main verb of a sentence.

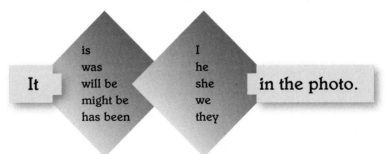

Because the forms of the verb *be* indicate that both pronouns refer to the same person, you should use a subject pronoun.

■ The top employees were she and I.
■ The thief is he.
■ It may have been they who called.

Prepositional phrases can occur anywhere in the sentence. Prepositions take pronouns from the object group. Just as in the earlier example, few would say, "This came from I." But it's not unusual to hear, "This came from Jan and I" rather than the correct pronoun case, "This came from Jan and me." Review the list of prepositions that follows. Once you are familiar with these prepositions, you can use object pronouns as the objects of these prepositions.

Common Prepositions				
about	around	during	of	under
above	at	except	off	until
across	before	for	on	up
after	behind	from	over	with
against	beside	in	through	without
along	between	into	to	
among	by	like	toward	

INCORRECT:	Between you and I, we shouldn't support her idea.
CORRECT:	Between you and me, we shouldn't support her idea.

Preposition   **Object Pronoun**

PRACTICE 18-10

Circle the correct pronoun case in parentheses. Answers are underlined below.

1. Jorge begged Carol and (I, <u>me</u>) not to reveal his secret.
2. Do you think it was (<u>she</u>, her) who received the award?
3. Are you and (<u>he</u>, him) working on the project together?
4. We asked Kim and (he, <u>him</u>) to the art exhibit.
5. I'm almost certain it was (<u>he</u>, him) who made the reservations.
6. This conversation is just between Ricky and (I, <u>me</u>).
7. My two friends and (<u>I</u>, me) decided it was time we stopped clowning around.
8. Everyone's attention slowly turned toward Tina and (I, <u>me</u>).
9. The group refused to do the presentation without Monica and (I, <u>me</u>).
10. The only choice left was between (she, <u>her</u>) and (he, <u>him</u>).

Using *Who* and *Whom*

The case of the relative pronouns *who* and *whom* depends on their function within their own clause. You need to determine whether the relative pronoun is the subject or the object of its clause. If it's the subject, use *who* or *whoever*; if it's the object of the verb, use *whom* or *whomever*.

PROBLEM:	We must find out (*who* or *whom*) left the message by the phone.

Focus on the relative clause:

> *(Who* or *Whom)* left the message by the phone

Is the relative pronoun the subject or the object of the clause?

> *(Who* or *Whom)* left the message by the phone

Subject   Verb

The clause needs a subject to complete its verb. *Who* can act as a subject. Test it by substituting a subject pronoun. Ask, "Who left the message by the phone?"

> <u>She</u> left the message by the phone.

Subject   Verb

The subject pronoun fits; therefore, *who* is the correct choice.

> **SOLUTION:**   We must find out <u>who</u> left the message by the phone.

Try another example:

> **PROBLEM:**   Mr. Jonathan Negrón consulted a lawyer (*who* or *whom*) he met in Miami.

Focus on the relative clause:

> *(who* or *whom)* he met in Miami

Is the relative pronoun the subject or the object of the clause?

> *(who* or *whom)* he met in Miami

Subject   Verb

The clause has a subject. Ask, "Who did he meet in Florida?" The answer is *him,* an object pronoun. *Whom* can act as an object pronoun. Also, test your answer by substituting a subject pronoun.

> He met him in Miami.

Verb   Object of the verb

The object pronoun fits; therefore, *whom* is the correct choice.

> **SOLUTION:**   Mr. Jonathan Negrón consulted a lawyer <u>whom</u> he met in Miami.

PRACTICE 18-11

Cross out any errors in the use of *who* and *whom* and *whoever* and *whomever* in the following items. Then write the correct form.

1. Let me know ~~who~~ you would recommend to replace our current administrative assistant. _whom_

2. ~~Whomever~~ wants to try this new, high-powered vacuum, please step forward. _Whoever_

3. As I stepped into the courtroom, I realized that the elderly woman who was sitting in the defendant's seat was my great aunt Hermie. _____

4. I handed the report to the employee, ~~whom~~ I assumed was Mr. Gonzales. _who_

5. To ~~who~~ should I return this report? _whom_

6. ~~Who~~ do you plan to hire? _Whom_

7. She was startled when she ran into her college roommate, ~~who~~ she hadn't seen in more than 20 years. _whom_

8. Working as a salesperson for a large publishing company is a demanding job as one must convince people ~~whom~~ are highly selective and choosy to purchase one's books. _who_

9. She tells her tale of adventure to ~~whomever~~ will endure her long narrative. _whoever_

10. The college plans to hire a new president ~~whom~~ they are convinced will improve student retention and student success. _who_

Pronoun Consistency

You have already seen how easy it is to create a shift in number by going from singular antecedent to a plural pronoun, or vice versa. A shift in person is yet another distracting pronoun error in writing. Readers are used to starting a reading from a certain perspective, such as the first person point of view, using *I*. If the writer shifts into *you* or into *he* or *she*, the perspective is changed and the reader is thrown off balance.

Make sure that all your pronouns are consistent in person with the antecedent you have established. In other words, unless you have a specific reason, if you start in second person, remain in second person; if you're writing in third person, don't suddenly shift to second person.

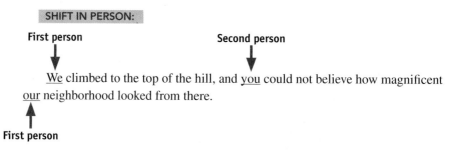

CONSISTENT:

First person

↓

First person

↓

<u>We</u> climbed to the top of the hill, and <u>we</u> could not believe how magnificent <u>our</u> neighborhood looked from there.

↑

First person

SHIFT IN PERSON:	<u>We</u> need to select a career carefully. <u>Your</u> entire future success depends upon <u>your</u> wise choice.
CONSISTENT FIRST PERSON:	<u>We</u> need to select a career carefully. <u>Our</u> entire future success depends upon <u>our</u> wise choice.
CONSISTENT SECOND PERSON:	<u>You</u> need to select a career carefully. <u>Your</u> entire future success depends upon <u>your</u> wise choice.
CONSISTENT THIRD PERSON:	<u>She</u> needs to select a career carefully. <u>Her</u> entire future success depends upon <u>her</u> wise choice.

A sudden shift to second person is probably the most common type of shift. As a rule, use the second person when you address the reader and third person for general statements.

| SHIFT IN PERSON: | <u>People</u> should be careful what they say. If <u>you're</u> not, <u>you</u> can hurt the people <u>you</u> care most about. |

Notice that the writer starts in third person plural and suddenly shifts to second person.

| CONSISTENT: | <u>People</u> should be careful what they say. If <u>they're</u> not, <u>they</u> can hurt the people <u>they</u> care most about. |

PRACTICE 18-12

On the line provided, revise each sentence to eliminate shifts in person. Answers will vary.

1. Everyone who wants to change their schedule should have your form already filled out.

   Everyone who wants to change his or her schedule should have the form already filled out.

2. If a person is a member of this club, you can meet some of the most interesting people.

   If you are a member of this club, you can meet some of the most interesting people.

3. One has to work hard to achieve what I want in life.

   I have to work hard to achieve what I want in life.

4. Someone who doesn't enjoy classical music has no clue what you're missing.

    Someone who doesn't enjoy classical music has no clue what she is missing.

5. Your essay may not receive a good grade if one does not take the time to revise.

    Your essay may not receive a good grade if you do not take the time to revise.

REVIEW 18-1

Edit the following essay for errors in fragments, run-ons, subject–verb agreement, and pronouns.

Jorge's: A Better Dining Experience

After spending all day packing our home to move to a new state. I was hungry and had a craving for Mexican cuisine, I knew an hour-old *chalupa* from Taco Bell just wouldn't do. I wanted authentic Mexican food, and at a decent price. Having lived in Pueblo the last 6 years, I have narrowed my Mexican restaurant favorites down to two establishments: Jorge's Sombrero and Nacho's. Both are owned by the same family, but Jorge's Sombrero was exactly what I had in mind. Although Jorge's Sombrero and Nacho's have similar cuisine and prices. Jorge's has far superior atmosphere and service.

Atmosphere is important when choosing a restaurant. When you walk into Jorge's Sombrero, immediately you can smell the flour tortillas, green chili, and cumin spice in the air, there are three "main" rooms in the restaurant, all painted a different color. The far left room is a bright green, the middle dining area a fuchsia color, and the far right, where the bar is located, a vibrant gold. Each of the rooms also have a wonderful décor: Mexican ritual masks, soccer jerseys mounted near the bar, and various paintings by Mexican artists. Jorge's also has an outdoor patio, which has comfortable dining in the spring and fall. Nacho's, however, is a bit different. The restaurant is in a downtown building. I'm not sure if anyone can say the

same, but the first thing I noticed about the restaurant was that there ~~is~~ no
^{are}

windows. The place seems stuffy and enclosed. There are few decorations

on the walls, nothing that stands out to me, anyway. The entire restaurant

is in one large room~~.~~ Stuffed with tables and booths. When Pueblo allowed
^{, s}

smoking in establishments~~.~~ The room had a smoky hue that hung in the air,
^{, t}

apparently from poor ventilation.

Service is possibly the most important factor when choosing a restaurant,

second only to the way the food tastes. Jorge's waitstaff and bussers are well

trained and courteous. First, you are greeted by a hostess who actually knows

the specials and waits by the door without having to be flagged down. The

bussers immediately follow the hostess by taking your drink and appetizer

order, and it is then the bartender ~~that~~ brings you your drinks, if you ordered
^{who}

from the bar. The waitperson is prompt in taking your order and makes the

proper suggestions and requests. The food service is also prompt and exactly

how you ordered~~,~~ in contrast~~.~~ Nacho's is lacking the service department. We
^{. I} [,]

were not greeted by a hostess promptly and had to wait by a door with a large

12-person party before we were asked if we had been helped. Once seated,

we didn't receive our drink order immediately and when ~~they~~ did come, the
^{the server}

majority of the people at the table had to swap drinks with the person sitting

next to ~~them~~. The food took approximately 45 minutes to arrive and either
^{him or her}

was cold or had been sitting under the heat lamp too long.

Whether you are entertaining out-of-town guests, looking for a quick

dining experience, or just have a craving for traditional Mexican cuisine,

I would recommend Jorge's Sombrero restaurant over Nacho's. Although the

cuisine and prices are similar, the atmosphere and service at Jorge's ~~is~~ far
^{are}

superior to that of Nacho's.

CHAPTER 19

Editing for Verb Use

YOUR GOALS

1. Use verb tenses correctly.

2. Recognize and use verb forms according to tense, voice, and mood.

3. Use troublesome verbs correctly.

4. Recognize and correct shifts in tense, voice, and mood.

5. Recognize and identify types of verbals.

"They've a temper, some

of them—particularly verbs:

they're the proudest—

adjectives you can do anything

with, but not verbs—however,

I can manage the whole lot

of them!"

■ **Lewis Carroll** ■

The following letter was written by an employee to her supervisor to find out why she did not receive a promotion.

Dear Mr. Burk,

I enjoyed the interview, and it was interesting to share my ideas with the management team. I'm sorry I did not get the vacant position, but I understand that you gotten many applications from qualified employees in our company. However, as my friend and my immediate supervisor, I wish you would tell me what I should of did differently so I can improve.

In my letter of application, I begun by explaining the qualities that make me a strong candidate for the position. I mention my experience, my people skills, and my organizational skills. I also, emphasized that I brang a lot of ideas that the company implemented and that I had went to most of the professional development workshops the company recommends.

During the interview, I focused on my motivation. I pointed out that no one would ever see me laying around when there's work to be done. Many times I could of took off for illness, but I came to work because I knew how important it is to meet our deadlines.

I trust your advice. I hope to hear from you soon.

Yours truly,

Norma Horvath

LET'S *warm up!*

You may have heard your international friends speak about how hard it is to learn English. One reason for this difficulty is the English verb system. For example, how would you explain the difference between "I eat" and "I'm eating"? After all, each seems to indicate present time. Think about a problem that most English learners would encounter when using verbs and tenses. Then write a paragraph explaining the difficulty and offering a possible solution.

Geri Engberg/Image Works

Companies, businesses, and organizations have certain expectations of the type of written communications appropriate to the profession. If the management team members read this letter filled with grammatical errors, they would probably feel that they had made the right decision in not giving Norma the promotion. Would Norma be taken seriously by other businesses or colleagues if she sent written communications containing similar errors?

Often, students don't realize their own difficulties in using verb forms. If you are such a writer, use this chapter to broaden your awareness of the English verb system.

UNDERSTANDING VERBS

Every complete sentence you write should contain at least one verb, whether stated or understood. Verbs are the hearts of sentences: they tell the reader what is happening, what has happened, and what will happen. Since verbs indicate both action and time, verbs change in form according to the idea you want to express: *speak, speaks, speaking, spoke, spoken.*

A verb expresses its point in three ways:

1. Physical actions: *speak, jump, climb, cook, clean, fight*
2. Mental or emotional expressions: *believe, think, love, hate*
3. No action but the state of the subject: *is, was, seem, appear*

Often, writers add suffixes, such as *-ify, -ize,* or *-en,* to change nouns and adjectives into verbs:

Beauty = Beautify   Final = Finalize   Weak = Weaken

As a writer, you should be able to recognize verbs, their function in your sentences, and their impact on your writing.

Verb Forms

The base of all verbs, with the exception of the verb *be,* takes four forms to express all tenses.

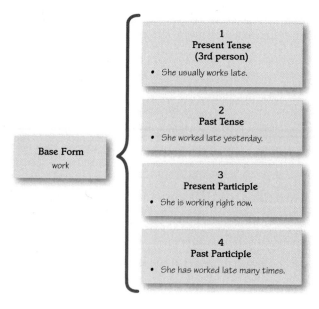

Base Form
work

1
**Present Tense
(3rd person)**
• She usually works late.

2
Past Tense
• She worked late yesterday.

3
Present Participle
• She is working right now.

4
Past Participle
• She has worked late many times.

The past tense and past participle of regular verbs are formed by adding the suffix *-ed* or *-d* (*wanted, traced*). Although most verbs are regular, English has many irregular verbs, which do not follow a consistent pattern as regular verbs do. The following list classifies irregular verbs by the types of changes they undergo in their past and past participle forms. This grouping may help you remember them, as well as help you spell them correctly.

Irregular Verbs by Types of Changes		
Group 1. The following verbs take *-en* in the past participle:		
Base/Present	**Past**	**Past Participle**
bite	bit	bitten
break	broke	broken
choose	chose	chosen
drive	drove	driven
eat	ate	eaten
forget	forgot	forgotten
get	got	gotten
give	gave	given
hide	hid	hidden
see	saw	seen
speak	spoke	spoken
steal	stole	stolen
write	wrote	written
Group 2. The following verbs take *-ought* or *-aught* in the past and the past participle:		
Base/Present	**Past**	**Past Participle**
bring	brought	brought
buy	bought	bought
teach	taught	taught
think	thought	thought
Group 3. The following verbs take *-ept* in the past and the past participle:		
Base/Present	**Past**	**Past Participle**
keep	kept	kept
sleep	slept	slept
sweep	swept	swept

Continued

Group 4. The following verbs change to *-ew* in the past and *-awn* or *-own* in the past participle:

Base/Present	Past	Past Participle
blow	blew	blown
grow	grew	grown
know	knew	known
throw	threw	thrown

Group 5. The following verbs change to *-ed* in the past and the past participle:

Base/Present	Past	Past Participle
feed	fed	fed
lead	led	led
speed	sped	sped

Group 6. The following verbs have the same present tense and past participle form:

Base/Present	Past	Past Participle
become	became	become
come	came	come
run	ran	run

Group 7. The past and past participle forms of the following verbs make minor spelling changes to the base:

Base/Present	Past	Past Participle
build	built	built
feel	felt	felt
find	found	found
hold	held	held
lose	lost	lost
make	made	made
meet	met	met
pay	paid	paid
send	sent	sent
stand	stood	stood
strike	struck	struck
swing	swung	swung
tell	told	told

Group 8. All three forms are the same for the following verbs:

Base/Present	Past	Past Participle
cost	cost	cost
cut	cut	cut
hit	hit	hit
hurt	hurt	hurt
put	put	put
read	read	read
shut	shut	shut
spread	spread	spread
wet	wet	wet

Group 9. Each tense has a different form for the following verbs:

Base/Present	Past	Past Participle
begin	began	begun
do	did	done
drink	drank	drunk
go	went	gone
ring	rang	rung
sing	sang	sung
swim	swam	swum
wear	wore	worn

PRACTICE 19-1

For each item, use the base of the verb given in parentheses to fill in the correct past or past participle form of the verb.

1. By the time you arrive, the guest speaker will have _given_ (give) her speech.
2. Yesterday, nobody _came_ (come) to pick up our mail.
3. I had already _begun_ (begin) my essay when she arrived.
4. My wife has _thrown_ (throw) out all my old, comfortable shirts.
5. The professor _froze_ (freeze) when he saw my 50-page report.
6. Yesterday, Mike _swam_ (swim) the length of the lake.
7. The barn has been _blown_ (blow) down by the hurricane.
8. My short story has been _chosen_ (choose) as the recipient of the award.
9. A few trees _fell_ (fall) on the shed during last night's strong wind.
10. Who has _drunk_ (drink) the wine I left in the refrigerator?

Auxiliary (Helping) Verbs

Another group of verbs is attached to main verbs to complete their meaning. They are called *auxiliary verbs* or *helping verbs*. Together with the main verb, they form the *verb phrase*. Auxiliary verbs are classified as either primary or modal.

Primary Auxiliary Verbs

Primary auxiliary verbs are combined with main verbs to help convey the tense of the main verb.

Base	Form		Function	Example
be	Present tense	*am, is, are*	1. Show continuous action	He is opening the window.
	Past tense	*was, were*		
	Present participle	*being*	2. Form passive voice	The window was opened by him.
	Past participle	*been*		
have	Present tense	*have, has*	Form the perfect tenses of verbs	I have seen this movie several times.
	Past tense	*had*		
	Present participle	*having*		
	Past participle	*had*		
do	Present tense	*do, does*	1. Form questions	Do you know him?
	Past tense	*did*	2. Form negatives	I did not know.
	Present participle	*doing*	3. Make emphasis	I do want you to leave.
	Past participle	*done*	4. Indicate concession	He was wrong, but he did apologize.

Modal Auxiliary Verbs

Modal auxiliaries add meaning to the main verb. They help the main verb express such judgments as necessity, obligation, or possibility about the occurrence of events.

Modal Form	Meaning	Example
can	1. Express ability 2. Express possibility	1. I can do this. 2. We can achieve these goals if we all work together.
could	1. Show ability in the past 2. Express possibility 3. Make a suggestion	1. I used to feel that I could do just about anything. 2. I could help you if you let me. 3. You could just ignore the problem.
may	1. Request permission 2. Express possibility	1. May I leave early? 2. I may leave early today.

Modal Form	Meaning	Example
might	Express possibility	I might leave early if no one notices.
will	1. Express future time 2. Show determination 3. Express a demand	1. He will leave tomorrow. 2. With my motivation, I will succeed. 3. You will follow my instructions immediately.
would	Make a polite request	Would you mind taking notes for me?
shall	1. Show future time (formal) 2. Show determination 3. Express a demand	1. I shall see you then. 2. We shall succeed. 3. You shall return my property.
should	1. Show expectation 2. Give advice	1. You should be able to download the information now. 2. You should talk to your adviser.
must	1. Show possibility 2. Give a command 3. Express necessity	1. You must have dialed the wrong number. 2. You must submit an application with your résumé. 3. We must get to the post office on time.
ought to	1. Give advice 2. Show expectation	1. You ought to apologize. 2. After studying, we ought to do well on the test.

Modal auxiliaries cannot act as main verbs. They can only support main verbs. A sentence such as "People must" would make no sense. Must *what?* The verb is incomplete. Also, the base of a verb, whether a main verb or a primary auxiliary, follows the modal.

He <u>may</u> <u>speak</u> to her.
He <u>may be</u> <u>speaking</u> to her now.

A verb phrase may have a maximum of three auxiliaries.

They <u>might have been</u> <u>taking</u> the test.

The diverse levels of meaning between and among modal auxiliaries are complex and thus confusing to many nonnative speakers of English. In some instances, modals are interchangeable and may have the same meaning in both present and past time, for example, *may* and *might.* The shades and subtle meanings of these auxiliaries are embedded into our culture.

PRACTICE 19-2

Underline the verb phrase in each of the following sentences. Remember that the verb phrase consists of the main verb and all auxiliary verbs.

1. They <u>did go</u> to Europe together.
2. You <u>should have seen</u> her performance.
3. As of next August, I <u>will have been working</u> here for 10 years.
4. Richard <u>has been revising</u> his essay all weekend.

5. You really <u>ought to invite</u> as many people as possible to tomorrow's charity.
6. Then <u>will</u> you <u>be delivering</u> the documents in person?
7. The check <u>may have been given</u> to him by mistake.
8. I<u>'ve been working</u> all night.
9. <u>Does</u> he <u>work</u> here?
10. We <u>must report</u> the incident to Human Resources as quickly as possible.

Note: In English, there are no word combinations such as *could of, should of, might of,* or *must of.* These types of errors are probably the result of the pronunciation of the contractions *could've, should've, might've,* and *must've.*

Constructing Verb Tenses

We use verbs to show when actions take place. For this purpose, verbs go through various transformations. For example, the verb *take* has three principal forms: *take, took,* and *taken.* With these three forms and the help of auxiliary verbs, you can construct all tenses.

	Person	Verb		Person	Verb
PRESENT TENSE	I	take	**PRESENT PROGRESSIVE**	I	am taking
	you	take		you	are taking
	he, she, it	takes		he, she, it	is taking
	we	take		we	are taking
	they	take		they	are taking
PAST TENSE	I	took	**PAST PROGRESSIVE**	I	was taking
	you	took		you	were taking
	he, she, it	took		he, she, it	was taking
	we	took		we	were taking
	they	took		they	were taking
FUTURE TENSE	I	will take	**FUTURE PROGRESSIVE**	I	will be taking
	you	will take		you	will be taking
	he, she, it	will take		he, she, it	will be taking
	we	will take		we	will be taking
	they	will take		they	will be taking
PRESENT PERFECT TENSE	I	have taken	**PRESENT PERFECT PROGRESSIVE**	I	have been taking
	you	have taken		you	have been taking
	he, she, it	has taken		he, she, it	has been taking
	we	have taken		we	have been taking
	they	have taken		they	have been taking

	Person	Verb			Person	Verb
PAST PERFECT TENSE	I	had taken	**PAST PERFECT PROGRESSIVE**		I	had been taking
	you	had taken			you	had been taking
	he, she, it	had taken			he, she, it	had been taking
	we	had taken			we	had been taking
	they	had taken			they	had been taking
FUTURE PERFECT TENSE	I	will have taken	**FUTURE PERFECT PROGRESSIVE**		I	will have been taking
	you	will have taken			you	will have been taking
	he, she, it	will have taken			he, she, it	will have been taking
	we	will have taken			we	will have been taking
	they	will have taken			they	will have been taking

UNDERSTANDING VERBS

English has six verb tenses to indicate when an action occurs (or doesn't occur), and each has a progressive form to indicate continuous action. With a few exceptions, the first three tenses—present, past, and future—offer little difficulty to most students. However, many students are easily confused and often avoid or misuse the three perfect tenses. With some practice and careful editing, these errors disappear.

Tense	Most Common Uses	Example
Present	1. Express habitual action 2. Present statements of fact 3. Convey an event that exists the moment you're speaking 4. Express the future in a clause beginning with *after*, *before*, or *when*	1. I go to class every Monday and Wednesday. 2. Water consists of hydrogen and oxygen. 3. I know who you are. 4. Before we meet, we'll ask Janet to research the problem.
Past	Express an action that started and concluded at a specific time in the past	I moved to Canada last month.
Future *will* + base	1. Express an action that will occur in the future 2. State a promise	1. They will leave sometime next week. 2. I'll wait here for you.

PRACTICE 19-3

Fill in the present, past, or future tense of the verb in parentheses. Be sure to use the correct form of the irregular verb.

The first time I __discovered__ (discover) my secret Shangri-La __was__ (is) this summer. I __was riding__ (ride) my horse in the woods on a sultry day when I __stumbled__ (stumble) upon a flat-topped rock about the size of a park bench. The rock __sat__ (sit) in the middle of a small clearing surrounded by aspen trees. I __was__ (is) hot and __decided__ (decide) to stop for a rest. As I __stopped__ (stop) to catch my breath, I __took__ (take) in my immediate surroundings. At the foot of the rock __lay__ (lie) a twisted mass of dense groundcover. The aspen trees at the edge of the clearing __glittered__ (glitter) with millions of silver, heart-shaped leaves that __fluttered__ (flutter) like butterflies in the breeze. Although blocked from my view, I __heard__ (hear) the lowing cattle in the valley below.

The perfect tenses are a bit more complicated. As you read the information, refer to the table that follows, which illustrates main uses of the perfect tenses.

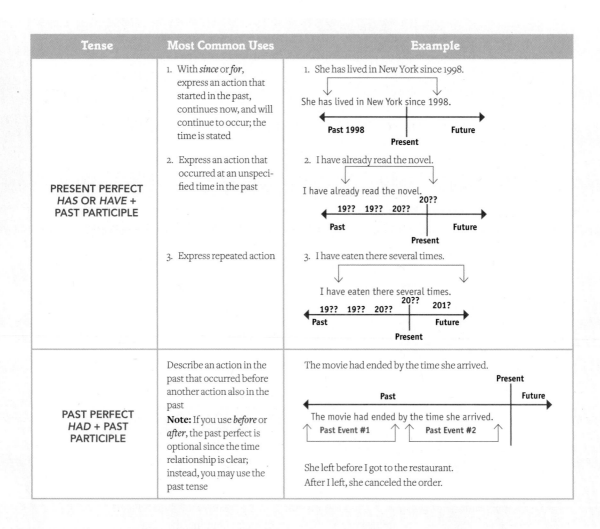

Tense	Most Common Uses	Example
PRESENT PERFECT *HAS* OR *HAVE* + PAST PARTICIPLE	1. With *since* or *for*, express an action that started in the past, continues now, and will continue to occur; the time is stated 2. Express an action that occurred at an unspecified time in the past 3. Express repeated action	1. She has lived in New York since 1998. 2. I have already read the novel. 3. I have eaten there several times.
PAST PERFECT *HAD* + PAST PARTICIPLE	Describe an action in the past that occurred before another action also in the past **Note:** If you use *before* or *after*, the past perfect is optional since the time relationship is clear; instead, you may use the past tense	The movie had ended by the time she arrived. She left before I got to the restaurant. After I left, she canceled the order.

Tense	Most Common Uses	Example
FUTURE PERFECT *WILL + HAVE +* *PAST PARTICIPLE*	1. Describe an action that will be completed in the future before another action takes place	1. I will have graduated by the time you return from Europe. **Present** Past — Future I will have graduated · · · by the time you return from Europe. Future Event #1 · · · Future Event #2
	2. Indicate an action that will be completed before a specific time in the future	2. I will have received my degree by next semester. **Present** Past — Future — 20?? I will have received my degree · · · by next semester. Future Event #1 · · · Future Event #2

Keeping Tense Consistent

The rule here is quite simple: don't shift tenses in the middle of a sentence or paragraph. As long as the time frame is the same, maintain tense consistency.

SHIFTS IN TENSE:	*Past* · · · *Past* · · · *Present* Once inside, he <u>hid</u> the package, <u>walked</u> toward the patio, and <u>calls</u> his wife.
CONSISTENT:	*Past* · · · *Past* · · · *Past* Once inside, he <u>hid</u> the package, <u>walked</u> toward the patio, and <u>called</u> his wife.

OR

Present · · · *Present* · · · *Present*
Once inside, he <u>hides</u> the package, <u>walks</u> toward the patio, and <u>calls</u> his wife.

However, when you clearly indicate a change in time frame from one action to another, it's necessary to shift tense.

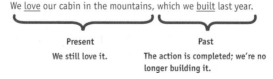

We <u>love</u> our cabin in the mountains, which we <u>built</u> last year.

Present — We still love it.

Past — The action is completed; we're no longer building it.

Most errors in shifts occur when a sentence has more than one clause.

SHIFTS IN TENSE:	*Past* · · · *Past* · · · *Past* When he <u>heard</u> that he <u>didn't</u> get the position, he <u>lowered</u> his *Present* head and <u>attempts</u> to smile.
CONSISTENT:	*Past* · · · *Past* · · · *Past* When he <u>heard</u> that he <u>didn't</u> get the position, he <u>lowered</u> his *Past* head and <u>attempted</u> to smile.

Check each sentence for shifts in tense. If the sentence is correct, write "C" for correct on the line provided; if the sentence contains a shift, cross out the shift and write the correct verb form on the line. Remember that when a sentence clearly indicates a change in time frame from one action to another, it needs to shift tense.

_____rang_____ 1. While Sara was taking the test, her cell phone ~~rings~~.

__will have visited__ 2. Most of us ~~will visit~~ the resort by the time the summer ends.

_____didn't_____ 3. The students constantly complained about the attendance policy, but when they had a chance to voice their feelings, they ~~don't~~ show up.

_____came_____ 4. I heard a loud crash after my roommate ~~comes~~ in to ask me for a loan.

_____C_____ 5. I stumbled over rocks and dried branches and then realized I was on the wrong path.

Action Verbs and Linking Verbs

You should now be quite familiar with auxiliary verbs and their role in building sentences, so we turn our attention to action and linking verbs. Recognizing action and linking verbs helps you proofread your essays for adjective, adverb, and pronoun usage, which we cover in later chapters.

Action Verbs: Transitive and Intransitive

You already know that verbs express action and that this action can be physical, mental or emotional, or a state of being rather than an actual action.

PHYSICAL:	Luke <u>sang</u> at the school's talent show.
MENTAL OR EMOTIONAL:	Sammy <u>loves</u> his iPod.
STATE OF BEING:	I <u>will</u> always <u>be</u> here for you.

Action verbs are classified as either transitive or intransitive. When a verb is *transitive*, the verb is followed by an object. This object, known as the *direct object*, receives or benefits from the action of the verb.

Verb   Direct Object

For her birthday, Steve <u>took</u> his <u>mother</u> to her favorite restaurant.

In this example, the subject (*Steve*) does the action (*took*) and the object (*mother*) receives the action.

Verb   Direct Object

The mechanic <u>repaired</u> my <u>car</u> quickly.

Here, the subject (*mechanic*) does the action (*repaired*) and the object (*car*) receives or benefits from the action.

This sentence pattern (subject + transitive verb + direct object) is not difficult to identify. A simple way to find the direct object of a verb is to ask *whom* or *what* of the verb. If you get an answer, you have a transitive verb.

> The salesclerk ignored the rude customer.
> [Read up to the verb and ask: The clerk ignored *whom?* A *customer;* therefore, the verb is transitive.]
> I purchased a car last year.
> [I purchased *what?* A *car;* the verb is transitive].

When you have two objects of a verb, don't mistake the indirect object for the direct object. Placed before the direct object, the indirect object indicates to whom or for whom the action of the verb is being done.

> Indirect Object   Direct Object
> The manager gave the <u>employees</u> a <u>raise</u>.

To have an indirect object, the sentence must first have a direct object. You can test the connection of the indirect and direct object by converting the indirect object into the object of the preposition.

> Prepositional Phrase
> The manager gave a raise [to the <u>employees</u>].

In a sense, an indirect object is a prepositional phrase in which the prepositions *to* and *for* are understood.

> I.O.   D.O.   I.O.   D.O.
> Jason bought <u>Lisa</u> a <u>car</u> but handed <u>me</u> the <u>keys</u>.

> D.O.   Prepositional Phrase   D.O.   Prepositional Phrase
> Jason bought a <u>car</u> [for <u>Lisa</u>] but handed the <u>keys</u> [to <u>me</u>].

Intransitive verbs also express action; however, they are not followed by an object. If you apply the whom/what test, you won't receive a correct answer; instead, you will get an answer to *how, when,* or *where,* or no answer since there's no object to receive the action of the verb:

> The child behaved rudely all evening.
> [The child behaved *whom? what?* There's no appropriate answer; the verb is intransitive.]
> Upset, the professor spoke harshly to the class.
> [The professor spoke *whom? what?* There's no appropriate answer.] Also, "to the class" is a prepositional phrase. The direct object is never the object of the preposition. [The verb is intransitive.]

Although there are many verbs that are either transitive or intransitive, some verbs can be both, depending on their context.

> Linda sang a beautiful song.
> Linda sang in front of a live audience.

By simply applying the whom/what test, you can quickly make the distinction:

- Linda sang *[whom? what?]* a beautiful song.
  [The verb is transitive.]
- Linda sang *[whom? what?]* in front of a live audience.
  [The verb is intransitive.]

Bridging Knowledge

See Chapter 20 for information on using adjectives with linking verbs.

Linking Verbs

Linking verbs form the final group of verbs. They differ in that they don't take direct objects; instead, the verb is followed by a *complement* (adjective or noun) that goes back to the subject, either identifying or describing the subject.

Gene is a computer hacker.
Subject   L. V.   Noun Complement

In the preceding sentence, the complement is a noun identifying the subject (*Richard = computer hacker*).

With computers, Gene is brilliant.
Subject   L. V. Adjective Complement

In the preceding case, the complement is an adjective describing *Gene*.

Unlike action verbs, English has a limited number of linking verbs. The following groups of words are often used as linking verbs:

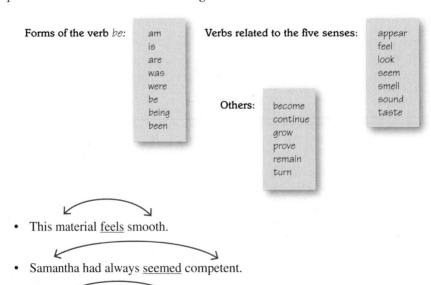

Forms of the verb *be*:	Verbs related to the five senses:	
am		appear
is		feel
are		look
was		seem
were		smell
be		sound
being	Others: become	taste
been	continue	
	grow	
	prove	
	remain	
	turn	

- This material *feels* smooth.

- Samantha had always *seemed* competent.

- Joe and Bob may *remain* friends.

- After much work, Susan will *become* our president.

However, the tricky part is that most linking verbs can also serve as action verbs.

- Jonathan <u>smelled</u> the cake.

- The cake <u>smelled</u> delicious.

In the first sentence, *cake* does not identify or describe the subject *Jonathan*. The verb *smelled* is an action verb; it's a transitive verb with a direct object, *cake*. In the second sentence, the adjective *delicious* describes the subject *cake*: the verb *smelled* is, therefore, a linking verb. Fortunately, there's also an easy way to determine whether a verb is action or linking. Try substituting the linking verb with the verb *am, is,* or *are.* If the sentence makes sense, most likely you have a linking verb:

> Sandy <u>looks</u> at the sauce curiously.
> [Is the verb linking or action? Substitute *is* for the verb.]
> Sandy <u>is</u> at the sauce curiously.
> [The meaning isn't logical; the complement does not identify or describe the subject. Therefore, this is an action verb; in fact, it's an intransitive verb.]
> Sandy <u>looks</u> curious.
> [Is the verb linking or action? Substitute *is* for the verb.]
> Sandy <u>is</u> curious.
> [The meaning is logical; the complement does identify or describe the subject. Therefore, this is a linking verb.]

Unfortunately, this test does not work with the verb *appear*:

> Sandy <u>appeared</u> at my door.
> Sandy <u>is</u> at my door.

The second sentence makes sense, so you need to examine the function of the verb. Is there a complement describing or identifying Sandy? Clearly, both verbs in these sentences are intransitive action verbs. Contrast the preceding sentences with the following:

Sandy <u>appeared</u> upset.
Subject   L. V.   Adjective Complement

PRACTICE 19-5

Underline the verb or verb phrase in each of the following sentences. On the line provided, label the verbs as AV for action verb or LV for linking verb.

_AV_ 1. During the storm, our cabin <u>didn't offer</u> much protection.

_LV_ 2. Having misplaced her paper, Virginia <u>became</u> depressed.

_AV_ 3. She <u>smelled</u> the delicious aroma coming from the restaurant's kitchen windows.

LV 4. The leaves <u>were turning</u> red, announcing the changing season.

AV 5. Spotting the prey, the hunter <u>sounded</u> his horn.

LV 6. Betsy <u>looked</u> uncomfortable in her new suit.

LV 7. I <u>have been</u> here for more than an hour.

AV 8. Although doubtful of Mike's culinary skills, Gayle <u>tastes</u> the soup.

AV 9. Confused and nervous, the students <u>looked</u> at the pop quiz.

AV 10. After his service learning experience, Miguel <u>decided</u> to become a social worker.

Working with Troublesome Verb Sets

Three sets of verbs give most students problems: *lie–lay*, *sit–set*, and *rise–raise*. However, by simply applying your knowledge of transitive and intransitive verbs, you no longer need to wonder whether you're using the correct form.

Lie versus *Lay*

Lie and *lay* give people more difficulty than any of the irregular verbs. *Lie* means to rest or recline, whereas *lay* means to place. Each verb has a different meaning and can't be used interchangeably, although they often are. *Lie* is an intransitive verb. Since you have to lie (rest) somewhere, the word or phrase that follows this verb often answers *where, how,* and *why* rather than *what;* there's no direct object.

- She lies [where?] on the couch.
- She lies [how?] quietly.
- She lies down [why?] to take a nap.

In contrast, *lay*, meaning to place or put, requires an object since something or someone has to be placed. This verb requires a receiver of the action, a direct object.

- He laid [who?] the baby in the crib.
- He lays [what?] the magazines on the table.

Compare the forms of *lie* and *lay* in the following conjugation.

Tense	Lie (rest) Intransitive Verb	Lay (place) Transitive Verb
Present	She lies on the beach often.	She lays the tiles with no difficulty.
Present progressive	She is lying on the beach now.	She is laying the tiles in the kitchen first.
Past	She lay on the beach last night.	She laid the tiles unevenly.
Past progressive	She was lying on the beach all night.	She was laying the tiles when the doorbell rang.

Tense	Lie (rest) Intransitive Verb	Lay (place) Transitive Verb
Future	She will lie on the beach tomorrow.	She will lay the tiles carefully.
Future progressive	She will be lying on the beach all afternoon.	She will be laying tiles all week.
Present perfect	She has lain there since yesterday.	She has laid the tiles with no assistance.
Present perfect progressive	She has been lying on the beach all day.	She has been laying the tiles since this morning.
Past perfect	She had lain on the beach all night.	She had just laid the final tile when she heard a crackling sound.
Past perfect progressive	She had been lying on the beach all night.	She had been laying the tiles until he walked in.
Future perfect	She will have lain on the beach for 6 hours by noon.	She will have laid the tiles for several hours.
Future perfect progressive	She will have been lying on the beach for 6 hours by noon.	She will have been laying the tiles for several hours.

Notice that the past tense of *lie* is *lay*, which is the present tense of *lay*. Don't let this similarity confuse you. Ask *who* or *what* to determine whether the verb is transitive or intransitive, and then make your choice.

Sit versus *Set*

Sit and *set* follow the same rules of transitive and intransitive verb. Just keep in mind that you have to sit (rest) somewhere and set (place) something.

- Dena sat [where?] outside the office all afternoon.
- Dena set [what?] the plates on the table.

Review some of the forms of this often-confused pair of verbs.

Tense	Sit (rest) Intransitive Verb	Set (place) Transitive Verb
Present	He sits quietly in class.	He set the essay on the shelf.
Present progressive	He is sitting quietly now.	He is setting the agenda for the meeting.
Past	He sat in the back of the room.	He set the time of the meeting.
Present perfect progressive	He has sat there for 3 hours.	He has set the clock for our trip.

Rise versus *Raise*

When something rises, it goes upward, ascends, increases, or elevates; when you raise something, you lift, increase, or elevate it. Although both *rise* and *raise* have the general meaning of moving upward, the main difference, as in the previous verbs, is that *rise* is intransitive and *raise* is transitive.

Rise (Intransitive):

- The sun rises [where?] in the east and sets in the west.
- The temperature rose [how?] another 10 degrees.
- Finally, Jay is rising [where?] from the sofa.
- My grandparents' business has risen [how?] unexpectedly.

Raise (Transitive):

- My grandparents raise [what?] cattle back in Kansas.
- The gas station raised [what?] the price of gas again.
- He is raising [whom?] the child above the water level.
- His solution has raised [what?] new problems.

Review the some of the forms of this troublesome pair of verbs.

Tense	Rise (move upward) Intransitive Verb	Raise (lift) Transitive Verb
Present	The smoke rises slowly.	She raises her hand to ask a question.
Present progressive	The smoke is rising slowly.	She raises her hand to speak.
Past	The smoke rose slowly.	She raised her hand to answer.
Present perfect progressive	The smoke has risen to the top.	She has raised her hand, so we called her forward.

PRACTICE 19-6

Edit the following paragraphs for incorrect use of verb forms, wrong choice of troublesome verbs, and shifts in tenses.

I was sitting down reading a letter when I remembered that my favorite

TV program was on. I ~~raised~~ ^{rose} from my seat and picked up the remote control,

which was ~~laying~~ ^{lying} on the floor. Just then, the phone rang. It was my wife,

Sophia, telling me that she wished she hadn't ~~went~~ ^{gone} to the conference. She

said that she had already ~~drove~~ ^{driven} 30 miles and still had a long way to go before

reaching Riverdale. She regretted having left in such a rush and lamented not having ~~drank~~ [drunk] the cup of coffee I prepared and laid on the counter this morn-

ing. I was sure she would take it if I ~~sat~~ [set] it there.

I could tell she was worried about the approaching storm. For the last

couple of days, the wind had ~~blew~~ [blown] hard and the clouds had ~~began~~ [begun] to drift in.

As a district manager, Sophia has to travel quite often. She really doesn't

mind. She enjoys working and plans to be president of her company within

5 years. Her hard work has ~~rose~~ [raised] the standards for all employees in her area,

and as a result, she has ~~rose~~ [risen] to a position of power and authority quickly. She

loves her job. She has received many job offers but has always ~~chose~~ [chosen] to stay

with her present company.

I decided to check the weather, so I ~~set~~ [sat] in front of my computer and

~~sat~~ [set] my remote control by the mouse so that I wouldn't misplace it. The

weather report didn't sound promising. Sophia was heading toward a tornado,

and here I was ~~laying~~ [lying] around the house in my bathrobe, worrying about

losing my remote control. Suddenly, the phone ~~rung~~ [rang]. What a relief. She heard

the weather report on the radio and decided to turn back. I ~~have~~ [had] better look

busy when she gets here.

Active versus Passive Voice

Verbs are said to be in the active voice when the subject does the action of the verb.

The manager <u>announced</u> the new policy.

However, a verb is in the passive voice when the action of the verb is not done by its subject but rather by some other agent either mentioned, implied, or unknown.

The new policy <u>was announced</u> today. ?

Most instructors prefer that you use the active voice when you write unless you have a specific reason for using the passive voice. Usually, students use the passive unknowingly, so an important step in editing your papers is to recognize an active sentence from a passive one. Three things happen when changing a sentence from active to passive voice:

1. The subject of the active sentence may become the object of the preposition in the passive voice. Sometimes the prepositional phrase containing the "doer" of the action may be omitted if the writer feels that naming the agent is unnecessary.
2. The object of the active voice becomes the subject of the passive voice.
3. The verb in the passive voice consists of a form of the verb *be* (*am, is, are, was, were, be, been*) plus the past participle form of the main verb.

Examine this transformation:

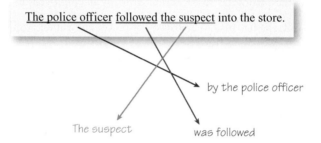

The police officer followed the suspect into the store.

by the police officer

The suspect

was followed

The suspect was followed by the police officer into the store.

Only transitive verbs can be transformed to the passive voice since the object of the verb becomes the subject. If you try to perform the preceding transformation on the following sentences, you can see that the results make no sense:

- We waited in the park all night. [intransitive verb; no passive possible]
- Ralph became president of the club. [linking verb; no passive possible]

Since the main verb of the passive voice is the past participle form, the verb *be* carries the tense of the action of the verb.

Tense	Passive Subject	Be Verb	Past Participle
Present	The ring	is	stolen.
Present progressive	The ring	is being	stolen.
Past	The ring	was	stolen.
Past progressive	The ring	was being	stolen.
Future	The ring	will be	stolen.
Present perfect	The ring	has been	stolen.
Past perfect	The ring	had been	stolen.
Future perfect	The ring	will have been	stolen.

As you probably noticed from the preceding conjugation, the passive transformation cannot be applied to all tenses or verbs. The passive voice in future progressive and perfect progressive is rare. Such constructions lead to awkward verb combinations such as *will be being, has been being,* or *will have been being.* In addition, some transitive verbs, such as *have, equal, mean,* and *lack,* cannot be used in the passive.

One weakness in many student essays is the overuse or ineffective use of the passive voice. Passive voice, if not used effectively, can make a writing style wordy and even obscure the meaning of the sentence.

PASSIVE VOICE:	The final exam was failed by only one student in our microbiology class.
ACTIVE VOICE:	Only one student in our microbiology class failed the final exam.

As you compare these two sentences, notice how wordy and awkward the passive voice is, whereas the active voice is more direct and focuses the reader's attention on what the student (the doer of the action) did, not on the object, the exam. Limiting your use of the passive voice does not mean you should always avoid it. It simply means that you should have a reason for its use; the passive voice, if used appropriately, can be quite effective. Therefore, once you have identified a passive construction in your essay, reconsider the choice you have made. Is there a reason you prefer the passive voice? Here are three basic justifications for using the passive voice:

1. To focus the reader's attention on the action rather than the agent.

> Every year, millions of people are given the wrong medication.

2. To describe an event where the agent is unknown.

> The trees were covered in ice.

3. To describe an event where the agent is unimportant.

> The results of the study were finally released this year.

The passive voice is more appropriate in technical writing, scientific writing, lab reports, or some mechanical process where the "doer" is not as important as the process itself. Compare the following:

PASSIVE VOICE:	Once the barrier was removed, the rate of water uptake was increased to 2.7 centimeters.
ACTIVE VOICE:	Once I removed the barrier, I increased the rate of water uptake to 2.7 centimeters.

PRACTICE 19-7

On the line provided, identify each sentence as A for active or as P for passive. If the sentence is passive, change it to active voice. **Hint:** Make sure that the sentence you identify as the passive voice has the three characteristics that signal a passive voice construction.

___P___ 1. The cake was sliced by Randy.

  Randy sliced the cake.

___P___ 2. Many novels were written by Ernest Hemingway.

  Ernest Hemingway wrote many novels.

  P   3. The salesclerk was bothered by the customer's sarcastic remarks.

      The customer's sarcastic remarks bothered the salesclerk.

  A   4. The class bully has intimidated my son on various occasions.

      _____

  P   5. The car was apparently vandalized by local teens during the night.

      Local teens apparently vandalized the car during the night.

Keeping Voice Consistent

Once you have determined the voice, make sure you're consistent; don't shift between active and passive voice without a reason. Examine the following example of a shift in voice.

SHIFT IN VOICE:	^{Active Voice} Leonard submitted his essay as soon as he was ^{Passive Voice} contacted by his instructor.
CONSISTENT:	^{Active Voice} Leonard submitted his essay as soon as his ^{Active Voice} instructor contacted him.

Verb Moods

A writer can express the action of a verb as a fact (ordinary statements), a command, or a possibility. The attitude that the verb expresses is known as *mood*. Verbs have three moods: indicative, imperative, and subjunctive.

Indicative

Most of your writing is in the indicative mood. When you state a fact, give an opinion, ask a question, or exclaim, you use the indicative mood.

FACT:	She bought a new outfit last week.
OPINION:	The outfit looks classy on you.
QUESTION:	Do you really think the outfit looks great?
EXCLAMATION:	How classy your outfit looks!

Imperative

You use the imperative mood when you give orders or instructions. Since the imperative is always in second person (*you*), the subject is usually omitted. This doesn't mean the sentence has no subject. The subject *you* is understood.

> <u>Leave</u> the room immediately.
>
> Please <u>hand out</u> these fliers.

One exception is a request using *let's*, meaning *let us*: "Let's leave immediately." The understood subject in this case is *we*.

Subjunctive

The subjunctive mood is slowly fading from the English language. However, in some situations, especially formal, the subjunctive mood is very much alive. Through the subjunctive, the verb can express an idea that is contrary to a fact, a wish, a desire, or a demand. This type of construction requires two clauses, and the subjunctive form of the verb occurs in the dependent clause. Generally, you can use the subjunctive in the following situations:

1. Use the subjunctive in *if* clauses to express conditions that are contrary to fact or not factual.

   > Lou would give you a raise <u>if he were manager</u>.
   > [Lou isn't the manager, so this condition isn't real.]

   > <u>If our country were to reduce its dependency on foreign oil</u>, our economy would be stable.
   > [This is merely a speculation and thus not real.]

   In this type of construction, the verb *were* is used in all persons:

   > If <u>I were</u> more assertive, I would get the promotion.
   > If <u>he were</u> a better dancer, his social life might improve.
   > If <u>we were</u> rich, we would be dining in Paris.
   > If <u>they were</u> interested, they would have applied.

2. Use the subjunctive in clauses starting with *as if* or *as though* when making judgments or speculating.

   > He acts <u>as if he were the manager.</u>
   > He talks <u>as though he were recording this conversation.</u>

3. Use the subjunctive in *that* clauses to express a wish; make a demand, suggestion, or request; or state urgency.

   > She wishes <u>that Joe were more responsible.</u>
   > I wish <u>(that) I were better prepared for this test.</u>

Note that sometimes the word *that* is understood.

The following verbs are used to make demands, suggestions, or requests. They are followed by the *that* clause and require the subjunctive. In this case, the subjunctive form is the base of the verb.

	advised	
	asked	
	commanded	**that** she **be** on time for the meeting.
	demanded	
	insisted	**that** she **find** another job.
Eugene	proposed	**that** she **do** the job according to the plan.
	recommended	
	requested	**that** she **be standing** there when we arrive.
	suggested	
	urged	

Some expressions indicating urgency or importance also take the subjunctive in the *that* clause.

	best	
	crucial	**that** she **be** on time for the meeting.
	essential	
It is	**imperative**	**that** she **find** another job.
	important	**that** she **do** the job according to the plan.
	necessary	
	urgent	**that** she **be standing** there when we arrive.
	vital	

4. Use the subjunctive in some common expressions.

Be that as it may   Please let me be
Come what may   Thanks be to God
Far be it from me

5. Use the negative correctly in the subjunctive.

The president proposed that all employees not accept gifts from clients.

6. Use the base of the verb *be* in the passive subjunctive.

The members demanded that you be nominated for the new position.

PRACTICE 19-8

On the line provided, identify whether the sentence is indicative, imperative, or subjunctive.

1. Let's go to the movies. <u>Imperative</u>
2. I really believed he was guilty. <u>Indicative</u>
3. Return the DVD by Friday. <u>Imperative</u>
4. The label states that there will be no penalty for late returns. <u>Indicative</u>
5. If I were you, I wouldn't risk it. <u>Subjunctive</u>
6. I suggest you leave the book on the desk. <u>Subjunctive</u>
7. Just leave us in peace while we get this project completed. <u>Imperative</u>
8. The officer demanded that I move my car immediately. <u>Subjunctive</u>
9. I wish that my essay were longer. <u>Subjunctive</u>
10. Scatter the seeds and wait for nature to take its course. <u>Imperative</u>

Keeping Mood Consistent

Just like tense and voice, mood also must be consistent. A shift in mood occurs when the writer starts writing on one mood and ends with another. The most common shifts are between indicative and imperative moods.

	Indicative Mood	Imperative Mood
SHIFT IN MOOD:	Law-abiding citizens generally follow social rules. For example, pay your taxes, pay your debts, and vote.	

	Indicative Mood	Indicative Mood

CONSISTENT: Law-abiding citizens generally follow social rules. For example, they pay their taxes, pay their debts, and vote.

SHIFT IN MOOD: *(Subjunctive Mood)* *(Indicative Mood)* If I were the governor, I am going to ban smoking in all public places.

CONSISTENT: *(Subjunctive Mood)* *(Subjunctive Mood)* If I were the governor, I would ban smoking in all public places.

PRACTICE 19-9

The following sentences contain shifts in tense, voice, or mood. Underline the shift and make the correction on the line provided.

1. Many superstitions abound in Chinese culture about brooms. Traditional Chinese culture holds that a spirit inhabits a broom, <u>so don't use it for games or in play</u>. Brooms should be only for cleaning the house, shop, or specific areas.

   <u>so the Chinese don't use it for games or in play</u>

2. Most Chinese will not use a broom for cleaning the household gods or altar; <u>they considered this disrespectful</u>.

   <u>they consider this disrespectful</u>

3. During the Spring Festival, Chinese custom prohibits the use of the broom for 3 days from New Year's Day since the Chinese <u>felt</u> that using it will sweep away the good luck the new year brings.

   <u>feel</u>

4. Beating a person with a broom will rain bad luck upon that person for years. However, if the person <u>were to rub</u> the injured part of the body, the curse will be lifted.

   <u>rubs</u>

5. The broom should never touch the head, <u>for bad luck will be brought by this</u>.

   <u>for this will bring bad luck</u>

Verbals

Verbals are verb forms, but they are not used as verbs. There are three types of verbals: infinitive, gerund, and participle. These verbal phrases function as adjectives, adverbs, or nouns. Since verbals consist of a verb form, occasionally students make the mistake of using a verbal as a complete sentence and thus causing a fragment, for example, "Believing that the problem was solved." An understanding of verbals can help you check your essay for fragments, edit for correctly placed modifiers, and punctuate your sentences correctly.

Infinitive Phrase

The *infinitive* is made up of the word *to* and the base of the verb: *to see, to run, to read.* The *infinitive phrase* is made up of the infinitive and its modifiers. The infinitive phrase can act as a noun, taking the position that nouns occupy in a sentence, or function as an adjective or an adverb. Review the following functions of the infinitive:

SUBJECT OF THE SENTENCE (NOUN):	To lie about my grade seemed pointless.
DIRECT OBJECT OF THE VERB (NOUN):	Jenny hopes to graduate this semester.
ADJECTIVE:	To get through his boring job, Rick thinks about the day he graduates.
ADVERB:	We are waiting to talk to the dean.

Occasionally, the *to* that signals the infinitive may be omitted.

Marvin doesn't dare [to] speak to his counselor about his grades.

The verb form of the infinitive may also be in the passive voice.

To be nominated for this position is a great honor.

Gerund Phrase

A *gerund* is a verb form used as a noun. The verb form of a gerund is in the present participle; thus, the gerund always ends in *-ing*. Since gerunds function as nouns, they occupy all positions that a noun occupies in a sentence.

SUBJECT OF A SENTENCE:	Talking loudly during a movie is rude.
OBJECT OF THE VERB:	She enjoys meeting new people.
OBJECT OF THE PREPOSITION:	Randy occupied his time by writing poetry.
SUBJECT COMPLEMENT AFTER A LINKING VERB:	His fondest memory was fishing in Colorado with his father.

The passive voice of the gerund takes the present participle form of the verb *be*.

Joshua hates being lectured to by his boss.

Participial Phrase

Participial phrases function as adjectives; thus, they modify nouns or pronouns. This type of verbal can take the present participle or the past participle form.

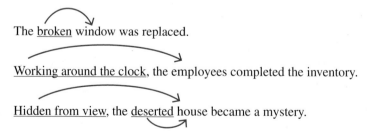

The broken window was replaced.

Working around the clock, the employees completed the inventory.

Hidden from view, the deserted house became a mystery.

The passive form of the participial phrase is often reduced to avoid a wordy style.

~~Having been~~ nominated various times, the candidate finally accepted.

PRACTICE 19-10

Underline the verbal phrase or phrases in each of the following sentences. On the line, indicate the type of verbal you underlined: I for infinitive, G for gerund, or P for participle.

<u>P</u>   1. <u>Hoping to be elected</u>, the candidate campaigned fiercely.

<u>G</u>   2. Ophelia always enjoyed <u>collecting flowers</u>.

<u>G</u>   3. <u>Identifying gerunds and participles</u> is an easy task.

<u>I</u>   4. <u>To watch the magician perform</u> is a great experience.

<u>P</u>   5. The car <u>approaching the stop sign</u> slowed down quickly.

<u>P</u>   6. We could see Dolores <u>sitting alone</u>.

<u>P</u>   7. <u>Acquitted by the jury</u>, the defendant was reinstated by the agency.

<u>P</u>   8. <u>Stumbling through the forest</u>, the camper finally found the trail.

<u>G</u>   9. My new lab partner does not like <u>writing his lab reports</u>.

<u>I</u>   10. Her plan <u>to increase student participation</u> shows great potential.

As you proofread your essay for verb use, address the following questions:
1. Are all your sentences in the correct tense?
2. Are the tenses consistent?
3. If you used various tenses, do you provide a context for the change in tense?
4. Did you use the correct forms of regular and irregular verbs?
5. Do you avoid unnecessary shifts in mood and voice?
6. If you used the passive voice, did you have a specific reason? Would the active voice be better?

REVIEW 19-1

Revise the following paragraphs for shifts in tense and errors in verb form and tense.

Scams on Our Highways

[1.]Consider this scenario: You're stuck in heavy traffic on a busy highway. [2.]Another car cuts off the driver in front of you, forcing him to slam on the brakes. [3.]You ~~tried~~ ^{try} to stop, but there's no time; you rear-end the guy in front of you. [4.]This may seem like an everyday accident, but not this time. [5.]It turns out that you've been had by a well-organized criminal ring that ~~sat~~ ^{set} the entire scam. [6.]This particular scam is called the *swoop and squat*. [7.]The first car "swoops" in while the second car "squats" in front of you. [8.]After the "accident," everyone in the car you rear-ended—usually crammed full of passengers—had ~~filed~~ ^{files} bogus injury claims with your insurance company. [9.]Each will complain ~~complains~~ of whiplash or other soft-tissue injuries, things difficult for doctors to confirm. [10.]These scammers may even go to crooked physical therapists, chiropractors, lawyers, or auto repair technicians to exaggerate their claims.

[11.]Staged accidents cost the insurance industry about $20 billion a year. [12.]These losses are ~~pass~~ passed on to all of us in the form of higher insurance rates. [13.]Consumers end up paying an average of $100 to 300 extra per car per year.

[14.]Similar "accident" scams abound. [15.] One scam to look out for is called the *drive down*. [16.]In this setup, you're attempting to merge when another driver waves you forward. [17.]Instead of letting you in, he slams into your car. [18.]When the police arrive, the other driver ~~denied~~ denies ever motioning to you. [19.]As a result, you're ticketed.

[20.]The *sideswipe* is equally effective. [21.]The scam ~~went~~ goes like this: as you round a corner at a busy intersection with multiple turn lanes, you drift slightly into the lane next to you. [22.]The car in that lane steps on the gas and sideswipes you. [23.]Again, you have ~~became~~ become a victim, although all evidence ~~indicate~~ indicates that you're responsible. [24.]Similar to the sideswipe, in the *T-bone* scam, you're crossing an intersection when a car coming from a side street accelerates and ~~hit~~ hits your car. [25.]When the police arrive, the driver and several planted "witnesses" ~~claimed~~ claim that you ran a red light or stop sign.

[26.]To help protect drivers from these schemes, law enforcement agencies have ~~ran~~ run their own cons. [27.]For example, last year in a sting called Operation Soft Tissue, a Chicago FBI agent posed as a corrupt lawyer and caught hundreds of these con artists and crooks red-handed. [28.]The subjects were tape recorded describing the manner in which they staged the collisions, how they ~~done~~ did the scheme with the participating attorneys and doctors, and how they divided the proceeds. [29.]The FBI has investigated more than 90 staged accident fraud cases over the past decade, and there's more to come.

(Adapted from http://www.fbi.gov, an official site of the U.S. Department of Justice, and http://sandiego.fbi.gov/twisted/twisted.htm).

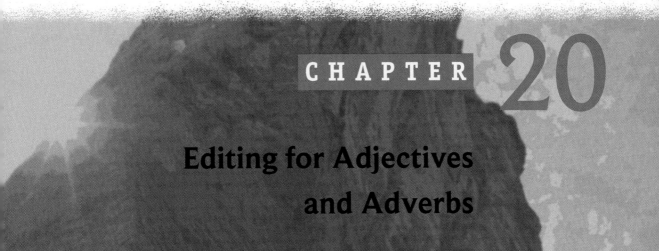

CHAPTER 20

Editing for Adjectives and Adverbs

YOUR GOALS

1. Identify adjectives and adverbs.

2. Use adjectives and adverbs correctly.

3. Revise sentences and paragraphs to correct errors in adjective and adverb usage.

"Don't tell me the moon is shining; show me the glint of light on broken glass."

■ Anton Chekhov ■

A college admissions officer has to assess the quality of the many high school applications that the school receives each year. The following paragraph is part of an application; the applicant is addressing her extracurricular activities in high school.

> I have been active at school and in the community during my junior and senior years in high school. For example, I am a starter on the women's soccer team, which did real good this past year, making it easy to reach the championship game of our league. My position is central defender, so I have to be ready to kick the ball firm and hard away from our goal if it goes past the midfield. Of the two central defenders, I am the best player. I also volunteer for the soup kitchen once a week, which entails cooking for people who can't hardly care for themselves. My other extracurricular activity is playing the piano for my church choir, my most favoritest activity of all. Not only do I attend rehearsals 3 days a week, but I also play every Sunday for our church services. As you can see, I am most proudest of my activities beyond the classroom.

LET's warm up!

Soccer is the most popular sport in the world. Study the action shot here and then describe the field, the players, and the action of the game. See the list of sensory words in Chapter 2, pages 23–24.

James Bosworth

This paragraph would have made a poor impression on the admissions officer because of its errors in adjective and adverb usage. The misuse of these two types of words can label the writer as uneducated and careless, creating a negative first impression. How many of you have winced when you heard such phrases as "He doesn't know nothing," "She performed good on her math test," or "She can't hardly spell her own name"? One error of this sort is enough for your reader or listener to assume that you lack the education and skills necessary for an academic or professional environment.

UNDERSTANDING ADJECTIVES AND ADVERBS

To help make writing concrete and effective, a writer relies on adjectives and adverbs. Nouns provide the content, and verbs provide the action; adjectives help the reader "see" the content by describing the nouns, and adverbs help the reader "feel" the action by emphasizing its intensity, frequency, and manner.

The following sentence consists mainly of nouns supplying the content and a verb providing the action:

> Content   Content Action   Content
> After his <u>comments</u>, the <u>manager</u> <u>left</u> the <u>employees</u>.

Below, note how the image of the first sentence builds as we add adjectives and adverbs.

> Adjective   Adjective   Adjective   Adverb
> After his <u>rude</u> and <u>inflammatory</u> comments, the <u>nervous</u> manager <u>very quickly</u>
> <u>left</u> the <u>angry</u> employees.   Adverb
>   Adjective

Notice how the final sentence paints a different picture than the first, more neutral and perhaps misleading, meaning. Through adjectives, we add concreteness to the content: the type of comments, the behavior of the manager, and the reaction of the employees. Through adverbs, we express the intensity and manner of the action.

Adjectives

Adjectives are the keys to specific and colorful writing, allowing you, as a writer, to specify size, shape, color, type, quantity, mood, and other general characteristics of the object, place, event, or person under discussion. You can identify adjectives easily by examining the position and the role they play in your sentences. As you review the examples and complete the practice exercises in this chapter, you'll be surprised by how much you already know about adjectives.

Describe or Modify Nouns

In grammar, the word *modify* means to limit or to qualify the meaning of a specific word. The main role of the adjective, then, is to limit and qualify nouns and pronouns.

> The smart consumer purchased three large plastic bins for the price of one.

Basically, adjectives accomplish their roles when performing one or more of the functions shown by the examples here.

1. Number	
Adjective	**Noun Modified**
three	pyramids
many	assignments
second	view
single	customer

2. Opinion or Judgment	
Adjective	**Noun Modified**
beautiful	day
difficult	task
noble	king
angry	manager

3. Size	
Adjective	**Noun Modified**
enormous	house
short	paragraph
brief	visit
tall	students

4. Age	
Adjective	**Noun Modified**
ancient	tomb
old	movie
contemporary	writer
new	edition

5. Shape	
Adjective	**Noun Modified**
rectangular	building
round	table
flat	box
square	room

6. Color	
Adjective	**Noun Modified**
gray	suit
dark	complexion
blond	hair
green	mug

7. Origin	
Adjective	**Noun Modified**
Greek	play
impressionistic	painting
Caribbean	music
Western	outfit

8. Material	
Adjective	**Noun Modified**
leather	boots
glass	table
cotton	dress
wooden	spoon

9. Purpose	
Adjective	**Noun Modified**
sleeping	bag
writing	paper
exercise	room
private	agenda

When several adjectives modify the same noun, the sequence of adjectives follows the order of the previously listed functions.

Number	Opinion	Size	Age	Shape	Color	Origin	Material	Purpose	Noun Modified
five	impatient		young			Irish			singers
three	magnificent	huge	ancient			Greek	bronze		statues
	reputable	small				Canadian		business	school
two				round	gold	18th century	wooden		frames

Of course, it would be awkward to pile up too many adjectives, but knowing these functions helps you punctuate a series of adjectives correctly.

PRACTICE 20-1

Underline the adjectives in each of the following sentences; then draw an arrow to the noun the adjective modifies.

1. She just finished an <u>exciting</u> <u>mystery</u> novel by the <u>famous</u> writer Agatha Christie.

2. Following the <u>long</u>, <u>tedious</u> lecture, the <u>20</u> students met with their <u>young</u> <u>Indian</u> tutor to review the <u>main</u> points.

3. If you plan to wear your <u>new</u> <u>plaid</u> skirt, be sure to put on a <u>colorful</u> blouse.

4. The Tour de France is a <u>difficult</u> <u>bike</u> race over hundreds of miles of the <u>French</u> countryside.

5. After <u>many</u> months of looking, we finally found the <u>perfect</u> house for our <u>imminent</u> retirement.

Describe Nouns and Pronouns

Adjectives do not always appear before the word they modify, nor do adjectives describe only nouns. Examine the following examples:

He is <u>wise</u> and <u>noble</u>, as a king should be.

They became <u>hesitant</u> and <u>fearful</u> after the accident.

We felt <u>exhilarated</u> and <u>energized</u> by their applause.

Your <u>house</u> looks <u>clean</u>.

My <u>grocery</u> list is <u>long</u>.

My uncle's stories are <u>wild</u> and <u>woolly</u>.

You probably recognized some of the verbs from Chapter 19 as linking verbs. Linking verbs connect the adjective to the subject. To review, the most common linking verbs are the forms of the verb *be*.

Forms of the verb *be* ⟶   am
is
are
was
were
be
being
been

> **Bridging Knowledge**
>
> **See Chapter 19** to review linking verbs.

Here are other common linking verbs that can be followed by an adjective to describe the noun in front of the verb:

appear	grow	seem	taste
become	look	smell	turn
continue	prove	sound	
feel	remain		

Describe Gerunds

Adjectives can also describe entire ideas represented by verb phrases known as gerunds. The verbs in gerunds always end in *-ing*.

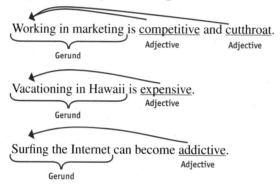

Working in marketing is <u>competitive</u> and <u>cutthroat</u>.
                Adjective   Adjective
Gerund

Vacationing in Hawaii is <u>expensive</u>.
                Adjective
Gerund

Surfing the Internet can become <u>addictive</u>.
                Adjective
Gerund

Participles

Some verbs (past participles) when used to modify a noun are also adjectives. Here are some examples:

broken promise	*drunk* driver	*published* novel
burned toast	*electrifying* performance	*relaxed* evening
chosen topic	*extended* vacation	*terrifying* moment
closed door	*eye-opening* revelation	*wanted* criminal

Participial phrases are adjectives since they modify nouns. A participle is a verb form like a gerund. The participle, just like a gerund, can end in *-ing*. However, the participial phrase can start with the past participle form of the verb, unlike a gerund. Review the following examples of participial phrases used as adjectives:

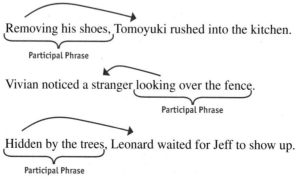

Removing his shoes, Tomoyuki rushed into the kitchen.
Participial Phrase

Vivian noticed a stranger looking over the fence.
Participial Phrase

Hidden by the trees, Leonard waited for Jeff to show up.
Participial Phrase

Use Nouns as Adjectives

A noun that modifies another noun may also be an adjective. Notice in the following examples how the first noun limits or qualifies the second (main) noun:

apple orchard	*file* folder	*pickle* jar
business plan	*house* boat	*student* center
festival time	*paper* towel	*tree* house

Possessive Adjectives

Possessive pronouns and possessive nouns are adjectives when they modify nouns.

> **Bridging Knowledge**
>
> **See Chapter 18** for a list of possessive pronouns.

a <u>father's</u> love	<u>my</u> <u>mother-in-law's</u> car	the <u>traders'</u> profits
<u>his</u> <u>counselor's</u> advice	the <u>owner's</u> house	<u>their</u> luck

PRACTICE 20-2

Read the following descriptive paragraph and underline all its adjectives. Then draw an arrow to the noun or pronoun that each adjective modifies.

Woodpeckers or flickers can be <u>annoying</u> pests, especially in the months of March to June when they are mating. The homeowner hears a <u>loud</u> knocking on the wood of the house, signaling the <u>woodpecker's</u> <u>bothersome</u> arrival. If the <u>nasty</u> bird is left to peck <u>large</u> holes in the <u>owner's</u> house, then <u>significant</u> damage will be done. Not only does the pecker make holes in the house, which <u>other</u> birds can nest in, but he also pulls out the insulation, which then must be replaced. There is no <u>foolproof</u> way of getting rid of these pests, besides killing them, which may be <u>illegal</u>. Some <u>temporary</u> relief can be had by attaching <u>large</u> <u>plastic</u> owls to the areas under attack, brushing a <u>sticky</u> substance on the <u>most visited</u> areas, broadcasting <u>distress</u> sounds of a flicker to scare it off, and building a nest for the woodpeckers to divert them from the <u>house's</u> <u>wood</u> siding. <u>One</u> <u>important</u> consideration, however, is to be sure to cover the holes quickly so that <u>other</u> birds don't nest in them, creating <u>another</u> <u>pest</u> problem. The <u>only</u> <u>dependable</u> solution is to replace <u>one's</u> <u>wood</u> siding with brick, stucco, or cement so that the woodpecker can't make his <u>enticing</u> <u>mating</u> call.

Comparatives and Superlatives

Most adjectives express three levels or degrees of comparison: positive, comparative, and superlative. You use the positive degree, the original form of the adjective, when you use *as . . . as* and *not as . . . as.*

> I'm <u>as</u> confident <u>as</u> Ralph.
> I'm <u>not as</u> humorous <u>as</u> Ralph.

Use the comparative degree to compare two people, objects, events, or ideas. When using the comparative, add the suffix *-er* for most one- and two-syllable adjectives (*easier, stronger, cleaner*) and use *more* in front of longer adjectives (*more intellectual, more troublesome, more interesting*).

> My lawn is <u>greener</u> than yours.
> This version of the movie is <u>more exciting</u> than the original.

Use the superlative degree to compare three or more people, things, events, or ideas. For most one- and two-syllable adjectives, use the suffix *-est* (*easiest, strongest, cleanest*); for longer adjectives, use *most* (*most intellectual, most troublesome, most interesting*).

> My lawn is the <u>greenest</u> in the cul-de-sac.
> This is the <u>most exciting</u> movie I've seen this year.

Unfortunately, these rules have many exceptions. For example, the word *eager* has two syllables, but would you say, "He is <u>eagerer</u> than John"? No, you would naturally say, "He is <u>more eager</u> than John." Therefore, if the word sounds awkward or strange, check your dictionary.

PRACTICE   20-3

For each of the following adjectives, write in the comparative and superlative forms. When in doubt, check your dictionary.

Adjective	Comparative	Superlative
messy	messier	messiest
greedy	greedier	greediest
wicked	wickeder	wickedest
suitable	more suitable	most suitable
cranky	crankier	crankiest
desperate	more desperate	most desperate
tricky	trickier	trickiest
impossible	more impossible	most impossible
green	greener	greenest

Absolute Adjectives

Some adjectives cannot be used in the comparative or superlative forms because they are already perfect or superlative as they are. For example, *unique* means one of a kind or unmatched. Adding more or most to it makes no sense. How can something or someone be more one of a kind than one of a kind? The same idea can be applied to the word *perfect*. *Perfect* means the best. How can something be *more perfect* or *more best*? Or *more priceless* or *straighter* or *most favorite*? It's like saying that a person was *sort of dead*.

Punctuating Adjectives in a Series

Often in our writing, we use several adjectives in a row to describe a person, place, or thing that we want the reader to envision in detail. Although we use commas to set off a list of items, in the case of adjectives, we have to distinguish between those that are coordinate and those that are cumulative.

Coordinate adjectives are separate and can be expressed with *and* between them; these adjectives are written with a comma to indicate their separateness.

> The chemistry course is <u>challenging, intriguing, and well taught.</u>

The course is challenging *and* intriguing *and* well taught. Each adjective describes a separate quality of the noun. Also notice that you can change the order of the adjectives. You determine the best order in which to present the series.

> The <u>professionally dressed, knowledgeable, articulate</u> professor lectured on the effects of globalization.

The professor is professionally dressed *and* knowledgeable *and* articulate; each adjective is separately describing the professor. Again, the order of the adjectives is up to the writer.

> The <u>knowledgeable, articulate, professionally dressed</u> professor lectured on the effects of globalization.

Therefore, if you separate the adjectives with *and* and if you can change the order of the adjectives, the adjectives are coordinate and should be set off by commas. Also, notice that you do not use a comma after the adjective placed just before the noun.

Cumulative adjectives add up gradually and are not separated by commas. The adjectives are in fixed positions because of their function.

> We gulped down the <u>fresh strawberry milk</u> shake.

Note that we didn't gulp down a shake that was fresh *and* strawberry *and* milk. We gulped down a fresh strawberry milk shake. Each adjective before *shake* describes the group of words after it.

> The <u>five international tennis</u> players held up their rackets in victory.

Note that there were five international tennis players, not five players. Also note that each adjective is in a fixed position. You would not hear a native English speaker say "tennis five international players." So when you write a series of adjectives that are in fixed positions, *don't* use commas.

PRACTICE 20-4

For the following items, decide whether the adjectives are coordinate or cumulative. If they are coordinate, add commas; if not, leave the commas as is. Carets show where commas should be inserted.

1. While skiing at Vail, she met an old college friend.
2. The editor composed a long detailed commentary on the local economy.
3. The pasta served at my favorite Italian restaurant is drenched in a rich creamy sauce.
4. The angry-looking 12-year-old skateboarder flew off the front steps and broke his nose on the sidewalk.
5. The daring adventuresome climber succeeded in scaling Mount Everest.
6. She chose a floor-length white sleeveless dress for her wedding.
7. The action-packed James Bond movie attracted huge crowds on its opening night.
8. Writing a long well-researched paper on global warming will take me months.
9. The tourists stared in awe at the colorful intricately designed mosaic on the mosque walls.
10. The long-winded preachy speech seemed to last forever.

Don't accumulate too many adjectives in front of one noun; such a sentence can become too cumbersome for the reader.

| INCORRECT: | The <u>sparkling, gold and silver, diamond-encrusted, $1,000</u> Dior bag hung ostentatiously from her left shoulder. |
| CORRECT: | The $1,000 Dior bag, encrusted with diamonds and colored gold and silver, hung ostentatiously from her left shoulder. |

Adverbs

Adverbs tell the reader how to do something—*slowly, quickly, carefully, extensively, determinedly, precisely, incrementally,* and so on. They tell when, where, why, under what conditions, and to what degree something happens or happened. Unlike adjectives, which modify nouns or pronouns, adverbs modify verbs, adjectives, or other adverbs.

VERB:	Ray walked <u>clumsily</u>. [How did he walk?]
ADJECTIVE:	The ring was <u>extremely</u> expensive. [How expensive?]
ADVERB:	Ray walked <u>very</u> slowly. [How slowly?]

An easy way to identify adverbs is to look for words ending in *-ly*. However, there are exceptions. Examine the following sentence:

She took a <u>leisurely</u> walk.

Leisurely is an adjective, describing the type of walk, which is a noun. *Lovely, lonely, motherly, friendly,* and *neighborly* are adjectives since they modify nouns.

It was a lovely day, so we walked through our friendly neighborhood.

Not all adverbs end in *-ly*. Such words as *here, there, everywhere,* and *somewhere* are adverbs indicating place (where?), *every, never, often, quite,* and *too* indicate frequency (how much or to what degree?), and *afterwards, again, early, first, now, later,* and *still* indicate time (when?). Also, some words, such as *fast, hard,* and *straight,* that are often used as adjectives may function as adverbs.

              Adverb   Adjective
He ran fast when he hit the fast ball.

Sylvia almost quit her job because she often gets depressed when she has to

get up early and work hard all day.

Tricky Verbs

Some verbs, such as *look, smell, feel,* and *taste,* can be tricky because they may be either action verbs or linking verbs. If they are used as action verbs, then an adverb describes them, but if they are linking, then they are followed by an adjective rather than an adverb. A good rule of thumb is that if the word following the verb describes the subject, then the verb is linking.

Carlos looks handsome in his new suit.
[*Handsome* describes Carlos, not the verb *looks;* thus, it is an adjective.]

Carlos was paid handsomely for his consulting work.
[*Handsomely* states how Carlos was paid; thus, it is an adverb. If the word following the verb describes the verb itself, then it is an adverb.]

Jordan looked strange with his spiked hair and purple nails.
[*Strange* describes Jordan; thus, it is an adjective.]

Jordan looked strangely at all of us as if he didn't recognize us.
[*Strangely* describes how Jordan looked and is an adverb.]

PRACTICE 20-5

For each item, draw an arrow from the underlined adjective or adverb to the word that it modifies. Then in the space to the left, write Adj or Adv.

Adj 1. I felt so cold in the meeting room that I had to put on my sweater and a jacket.

Adv 2. The priest stared coldly at the congregation as he chastised them for their sins.

Adj 3. The toast smells burnt; you left it in the toaster oven too long.

Adv 4. The dog smelled <u>cautiously</u> at the mouse hole.

Adv 5. The manager looked <u>calmly</u> around the meeting room before she began her opening remarks.

PRACTICE 20-6

For each of the following sentences, change the underlined adjective to an adverb and rewrite the sentence. Answers will vary.

Example: I watched a <u>slow</u> man walk across the street.

Correction: A man walked slowly across the street.

1. She kicked a <u>direct</u> ball into the goal.

Revised: She kicked the ball directly into the goal.

2. I took a <u>sharp</u> hit to my shins.

Revised: I was hit sharply in my shins.

3. We fought a <u>hard</u> match to win.

Revised: We fought hard to win the match.

4. The toddler gave her father a <u>sweet</u> smile as she bounded toward him.

Revised: The toddler smiled sweetly at her father as she bounded toward him.

Be careful not to rely too much on adverbs to carry the weight of the action; instead, focus on strong verbs, reserving adverbs for more detail when necessary. For example, study the following sentences:

Greg <u>walked slowly</u> down the street.
Greg <u>ambled</u> down the street.

The first sentence relies on the adverb to clarify how Greg walked; the second sentence offers a strong verb that tells the reader precisely how Greg moved down the street.

PRACTICE 20-7

Identify the adverbs in the following sentences; then rewrite each sentence, substituting a more vivid, stronger verb to make the sentence more concise and more forceful.

1. The poodle jumped <u>way up</u> in the air to catch the ball. Answers will vary.

Revised: The poodle leapt into the air to catch the ball.

2. Marvin ran <u>quickly</u> from the house when he heard a police siren approaching.

Revised: Marvin sprinted from the house when he heard a police siren.

3. Calvin stared <u>glumly</u> at the low grade on his research paper.

Revised: <u>Calvin glowered (frowned) at the low grade on his research paper.</u>

4. The front door opened <u>loudly</u>, and Hamad came <u>suddenly</u> into the room.

Revised: <u>The front door banged, and Hamad raced into the room.</u>

5. He treated her <u>badly</u> by never paying her much attention.

Revised: <u>He mistreated her by never paying her much attention.</u>

Comparatives and Superlatives

Like adjectives, adverbs take comparative and superlative forms, usually using *more* and *most.*

> I drive a manual transmission <u>more smoothly</u> than Beth does.

Adverbs ending in -*ly* always use *more* or *most* for comparative and superlative (*more speedily, most speedily*).

Some one-syllable adverbs, such as *fast,* add -*er* for the comparative form and -*est* for the superlative form.

> She finishes her calculus problems <u>the fastest</u> of any of her classmates.

PRACTICE 20-8

Fill in the comparative and superlative forms of the given adverbs.

	Comparative	Superlative
easily	more easily	most easily
creatively	more creatively	most creatively
angrily	more angrily	most angrily
far	farther	farthest
hard	harder	hardest

Frequently Confused Adjectives and Adverbs

When you edit your writing, pay close attention to four pairs of often-misused adjectives and adverbs: *good–well, bad–badly, fewer–less,* and *real–really.* Apply the basic rules of usage, and you can't go wrong.

Good versus *Well*

Good is an adjective and *well* is an adverb; thus, each must follow the rules of modification: *good* modifies adjectives and adverbs, whereas *well* modifies verbs, adjectives, and other adverbs. To help you make this distinction, just keep in mind that you can do something well but that something is good.

INCORRECT:	The team performed so <u>good</u> at the tournament that it placed second overall.
CORRECT:	The team performed so <u>well</u> at the tournament that it placed second overall.
INCORRECT:	I did <u>good</u> on the last history exam, despite my fears.
CORRECT:	I did <u>well</u> on the last history exam, despite my fears.

As adverbs, each use of *well* modifies the verb, explaining *how*. However, some verbs require your careful judgment. Forms of the verb *be* (*am, is, are, be, been*) and words of sensation (*feel, look, smell, sound, touch*) can take either an adjective or an adverb, depending on your meaning.

| INCORRECT: | The food smells <u>well</u>. |

The meaning here is that the food has a nose, not a pleasant picture.

| CORRECT: | The food smells <u>good</u>. |

As a rule, use *well* when referring to health:

I am <u>well</u> now after my recent bout with the flu.
How do you feel? You look *well*, so you must feel *well*.

However, it is correct to use *good* to refer to your overall well-being, both physical and emotional. For example, after getting an A on an essay, you might exclaim, "I feel good!"

Although we often use *good* and *well*, especially in speech, keep in mind that in your writing, *good* and *well* may be vague descriptors: they are too general and often overused, communicating little to the reader. Therefore, where possible, use clear adjectives and adverbs that your audience does not need to interpret.

PRACTICE 20-9

Cross out any incorrect use of *good* and *well* in the following sentences and write the correct word on the line provided. If the sentence is correct, write *Correct* on the line.

1. The annual report this year was ~~well~~.   <u>good</u>
2. Minerva was sick yesterday, but now she feels ~~good~~.   <u>well</u>
3. Our stocks performed well during the last quarter.   <u>Correct</u>
4. I'm proud of myself. I did so ~~good~~ on yesterday's pop quiz.   <u>well</u>
5. Regis doesn't hide his anger very well.   <u>Correct</u>

Bad versus *Badly*

Similar to *good* and *well, bad* and *badly* are often misused. Again, the trick is to follow the rules of modification and not rely on the way it sounds. *Bad* is an adjective, whereas *badly* is an adverb.

Juan took a <u>bad</u> fall, spraining his ankle.

Juan did <u>badly</u> on his physics exam and had to retake it.

Do not use *bad* to describe a verb.

| INCORRECT: | Trini did <u>bad</u> in her first marathon. |

| CORRECT: | Trini did <u>badly</u> in her first marathon. |

As with all adjectives, watch out for verbs that can be linking.

| INCORRECT: | Jason <u>felt</u> <u>badly</u> about shouting at her. |

| CORRECT: | Jason <u>felt</u> <u>bad</u> about shouting at her. |

PRACTICE 20-10

Cross out any incorrect use of *bad* and *badly* in each of the following sentences and write the correct word on the line provided. If the sentence is correct, write *Correct* on the line.

1. Sharon knew immediately that she had done ~~bad~~ on the unit quiz. _badly_
2. The toddler was so bad at the grocery store that the father refused to take her there again. _Correct_
3. The nurse felt ~~badly~~ for the family as they mourned their father. _bad_
4. The theatre group acted badly on the opening night of the play. _Correct_
5. After a sleepless night, he looked ~~badly~~. _bad_

Fewer versus *Less*

Although *fewer* and *less* have the same meaning, they have different uses. *Fewer* is used for words that can be counted: *fewer pencils, fewer houses, fewer people.* Less is used for words that can't be counted: *less coffee, less information, less ice cream.*

I lost <u>fewer pounds</u> than I had hoped even though I ate <u>less food</u> than I was used to.

We can count 1 pounds, 2 pounds, 3 pounds, and so on. We can't count one food, two food, three food.

PRACTICE 20-11

Write either fewer or less in front of the words given here.

1. fewer_____ calories
2. less_____ ketchup
3. fewer_____ misunderstandings
4. less_____ stress
5. less_____ liver sausage

Real versus *Really*

Real is an adjective, meaning genuine or authentic; and *really* is an adverb, meaning very, extremely, or exceedingly. To determine the correct word, try substituting *genuine* or *authentic* and *very* or *extremely* in place of *real* and *really*, respectively.

> The historical novel includes some <u>real</u> events that took place during the Battle of Gettysburg. I <u>really</u> enjoyed reading the novel.

Real is sometimes used incorrectly as an adverb.

INCORRECT: She was <u>real sure</u> that her testimony was accurate.

CORRECT: She was <u>really sure</u> that her testimony was accurate.

PRACTICE 20-12

Cross out any incorrect use of *real* and *really* in the following sentences and write the correct word on the line. If the sentence is correct, write *Correct* on the line.

1. My car was just tuned and runs ~~real~~ well now. really_____
2. Have a ~~real~~ nice day. really_____
3. The manager is really pleased with your work. Correct_____
4. Leo prefers a jacket made of real leather to one made of synthetic leather. Correct____
5. Be sure to drive ~~real~~ carefully on icy roads. really_____

When you edit your writing, keep in mind that *really* is an overused adverb. Your instructor might prefer that you use other adverbs, if needed, such as *extremely* or *exceedingly*. Your job as a writer is to make effective word choices.

Irregular Adjectives and Adverbs

The following adjectives and adverbs are irregular: their degree of comparison is not formed by merely adding a suffix (*-er* or *-est*). Even more so than some irregular verbs that you practiced using in Chapter 19, the irregular adjective and adverb forms undergo a complete change. Make sure you know the correct form to apply when using any of the three levels of comparison: positive, comparative, and superlative.

Positive	Comparative	Superlative
good	better	best
well	better	best
bad	worse	worst
badly	worse	worst
little	less	least
much	more	most

Double Negatives

The word *no* is usually used as an adjective or an adverb. Although its meaning is quite clear, the problem in usage occurs when two negatives (*no, not, never, none, nothing,* or a minimizing adverb such as *barely, hardly,* or *scarcely*) are used in the same phrase or clause. Such double negatives are viewed by many professionals as an obvious sign of a lack of education. This assumption may be incorrect, but this is the impression made by a person who uses double negatives. As a rule, avoid double negatives. Do not use such expressions as the following:

> **INCORRECT:** I <u>don't</u> know <u>nothing</u> about the Renaissance.
> [Note that *don't* and *nothing* are both negative.]
> **CORRECT:** I <u>don't</u> know <u>anything</u> about the Renaissance.
> OR
> **CORRECT:** I <u>know</u> <u>nothing</u> about the Renaissance.

> **INCORRECT:** We <u>don't</u> know <u>none</u> of those people who attended the meeting.
> **CORRECT:** We <u>don't</u> know <u>any</u> of those people who attended the meeting.
> OR
> **CORRECT:** We <u>know</u> <u>none</u> of those people who attended the meeting.

When you write, be aware of negative modifiers such as *never, no, none, no one, nobody, not,* and *nothing.* Don't pair them with other negative modifiers. Also, remember that *barely, hardly,* and *scarcely* should *not* be used with the negative as they already express negativity.

> **INCORRECT:** She <u>doesn't</u> have <u>hardly</u> any money left to spend on her trip.
> **CORRECT:** She <u>hardly</u> has any money left to spend on her trip.

PRACTICE 20-13

Rewrite the following sentences so that none of them contain double negatives.

1. I'm sure that the change in policy will not last barely a month.

Revised: I'm sure that the change in policy will last barely a month (will not last a month).

2. Our instructor decided not to offer extra credit because none of the students hardly showed interest.

Revised: Our instructor decided not to offer extra credit because none of the students showed interest (because the students hardly showed interest).

3. Since its last CD, the band has not had no requests to perform at concerts.

Revised: Since its last CD, the band has not had any requests to perform at concerts (has had no requests to perform at concerts).

4. Matt realized that their research place did not have none of the sources that the professor required.

Revised: Matt realized that their research place did not have any of the sources that the professor required (had none of the sources that the professor required).

5. Last weekend I couldn't think of nowhere to go.

Revised: Last weekend I couldn't think of anywhere to go (could think of nowhere to go).

REVIEW 20-1

Edit the following essay for errors in run-ons, pronouns, verb forms, verb tense, adjectives, and adverbs.

The Gas Chamber

I was never as nervous as I was while I awaited my turn to enter the gas chamber. This is one of the final requirements for graduation from the U.S. Army Basic Training Camp, this training will assist the soldier in gaining confidence in the military-issued gas mask. With only a week until graduation, each soldier knew that the gas chamber was their final step.

We were loaded into a cattle car, which was nothing short of an 18-wheel semi used for moving cattle, and then trucked into a secluded area of Fort Jackson, South Carolina. When we arrived at the area, the instruction began.

First, the drill sergeant ~~orders~~ (ordered) the platoon to exit the truck and form a line in front of a cabin. The bleak, shabby cabin with no windows stood ~~innocent,~~ (innocently) unaware of the hellish tests being performed inside ~~their~~ (its) walls. ~~Lucky~~ (Luckily) for me, I was near the end of the line. I watched as the soldiers before me staggered out the back door of the cabin, after what ~~seems~~ (seemed) like minutes inside the chamber, coughing, spitting, and gasping for ~~air, they~~ (air. They) had tears in their eyes, reddish skin, and a look of terror on their faces. They ~~can't~~ (could) hardly breathe.

Once a group of soldiers ~~departs~~ (departed) the chamber, the next group immediately ~~prepares.~~ (prepared) The line moved forward as we continued standing, waiting, not knowing what we ~~are~~ (were) headed for. The results ~~are real~~ (were really) apparent as our predecessors ~~depart~~ (departed) the chamber. After all the military training, we stood overwhelmed that this was our last major obstacle and all we had to do was ~~survive, then~~ (survive. Then) my group ~~is~~ (was) called.

We were instructed to don our gas masks and enter the chamber ~~slow.~~ (slowly) As we ~~walk~~ (walked) through the entrance, the vapors ~~become~~ (became) visual. Immediately, we ~~are~~ (were) compelled to inhale just for some reassurance. Next, we ~~are~~ (were) instructed to form a line, standing shoulder to ~~shoulder, we are~~ (shoulder. We were) then instructed to remove our masks and state our names, ranks, and serial numbers. Our hearts ~~race;~~ (raced) adrenaline ~~flows free~~ (flowed freely) through our veins as the drill sergeant ~~prepares~~ (prepared) to give the signal. The mask ~~is~~ (was) off; we ~~spew~~ (spewed) out the required information as our lungs and bodies ~~are~~ (were) rapidly engulfed with the burning gases. Finally, it was over, and just as those before me, my reaction was the same: I did ~~good~~ (well) and passed the test.

Although this was one of the ~~worse~~ (worst) experiences of my life, it has given me the courage to face any obstacle without giving into overwhelming fear or anxiety.

Editing for Style

PART 4

CHAPTER 21

Writing Clear Sentences

YOUR GOALS

1. Identify and correct misplaced and dangling modifiers.

2. Identify and correct mixed constructions.

3. Recognize and revise errors in parallelism.

"Words have to be crafted, not sprayed. They need to be fitted together with infinite care."

▪ Norman Cousins ▪

How often have you started an explanation with the words *I meant?* Usually, this opening indicates that you failed to express your meaning the first time. When does miscommunication happen? It often starts at the sentence level. In a sentence, every word has its place. If we don't follow certain rules, miscommunication may result. The following newspaper ads illustrate the unintentional meanings that may result when words or phrases are not in the correct order:

- For sale: Antique desk suitable for lady with thick legs and large drawers.
- Now is your chance to have your ears pierced and get an extra pair to take home, too.
- Tired of cleaning yourself? Let me do it.
- Dog for sale: eats anything and is fond of children.
- Used cars: Why go elsewhere to be cheated? Come here first!
- Wanted: Man to take care of cow that does not smoke or drink.

LET's warm up!

Think of a time when you misspoke or someone misinterpreted something you said or wrote. How frustrating was it to clarify or correct the situation? What consequences did it bring? Write a paragraph about such an experience.

George Doyle/Getty Images

When proofreading, don't overlook the most basic component of writing, the sentence. If you're not careful, silly and nonsensical meanings can crop up in your writing, whether for college or in your profession. When you write, you know what you mean, but don't assume that everyone else does. Make your sentences clear.

UNDERSTANDING SENTENCE CLARITY

Words, phrases, and clauses pack our sentences with essential information so that the reader understands the point we're making. Often, we concern ourselves more with including details that we consider important than with placing the details correctly in the sentences. As you move from rough draft to final draft, your revising goal is to make sure that the ideas in your sentences say exactly what you mean. Consider the following sentence:

> Ray revised his psychology paper on abnormal behavior in the school's writing lab, and he found that writing multiple drafts often improves the content, style, and makes the paper interesting.

Overall, your reader can understand the points that this sentence makes, but upon closer examination of the modifiers, you can easily detect some major problems that not only may be confusing and distracting to your reader but also may hurt your credibility. Examine the underlined modifiers:

> Ray revised his psychology paper on abnormal behavior <u>in the school's writing lab,</u> and he found that writing multiple drafts <u>often</u> improves <u>the content, style, and makes the paper interesting.</u>

- **Problem #1:** Is the topic of Ray's paper "abnormal behavior in the school's writing lab," or is the topic simply "abnormal behavior" and Ray worked on it in the writing lab?
- **Problem #2:** Did Ray write multiple drafts *often,* or did he find that writing more than one draft *usually* improves his paper?
- **Problem #3:** Ray found that drafts improved three things: "the content, style, and makes the paper interesting." Notice how awkward, even distracting, the last item of the series sounds?

Effective writing should be clear, not ambiguous or distracting. However, the problem with modifiers usually occurs because the writer can't readily see what the reader might find confusing when the idea is so clear to the writer. Your job as the writer is to proofread your essay to avoid these types of errors. Learn to recognize basic errors that can occur at the sentence level to revise for sentence clarity.

> In the writing lab, Ray revised his psychology paper on abnormal behavior, and he found that writing multiple drafts can improve the content, style, and interest level of his paper.

Misplaced Modifiers

Modifiers are words, phrases, or clauses that provide information to complete the main idea of your sentence. Modifiers clarify, identify, limit, describe, define, or explain a word, phrase, or idea in your sentence.

> My <u>youngest</u> brother would always brag about his <u>athletic</u> achievements.

The modifier *youngest* identifies which brother, and the modifier *athletic* limits the type of achievement the brother would brag about.

Misplaced modifiers are the errors most likely to confuse your reader. If you place a word, phrase, or clause in the wrong position in the sentence, you may give your sentence more than one meaning, an unintended meaning, or a silly meaning that makes the reader chuckle rather than focus on the importance or seriousness of your ideas. Don't permit the arrangement of information in your sentences to communicate the wrong ideas and reflect on you as a careless writer. Start with a basic principle of sentence clarity.

> **Place modifiers as near as possible to the word they modify.**

When you insert a modifier near a word it does not modify, you destroy the clarity of your sentence. Errors in modification are likely to pop up in your first draft, but you can catch them when you revise your draft. Examine some common types of misplaced modifiers.

Misplaced Words

Such words as *almost, even, exactly, hardly, just, merely, nearly, not, only, scarcely,* and *simply* limit the meaning of the word they modify. As a result, they may change the meaning of the sentence according to the position they occupy in the sentence.

Only the coach wanted Jamie to win.
[Meaning: No one else wanted Jamie to win.]

The coach only wanted Jamie to win.
[Meaning: This is all the coach wants, and the coach is not expecting anything else.]

The coach wanted only Jamie to win.
[Meaning: The coach doesn't want anyone except Jamie to win.]

Notice how the idea of each sentence is different. This type of modifier limits the word it precedes; thus, inserting a limiting modifier in the wrong position may create confusion or misunderstanding.

A single-word modifier, with its ability to sound right in almost any position in a sentence, can also end up describing both the word that precedes the modifier and the word that follows it. These *two-way modifiers,* also known as *squinting modifiers,* can cause much confusion.

TWO-WAY MODIFIER: The bridge that was repaired <u>partially</u> was destroyed by the storm.
[What's the meaning? Was it partially repaired, or was it partially destroyed?]

BETTER: The bridge that was <u>partially</u> repaired was destroyed by the storm.

OR

The bridge that was repaired was <u>partially</u> destroyed by the storm.

Unlike speech, where the rise of your intonation helps determine the word the modifier describes, writing must be clear and not offer the reader an either/or choice of interpretation.

In particular, be careful with the limiting word *not*.

> **INCORRECT:**   All exercise programs are <u>not</u> beneficial.

This sentence means that there are no exercise programs that are beneficial, which may not be what the writer intended to say.

> **CORRECT:**   <u>Not</u> all exercise programs are beneficial.

What meaning does the following sentence have?

> Liz <u>just</u> worked on her essay for 10 minutes.

Did Liz "just work" as opposed to read or plan the essay? Or did the writer mean to place *just* before the phrase "her essay" to indicate that Liz worked on nothing but her essay? Perhaps the writer meant that Liz worked for "just 10 minutes" when she should have spent more time. The reader shouldn't have to assume; your sentence should be clear.

PRACTICE 21-1

Revise the following sentences by changing the position of any two-way modifier. If the sentence is correct as written, write *Correct* on the line. Answers will vary.

1. Students who attend classes rarely are unsuccessful.

   <u>Students who rarely attend classes are unsuccessful.</u>

2. The police officers are permitted to pursue a driver only after requesting backup.

   <u>The police officers are permitted only to pursue a driver after requesting backup.</u>

3. What people read in the newspaper often they will believe.

   <u>What people read often in the newspaper, they will believe.</u>

4. Beginning swimmers who often practice the backstroke will improve their skills.

   <u>Correct</u>

5. Our adviser told us eventually our financial aid check would arrive.

   <u>Our adviser told us that our financial aid check would arrive eventually.</u>

Misplaced Phrases

As you revise your essay, also check the position of your phrases; they, too, can modify the wrong word or phrase. The position of your prepositional phrases and verbal phrases (participial and infinitive phrases) requires your careful attention.

> **INCORRECT:**   Margaret plans to travel before she attends college <u>for a little while</u>.

 With the modifying phrase placed where it is, the sentence can have two meanings. If the writer means to say that Margaret will travel for a little while before attending college, the modifier should be placed next to "travel." If the writer means that she will attend college for a little while, it might be best to rewrite the sentence.

> CORRECT: Margaret plans to travel before she spends <u>a little time</u> at college.

> CORRECT: Margaret plans to travel <u>for a little while</u> before she attends college.

To avoid ambiguity, place your prepositional phrases as close as possible to the word that conveys your intended meaning.

Another problem that interferes with the clarity of a sentence occurs when students insert examples too far from the idea that the examples illustrate.

> INCORRECT: The consequences of depression are frequently overlooked, <u>such as low self-esteem and suicide</u>.

> CORRECT: The consequences of depression, <u>such as low self-esteem and suicide</u>, are frequently overlooked.

PRACTICE 21-2

Locate and underline the misplaced prepositional phrase in each of the following sentences. Then revise each sentence on the line provided. If the sentence is correct, write *Correct* on the line.   Answers will vary.

1. Gayle found Rick's missing sociology notes <u>on the way to class</u>.

    On the way to class, Gayle found Rick's missing sociology notes.

2. By mistake, he hit the neighbor's dog with his bike <u>on the nose</u>.

    By mistake, he hit neighbor's dog on the nose with his bike.

3. Vacationing in Mexico proved to be the most exciting experience I've ever had.

    Correct

4. I read that the cat burglar has been apprehended <u>in today's paper</u>.

    I read in today's paper that the cat burglar has been apprehended.

5. We stared at the student in the back row <u>with a raccoon coat</u>.

    We stared at the student with a raccoon coat in the back row.

Misplaced Participial Phrases

A participial phrase adds concreteness to your writing by providing the reader with additional information about the word it modifies. However, placing a participial phrase near the wrong word can create confusion and give your sentences unintentional, and at times embarrassing, humor.

> INCORRECT: Jorge bought a jacket for his girlfriend <u>trimmed in rhinestones</u>.

Does the writer mean that Jorge's girlfriend is trimmed in rhinestones? This example illustrates how humorous some misplaced modifiers can be.

> **CORRECT:** Jorge bought a jacket <u>trimmed in rhinestones</u> for his girlfriend.

When you start your sentence with a participial phrase, make sure that the word that follows the comma is doing the action described in the participial phrase. A misplaced introductory participial phrase refers to another word in the sentence, not the subject.

> **INCORRECT:** <u>Dangling from the flagpole</u>, Ruben spotted his Nike shoes.

It is unlikely that Ruben was hanging from the flagpole.

> **CORRECT:** Ruben spotted his Nike shoes <u>dangling from the flagpole</u>.

To find misplaced phrases in your essays, whether prepositional or participial, start by underlining each such phrase in your sentences and drawing an arrow to the word it modifies. If the phrase distorts the meaning of the sentence, then move the phrase closer to the word it explains.

> **INCORRECT:** <u>Being an organized person</u>, Mathew, <u>not wanting to burden his family</u>, requested that he be cremated <u>before his death</u>.

Right away the misplaced phrase sticks out. You can be certain that Matthew does not want to be cremated while still alive.

> **CORRECT:** <u>Before his death</u>, Mathew, <u>being an organized person and not wanting to burden his family</u>, requested that he be cremated.

PRACTICE 21-3

The following sentences contain misplaced modifiers: prepositional or participial phrases. Underline the misplaced modifier and revise the sentence on the line provided. *Answers will vary.*

1. I slowed down to read the signs <u>driving on the interstate</u>.
   Driving on the interstate, I slowed down to read the signs.

2. He prepared a special plate of spaghetti for his brother <u>loaded with meatballs</u>.
   He prepared a special plate of spaghetti loaded with meatballs for his brother.

3. A box was left at her front door <u>with a large red bow</u>.
   A box with a large red bow was left at her front door.

4. <u>Burying the bone in the backyard</u>, Mother watched the dog.
   Mother watched the dog burying the bone in the backyard.

5. The candidate was falsely accused of covering up a crime <u>by the media</u>.
   The candidate was falsely accused by the media of covering up a crime.

Misplaced Clauses

Misplaced dependent clauses also create confusion. As with all modifiers, place dependent clauses as close as possible to the word they modify. Dependent clauses should add depth to your ideas, not obscure them; they should flow smoothly, not awkwardly.

MISPLACED CLAUSE:	Renaldo lost an important account <u>after he was hired and was fired</u>.
	[According to the placement of the dependent clause, first Renaldo was hired and fired and then he lost the account. But he wasn't employed then. The time sequence of this sentence doesn't make sense.]
BETTER:	<u>After he was hired</u>, Renaldo lost an important account <u>and was fired</u>.

Relative clauses (dependent clauses introduced by *who, whom, whoever, whomever, which, whose,* or *that*) can easily fall in the wrong position if you're not careful.

INCORRECT:	The officer <u>handcuffing the suspect who was reading him his Miranda rights</u> is a new recruit.
CORRECT:	The officer <u>handcuffing the suspect</u> and <u>reading him his Miranda rights</u> is a new recruit.

Don't place clauses in a position that would interrupt the flow of ideas in the sentence.

INCORRECT:	The company, <u>because of recent complaints filed by employees</u>, was audited.
CORRECT:	<u>Because of recent complaints filed by employees</u>, the company was audited.

A dependent clause can also be a two-way modifier if the clause can modify two different ideas, forcing the reader to guess which idea the writer intended to modify.

TWO-WAY MODIFIER WITH CLAUSE:	Sara told the president <u>when the meeting was over she would submit the latest figures</u>.
	[When did Sara offer to submit the latest figures? Was it after the meeting, or was it during the meeting? Both possibilities exist.]
BETTER:	<u>When the meeting was over</u>, Sara told the president <u>that she would submit the latest figures</u>.

OR

Sara told the president that <u>when the meeting ended, she would submit the latest figures</u>.

Underline the dependent clauses in each of the following sentences. If a dependent clause is misplaced, is interruptive, or could be read in two ways, revise the sentence on the line provided. Answers will vary.

1. They flew to San Juan in their private jet <u>where they always escape for the winter</u>.
   In their private jet, they flew to San Juan, where they always escape for the winter.

2. We laughed at the picture of Rita on a roller coaster <u>that she sent the office</u>.
   We laughed at the picture that Rita sent the office of her on a roller coaster.

3. The professor found the research paper in the writing lab <u>that she lost</u>.
   In the writing lab, the professor found the research paper that she lost.

4. George showed the photos to the client <u>that he shot last week in Santa Fe</u>.
   George showed the client the photos that he shot last week in Santa Fe.

5. They both agreed <u>after the contract was signed</u> to renegotiate some of the conditions.   After the contract was signed, they both agreed to renegotiate some of the conditions.

Split Infinitives

An infinitive phrase is made up of the word *to*, the base of the verb, and any modifiers that complete the phrase. Although the infinitive is a verb form, it is not considered a verb since it functions as a noun, adjective, or adverb. However, many people treat the infinitive as a verb, especially in speech, and split the infinitive by placing modifiers directly between the *to* and the verb. As a rule, avoid splitting an infinitive when possible.

SPLIT INFINITIVE (SINGLE-WORD MODIFIER):	Gene promised <u>to never reveal</u> the code.
CORRECT:	Gene promised <u>never</u> <u>to reveal</u> the code.
SPLIT INFINITIVE (PHRASE MODIFIER):	The committee hopes <u>to, with a lot of help with from the community, raise</u> enough money for the new project.
CORRECT:	<u>With a lot of help with from the community</u>, the committee hopes <u>to raise</u> enough money for the project.
	OR
CORRECT:	The committee hopes <u>to raise</u> enough money for the project <u>with a lot of help with from the community</u>.

It's becoming increasingly acceptable to split the infinitive even in formal writing. As a rule, if you insert a long modifier, place it outside the infinitive since the split may be disruptive to the reader. However, before you decide to split an infinitive, consider your audience. How will your reader react? How will your instructor react? If in doubt, don't split the infinitive.

Even so, you may find certain situations in which not splitting the infinitive would make the sentence awkward. In this case, it's preferable to split your infinitive.

> **SPLIT INFINITIVE (SINGLE-WORD MODIFIER):** After she reviewed the report, she decided to <u>personally</u> supervise the revisions.

This example might be acceptable to most readers. It likely wouldn't sound awkward to most. It might even add a stronger emphasis to the verb form *supervise*. If this is acceptable to your reader and purpose, then it wouldn't be an issue. But if you're writing to a more formal audience, to an academic community, or to an unknown audience, it might be better not to split the infinitive.

> **CORRECT:** After she reviewed the report, she decided to supervise <u>personally</u> the revisions.

If this revision seems awkward to you, try recasting the sentence.

> **CORRECT:** After she reviewed the report, she decided <u>she would personally supervise</u> the revisions.

PRACTICE 21-5

Underline the words or phrases that split the infinitives in the given sentences. Then revise the sentences to eliminate the split infinitives. Answers will vary.

1. A bad experience does not need to <u>necessarily</u> be traumatic.
   A bad experience does not necessarily need to be traumatic.

2. Although he received numerous reminders, he failed to <u>for more than 6 months</u> contact the vendor. Although he received numerous reminders, he failed to contact the vendor for more than 6 months.

3. The student was able to <u>quickly and quietly</u> find a seat before the guest speaker began her presentation. Quickly and quietly, the student was able to find a seat before the guest speaker began her presentation.

4. To <u>safely</u> roller skate, a skater should wear knee pads, elbow pads, and a helmet.
   To roller skate safely, a skater should wear knee pads, elbow pads, and a helmet.

5. Pedro plans to <u>immediately</u> withdraw from his classes before the drop period.
   Pedro plans to withdraw immediately from his classes before the drop period.

Dangling Modifiers

The dangling modifier usually comes at the beginning of the sentence. Unlike other misplaced modifiers that you can revise by placing them near the words they modify, the dangling modifier may not have a logical correlation to any word in the sentence. The word it modifies is usually implied. Always keep in mind that when a sentence starts with a modifying word, phrase, or clause, the start of the main clause must be the word that the modifier explains. A dangling modifier can occur with a prepositional phrase, a participial phrase, an infinitive phrase, a gerund, or an elliptical clause. Examine the following examples of dangling modifiers. Notice that there's no word in the sentence that the modifier explains.

1. **Dangling participial phrase.**

   INCORRECT:　Knowing that the accident occurred earlier, the report was incorrect.
   [The report *knew that the accident occurred earlier?* This makes no sense.]

   CORRECT:　Knowing that the accident occurred earlier, I realized that the report was incorrect.

   INCORRECT:　Worried about accumulating late fees, the documents were submitted extra early.
   [The documents *were worried?* This is definitely dangling. Be careful with passive constructions.]

   CORRECT:　Worried about accumulating late fees, the tenants submitted the documents extra early.

2. **Dangling infinitive phrase.** Remember than an infinitive is *to* plus the base of the verb.

   INCORRECT:　To receive the tickets quickly, a self-stamped envelope should accompany your request.
   [The self-stamped envelope will *receive the tickets?* This isn't logical.]

   CORRECT:　To receive the tickets quickly, submit a self-stamped envelope with your request.
   [The main sentence is imperative: the phrase modifies the understood subject *you.*]

3. **Dangling gerund phrase.** The present participle is functioning as a noun.

   INCORRECT:　After studying all night, the test was easy.
   [The test was *studying all night?* Notice that the gerund acts as the object of the preposition *after.*]

   CORRECT:　After I studied all night, the test was easy.
   [The gerund is transformed to a dependent clause.]

   OR

   CORRECT:　After studying all night, I found the test easy.

4. **Dangling elliptical clause.** An *elliptical clause* is a clause in which the subject, the verb, or both have been omitted. For example, "when she is alone" becomes "when alone." Since the missing words and the logic of the sentence are clear to us, we assume that it will be just as clear to the reader. However, if the implied subject of the elliptical clause is not the same as the subject of the main clause, you have written a dangling modifier.

INCORRECT:	When alone, the house sounds scary.
CORRECT:	When I'm alone, the house sounds scary.

[Put back the missing words.]

OR

When alone, I'm scared by the sounds in the house.

You can repair dangling modifiers in two ways:

1. Leave the modifier as it is, but create a subject that the modifier can logically modify. This will prevent it from dangling.

DANGLING MODIFIER:	Approaching Santa Fe, the distant view of the city was exciting.
ADD A LOGICAL SUBJECT:	Approaching Santa Fe, we grew excited by the distant view of the city.

2. Change the dangling modifier into a clause, adding a subject and a verb.

DANGLING MODIFIER:	Having been out all weekend, my apartment was burglarized.
TRANSFORM TO CLAUSE:	Since I had been out all weekend, my apartment was burglarized.

PRACTICE 21-6

Examine the following sentences. If the sentence contains a dangling modifier, underline it and revise the sentence on the line provided. If the sentence is correct as written, write *Correct* on the line. Answers will vary.

1. After rereading several poems, the symbolism still puzzled me.
    After rereading several poems, I was still puzzled by the symbolism.

2. Pausing briefly to answer Jane's question, the discussion continued.
    Pausing briefly to answer Jane's question, the instructor continued the discussion.

3. Having submitted his last essay, Alfonso was able to enjoy spring break.
    Correct

4. <u>When 3 years old</u>, his father showed Brian how to play golf.
    When Brian was 3 years old, his father showed him how to play golf.
5. <u>Having driven all day</u>, the hotel was a welcoming site.
    After the family had driven all day, the hotel was a welcoming site.

Mixed Constructions

Occasionally, while writing one sentence, a writer inserts part of another sentence, and the two sentences become confused. In such a case, the result is likely to be a mixed construction. Examine five common types of mixed constructions.

1. **Mixed constructions with dependent clauses.** In this type of construction, the writer starts the sentence with a dependent clause, which is a good style, but what happens next creates a confusing structure.

    > INCORRECT: Although the class had not yet begun has caused the students to worry about the test.

    Examine the two parts of this sentence closely. The reader expects a comma after the main clause, but see what happens? Instead of a dependent clause, the writer starts with a verb and the rest of a sentence, incorrectly making the dependent clause the subject of the sentence.

    Dependent clauses that begin with subordinating conjunctions cannot act as subjects of sentences.

    > CORRECT: Although the class had not yet begun, the students were worried about the test.

    In the revision, place the comma after the clause and then complete the second idea by inserting a logical subject to create a dependent clause.

2. **Mixed constructions with prepositional phrases.** If the writer isn't careful, mixed constructions can result when you start a sentence with a prepositional phrase.

    > INCORRECT: During the confusion of this morning's accident rushed into the room and yelled that we needed to file an incident report.

    The writer uses the prepositional phrase as the subject of the sentence, creating confusion when the reader gets to the main part of the sentence. A prepositional phrase can never serve as the subject of the sentence. This construction creates a long fragment.

    > CORRECT: <u>During the confusion of this morning's accident, the manager</u> rushed into the room and yelled that we needed to file an incident report.

    To revise this type of error, you can complete the main clause, or you can place the prepositional phrases in another part of the sentence where it makes sense as in the next sentence.

CORRECT: The <u>manager</u> rushed into the room <u>during the confusion of this morning's accident</u> and yelled that we needed to file an incident report.

The prepositional phrase should modify the verb to indicate a time frame. Placing the prepositional phrases at the end of the sentence would create a misplaced modifier.

3. **Mixed constructions with complete sentences.** A mixed construction can also result when you have a complete sentence and then tag on another idea.

INCORRECT: During the initial phase, we decided to emphasize the growth of this profession, <u>examined the employment trend for the last 5 years</u>.

In this type of mixed construction, the writer is treating the complete sentence as the subject of the sentence.

CORRECT: During the initial phase, we decided to emphasize the growth of this profession. <u>We examined the employment trend for the last 5 years</u>.

4. **Mixed constructions with gerunds.** A common type of mixed construction occurs when you start a sentence with a gerund in the form of a prepositional phrase and treat it as the subject of the sentence.

INCORRECT: <u>By revising your essay carefully</u> assures a good grade.
CORRECT: <u>Revising your essay carefully</u> assures a good grade.

Simply change the prepositional phrase to a noun subject to fix the problem.

5. **Mixed constructions resulting from illogical verb complements.** Sometimes the subject of the sentence and its complement do not logically connect. This type of mixed construction is known as *faulty predication*. The most common instances of faulty predication occur when a linking verb, usually the verb *be* (*am, is, are, was, were, be,* or *been*), is followed by a dependent clause introduced by the subordinating conjunction *when, where, if,* or *because*. These subordinating conjunctions are not nouns and, therefore, cannot serve as the complement of the linking verb.

> **Bridging Knowledge**
>
> **See Chapter 19** for a full explanation of linking verbs.

INCORRECT: Claustrophobia <u>is when a person has an abnormal fear of being in narrow or enclosed spaces</u>.
CORRECT: Claustrophobia <u>is an abnormal fear</u> of being in narrow or enclosed spaces.

INCORRECT: <u>The reason why</u> they lost the game <u>was because they couldn't work as a team</u>.
CORRECT: They lost the game <u>because they couldn't work as a team</u>.

OR

| CORRECT: | The reason they lost the game <u>was</u> <u>that they couldn't work as a team</u>. |

When you proofread your writing, be sure to revise sentences that use the following connectors: *is when, is where, is if, the reason . . . is because*, and *the reason why . . . is because*.

PRACTICE 21-7

Revise the sentences with mixed constructions. If the sentence is correct, write *Correct* on the line. Answers will vary.

1. By keeping up with all assignments helped him succeed in the course.

   Keeping up with all assignments helped him succeed in the course.

2. The reason Marie lost her job was because she was usually late.

   Marie lost her job because she was usually late.

3. Because we both love sports made our connection stronger.

   Our love for sports made our connection stronger.

4. The reason I changed my schedule was that I got a part-time job.

   Correct

5. Although we gave her additional time, she never returned the files she borrowed.

   Correct

Parallel Constructions

Which one of the following is the oddball in the following group of occupations?

writer   manager   pharmacist

drives trucks   butler

Now, try this group; which item does not fit in?

baking   roasting

broiling   fry chicken

If you answered *drives trucks* and *fry chicken*, you already understand the concept of parallelism. The principle of parallelism is simple: when you are writing and list two or more words, phrases, or clauses in a sequence, each item must be the same grammatical form. You must choose verbs, nouns, adjectives, verbals, dependent clauses, independent clauses, and so forth, but you can't combine them. Using the same form adds smoothness to your writing. Don't permit your reader to stop and focus on the break in the flow of your writing; your reader expects consistency.

Parallelism in a Series

Repeating the same grammatical form in a series adds balance to your sentences and shows that each idea in the series is of equal importance. Observe what happens when a writer violates the rule of parallelism:

> **INCORRECT:**   After working all night on his backyard, Eric came in tired, hungry, and needing a bath.

Does the last item sound harsh to the ear? The writer starts the series with adjectives (*tired, hungry*) and then shifts to a participle (*needing*). As a result, the rhythm of the sentence is broken. Compare this sentence with the following balanced sentence:

> **CORRECT:**   After working all night on his backyard, Eric came in tired, hungry, and filthy.

Review the following common parallel patterns. Pay close attention to the consistency of the items in the series.

Parallel Patterns	Examples
Nouns	The variety of <u>trees</u>, <u>plants</u>, <u>flowers</u>, and <u>shrubs</u> gave the yard the illusion of an enchanted garden.
Verbs	
Present tense	Once you <u>plan</u>, <u>draft</u>, and <u>revise</u> your essay, submit it to your instructor for additional feedback.
Past tense	At last night's meeting, we <u>discussed</u>, <u>debated</u>, <u>developed</u>, and <u>generated</u> ideas that would move the company into the next century.
Adjectives	After the trial period, the manager found her <u>competent</u>, <u>reliable</u>, <u>respectful</u>, and <u>trustworthy</u>.
Adverbs	He worked on the project <u>cautiously</u>, <u>conscientiously</u>, and <u>responsibly</u>.
Prepositional Phrases	In my panic, I search for my research paper <u>in my room</u>, <u>under my bed</u>, and <u>in my car</u>.
Verbal Phrases	
Infinitive	Glen expected to accomplish three things in college: <u>to develop</u> his communication skills, <u>to learn</u> a profession, and <u>to meet</u> people.
Gerund	<u>Writing</u> poetry, <u>singing</u> karaoke, <u>dancing</u> salsa, and <u>skiing</u> are his favorite pastimes.
Participle	Poorly <u>written</u>, <u>unorganized</u>, and <u>filled</u> with grammatical errors, his report received much criticism at the meeting.
Dependent Clauses	<u>How she left</u>, <u>where she went</u>, and <u>whom she met</u> remained a mystery to all.
Independent Clauses	The president's plan faced three major obstacles: <u>his Cabinet had no input in the planning</u>, <u>his party did not support it</u>, and <u>the taxpayers did not understand it</u>.

PRACTICE 21-8

Underline any faulty parallelism. On the line provided, revise the sentence. If the sentence is correct, write *Correct* on the line. Answers will vary.

1. As a journalist in the Middle East, Janet Trujillo observed direct combat, civilian casualties, and <u>reporting on civilians' daily hardships</u>.

    As a journalist in the Middle East, Janet Trujillo observed direct combat, civilian casualties, and civilians' daily hardships.

2. Three elements are particularly crucial when writing a comparison or contrast essay: maintaining a focus, <u>to write to a specific audience</u>, and providing enough detail to be convincing.

    Three elements are particularly crucial when writing a comparison or contrast essay: maintaining a focus, writing to a specific audience, and providing enough detail to be convincing.

3. The equipment may be leased by the week, by the month, or <u>the customer could pay on a yearly plan</u>.

    The equipment may be leased by the week, by the month, or by the year. OR The equipment may be leased weekly, monthly, or yearly.

4. She is healthy, she is educated, and <u>knows a lot about major world issues</u>.

    She is healthy, educated, and knowledgeable about major world issues.

5. Destroying his marriage, alienating his children, and quitting his job, Greg soon fell into a state of despair.

    Correct

Parallelism in Pairs

As you have seen, repeating similar elements in a series adds clarity and coherence to your sentences. However, you can easily miss faulty parallelism during revision if you're not careful.

Compare the following sentences:

> INCORRECT: The family's unity is jeopardized <u>because the household faces serious financial difficulties</u> and <u>the changing values of the children</u>.
>
> CORRECT: The family's unity is jeopardized <u>because the household faces serious financial difficulties</u> and <u>because the values of the children are changing</u>.

The two main points in the second sentence are clear and have a sense of balance: each cause shares the same importance. Pay close attention to words such as *and, or, yet, but, than, rather than,* and *whereas.* They often signal the need for parallel structure.

Gerund Phrase

> INCORRECT: Jorge decided that <u>getting married next year</u> would be more beneficial than to get married this year.
> Infinitive

Gerund Phrase

CORRECT: Jorge decided that <u>getting married next year</u> would be more beneficial [than] <u>getting married this year</u>.

Gerund Phrase

Dependent Clause

INCORRECT: Our main concern was <u>that he would seek another job</u> [or] <u>giving away confidential information</u>.

Participial Phrase

Dependent Clause

CORRECT: Our main concern was <u>that he would seek another job</u> [or] <u>that he would give away confidential information</u>.

Dependent Clause

Correlative Conjunctions

Correlative conjunctions are used in pairs:

both ... and   either ... or   whether ... or

neither ... nor   not only ... but also

These conjunctions should act as signposts to the need for parallel constructions. The word, phrase, or clause following each part of the conjunction should be parallel.

[Either] we move to New York this year [or] we move to Kansas next year.

Verb   Verb

We [either] move to New York this year [or] move to Kansas next year.

Prepositional Phrase   Prepositional Phrase

We move [either] to New York this year [or] to Kansas next year.

Consider the following nonparallel conjunctions and their revisions.

Infinitive Phrase   Verb

INCORRECT: Renee can't decide <u>whether</u> to go into medicine <u>or</u> be a lawyer.

Infinitive Phrase   Infinitive Phrase

CORRECT: Renee can't decide <u>whether</u> to go into medicine <u>or</u> to go into law.

OR

Infinitive Phrase   Infinitive Phrase

CORRECT: Renee can't decide <u>whether</u> to become a doctor <u>or</u> to become a lawyer.

Verb

INCORRECT: We must <u>not only</u> join the opposition <u>but also</u> we must distance ourselves from the issue.

Independent Clause

Verb   Verb

CORRECT: We must <u>not only</u> join the opposition <u>but also</u> distance ourselves from the issue.

PRACTICE 21-9

Underline any faulty parallelism. On the line provided, revise the sentence. If the sentence is correct, write *Correct* on the line. Answers will vary.

1. I spent last evening <u>researching my topic</u> and <u>in preparing a tentative outline</u>.

   I spent last evening researching my topic and preparing a tentative outline.

2. I would like to congratulate both the evening staff and their manager for the time they've spent on this special project.

   Correct

3. He not only <u>brought home his best friend</u> but also <u>the neighbor's dog</u>.

   He brought home not only his best friend but also the neighbor's dog.

4. My neighbor uses her van <u>to chauffer her teenagers</u> and <u>for shopping</u>.

   My neighbor uses her van to chauffer her teenagers and to go shopping.

5. Mr. Uliberri will either <u>ask you</u> or <u>me</u> to join him for lunch.

   Mr. Uliberri will ask either you or me to join him for lunch.

Effective Repetition to Emphasize Ideas

For conciseness, it's not necessary to repeat words in a series.

> Usually, we look forward to hearing his jokes, ~~hearing his~~ stories, and ~~hearing his~~ songs.

However, some writers and public speakers repeat words in parallel structures for emphasis or for a certain effect. Many great speeches have used parallelism effectively to bring out an important message. Imagine the audience's reaction when Abraham Lincoln spoke these resounding words in his Gettysburg Address:

> "But in a larger sense, we cannot dedicate—we cannot consecrate—we cannot hallow—this ground."

Without the repetitions of words, this sentence would be less forceful, lose its momentum, and probably not be as memorable: "But in a larger sense, we cannot dedicate—consecrate—hallow—this ground."

PRACTICE 21-10

Underline the parallel structures in the following famous quotations. Indicate additional parallel items within the same sentence by using double underlines. Answers will vary.

1. "We hold these truths to be self-evident, <u>that all men are created equal</u>, <u>that they are endowed by their Creator with certain inalienable Rights</u>, <u>that among these are <u>Life</u>, <u>Liberty</u>, and <u>the pursuit of Happiness</u></u>." Thomas Jefferson, *The Declaration of Independence* (Dependent clauses are parallel and the series of nouns in the last clause are parallel.)

2. "It is rather for us to be here dedicated to the great task remaining before us—<u>that from these honored dead we take increased devotion to that cause for which they gave the last full measure of devotion</u>; <u>that we here highly resolve that these dead shall not have died in vain</u>; <u>that this nation, under God, shall have a new birth of freedom</u>; and <u>that government of the people</u>, <u>by the people</u>, <u>for the people</u> shall not perish from the earth." Abraham Lincoln, *The Gettysburg Address* (Dependent clauses are parallel and the series of prepositional phrases in the last clause are parallel.)

3. "Never in the field of human conflict was <u>so much</u> owed by <u>so many</u> to <u>so few</u>." Winston Churchill

4. "Ask not <u>what your country can do for you</u> but rather <u>what you can do for your country</u>." Marcus Tullius Cicero, 63 B.C.

5. "<u>We are not satisfied</u>, and <u>we will not be satisfied</u> until <u>justice rolls down like waters</u> and <u>righteousness like a mighty stream</u>." Martin Luther King Jr.

Here are some tips to help you write clear sentences:

1. Until you can identify modifiers quickly and accurately, underline the modifiers in your essays to make it easier for you to check their placement.
2. Make sure your modifiers are as close as possible to the word they modify.
3. Make sure that your modifiers refer to words that are actually in the sentence.
4. Be careful when you insert limiting modifiers (*almost, even, exactly, hardly, just, merely, nearly, not, only, scarcely,* and *simply*). Be sure to place them next to the words they modify.
5. Check that items in pairs or in a series are parallel.
6. Look for correlative conjunctions that signal parallel constructions.

REVIEW   21-1

Revise the following essay for modifiers and parallel constructions. Cross out any errors and add or change any words as necessary.

My Dearest Cheapskate

I met my prince charming in the summer of 1987. He possessed all of

the qualities of the perfect man: he was kind, considerate, handsome, and

a fantastic cook

~~he cooked fantastically~~. Because love is blind, I viewed his imperfections as

thriftiness

strengths and his stingy attitude as ~~being thrifty~~. If hindsight is 20/20, I can

now reflect on our first date with a different view. Impressed by his invitation to our city's reservoir, _{I was sure} ~~it was obvious to me~~ that his love for nature couldn't

keep him away. Actually, he was drawn by the $1 admission. I was impressed

with his motivation to pack a picnic lunch complete with fried chicken,

potato salad, and ~~included~~ red wine. He raided his mother's refrigerator and

applied his employee discount to the wine _{while working at Loco Liquors} ~~while working at Loco Liquors~~

that he bought.

_{When I arrived} ~~Upon arriving at~~ home to brag to my mom about my dream date,

my mom provided me with the insight of what she termed a *cheapskate*.

According to my mom, a cheapskate is one whose number one priority is

to ~~no matter what~~ avoid his share of the cost _{no matter what}. She added a cliché of advice:

"You can't squeeze blood out of a turnip." Then she warned, "Honey, I don't

want to have to say I told you so." However, convinced ~~in a prior life~~ that I

was a phlebotomist _{in a prior life}, I thought I was the one who could squeeze blood out of

this turnip.

Love knows no bounds. However, although I continue to tolerate his

oddities _{, his behavior} has caused me much concern. Being thrifty is a trait I admire in a

person, but he can carry things a little bit too far. I didn't mind that he saved

every scrap of food ~~for the dog~~ that we left on our plates _{for the dog}. However, the icing

on the cake was when he decided he could save money ~~really~~ in the bath-

room. He instructed us that we would only be allowed to take "Navy show-

ers," and what's more, he bought 4-ply toilet paper (on sale, of course) and

separated it into 2-ply sheets so he could get twice as much for his money.

As I look back over the last 17 years, I can now say I know the true

meaning of a cheapskate. My husband is one who hoards money just for the

sake of doing so. ~~The reason that I remain in this situation is because~~ _{I remain in this situation because} I have

come to accept that I will never be able to squeeze blood out of my turnip

and, to make matters worse, I will always be able to hear my mother's

unspoken words, "I told you so; I told you so."

CHAPTER 22

Writing Varied Sentences

YOUR GOALS

1. Identify and use different types of sentence structures to enrich and add variety to your writing style.

2. Combine clauses and phrases.

3. Apply basic rules of punctuation when combining clauses and phrases.

4. Edit and revise sentences and paragraphs for sentence variety, sentence correctness, and punctuation.

One of our students described her writing experience as follows:

> I immediately break out in a cold sweat at the thought of writing an essay for class or any kind of lengthy writing assignment for that matter. How do I start? What will my instructor think about me? Why doesn't it sound grown up? I feel as if I'm still in elementary school; I sound like my children. Gosh, my elementary school child writes better than I do! I don't think in terms of short, disconnected ideas, but when I write my ideas down, that's what I end up with. They really sound dumb.

This frustration is true about many writers, both students and professionals. How we present our ideas on paper determines how well we communicate our ideas to others and how seriously the reader takes us. Your ideas may be logical, energetic, and interesting; but when you create your sentences, will these ideas continue to be logical, energetic, and interesting?

Worried about committing grammatical errors, some students try to play it safe by writing mostly in short, simple sentences. As a result, the writing style is choppy and boring. By contrast, some students, as well as some professionals, believe that their writing sounds more mature and professional if they use longer, more complex sentences. Read the following note sent by a nurse to her director:

LET's warm up!

We all have a writing style. How would you describe your writing style? Think about the writing style of other people you know. How is your writing style different? Write a paragraph describing your writing style.

Art Vandalay/Getty Images

Dear Mr. Naidu,

At our last staff meeting, you encouraged us to voice some of our concerns. Although I did not volunteer any comments since I felt that many of my workers might feel I was referring to them and become uncomfortable and that mentioning it toward the end of the meeting when everyone wants to leave after a long day working with patients would not lead to a productive exchange of opinions, I'm expressing my concerns to you now.

As you're aware, several nurses on our floor are smokers and take constant breaks to go outside to smoke. It's bad enough that one nurse leaves, but when she is accompanied by other nurses who also smoke, the nurses left on the floor must attend to the smokers' patients, which affects our duties to our own patients, especially when the smokers continue to gossip and the 10-minute breaks turn into half-hour breaks and are repeated several times in the day, increasing the workload of nonsmokers. I understand the addiction a smoker battles every day, and I'm not insensitive to the needs of my colleagues, but when it affects the workplace, then this addiction touches all of us, so we nonsmokers would appreciated it if you address this issue before our next staff meeting.

Thank you for your time,

Dena Rosca, RN

Using excessive coordination and subordination to combine ideas shows a misunderstanding of what constitutes style in writing. You don't need long sentences to prove to your instructor or employer that you're a good writer. Effective writing is made up of a balance among a variety of sentences. A short sentence can be as strong and as effective as a long one.

UNDERSTANDING SENTENCE VARIETY

We all have a unique writing style. Our choice of words, the way we arrange words and sentences, our attitudes about our topic, and the effect we want our writing to have on our audience are some factors that determine our style. Since style is a personal quality, there really is no right or wrong style of writing. However, the quality of your writing depends on your skills in presenting your ideas—your maturity as a writer. Thus, improving your writing style and developing a more effective and mature style start at the most basic element of writing: the sentence.

Identifying and Using Basic Types of Sentences

Sentences are classified according to their structure. Depending on the number and types of clauses they contain, sentences are classified as simple, compound, complex, or compound-complex. Effective writers pay close attention to sentence variety, focusing on how sentences work together within each paragraph. Blending different sentence lengths and different sentence types holds the reader's interest. As you learn to recognize and practice manipulating these four basic types of sentences in your writing, you will be on your way to developing a stronger, more mature writing style.

The Simple Sentence

As you may recall from Chapter 15, a complete sentence that can stand alone is called an *independent clause*. A *simple sentence* is one independent clause.

Mike left the conference early.

Notice that this clause is one complete idea containing a subject and a verb. Of course, you can *compound,* or add, another subject.

Mike <u>and Sophia</u> left the conference early.

You still have a simple sentence. You can also compound the verb.

Mike and Sophia <u>gathered</u> their notes and left the conference early.

The sentence continues to be a simple sentence. The length of the sentence does not change its classification. In classifying sentences, you examine only the clauses, not the number of words or phrases. For example, adding phrases (verbal or prepositional) does not change the classification of the sentence:

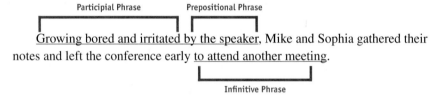

This sentence continues to be a simple sentence since the sentence still has one independent clause.

A simple sentence can consist of one word that expresses a complete idea.

Go! [Meaning: You go!]

Or it can be filled with phrases, adjectives, and adverbs that help build a complete idea. The simple sentence, if used effectively, can express a strong emotion or emphasize an idea that you feel the reader should focus solely on. Don't disregard the simple sentence as too elementary. Ending a paragraph or an important point with a strong simple sentence can be an effective technique. However, too many simple sentences can make your writing choppy and childish and can prevent your ideas from flowing smoothly.

The Compound Sentence

Unlike the simple sentence that focuses on one main idea, a *compound sentence* emphasizes the relationship of two or more main ideas. The compound sentence is most effective when you wish to present several ideas that you feel are equal in importance. A compound sentence consists of two or more independent clauses. A compound sentence has three patterns, which you may recall from Chapter 16. (Pay close attention to the punctuation in each pattern.)

Coordinating Conjunctions

Two independent clauses are connected by a coordinating conjunction.

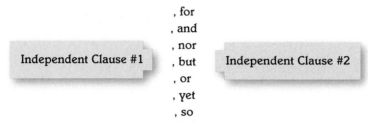

Emilia heard the news,_ and_ she immediately called her manager.

Notice that there is a complete sentence on each side of the conjunction. If the writer were to leave out the subject *she* in the second independent clause, the sentence would no longer be compound, and a comma could not be used before the conjunction.

Emilia heard the news _and_ immediately called her manager.

The preceding example is a simple, not a compound, sentence since it has only one independent clause made up of one subject, *Emilia,* and two verbs, *heard* and *called.* The original compound sentence was made up of two independent clauses, each with its own subject and verb.

Conjunctive Adverbs or Transitional Expressions

Two independent clauses are connected by a conjunctive adverb or transitional expression.

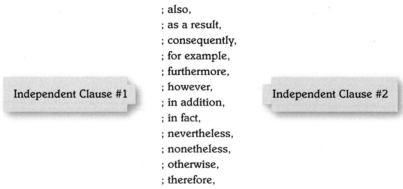

Emilia heard the news;_ therefore,_ she immediately called her manager.

Note: Be sure to place the semicolon before, not after, the conjunction and the comma after the conjunction. Don't capitalize the word after a semicolon unless it's a proper noun (a word that is always capitalized).

> **Bridging Knowledge**
>
> **See Chapter 16** for methods of revising comma splices and fused sentences.

Semicolons

Two independent clauses are connected by a semicolon.

> Emilia heard the news; she immediately called her manager.

Notice how the semicolon establishes a relationship between both main ideas. The semicolon provides a shorter pause than the period, emphasizing the close connection of the second sentence to the first sentence.

Too many compound sentences can weaken your writing. Avoid excessive coordination.

EXCESSIVE:	Emilia heard the news, and she immediately called her manager, but the manager refused to hear any bad news, so he asked her to return to her office, and he asked her to send him an e-mail.
BETTER:	Hearing the news, Emilia immediately called her manager; however, the manager refused to hear any bad news. He asked her to return to her office and send him an e-mail.

The revision uses a combination of simple and compound sentences.

PRACTICE 22-1

On the lines provided, classify each of the following sentences as S for simple or CP for compound.

_S_ 1. Many people still believe in old superstitions.

_S_ 2. For example, some average citizens shudder at the thought of opening an umbrella indoors.

_S_ 3. My mother is one of these people and would order everyone to close all umbrellas once inside the house.

_CP_ 4. All superstitions die hard, so I often feel uncomfortable seeing an umbrella inside the house.

_CP_ 5. During this period, sun worshipping wasn't a new faith; however, Akhenaton changed the belief from a polytheistic religion to a monotheistic one.

The Complex Sentence

A *complex sentence* contains one independent clause and one or more dependent clauses. If you recall from Chapter 15, a dependent clause cannot stand alone and is introduced by either a subordinating conjunction or a relative pronoun.

Common Subordinating Conjunctions				
after	before	rather than	though	where
although	even though	since	unless	whether
as	how	so that	until	while
as if	if	than	when	why
because	in order that	that		

Continued

Relative Pronouns				
that	whatever	who	whom	whose
what	which	whoever	whomever	

Consider the following dependent clause:

After I resigned

If this dependent clause is not attached to an independent clause (a complete sentence), a fragment results; but once an independent clause is added, the new structure becomes a complex sentence. The following is a complex sentence; it has one dependent clause and one independent clause.

Bridging Knowledge

See Chapter 15 for a review and examples of dependent and independent clauses.

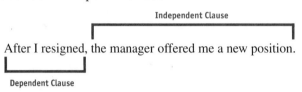

A complex sentence can have more than one dependent clause, but it always has only one independent clause.

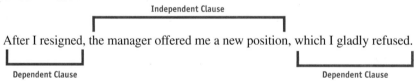

Note: Don't forget to use a comma when you place a dependent clause in front of the independent clause.

The complex sentence is the most frequently used sentence type among writers. Since dependent clauses add information to help the reader understand the main sentence, using a complex sentence adds clarity to the main ideas. Contrast the preceding sentence with the following group of simple sentences.

I resigned. The manager offered me a new position. I gladly refused.

Without subordinating ideas, the reader has to determine the relationship among these sentences: Did this person resign because she was offered a new position? What and why did she refuse? Complex sentences indicate clear and specific relationships between ideas, and since complex sentences contain only one independent clause, the reader clearly knows which ideas are most important.

Avoid excessive subordination. Making a sentence long with many subordinate (dependent) ideas adding information to the main idea creates a confusing sentence.

The Compound-Complex Sentence

The *compound-complex sentence* contains at least two independent clauses and at least one dependent clause. As the name implies, this type of sentence structure is a combination of a compound and a complex sentence. Examine the following examples of compound-complex sentences; each has a different pattern of the compound sentence.

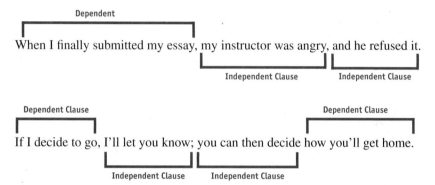

The compound-complex sentence is effective when you want to show relationships among several main ideas. Since this type of sentence is the most stylish, applying it to your writing reflects a more mature and sophisticated writer. Note that compound-complex sentences are typically longer than most sentences, so it's important that you punctuate them correctly.

PRACTICE 22-2

On the lines provided, classify each of the following sentences as CX for complex or CP-CX for compound-complex.

CP-CX 1. Before the year ends, we should plan our family reunion, for we have so many new members of the family whom we have yet to meet.

CX 2. When our grandparents were growing up, they lived in traditional nuclear families.

CX 3. The boss fired the shipping clerk since he took too many coffee breaks.

CP-CX 4. Although Cecilia is known to procrastinate, she always comes through, so when she offered to write the report, everyone on the team approved.

CX 5. When Laura returned from college, her friends were excited and threw her a party.

The following chart can help you identify the various sentence types:

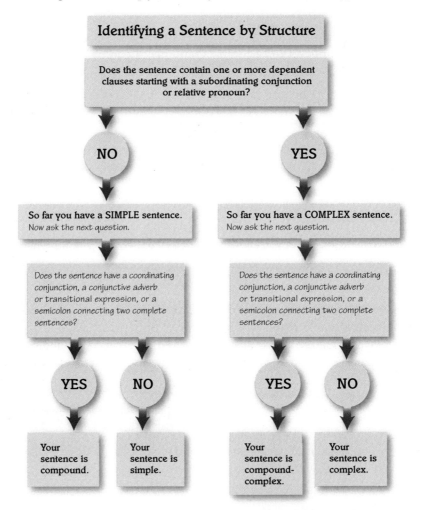

Identifying a Sentence by Structure

Does the sentence contain one or more dependent clauses starting with a subordinating conjunction or relative pronoun?

NO

So far you have a SIMPLE sentence. Now ask the next question.

Does the sentence have a coordinating conjunction, a conjunctive adverb or transitional expression, or a semicolon connecting two complete sentences?

YES — Your sentence is compound.

NO — Your sentence is simple.

YES

So far you have a COMPLEX sentence. Now ask the next question.

Does the sentence have a coordinating conjunction, a conjunctive adverb or transitional expression, or a semicolon connecting two complete sentences?

YES — Your sentence is compound-complex.

NO — Your sentence is complex.

PRACTICE   22-3

Using the following letters, classify each of the following sentences as follows:
S for simple, CP for compound, CX for complex, and CP-CX for compound-complex.

___CX___ 1. Leo still insisted that he did not plagiarize his research paper.

_CP-CX_ 2. Mr. Morelli, who was angry with his daughter, grounded her for a month; he soon regretted his rashness.

___CX___ 3. The completion of our Student Center will be delayed unless funds become available.

_CP-CX_ 4. Consider your decision carefully before you make the announcement; your decision will be final.

___S___ 5. This year, either Tony or Lydia will be inducted into the Honor Society.

Combining Phrases and Clauses

The most apparent element of a writer's style is probably the writer's sentence structure. When you finish your essay, critically examine your writing style and consider the many options you have for effectively varying your sentence structures. This section reviews some of these stylistic options.

Vary the Beginning of Your Sentences

Introductory Participial Phrases

Participial phrases make interesting lead-ins to the main ideas of your sentences. Use the present participle, which always ends in *-ing,* or the past participle, ending in *-d, -ed, -en, -en,* or *-t.* (See the participle forms of irregular verbs on page 531.)

SIMPLE SENTENCES:	Dave is waiting for the bus. Dave fell asleep.
PRESENT PARTICIPIAL PHRASE:	Waiting for the bus, Dave fell asleep.
SIMPLE SENTENCES:	The mayor was surrounded by reporters. He stopped to answer their questions.
PAST PARTICIPIAL PHRASE (REGULAR VERB):	Surrounded by reporters, the mayor stopped to answer their questions.
SIMPLE SENTENCES:	Ray is known for his rude remarks. No one was surprised at the meeting.
PAST PARTICIPIAL PHRASE (IRREGULAR VERB):	Known for his rude remarks, Ray did not surprise anyone at the meeting.

Notice that a comma follows the introductory participial phrase.

Note: When starting your sentences with participial phrases, be careful you don't create dangling modifiers. Participial phrases function as adjectives; therefore, they should be placed as closely as possible to the nouns or pronouns they modify.

PRACTICE 22-4

Each group of simple sentences in this activity can be combined by using a participial phrase. Start your new sentence with a participial phrase and make sure that your new sentence is logical. Don't forget to punctuate correctly.

1. My brother was searching my room. He found out where I hid my money.
   <u>While searching my room, my brother found out where I hid my money.</u>
2. The children were frightened by the storm. They quickly hid in the closet.
   <u>Frightened by the storm, the children quickly hid in the closet.</u>
3. The governor rushed into the building. He waved to the crowd.
   <u>Rushing into the building, the governor waved to the crowd.</u>

4. The hotel room was perfect. It overlooked the Eiffel Tower.

   <u>Overlooking the Eiffel Tower, the hotel room was perfect.</u>

5. This essay was given as an example for us to follow. It is hard to understand.

   <u>Given as an example for us to follow, this essay is hard to understand.</u>

Introductory Dependent Clauses

Starting your sentence with a dependent clause highlights the main idea. When you start with a dependent clause, determine the main idea you want your reader to focus on and let the dependent clause lead to this one idea.

SIMPLE SENTENCES:	Rita joined the debate team. She became popular.
INTRODUCTORY SUBORDINATE CLAUSE:	<u>When Rita joined the debate team</u>, she became quite popular. <u>When Rita became quite popular</u>, she joined the debate team.

Notice that each of these sentences expresses a different idea since the main clause and the dependent clause differ.

When you start your sentence with a dependent clause, use a comma after the dependent clause when an independent clause follows it. Not doing so may change your meaning.

INCORRECT:	While John was eating his cat jumped on the table.

If the reader doesn't pause after the subordinate clause, the sentence states that John is eating his cat. The reader then has to stop and locate the main idea. The writer should be using a comma to guide the reader.

CORRECT:	While John was eating, his cat jumped on the table.

The following conjunctions introduce subordinate clauses. Pay close attention to the comma that sets off the introductory subordinate clause from the main clause.

After
Although
As (if)
Because
Before
Even though
If
Since   Dependent Clause **,** Independent Clause
So that
Though
Unless
Until
When
Whether   **If** <u>she needs my help</u>, she'll call me on my cell.
While   **Dependent Clause + Independent Clause**

PRACTICE 22-5

Each group of simple sentences in this activity can be combined into a complex sentence. Start your new sentence with a dependent clause, vary your conjunctions, and make sure that your new sentence is logical. Don't forget to punctuate correctly.

1. I heard that Luther was in the hospital. I called his wife to find out how he's feeling.

   When I heard that Luther was in the hospital, I called his wife to find out how he's feeling.

2. Ray was trying hard to pass chemistry. He hired a tutor for the semester.

   Since Ray was trying hard to pass chemistry, he hired a tutor for the semester.

3. I did not want to inconvenience my friend by asking her to drive me to school. I decided to take the bus.

   Because I did not want to inconvenience my friend by asking her to drive me to school, I decided to take the bus.

4. Mark didn't have all the necessary information. He felt confident that he would be able to complete the assignment.

   Even though Mark didn't have all the necessary information, he felt confident that he would be able to complete the assignment.

5. Paul was convinced that he would never learn to speak French. He dropped his French class.

   Since Paul was convinced that he would never learn to speak French, he dropped his French class.

Vary Your Method of Combining Sentences

Use Subordinate Clauses

As you have already seen, subordinate clauses establish clear relationships between ideas. You may use a subordinating conjunction to indicate the following relationships:

1. Time (*when?*)	after, as, as soon as, before, since, until, when, whenever, while
2. Place (*where?*)	where, wherever
3. Reason or cause (*why?*)	as, because, since, whereas
4. Purpose or result	in order that, so that
5. Manner (*how?*)	as if, as though
6. Condition or contrast	although, if, though, unless
7. Extent	as far as, as long as

Unlike an introductory dependent clause, which you punctuate to separate it from the main clause, you do not punctuate a dependent clause when it comes at the end of your sentence.

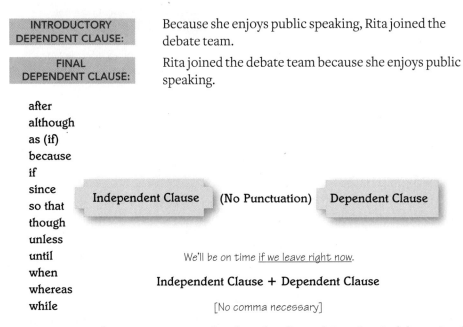

INTRODUCTORY DEPENDENT CLAUSE:	Because she enjoys public speaking, Rita joined the debate team.
FINAL DEPENDENT CLAUSE:	Rita joined the debate team because she enjoys public speaking.

after
although
as (if)
because
if
since
so that
though
unless
until
when
whereas
while

Independent Clause   (No Punctuation)   Dependent Clause

We'll be on time *if we leave right now*.

Independent Clause + Dependent Clause

[No comma necessary]

Not every one of your sentences needs to be subordinated. Bear in mind that a simple sentence can be quite effective; however, short sentences call readers' attention to themselves, so you should use them primarily for emphasis. Too many short sentences or repetition of the same sentence type can create a choppy style, making your writing sound almost telegraphic. As you revise your essay for style, consider the many options you have learned so far to help you make your ideas clear and your presentation more mature and sophisticated.

Simple Sentences:

- We have enough money to attend the concert. We have been saving money for a week.
- Having saved money for a week, we have enough to attend the concert.

Compound Sentences:

- We have enough money to attend the concert; we have been saving for a week.
- We have been saving money for a week; therefore, we have enough to attend the concert.

Complex Sentences:

- Since we have been saving money for a week, we have enough to attend the concert.
- We have enough money to attend the concert since we have been saving for a week.

Compound-Complex Sentences:

- Because we have been saving money for a week, we have enough to attend the concert, so we're buying tickets today.

PRACTICE 22-6

Each item here contains two simple sentences. Determine the relationship between the sentences and combine each pair in three different ways, using the conjunctions or conjunctive adverbs given in parentheses. Make sure your sentences are logical. Punctuate correctly.

1. This car is quite expensive. It is a classic model.

    (For) This car is quite expensive, for it is a classic model.

    (Because) This car is quite expensive because it is a classic model.

    (Therefore) This car is a classic model; therefore, it is quite expensive.

2. Our manager stormed out of the office. We laughed nervously.

    (When) When our manager stormed out of the office, we laughed nervously.

    (And) Our manager stormed out of the office, and we laughed nervously.

    (As a result) Our manager stormed out of the office; as a result, we laughed nervously.

3. Carl has brilliant and creative ideas. He is too shy to present them.

    (However) Carl has brilliant and creative ideas; however, he is too shy to present them.

    (Yet) Carl has brilliant and creative ideas, yet he is too shy to present them.

    (Although) Although Carl has brilliant and creative ideas, he is too shy to present them.

Reduce Clauses to Phrases

You can reduce some dependent clauses to participial phrases and retain the subordinating conjunction. When a subordinating conjunction related to time clarifies the ideas in a sentence, it's generally best to keep it. As long as the meaning remains clear, phrases can offer a more concise method of expressing two ideas.

| DEPENDENT CLAUSE: | While I was coming to class this morning, I witnessed an accident. |
| PARTICIPLE PHRASE: | While coming to class this morning, I witnessed an accident. |

Notice that you're creating a participial phrase but maintaining the subordinating conjunction to keep the relationship of the clauses clear.

When you reduce a clause to a phrase, make sure the subject of the main clause and the subject of the participial phrase (*who* or *what* performed the action of the participle) are the same. Dangling participles can easily occur.

DEPENDENT CLAUSE:	While I was taking a shower, the bell rang.
INCORRECT:	While taking a shower, the bell rang.
	[Was the bell taking a shower?]
CORRECT:	While taking a shower, I heard the bell ring.

For each of the following sentences, reduce the subordinate clause to a phrase. Be sure to punctuate correctly. If the clause cannot be reduced, write "Creates a dangling modifier" on the line to indicate the reason the clause couldn't be reduced.

1. When Carmen opened the box, she gasped at the size of the diamond.
    When opening the box, Carmen gasped at the size of the diamond.

2. I fell asleep while I was waiting for the bus.
    I fell asleep while waiting for the bus.

3. Since Leo has been playing baseball, his self-esteem has increased.
    Creates a dangling modifier

4. Before he left the house, Sammy remembered to grab his cell phone.
    Before leaving the house, Sammy remembered to grab his cell phone.

5. Before I left for college, my father bought me a computer.
    Creates a dangling modifier

Join Ideas with Relative Clauses

So far you have combined sentences using subordinate clauses. Another type of dependent clause is the relative clause. This type of dependent clause begins with one of the following *relative pronouns:*

that	whichever	whom
where (sometimes)	who	whomever
which	whoever	whose

Use relative clauses when you want to give necessary or additional information about someone or something.

> Mr. Richardson, <u>who was the governor of New Mexico,</u> visited our town last year.

This example is a combination of the following two simple sentences.

> Mr. Richardson visited our town last year. Mr. Richardson was the governor of New Mexico.

Writing it as two separate sentences would draw unnecessary attention to an idea that you have no intention of developing—that Mr. Richardson is the governor of New Mexico. Since the purpose of the second sentence is to identify Mr. Richardson for a reader who may not be familiar with this person, this clause should be treated as added information that's nonessential to the meaning of the main idea.

As a rule, place the relative clause as close as possible to the person, place, or thing that you are identifying or explaining to avoid confusing, silly, and sometimes nonsensical meanings to your sentences.

INCORRECT: Mark moved to New York City, <u>who grew up in a small town</u>.

CORRECT: Mark, <u>who grew up in a small town</u>, moved to New York City.

Note: Use *who* or *whom* when you refer to people; use *which* and *that* when you refer to things.

PRACTICE 22-8

Combine each set of sentences into one sentence containing a relative clause. All relative clauses in this activity require commas, so make sure you don't omit the commas.

1. My grandma is giving me guitar lessons. She was in a band during the 1930s.
   My grandma, who was in a band during the 1930s, is giving me guitar lessons.

2. This shopping center has more than 300 stores. It attracts much tourism.
   This shopping center, which has more than 300 stores, attracts much tourism.

3. Reading is my favorite pastime. It provides an escape after a busy day.
   Reading, which is my favorite pastime, provides an escape after a busy day.

4. Arabic is a difficult language to learn. It has a complicated verb system.
   Arabic, which is a difficult language to learn, has a complicated verb system.

5. Hilda speaks fluent Spanish. She grew up in Santa Domingo. Spanish is a musical language.
   Hilda, who grew up in Santa Domingo, speaks fluent Spanish, which is a musical language.

Not all relative clauses are set off by commas. To determine which relative clauses should be punctuated, you need to understand the difference between restrictive and nonrestrictive clauses.

A *restrictive clause* carries information that is important or essential to the meaning of the main idea of the sentence.

The students who failed the final exam will have to repeat the course.

The relative clause *who failed the final exam* is important to the meaning of this sentence. If you were to leave it out, you would be saying that *all* students have to repeat the course. We need the relative clause to restrict the word *the students* and let the reader know exactly which students. There are no commas setting off the restrictive clause because this information is important.

In contrast, a *nonrestrictive clause* offers nonessential or additional information to the main idea of the sentence.

Miguel, who failed the final exam, will have to repeat the course.

In this case, we know exactly who will be repeating the course; therefore, the relative clause is serving as additional information. This clause is set off by commas, indicating that the information is not necessary for the understanding of the main idea of the sentence.

Since your decision to punctuate or not punctuate restrictive clauses provides your reader with information that may be important, it's crucial that you punctuate correctly. What difference in meaning do the following sentences provide the reader?

> My brother who lives in Florida was arrested for leading a protest march.
> My brother, who lives in Florida, was arrested for leading a protest march.

In the first sentence, the relative clause is not set off by commas, signaling important information to the meaning of the sentence. The reader can then assume that the writer has more than one brother and it was the one who lives in Florida who was arrested, not the one living somewhere else. In this case, the information is necessary to restrict the phrase *my brother*. However, the commas enclosing the relative clause in the second sentence imply added information. This information, if omitted, wouldn't change the meaning of the sentence. In reading the second sentence, the reader assumes that Miguel has only one brother.

In most writing, determining which relative clauses are restrictive and which are nonrestrictive is a relatively easy process, but first you must review four terms that you need to consider: proper nouns, indefinite pronouns, and general and specific nouns.

A *proper noun* is a word that is capitalized. It can be someone's name (Ruth, President Clinton, Captain Picard), a place (Colorado, Denver, Newark, Asia, Pacific Ocean), or a thing (Empire State Building, Boy Scouts of America, NATO).

It is also important that you are able to identify *indefinite pronouns:*

> **Bridging Knowledge**
>
> **See Chapter 27** for a full explanation and examples of proper and common nouns.

all	everybody	nobody
any	everyone	none
anybody	few	one
anyone	many	several
both	most	some
each	neither	somebody
every	no one	someone

In addition, you should know the difference between a specific noun and a general noun. A *general noun* refers to a broad class of things, whereas a *specific noun* is a part of that broad or general category. For example, the noun *flower* is also a general noun, whereas the noun *rose* is specific since it is part of a broader class.

Now, with the preceding information in mind, carefully read the following table, which can help you identify restrictive and nonrestrictive clauses.

Restrictive Clause	Nonrestrictive Clause
(Important information: No commas)	(Added information: Use commas)
1. Do not use commas if the relative clause refers to a general noun. **Example:** Flowers <u>that bloom in March</u> are rare.	1. Use commas if the relative clause refers to a specific noun. **Example:** The black rose, <u>which blooms in May</u>, is rare.
2. Do not use commas if the relative clause refers to an indefinite pronoun. **Example:** Everyone <u>who was interested in the class</u> remained seated.	2. Use commas if the relative clause refers to a proper noun. **Example:** Leo, <u>who left early</u>, is irresponsible.
3. Use the relative pronoun *that* only with restrictive clauses. **Example:** The house <u>that was sold last week</u> is occupied.	3. Use possessive pronouns, such as *my, his, our,* and *their;* demonstrative pronouns, such as *this, these,* and *those;* and possessive nouns (the *boy's* book) to make a general noun specific. **Examples:** • <u>This</u> house, <u>which was sold last week</u>, is occupied. • <u>Ed's</u> parents, <u>who live in Denver</u>, arrived yesterday.

Always examine the word or words in front of the relative clause (the word or phrase the clause modifies) to determine whether to set the clause off with commas.

PRACTICE 22-9

Underline the relative clause in each of the following sentences. If the relative clause is restrictive, write *C* for Correct on the space provided to indicate that no commas are necessary; however, if the clause is nonrestrictive, insert the necessary commas.

__C__ 1. "People <u>who live in glass houses</u> shouldn't throw stones."

__C__ 2. Employees <u>who are overworked</u> cannot be productive.

_____ 3. Ricky, <u>who is repeating this course</u>, wants to graduate with honors.

__C__ 4. The building <u>that I live in</u> is filled with extraordinary individuals.

_____ 5. These parties, <u>which are quite popular on campus</u>, break up rather late.

Reduce Relative Clauses to Phrases

Just as you are able to reduce subordinate clauses to phrases, so are you able to reduce relative clauses to phrases. Thus, rather than rely solely on relative clauses to identify, explain, or give additional information, you can reduce the relative clauses to an appositive for greater sentence variety and conciseness. *Appositives,* then, are nouns or noun phrases that define or explain nouns or pronouns.

Simple Sentences: Ramon wants to leave the city. He is a student at NYU.	• Appositive phrases do not start with a verb form.
Relative Clause: Ramon, who is a student at NYU, wants to leave the city.	• Appositive phrases are usually nonrestrictive since they define or identify specific nouns and therefore must be set off by commas; however, they follow the same restrictive and nonrestrictive rules as relative clauses.
Reduction: Ramon, ~~who is~~ a student at NYU, wants to leave the city.	
Appositive: Ramon, <u>a student at NYU</u>, wants to leave the city.	

PRACTICE 22-10

Rewrite the following sentences, reducing each relative clause to an appositive phrase. Punctuate accordingly.

1. The Royale, which is a new theater, is located near the old courthouse.
   <u>The Royale, a new theater, is located near the old courthouse.</u>

2. That door, which is the one with a star on it, leads to Beyoncé's dressing room.
   <u>That door, the one with a star on it, leads to Beyoncé's dressing room.</u>

3. She will be going to CU, which is a highly competitive institution.
   <u>She will be going to CU, a highly competitive institution.</u>

4. Tomiko, who is my friend from Japan, will be staying with me this week.
   <u>Tomiko, my friend from Japan, will be staying with me this week.</u>

5. Ben, who is a rather short person, decided not to pick a fight with the school's champion wrestler.
   <u>Ben, a rather short person, decided not to pick a fight with the school's champion wrestler.</u>

You can also change relative clauses to participial phrases just as you did with dependent clauses.

Example #1	
Relative Clause: The man who is walking with Jay is from Pueblo. **Reduction:** The man ~~who is~~ walking with Jay is from Pueblo. **Participial Phrase:** The man <u>walking with Jay</u> is from Pueblo.	• There is no difference in meaning between a relative clause and its reduced forms (participial or appositive phrase).
Example #2	
Relative Clause: Anyone who wants to come must sign the form. **Reduction:** Anyone ~~who~~ wants to come must sign the form. **Participial Phrase:** Anyone <u>wanting to come</u> must sign the form.	

Example #3	
Relative Clause: The ideas that are presented in this book are challenging. **Reduction:** The ideas ~~that are~~ presented in this book are challenging. **Participial Phrase:** The ideas <u>presented in this book</u> are challenging.	• If the relative clause is restrictive, the reduction to participial phrase will also be restrictive and no commas should be used.
Example #4	
Relative Clause: Spanish has an alphabet that consists of 29 letters. **Reduction:** Spanish has an alphabet ~~that~~ consists of 29 letters. **Participial Phrase:** Spanish has an alphabet <u>consisting of 29 letters.</u>	
Example #5	
Relative Clause: This pamphlet, which is being distributed around campus, argues against five major changes in policy. **Reduction:** This pamphlet, ~~which is~~ being distributed around campus, argues against five major changes in policy. **Participial Phrase:** This pamphlet, <u>being distributed around campus,</u> argues against five major changes in policy.	• If the relative clause is nonrestrictive, its participial phrase form will also be nonrestrictive and should therefore be set off by commas.

PRACTICE 22-11

Rewrite the following sentences, reducing each relative clause to a participial phrase. Be sure to punctuate correctly where necessary.

1. The people who are waiting for the bus are getting impatient.

   The people waiting for the bus are getting impatient.

2. Pueblo is a city that is located in the southeastern part of Colorado.

   Pueblo is a city located in the southeastern part of Colorado.

3. Students who attend community colleges receive a good education.

   Students attending community colleges receive a good education.

4. Do you know the reputation of the person who is handling the political campaign?

   Do you know the reputation of the person handling the political campaign?

5. The police officer who is investigating the case is baffled by the evidence.

   The police officer investigating the case is baffled by the evidence.

Final Advice for Improving Your Style

1. The more you write, the better your style becomes, so write, write, and write some more. Every time you write something new, you improve your style.

2. Don't forget that you may just now be discovering your unique style. Continue to experiment with words and sentence structures until you achieve the variety you want and until you start to feel confident about your writing.

3. **Review the many options you have for varying your sentences.** Refer to these options when you are revising your paper.

4. **The revision stage of writing is crucial.** First, get all your ideas down. After you've completed your draft, start to revise. Focus on each group of sentences. Explore how you can improve them. Do this for half an hour. Then put the paper away and come back the next day and revise it again. Keep revising it until you feel your sentences communicate what you want to say.

5. **Use a voice recorder to record your essay.** Judge your style. Are sentences too long? Are they clear? Does the writing sound choppy? Did you detect any sentences that should be improved?

6. **You can learn by mimicking other authors.** To practice, find writings by authors whose style you admire. Copy their sentences, paragraph by paragraph, until you start to feel or understand each writer's style. Then practice revising your writing using their style. At first you may feel that you're copying someone's style, but you will soon realize that there are unique differences among styles; your style is just evolving.

7. **Have people whose opinion you trust critique your style.** Listen, smile, and try their suggestions. No suggestion is a waste of time. The worst that can happen is that you will learn what not to do.

REVIEW   22-1

The following essay is made up mostly of simple sentences. On a separate piece of paper, revise the essay by varying the types of sentences and by combining sentences to include both clauses and phrases. Feel free to add, delete, or change words as you change the structure of the sentences. As you make changes, make sure that the relationships between ideas are logical. Don't forget to punctuate correctly. Answers will vary.

Life Is One Page at a Time

Where are your old photos? Are they still in the envelopes from the photo lab? Perhaps they are just sitting in a drawer somewhere. This summer my cousin dragged me to a scrapbooking party. I was so impressed by the hostess's presentation. I was immediately hooked. I got home that evening. I gathered up my photos. I gathered my newly purchased scrapbooking gear. I went to work. I soon discovered why so many people put so much time and effort into this hobby.

Scrapbooking has been a satisfying way to preserve my most precious memories. For example, I made a scrapbook of my daughter's first year of life. On the first page, I had her newborn picture. I had our hospital identification bracelets and window sign. The pages after that were filled with several other snapshots. They were filled with special trinkets. I had saved them.

I look at that album. My heart is filled with so much joy. I relive those precious moments. My daughter is already in kindergarten. Time goes fast. I realize how important it is to preserve those treasured memories.

I have also found that scrapbooking gives me the opportunity to share a part of my life with others. I let other people look at the album. They can see us in Maui. We vacationed there. We had so much fun. Each page tells a different story. Another page shows a family reunion. Another one shows my sister's wedding. The memories I include are not only of joyous occasions. I also include the tragedies in my life. I dedicated a page to each of my parents. It was my way to celebrate their lives. It helped with the grieving process. I cherish these memories. I hold them close to my heart.

Scrapbooking actually lets time stand still. Scrapbooks are filled with fabulous stories. They are filled with memories worth sharing. These albums can be passed on for generations to come. These albums will tell our stories. Through these stories, our legacy will go on.

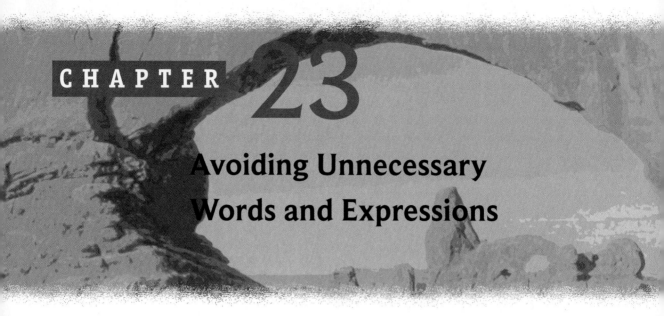

CHAPTER 23

Avoiding Unnecessary Words and Expressions

YOUR GOALS

1. Recognize and revise wordiness.
2. Identify and edit for clichés.
3. Identify and edit for slang.
4. Identify and edit for offensive language.

"Our writers are full of clichés just as old barns are full of bats. There is obviously no rule about this, except that anything that you suspect of being a cliché undoubtedly is one and had better be removed."

▪ **Wolcott Gibbs** ▪

Trent, a student in a marketing class, has been assigned to write an advertisement promoting his college with the goal of increasing enrollment at the college. The ad will appear in a sleek brochure that the college plans to send to graduating high school students and their parents, as well as working adults in the community who might want to return to college for retraining or for a degree. Here is the ad copy that Trent turns in to his instructor.

It is a fact that you men out there will love this college as the ratio of women to men is 70 to 30 and lots of the women are real lookers. No problems with your dating lives, dudes! You girls will appreciate the comfy new student hangout and the low-cal food in the cafeteria, as well as the finely decorated bookstore with its stuffed animals, cute clothing, and greeting cards. Other cool stuff includes the awesome fitness center; the monster, two-story library with tons of computers for Internet surfing; and the bad coffee carts in the entryway of each campus building.

It doesn't stop here. The dorms are so rad and stylish that you feel like you are living in a posh bachelor pad. Each suite has a common living space, a corner for food prep, and two or three bedrooms. Who wouldn't want to escape Mom and Pop's house to live in this kind of setup?

Last, but not least, you are going to college to get an education, so you need to know about the profs. Some are as dull as dirt; others are as smooth as silk. You just gotta check online at *RateMyProfessor.com* to figure out which prof to take and how to get the most out of your classes so that you can be successful, have an effect on the planet, and move on to greater heights and the next level. It is a fact that college is the place to be! Check it out!

LET's warm up!

Ideally, we write because we feel strongly about a topic and want to make a memorable impression on the reader. However, sometimes we fall into "automatic" patterns of expression—stock phrases, clichés, slang, or offensive language—and these patterns of expression work against our purpose. Write a paragraph in which you try to use as many slang expressions as you can. (*Slang* is the kind of language we use when talking to friends informally: *cool, sick, dude,* and so on.) Choose any topic. Read your paragraph aloud to a classmate or friend and observe the reaction.

Yevgen Timashov/istockphoto.com

In Trent's choice of words and phrases and his informal style, he has not considered the impression he makes on his audience. The text provides some useful information to potential students and their parents, but it does so in such an informal, slangy, and sexist way that most recipients of the brochure will look elsewhere for their higher education.

UNDERSTANDING PROBLEMATIC PATTERNS OF EXPRESSION

Your job as a writer is to write clearly and concisely. See how you can slim down long sentences and clarify your diction by eliminating empty or inflated words and phrases. Eliminate jargon, slang, and words or expressions that may be offensive to your audience.

In this chapter, we look closely at the words and phrases you use to express your ideas. We focus on avoiding problematic expressions, allowing you to pare your writing down to just the words and phrases that convey your message most powerfully. Fortunately, you can learn to identify most of these expressions, for they fall into several easily recognized categories: wordiness, clichés, slang, and offensive language.

Eliminating Wordiness

When some students are assigned papers with a required number of words, they may naturally fall back on wordy expressions as "fillers" to meet the word requirement. As a writer, you can learn to recognize many of these fillers and eliminate them or replace them with shorter, more meaningful words or phrases. This section helps you examine several common practices that lead to wordiness and lets you practice ways to avoid them.

Avoid Stock Phrases, or "Deadwood"

Stock phrases are expressions that come from a large "stock" of ready-to-use words and phrases. You hear and read these expressions so often that you may be tempted to employ them in your own writing. "Deadwood" is a colorful term for these types of phrases—just like actual deadwood in a garden, stock phrases need to be cleared out.

> **WORDY:** It is a fact that a low grade on a test can be incredibly discouraging to the poor student who receives it.
>
> **SOLUTION:** A low grade on a test can discourage a student.

Learn to recognize deadwood. For example, rather than simply writing *because, since,* or *if,* some students feel compelled to clutter their sentences with empty phrases. Here are some common stock phrases that an inexperienced writer might choose instead of using one word that conveys the same meaning:

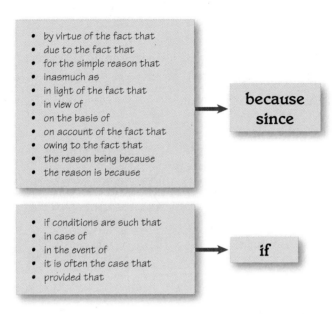

- by virtue of the fact that
- due to the fact that
- for the simple reason that
- inasmuch as
- in light of the fact that
- in view of
- on the basis of
- on account of the fact that
- owing to the fact that
- the reason being because
- the reason is because

→ **because since**

- if conditions are such that
- in case of
- in the event of
- it is often the case that
- provided that

→ **if**

Avoid the following expressions, which may clutter your paper, and replace them with clear and precise words.

Phrase to Avoid	Words or Phrases That Fix the Error	Phrase to Avoid	Words or Phrases That Fix the Error
at that point in time	then	it is possible that	perhaps, maybe
at the present time	now	on the part of	for
by means of	by	past experience	experience
concerning the matter of	about	regardless of the fact that	although
during the course of	during	subsequent to	after
for a period of a month	for a month	the question as to	whether
for the purpose of	for	12 midnight	midnight
in close proximity to	near	12 noon	noon
in the near future	soon	until such time as	until
in the process of	during, while	we would appreciate	please
in this day and age	currently, now, today	with reference to	about, concerning
it is our opinion that	we believe, we think	with the exception of	except

In addition, some expressions repeat the same idea. Avoid such redundancies.

> **WORDY:**   The <u>real</u> truth is that during the <u>grave</u> crisis, he used his <u>past</u> experiences to offer a solution.
> [Note that each of the underlined adjectives repeats the idea of the word it modifies.]

> **BETTER:**   The <u>truth</u> is that during the <u>crisis</u>, he used his <u>experiences</u> to offer a solution.

Learn to spot these types of expressions by familiarizing yourself with the following common phrases.

Redundant Phrase	Words or Phrases That Fix the Error	Redundant Phrase	Words or Phrases That Fix the Error
at an early time	earlier	new innovations	innovations
circle around	circle	past experience	experience
common similarities	similarities	personal opinion	opinion
completely unanimous	unanimous	real truth	truth
enclosed herewith	enclosed	reddish color	reddish
end result	result	throughout the course of	throughout
every single one	each, every one	through the use of	through
exactly identical	exactly	to a further extent	further
each and every	each, every	total annihilation	annihilation
future plans	plans	totally obvious	obvious
general consensus	consensus	true facts	facts
honest in character	honest	unusual in nature	unusual
I myself	I	witnessed firsthand	witnessed

Also, omit expressions that contribute nothing to your sentence. They only clutter your ideas.

all things considered	as the case may be	it goes to show that
as a matter of fact	by leaps and bounds	it should be noted that
as far as I'm concerned	it can be seen that	kind of/sort of

Whenever possible, be economical with your words so that you don't bog the reader down and waste the reader's time with empty phrases such as "it is my opinion that." The careful and interested reader becomes annoyed by unneeded wordiness, causing you to lose credibility and clarity.

PRACTICE 23-1

For each of the phrases that follow, write a word that expresses the same idea but more economically. If the phrase should be omitted, write *Omit*. Answers will vary.

1. it is a fact that ___Omit___
2. due to the fact that ___because___
3. because of the fact that ___because___
4. despite the fact that ___although___
5. at this point in time ___now___
6. nowadays ___now___
7. in our society today ___today___
8. in the year 2015 ___in 2015___
9. kind of sweet ___sweet___
10. rather trendy ___trendy___

Reduce Wordy Verbs

As you are revising your writing, be aware of verb-plus-noun phrases that might be expressed as just one verb. Here are some common phrases that can be reduced to just the verb.

Wordy	Reduced
are indications of	indicate
ascertain the location of	find
ask the question	ask
assembled together	assembled
be in receipt of	have
come to a realization	realize, recognize
give consideration to	consider

Wordy	Reduced
is aware of the fact that	knows
is capable of	can
is found to be	is
is suggestive of	suggests
put an end to	end
reach the conclusion that	conclude
serve the function of being	is

Be careful with verbs such as *make* and *have*. They often can be left out to focus the sentence on a more powerful verb.

> **WORDY:** I <u>have a feeling</u> that she dislikes me.
> **SOLUTION:** I <u>feel</u> that she dislikes me. [Use one strong verb.]

Wordy	Reduced
make an arrangement, decision, correction, inquiry, plan	arrange, decide, correct, inquire, plan
make an inquiry regarding	ask about
have an understanding, desire, hope, wish	understand, desire, hope, wish

Choose Strong Verbs Rather Than Attach Adverbs

Another danger spot is a verb plus an adverb. Often, you can use one powerful verb, rather than a weaker verb with a tacked-on adverb, to infuse the sentence with strength.

WORDY:	He <u>pulled strongly</u> on the tow rope.
SOLUTION:	He <u>yanked</u> on the tow rope. [Use one strong verb.]

PRACTICE 23-2

Cross out the wordy phrase in each sentence and rewrite that sentence by substituting one strong verb. Answers will vary.

1. The thief ~~moved stealthily~~ around the corner and into the den.
   The thief snuck around the corner and into the den.

2. The children ~~made a mess of~~ the family room with their Transformers and building blocks.
   The children cluttered the family room with their Transformers and building blocks.

3. The out-of-control bus ~~ran directly~~ into the department store window, which shattered into millions of pieces.
   The out-of-control bus smashed into the department store window, which shattered into millions of pieces.

4. He ~~had a feeling~~ that she might stand him up, but he kept waiting for her.
   He felt that she might stand him up, but he kept waiting for her.

5. Patients must ~~put their trust in~~ their physicians.
   Patients must trust their physicians.

6. The police ~~put a halt to~~ the riot with tear gas.
   The police halted the riot with tear gas.

7. The teens ~~had a party~~ in their parents' basement.
   The teens partied in their parents' basement.

8. The prosecutor ~~expressed an objection~~ to the defense lawyer's line of questioning.
   The prosecutor objected to the defense lawyer's line of questioning.

9. The onlooker ~~made a move~~ to help the stranded pedestrian.
   The onlooker rushed to help the stranded pedestrian.

10. She ~~tried hard~~ to overcome the obstacles in her life.
    She struggled to overcome the obstacles in her life.

Avoid Overusing Relative Clauses

Who, that, and *which* clauses may lead to unnecessary wordiness. When possible, omit or reduce relative clauses.

WORDY:	The camp director <u>who worked the hardest</u> is Marissa Harris.

> **Bridging Knowledge**
>
> **See Chapter 22** for an explanation and practice in reducing relative clauses to phrases.

SOLUTION: The hardest-working camp director is Marissa Harris.
[Omit the clause and put an adjective before the noun.]

WORDY: Jean Darling, <u>who has worked for the city for 25 years</u>, plans to retire in the summer.

SOLUTION: Jean Darling, a 25-year employee of the city, plans to retire in the summer.
[Use an appositive phrase after the noun.]

WORDY: Hemingway's novel <u>that is titled *The Sun Also Rises*</u> takes place in Spain.

SOLUTION: Hemingway's novel *The Sun Also Rises* takes place in Spain.
[Use a one-word appositive.]

Avoid Overusing *Be* Verbs

Unless necessary, avoid using the verb *be* (*am, is, are, was, were*) as the main verb of your sentence. This verb may lead to wordy sentences. If possible, reduce the sentence so that the main verb is more specific.

WORDY: Jose is the architect who designed our new civic center.

SOLUTION: Jose, an architect, designed our new civic center.
[Use an appositive.]

WORDY: Marisol is the one who rejected all suggestions.

SOLUTION: Marisol rejected all suggestions.
[Reduce the sentence to a simple sentence and use the verb of the relative clause as the main verb.]

PRACTICE 23-3

Reduce the wordiness in the following sentences by substituting appositives, adjectives, or vivid verbs as appropriate. Refer to the earlier examples. Answers will vary.

1. The man who is standing on the corner looks suspicious.
   The suspicious-looking man is standing on the corner.

2. Marketing, which is my chosen field of study, offers many employment possibilities.
   Marketing, my chosen field of study, offers many employment possibilities.

3. The pilot, who is exhausted, could not fly more hours until he had a good night's sleep.
   The exhausted pilot could not fly more hours until he had a good night's sleep.

4. Tricia, who is the most popular member of our staff, is upbeat, energetic, and creative.
   Tricia, the most popular member of our staff, is upbeat, energetic, and creative.

5. Anthony is the soldier who will most effectively lead the troops into battle.
   Anthony, a soldier, will most effectively lead the troops into battle.

Avoid Overusing Passive Voice

Since the passive voice may lead to wordy sentences, avoid it unless you have a specific reason for its use. The following are three main uses of the passive:

Bridging Knowledge

See Chapter 19 for an explanation of the effective use of the passive voice.

1. To focus the reader's attention on the action rather than the agent or doer of the action.
2. To describe an event for which the agent is unknown.
3. To describe an event for which the agent is unimportant.

PASSIVE:	The child was rescued by the neighbor from the burning house.
ACTIVE:	The neighbor rescued the child from the burning house.

Avoid Overusing Expletive Constructions

Expletive constructions begin a sentence with *it is, it was, there is, there are, there was,* or *there were*. Although expletives occupy the subject position, they are not the subjects of sentences; they act as empty fillers. Unless you have a specific reason for using expletive constructions, avoid them since they may delay and obscure the subjects of sentences.

WORDY:	It was her last comment that caught our attention.
SOLUTION:	Her last comment caught our attention.
	[Omit *it was* and rewrite the sentence as necessary.]

WORDY:	There is a local country-western band that plays at the arts center every Friday night.
SOLUTION:	A local country-western band plays at the arts center every Friday night.
	[Omit *there is* and rewrite the sentence as necessary.]

Wordiness often occurs during the initial drafting stage, when you are trying to generate as many ideas as possible. Before you consider submitting your paper, whether in college or in your profession, examine your sentences. If you find that you're writing long sentences, there's a good chance that you're being wordy.

PRACTICE 23-4

Rewrite the following wordy sentences to make them more concise. Answers will vary.

1. In spite of all of the worries that she had about her trip to Spain, everything went rather smoothly for her.

   Despite her worries about her trip to Spain, everything went smoothly.

2. It was agreed upon by every member of the committee that elections for those who wanted to be officers would occur next fall.

   The committee agreed that officer elections would occur next fall.

3. The dog moved furtively to the side of his master after taking a large bite out of the birthday cake.

   The dog slunk to his master's side after taking a large bite from the birthday cake.

4. It was kind of strange that she chose the green dress for her wedding.

   Strangely, she chose the green wedding dress.

5. It is indeed a fact that you should not leave your engine running while you are stuck in a traffic jam in order not to waste gas.

   To avoid wasting gas, do not leave your engine running in a traffic jam.

Avoiding Clichés

A cliché is a worn-out expression, used so often that it has lost its power, its specificity, and its freshness. Writers who use clichés lose their reader's confidence as their reader realizes they lack originality and thoughtfulness. Like an overused chair with its stuffing falling out, clichés should be avoided. Here are some examples of commonly used clichés:

Clichés to Avoid		
as big as a house	fit as a fiddle	put your best foot forward
at a loss for words	get the ball rolling	sad but true
better late than never	green with envy	short and sweet
butterflies in her stomach	hit the ground running	sleeps like a log
can't fight city hall	keep your chin up	sly as a fox
cold facts	last but not least	start from scratch
dance around the subject	let the dust settle	step forward or backward
don't rock the boat	like a bull in a china shop	sweep it under the rug
draw the line	the lion's share	throw light on the subject
drinks like a fish	look over his shoulder	tried and true
dumb as an ox	make ends meet	under the weather
easier said than done	my pay is chicken feed.	wide as a barn
eats like a pig (bird)	one in a million	work like a dog
fair shake	pretty as a picture	wrapped him (her) around her (his) finger
fall on deaf ears	push the envelope	wrestle with the problem

These phrases and expressions have been so overused that they have lost their intended impact on the reader. Clichés weaken your writing by making your points flat and boring, reflecting poorly on you as a writer. Instead, use fresh, more creative expressions that perk up your writing and reflect your skills as a writer and critical thinker. Your writing doesn't always have to sound fresh and inventive, but it should be appropriate for its context. Clichés are typically out of place in most college and business writing situations.

Underline the clichés and wordiness in the following sentences. On the lines provided, rewrite the sentences by substituting fresher, or more appropriate, expressions. Answers will vary.

1. When my boss assigned me a new project, I <u>ran with it</u>, realizing that my success depended on my <u>blowing my boss away with my impressive results</u>.

   When my boss assigned me a new project, I eagerly took it on, realizing that my success depended on my demonstrating motivation, as well as ability.

2. <u>It is a known fact that</u> no matter how hard you <u>dig in your heels and work like a dog</u>, you need the help of others.

   No matter how hard you apply yourself, you need the help of others.

3. The sprinter was swift <u>as an arrow</u> as he completed the first lap of the race.

   The sprinter was swift as a startled antelope as he completed the first lap of the race.

4. <u>Try as you may, you must always keep in mind that a bird in the hand is worth two in the bush</u>.

   Sometimes it's better to avoid risk and be satisfied with what you have.

5. <u>Don't fight fire with fire</u>; if people slander you, don't slander them back.

   Don't use the same tactics as your opponent; if people slander you, don't slander them back.

Avoiding Slang

Slang is one of the most colorful, creative, and interesting manifestations of spoken language. Most slang words and expressions are short lived: they are restricted to a specific time and a specific group. Since slang is limited to a certain audience, it is not appropriate for formal writing—biology reports, English essays, history papers, scholarship and job applications, and so on. If you don't edit carefully, slang can easily sneak into your writing since slang is so embedded in our culture. Avoid expressions such as the following in your college and professional writing (in everyday writing, you could find special uses for slang).

Popular Slang to Avoid (Some definitions are provided in parentheses.)		
all nighter	bad (meaning *good*)	blow a fuse
all that (*superior*)	barf	blown away
awesome, cool, dope, fresh, phat	bent out of shape	booze

bummer	earful	peace out (*good-bye*)
check out	easy mark	pig out
cheesy	flaky	po po (*police*)
chillaxin (*chill* and *relax*)	fo'shizzle (*for sure*)	pro
chill out	glazing	puke
cram	I hear that (*I agree*)	screw around
crib (*house*)	jerk someone around	sucker
croak	junkie	sweet (meaning *nice*)
cuz, dawg, homie (*friend*)	kick butt	tight
deep pockets	late (*later*)	24/7
dis (*disrespect*)	loser	whack
dork	make waves	up for grabs
dude	my bad, my bust	

Text messaging has become a popular way of communicating. Since text messages are limited to no more than 160 characters per message, writers often shorten words to insert as much information as possible. This type of shorthand includes removing apostrophes (*DONT* or *DNT* for *don't*), omitting vowels (*THS* for *this* or *these* or *PPL* for *people*), using symbols (@ for *at*, *2* for *to* or *too*, or *l8tr* for *later*), using sounds to represent the words (*U* for *you* or *8* for *ate*), and, most commonly, abbreviating words and phrases (*IDK* for *I don't know*, *BTW* for *by the way*, or *PLZ* for *please*). Although such shorthand texting is appropriate and convenient between cell phones, don't permit it to slip into your papers in college or professionally. It's not acceptable.

PRACTICE 23-6

The following sentences use some common slang words and expressions and some clichés. First, underline the slang expressions and clichés. Then, replace the underlined expressions with standard words that a general audience can easily understand. Make sure the form of the new words fits the sentence. Answers will vary.

1. Mr. James Zorrer, a collector of rare books, has a <u>phat</u> collection of first editions that is available to the public <u>24/7</u>.

   Mr. James Zorrer, a collector of rare books, has an exceptional collection of first editions that is always available to the public.

2. Accounting is such a <u>dorky</u> field because all you do all day is work with numbers and spreadsheets and face horrible time crunches.

   Accounting is such a difficult field because all you do all day is work with numbers and spreadsheets and face horrible time crunches.

3. I asked <u>my better half</u> to retire to Florida with me, but she <u>put her foot down</u> <u>and</u> refused.

    I asked my wife to retire to Florida with me, but she refused.

4. I can't believe she <u>dissed</u> you! That's really <u>whack</u>.

    I can't believe she insulted you! That's displeasing.

5. Her tattoo was so <u>awesome</u> that I <u>trucked</u> right over to the tattoo parlor and got myself one.

    Her tattoo was so artistic that I drove right over to the tattoo parlor and got myself one.

Avoiding Offensive Language

Language is more than just a sequence of words with definite meanings. Words and phrases carry connotations that give them meanings based on how they have been used over time and what emotional associations they carry. If not careful, you may unintentionally imply that some people are inferior to others by using language that excludes people or reinforces stereotypical attitudes. Thus, you want to be aware of writing in an unbiased and all-inclusive manner so that no reader feels insulted, excluded, or unfairly labeled or stereotyped.

Avoid Insulting Language

No careful, sensitive writer wants to offend the reader by using degrading or insulting expressions that show bias in terms of race, gender, nationality, age, disability, or sexual orientation. Note the following list of inappropriate words or phrases and then some possible substitutes.

	Offensive	Acceptable
AGE	old people, the elderly	senior citizens, people over 65, retirees, octogenarians
	your loved ones	relatives
DISABILITY	able-bodied, normal, healthy	nondisabled
	birth defect	congenital disability
	disabled	people with disabilities
	disabled toilet	accessible toilet
	down syndrome child, mongoloid	person with Down syndrome
	dumb	person with a speech impairment
	learning disabled	person with a specific learning disability
	handicapped, crippled, deformed	disabled
	psycho, mentally ill, crazy	person with mental illness
	retarded	person who has a developmental delay

GENDER	engineers and their wives	engineers and their spouses
	female or woman judge (lawyer, doctor, and so on)	judge (lawyer, doctor, and so on)
	girl or gal (for an adult woman)	female, woman, lady
	housewife	housekeeper, homemaker
	male nurse	nurse
	Miss, Mrs.	Ms.
SEXUAL ORIENTATION	homosexual	gay man, lesbian (specify)
	homosexual couple	couple
	homosexual relationship	relationship
	sexual preference	sexual orientation

Writers who use offensive language usually do so out of habit, not really intending to offend. However, your reader will not consider ignorance an excuse. As you choose and revise your words, be sure to avoid words that may be construed as sexist, ageist, or racist. Using words that demean people because of their gender, age, or origin is a sure way to alienate your audience and damage your credibility as a writer.

For instance, using ageist phrases such as "driving like a senior citizen" or "driving like a teenager" may alienate either group of readers—senior citizens or teenagers. "Haggard as an old crone" as a concrete description may only jeopardize your purpose in writing, even when your intentions are good.

One variation of offensive language is tagging an adjective to a specific group for no particular purpose. For example, why refer to a *male* nurse, *woman* doctor, *gay* mayor, *Jewish* lawyer, *female* truck driver, or *blind* musician? Is the implication that this person is less qualified or competent? Your reader will question your motive for drawing unnecessary attention to a specific characteristic. These types of expressions are insulting and should be avoided.

Offensive	Acceptable
black athlete	athlete
blind man	the man who is blind
disabled lawyer	lawyer
fat person	a person who is overweight

Also avoid words and expressions that reinforce stereotypes. Such generalities are usually the results of our lack of knowledge or understanding of other people, groups, or cultures. For example, stating that a person *looks gay* indicates that all gays have the same physical characteristics or behavior. Similarly, claiming that a man is complaining *like a woman* is offensive since the phrase stereotypes women and attempts to equate female behavior as negative or inferior, whereas the phrase *you think like a man* implies that males are better analytical thinkers. Similarly, when a writer refers to someone as a *jock* and *redneck*, the writer presumes that the reader shares the same assumptions about the group.

Language That Reinforces Stereotypes	
babe	Mafioso type
foxy manager	out of date
geriatric	over the hill
hen-pecked	(smart, fast, and so on) for a woman
hot-blooded Latin	the weaker sex
little lady	too old to change

Avoid Excluding Language

One danger in writing that creates a negative tone is using sexist language that excludes women or men. Avoid using masculine or feminine terms to refer to people who may be either male or female. The following list should help you become familiar with such words or expressions.

Offensive	Acceptable
actress	actor
anchorman	anchor
bellboy	bellhop
businessman	business person
cameraman	camera operator
chairman	chairperson or chair
cleaning woman	house or office cleaner, custodian
common man	average citizen
congressman	congressional representative
Dear Sir	Dear Sir/Madam
mailman	mail carrier, postal worker
mankind	humans, human beings, human race
manmade	manufactured, machine-made
paperboy	paper carrier
poetess	poet
policeman	police officer
spokesman	spokesperson, representative
steward, stewardess	flight attendant
workman	worker

PRACTICE 23-7

For each of the following words or phrases, write an inoffensive substitute. Answers will vary.

1. salesman ___salesperson___
2. fireman ___fire fighter___
3. female truck driver ___truck driver___
4. female astronaut ___astronaut___
5. deaf woman ___hearing-impaired woman___
6. stewardess ___flight attendant___
7. male hairdresser ___hairdresser___
8. Mr. Chavez and Miss Hernandez ___Mr. Chavez and Ms. Hernandez___
9. Oriental woman ___Chinese woman___
10. janitress ___janitor___

Because of the nature of our language, pronouns present a special problem. English does not have a personal pronoun that is gender neutral. As a result, writers have used the masculine pronoun to indicate both male and female. Your reader may find this practice sexist and exclusive.

EXCLUSIVE:	Each of the soldiers was praised for <u>his</u> valor.
BETTER:	The soldiers were praised for <u>their</u> valor.
EXCLUSIVE:	If a physician wants to make an accurate diagnosis, <u>he</u> must listen carefully to his patient.
BETTER:	If physicians want to make accurate diagnoses, <u>they</u> must listen carefully to their patients.

Although some writers may use a he/she type of construction to avoid sexist language, this practice can be distracting when repeated too often. Where possible, avoid identifying the gender, use plural references to make your pronouns plural, or use more inclusive forms of the words.

PRACTICE 23-8

Edit the following sentences for offensive language by crossing out the offensive words or phrases and rewriting the sentences on the lines provided. Change pronouns where necessary. Answers will vary.

1. The ~~gal~~ who helps run the office is efficient, hard working, and dependable.
    The woman who helps run the office is efficient, hard working, and dependable.

2. The building was redesigned so that the ~~crippled~~ are better able to access the various offices.

    The building was redesigned so that people with disabilities are better able to access the various offices.

3. Kristin plays hockey well ~~for a girl~~.

    Kristin plays hockey well.

4. ~~Normal people~~ should have no problem figuring out how to install laminate flooring.

    The average person should have no problem figuring out how to install laminate flooring.

5. Our TV station conducted interviews with the ~~man~~ in the street to determine how ~~he~~ feels about the upcoming presidential election.

    Our TV station conducted interviews with the people in the street to determine how they feel about the upcoming presidential election.

Use Groups' Preferred Names

Choosing the correct reference for a group may be troublesome for some students. For example, although the words *Latino* and *Hispanic* are often used interchangeably, they have different meanings. *Hispanic* is used more broadly to include all people who share the same language, Spanish. This broader reference also includes people from Spain. However, the word *Latino* refers to people of Latin American origin, which does not include Spain. As a rule, find out the name the group has chosen for itself, but preferably, be specific. For example, specifying *Cuban Americans, Mexican Americans,* or *Puerto Ricans* does not assume that all Spanish-speaking groups are identical.

Offensive	Acceptable
Eskimo	Inuit, Alaska Native
Indian (for an American Indian)	Native American (where possible, use more specific names: Iroquois, Hopi, Navajo, and so on)
Latins	Hispanics, Latinos and Latinas, Chicanos and Chicanas (for Mexican Americans; where possible, use more specific names)
Negro, Afro-American, colored person	African American, black
Oriental, Asiatic	Asian (where possible, use more specific names: Korean, Chinese, and so on)

REVIEW 23-1

Cross out any offensive language and slang. Where necessary, substitute acceptable language above the words or phrases you eliminate. If you change pronouns, make sure you follow the rules of subject–verb and pronoun–antecedent agreement. Answers will vary.

To: Convenience Store Managers

RE: Preparing Employees for Possible Robbery

Any business can be targeted for a robbery. But the consequences of ~~this hairy~~ <u>robbery</u> ~~event~~ can be minimized by having your employees follow a simple procedure. First, let your employees know that the goal is to protect themselves and the customers. In the event of a robbery, all employees, ~~especially female cashiers,~~ should remain calm. A ~~customer~~ <u>Customers</u> may easily ~~freak out~~ <u>lose their composure</u> if ~~she sees~~ <u>they see</u> an employee panic. In particular, ~~old timers~~ <u>senior citizens</u> are ~~fussy and~~ quick to overreact in most strange situations. Ask these customers to ~~chill~~ <u>remain calm</u>. Most importantly, emphasize to your employees that they do exactly what the thieves demand and nothing more.

The personal safety of our employees and that of the customers is far more important than all the ~~bucks~~ <u>money</u> or merchandise the thieves might take. Advise your employees not to communicate with the robbers; the employees should speak only when spoken to. Talking to the offenders only prolongs the event.

As the robbery progresses, the ~~creeps~~ <u>robbers</u> will most likely be nervous and tense. Therefore, if ~~an employee needs~~ <u>employees need</u> to make any sudden movements, ~~she~~ <u>they</u> should explain what ~~she's~~ <u>they are</u> going to do in advance, for example, "I'm going to move toward the cash register." It's often difficult to predict whether the criminal is really ~~packing heat or carrying a blade~~ <u>carrying a weapon</u>. In addition, let the ~~employee~~ <u>employees</u> know that ~~she is~~ <u>they are</u> to avoid eye contact with the robbers at all times. Finally, encourage your employees to remember as much information as they possibly can about the lawbreakers so that they can help the ~~policemen nail the~~ <u>police officers identify</u> ~~jerks~~ <u>them later</u>.

Using the Correct Words

PART 5

CHAPTER 24

Frequently Confused Words

YOUR GOALS

1. Distinguish among closely related words.

2. Revise sentences and paragraphs to correct errors in frequently confused words.

"How often misused words

generate misleading thoughts."

■ Herbert Spencer ■

Mr. Peter Allan, a food inspector, turns in the following report on a fast-food restaurant that he inspected the previous day.

My overall rating of Tacos To Go is poor because of the following infractions:

1. Some of it's employees did not have there hair properly pulled back and secured.

2. Some of the employees' cloths were dirty and food spattered.

3. The butcher-block workspace had moldy food setting on it.

4. Customers could see overflowing trash cans threw the doors too the kitchen.

5. Buy the sink were sponges full of bacteria.

6. A large amount of cockroaches were laying under the sink.

7. Between the five cooks, only one washed his hands frequently.

8. Much of the floor, accept for the stove area, was covered with food scraps.

9. It was difficult to breath in the kitchen do to the lack of proper ventilation.

In general, the sight was way below standard.

LET's warm up!

Some English words sound or look almost exactly alike and therefore are easily confused, such as *your* and *you're*. It is easy to misuse these words as you are busily typing an e-mail, writing a research paper, or composing a lab report. Because these words are simple and frequently used, however, their misuse is particularly glaring; thus, you as a writer must be sure to proofread to correct them before hitting the send button or turning a paper or report in to your instructor or supervisor. Write a paragraph that offers some strategies to help writers avoid errors in words that look and sound alike. Be as specific as possible.

Enrico Fianchini/istockphoto.com

In this report, it is difficult to focus on the inspector's evaluation because the errors in word choice are so obvious. Most people are aware of the writing problems they have, but ignoring the problems says much about such people as professionals. English contains words that sound alike, look alike, or both yet are used differently. When writers confuse these words, the errors are glaring for the discriminating reader and detract from the writer's credibility. Mr. Allen should have taken time to read over the report. Simply reviewing for commonly confused words would have made a big difference in his report and in his reputation as a professional.

UNDERSTANDING FREQUENTLY CONFUSED WORDS

English is probably the most linguistically diverse language in the world. English borrows words from Latin, Greek, French, Spanish, Italian, and other languages and sometimes incorporates the spelling patterns of those languages. This quality makes English rich and dynamic, but it also can make choosing the right word confusing. Some factors that contribute to this confusion are the following characteristics of English words:

- English has the ability to change a word to different parts of speech, changing the pronunciation but maintaining the same spelling: "Your <u>conduct</u> is exemplary since you <u>conduct</u> yourself like a professional."
- Some words may have the same sound but different spelling and meaning: "I had a strong desire to <u>see</u> the <u>sea</u>."
- Two words can mean basically the same thing but are used differently, for example: <u>Between</u> the two, he was the funniest; but <u>among</u> the four comedians, he couldn't raise a smile.

You can probably think of other reasons that make choosing the wrong word easy. Start by identifying the words you usually confuse. Then try to understand the reasons you find these words difficult, and finally, edit your writing for precisely these words. This chapter examines the most frequently confused words. See whether some of your common errors are among them and develop you own checklist. The next time you need to proofread what you write, pull out your checklist.

Words Frequently Confused

For each set of words, first read the Preview the Context example. Try to determine the difference in the way each word is used. Then read the definitions and examples of each separate word. Finally, test your understanding by filling the correct words in the Practice the Context sentences. You can check your answers in Appendix A.

1. **A lot/allot**

   PREVIEW THE CONTEXT: Don't <u>allot</u> <u>a lot</u> of time to introductions of the speakers.

   - *A lot* is two words meaning a large quantity. Do not write *a lot* as one word.
       We have <u>a lot</u> of reading to do for tomorrow.
   - *Allot* is a verb meaning to portion out.
       The council will <u>allot</u> each farmer 10 bags of seed.
       The pie graph showed how the tax revenue was <u>allotted</u>.

   PRACTICE THE CONTEXT: _____ of the graphs and charts illustrate ways our legislators plan to _____ the tax revenue.

2. **Accept/except**

   PREVIEW THE CONTEXT: You should <u>accept</u> the fact that the college will admit all students <u>except</u> those with low test scores.

   ■ *Accept* is a verb meaning to receive or to agree with.
   He <u>accepted</u> the package.
   We <u>accepted</u> the terms of the contract.
   ■ *Except* is a preposition meaning excluded or but.
   Everyone <u>except</u> Jay was invited to the anniversary celebration.

   PRACTICE THE CONTEXT: When we found out that all the employees _____ union employees were willing to _____ the new contract, we were angry.

3. **Advice/advise**

   PREVIEW THE CONTEXT: You did <u>advise</u> him to drive slowly within city limits, but your <u>advice</u> was not well taken.

   ■ *Advice* is a noun, meaning an opinion or a recommendation.
   I can always count on you to give me sound <u>advice</u>.

   ■ *Advise* is a verb that means to give an opinion or recommendation or to counsel.
   Ms. Randall will <u>advise</u> me again next week.

   PRACTICE THE CONTEXT: I will bluntly _____ him to keep his meddling _____ to himself.

4. **Affect/effect**

   PREVIEW THE CONTEXT: The patient feared that the <u>effects</u> of the treatment will eventually <u>affect</u> his social life, which will <u>effect</u> changes in his career plans.

   ■ *Affect* is a verb, meaning to influence or to change.
   Working the graveyard shift can <u>affect</u> your schoolwork.
   ■ *Effect* is a noun, meaning the result or consequence of a cause or an influence.
   Working the graveyard shift has had an <u>effect</u> on my schoolwork.
   ■ *Effect* can also function as a verb to mean bring about.
   The newly elected mayor swore to <u>effect</u> major changes in zoning laws during his term.

   PRACTICE THE CONTEXT: The new vaccine is able to _____ a cure with only one side _____ that will not _____ most people's lifestyles.

5. **All ready/already**

   PREVIEW THE CONTEXT: She <u>already</u> announced she is <u>all ready</u> to lead the organization.

■ *All ready* is an adjective, meaning completely prepared.
  The students were <u>all ready</u> to start the exam.
■ *Already* is an adverb meaning previously.
  They've <u>already</u> completed today's assignment.

PRACTICE THE CONTEXT: I was _____ to call my dentist when I remembered I had _____ canceled my appointment.

6. All right/alright

PREVIEW THE CONTEXT: Despite his injuries, he is <u>all right</u>.

■ *All right* means okay or adequate. *All right* is the only correct form.
  He promised that everything would be <u>all right</u> if I called.
■ *Alright* is a misspelling of the word *all right*. The form *alright* does not exist.

PRACTICE THE CONTEXT: I knew it would be _____ with Mike, but it wasn't _____ with his wife.

7. Among/between

PREVIEW THE CONTEXT: <u>Among</u> my friends, I am the most gregarious; but <u>between</u> my husband and me, he is the more outgoing.

■ *Among* refers to more than two people, items, places, and so on.
  He was <u>among</u> the many customers who filed a complaint.
■ *Between* is limited to two people, items, places, and so on.
  <u>Between</u> the two, she seems the more level headed.

PRACTICE THE CONTEXT: We wanted to divide the pizza _____ the two of us, but we decided to join the other group and divide it _____ the four of us.

8. Amount/number

PREVIEW THE CONTEXT: The <u>amount</u> of food at the party was excessive considering the small <u>number</u> of guests.

■ *Amount* is used with things that can't be counted, like money, food, and stress.
  The <u>amount</u> of rain we got this year set a record.
■ *Number* is used with things that can be counted, such as friends, dollars, and visits.
  We were amazed at the <u>number</u> of students who attended the study session.

PRACTICE THE CONTEXT: When a large _____ of lumber was returned to the store, the manager had a large _____ of questions.

9. Are/our

PREVIEW THE CONTEXT: We transferred <u>our</u> money so that all of <u>our</u> funds <u>are</u> in one financial institution.

■ *Are* is a form of the verb *be*.
  I believe most of us <u>are</u> due for a salary increase this year.

■ *Our* is the possessive form of *we.*
We couldn't understand how <u>our</u> instructor calculated <u>our</u> grades.

PRACTICE THE CONTEXT: _____ manager wants us to pick up the cans that _____ on the shelf.

10. Assure/ensure/insure

PREVIEW THE CONTEXT: The agent <u>assured</u> my parents that if they <u>insure</u> their house with his agency, he would <u>ensure</u> them a discount when they <u>insure</u> their automobiles.

■ *Assure* means to make sure or certain or to give confidence.
Our professor <u>assured</u> us that if we revised our essays as indicated, we would receive a passing grade.
■ *Ensure* means to guarantee.
The manager took necessary steps to <u>ensure</u> quality service.
■ *Insure* is to obtain an insurance policy.
It is always safe to <u>insure</u> your property against theft.

PRACTICE THE CONTEXT: Rushing to _____ his motorcycle, Larry double-checked to _____ himself that his documents were in order since he needed proof of insurance to _____ his entry in tonight's bike race.

PRACTICE 24-1

Underline the correct word in each sentence.

1. (<u>Among</u>/between) all of the choices, the last option fits me best.
2. Students must (<u>accept</u>/except) that they can always be studying something.
3. Although the (amount/<u>number</u>) of relatives that she has is small, they are a close and supportive group.
4. Do not (<u>allot</u>/a lot) too many resources to just one project.
5. A week's camping trip requires a large (<u>amount</u>/number) of food.
6. The weather is (<u>all right</u>/alright) as long as you enjoy heat and dryness.
7. She enjoys most Greek food (accept/<u>except</u>) moussaka.
8. Working with a tutor has had a positive (affect/<u>effect</u>) on my grades.
9. Teachers spend (allot/<u>a lot</u>) of their time preparing lessons and grading papers.
10. (Among/<u>between</u>) my two children, my younger son is calmer and easier to control.

11. Beside/besides

PREVIEW THE CONTEXT: <u>Besides</u> his own feelings of guilt, he felt it was his duty to stay <u>beside</u> her throughout the ordeal.

■ *Beside* is a preposition meaning along the side of.

Waiting for the driver to change the tire, the passengers remained <u>beside</u> the taxi.

■ *Besides* means in addition to.

I don't see the point in incorporating tables and charts into my report; <u>besides,</u> I don't have the time.

PRACTICE THE CONTEXT: _____ that stack of boxes, you'll also need to move those barrels _____ the exit sign.

12. Brake/break

PREVIEW THE CONTEXT: The mechanic was just about to fix my <u>brakes</u> before they <u>break</u> but decided first to take his <u>break</u>.

■ *Brake* as a verb means to slow or to stop. As a noun, it's the name of the device to slow or stop the motion of a mechanism.

Sometime it's dangerous to step on the <u>brake</u> and <u>brake</u> unexpectedly.

■ *Break* as a verb means to shatter, to come apart, or to split.

If you drop it, you'll <u>break</u> it.

■ *Break* is also used as a noun to mean an interruption from one activity to do something else.

We all agreed to stop for a coffee <u>break</u>.

PRACTICE THE CONTEXT: All of a sudden, Jeff decides to _____ in front of Starbucks and take an early _____ even though this will _____ his routine.

13. Breath/breathe

PREVIEW THE CONTEXT: I needed a <u>breath</u> of fresh air after I had to <u>breathe</u> indoor air all day at the conference.

■ *Breath* is a noun referring to respiration. It can also refer to a light breeze.

Take a deep <u>breath</u> and enjoy the smell of freshly brewed coffee.

■ *Breathe* is a verb, meaning to take air in and out from the lungs.

<u>Breathe</u> deeply three times to calm yourself when you're angry.

PRACTICE THE CONTEXT: I hate when they _____ next to me; their _____ smells like an ashtray.

14. By/buy

PREVIEW THE CONTEXT: I'll <u>buy</u> it if you ship it <u>by</u> tomorrow.

■ *By* is a preposition meaning next to or via (as in "by train"). It can also mean as of a certain time (for example, "by then" or "by tomorrow").

My boss walked <u>by</u> me and didn't even acknowledge seeing me.

■ *Buy* is a verb meaning to purchase.

You'll never save money if you <u>buy</u> everything you see.

PRACTICE THE CONTEXT: My wife and I decided to _____ the old house _____ the creek.

15. Capital/capitol

PREVIEW THE CONTEXT: The Capitol Building, the seat of government, is located in our nation's capital, Washington, D.C.

- *Capital* is the correct form for all uses (state and country capitals, capital crime, capital letters) except to indicate a government building.

  Many gathered in Austin, the capital of Texas, to protest capital punishment.
- *Capitol* refers only to the government building. Sometimes the word is capitalized.

  We decided to visit the state capitol to see our legislators in action.

PRACTICE THE CONTEXT: Since we were touring the nation's _____, we decided to visit the _____ building to hear the debate.

16. Choose/chose

PREVIEW THE CONTEXT: Frank chose not to participate in the activities; therefore, he shouldn't be allowed to choose the winner.

- *Choose* is the present tense of the verb, meaning to pick or select.

  Once you choose your courses, fill out the forms.
- *Chose* is the past tense of *choose*. Although both words are pronounced differently, some students tend to mix the forms.

  We thought it strange that he chose not to vote this year.

PRACTICE THE CONTEXT: Yesterday, Gina _____ to stay home, whereas today she may _____ to wander the city streets.

17. Cite/sight/site

PREVIEW THE CONTEXT: After arriving at the site, the project manager caught sight of a potential problem that he knew he needed to cite in his report.

- *Cite* means to give credit or list examples.

  Be sure to cite all of the sources that you used in your research paper.
- *Sight* refers to vision.

  The sight of the jets in formation was impressive.
- *Site* refers to a place.

  The police searched the site of the murder.

PRACTICE THE CONTEXT: The archeologist can _____ several instances in which an ancient _____ has been plundered for the _____ of buried treasures.

18. Clothes/cloth

PREVIEW THE CONTEXT: The <u>cloths</u> we use to decorate our tables may be used to sew <u>clothes</u> for orphans.

■ *Clothes* are garments that we wear.
   When he heard the banging on the door, he jumped out of bed, put on his <u>clothes,</u> and ran downstairs.
■ *Cloth* is material to make clothing, covers, and so on.
   The scratchy <u>cloth</u> of her wool jacket made her arms itch.

PRACTICE THE CONTEXT: We will create stylish _____ made from the finest choice of _____ for tailoring.

19. Compliment/complement

PREVIEW THE CONTEXT: The colors in the room <u>complement</u> the style of furniture; therefore, I receive many <u>compliments</u> on my good taste in decorating.

■ *Complement* means to go with or complete.
   The shoes <u>complement</u> your dress perfectly.
■ *Compliment* as a verb means to flatter or praise; as a noun, it means flattery or praise.
   His false and excessive <u>compliments</u> were obvious to the interviewer.

PRACTICE THE CONTEXT: People would often _____ our teamwork and would praise how our personalities _____ each other.

20. Criterion/criteria

PREVIEW THE CONTEXT: The <u>criteria</u> for a good action film are an exciting plot, clever action scenes, and good cinematography. A <u>criterion</u> that is not necessary is character development.

■ *Criterion* means one standard of evaluation.
   One <u>criterion</u> that the workers objected to was their requirement to willingly work overtime.
■ *Criteria* is the plural form of *criterion,* meaning several standards.
   The students wanted to know the <u>criteria</u> their instructor would use to evaluate their essays.

PRACTICE THE CONTEXT: We accepted the _____ she established to evaluate our performance except one _____, which we felt was unfair.

PRACTICE 24-2

Underline the correct word in each sentence.

1. Most women try to buy (<u>clothes</u>/cloths) that flatter their figure.

2. My coworker (<u>complimented</u>/complemented) me on my new suit.

3. The (cite/<u>sight</u>/site) of a man dangling from the scaffolding terrorized the onlookers below.

4. Researchers must always (<u>cite</u>/sight/site) their sources to acknowledge the work of others.

5. Last night, the search committee finally (choose/<u>chose</u>) three candidates to interview for the philosophy position.

6. To pay their respects to those who lost their lives, many people visit the (cite/sight/<u>site</u>) of the mining disaster.

7. (<u>By</u>/Buy) now, the families have been notified of the accident.

8. His suit is made of some of the finest linen (clothes/<u>cloth</u>) available in Egypt.

9. If buyers (chose/<u>choose</u>) carefully, they can save on their electronic purchases.

10. The interior designer pointed out that the earth tones on the walls (compliment/<u>complement</u>) the African print furniture.

21. Dessert/desert

PREVIEW THE CONTEXT: I was afraid our guide would <u>desert</u> us in the <u>desert</u>, so we offered him dinner and promised him apple pie for <u>dessert</u>.

■ *Dessert* is the sweet you want after dinner. Think of the double *s* in this word as standing for two helpings of dessert.

Strawberry cheesecake is my favorite <u>dessert</u>.

■ *Desert* is a verb that means to withdraw from, leave, or abandon.

Before I testified, I did not realize that my friends would <u>desert</u> me.

■ *Desert* is also a noun to describe an arid, barren land.

As we drove across the hot <u>desert</u>, we were afraid that the car might break down.

PRACTICE THE CONTEXT: Dora couldn't understand why the people she trusted most would _____ her. Feeling as if she were alone in a vast _____, her only comfort was to nibble on her chocolate _____.

22. Do/due

PREVIEW THE CONTEXT: We decided that it would be in our interest to <u>do</u> the job a week before it is <u>due</u>.

■ *Do* is a verb meaning to make, construct, carry out, prepare, or complete.

Once you <u>do</u> your homework, review it before submitting it to your instructor.

■ *Due* is when something is scheduled for a certain time or is a promise of payment by a certain date.

The rent is usually <u>due</u> at the beginning of the month.

PRACTICE THE CONTEXT: Although it was _____ this week, he did not want to _____ the project just yet.

23. Farther/further

PREVIEW THE CONTEXT: The <u>farther</u> the mountain climber hiked, the <u>further</u> he exhausted his lungs.

■ *Farther* refers to physical distance.
  How much <u>farther</u> do we need to walk?
■ *Further* means to extend more or to go beyond a certain time or degree.
  Our professor extended the due date <u>further</u> than the students expected.

PRACTICE THE CONTEXT: Since the site of the cabin is much _____ in the hills than we anticipated, we had to stop and _____ study the road map to avoid getting lost.

24. Fewer/less

PREVIEW THE CONTEXT: As one takes on more commitments, one has <u>less</u> time and <u>fewer</u> opportunities for recreation.

■ *Fewer* describes items or people who can be counted. Use *fewer* if you can substitute the word *many*.
  <u>Fewer</u> complaints mean happier customers.
■ *Less* describes things that can't be counted. It refers to amount and degree.
  My fiancé needs to spend <u>less</u> money on his hobby and <u>less</u> time with his friends.

PRACTICE THE CONTEXT: The _____ you exercise, the _____ calories you will burn.

25. Former/latter

PREVIEW THE CONTEXT: We had to decide whether to dine at the Chinese or Italian restaurant. Ben loves egg rolls and thus voted for the <u>former</u>, but I was in the mood for lasagna and insisted on the <u>latter</u>.

■ *Former* refers to the first of two items mentioned in the sentence.
  When offered free tickets to either the football or the soccer game, Gloria, whose husband plays football for the Broncos, chose the <u>former</u>.
■ *Latter* refers to the second of two items mentioned in the sentence.
  When offered free tickets to either the football or the soccer game, Nathaniel, who once played soccer for the Rapids, chose the <u>latter</u>.

PRACTICE THE CONTEXT: We had a choice of two topics to research: legalized gambling or global warming. Since I'm a science major with a strong interest in ecological issues, I chose the _____; however, my roommate, who had just returned from Las Vegas, chose the _____.

26. Hear/here

PREVIEW THE CONTEXT: Here at the opera house is a place to hear some of the finest sopranos of our time.

- *Hear* is a verb meaning to perceive with the ear. Notice that the last three letters spell *ear*, indicating the correct word choice.
    She spoke so softly that I could barely hear her.
- *Here* indicates a place or location; it tells where.
    We need you here to write up the final report.

PRACTICE THE CONTEXT: When he finally arrived _____, she was so excited to _____ that she had won the music award.

27. Heard/herd

PREVIEW THE CONTEXT: The buffalo herd was heard lowing in the pasture.

- *Heard* is the past tense of *hear*.
    I heard you were leaving the firm.
- *Herd* is a group of animals.
    The cowboys rounded up the herd of cattle and headed them back to the ranch.
- *Herd* is also a verb meaning to gather together.
    The suspects were herded into one room for questioning.

PRACTICE THE CONTEXT: We _____ the _____ of cattle in the distance.

28. Hole/whole

PREVIEW THE CONTEXT: There's a hole in the wall that needs to be repaired, but we may have to do the whole wall so that the repair isn't noticeable.

- *Hole* is an empty or hollow space or a gap in an object or surface.
    The heavy rain filled the hole with water.
- *Whole* means entire, complete, or healthy.
    We were surprised that he ate the whole pizza.

PRACTICE THE CONTEXT: He attempted to cover the _____ in his shirt as he got on the stage to address the _____ student body.

29. Imply/infer

PREVIEW THE CONTEXT: The politician implied that if school funding were raised, the town would need to increase taxes; the audience inferred that raising taxes would be difficult.

- *Imply* means to suggest or state indirectly.
    Although she denied it, Nydia implied that she would quit if she didn't get the promotion.

■ *Infer* means to conclude or draw a conclusion based on evidence.
   After hearing the dismal state of our budget, we could only <u>infer</u> that salaries would be frozen this year.

PRACTICE THE CONTEXT: From his accent, she _____ that he was from Boston;
however, she was bothered when he _____ that
Boston was the center of culture in the United States.

30. Its/it's

PREVIEW THE CONTEXT: <u>It's</u> a fact that the dog used <u>its</u> teeth to gnaw through the
fence.

■ *Its* expresses possession. This possessive pronoun needs no apostrophe.
   The company decided to outsource some of <u>its</u> production jobs.
■ *It's* is short for *it is* or *it has.*
   I'm not totally convinced <u>it's</u> the right decision, but I will support it.

PRACTICE THE CONTEXT: The agency has always provided all _____ members
the opportunity to voice their concern, but _____
been slow in making any significant changes.

PRACTICE 24-3

Underline the correct word in each sentence.

1. In an open field on the way to our cabin, we saw a (heard/<u>herd</u>) of antelope
   grazing on the grasses.

2. The cat stuck (<u>its</u>/it's) paw into the spilled juice.

3. In her criticism of the movie, the critic (<u>implied</u>/inferred) that it was overly violent.

4. Our political science professor assigned us (farther/<u>further</u>) reading in the
   chapter.

5. The (<u>farther</u>/further) we drove down the country road, the more worried we
   became that we were lost.

6. The (<u>fewer</u>/less) courses that you enroll in now, the longer (its/<u>it's</u>) going to take
   you to complete your degree.

7. The audience (implied/<u>inferred</u>) from the politician's speech that she supported
   physician-assisted suicide.

8. The instructor received (<u>fewer</u>/less) complaints once she offered students
   retakes on their quizzes if they did poorly the first time.

9. Even though I was not hungry, I ate my (hole/<u>whole</u>) lunch since I didn't want to
   fix the (<u>hole</u>/whole) in the door just yet.

10. While Juan was studying abroad, he (<u>heard</u>/herd) from his girlfriend only twice.

31. Knew/new

PREVIEW THE CONTEXT: I <u>knew</u> the minute that she sailed into the room that she was wearing a <u>new</u> outfit.

- *Knew* is the past tense of *know*. The word comes from *knowledge*, and both of these words start with the letter "k."
  Eli <u>knew</u> the answer but didn't want to raise his hand.
- *New* is an adjective, meaning the opposite of *old*.
  He decided to create a <u>new</u> climax for this story since the old one was too predictable.

PRACTICE THE CONTEXT: Richard _____ from the start that the _____ strategy would not increase sales.

32. Lay/lie

PREVIEW THE CONTEXT: After I <u>lay</u> my books on the dining room table, I will <u>lie</u> down for a nap.

- *Lay* means to put. It can also mean the past tense of *lie*, to recline.
  I asked the driver to <u>lay</u> the lumber in the driveway, and then I <u>lay</u> down on the couch to watch TV.
- *Lie* means to recline.
  I felt dizzy and had to <u>lie</u> down for a while.

PRACTICE THE CONTEXT: I'll _____ here until they _____ the packages where they belong.

33. Lead/led

PREVIEW THE CONTEXT: The new manager <u>led</u> the workers to the exact place where they should place the <u>lead</u> pipes.

- *Lead* is a noun that refers to the metal. This word rhymes with *dead*.
  The <u>lead</u> box was so heavy that two employees had to carry it.
- *Lead* is also a verb that means to go first as a guide or to conduct. This word rhymes with *bead*.
  We need a new leader; someone who will <u>lead</u> us through new directions.
- *Led* is the past and past participle form of the verb *lead*. If the action of the verb did not take place in the past, then use *lead*.
  As mayor of our town, Ms. Hamilton <u>led</u> the parade.

PRACTICE THE CONTEXT: Yesterday's protest, _____ by a tall man waving a _____ pipe, must be addressed promptly or it may _____ to unforeseeable problems.

34. Lose/loose

PREVIEW THE CONTEXT: Although Carmela tried not to <u>lose</u> her car keys, they fell off her <u>loose</u> key chain and dropped into the stream.

- *Lose* means to misplace something or someone. It can also mean to fail to win (the opposite of *win*).

  Follow the map so that you don't <u>lose</u> your way.
- *Loose* means free, not fastened, or not tight-fitting (the opposite of *tight*).

  After only 2 weeks on the new diet, his pants felt <u>loose</u>.

PRACTICE THE CONTEXT: Since all the pages in your report are _____, you just might _____ part of it.

35. Moral/morale

PREVIEW THE CONTEXT: When we criticized the lack of <u>morals</u> in their behavior, the employees' <u>morale</u> decreased dramatically.

- *Moral* refers to the rules of right or wrong conduct. Also, *moral* is a lesson of conduct.

  Since she wanted her son to grow up to be a <u>moral</u> person, every night she would tell him stories with a <u>moral</u> that they would then discuss.
- *Morale* refers to a person's or group's mental condition or spirit.

  Our company's latest climate survey indicates that <u>morale</u> is fairly low.

PRACTICE THE CONTEXT: Everyone's _____ will increase if we make sure that all employees adhere to a strict _____ code.

36. Passed/past

PREVIEW THE CONTEXT: In the <u>past</u> several years, I have been <u>passed</u> over for a promotion at work.

- *Passed* is the past tense of the verb *pass*. It means to succeed or to hand something to someone.

  Since I had reviewed all the handouts my professor <u>passed</u> out, I was sure I had <u>passed</u> the course.
- *Past* is a noun referring to a time before the present. Also, it means to go by someone or something.

  As my professor walked <u>past</u> me, he uttered, "If we wish to truly understand the present, we must study the <u>past</u>."

PRACTICE THE CONTEXT: In the _____, I _____ all special training programs mandated by my company.

37. Peace/piece

PREVIEW THE CONTEXT: The Israelis and the Palestinians hope for <u>peace</u> after years of fighting over a <u>piece</u> of land in the Golan Heights.

- *Peace* means to be calm or be free of war.

  The <u>peace</u> and serenity we experienced in the mountains was worth the long trip.

■ *Piece* refers to a part. Notice that the word *piece* starts with *pie*, as in a piece of pie.

> Through our research, we solved a <u>piece</u> of the puzzle.

PRACTICE THE CONTEXT: To maintain the _____ among the quarreling siblings, I gave each some sound _____ of advice.

38. Principle/principal

PREVIEW THE CONTEXT: At the beginning of the school year, the <u>principal</u> outlined to all parents the basic <u>principles</u> by which he planned to lead the school.

■ *Principle* is the basis of a law or standard of conduct on which other rules are based.

> The <u>principle</u> of the matter should be considered.

■ *Principal* when used as an adjective means main component or first in rank. As a noun, it means the head of a group, for example, a school. (Remember that the principal is a "pal.")

> The <u>principal</u> outlined the <u>principal</u> changes in the school that occurred this year.

PRACTICE THE CONTEXT: The _____ addressed the students during assembly and stated that the _____ quality of people is how they embrace honesty as the most important _____.

PRACTICE 24-4

Underline the correct word in each sentence.

1. While traveling, you should wear (lose/<u>loose</u>) clothing for more comfort.
2. The (principle/<u>principal</u>) reason for opening a 401K is to ensure sufficient savings for one's retirement.
3. If you continue to live in the (<u>past</u>/passed), you will never appreciate the present.
4. It was both rude and arrogant of him to question my (<u>morals</u>/morale).
5. The quiz show contestant assumed that he (<u>knew</u>/new) the answer.
6. The shopper (past/<u>passed</u>) the (knew/<u>new</u>) jackets, which (<u>lay</u>/lie) temptingly on several tables in the middle of the store.
7. The (principle/<u>principal</u>) of the school spoke briefly at the ceremony.
8. When we drove (passed/<u>past</u>) your car, we noticed the dent.
9. The (<u>moral</u>/morale) of this story is that people will always admire and respect a (<u>moral</u>/morale) person.
10. The tennis star may (<u>lose</u>/loose) the match unless she starts serving the ball harder.

39. Quiet/quite

PREVIEW THE CONTEXT: In the <u>quiet</u> of her research lab, she made <u>quite</u> a surprisingly discovery.

- *Quiet* means silent, peaceful, or free from noise.
  I can't hear the lecture if you're not <u>quiet</u>.
- *Quite* means very, entirely, really, or rather.
  He was <u>quite</u> certain that he wasn't <u>quite</u> ready for the test.

PRACTICE THE CONTEXT: What the panel understood wasn't _____ what he meant, so he was _____ for _____ a while and then explained.

40. Real/really

PREVIEW THE CONTEXT: This is a <u>real</u> diamond, and it's <u>really</u> pretty.

- *Real* means factual or genuine.
  The story was <u>real</u>, but no one believed it.
- *Really* means very.
  When I explained the situation, she was <u>really</u> understanding.

PRACTICE THE CONTEXT: I found it _____ offensive that he wouldn't discuss the _____ issues and resorted to complete fabrications.

41. Right/rite/write

PREVIEW THE CONTEXT: As you <u>write</u> your essay, remember that the <u>right</u> attitude is to respect each religion's special <u>rites</u>.

- *Right* means correct or proper, opposite of *left*, or something owed to someone.
  You are <u>right</u> to suggest that the <u>right</u> lane is the most dangerous.
- *Rite* is a special or religious ceremony, practice, initiation, or tradition.
  It's hard for us to understand some marriage <u>rites</u> that are so different from our own culture.
- *Write* means to put words on paper.
  I decided to <u>write</u> on a local issue.

PRACTICE THE CONTEXT: He made the _____ decision to _____ a scandalous short story recounting his _____ of passage into manhood.

42. Rise/raise

PREVIEW THE CONTEXT: When citizens are dissatisfied with a country's economy, they may <u>rise</u> up in protest and demand that politicians <u>raise</u> the standard of living.

- *Rise* means to move upward.
  The balloon continued to <u>rise</u> in the air until it was out of view.
- *Raise* means to lift something up, elevate, or increase.
  Please <u>raise</u> your hand if you plan to attend the concert.

PRACTICE THE CONTEXT: It seems as if every time the price of gas _____ businesses _____ the price of food.

43. Sit/set

PREVIEW THE CONTEXT: After the standing ovation, the audience <u>sits</u> down. Then the conductor <u>sets</u> his music on the music stand and walks off the stage.

- *Sit* is the action of being in a chair, couch, and so on.
  The 5-year-old found it difficult to <u>sit</u> still during the entire Disney movie.
- *Set* means to put something down.
  Susan carelessly <u>set</u> her wedding band near the sink, where the slightest movement could cause it to fall down the drain.

PRACTICE THE CONTEXT: He had to _____ and wait for his interview, so he _____ his jacket aside and opened a book.

44. Then/than

PREVIEW THE CONTEXT: We would rather go to the movies <u>than</u> go shopping; <u>then</u> we can go out for dinner.

- *Then* means next or at that time.
  I raced to my office; <u>then</u> I called my wife.
- *Than* refers to a comparison between two people, objects, places, or events.
  This course seems to be less stressful <u>than</u> my previous one.

PRACTICE THE CONTEXT: My schedule this semester is tighter _____ ever, and _____ I have to run to work.

45. Their/there/they're

PREVIEW THE CONTEXT: <u>Their</u> personal trainer announced that <u>they're</u> out of shape and thus should work out <u>there</u> at the gym at least 5 days a week.

- *Their* shows ownership.
  Ralph and Janice led <u>their</u> team to victory.
- *There* points to a place, object, or person.
  Go <u>there</u> when you get a chance.
- *There* is also a neutral word followed by a form of the verb *be*: *is, are, was, were, will be, has been, have been,* and *had been.*
  <u>There</u> is no way I'll let you do that.
- *They're* is the contraction for *they are.*
  <u>They're</u> not exactly the hardest workers here.

PRACTICE THE CONTEXT: _____ is a place over _____ where people go to enjoy _____ favorite sports if _____ willing to spend the money.

46. Through/threw

PREVIEW THE CONTEXT: Tad accidentally <u>threw</u> the ball <u>through</u> the window.

- *Through* means to go from one side to the other. It also means finished.
  Leonard took a shortcut <u>through</u> the woods.
- *Threw* is the past tense of *throw*. It means to toss.
  We were surprised when he finally <u>threw</u> out all his old shirts.

PRACTICE THE CONTEXT: We all thought we were _____, but the guide told
us we still had to go _____ the fields. Therefore,
we _____ all unnecessary supplies away to lighten
our load.

47. To/too/two

PREVIEW THE CONTEXT: <u>To</u> juggle more than <u>two</u> balls at a time is <u>too</u> challenging
for me.

- *To* is a preposition meaning toward.
  I'll be heading <u>to</u> the lake if you want to meet me there.
- *Too* means very, overly, or also.
  The tea is <u>too</u> hot to drink, so I'll have to leave it, <u>too</u>.
- *Two* is the number 2.
  I had only <u>two</u> hours left to finish my project.

PRACTICE THE CONTEXT: If you want gas under _____ dollars, head
_____ the next town _____ miles south; you
can go _____ the next state, _____.

48. Weather/whether

PREVIEW THE CONTEXT: <u>Whether</u> the mountain climbers start their climb
tomorrow depends on the <u>weather</u>.

- *Weather* refers to atmospheric condition.
  We had wonderful <u>weather</u> all last week, so we were able to enjoy the
  outdoors.
- *Whether* indicates a choice or option. It introduces a possibility.
  The candidate wasn't sure <u>whether</u> he'll accept the nomination.

PRACTICE THE CONTEXT: _____ we drive or take a plane depends on
tonight's _____ forecast.

49. Were/we're/where

PREVIEW THE CONTEXT: The mourners <u>were</u> standing close to <u>where</u> <u>we're</u>
filming the scene.

- *Were* is the past form of *are*.
  Both paintings <u>were</u> identical in every way; the art dealers <u>were</u> confused.
- *We're* is the contraction for *we are*.
  <u>We're</u> leaving Seattle at noon, and <u>we're</u> hoping to be with you by midnight.

■ *Where* indicates location.

Where were you? We had no clue where you went.

PRACTICE THE CONTEXT: _____ really sorry you _____ unable to find _____ _____ located.

50. Who's/whose

PREVIEW THE CONTEXT: Julie Madison, who's our Hollywood tourist guide, couldn't tell us whose house is believed to be haunted.

■ *Who's* is the contraction for *who is* and *who has*.

We're trying to find out who's the author of this insulting letter.

■ *Whose* indicates ownership or possession.

Whose textbook is this?

PRACTICE THE CONTEXT: He stormed into the kitchen and accusingly asked, " _____ wine glass is this, and _____ been using my shaver?"

51. Your/you're

PREVIEW THE CONTEXT: Your tax return looks questionable, so you're probably going to be audited by the IRS.

■ *Your* expresses ownership or possession; it means belonging to you.

You left your cell phone at the coffee shop.

■ *You're* is the contraction for *you are*.

I'm still wondering if you're planning to attend the reception.

PRACTICE THE CONTEXT: _____ asking me for _____ iPod, but you forget that _____ the one who told me to leave it by _____ car.

PRACTICE 24-5

Underline the correct word in each sentence.

1. The employees asked for a (rise/<u>raise</u>) for next year, but management turned them down.

2. Voting is a basic (<u>right</u>/rite/write) for all U.S. citizens.

3. Don't (<u>sit</u>/set) around complaining about the neighborhood; go out and clean it up.

4. Mass is a sacred (right/<u>rite</u>/write) for Catholics.

5. The (<u>rise</u>/raise) in gas prices has led to an increase in many consumer goods.

6. Some dorms enforce (<u>quiet</u>/quite) hours to make sure that students can study and sleep.

7. The shipment of generators was (quiet/<u>quite</u>) large compared to the one we received last month.

8. The kindergarteners were (real/<u>really</u>) excited when the clown visited their classroom.

9. When the professor asked (who's/<u>whose</u>) turn it was to open the discussion, the room was (<u>quiet</u>/quite). (Their/<u>There</u>/They're) was no one (their/<u>there</u>/they're) who would volunteer.

10. (Weather/<u>Whether</u>) you prefer math or English, you must master both to succeed in your other studies.

REVIEW   24-1

Read the following paragraph and cross out any incorrect words, replacing each with the correct one.

      Hunting is sometimes frowned upon as a senseless and even cruel

activity. Why would someone want to go out in nature to purposefully kill

innocent animals? Doesn't a hunter have to be a bit sadistic to stalk, aim at,

and shoot a poor beast of nature? I've ~~herd~~ ^{heard} these comments enough to want

to counter them with what makes hunting a viable activity. Hunting takes

us back to primordial times when it was a necessity for survival. ~~They're~~ ^{There}

were no grocery stories, delis, or butcher shops to provide meat ~~too~~ ^{to} humans,

so ~~weather~~ ^{whether} or not they wanted to, they had to track down ~~there~~ ^{their} food. Today,

many hunters butcher, freeze, and eat the meat that they capture. Another

aspect of hunting is the physicality that is required—more ~~then~~ ^{than} some non-

hunters would suspect. ~~Its real~~ ^{It's really} crucial that the hunter is in top condition to

walk, run, stoop, ~~rise~~ ^{raise} a gun, and fire quickly when the prey is close. In addi-

tion, hunting is almost a ~~right~~ ^{rite} of passage to adulthood for many boys and

some girls. ~~Buy~~ ^{By} going ~~threw~~ ^{through} the experience of the hunt, ~~their~~ ^{they're} learning skills

of independence, quick decision making, and teamwork. Finally, ~~their~~ ^{there}

will always be those who object to hunting and to whom hunting is an

objectionable activity; however, ~~there~~ ^{they're} the minority who ~~loose site~~ ^{lose sight} of the

larger picture of hunting as central to ~~are~~ ^{our} ancient ~~passed~~ ^{past} and to ~~are~~ ^{our} current

connection ~~too~~ ^{to} nature.

CHAPTER 25

Improving Your Spelling

YOUR GOALS

1. Develop strategies to improve spelling.

2. Review and apply basic spelling rules.

3. Proofread to correct spelling errors.

"My spelling is Wobbly. It's good spelling but it Wobbles, and the letters get in the wrong places."

■ A. A. Milne

(*Winnie the Pooh*, Chapter 6) ■

A college student taking an introduction to literature class online must participate in weekly discussions. In the first week of class, Jennifer writes the following response to a question about the short story "A Rose for Emily."

> Miss Emily's caracter is complex. On the one hand, you gotta love her as she's strong and ferm abut taking charge of her own live and refusing to let the gosipy townspeople run her live. On the other hand, she's so excentric that you wander if anyone culd stand to live around her. You can sea how Homer Barron would have been afraid to take her on. She killd Homer cuz she new that Homer would never mary her; this was the only way Miss Emily culd hold on to a men and keep her sef respect.

The instructor and other students who read her response could find themselves so distracted by the spelling errors that her ideas become lost in the sloppiness of her words.

Although we now have spell-check tools on computers, it is still important to know basic spelling rules and be aware of when to check the dictionary for commonly misspelled words. Many students rely too much on spell-check tools; however, the tools themselves do not replace careful proofreading, as illustrated by the following poem:

Eye halve a spelling chequer
It came with my pea sea
It plainly marques four my revue
Miss steaks eye kin knot sea.

Eye strike a key and type a word
And weight four it two say
Weather eye am wrong oar write
It shows me strait a weigh.

As soon as a mist ache is maid
It nose bee fore two long

LET's warm up!

Think back to your own years in elementary school and how you first learned how to spell. Write a paragraph responding to the following questions:

- What spelling rules do you still remember and can you still recite?
- How would you rate your spelling abilities?
- What specific words have given you the most problems through the years and what strategies do you use to check your spelling?

CenLu/Alamy Limited

And eye can put the error rite
Its rare lea ever wrong.

Eye have run this poem threw it
I am shore your pleased two no
Its letter perfect awl the weigh
My chequer tolled me sew.

———————————————

(Author unknown. This poem has been published many times on the Internet. It may be an adaptation from "Candidate for a Pullet Surprise," written in 1992 by Jerry Zar, retired dean of Northern Illinois University Graduate School.)

UNDERSTANDING YOUR PROBLEMS WITH SPELLING

Some students feel that a person is either a good or bad speller. Is this a myth or a fact? English has borrowed words from Latin, Greek, Spanish, French, and other languages. In addition, new discoveries, inventions, and technology add additional words to the English language. Although English pronunciation has changed over the centuries, spelling conventions have remained relatively stable; thus, attempting to write the word by the way it's pronounced is hit or miss, frustrating many people.

Using Basic Spelling Rules

The word *rule* implies little exception; however, when it comes to spelling, many rules carry some exceptions. Nevertheless, these rules offer enough accuracy to make them worth learning. As the exceptions creep up, learn them. You might even want to take time to find out why a particular rule has exceptions. The more you learn about the nature of words, the better speller you're likely to be.

Some spelling rules ask you to distinguish vowels from consonants. Therefore, before you start learning the rules, keep in mind that there are five vowels: *a, e, i, o, u.* All other letters are consonants. The letter *y* can be either a consonant or a vowel: it is a consonant when it comes at the beginning of a word, e.g. *yogurt*, but when it occurs anywhere else in a word, *y* is a vowel, e.g. *gym* or *sky*.

Deciding Between *ie* and *ei*

Choosing between *ie* and *ei* can seem challenging but is not impossible. First, pronounce the word. If the sound is a long $\bar{e}$, use *ie* except after *c*.

Believe, belief, chief, fierce, grief, niece, relief, thief

BUT

ceiling, conceive, deceive, receive

EXCEPTIONS: either, foreign, leisure, neither, seized, weird

However, if the *c* has a "she" or "sheh" sound, then use *ie*.

ancient, conscience, deficient, efficient, glacier, proficient, species, sufficient

Use *ei* when the sound is not a long *ē*, especially when the sound is a long *ā* (*ay*).

freight, neighbor, veil, weigh

Although you can find many exceptions to this rule, most words conform to this rule. The odds are in your favor. If in doubt, look it up in the dictionary.

PRACTICE   25-1

Complete the spelling of the following words by inserting *ie* or *ei*.

1. ach__ie__ve
2. f__ie__nd
3. rec__ei__pt
4. p__ie__rce
5. hyg__ie__ne

6. gr__ie__vance
7. bes__ie__ge
8. w__ie__ld
9. pat__ie__nce
10. n__ei__ther

Choosing among *-cede, -ceed,* and *-sede*

Another dilemma may occur with a simple word such as *proceed*. Or is it *procede*, or maybe *prosede*? The answer is quite simple:

- English has only one *-sede* word: *supersede*
- English has only three *-ceed* words: *exceed, proceed, succeed*
- For all other words, use *-cede*: *concede, precede,* and so on

Attaching Prefixes

Prefixes are added to the beginning of words to make a new word with a new meaning. Spelling errors occur when the writer drops a letter when adding a prefix. As a rule, when adding a prefix to a word, don't drop a letter or change the spelling of the original word.

INCORRECT:	mis- + spell = mispell
CORRECT:	mis- + spell = misspell

INCORRECT:	re- + elect = relect
CORRECT:	re- + elect = reelect

Be careful with such prefixes as *dis-, il-, im-, in-, ir-, mis-, re-,* and *un-*. The rule is simple: don't drop any letters. There are no exceptions.

PRACTICE 25-2

On the line provided, write the new word formed with the given prefix.

1. il- + legible = ___illegible___
2. dis- + similar = ___dissimilar___
3. re- + appraise = ___reappraise___
4. un- + acceptable = ___unacceptable___
5. over- + look = ___overlook___
6. in- + appropriate = ___inappropriate___
7. in- + sensitive = ___insensitive___
8. extra- + ordinary = ___extraordinary___
9. im- + partial = ___impartial___
10. dis- + satisfied = ___dissatisfied___

Attaching Suffixes

Suffixes are added to the ending of words to change the grammatical function of the word in a sentence. For example, the word *read* can be used as a verb as in "I want to read the book"; however, adding *-er* to the end of the verb changes the verb to a noun ("He's a good reader"), whereas adding *-able* makes the word an adjective ("The file is readable").

When adding a suffix, your first step to spelling words correctly is to determine whether the suffix starts with a vowel or a consonant. Then follow three basic rules.

Attaching Suffixes *-ness* and *-ly* to a Word

When you add the suffixes *-ly* or *-ness* to a word, don't drop any letters.

final + -ly = finally	lean + -ness = leanness
sincere + -ly = sincerely	mean + -ness = meanness
truthful + -ly = truthfully	sudden + -ness = suddenness

However, if the original word ends in *y*, then change the *y* to *i* and then add *-ly* or *-ness*.

busy + -ly = busily	happy + -ness = happiness
crazy + -ly = crazily	kindly + -ness = kindliness
steady + -ly = steadily	sturdy + -ness = sturdiness

> **EXCEPTION:** Generally, for one-syllable adjectives ending in *y*, don't drop the *y*; simply add the suffixes *-ly* and *-ness*.
>
> | | |
> |---|---|
> | dry + -ly = dryly | dry + -ness = dryness |
> | shy + -ly = shyly | shy + -ness = shyness |

Keeping or Dropping the Final *e*

Many words end in silent *e*. Sometimes, students are tempted to drop the *e* when adding a suffix. The rule is simple: keep the final *e* if the suffix begins with a consonant.

accurate + -ly = accurately   use + -ful = useful

> **EXCEPTION:** Sometimes, when the *e* is preceded by another vowel, the *e* may be dropped.
>
> argue + -ment = argument   true + -ly = truly

However, drop the final *e* when the suffix begins with a vowel or a *y*, whose sound functions as a vowel in this case.

advise + -able = advisable   sense + -ible = sensible

believable + -y = believably   surprise + -ing = surprising

guide + -ance = guidance

> **EXCEPTION:** If a suffix starts with an *a* or *o* and you need to retain the sound of the soft *c* or *g* preceding the *e*, then keep the final *e*.
>
> change + -able = changeable   knowledge + -able = knowledgeable
>
> courage + -ous = courageous   manage + -able = manageable

Try pronouncing the preceding words without the *e*. Another exception also arises when it's necessary to keep the final *e* to prevent confusion or mispronunciation.

dye + -ing = dyeing   [changing color, not to be confused with *dying*]

mile + -age = mileage   [avoid pronouncing as *milage*]

agree + -able = agreeable   [avoid pronouncing as *agreable*]

Changing the *y* to *i* in Words Ending with *y*

When a *y* at the end of a word is preceded by a consonant, change the *y* to *i* before adding the suffix.

beauty + -ful = beautiful   mystery + -ous = mysterious

lively + -ness = liveliness

However, if the suffix begins with *i*, keep the *y*.

bury + -ing = burying   pry + -ing = prying

Common Suffixes				
Beginning with Vowels			Beginning with Consonants	
-able	-an	-ar	-cess	-less
-age	-ance	-ed	-ful	-ly
-al	-ant	-er	-hood	-ment

Continued

UNDERSTANDING YOUR PROBLEMS WITH SPELLING

Common Suffixes				
Beginning with Vowels			**Beginning with Consonants**	
-es	-ism	-or	-ness	-wise
-est	-ist	-ous	-ry	
-ing	-ive	-y	-ty	
-ish	-on		-ward	

PRACTICE   25-3

On the line provided, fill in the new form of each word as indicated.

1. entire + -ly = ___entirely___
2. virtue + -ous = ___virtuous___
3. friendly + -ness = ___friendliness___
4. service + -able = ___serviceable___
5. body + -ly = ___bodily___
6. force + -ible = ___forcible___
7. battle + -ing = ___battling___

8. nerve + -ous = ___nervous___
9. bury + -al = ___burial___
10. malice + -ious = ___malicious___
11. force + -ful = ___forceful___
12. sincere + -ly = ___sincerely___
13. love + -able = ___lovable___
14. fame + -ous = ___famous___

Doubling a Final Consonant

Whether or not to double the final letter of a word when adding a suffix can be quite a dilemma. Generally, double the final consonant before a suffix that *begins with a vowel* if the original word meets both of the following conditions.

1. The word has only one syllable, or the word has more than one syllable and ends in a stressed syllable. *Stressed syllable* simply means that its strength of pronunciation falls on the final syllable. For example, in the word *conduct,* meaning behavior, as in "his conduct is unacceptable," the stress is on the first syllable, *con-*. However, in *conduct* meaning to lead, direct, or act, the stress is on the second syllable, "He promised to conduct himself appropriately."

2. The word ends in a single consonant. The pattern is consonant–vowel–consonant (a C + V + C pattern).

    spin + -ing

    [*spin* is one syllable and it ends in C + V + C; therefore, you need to double the final consonant: *spinning.*]

    omit + -ing

    [The word *omit* has more than one syllable, but the accent is on the final syllable: your intonation rises on the second syllable *-mit*, not on the *o-*. Try pronouncing it both ways and get a feel for stressed syllables. In addition, the word ends in a C + V + C pattern; thus, the correct spelling of the new word is *omitting.*]

rain + -ing
[The word is one syllable, but it ends in a consonant preceded by two vowels (V + V + C). Don't double the final consonant when adding the suffix: *raining*.]
hang + -er
[The word in one syllable, but it ends in a V + C + C pattern. Therefore, don't double the final consonant: *hanger*.]

> **EXCEPTION:** Be careful with words ending in *x, w,* or *y*. Some do not follow the doubling rule. If in doubt, consult your dictionary.

blow + -ing = blowing   box + -er = boxer   know + -ing = knowing

PRACTICE   25-4

On the line provided, fill in the new form of each word as indicated.

1. begin + -er = ___beginner___
2. differ + -ence = ___difference___
3. refer + -al = ___referral___
4. develop + -ed = ___developed___
5. drop + -ed = ___dropped___
6. bag + -age ___baggage___
7. pin + -ing = ___pinning___
8. hit + -er = ___hitter___
9. hop + -ing = ___hopping___
10. benefit + -ed = ___benefited___
11. repel + -ent = ___repellent___
12. shovel + -ing = ___shoveling___
13. suffer + -ance = ___sufferance___
14. conceal + -ed = ___concealed___

Spelling the Plurals of Nouns Correctly

The plurals of most nouns are formed by simply adding an *s* at the end of the noun; however, forming the plural of some nouns can be troublesome since the spelling may change. The following rules can help. Nonetheless, when in doubt, always consult your dictionary.

Forming the Plural by Adding *s*

In general, to form the plural of nouns, simply add an *s*.

assignment → assignments   solution → solutions

However, for pronunciation, add *es* to form the plural of a noun ending in *s, x, z, ch,* or *sh*.

box → boxes   patch → patches

bush → bushes   waltz → waltzes

Forming the Plural of a Noun Ending in *y*

As you saw earlier, adding a suffix to a word ending in *y* requires a little attention. If the *y* is preceded by a vowel, simply add an *s*.

essay + -s = essays   valley + -s = valleys

However, if the *y* is preceded by a consonant, change the *y* to *i* and add *es*.

city + -s = cities   property + -s = properties

Forming the Plural of a Noun Ending in *f* or *fe*

Add *s* to form the plural of most nouns ending in *f* or *fe*.

belief + -s = beliefs   gulf + -s = gulfs

chief + -s = chiefs   roof + -s = roofs

giraffe + -s = giraffes   safe + -s = safes

However, in many cases, change the *f* or *fe* to *v* and then adding *es*.

knife + -s = knives   life + -s = lives

leaf + -s = leaves   yourself + -s = yourselves

To determine whether the word takes an *s* or *ves*, say the word out loud. If the plural sounds like an *s*, add the *s*; if the plural sounds like a *ves*, change the *f* or *fe* to *v* and add *es*.

Forming the Plural of a Noun Ending in *o*

Forming the plural of nouns ending in *o* can sometimes be tricky. Some plurals are formed by adding *s*, others are created by adding *es*, and many can take either *s* or *es*. Of course, this doesn't mean that you should play it safe by adding *es* to all nouns ending in *o*. You should consult your dictionary. Here are three simple rules that can guide you:

1. If a noun ending in *o* is preceded by a vowel, simply add *s* to form the plural.

   pat<u>io</u> + -s = patios   z<u>oo</u> + -s = zoos

2. For most nouns ending in *o* preceded by a consonant, add *es*.

   he<u>ro</u> + -s = heroes   torpe<u>do</u> + -s = torpedoes

3. For words ending in *o* that refer to musical terms, form the plural by adding *s*.

   alto → altos   solo → solos

   cello → cellos   soprano → sopranos

   EXCEPTION: Unfortunately, these rules contain many exceptions. If you find that the spelling seems awkward, check your dictionary. Here are some common words ending in *o* whose plural form can be either *s* or *es*.

   avocado → avocados/oes   motto → mottos/oes

   cargo → cargos/oes   tornado → tornados/oes

   domino → dominos/oes   volcano → volcanos/oes

   ghetto → ghettos/oes   zero → zeros/oes

   mosquito → mosquitos/oes

PRACTICE   25-5

On the line provided, write the plural form of the given nouns.

1. donkey __donkeys__

2. half __halves__

3. fly __flies__

4. auto __autos__

5. comedy __comedies__

6. church __churches__

7. ditch __ditches__

8. stereo __stereos__

9. chef __chefs__

10. baby __babies__

Forming the Plural of a Compound Noun

Compound nouns consist of a noun and its modifier. For example, the compound noun *brother-in-law* consists of the main noun *brother* and the modifier *in-law*. Compound nouns are hyphenated (*commander-in-chief*), written as separate words (*lieutenant colonel*), or combined as one word (*castaway*). You may need to consult your dictionary if you're not sure how the compound word is represented. Here are some general rules that may help you pluralize compound words:

1. Add an s to the main noun of most compound nouns followed by a prepositional phrase.

INCORRECT:	brother-in-laws
CORRECT:	brothers-in-law

Add *s* to most compound nouns referring to people and ending with an adverb.

INCORRECT:	runner-ups
CORRECT:	runners-up

INCORRECT:	passerbys
CORRECT:	passersby

EXCEPTION:	The plural of some compound nouns is irregular.

drive-in = drive-ins   two-year-old = two-year-olds

As you gain more experience working with compound nouns, you should quickly memorize their spelling.

Forming the Plural When Referred to as a Word

Form the plural of numbers by adding *s*. Do not use apostrophes since there is no possibility of misreading.

The suspect is in his 20s.
My cell phone number has four 6s.
The 1960s and '70s brought many changes to the music industry.

To pluralize letters, italicize (or underline) the letter and then add *s*. Don't italicize the *s*, and don't italicize academic grades.

The two *R*s on his jacket stand for Ray Reed.
He received Bs in both assignments.

However, use apostrophes for lowercase letters and capital *A* and *I* to avoid misreading.

How many A's did you receive this semester?

The word *Mississippi* has a total of four *i*'s, four *s*'s, and four *p*'s but no *a*'s.

When you mention a word as a word, as we have been doing throughout this chapter, italicize (or underline) the word and then add the *s*, not italicized, to make it plural.

When you start building sentences with too many *and*s, *but*s, and *yet*s, you have excessive coordination.

Enough with all the *if*s; let's make decisions.

His presentation was distracting because it was filled with *uh*s, *okay*s, and *you knows*.

Note: Some people prefer to use apostrophes in all cases. If you choose to do this, first check with your instructor, but be consistent:

He received C's on his presentations since all were filled with numerous *uh*'s, *okay*'s, and *you know*'s.

Recognizing Irregular Plurals

Make sure you use the correct form of irregular plurals. The following plurals do not take *s* but change their spelling from singular to plural:

child → children	mouse → mice
foot → feet	ox → oxen
goose → geese	tooth → teeth
louse → lice	woman → women
man → men	

There are also nouns whose singular and plural forms are the same. The following nouns do not change:

Chinese	fish	salmon	sheep	species
deer	means	series	shrimp	

Some words derived from Italian, Greek, Latin, or French form their plural as in their original language:

alumnus → alumni	curriculum → curricula
analysis → analyses	datum → data
bacterium → bacteria	diagnosis → diagnoses
basis → bases	hypothesis → hypotheses
beau → beaux	medium → media
crisis → crises	memorandum → memoranda
criterion → criteria	paralysis → paralyses

parenthesis → parentheses

phenomenon → phenomena

radius → radii

stimulus → stimuli

synopsis → synopses

synthesis → syntheses

thesis → theses

vertebra → vertebrae

Note: Since language is dynamic and constantly changing, it may be acceptable to use *s* to form the plural of some irregular verbs, for example, *fish–fishes* or *curriculum–curriculums*. Before making your own decision, consult your dictionary, and above all consider your audience. How would your audience react?

PRACTICE 25-6

Revise the following paragraphs for spelling errors. Cross out each misspelled word and write the correct word above it.

Yesterday I was ~~waitting~~ *waiting* for the train to Washington Square. The ~~passerbys~~ *passersby* rushed ~~hurryedly~~ *hurriedly* to get to their jobs, paying little attention to the group of musicians setting up ~~thier~~ *their* instruments. ~~Clumsyly~~ *Clumsily*, the musicians finished ~~organizeing~~ *organizing* the instruments. The first composition was an old Cuban ballad. Its soft melody ~~succeded~~ *succeeded* in slowing the commuters. The song filled me with nostalgia, ~~makeing~~ *making* me ignore my train's arrival. I ~~wisht~~ *wished* that my three ~~sister-in-laws~~ *sisters-in-law* were here. I had no doubt that the haunting words of the song would fill them with visions of the Cuba of the ~~50,~~ *1950s or '50s* the Cuba our parents spoke so much about: its art, its music, and its people.

Two professors from NYU also ~~stoped~~ *stopped*. One was a music instructor. She observed the crowd's reactions and realized what was missing from her Music 205 course ~~curricula~~ *curriculum*. She spoke of ~~infuseing~~ *infusing* the course with passion by ~~introduceing~~ *introducing* more cultural ~~peices~~ *pieces*. She even thought of ~~inviteing~~ *inviting* the musicians to her class. The other professor, a literature instructor, agreed. He said that he was currently teaching an ethnic poetry class. He ~~beleived~~ *believed* that ~~bringging~~ *bringing* the musicians into the class would bring the poetry of that period to life. The thought of his students reading and ~~enjoing~~ *enjoying* poetry rather than just throwing the textbooks on their ~~shelfs~~ *shelves* excited the professor. "This will be better than the old historical ~~videoes~~ *videos* I've been showing all year," he stated.

Another train came to a halt. I entered, leaving the magic of the moment

behind. I ~~tryed~~ tried to get one last glimpse of the musicians, ~~grining~~ grinning as they

shared their art.

Being Watchful for Commonly Misspelled Words

Many times, we ignore correct spelling for speedy or catchy expressions. We, as well as the media, change, clip, or abbreviate words to quickly get message across. Commercials, advertisements, e-mails, and text messages are filled with inventive and simplified words, misspelled words, and obscure acronyms. Although these expressions may be appropriate if the writer and the audience share similar styles, often writers carry these words and expressions to other audiences and other modes of communication, annoying the audience. Instructors are increasingly finding errors that are unacceptable in academic or professional settings. Avoid such simplification of words as *thru, tuff, nite, lite,* and *brite.* Spell them correctly: *through, tough, night, light,* and *bright.* Also, don't carry informal writing habits from personal e-mail and text messaging into academic or professional settings, for example, *i* (*I*) and *UR* (*You are*).

In addition, some words are commonly misspelled because the rules are difficult to remember or apply. The list that follows includes many of these words.

Commonly Misspelled Words				
absence	arctic	commitment	despise	entrance
accidentally	argument	committed	develop	environment
accommodate	athlete	conceive	different	especially
acknowledgment	attendance	conscience	dilemma	exaggerate
acquire	basically	conscientious	disappear	exercise
address	beginning	conscious	disappoint	existence
advice	benefited	consistent	disastrous	explanation
affect	bureaucracy	curiosity	duel	familiar
aggressive	business	criticize	ecstasy	fascinate
all right	calendar	decision	effect	fiend
amateur	candidate	definitely	eighth	fiery
answer	cannot	descendant	eligible	fluorescent
apology	cemetery	describe	embarrass	foreign
apparently	challenge	description	eminent	foresee
appearance	column	desperate	emphasize	formerly

forty	lightning	parallel	regard	succeed
fourth	loneliness	pastime	relevant	success
frustrated	magnificent	perceive	relief	surprise
fulfill	maintenance	permanent	religion	temperature
government	maneuver	permissible	reminiscence	thorough
grammar	marriage	perseverance	repetition	threshold
guard	mathematics	persuade	restaurant	tomorrow
harass	memento	pigeon	rhyme	tragedy
hindrance	millennium	playwright	rhythm	transferred
humorous	minuscule	possess	ridiculous	truly
hypocrisy	mischievous	possession	roommate	undoubtedly
immediately	modern	precede	sacrifice	unnecessarily
incidentally	murmur	prejudice	sacrilegious	until
indispensable	narrator	privilege	schedule	usage
inevitable	necessary	probably	secretary	vacuum
infinite	niece	pronunciation	seize	vengeance
ingenious	nonexistent	pursue	self-conscious	villain
intelligence	noticeable	questionnaire	separate	warrant
irrelevant	obstinate	quiet	sergeant	weird
irresistible	occasion	quite	siege	whether
jealousy	occurred	quizzes	significant	withhold
judgment	occurrence	receive	similar	writing
laboratory	omission	recommend	sincerely	written
latter	opposite	reference	strictly	
license	original	referred	subtly	

Strategies for Improving Your Spelling

Getting rid of old habits is never an easy matter. Nevertheless, with some effort, it can be done. The following strategies can help you become a better speller:

Put your mouse on **Computer tip** the word and right-click for correct spellings.

1. Use the spell-check tool on all of your documents, but remember that the tool cannot find certain errors in words that look or sound alike, such as *then* and *than*, *your* and *you're*, or *effect* and *affect*.
2. Use the dictionary if you are unsure of how to spell a word.

3. Keep a personal spelling list of the words that you commonly misspell. When your instructor identifies misspelled words in your essay, add them to your personal spelling list.

4. Keep a list of common terms associated with your major field, the classes that you are taking, or both as you will be using these words and phrases often in your writing, on exams, and in your profession.

5. Don't worry about spelling when you are brainstorming and writing your first draft; however, circle or mark questionable spellings to check later during the revision and editing process.

6. Read a lot. If you see words frequently, you are more likely to spell them correctly.

7. Have a friend, fellow student, or family member read your final draft for one last check for spelling errors.

8. Occasionally review the basic spelling rules to help reduce your spelling errors.

9. Most professions share a common vocabulary. Learning the correct spelling of these words is crucial; it's *your* profession.

REVIEW   25-1

Cross out any misspellings, frequently confused words, or typos in the following paragraph and write the correction above the word.

I enjoy the seclusion that ~~hikeing~~ hiking offers. It gives me a chance of ~~geting~~ getting away from the hustle and bustle of everyday ~~live~~ life. I do not feel ~~rushd~~ rushed or as if I have to ~~met~~ meet a deadline because nobody is bothering or ~~judgeing~~ judging me. I can feel and act any way I want to. I am surrounded by a sense of peace and ~~quite~~ quiet. It ~~offeres~~ offers a chance to calm my mind and to focus on whatever is ~~realy~~ really important to me. No experience compares to being the only one on a mountainside. At the same time, I am aware of a sense of ~~lonliness~~ loneliness, a ~~humbleing~~ humbling experience. For me, this is a stress ~~releiver~~ reliever. The few people whom I do meet while ~~hikeing~~ hiking seem to be a ~~diffrent~~ different breed ~~then~~ than the rest of mankind. They are ~~freindlyer~~ friendlier, always greeting me with a smile. I never know if I might need that person's help if trouble ~~striks~~ strikes.

One of the most remote places that I have been was the Boundary Waters Canoe Area in northern Minnesota. Some places there have never been touched by human ~~feat~~ feet. At ~~nite~~ night, the sky was lit up with trillions of stars, and the aurora borealis ~~wood~~ would dance across the heavens. I was awed at the ~~site~~ sight and realized that I could never have witnessed this marvel of nature if I were near civilization.

Using Punctuation and Capitalization

PART 6

CHAPTER 26

Using Commas, Semicolons, and Colons

YOUR GOALS

1. Apply basic rules for the use of commas.

2. Use the semicolon correctly.

3. Use the colon correctly.

4. Revise sentences, paragraphs, and essays for errors in commas, semicolons, and colons.

"The writer who neglects punctuation, or mispunctuates, is liable to be misunderstood. . . . For the want of merely a comma, it often occurs that an axiom appears a paradox, or that a sarcasm is converted into a sermonoid."

■ **Edgar Allan Poe** ■

We often underestimate the importance of punctuation. After all, we tend to rationalize that the reader knows what we mean. However, this conclusion is not necessarily true. Commas, semicolons, and colons not only clarify our ideas but also express meaning.

Examine the following versions of the same letter. All words remain the same in both versions, but the punctuation marks are different. Notice how the use of punctuation can turn the following love letter to a "dear John" letter.

I. Rozenbaum & F. Cirou/Blend Images LLC

Love Letter:

Dear Ralph,
I need someone who understands what love is all about. You are giving, sincere, warm. Men who are different from you confess to being lazy and no good. Ralph, you have devastated my feelings for other men. I long for you. I feel nothing when we are separated. I can be eternally elated. Please let me be yours,

Gloria

Break Up Letter:

Dear Ralph,
I need someone who understands what love is. All about you are giving, sincere, warm men who are different from you. Confess to being lazy and no good, Ralph. You have devastated my feelings. For other men, I long. For you, I feel nothing. When we are separated, I can be eternally elated. Please let me be.

Yours, Gloria

(Dr. Emily Golson, University of Northern Colorado)

In the professional world, a misused or misplaced punctuation mark can change the meaning of a sentence so drastically that it can lead to misunderstandings, confusion, disagreements, and even misinterpretation of legal agreements.

If you can imagine lawyers searching legal documents to find ambiguities resulting from faulty punctuation, you can understand the importance of correct punctuation.

UNDERSTANDING COMMAS, SEMICOLONS, AND COLONS

Don't confuse your reader by cluttering your writing with too many punctuation marks. Use commas, semicolons, and colons when specific rules require them. Your reader should be able to read your message with ease, and your writing should flow smoothly; thus, each punctuation mark you use should guide your reader through your text in the same way that transitional words and expressions give coherence to your essays. Even in the case of punctuation, your goal as a writer is to communicate your ideas clearly.

Commas

Don't sprinkle your writings with commas that serve no purpose or with commas that obscure your ideas rather than clarify them. The rules for using commas are clear. Don't use commas, as some students do, to give the reader time to breathe; you won't find this notion in any of the comma rules. Use a comma when a rule specifically calls for it or when the comma clarifies the meaning of a sentence. If you're not sure whether to use a comma, leave it out. Start by learning the rules and tying your use of commas to specific rules.

In previous chapters, when you revised sentences or paragraphs for fragments, comma splices, and fused sentences or when you combined sentences for style, you also applied basic rules of punctuation. We start by reviewing and enriching the rules with which you are already familiar.

> **Bridging Knowledge**
>
> See Chapter 15 for complete information on independent clauses, see Chapter 16 to review the use of coordination to revise comma splices and fused sentences, and return to Chapter 22 to review compound sentences as a way to vary sentence type.

Connecting Independent Clauses

Use a comma before a coordinating conjunction that connects two complete sentences (independent clauses).

Independent Clause #1	, for , and , nor , but , or , yet , so	Independent Clause #2

Independent Clause #1   Independent Clause #2
■ I called her up, **and** I apologized for my insensitive remark.

Independent Clause #1   Independent Clause #2
■ We remained seated, **but** the noise grew louder.

Don't use a comma if you do not have two complete sentences.

Independent Clause #1   Not an Independent Clause
I called her up **and** apologized for my insensitive remark.

Since the subject is missing in the phrase after the coordinate conjunction, no comma is necessary. Also, be careful with long complex sentences.

Not an Independent Clause   Not an Independent Clause

- Because we were not familiar with her idea **and** she was unable to address my associates, I gave them the wrong information.

In this example, the subordinate conjunction *because* is understood after *and*: "[because] she was unable to address my associates." Be careful not to confuse this type of structure for an independent clause.

Also, don't place a comma after the coordinate conjunction as a way to separate independent clauses.

> INCORRECT: Jeff was unwilling to share information <u>and</u>, he wanted to work alone.
>
> CORRECT: Jeff is unwilling to share information, <u>and</u> he prefers to work alone.

If you have short independent clauses joined by *and, but,* or *nor* and if there's no danger of misreading the sentence, it is not necessary to use a comma.

- I called **and** <u>she answered</u>.

However, for clarity, do not omit the comma after short independent clauses joined by *yet* and *for*.

- <u>I offered</u>, **yet** <u>she refused</u>.
- <u>We left</u>, **for** <u>the store was closed</u>.

If you're not sure whether to insert a comma in any of these cases, insert it; it will always be correct.

When you proofread your papers for commas, skim through quickly and stop at every coordinating conjunction. Then determine whether a comma is necessary to meet the conditions of the preceding rules.

PRACTICE 26-1

For the following sentences, insert necessary commas and remove any unnecessary commas. If a sentence is correct, write C for correct on the line provided.

__C__ 1. That he was unable to complete his assignment and that he would probably be absent for over a week demonstrated his priorities.

_____ 2. A schedule is useful for organization, but the willingness to follow a schedule determines its success.

_____ 3. Our family had more than a dozen things to do to get ready for our trip, but there wasn't enough time or cooperation from anyone.

__C__ 4. We took the biology exam early and passed it with ease.

_____ 5. We rushed to the airport, for, no one would be admitted after the boarding time.

_____ 6. A few fans tried to jump on the stage, but the police prevented their attempts.

_____ 7. Employees today are working more hours than employees in the past, yet many still find it possible to spend quality time with their children and take family vacations.

_____ 8. Beverly said she did not feel comfortable peer reviewing an essay, nor, did she want to write comments on her classmate's paper.

_____ 9. Although our manager would not approve overtime, some employees worked late last Wednesday and came in early the next morning, yet the next day the manager said nothing.

_____10. My professor knew how long I've been waiting and how anxious I was to speak to her, for she kept looking at her watch and smiling at me during her phone conversation.

Adding Introductory Elements

As you may recall from Chapter 22, introductory elements enrich your writing style by adding variety. Now, pay closer attention to punctuating introductory elements.

> **Bridging Knowledge**
>
> **See Chapter 15** to review information on dependent clauses, and see Chapter 16 to review the use of subordinating conjunctions to revise comma splices and fused sentences.

Setting Off an Introductory Dependent Clause

The following subordinating conjunctions can signal the beginning of an introductory dependent clause:

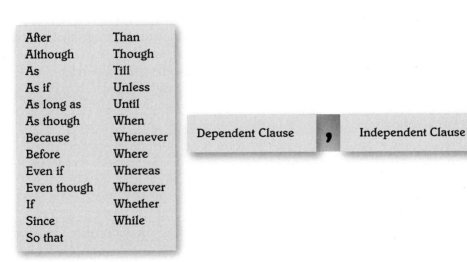

After	Than
Although	Though
As	Till
As if	Unless
As long as	Until
As though	When
Because	Whenever
Before	Where
Even if	Whereas
Even though	Wherever
If	Whether
Since	While
So that	

Dependent Clause **,** Independent Clause

Dependent Clause   Independent Clause
■ **After I read the newspaper article,** I quickly wrote a letter to the editor.

The comma lets the reader know that the main idea of the sentence is about to begin. However, don't use a comma if the dependent clause is at the end of the sentence.

Independent Clause   Dependent Clause
I quickly wrote a letter to the editor **after I read the newspaper article.**

Be extra careful when punctuating introductory clauses that may appear within another dependent clause in a complex sentence.

Dependent Clause   Dependent Clause
While we were driving through Nevada, we met a family **who told us that if we continued on the same road,** we would run into a ghost town.

Independent Clause   Independent Clause

Dependent Clause

Do not use a comma after the subordinating conjunction.

INCORRECT:	**Although,** we tried, we couldn't meet the deadline.
	OR
	We couldn't meet the deadline **although, we tried.**
CORRECT:	**Although we tried,** we couldn't meet the deadline.
	OR
	We couldn't meet the deadline **although we tried.**

Don't use a comma if the dependent clause is not followed by an independent clause.

Dependent Clause   Dependent Clause
| INCORRECT: | **When you leave** or **where you go,** is of no concern to me. |

Here, the two dependent clauses are both subjects of the sentence. Using a comma separates the verb from its subject.

| CORRECT: | **When you leave** or **where you go** is of no concern to me. |

When you proofread your paper for commas after introductory clauses, quickly look at the first couple of words of each sentence. If the sentence starts with one of the subordinating conjunctions listed earlier, place the comma at the end of the dependent clause if it is followed by a complete sentence (an independent clause).

Setting Off a Verbal

As you already know, a *verbal* consists of a verb form. It can be a present participle (verb + -ing), a past participle (the third form of verbs), a gerund (a verb form ending in -ing and used as a noun), or an infinitive (to + the base of the verb). If you start a sentence with a verbal, insert a comma at the end of the verbal to indicate that the main idea of the sentence is starting.

1. **Introductory present participial phrase.** The present participle can be used in an introductory phrase as follows.

Present Participial Phrase (-ing)		Independent Clause

- **Noticing that no one wanted to be first,** Sarah raised her hand.

Make sure that you have an independent clause following the present participial phrase. If not, don't insert a comma. Most likely, you have a gerund and not a participial phrase.

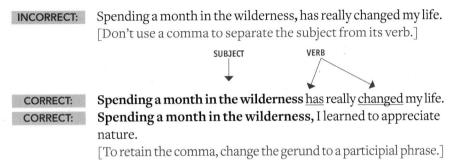

INCORRECT: Spending a month in the wilderness, has really changed my life.
[Don't use a comma to separate the subject from its verb.]

SUBJECT   VERB

CORRECT: **Spending a month in the wilderness** <u>has</u> really <u>changed</u> my life.
CORRECT: **Spending a month in the wilderness,** I learned to appreciate nature.
[To retain the comma, change the gerund to a participial phrase.]

2. **Introductory past participial phrase.** The past participle as an introductory phrase is followed by a comma.

Past Participial Phrase **,** Independent Clause

- **Delivered to the wrong address,** the package remained on the porch for more than a week.
- **Known for his negative attitude,** Fred wasn't invited to the meeting.

3. **Introductory gerund phrase used as the object of the preposition.** A preposition followed by a gerund and a comma can be used in an introductory phrase as follows:

Preposition + Gerund (-ing) **,** Independent Clause

- **Without hesitating,** John offered to pay for the damage.

4. **Introductory infinitive phrase.** An infinitive can also begin a sentence.

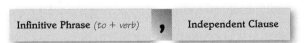

Infinitive Phrase (to + verb) **,** Independent Clause

- **To get the best estimate possible,** we consulted an expert.

Sometimes, the infinitive phrase functions as a noun. As a result, a verb, rather than an independent clause, follows the infinitive phrase. In such cases, don't insert a comma since it would separate the subject from its verb. Always make sure that you have an independent clause following the infinitive.

Infinitive Phrase   Verb

INCORRECT: **To reach the top of the mountain,** became his one obsession.

When you proofread your paper for commas after introductory elements, stop if the phrase begins with a verb that ends in *-ing*, is in past participle form, or is in infinitive form (*to* + verb). If the phrase is followed by an independent clause, insert a comma.

Setting Off a Long Phrase

Use a comma to set off a long or a succession of prepositional phrases.

Common Prepositions			
About	Below	In	Toward
Above	Beneath	Inside	Under
According to	Beside	Into	Underneath
Across	Between	Like	Until
After	Beyond	Near	Up
Against	By	Of	Upon
Along	Despite	Off	Via
Among	Due to	On	With
Around	During	Outside	Within
At	Except	Over	Without
Before	For	Through	
Behind	From	To	

, Independent Clause

LONG PREPOSITIONAL   <u>In his long opening speech</u>, the president blamed the man-
PHRASE: agers for the decrease in profits.

A prepositional phrase of more than four words may be considered long. Even with four words, use your judgment. Is the meaning clear? Can the reader read the sentence with ease?

MORE THAN ONE   <u>At the second exit</u> <u>on the interstate</u>, his car came to a
PREPOSITIONAL PHRASE: screeching halt.

Don't insert a comma after prepositional phrases that start inverted sentences. In such sentences, what follows the prepositional phrase is not a dependent clause but a verb. The subject follows the verb.

Subject   Prepositional Phrases

NORMAL WORD   The abandoned car lay **at the end of the dirt road.**
ORDER: Verb

Prepositional Phrases   Verb   Subject

INVERTED SENTENCE   **At the end of the dirt road,** lay the abandoned car.
INCORRECTLY PUNCTUATED:

CORRECT: At the end of the dirt road lay the abandoned car.

If there is no danger of misreading the sentence, you may choose to omit the comma after a short prepositional phrase.

| CLEAR: | **In the library** we heard the students whispering. |
| UNCLEAR: | **In the library books** were left unorganized on the shelves. |

In the second sentence, the reader may initially start reading "In the library books" and then realize the sentence isn't making sense. Most likely, the reader may need to start the sentence again. Your sentences should be clear, and correct punctuation provides this clarity.

| CORRECT: | **In the library,** books were left unorganized on the shelves. |

Setting Off a Transitional Word or Expression

Use a comma when you start a sentence with one of the following conjunctive adverbs or transitional expressions:

Conjunctive Adverbs	Some Transitional Words and Expressions
Accordingly,	Also,
Consequently,	As a matter of fact,
Furthermore,	As a result,
Hence,	At the same time,
Henceforth,	Finally,
However,	For example,
Incidentally,	For instance,
Moreover,	In addition,
Nevertheless,	In fact,
Nonetheless,	In summary,
Otherwise,	On the other hand,
Therefore,	(See Appendix C for a more
Thus,	complete list of transitional words and expressions.)

| CORRECT: | Jeff was already late for work. **However,** he stopped at the club for a quick swim. |
| CORRECT: | Martha is usually late for her appointments. **On the other hand,** her twin sister is always on time. |

However, if the transitional word or words or the conjunctive adverb is not the first word or phrase of the sentence, set it off with commas.

| INCORRECT: | Jeff was already late for work. He **however,** stopped at the club for a quick swim. |
| CORRECT: | Jeff was already late for work. He, **however,** stopped at the club for a quick swim. |

For the following sentences, insert necessary commas and remove any unnecessary commas. If a sentence is correct, write C for correct on the line provided. Some sentences may require more than one comma.

_____ 1. Since my parents were coming over for dinner, I canceled my plans.

_____ 2. Asking for some kind of explanation, the father grew impatient with his son.

_____ 3. Exhausted after a long trip, Kent turned off his cell phone and went to bed.

_____ 4. In fact, written in 1905, the novel was an instant success.

___C___ 5. Seeing what had just happened made him nervous.

_____ 6. Within the last 30 minutes of class, we started the test.

_____ 7. Not knowing how to answer her questions, Jacob attempted to leave the room. However, she called him before he could leave.

_____ 8. Expecting no one to arrive, Greg fell asleep in front of the TV.

_____ 9. When I was 6, my parents decided to leave Hoboken and move to Patterson, New Jersey.

_____10. Speeding to beat the rushhour traffic, Mari lost control of her car.

Setting Off Nonrestrictive Elements

Commas around dependent clauses or phrases indicate that the information is not necessary to the meaning of the sentence; it is nonrestrictive. Leaving the information out does not affect the meaning of the sentence. However, not placing commas around a dependent clause or phrase lets the reader know that the information in the sentence is crucial to the meaning of the sentence: it is restrictive. Leaving out the information would change the idea of the sentence. Therefore, your first task is to determine whether the information is restrictive (essential) or nonrestrictive (nonessential). Although on occasion the decision is yours to make, here's an easy process to determine whether the clause or phrase should be punctuated. Throughout this section, refer to the chart that follows as we discuss restrictive and nonrestrictive clauses and phrases.

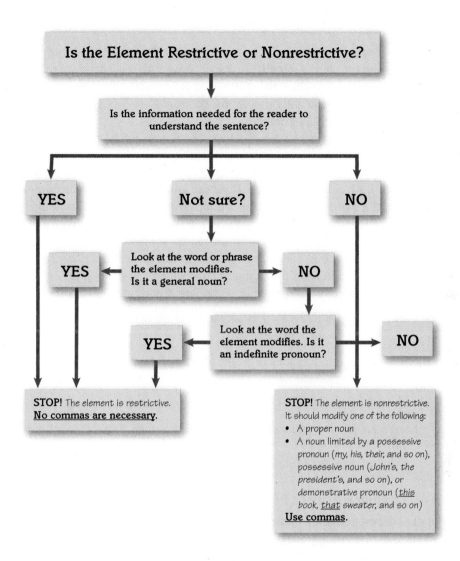

Is the Element Restrictive or Nonrestrictive?

Is the information needed for the reader to understand the sentence?

YES Not sure? NO

YES Look at the word or phrase the element modifies. Is it a general noun? NO

YES Look at the word the element modifies. Is it an indefinite pronoun? NO

STOP! The element is restrictive. **No commas are necessary.**

STOP! The element is nonrestrictive. It should modify one of the following:
• A proper noun
• A noun limited by a possessive pronoun (*my, his, their,* and so on), possessive noun (*John's, the president's,* and so on), or demonstrative pronoun (<u>*this*</u> book, <u>*that*</u> sweater, and so on)
Use commas.

Restrictive and Nonrestrictive Relative Clauses

Use commas to set off all nonrestrictive relative clauses. Relative clauses are introduced by one of the following relative pronouns:

that	which	whoever	whose
where	whichever	whom	whosever
wherever	who	whomever	

Consider the following sentence:

Ruth decided to ask the man <u>who was standing by the booth</u>.

To determine whether to set off the relative clause, first see whether the meaning of the sentence would change if the clause is omitted.

Ruth decided to ask the man.

Since the word *man* is too general, we must keep the relative clause for the meaning of the sentence to be complete. After all, Ruth doesn't want to ask just any man but only the one standing by the booth. Thus, the relative clause is restrictive, necessary to restrict the meaning of *man*. The clause does not require a comma.

Now, examine the following sentence:

Ruth decided to ask Mr. Rivera <u>who was standing by the booth</u> to join them.

Unlike the first example, if we remove the relative clause, the meaning of the sentence is still clear: "Ruth decided to ask Mr. Rivera to join us." The rest of the information is simply additional information, not essential: "By the way, he was standing by the booth." In addition, *Mr. Rivera* is a proper noun, which would usually indicate that the information in the clause is not necessary for the reader to understand who *Mr. Rivera* is. (Refer to the figure on page 691.) The relative clause in this sentence is nonrestrictive and should be set off by commas. By not punctuating the clause, the writer implies that there were other *Mr. Riveras* and that *Ruth* asked only the one standing by the booth.

CORRECT: Ruth decided to ask Mr. Rivera, **who was standing by the booth,** to join them.

If the nonrestrictive relative clause is in the middle of the sentence, be sure to use commas around the entire clause.

Ruth's husband**,** who lives in Newark**,** refused to support our decision.

Note: Use the relative pronoun *that* for restrictive clauses only. Don't use commas. The relative pronoun *which* is usually used for nonrestrictive clauses. Always examine the word or words the relative clause modifies to determine whether to punctuate the clause.

Restrictive and Nonrestrictive Phrases

The same rules of restrictive and nonrestrictive elements we used for clauses may be applied to phrases within a sentence.

1. **Participial phrases.** Participial phrases can be restrictive or nonrestrictive.

RESTRICTIVE PARTICIPIAL PHRASE: The closet was filled with books **dating from 1810.**

Notice that the participial phrase, "dating from 1810," is necessary to restrict the meaning of the noun *books*. This phrase is necessary for the reader to understand the meaning of the sentence, perhaps emphasizing that the books are valuable. This phrase is restrictive and does not require a comma.

NONRESTRICTIVE PARTICIPIAL PHRASE: These books, **dating from 1810,** take up all the closet space.

Unlike the previous sentence, the word *these* makes *books* specific. Without the participial phrase, the main idea of the sentence would not be changed. (Refer to the figure on page 691.)

PRACTICE 26-3

On the lines provided, determine whether the underlined clauses and participial phrases are restrictive (R) or nonrestrictive (N). If nonrestrictive, insert commas. Use the chart on page 691 to help you determine whether the clauses or phrases should be set off by commas.

R 1. Everyone <u>who wanted to attend the concert</u> remained after class.

R 2. The cake <u>baked by the Culinary Arts department</u> is destined to win first place in the cooking contest.

N 3. My favorite place to socialize is The Cabaret, <u>which is located on Lexington Avenue</u>.

R 4. The guy <u>whom my sister married</u> is annoying.

N 5. His essay, <u>submitted late and unrevised</u>, received a failing grade.

N 6. The Lake Avenue Firehouse, <u>abandoned in the '70s</u>, will be renovated and will open as a nightclub.

R 7. The jewelry store <u>robbed last Friday</u> will close permanently by the end of the month.

N 8. Creative Writing 212, <u>which is my favorite course this semester</u>, meets on Friday nights and every other Saturday.

R 9. I'm envious and somewhat jealous of the person <u>who won last semester's poetry contest</u>.

R 10. The cabin <u>that we rented last year for the entire summer</u> burned down last week.

2. **Restrictive and Nonrestrictive Appositive Phrases.** *Appositives* rename, define, or intensify the noun or pronoun they modify. The appositive phrase can be made up of a noun and its modifiers or a verbal (infinitive or gerund phrase) that functions as a noun. Most appositives are nonrestrictive and should, therefore, be set off by commas.

NONRESTRICTIVE APPOSITIVES:

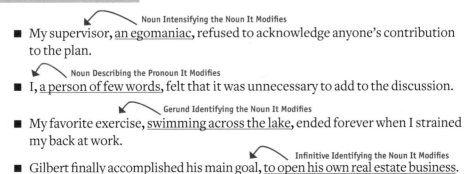

Noun Intensifying the Noun It Modifies
■ My supervisor, <u>an egomaniac</u>, refused to acknowledge anyone's contribution to the plan.

Noun Describing the Pronoun It Modifies
■ I, <u>a person of few words</u>, felt that it was unnecessary to add to the discussion.

Gerund Identifying the Noun It Modifies
■ My favorite exercise, <u>swimming across the lake</u>, ended forever when I strained my back at work.

Infinitive Identifying the Noun It Modifies
■ Gilbert finally accomplished his main goal, <u>to open his own real estate business</u>.

However, some appositives are restrictive and do not require commas. If the noun or pronoun it modifies is too general, then the appositive is essential to its meaning. Your decision to punctuate or not punctuate determines the meaning of your sentences.

My uncle <u>Dave</u> gave us free passes to tonight's game.

The assumption in the preceding sentence is that the writer has more than one uncle; thus, the appositive is essential to restrict the meaning of *my uncle*.

> INCORRECT: My wife Carmen enjoys dancing.

Without commas, the sentence implies that the writer may be a bigamist. The appositive is nonrestrictive.

> CORRECT: My wife, Carmen, enjoys dancing.

PRACTICE   26-4

Underline the appositives and punctuate as necessary. One sentence does not contain an appositive.

1. Rita's car, <u>a total wreck</u>, finally drove its final mile last night.
2. The Tower of London, <u>once a fortress, royal palace, prison, place of execution, and arsenal</u>, is England's leading historic attraction.
3. Isadora Duncan was a great dancer of the early 20th century. No appositive
4. Because of her many family obligations, Professor Cordero, <u>my favorite art teacher</u>, had to sacrifice her greatest desire, <u>to live in Paris and paint</u>.
5. Her favorite pastime, <u>playing video games until midnight</u>, led to her failing three of her courses.

3. **Absolute phrases.** Unlike appositive phrases, absolute phrases do not modify any specific word. Instead they add information to the entire idea of the sentence in which they are inserted. Absolute phrases, usually appearing at the beginning or at the end of sentences, are nonrestrictive and should be punctuated. Most absolute phrases consist of a noun or pronoun, which acts as the subject of the absolute phrase, and possibly a participle and its modifiers.

Subject   Participle   Independent Clause
His reelection secured, Fredrick decided to take a long vacation.

Independent Clause   Subject
The debate team entered the classroom after the contest, **their faces beaming with pride**.
Participle and Modifiers

However, writers often leave out the participle of the absolute phrase when the participle is a form of the verb *be*, such as *being* and *having been*. In these cases, the participle is understood:

■ **The game ~~being~~ over,** the team walked sadly to the lockers.
■ **The game over,** the team walked sadly to their lockers.

Occasionally, an absolute phrase may be placed after a noun to enhance the idea of the main clause. Nonetheless, since the absolute phrase is not essential to the meaning of sentence, you should place commas around it.

Subject   Subject

Our manager, **his face red with anger and his fist clenched,** let us know that our jobs depended on the success of the new campaign.

Note: Absolute phrases contain a subject, so when editing your essay, don't confuse an absolute phrase with a complete sentence. If you place a period or a semicolon after the absolute phrase, you create a fragment.

PRACTICE 26-5

Underline the absolute phrase in the following sentences and punctuate accordingly.

1. The nurse paused a moment in front of the patient, his mind considering different possibilities for the patient's sudden change of behavior.
2. The climbers rested for a moment, their eyes fixed at the distance they had yet to climb.
3. The play finally over, the irritated audience rose quickly to leave.
4. The customer, her questions ignored by unsympathetic clerks, left the store angrily.
5. Their motivation rising to a new level, the team members prepared their most creative proposal.

Separating Coordinate Adjectives

Use commas to separate two or more coordinate adjectives not joined with *and*. To determine whether the two or more adjectives in front of a noun need commas, try the following tests:

- Reverse the order of the adjectives. If the sentence makes sense, the adjectives are coordinate and should be set off by commas.
- Add the word *and* between each adjective. If the sentence makes sense, the adjectives are coordinate, so punctuate.

COORDINATE OR CUMULATIVE?   We prepared ourselves for a dangerous treacherous journey.

If you reverse the adjectives and read the sentence as "treacherous and dangerous journey," the sentence still makes sense. If you add the conjunction *and* between the adjectives, "treacherous and dangerous journey," the sentence still makes sense. Therefore, you need to insert a comma.

COORDINATE = ADD COMMA: We prepared ourselves for a dangerous, treacherous journey.

COORDINATE OR CUMULATIVE?   They purchased two blue jackets for the show.

Try reversing the order: "They purchased blue two jackets for the show." The sentence doesn't make sense. Try inserting *and* between the adjectives: "They purchased two and blue jackets for the show." It still doesn't make sense. The adjectives are cumulative: they must remain in fixed position for the sentence to make sense. No comma is necessary.

Don't punctuate the adjective before the noun.

INCORRECT:	He had to think twice before entering the dark, empty, creepy, alley.
CORRECT:	He had to think twice before entering the dark, empty, creepy alley.

Separating Items in a Series

When you have a series consisting of three or more words, phrases, or clauses, place a comma after each item except the last.

WORDS:	We felt **anger, frustration, and humiliation** when we heard his explanation.
PHRASES (PREPOSITIONAL):	Josh marched **through the park, around the block, and up the stairs** to file his complaint.
PHRASES (GERUND):	The child would not stop **screaming, running, or throwing** his toys.
CLAUSES (DEPENDENT):	Carla was trying to decide **where she would live, when she should marry, and what profession she should pursue.**
CLAUSES (INDEPENDENT):	Before leaving, **Rita washed the van, Jeff packed the luggage, and Ben secured the house.**

When the last two items of the series are joined by *and*, you may leave out the comma if there is no chance the sentence may be misread. However, we suggest that you always insert the comma; it will always be correct.

CLEAR:	Martha **created, designed, revised and updated** our new website.
UNCLEAR:	Next semester, Martha will be taking English Composition I, General Biology, Abnormal Psychology and Human Sexuality.

Is the list made up of three or four courses? Might the reader read "Abnormal Psychology and Human Sexuality" as one course rather than two? Correct punctuation prevents any confusion.

CLEAR:	Next semester, Martha will be taking English Composition I, General Biology, Abnormal Psychology, and Human Sexuality.

| UNCLEAR: | Security guards apprehended two shoplifters, a cashier and a stock clerk. |

Did the security guards arrest a total of four people, or are the words "a cashier and a stock clerk" an appositive to define the two shoplifters? A simple comma prevents the possibility of misreading the sentence.

| CLEAR: | Security guards apprehended two shoplifters, a cashier, and a stock clerk. |

PRACTICE 26-6

Where necessary, punctuate the series in the following sentences.

1. Leaving early, taking long breaks, and making personal calls are the main reasons that he lost his job.

2. I can't find my wallet, my checkbook, or my car keys.

3. The unpaved, muddy road took us directly to the cabin.

4. Her husband gave her two nervous little white Maltese puppies for her birthday.

5. The stargazers stared at the dark blue sky, waiting for the total eclipse.

6. They repaired the car, painted the house, and fixed the fence.

7. Chris has always been cautious of what he says, where he says it, and how he says it.

8. After putting on sterile gloves, a white gown, and a cap, Marta was ready to visit her father in the ICU.

9. She purchased several white silk blouses to take on her trip.

10. We need a person who's a team player, has excellent communication skills, and can motivate others.

Separating Words That Interrupt Sentence Flow

Writers use words and phrases that interrupt the flow of the sentence to emphasize, clarify, or verify ideas. Since these interrupters do not add any essential meaning to a sentence, they should be set off by commas.

Using Parenthetical Expressions

Parenthetical expressions interrupt the flow of the sentence by providing information that's not essential to the meaning of the sentence. Since they appear as afterthoughts, brief digressions, or supplemental comments or information, parenthetical expressions are nonrestrictive and should be set off by commas.

■ The sudden drop in profits, **I'm sorry to say,** will mean a freeze in salaries.

■ **Believe it or not,** I had no clue that you would be here.

Common Parenthetical Expressions			
, after all,	, I assure you,	, it seems to me,	, to begin with,
, all things considered,	, I'm sorry to say,	, it would seem,	, to be honest,
, as a matter of fact,	, in case you didn't know,	, needless to say,	, to tell the truth,
, as far as we know,	, in fact,	, of course,	, unfortunately,
, believe it or not,	, in my opinion,	, on the other hand,	, without a doubt,
, by the way,	, in other words,	, so it seems,	, you know,
, fortunately,	, in reality,	, surprisingly enough,	
, I am sure,	, I suppose,	, to be frank,	

Some of the preceding phrases may be used as part of the sentence and not parenthetical, so be sure that the expressions you set off with commas do indeed interrupt the flow of the sentence and appear as afterthoughts or asides.

PARENTHETICAL:	Soccer, **I am sure**, is an exciting sport.
NOT AN INTERRUPTER:	**I am sure** that soccer is an exciting sport.
PARENTHETICAL:	Our instructor, **after all**, expects that we be there on time.
NOT AN INTERRUPTER:	**After all** our instructor has done, we should be there on time.

It is not necessary to place a comma in front of the parenthetical expression when the phrase comes after the coordinating conjunction in a compound sentence.

■ Leo decided to help raise the money, and **of course**, we were all delighted.

A comma in front of the word *of* is unnecessary.

PRACTICE   26-7

Insert commas to set off parenthetical expressions.

1. Gilbert possesses it would seem an unusual talent to exaggerate the facts.
2. The employee is in fact the one person we really want to promote. Surprisingly, however, he wants to remain in his present position.
3. This building as a matter of fact dates back to 1860, a period which I'm sorry to say was filled with violence and political deceit.
4. Her mother by the way will join us for dinner; I of course will pick up the tab.
5. My favorite candidate was needless to say doing exceptionally well during the first part of the debate. Of course she had all the answers when the question on the economy came up, but she unfortunately was vague on health care issues.

Expressing Contrast

Phrases expressing contrast usually begin with one of the following words: *never, not,* or *unlike.* If you need to stop the flow of a sentence to negate, contrast, or state an exception, place commas around these expressions.

- It was the plot, **not the characters or the setting,** that kept me glued to the movie.
- Carol seemed always interested, **never bored**.

Addressing a Person Directly

When you address a person or group directly, insert commas around the name, title, or phrase.

- **Tina,** did you complete the project?
- Showing your support, **sir,** will indicate the importance of this campaign.
- I, **my good friend,** will be surfing in Hawaii.

Notice that in each of the preceding examples, the writer must be talking directly to the person, not about the person.

Using Mild Interjections

Interjections are words that express surprise or other emotions. Strong interjections, such as *wow, ouch,* or *darn,* are usually followed by an exclamation point. However, when such mild exclamatory words such as *yes, no, well,* and *oh* start a sentence, they are usually set off from the rest of the sentence by commas.

- **No,** you shouldn't make the suggestion.
- **Oh,** I wasn't expecting an answer so quickly.

Using Interrogative Tags

An *interrogative tag* is a word or phrase that turns a statement into a question. The interrogative tag may verify or confirm the information in the statement, or it can express politeness, emphasis, or sarcasm. A tag question is usually placed at the end of a sentence and should be set off from the rest of the sentence by a comma.

- You enjoyed the course, **didn't you?**
- You are going to vote for me, **right?**
- It was a shock, **wasn't it,** to hear the verdict?

Although words and phrases that interrupt the flow of your ideas may help clarify and even add to the meaning of your sentences, avoid cluttering your sentences with too many or unnecessary interrupters. Overusing such expressions may be distracting or confusing to the reader. As a writer, always keep in mind that your goal is to communicate your ideas clearly.

PRACTICE 26-8

Insert commas to set off contrasting words, direct addresses, mild interjections, and interrogative tags.

1. Miguel, unlike Ray, is willing to help, but I prefer Ray since he's organized.
2. Diane, you did say you were coming, didn't you?
3. Rose talks to me as a colleague, not like her helper.
4. Oh, you really thought it would be a good idea to wait until the last moment to stop for gas, didn't you? Well, my friend, here we are somewhere in the desert.
5. It is my sense of duty, not my love for this company, that motivates me to work late.

Setting Off Quoted Elements

Expressions such as *said, state, writes, explains, asserts,* and so on may signal a direct quotation, the writer's or speaker's actual words, unedited by you, which are placed in quotation marks. Insert commas after such introductory words.

■ The candidate clearly said, "There will absolutely be no more new taxes."

■ Without hesitating, the clerk said, "I'll get you the samples right away."

Also, place the comma after the quotation when a reference to the speaker follows the quotation.

■ "I'm not sure they want me to stay," he said nervously.

However, if you place an acknowledgement of the speaker in the middle of the direct quotation, then place commas on both sides of the reference. This rule is especially important in research when you want to vary your style as you quote information from your sources.

■ "The problem is," said Shanda, "we won't be in town that week."

Make sure that both sides of the direct quotation make up one sentence, not two complete sentences. If you use a comma for two complete sentences, you may have created a comma splice.

| INCORRECT: | "The problem is the schedule," said Shanda, "we won't stand for it." |
| CORRECT: | "The problem is the schedule," said Shanda. "We won't stand for it." |

Note: Throughout all preceding examples commas and periods are placed inside the quotation marks.

However, don't insert a comma if the direct quotation is introduced by the word *that,* and don't capitalize the first letter of the word in the quotation.

■ He often says that "money is the root to all evil." I say, "Give me some evil!"

PRACTICE 26-9

In the following paragraphs, insert commas for parenthetical expressions, direct addresses, contrasting words, mild interjections, and interrogative tags.

Most people don't appreciate what they have until they lose it. Yes this saying may be a cliché, but it still holds true. Last week, my best friend, Rick came over to visit not a good time for me, but of course I didn't say anything. He was upset that he didn't get the salary increase that he wanted. Yelling and cursing, Rick complained not surprisingly that now all his future plans were on hold. "What plans Rick?" I asked. "Well buddy my plasma TV for one" he shot back.

I stared at him for a moment. I finally said "Rick you really think you've lost a lot don't you?" He stared at me in disbelief. Yes I knew he expected me to be supportive. After all he was supportive when last year I told him I was going to purchase a Jaguar. In fact he encouraged me not to think about it and just do it. As a matter of fact he I'm embarrassed to say offered to take me to the dealership. Fortunately I decided to wait until the end of the year. Rick simply said "You'll call me when you decide won't you? I unlike you have more experience negotiating with car dealers. In fact in my opinion I can probably save you a bundle." No doubt Rick is a true friend.

Needless to say he was still waiting for a response. Finally I said "Rick last week I demanded a raise, and yes believe it or not I was fired. Right now I would welcome half of my previous salary wouldn't you?" Rick was quiet for a moment and then answered "I guess I really don't need an iPhone do I?"

Using Commas with Special Elements

Although often ignored by students, the following rules help guide the reader through special elements.

Dates

Use commas to separate the month and its date from the year and to separate the year from the rest of the sentence. If you include the day of the week, separate it as well.

- Our vacation started on March 15, 2007, and continued through April 2, 2007.
- Monday, August 25, 1964, is the date my grandparents left Poland.

However, don't insert a comma to set off a one-word date preceded by a preposition (*at, from, in, near, on,* and so on) or if the month or year is used by itself.

- The governor plans to be in Boston **in May 2010**.

Also, don't insert a comma between or after an inverted date or between the season and the year.

- The last payment on our mortgage will be on **25 April 2012**.
- **Fall 1995** was the turning point of my career.

Addresses

When punctuating addresses, don't split each component with a comma. Rather, insert the comma after each of the following elements:

- Mail your rebate form to **Ms. Tina Sandoval, 13 Maple Drive, Roanoke, Virginia 24008,** for immediate handling.
- **Santa Fe, New Mexico,** is known for the art of Georgia O'Keeffe.

Similar to dates, don't use a comma with a one-word address preceded by a preposition.

- We moved **to Georgia** to be with our family.
- We visited the Metropolitan Museum of Art **in New York** last year.

Also, when the state is used in the possessive form, don't include the comma for the rest of the sentence.

- **Las Vegas, Nevada's** grand casinos entice even the most conservative of tourists.

Titles

Use commas after a name followed by degrees or titles such as M.D., Ph.D., and so on. If the title is in the middle of the sentence, use commas around the title. However, if the title ends the sentence, insert the comma before the title.

- Tanya Gregory, **M.D.,** has accepted the new position.
- To receive the check, we need the signature of Joe Easton, **Accounts Payable Manager.**

Long Numbers

When writing a number of more than four digits, use a comma to separate a number in groups of three, counting from the right. The comma is optional with numbers of four digits.

- We paid $1500.   OR   We paid $1,500.

However, don't insert the comma if the number is a year, such as 1776 or 2010. Also, don't use commas in street addresses, zip codes, or page numbers.

- The flowchart on page 1205 of the journal describes the process.
- The robbery took place at 1313 Wayne Street.

Salutation and Closing of Friendly Letters

Use a comma after the salutation of a friendly letter (business letters often use a colon instead of the comma).

- Dear Sophia,
- Dear Aunt Betsy,

However, whether you're writing a business letter or a friendly letter, use a comma after the closing.

- Yours truly,
- Sincerely,

Ensuring Clarity

Use commas for clarity (to help readability).

| CLEAR: | **Inside the house** he heard the familiar laughter. |
| UNCLEAR: | **Inside the house** was lavishly decorated. |

In the second sentence, the reader may initially read "Inside the house"; then realize it doesn't make sense. Correct punctuation provides clarity.

| CORRECT: | **Inside,** the house was lavishly decorated. |

When editing your essays for commas, stop at each comma you used in your paper. If you can't justify the comma by citing a rule or if the comma is not necessary for clarity, remove it. Too many or needless commas can be distracting to the reader.

Semicolons

When you revised fragments and run-ons in Chapters 15 and 16 and when you combined sentences for variety in Chapter 22, you became familiar with the semicolon. The first two rules of this section review what you already know and then enrich your knowledge by providing rules that may not be so familiar.

> **Bridging Knowledge**
>
> **See Chapter 15,** Chapter 16, and Chapter 22 for more information on the semicolon.

Without a Coordinating Conjunction

Use a semicolon when the content of both independent clauses is closely related but is not connected by a coordinating conjunction.

■ The report made three recommendations; only one was reasonable.

Don't place a semicolon after a dependent clause. If you do so, you create a sentence fragment. Generally, if you can't use a period, don't use a semicolon.

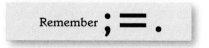

Remember ; = .

| INCORRECT: | Although we qualified; the manager refused to lease us the apartment. |
| CORRECT: | Although we qualified, the manager refused to lease us the apartment. |

Don't capitalize the first letter of the word following the semicolon. Also, unless you're adding a specific rule, don't use a semicolon before a coordinating conjunction.

| WRONG: | We wanted to go to the reception; but we weren't invited. |
| CORRECT: | We wanted to go to the reception, but we weren't invited. |

However, if the clauses are long and one or both clauses contain commas, using a semicolon in front of the coordinating conjunction is acceptable.

■ As I was leaving the office, I met Jake, who wanted to discuss the agenda; but I didn't have the time.

Notice how the semicolon points the reader's attention to the next main idea of the sentence.

With a Transitional Word or Expression

When you use a conjunctive adverb or transitional expression to connect two complete sentences, you may use a semicolon rather than a period to end the first sentence.

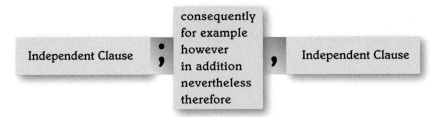

Independent Clause **;** consequently / for example / however / in addition / nevertheless / therefore **,** Independent Clause

■ Ricardo left the meeting early; therefore, he was unable to complete the report.

Don't reverse the order of the semicolon and the comma. Doing so may change the meaning of the first sentence.

> INCORRECT: The parents' position should be supported, however; some restrictions are necessary.
>
> CORRECT: The parents' position should be supported; however, some restrictions are necessary.

Avoid overusing the semicolon. Have a purpose for using a semicolon.

With Items in a Series That Also Contain Commas

Normally, you use commas to separate the items in a series; however, when one or more items contain a comma, substitute a semicolon to help the reader understand the grouping of the series.

■ The vice president was accompanied by his brother-in law, an insurance agent; his wife, a corporate lawyer; and his daughter, a computer engineer.

The semicolon helps tie each item to its appositive to prevent the reader from assuming that the president was accompanied by six people.

> CONFUSING: To conduct research for his book, Mr. Engle visited Nairobi, Kenya, Lusaka, Zambia, Luanda, Angola, and Accra, Ghana.

A reader who is unfamiliar with these cities and countries would find this listing confusing. How many places did Mr. Engle visit? By substituting semicolons for commas to group the items in the series, the reader can easily associate the city with its country.

> BETTER: To conduct research for his book, Mr. Engle visited Nairobi, Kenya; Lusaka, Zambia; Luanda, Angola; and Accra, Ghana.

Use semicolons and commas to revise the following sentences. Cross out any unnecessary commas.

1. No one knows where he went; he disappeared mysteriously.

2. While in Norway, Nathaniel bought Crystal three gifts: a necklace, which she admired at the jewelry store; a jacket, made of genuine leather; and a broach, a family heirloom.

3. Catherine saw smoke coming from the room; she immediately dialed 911.

4. I always felt confident when making a presentation; however, I forgot to analyze my audience this time.

5. The following employees were dismissed from the company: Jay Johnson, the accounts payable supervisor; Rita Moreno, the accounts receivable clerk; and Mark Lane, the payroll clerk.

Colons

Most students are familiar with some basic uses of the colon. We often use the colon after the salutation in a business letter (*Dear Dr. Mercer:*), between the hour and the minute (*7:30 a.m.*), for ratios (*4:1*), or in a memo (*From: To: Subject:*). Nonetheless, the colon is a punctuation mark that is rarely used or often misused by many composition students. The following four simple rules describe the major uses of the colon.

1. **Use a colon after an independent clause to let the reader know that an explanation follows.** When you place the colon between two independent clauses, the second sentence explains or summarizes the first.

   ■ Frank volunteered to head the project for only <u>one reason</u>: he wanted to <u>advance his career</u>.

   Notice that the phrase "advance his career" explains the phrase "one reason" in the main clause. Also notice that the first letter after the colon is not capitalized. The decision to capitalize the independent clause that follows the colon is up to you: both ways are correct. Not capitalizing a short sentence gives the first sentence a sense of continuity. However, if the explanation following the colon consists of more than one sentence, capitalizing is preferable.

   ■ The consultant provided two reasons for the loss of sales: <u>First</u>, the product was poorly packaged. Second, the low advertisement budget made it difficult to reach a broader market.

   Since many instructors prefer that students always capitalize after a colon, consult your instructor.

2. **Use a colon after an independent clause to note a list of items.** Use the colon to introduce a list.

   ■ To apply for this position, you must possess three important qualities: assertiveness, patience, and commitment.

   If you use such expressions as *the following* or *as follows* to introduce the list, use a colon. The list must immediately follow these types of constructions.

   ■ Please submit the following: a current résumé, a completed application, and two letters of recommendation.

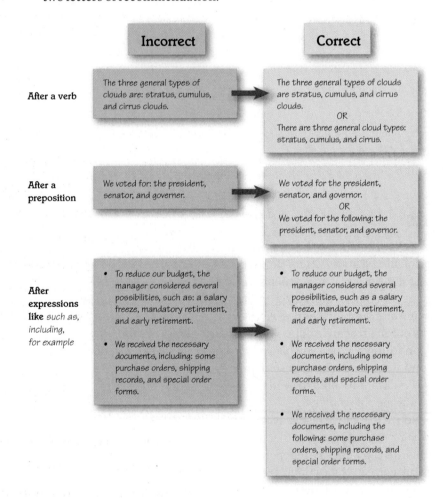

	Incorrect	Correct
After a verb	The three general types of clouds are: stratus, cumulus, and cirrus clouds.	The three general types of clouds are stratus, cumulus, and cirrus clouds. OR There are three general cloud types: stratus, cumulus, and cirrus.
After a preposition	We voted for: the president, senator, and governer.	We voted for the president, senator, and governor. OR We voted for the following: the president, senator, and governor.
After expressions like *such as, including, for example*	• To reduce our budget, the manager considered several possibilities, such as: a salary freeze, mandatory retirement, and early retirement. • We received the necessary documents, including: some purchase orders, shipping records, and special order forms.	• To reduce our budget, the manager considered several possibilities, such as a salary freeze, mandatory retirement, and early retirement. • We received the necessary documents, including some purchase orders, shipping records, and special order forms. • We received the necessary documents, including the following: some purchase orders, shipping records, and special order forms.

3. **Use a colon to signal an appositive.** Although a comma is normally used to set off an appositive phrase, using a colon gives the appositive greater emphasis.

   ■ I nervously read my final biology grade: D−.
   ■ The president made the final decision: immediate foreclosure.

4. **Use a colon to present a formal quotation or an extended quotation.** If you introduce a quotation with a colon, use the main sentence to set the context for the quotation.

▪ Martin Luther King, Jr., forced us to examine our values as a nation: "A nation that continues year after year to spend more money on military defense than on programs of social uplift is approaching spiritual doom."

When the colon introduces a quotation, always capitalize the first letter of the word after the colon.

PRACTICE 26-11

Insert colons where necessary. If the sentence does not require a colon, write C for correct on the line provided.

_____ 1. He made a tempting offer: he would pay the airfare and hotel expenses if I would write up the annual report.

_____ 2. The new technician will have to perform the following duties: upgrade all office computers, service existing computers, and train new employees.

_____ 3. In her poem "Coda," Dorothy Parker, best known for her sarcastic wit, voiced the feelings of her time: "Art is a form of catharsis, / And love is a permanent flop."

_____ 4. After some discussion, the parents made a decision: the Internet will be off limits for the rest of the summer.

___C___ 5. When selecting a candidate, we considered experience, education, and philosophy.

REVIEW 26-1

Examine each of the following sentences and determine whether the positions marked *a, b, c,* and *d* are punctuated correctly or lack punctuation. If any one of the positions is either punctuated incorrectly or not punctuated where it should be, circle the corresponding letter. If the sentence is correct, choose *e*. (Each sentence has either one error or no errors.)

1. After we completed the job[a] we went out to dinner[b] and ordered wine,[c] cold soup,[d] and cake. [e] NO ERROR

2. While discussing[a] the salary freeze[b] all of the employees became angry[c] and marched[d] to the president's office. [e] NO ERROR

3. Well[a] failing one test[b] doesn't determine the outcome of the entire semester,[c] but[d] it sure is depressing. [e] NO ERROR

4. The waiter suggested[a] that we order Sangria[b] and[c] that[d] we try the exquisite paella. [e] NO ERROR

5. The stuntman[a] survived a two-story fall,[b] however,[c] he was never[d] quite the same again. [e] NO ERROR

6. Whenever we get spring southern winds,[a] our house,[b] a rather old one[c] creaks[d] and groans. [e] NO ERROR

7. He completed his internship on[a] September,[b] 2007[c] and received a job offer,[d] which he refused. [e] NO ERROR

8. Because of its condition[a] and selling price,[b] the house, which is located on my grandfather's farm, [d] stood empty for years,[c] no one would buy it. [e] NO ERROR

9. Pueblo,[a] Colorado,[b] has many cultural[c] festivals[d] during the summer. [e] NO ERROR

10. There was a blizzard[a] the day[b] that I arrived home from college,[c] and Jason, who was such a pessimist[d] thought that I would turn back. [e] NO ERROR

CHAPTER 27

Other Punctuation and Capitalization

YOUR GOALS

1. Apply basic rules for the use of apostrophes.

2. Use quotation marks correctly.

3. Use parentheses and dashes correctly.

4. Apply basic rules for correct capitalization.

5. Use underlining or italics correctly.

"Cut out all those exclamation marks. An exclamation mark is like laughing at your own joke."

■ **F. Scott Fitzgerald** ■

The community of Cañon City, Colorado, recently built a new stadium. Since it was paid for by local tax dollars, the builders wanted to acknowledge that the stadium was funded by the citizens of the city. Thus, the following was sandblasted into the walls of the stadium: *Citizen's Stadium*. Soon after completion of the stadium, one of the city's citizens wrote to the local newspaper asking which citizen owned the stadium since *Citizen's* indicates one person. This mistake was expensive. More public funds had to be used to erase the apostrophe before the *s* and to put it after the *s* to make the correction: *Citizens' Stadium*.

Some errors may not be as expensive as the one in Cañon City, but the professional should be aware of the difference a punctuation mark can make. Misused punctuation not only can cause you or your employer embarrassment but also can cost you your job or position if the error results in financial loses.

Whether you're writing for college, writing in your profession, or even creating a business or personal web page, you cannot ignore the importance of punctuation if you want to be taken seriously.

LET's warm up!

Write a paragraph summarizing your understanding of the uses of apostrophes, quotation marks, exclamations, and capitalization. Which writing convention gives you the most trouble and why?

Ed Holden

UNDERSTANDING PUNCTUATION MARKS AND CAPITALIZATION

In the writing process, we usually address punctuation in the proofreading stage. Unfortunately, some students interpret this practice as indicating that punctuation is the least important part of writing and that they may, as a result, speed through this stage carelessly. Think of punctuation as your audience's guide to reading, understanding, and interpreting your writing. Punctuation tells the reader when to stop, where to pause, what to stress, and how ideas are related. Through punctuation, you make your text come alive. An effective writer knows the rules of punctuation.

Not understanding the value and power of punctuation may harm or even destroy the purpose of your writing. You're already aware of the importance of commas, semicolons, and colons in your writing. This chapter covers the basic rules for apostrophes, quotation marks, and other more sophisticated punctuation marks, such as dashes and parentheses. The variety of punctuation marks offers you plenty of choices to help you communicate your ideas effectively and vigorously. This chapter concludes with a review of and practice in capitalization.

Apostrophes

For such a small mark, apostrophes have a number of uses: they show possession, indicate an omission of letters in words, and help form the plurals of some nouns. Examine each of these uses closely.

Showing Ownership

An apostrophe shows ownership or possession. It tells the reader that something belongs to a person or thing. Use apostrophes in the following situations.

Nouns Not Ending in *s*

To show ownership (possession) of singular or plural nouns not ending in *s*, add an apostrophe + -*s* (*'s*) to the noun that claims ownership, not to the word that is owned:

Belongs to   What is owned
friend's car

However, before adding an apostrophe, first make sure that the noun is possessive.

INCORRECT: The committee considered the first applicants suggestion.

Question: Is there more than one applicant with a suggestion?
Analysis: Invert the two words and add *of* or *belongs to:*
The committee considered the suggestion **of** the <u>applicant</u>.
[The meaning is clearly possessive; therefore, add the apostrophe before the *s*.]
The committee considered the first <u>applicant</u>**'s** suggestion.
He permitted the students to submit the projects late.

Question: Is the word *students* in this case a plural noun or a noun expressing possession?
Analysis: Form an *of the* or *belongs to* phrase:
He permitted to submit **of (or belonging to)** the <u>students</u> the projects late.
[This sentence doesn't make sense since there's no noun for the word *students* to express ownership of; therefore, the noun is plural, not possessive. No apostrophe is necessary.]

CORRECT: He permitted the <u>students</u> to submit the projects late.

Here are other examples. Note that some of the nouns are singular and others are plural but that none end in *s.*

the car belonging to Tracy	=	Tracy's car
the toy of the cat	=	the cat's toy
the microscope belonging to the doctor	=	the doctor's microscope
the jackets belong to the men	=	the men's jackets
the stories of the children	=	the children's stories

Singular Nouns Ending in *s*

Add an apostrophe + -*s* (*'s*) to nouns that are singular and end in *s.*

- Jamie Bruss**'s** new play opens in Denver next month.
- The dress**'s** length was just perfect for her short stature.

When the extra syllable is pronounced, the apostrophe + -*s* is acceptable to most writers; however, some writers may not pronounce the extra syllable, in which case the *s* may be omitted. For example, *James's car* and *James' car* are both correct, depending on which pronunciation the writer intends.

On the other hand, if the extra syllable makes the word sound awkward, confusing, or difficult to pronounce, it is acceptable to omit the *s.*

- Socrates**'** final days were spent in prison, awaiting execution.
- Lloyd Bridges**'** career started on Broadway.
- For goodness**'** sake, close the darn door!

If you try to pronounce each of the preceding sentences with the added syllable (*Socrates's, Bridges's, and goodness's*), you might hear the awkwardness. However, some writers feel that there should be no exception and that, regardless of pronunciation, apostrophe + -*s* should be added. Consult your instructor if necessary, but above all, be consistent in your writing.

Indefinite Pronouns

Add apostrophe + -*s* (*'s*) to make an indefinite pronoun possessive.

- This is anybody**'s** game.
- The supervisor posted everyone**'s** schedule.
- One**'s** goal in life must be fulfilled.

Basically, add apostrophe + -*s* to indefinite pronouns ending in -*one* or -*body.* If you combine the word *else* with an indefinite pronoun to express ownership, add apostrophe + -*s* to *else*, not to the indefinite pronoun.

- This is someone else**'s** responsibility.

However, the pronoun *other* follows the same rules of singular and plural nouns:

- In class, we read each other**'s** essay.
  [Invert the phrase to see that the use is singular: *the essay of each other.*]
- At the dorm we visited one another**'s** rooms.
  [Invert the phrase to see that the use is singular: *the rooms of one another.*]

■ Afterward, we heard the <u>others'</u> proposals.

[Invert the phrase to see that the use is plural: *the reports of the others.*]

This rule applies only to indefinite pronouns, never to possessive pronouns. Since the form of a possessive pronoun already shows ownership, it is not necessary to use an apostrophe. Although the following pronouns end in *s*, do not make the mistake of using an apostrophe with any of them:

hers	its	theirs
his	ours	yours

Plural Nouns Ending in *s*

Add only an apostrophe to the end of plural nouns that end in *s*:

■ I hate receiving <u>marketers'</u> telephone calls while I'm eating dinner.

■ The <u>athletes'</u> fitness level is already quite high.

the telephone calls of the marketers	=	the marketers' telephone calls
the condominium of the Joneses	=	the Joneses' condominium
the roofs of the houses	=	the houses' roofs
a vacation of 3 weeks	=	3 weeks' vacation

PRACTICE 27-1

Change each phrase into its possessive form, using apostrophe or apostrophe + *-s* as necessary. Write each phrase on the line provided.

1. the show of the stars ___the stars' show___
2. the pay of 3 weeks ___3 weeks' pay___
3. the entrance of the cave ___the cave's entrance___
4. the dispute of the referees ___the referees' dispute___
5. the book by Doris Kearns ___Doris Kearns's (Kearns') book___
6. the ticket belonging to James ___James's (James') ticket___
7. the concerns of the faculty members ___the faculty members' concerns___
8. the feats of the Vikings ___the Vikings' feats___
9. the arguments of my sisters ___my sisters' arguments___
10. the objections of the lawyer ___the lawyer's objections___

Compound Nouns

Add apostrophe + *-s* (*'s*) to the last word of a compound noun:

■ I love <u>my mother-in-law**'s**</u> cooking.

■ Todd borrowed <u>his brothers-in-law**'s**</u> rifles for the weekend.

Since the first word of the compound noun indicates the number (singular or plural), the apostrophe + *-s* is all that's needed to show ownership.

Multiple Nouns

Add apostrophe + -*s* (*'s*) to the last noun to show joint possession.

■ Mark and Juanita**'s** house is on the historic registry of their town.

The use of apostrophe in the preceding sentence indicates to the reader that Mark and Juanita own one house together.

■ Mark and Juanita**'s** houses are on the historic registry of their town.

The preceding sentence indicates that Mark and Juanita own various houses jointly. However, by using apostrophe + -*s* after each noun, we can change the meaning of the sentence to indicate individual ownership.

■ Mark**'s** and Juanita**'s** houses are on the historic registry of their town.

Mark and Juanita each own a house or houses.

PRACTICE 27-2

Insert apostrophes where necessary.

1. To everyone's amazement, Ralph ate eight hot dogs for lunch.
2. Gabriela left her sisters-in-law's contracts on her car's hood and drove off.
3. We saw the Smiths' light go on, but we knew the Smiths were on vacation.
4. To escape his boss, who is pressuring him to finish a project, Jeff sneaks into the men's room.
5. The store's policy has always been that no children's toy should be sold until we receive our president's approval.
6. The three top employees participated in each other's committees, but Sharon's report indicates that the committees were not efficient.
7. Paul's anger is due to receiving 3 days' wages for 1 week's work regardless of his manager's promise to pay him at three times his hourly rate.
8. Linda Yarnell's book, *One Last Breath*, was a tribute to her son's memory.
9. The storm's approach prevented me from going out, so I reread my three friends' letters three times.
10. Somebody's jacket was stolen during last night's meeting, but the surveillance cameras were off.

Indicating Omissions of Letters and Numbers

English, especially when the diction is informal, uses many contractions. Learn these contractions and use an apostrophe to indicate the position of the missing letters:

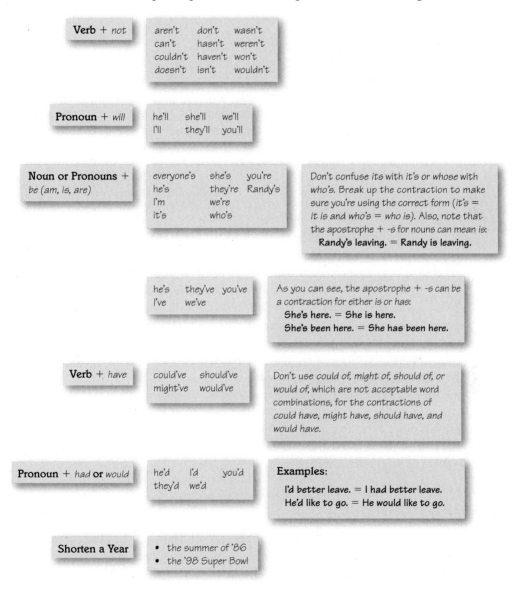

| **Verb** + *not* | aren't don't wasn't
can't hasn't weren't
couldn't haven't won't
doesn't isn't wouldn't |

| **Pronoun** + *will* | he'll she'll we'll
I'll they'll you'll |

| **Noun or Pronouns** +
be (am, is, are) | everyone's she's you're
he's they're Randy's
I'm we're
it's who's | Don't confuse *its* with *it's* or *whose* with *who's*. Break up the contraction to make sure you're using the correct form (*it's* = *it is* and *who's* = *who is*). Also, note that the apostrophe + *-s* for nouns can mean *is*:
Randy's leaving. = Randy is leaving. |

| | he's they've you've
I've we've | As you can see, the apostrophe + *-s* can be a contraction for either *is* or *has*:
She's here. = She is here.
She's been here. = She has been here. |

| **Verb** + *have* | could've should've
might've would've | Don't use *could of, might of, should of,* or *would of*, which are not acceptable word combinations, for the contractions of *could have, might have, should have,* and *would have*. |

| **Pronoun** + *had* **or** *would* | he'd I'd you'd
they'd we'd | **Examples:**
I'd better leave. = I had better leave.
He'd like to go. = He would like to go. |

| **Shorten a Year** | • the summer of '86
• the '98 Super Bowl |

Avoiding Apostrophes When Forming the Plural of Numbers and Letters

As a rule, do not use apostrophes to form the plural of numbers and letters.

■ During the 1990s, the Internet grew 100% every year.
■ Since he received two Cs and three Ds this semester, he lost his scholarship.

Note: Do not italicize academic grades. Also, although it is not necessary to use apostrophes to form the plurals of uppercase letters, an apostrophe to form the plural of lowercase letters and capital letters *A* and *I* may prevent confusion or misreading.

- Don't forget to dot your *i*'s and cross your *t*'s.
  [The letter is italicized, but the apostrophe + -*s* is not.]
- I received three A's and two Bs this semester.

Proofreading for Apostrophes

When you proofread your paper for apostrophes, check every word that ends with *s* to make sure that it's not possessive. If it is, you'll need an apostrophe. Also, if you find yourself using too many apostrophes, this may be a signal that you're misusing the apostrophe. Check each one and tie your use of the apostrophe to a rule discussed in this section.

PRACTICE 27-3

Add apostrophes where needed in the following passage.

Rubbernecking is the practice of slowing down and sticking one's neck out the window to get a closer look at a highway accident. This practice tests many drivers' patience, especially those who have appointments to keep. Rubbernecking represents people's curiosity about accidents and catastrophes, but it's not just an irritating behavior. It disrupts traffic flow and endangers others' lives as drivers' attention is diverted from the highway ahead to the accident along the roadside. For example, I remember in the late '90s I was driving to Indianapolis with my cousin's boyfriend to pick my cousin up at the airport. Suddenly, I had to put on my brakes because of the rubberneckers' curiosity about an accident ahead of us. Unfortunately, other drivers' reflexes weren't as good as mine were, and I was rear-ended by the car behind me. Luckily, my car's bumper protected the passengers and vehicle from any serious injury or damage, but other drivers weren't as lucky. Therefore, drivers need to be made more aware of the perils of this behavior.

Quotation Marks

The use and placement of quotation marks can cause confusion. Do the punctuation marks, questions marks, and periods go inside or outside the quotation marks? When do you use a single rather than a double quotation mark? What types of information require quotation marks?

Before inserting quotation marks, learn to distinguish between direct and indirect quotations. A *direct quotation* uses a speaker's or a writer's exact words—word for word. Therefore, you must use quotation marks to let the reader know that the information is not your writing but the writing of the source you're using. However, if you are rephrasing someone's writing or speech—that is, if you are making an *indirect quotation*—no quotation marks are necessary.

DIRECT QUOTATION:	In his famous Gettysburg Address, Abraham Lincoln states that our nation was **"conceived in liberty and dedicated to the proposition that all men are created equal."**
INDIRECT QUOTATION:	In his famous Gettysburg Address, Abraham Lincoln states that our nation was **created and based on the principles of freedom and equality for all.**

Since indirect quotations do not use the exact words of the writer or speaker (the verb tense usually changes), they require no commas.

Direct Quotations

Use quotation marks for direct quotes or speech. Make sure that the quotation marks enclose the entire phrase or sentence that you are quoting.

- In his *Letter from Birmingham Jail* in 1963, Martin Luther King Jr. made his case for peaceful protest marches: "Injustice anywhere is a threat to justice everywhere."
- The Republican candidate stated, "I promise to lower taxes if I am elected."

Note that when you use quotation marks, you are promising the reader that the words between the quotes are what the person said word for word. You cannot change anything even if the statement contains grammatical, punctuation, or usage errors.

Quotations Within Quotations

For quotations within quotations, use single quotation marks. If the information you're using has quotation marks, change the source's quotation marks to single quotes when you place the information within your double quotes.

- In Nancy Mairs's definition essay "On Being a Cripple," she protests: "But I don't care what you call me, so long as it isn't 'differently abled,' which strikes me as pure verbal garbage designed, by its ability to describe anyone, to describe no one."
- The president addressed his staff: "I will not tolerate negativism, nor do I want anybody to say, 'It can't be done.'"

PRACTICE 27-4

Add quotation marks where needed in the following sentences. Two sentences do not require quotation marks.

1. Mr. Connors told me that I should study harder and spend less time on the basketball court. Correct

2. In 1982 the feminist Gloria Steinem stated in *MS* magazine, "Now, we are becoming the men we wanted to marry."

3. The *New York Times* quotes a Florida mother of three: "After paying into my plan for 12 years, I never expected my insurance company to say, 'You realize, Mrs. Rios, that your child's surgery is not covered by your policy?'"

4. These are the exact words that the doctor used at the end of my annual exam: "Exercise is the one best medicine for good health."

5. The platoon leader ordered his troops to prepare for a major battle. Correct

Titles of Short Works

Use quotes for titles of short works, such as short stories, poems, one-act plays, articles in magazines and newspapers, essays, chapter titles in books, songs, and specific TV episodes.

■ My favorite short story is "The Lottery," and my favorite poem is "My Papa's Waltz."

■ One of the funniest episodes from *Seinfeld* is called "The Fix-Up," in which George is set up on a blind date.

■ The *New Yorker* magazine's articles always start with the section "The Talk of the Town," which contains short articles on politics, culture, sports, and finance.

Words as Words

Use quotes when referring to words as words; italics are also acceptable.

■ Students seem to have trouble with "then" and "than" and "its" and "it's."

OR

■ Students seem to have trouble with *then* and *than* and *its* and *it's*.

Don't use quotes to emphasize a word or phrase.

INCORRECT:	The "soccer mom" represents the upper-middle-class woman who drives a van or SUV and has a lot of political clout.
CORRECT:	The soccer mom represents the upper-middle-class woman who drives a van or SUV and has a lot of political clout.

Quotation Marks and End Punctuation

Apply the following rules when using commas and end marks with quotation marks:

1. Generally, commas and periods are put inside quotation marks, both double and single quotes.

■ "It is a good thing for an uneducated man to read books of quotations," advised Winston Churchill in his autobiography titled *My Early Life*.

■ I had difficulty understanding the technical terms in "DNA and the Human Genome," an article in *Scientific American*.

■ Michael Specter, a *New Yorker* writer on science and health, reports: "It takes less than two per cent of our genome to create all the proteins necessary for us to live" (64).

Note the exception in the MLA style when you are crediting sources at the end of the information. The period goes after the parentheses.

2. Colons and semicolons go outside quotes.

- One of Nancy Mairs's most dramatic essays about her struggles with multiple sclerosis is "On Being a Cripple"; she asserts in this essay that she does not want to be identified mainly by her disease.

3. In general, question marks and exclamation points go inside quotes except when they are a part of the entire sentence.

Bridging Knowledge

See Chapter 13 for additional explanation, examples, and practice punctuating direct quotations.

- Our philosophy professor asked the class last week, "How do you define existence?"
  [The question mark is part of the quotation.]
- What is the meaning of the saying "A bird in the hand is worth two in the bush"?
  [The sentence itself is a question, so the question mark is not part of the actual quotation.]

  INCORRECT: Was it Marc Antony who states, "Friends, Romans, countrymen?" [The question mark inside the quotation mark indicates that Marc Antony asked a question when actually he made a statement.]

  CORRECT: Was it Marc Antony who states, "Friends, Romans, countrymen"? [The question mark outside the quotation indicates that the quotation is a statement but that the writer is asking a question: "Is this what he said?"]

4. Use a colon to present a line of poetry and slashes to separate two lines of poetry.

- In "Sonnet 43," Elizabeth Barrett Browning captures her intense love for her husband-to-be, Robert Browning: "I love thee to the depth and breadth and height / My soul can reach, when feeling out of sight."

If you quote three or more lines of poetry, set it off in the text as you would long quotations. Don't use quotation marks.

PRACTICE 27-5

Add or remove quotation marks and punctuation marks in the following sentences to correct them.

1. In his *Narrative of the Life of Frederick Douglass,* the section titled "Learning to Read and Write" illustrates Douglass's struggle to become literate.

2. The poem "Stopping by Woods on a Snowy Evening" is one of Robert Frost's most famous verses.

3. The word "success" has different meanings depending on whom you talk to.

4. "A Rose for Emily," a short story by William Faulkner, represents the genre of Southern Gothic fiction.

5. We shouldn't "always believe" the saying: "It takes two to tango."

Quotation Marks in Dialogue

When you use quotation marks in dialogue, apply the following rules:

1. Start by paragraphing correctly. Whenever you change speakers, begin a new paragraph. It doesn't matter if the speaker utters one small word or sound; place it in its own paragraph. Doing so makes it easier for the reader to follow the conversation between or among characters.

> **INCORRECT:**   "Mike, I can't be involved in this situation," Emilia whispered. "Yes, I know," Mike tried to reassure her. "It'll be strictly confidential. No one needs to know where the information comes from." "I don't think you realize how serious and damaging this information is," Emilia cautioned.
>
> **CORRECT:**   "Mike, I can't be involved in this situation," Emilia whispered.
>
> "Yes, I know," Mike tried to reassure her. "It'll be strictly confidential. No one needs to know where the information comes from."
>
> "I don't think you realize how serious and damaging this information is," Emilia cautioned.

If a speaker's discourse continues beyond a paragraph, start each paragraph with a quotation mark but don't close the paragraph with an end quotation mark until the final paragraph of that speaker's speech.

2. When you introduce a quotation with a dialogue tag ("he said" or "George shouted"), place a comma before the quotation.
   - Marie said, **"**I'm glad we can finally get together.**"**
3. If the dialogue tag comes after the quotation, place a comma inside the closing quotation mark.
   - "I'm glad we can finally get together," said Marie.
4. If you interrupt a sentence with a dialogue tag, place commas before and after the tag.
   - "I'm glad," said Marie, "we can finally get together."
5. Place question marks and exclamation points inside the quotation mark when they are part of the conversation.
   - "No way!" exclaimed Marie. **"**Did you really think I would agree?**"**

PRACTICE   27-6

In the following sentences, insert quotation marks, commas, and periods where necessary. Two sentences are indirect quotations.

1. "I can see the overall improvement in your work" the professor told Paula.

2. "No" the customer told the salesclerk "I will not settle for another style."

3. "I know" explained Tracy "that you want to leave early, but we have a presentation to make."

4. My art instructor told me that I will not pass the course if I don't turn in my project. Correct

5. Sue asked, "what are the requirements for the dental hygiene program?"

6. When did Roosevelt say, "we have nothing to fear but fear itself"?

7. When Michael told us that he needed to see us, we ignored him. Correct

8. Last night, Randy called the human resources director and said, "I will need to file a grievance against my supervisor." Then almost as an afterthought he added, "The incident happened a year ago. Is it too late?"

9. "Of course," Ms. Rodriquez answered, "all you need to do is fill out this form and request your refund. Don't forget that you have only 3 days left."

10. Ms. Ballard examined the documents carefully and finally asked, "Do you realize what this plan will cost the company?" No one dared to answer.

Dashes and Parentheses

In Chapter 26, you practiced using commas to set off phrases and clauses that interrupted the flow of a sentence. Similarly, dashes and parentheses can indicate various kinds of extra information in a sentence.

Dashes

The expressions that dashes introduce can seem like commentaries or expansions on the main idea of a sentence. Use an em dash (—) when the slight pause of a comma is not emphatic enough to highlight the indicated interrupters.

A dash can be used to do the following:

1. **Indicate a sudden shift in thought.**
   - I spent all night writing my essay and reviewing for a math test—but I'm sure that's not what you want to hear.
   - I was ready to deliver my graduation speech and then—good grief!—I froze and couldn't utter a syllable.

2. **Emphasize an idea.**
   - Professor Vidmar is in her creative mode—if you know what I mean.

3. **Present an aside or minor digression.**
   - Michael interrupted the president and demanded an apology—so he claims.

4. **Help guide the reader when too many commas may be confusing.**

| CONFUSING: | Overly sentimental movies, *The Notebook*, for example, highlight the seriousness of certain conditions. |
| CLEARER: | Overly sentimental movies—*The Notebook*, for example—highlight the seriousness of certain conditions. |

| CONFUSING: | The supervisor had the necessary qualities, motivation, creativity, and competency, needed to complete the task. |
| CLEARER: | The supervisor had the necessary qualities—motivation, creativity, and competency—needed to complete the task. |

Dashes are a good way to guide the reader through your shifts of ideas. However, before you start inserting dashes in your paper, keep in mind that for dashes to be effective you should not overuse them. Unless you have a reason, why use a dash when a comma, colon, or semicolon works? Also, papers filled with interrupters can be distracting, disjointed, and confusing.

PRACTICE 27-7

On the line provided, rewrite each of the following sentences by inserting dashes to clarify the ideas. Remove commas where necessary.

1. His explanation and I must admit that I had to swallow hard for this one was that no one called him to remind him. His explanation—and I must admit that I had to swallow hard for this one—was that no one called him to remind him.

2. The vice president lost his temper at the meeting he threw pencils, screamed, and pointed his finger at us and all we could do was look at one another. The vice president lost his temper at the meeting—he threw pencils, screamed, and pointed his finger at us—and all we could do was look at one another.

3. When the manager opened his office door, he came face to face with his employees, all 37 of them, waiting for their bonuses. When the manager opened his office door, he came face to face with his employees—all 37 of them—waiting for their bonuses.

4. Everything about the movie, especially the flashback to the characters' childhood experiences, kept me at the edge of my seat. Everything about the movie—especially the flashback to the characters' childhood experiences—kept me at the edge of my seat.

5. I demand three things from you, respect, professionalism, and integrity. I demand three things from you—respect, professionalism, and integrity.

Parentheses

Use parentheses to set off supplemental information or explanations that might help the reader better understand your point. Although less emphatic than dashes, parentheses also set off such interrupters and asides. However, just as with the dash, don't overuse parentheses in your writing: have a reason for their use. Examine the following example:

■ He had to go through the usual procedure to go through airport security (provide identification, empty his pockets, take off his shoes, and go through metal detectors).

Since the colon, dash, and parentheses are all acceptable punctuation marks in this sentence, the writer must choose which one would be the most effective. A colon would give the list more importance if the writer felt the reader needed to understand the procedure; the dash would add stronger emphasis to the list, perhaps indicating to the reader that it's an inconvenient yet necessary procedure. However, since the sentence states that this is "the usual procedure," the writer felt that the list should be presented as an aside or as supplemental information and that the parentheses would convey that meaning. In your writing, you face similar choices, so it's important that you understand the subtle meaning that each choice conveys.

The information in the parentheses may consist of a phrase, a sentence, or several sentences (although it's not advisable to present large amounts of information within parentheses), so it's important that you punctuate correctly. Follow these simple rules:

1. When you place the nonessential information within a sentence, don't capitalize the first letter of the parenthetical sentence or end the sentence with a period. (Of course, if the first word is the pronoun *I* or a proper noun, it must be capitalized.)
   ■ The committee decided to reexamine the concerns regarding merit pay (most issues have not been resolved within the last 10 years) and offer some practical recommendations.
2. If the parenthetical sentence is a question or exclamation, then capitalize the first letter and place the question mark or exclamation point at the end of the parenthetical sentence—before the final parenthesis.
   ■ We were amazed by his suggestion (<u>H</u>ave you ever heard him express an original or creative idea?) and even more impressed by his presentation.
3. If the main sentence is a question or exclamation, place the end punctuation after the parentheses.
   ■ Do you really want to confront the president (five executives fired this month alone)?
4. If the parenthetical phrase or sentence that's within another sentence requires a comma, place the comma after the parentheses, not before.
   ■ The president made a terrible decision (the most irrational one ever), and he expects all of us to promote the plan.
5. If the parenthetical sentence or sentences are separated from another sentence—either between two sentences or at the end of a paragraph—capitalize the first letter and place the correct end mark (period, question mark, or exclamation point) at the end of the sentence inside the parentheses.
   ■ I met with the president to object to his decision. (<u>I</u>t was a big gamble, but one I had to take.) I then outlined the consequences of his plan.

PRACTICE 27-8

On the line provided, rewrite each of the following sentences by using parentheses. Be sure to delete unnecessary commas and if needed, add commas, end marks, or capitalization. Answers will vary.

1. I decided not to attend the meeting. Life is too short. I decided to go to the gym instead. <u>I decided not to attend the meeting. (Life is too short.) I decided to go to the gym instead.</u>

2. I went to the end of the line isn't this what's expected and waited my turn while everyone just passed me by. <u>I went to the end of the line (Isn't this what's expected?) and waited my turn while everyone just passed me by.</u>

3. The manager decided to give Jennifer an early raise, her child was in the hospital and her husband was unemployed, to ease her financial burden. _The manager decided to give Jennifer an early raise (her child was in the hospital and her husband was unemployed) to ease her financial burden._

4. After her bagel, cheese omelet, and hot tea, her usual lunch, she joined the other tourists. _After her bagel, cheese omelet, and hot tea (her usual lunch), she joined the other tourists._

5. My professor dislikes, I should really say he abhors, late papers. _My professor dislikes (I should really say he abhors) late papers._

Capitalization

Most students are familiar with the general rules of capitalization. However, the rules of capitalization are extensive, making it impractical to cover every imaginable condition that may call for capitalization. The following section examines the most common rules. Always consult a dictionary when in doubt.

Sentence Beginnings

Unless the sentence follows a semicolon or colon (where capitalization is optional), always capitalize the first letter of a sentence.

■ The employees were most productive during the summer.

Note: Capitalize the first person pronoun *I* wherever it occurs. During speedy communications such as e-mails and text messages, some people may ignore this rule. Although there is no exception to this rule, keep your audience in mind should you decide to break it.

Proper Nouns

Capitalize proper nouns; do not capitalize common nouns. A proper noun names a specific person, place, or thing. Make sure you can distinguish between these two types of nouns. The following list names the types of proper nouns that should be capitalized and in the last column illustrates a related common noun that should not be capitalized.

	Capitalize Proper Nouns	**Do Not Capitalize Common Nouns**
People	■ Toni Morrison ■ Bill Ritter	■ a writer ■ a governor
Countries	England	a land
Nationalities	French	a citizen
Races	Native American	an ethnic group
Language	Spanish	a dialect

	Exception: Do not capitalize a prefix or word added to a proper noun: ■ anti-American sentiments ■ French-like behavior ■ Spanish speaker ■ pro-Russian **Exception:** In most cases, do not capitalize a word derived from a proper noun if the word does not depend on the proper noun for its meaning: ■ bone china ■ china cabinet ■ french fries ■ vienna sausages However, Italian bread, Russian dressing, and Irish whiskey would be capitalized since they indicate a specific type. When in doubt, consult your dictionary.	
Religions Denominations Religious figures Sacred books	Islam Catholic the Pope the Torah	a belief a sect a church leader a holy book
Months Days	September Wednesday	a month a day
	Exception: Do not capitalize the seasons (spring, summer, fall, autumn, winter) unless you use another noun to make the name of the season specific, thus functioning as a proper noun. The Fall 2008 semester begins next week.	
Holidays	Thanksgiving Day	a holiday
Documents	Treaty of Versailles	a treaty
Organizations		
Social Business Political Cultural Sporting	Boy Scouts of America General Motors Corporation Democrats Nebraska State Historical Society National Football League	a club a corporation, a business a political party a cultural group a football team
Awards	■ Oscar ■ Purple Heart	■ a trophy ■ a medal
Historical		
Events Periods Streets Cities and states Buildings Public offices Agencies Meeting rooms Monuments	the Civil War Victorian Era Kennedy Boulevard Austin, Texas the White House Electoral Commission the Bureau of Labor Statistics Room 222 Statue of Liberty	a civil war the 19th century a boulevard, an avenue a city and state a house an office an agency a room a statue

Continued

	Capitalize Proper Nouns	Do Not Capitalize Common Nouns
Geographical		
Locations	North Pole	north of here
Features	▪ Mississippi River	▪ a river
	▪ Atlantic Ocean	▪ an ocean, a sea

Exception: Capitalize compass directions (north, south, west, and east) when they are part of a name (North Carolina or the Middle East). However, do not capitalize the directions when they are not part of a name or not referring to a specific place:
- We moved to the south side of town.
- After 10 years living in the South, we drove west in search of new adventures.

Products	Kleenex	a tissue
Brands	Maytag	a refrigerator
Vehicles	Ford	a car
Models	Escort	the make, the model

Spacecraft	*Challenger*	a space shuttle
Aircraft	*The Spirit of St. Louis*	an airplane
Ships	USS *Abraham Lincoln*	a ship
Trains	*Eurostar*	a train

Celestial bodies	▪ Venus, Neptune, Mars	▪ a planet
	▪ Milky Way	▪ a galaxy

Exception: Do not capitalize earth, moon, and sun unless any of these words appears in context with other celestial bodies that are capitalized:
What's the distance between Earth and Mars, and how close is Mercury to the Sun?

School courses	History 101	a history class

Titles of people		
Status	Mrs. Daugherty	a woman
Professions	Dr. Atkins	a doctor
Rank	President Clinton	a president
Epithets	Ivan the Terrible	a leader

Exception: Do not capitalize the title when it follows the name:
- Thomas Jefferson, president of the United States
- Elizabeth II, queen of England

PRACTICE 27-9

Cross out any error in capitalization and write the correct uppercase or lowercase letter.

1. the senator from boston rose from his seat to deliver an eloquent speech
    regarding the new trade treaty with china.

2. After i gave my oral presentation on the great depression, i was surprised that
    few students in my economics 101 class were even aware of this historical period.

3. Last Spring, i bought a Raffle ticket while passing through atlantic city and won a chevy impala.
   [corrections above: Spring→s, i→I, Raffle→r, atlantic→A, city→C, chevy→C, impala→I]

4. Named after christopher columbus, the knights of columbus was founded in 1882. it is the world's largest roman catholic, Fraternal service Organization, with more than 1.7 Million members.
   [corrections above: christopher→C, columbus→C, knights→K, columbus→C, it→I, roman→R, catholic→C, Fraternal→f, Organization→o, Million→m]

5. Many Ancient Societies worshipped the Earth, Moon, and Sun. as knowledge of astronomy grew, we learned that the eight Planets, such as mercury, venus, earth, and mars, rotate around the sun.
   [corrections above: Ancient→a, Societies→s, Earth→e, Moon→m, Sun→s, as→A, Planets→p, mercury→M, venus→V, earth→E, mars→M, sun→S]

Titles of Works

Capitalize all main words in titles of works. Adjectives, adverbs, nouns, pronouns, verbs, and subordinate conjunctions (*although, because, since,* and so on) are considered main words in a title. These types of words should always be capitalized. However, don't capitalize the following:

- Prepositions (some authorities prefer that you capitalize prepositions consisting of five or more letters, so ask your instructor)
- Coordinating conjunctions (*and, or, nor, but, for, yet, so*)
- Articles (*a, an, the*) unless they begin or end the title
- The word *to* in front of a verb (infinitive)

Type	Example
Books	Our first required reading this semester is *The Catcher in the Rye.*
Periodicals: Journals, magazines, newspapers	▪ Our next assignment is to review three articles from the *Journal of Abnormal and Social Psychology.* ▪ A cup of coffee, a bagel, and the *Chicago Sun-Times* make up the start of a great morning. **Exception:** Do not capitalize the word *the* in front of the title of a periodical unless, of course, the word starts the sentence.
Articles, essays	I found Alice Nobel's "DNA Fingerprinting and Civil Liberties" the most useful article for my research paper.
Poems	I was so impressed when I first read Keats's "Ode on a Grecian Urn."
Plays	I was intrigued by the characters in Tennessee Williams's *Cat on a Hot Tin Roof.*
Films	*The Sound of Music* is still my favorite movie.
Paintings	Our assignment was to write a narrative about Raphael's painting *St. George and the Dragon.*
Songs	Celine Dion and Peabo Bryson's performance of "Beauty and the Beast" brings out the beauty in this piece of music.

Family Relationship Titles

When you assign a title to a person's name that indicates a family relationship, such as aunt, uncle, or cousin, capitalize the title.

> INCORRECT: I ran the idea by uncle Raymond.
> CORRECT: I ran the idea by Uncle Raymond.

Also, capitalize the word that indicates the family relationship when the word is a substitute for the name of the person.

- I proposed the business deal to Dad, and he'll let me know as soon as he speaks to Mom.
- I don't know why Grandma refuses to answer her e-mails promptly.

However, if the word is modified by a personal pronoun (*my, his, her, their, our*), do not capitalize the word.

> INCORRECT: I stopped to see whether my Grandmother received the package.
> CORRECT: I stopped to see whether my grandmother received the package.

PRACTICE 27-10

Cross out any error in capitalization and write the correct uppercase or lowercase letter.

1. The rawlings public library has a new paperback copy of *the rise and fall of the roman empire,* but I can't bring myself to read such a lengthy History.
   (corrections: R, P, L; T, R, F; R, E; h)

2. The beatles' song *I want to hold your hand* is a classic.
   (corrections: B; W, H, Y, H)

3. Josie has a large family, but her favorite relatives are aunt Tillie and granddad Edward.
   (corrections: A; G)

4. In high school we read shakespeare's *othello,* but it wasn't until we studied the play in depth at arapahoe community college that I really understood it.
   (corrections: S, O; A, C, C)

5. For our Political Science course, we are required to read the *new york times* and the *economist.*
   (corrections: p, s; N, Y, T; E)

Italics and Underlines

If you were handwriting a paper, you would underline the title of a book. However, word processing programs permit us to use italics for the same purpose. Thus, underlining and italicizing are synonymous. Check your instructor's preference, but whichever method you choose, be consistent throughout your document. Use underlining or italics in the following cases.

Titles of Works	
Type	**Example**
Books	I have read Chinua Achebe's *Things Fall Apart* five times and have enjoyed it each time. **Exception:** Do not italicize, underline, or use quotation marks with titles of sacred books (Bible, Torah, Koran, Exodus, Revelation, and so on). Also, do not include end marks (periods, question marks, or exclamation points), parentheses, or possessive forms (apostrophe + *-s*) when you italicize or underline a word unless those punctuation marks are part of the title, name, or word you're italicizing.
Plays	Tennessee Williams's *Suddenly Last Summer* contained themes that are still relevant today.
Long poems	Milton's *Paradise Lost* is required reading in most introductory literature courses.
Periodicals: Newspapers, magazines, journals	■ As a psychology major, I subscribe to *Psychology Today.* ■ The *Arizona Journal of Hispanic Cultural Studies* provides in-depth information on the effects of economics and politics on the cultures of Spanish-speaking countries and societies. **Exception:** Do not italicize or underline the article *the* in front of the title of a periodical even if the article is part of the title, for example, the *New York Times.*
Pamphlets	While at my doctor's office, I picked up a copy of *Coping with Stress.* **Exception:** Do not italicize, underline, or use quotation marks with titles of legal documents such as charters, treaties, acts, statutes, or reports, for example, The Declaration of Independence.
Movies, videos	Although I'm usually critical of most Batman movies, I really enjoyed *The Dark Knight.*
Long musical works, recordings	I prefer the Broadway recording of *Hairspray* with the original cast to the 2007 movie soundtrack.
Television programs	I miss not watching *Stargate SG-1,* so now I watch *Stargate Atlantis.*
Radio programs	*The Opie and Anthony Show* is a highly rated talk radio program that comments on American social and popular culture.
Visual works, art	Rodin's *The Thinker* has always fascinated me.
Websites	*MySpace* is one of the most popular English-language websites on the Internet.
Electronic databases	To start my research, I first accessed EBSCOhost and searched in *Academic Search Premier,* a database containing more than 8,000 journals.
Electronic games	*Super Mario Galaxy* has Mario exploring bizarre planets all across the galaxy. **Exception:** Do not italicize, underline, or use quotation marks with titles of computer software such as WordPerfect, Microsoft Word, or Adobe Photoshop.

Don't forget that shorter works, such as the titles of chapters in books, articles, short stories, poems, songs, and TV episodes should be placed within quotation marks, not italicized or underlined.

■ "The Economist" from the fourth season of *Lost* is still my favorite episode.

When you have a title, name, or word that should be italicized within another title that should be italicized (italics within italics), you can do one of the following:

1. Use standard type (not italics) for the second item.
   ■ The article *Symbolism and Contradictions in* Hamlet: *An Exercise in Madness* helped me understand the beauty of this play.
2. Underline the second item.
   ■ The article *Symbolism and Contradictions in <u>Hamlet</u>: An Exercise in Madness* helped me understand the beauty of this play.

Use the form least confusing to your reader.

Names of Aircraft, Spacecraft, Ships, and Trains	
Type	**Example**
Spacecraft	In 1986, the explosion of the space shuttle *Challenger* was witnessed by millions on live television.
Aircraft	The president waved at reporters as he boarded *Air Force One.*
Ships	The *Bounty* set sail on December 23, 1787, under the command of the infamous Captain Blight. **Exception:** Do not italicize or underline the SS or USS before the name of a ship: The crew members of the USS *Ronald Reagan* were ready to depart.
Trains	*The Orient Express,* a long-distance passenger train, has become synonymous with intrigue and decadence.

Unfamiliar Foreign Words and Phrases

English permits many words and phrases to enrich the language. Because of frequent use and broader public knowledge of these words and phrases, we don't italicize or underline them in writing. The following words, most of which you should recognize, are a few examples of foreign words that are often used and have, as a result, become part of standard usage; thus, you should not italicize or underline them:

ambiance	carte blanche	fait accompli	siesta
avant-garde	champagne	laissez-faire	status quo
bon voyage	coup	per diem	subpoena
bourgeois	cul-de-sac	résumé	wok

However, to capture just the right meaning or feeling, we use foreign words and phrases that are less common and not in everyday use. Such words or phrases should be italicized or underlined.

■ She has a certain *je ne sais quoi* about her.

Since the phrase *je ne sais quoi* is not commonly used in English, italics or underline is necessary. Although some words are more familiar to us, they may not have yet made it into common use.

■ I have often wondered about the phenomenon of *déjà vu.*

As you can see, it may sometimes be difficult to determine which words are standard usages. It's a matter of judgment and experience. When in doubt, ask your instructor.

Words, Letters, and Numbers Talked About	
Type	**Example**
Words mentioned as words	Some people confuse the word *emigrant,* which means one who moves out, with the word *immigrant,* which means one who moves in in. **Note:** It is also acceptable to use quotation marks for words mentioned as words.
Letters mentioned as letters	The word *committee* is often misspelled because it has two *m*'s, two *t*'s and two *e*'s. **Note:** Italicize or underline only the letter mentioned as a letter, not the *s* to indicate plural. Although MLA recommends using an apostrophe for the plural of letters (in either uppercase or lowercase), it is not necessary unless its absence would confuse the reader.
Numbers mentioned as numbers	I end my signature with a *7* because it is my lucky number.

Emphasized Words

Italicize or underline a word that you want to emphasize or stress in a sentence either because you want to point the reader's attention to the word or because you want the reader to stress the word during the reading.

■ It is *you* I want here.

By italicizing the pronoun *you,* the writer forces the reader to stress the word. When reading the sentence aloud, the reader raises the intonation on this word.

■ I asked you to *speak up* when you disagree, not yell at or insult the person.

In the preceding example, the writer wants the reader to stress the action "speak up" and contrasts it with "yell at or insult." Read this sentence aloud and feel the emphasis on the italicized word. However, don't italicize the word if the stress is obvious. In fact, avoid excessive italicizing or underlining for emphasis. Excessive use of emphasis can become distracting and ineffective.

PRACTICE 27-11

Revise the following sentences by underlining words that should be either underlined or italicized.

1. With more maps, more missions, and a great crew of war heroes, <u>Metal Gear Solid: Portable Ops Plus</u> is an incredible action game.

2. Will <u>Harry Potter and the Deathly Hallows</u> really be the final book of the Harry Potter series?

3. The official song of the state of Oklahoma is <u>Oklahoma</u>, which originated from the movie <u>Oklahoma</u>.

4. Since the media sensationalized the crime, the lawyer committed a <u>faux pas</u> when he consented to take the case <u>pro bono</u>.

5. According to <u>Merriam-Webster's Collegiate Dictionary</u>, the word exobiology means "a branch of biology concerned with the search for life outside the earth."

REVIEW   27-1

Revise the following paragraph by inserting missing quotation marks, commas, colons, periods, and question marks and by crossing out errors.

Students in introduction to literature classes study three genres of literature: fiction, poetry, and drama. Poetry is the genre that students sometimes find the most challenging as they assume that they will struggle to figure out the meanings of the poems. One pair of works, however, that seems straightforward is Edwin Arlington Robinson's poem "Richard Cory" and the song by Paul Simon also titled "Richard Cory." In Robinson's poem, we read about a man who is "quietly arrayed" and "always human when he talked," whereas in Simon's version he "had the common touch." Robinson's Cory is almost kinglike: "He was a gentleman from sole to crown."

Now for the following paragraph, cross out any errors in capitalization and write the correct uppercase or lowercase letter.

The international organization ~~a~~mnesty ~~i~~nternational had its beginnings in 1961. Its ~~M~~ission is to raise awareness of ~~H~~uman ~~R~~ights abuses around the ~~W~~orld, including citizens jailed for voicing their political opinions, violence against women, and the death penalty. Amnesty ~~i~~nternational members worldwide write letters to ~~G~~overnments in support of political prisoners. One example is ~~m~~esfin ~~w~~oldemariam, who spoke out for human rights in ~~e~~thiopia. Another example is ~~m~~a ~~k~~hin ~~k~~hin ~~l~~eh, who was jailed for peacefully demonstrating in ~~m~~yanmar. Recently ~~a~~mnesty ~~i~~nternational celebrated the 20th ~~A~~nniversary of the ~~u.n.~~ ~~c~~onvention against torture, which takes a stance against torture no matter where it is in the ~~W~~orld.

Reading Critically

PART 7

CHAPTER 28

Reading Critically

YOUR GOALS

1. Demonstrate an understanding of effective reading strategies.

2. Increase your vocabulary.

3. Analyze readings for comprehension, structure, tone, and style.

4. Show a personal connection to topics introduced by professional writers.

"The real importance of reading is that it creates an ease and intimacy with the process of writing. . . ."

■ **Stephen King** ■

UNDERSTANDING HOW TO READ CRITICALLY

When many of us take up our biology or philosophy textbooks to complete a reading assignment, we plunge right in, reading the first sentence, then the next, and so on. Sometimes, because this approach forces us to create the context of the reading as we go along, we find our minds wandering to personal thoughts and daydreams. This approach is not the most effective use of our time; instead, try several of the strategies listed here to help you become a more efficient and more active reader:

- **Preview your reading.** Instead of starting with the first line, study the title, headings, and subheadings of the reading. Flip to the end to find out if there is a summary, glossary of terms, and/or study questions that can help you focus on the most important information.
- **Question.** Start reading with some questions in mind that you assume the reading answers; doing so keeps your mind focused on the material. Jot down your questions beforehand, and as you read, record your answers to those questions.
- **Skim before reading in more depth.** Read the topic sentences of each paragraph to familiarize yourself with the structure of the reading.
- **Mark your text (annotate).** Read actively by highlighting interesting and important information, and new vocabulary. Write in the margins to summarize key information and to note areas that are unclear or that you want further information about. The more physically active you are when you read, the more you retain.
- **Take notes.** Have paper, note cards, or a computer handy so that you can write down significant information. Later you can use these notes to study from so that you rarely have to refer back to the text.
- **Review.** Carefully go over your questions, notes, and marginal notations to assess how much you have learned and what information you may need to reread. Quiz yourself to put the information in your long-term memory.

The following readings and exercises give you an opportunity to practice these critical reading strategies. They also represent professional models of the types of essays that you have been writing for this course. Each selection gives you a brief biography of the writer, a warm-up question to ponder, vocabulary items that might be new to you, and questions at the end to test your comprehension and skills in identifying audience, tone, style and structure.

Description

The Inheritance of Tools by Scott Russell Sanders

Scott Russell Sanders, born in 1945 in Memphis, earned a Ph.D. in English from Cambridge University in 1971. Since then he has taught at Indiana University and won numerous teaching awards. He writes both fiction and essays and has published 19 books. His work has been selected for *The Best American Essays*. The focus of his writing is nature, community, spirituality, and social justice.

LET's warm up!

Ponder the tools that you may have inherited from a parent, relative, or friend—a sewing machine, a table saw, an ice cream maker, a pocketknife. How do these tools connect you to the original owner? When you use the tool, what thoughts about the original owner come to mind?

Increasing Your Vocabulary

- **Joist:** a horizontal beam to support the boards of a ceiling or floor
- **Drawknife:** a knife with a handle at each end of the blade, used for shaving a surface
- **Nautilus:** a mollusk with a spiral shell
- **Joint:** a place where two parts are connected
- **Awl:** a pointed tool to make holes in wood or leather
- **Plumb:** vertical
- **Framing square:** a tool for making cuts to ensure 90-degree angles
- **Aphorism:** a statement of truth
- **Clasp knife:** a pocketknife whose blade folds
- **Gouge:** a type of chisel with a blade shaped like a trough

1   At just about the hour when my father died, soon after dawn one February morning when ice coated the windows like cataracts, I banged my thumb with a hammer. Naturally I swore at the hammer, the reckless thing, and in the moment of swearing I thought of what my father would say: "If you'd try hitting the nail it would go in a whole lot faster. Don't you know your thumb's not as hard as that hammer?" We both were doing carpentry that day, but far apart. He was building cupboards at my brother's place in Oklahoma; I was at home in Indiana, putting up a wall in the basement to make a bedroom for my daughter. By the time my mother called with news of his death—the long-distance wires whittling her voice until it seemed too thin to bear the weight of what she had to say—my thumb was swollen. A week or so later a white scar in the shape of a crescent moon began to show above the cuticle, and month by month it rose across the pink sky of my thumbnail. It took the better part of a year for the scar to disappear, and every time I noticed it I thought of my father.

The hammer had belonged to him, and to his father before him. The three of us have used it to build houses and barns and chicken coops, to upholster chairs and crack walnuts, to make doll furniture and bookshelves and jewelry boxes. The head is scratched and pockmarked, like an old plowshare that has been working rocky fields, and it gives off the sort of dull sheen you see on fast creek water in the shade. It is a finishing hammer, about the weight of a bread loaf, too light, really, for framing walls, too heavy for cabinetwork, with a curved claw for pulling nails, a rounded head for pounding, a fluted neck for looks, and a hickory handle for strength.

The present handle is my third one, bought from a lumberyard in Tennessee, down the road from where my brother and I were helping my father build his retirement house. I broke the previous one by trying to pull sixteen-penny nails out of floor **joists**—a foolish thing to do with a finishing hammer, as my father pointed out. "You ever hear of a crowbar?" he said. No telling how many handles he and my grandfather had gone through before me. My grandfather used to cut down hickory trees on his farm, saw them into slabs, cure the planks in his hayloft, and carve handles with a **drawknife.** The grain in hickory is crooked and knotty and therefore tough, hard to split, like the grain in the two men who owned this hammer before me.

After proposing marriage to a neighbor girl, my grandfather used this hammer to build a house for his bride on a stretch of river bottom in northern Mississippi. The lumber for the place, like the hickory for the handle, was cut on his own land. By the day of the wedding he had not quite finished the house, and so right after the ceremony he took his wife home and put her to work. My grandmother had worn her Sunday dress for the wedding, with a fringe of lace tacked on around the hem in honor of the occasion. She removed this lace and folded it away before going out to help my grandfather nail siding on the house. "There she was in her good dress," he told me some forty odd years after that wedding day, "holding up them long pieces of clapboard while I hammered, and together we got the place covered up before dark." As the family grew to four, six, eight, and eventually thirteen, my grandfather used this hammer to enlarge his house room by room, like a chambered **nautilus** expanding its shell.

5   By and by the hammer was passed along to my father. One day he was up on the roof of our pony barn, nailing shingles with it, when I stepped out the kitchen door to call him for supper. Before I could yell, something about the sight of him straddling the spine of that roof and swinging the hammer caught my eye and made me hold my tongue. I was five or six years old, and the world's commonplaces were still news to me. He would pull a nail from the pouch at his waist, bring the hammer down, and a moment later the thunk of the blow would reach my ears. And that is what had stopped me in my tracks and stilled my tongue, the momentary gap between seeing and hearing the blow. Instead of yelling from the kitchen door, I ran to the barn and climbed two rungs up the ladder—as far as I was allowed to go—and spoke quietly to my father. On our walk to the house he explained that sound takes time to make its way through air. Suddenly the world seemed larger, the air more dense, as if sound could be held back like any ordinary traveler.

By the time I started using this hammer, at about the age when I discovered the speed of sound, it already contained houses and mysteries for me. The smooth handle was one my grandfather had made. In those days I needed both hands to swing it. My father would start a nail in a scrap of wood, and I would pound away until I bent it over.

"Looks like you got ahold of some of those rubber nails," he would tell me. "Here, let me see if I can find you some stiff ones." And he would rummage in a drawer until he came up with a fistful of more cooperative nails. "Look at the head," he would tell me. "Don't look at your hands, don't look at the hammer. Just look at the head of that nail and pretty soon you'll learn to hit it square."

Pretty soon I did learn. While he worked in the garage cutting dovetail **joints** for a drawer or skinning a deer or tuning an engine, I would hammer nails. I made innocent blocks of wood look like porcupines. He did not talk much in the midst of his tools, but he kept up a nearly ceaseless humming, slipping in and out of a dozen tunes in an afternoon, often running back over the same stretch of melody again and again, as if searching for a way out. When the humming did cease, I knew he was faced with a task requiring great delicacy or concentration, and I took care not to distract him.

He kept scraps of wood in a cardboard box—the ends of two-by-fours, slabs of shelving and plywood, odd pieces of molding—and everything in it was fair game. I nailed scraps together to fashion what I called boats or houses, but the results usually bore only faint resemblance to the visions I carried in my head. I would hold up these constructions to show my father, and he would turn them over in his hands admiringly, speculating about what they might be. My cobbled-together guitars might have been alien spaceships, my barns might have been models of Aztec temples, each wooden contraption might have been anything but what I had set out to make.

10   Now and again I would feel the need to have a chunk of wood shaped or shortened before I riddled it with nails, and I would clamp it in a vise and scrape at it with a handsaw. My father would let me lacerate the board until my arm gave out, and then he would wrap his hand around mine and help me finish the cut, showing me how to use my thumb to guide the blade, how to pull back on the saw to keep it from binding, how to let my shoulder do the work.

"Don't force it," he would say "just drag it easy and give the teeth a chance to bite." As the saw teeth bit down, the wood released its smell, each kind with its own fragrance, oak or walnut or cherry or pine—usually pine because it was the softest, easiest for a child to work. No matter how weathered and gray the board, no matter how warped and cracked, inside there was this smell waiting, as of something freshly baked. I gathered every smidgen of sawdust and stored it away in coffee cans, which I kept in a drawer of the workbench. When I did not feel like hammering nails, I would dump my sawdust on the concrete floor of the garage and landscape it into highways and farms and towns, running miniature cars and trucks along miniature roads. Looming as huge as a colossus, my father worked over and around me, now and again bending down to inspect my work, careful not to trample my creations. It was a landscape that smelled dizzyingly of wood. Even after a bath my skin would carry the smell, and so would my father's hair when he lifted me for a bedtime hug.

I tell these things not only from memory but also from recent observation, because my own son now turns blocks of wood into nailed porcupines, dumps cans full of sawdust at my feet, and sculpts highways on the floor. He leans how to swing a hammer from the elbow instead of the wrist, how to lay his thumb beside the blade to guide a saw, how to tap a chisel with a wooden mallet, how to mark a hole with an **awl** before starting a drill bit. My daughter did the same before him, and even now, on the brink of teenage aloofness, she will occasionally drag out my box of wood scraps and carpenter something. So I have seen my apprenticeship to wood and tools reenacted in each of my children, as my father saw his own apprenticeship renewed in me.

The saw I use belonged to him, as did my level and both of my squares, and all four tools had belonged to his father. The blade of the saw is the bluish color of gun barrels, and the maple handle, dark from the sweat of hands, is inscribed with curving leaf designs. The level is a shaft of walnut two feet long, edged with brass and pierced by three round windows in which air bubbles float in oil-filled tubes of glass. The middle window serves for testing if a surface is horizontal, the others for testing if a surface is **plumb,** or vertical. My grandfather used to carry this level on a gun rack behind the seat in his pickup, and when I rode with him I would turn around to watch the bubbles dance. The larger of two squares is called a **framing square,** a flat steel elbow so beat up and tarnished you can barely make out the rows of numbers that show how to figure the cuts on rafters. The smaller one is called a try square, for marking right angles, with a blued steel blade for the shank and a brass-faced block of cherry for the head.

I was taught early on that a saw is not to be used apart from a square: "If you're going to cut a piece of wood," my father insisted, "you owe it to the tree to cut it straight."

¹⁵   Long before studying geometry, I learned there is a mystical virtue in right angles. There is an unspoken morality in seeking the level and the plumb. A house will stand, a table will bear weight, the sides of a box will hold together, only if the joints are square and the members upright. When the bubble is lined up between two marks etched in the glass tube of a level, you have aligned yourself with the forces that hold the universe together. When you miter the corners of a picture frame each angle must be exactly forty-five degrees, as they are in the perfect triangles of Pythagoras, not a degree more or less. Otherwise the frame will hang crookedly, as if ashamed of itself and of its maker. No matter if the joints you are cutting do not show. Even if you are butting two pieces of wood together inside a cabinet, where no one except a wrecking crew will ever see them, you must take pains to ensure that the ends are square and the studs are plumb.

I took pains over the wall I was building on the day my father died. Not long after that wall was finished—paneled with tongue-and-groove boards of yellow pine, the nail holes filled with putty and the wood all stained and sealed—I came close to wrecking it one afternoon when my daughter ran howling up the stairs to announce that her gerbils had escaped from their cage and were hiding in my brand new wall. She could hear them scratching and squeaking behind her bed. Impossible! I said. How on earth could they get inside my drum-tight wall? Through the heating vent, she answered. I went downstairs, pressed my ear to the honey-colored wood, and heard the scritch, scritch of tiny feet.

"What can we do?" my daughter wailed. "They'll starve to death, they'll die of thirst, they'll suffocate."

"Hold on," I soothed. "I'll think of something."

While I thought and she fretted, the radio on her bedside delivered us the headlines: Several thousand people had died in a city in India from a poisonous cloud that had leaked overnight from a chemical plant. A nuclear-powered submarine had been launched. Rioting continued in South Africa. An airplane had been hijacked in the Mediterranean. Authorities calculated that several thousand homeless people slept on the streets within sight of the Washington Monument. I felt my usual helplessness in the face of all these calamities. But here was my daughter, weeping because her gerbils were holed up in a wall. This calamity I could handle.

²⁰   "Don't worry," I told her. "We'll set food and water by the heating vent and lure them out. And if that doesn't do the trick, I'll tear the wall apart until we find them."

She stopped crying and gazed at me. "You'd really tear it apart? Just for my gerbils? The wall?" Astonishment slowed her only for a second, however, before she ran to the workbench and began tugging at drawers, saying, "Let's see, what'll we need? Crowbar. Hammer. Chisels. I hope we don't have to use them—but just in case."

We didn't need the wrecking tools. I never had to assault my handsome wall, because the gerbils eventually came out to nibble at a dish of popcorn. But for several hours I studied the tongue-and-groove skin I had nailed up on the day of my father's death, considering where to begin prying. There were no gaps in that wall, no crooked joints.

I had botched a great many pieces of wood before I mastered the right angle with a saw, botched even more before I learned to miter a joint. The knowledge of these things resides in my hands and eyes and the webwork of muscles, not in the tools. There are machines for sale—powered miter boxes and radial-arm saws, for instance—that will enable any casual soul to cut proper angles in boards. The skill is invested in the gadget instead of the person who uses it, and this is what distinguishes a machine from a tool. If I had to earn my keep by making furniture or building houses, I suppose I would buy powered saws and pneumatic nailers; the need for speed would drive me to it. But since I carpenter only for my own pleasure or to help neighbors or to re-make the house around the ears of my family, I stick with hand tools. Most of the ones I own were given to me by my father, who also taught me how to wield them. The tools in my workbench are a double inheritance, for each hammer and level and saw is wrapped in a cloud of knowing.

All of these tools are a pleasure to look at and to hold. Merchants would never paste NEW NEW NEW! signs on them in stores. Their designs are old because they work, because they serve their purpose well. Like folk songs and **aphorisms** and the grainy bits of language, these tools have been pared down to essentials. I look at my claw hammer, the distillation of a hundred generations of carpenters, and consider that it holds up well beside those other classics—Greek vases, Gregorian chants, Don Quixote, barbed fishhooks, candles, spoons. Knowledge of ham-mering stretches back to the humans who squatted beside fires, chipping flints. Anthropolo-gists have a lovely name for those unworked rocks that served as the earliest hammers. "Dawn stones," they are called. Their only qualification for the work, aside from hardness, is that they fit the hand. Our ancestors used them for grinding corn, tapping awls, smashing bones. From dawn stones to this claw hammer is a great leap in time, but no great distance in design or imagination.

25   On that iced-over February morning when I smashed my thumb with the hammer, I was down in the basement framing the wall that my daughter's gerbils would later hide in. I was think-ing of my father, as I always did whenever I built anything, thinking how he would have gone about the work, hearing in memory what he would have said about the wisdom of hitting the nail instead of my thumb. I had the studs and plates nailed together all square and trim, and was lifting the wall into place when the phone rang upstairs. My wife answered, and in a moment she came to the basement door and called down softly to me. The stillness in her voice made me drop the framed wall and hurry upstairs. She told me my father was dead. Then I heard the details over the phone from my mother. Building a set of cupboards for my brother in Oklahoma, he had knocked off work early the previous afternoon because of cramps in his stomach. Early this morning, on his way into the kitchen of my brother's trailer, maybe going for a glass of water, so early that no one else was awake, he slumped down on the linoleum and his heart quit.

For several hours I paced around inside my house, upstairs and down, in and out of every room, looking for the right door to open and knowing there was no such door. My wife and children followed me and wrapped me in arms and backed away again, circling and staring as if I were on fire. Where was the door, the door, the door? I kept wondering. My smashed thumb turned purple and throbbed, making me furious. I wanted to cut it off and rush outside and scrape away at the snow and hack a hole in the frozen earth and bury the shameful thing.

I went down into the basement, opened a drawer in my workbench, and stared at the ranks of chisels and knives. Oiled and sharp, as my father would have kept them, they gleamed at me like teeth. I took up a **clasp knife,** pried out the longest blade, and tested the edge on the hair of my forearm. A tuft came away cleanly and I saw my father testing the sharpness of tools on his own skin, the blades of axes and knives and **gouges** and hoes, saw the red hair shaved off in patches from his arms and the backs of his hands. "That will cut a bear," he would say. He never cut a bear with his blades, now my blades, but he cut deer, dirt, wood. I closed the knife and put it away. Then I took up the hammer and went back to work on my daughter's wall, snugging the bottom plate against a chalk line on the floor, shimming the top plate against the joists overhead, plumbing the studs with my level, making sure before I drove the first nail that every line was square and true.

Understanding the Reading

1. List the items, people, events, and processes that Sanders describes in detail.

2. Find examples of the use of sensory details, particularly sight, sound, touch, and smell. How do these details enhance the essay?

3. Write down three or four figures of speech—similes, metaphors—and comment on their contribution to the essay.

4. Why is the title of the essay so appropriate? What did Sanders inherit in addition to the tools?

5. The essay begins and ends with the death of Sanders's father. What does the final paragraph emphasize about Sanders's father and his tools?

Understanding the Structure, Style, and Tone

1. What is the essay's dominant impression or tone? How do you think that Sanders wants the reader to feel after finishing the essay?

2. How does Sanders order his descriptions?

3. Note where Sanders uses dialogue. Why is it particularly effective?

Making a Personal Connection

1. Choose an item that you have inherited from a special person and describe it in such a way that your reader can visualize it and appreciate its importance to you.

2. Describe several items that reinforce a person's influence in your life. Follow Sanders's model by giving their history, usefulness, and life lessons.

LET's warm up!

Reflect on your experiences in a foreign language classroom in either high school or college. What was your instructor like? What embarrassing moments do you remember? What misunderstandings resulted in humorous interchanges? What qualities did it take to learn a foreign language thoroughly and efficiently?

Narration

Me Talk Pretty One Day by David Sedaris

David Sedaris was born in 1956 in Johnson City, New York, and grew up in North Carolina. He is one of the best-known humor essayists writing today. His collections of essays, including *Naked* (1998), *Me Talk Pretty One Day* (2000), and *Dress Your Family in Corduroy and Denim* (2004), make fun of popular culture, family dynamics, and political correctness. *Time* magazine recognized Sedaris as the "Humorist of the Year" in 2001. He is a regular on the National Public Radio show *This American Life*. The following essay appears in his book *Me Talk Pretty One Day*.

Increasing Your Vocabulary

▪ **Debutante:** a young woman who is formally presented to society	▪ **Belittle:** to make to feel inferior and unimportant
▪ **Stegosaurus:** a plant-eating dinosaur	▪ **Cesarean section:** cutting through the abdomen and uterus to deliver a baby
▪ **Forge on:** to keep moving ahead gradually	▪ **Diatribe:** criticism, rantings against someone or something
▪ **Mastermind:** to plan, supervise, oversee	
▪ **Dermatological:** related to the skin	

1   At the age of forty-one, I am returning to school and have to think of myself as what my French textbook calls "a true **debutante.**" After paying my tuition, I was issued a student ID, which allows me a discounted entry fee at movie theaters, puppet shows, and Festyland, a far-flung amusement park that advertises with billboards picturing a cartoon **stegosaurus** sitting in a canoe and eating what appears to be a ham sandwich.

I've moved to Paris with hopes of learning the language. My school is an easy ten-minute walk from my apartment, and on the first day of class I arrived early, watching as the returning students greeted one another in the school lobby. Vacations were recounted, and questions were raised concerning mutual friends with names like Kang and Vlatnya. Regardless of their nationalities, everyone spoke in what sounded to me like excellent French. Some accents were better than others, but the students exhibited an ease and confidence I found intimidating. As an added discomfort, they were all young, attractive, and well dressed, causing me to feel not unlike Pa Kettle trapped backstage after a fashion show.

The first day of class was nerve-racking because I knew I'd be expected to perform. That's the way they do it here—it's everybody into the language pool, sink or swim. The teacher marched in, deeply tanned from a recent vacation, and proceeded to rattle off a series of administrative announcements. I've spent quite a few summers in Normandy, and I took a monthlong French class before leaving New York. I'm not completely in the dark, yet I understood only half of what this woman was saying.

"If you have not *meimslsxp* or *Igpdmurct* by this time, then you should not be in this room. Has everyone *apzkiubjxow?* Everyone? Good, we shall begin." She spread out her lesson plan and sighed, saying, "All right, then, who knows the alphabet?"

5   It was startling because (a) I hadn't been asked that question in a while and (b) I realized, while laughing, that I myself did *not* know the alphabet. They're the same letters, but in France they're pronounced differently. I know the shape of the alphabet but had no idea what it actually sounded like.

"Ahh." The teacher went to the board and sketched the letter *a*. "Do we have anyone in the room whose first name commences with an *ahh?*"

Two Polish Annas raised their hands, and the teacher instructed them to present themselves by stating their names, nationalities, occupations, and a brief list of things they liked and disliked in this world. The first Anna hailed from an industrial town outside of Warsaw and had front teeth the size of tombstones. She worked as a seamstress, enjoyed quiet times with friends, and hated the mosquito.

"Oh, really," the teacher said. "How very interesting. I thought that everyone loved the mosquito, but here, in front of all the world, you claim to detest him. How is it that we've been blessed with someone as unique and original as you? Tell us, please."

The seamstress did not understand what was being said but knew that this was an occasion for shame. Her rabbity mouth huffed for breath, and she stared down at her lap as though the appropriate comeback were stitched somewhere alongside the zipper of her slacks.

10   The second Anna learned from the first and claimed to love sunshine and detest lies. It sounded like a translation of one of those Playmate of the Month data sheets, the answers always written in the same loopy handwriting: "Turn-ons: Mom's famous five-alarm chili! Turnoffs: insecurity and guys who come on too strong!!!!"

The two Polish Annas surely had clear notions of what they loved and hated, but like the rest of us, they were limited in terms of vocabulary, and this made them appear less than sophisticated. The teacher **forged on,** and we learned that Carlos, the Argentine bandonion player, loved wine, music, and, in his words, "making sex with the womens of the world." Next came a beautiful young Yugoslav who identified herself as an optimist, saying that she loved everything that life had to offer.

The teacher licked her lips, revealing a hint of the saucebox we would later come to know. She crouched low for her attack, placed her hands on the young woman's desk, and leaned close, saying, "Oh yeah? And do you love your little war?"

While the optimist struggled to defend herself, I scrambled to think of an answer to what had obviously become a trick question. How often is one asked what he loves in this world? More to the point, how often is one asked and then publicly ridiculed for his answer? I recalled my mother, flushed with wine, pounding the tabletop late one night, saying, "Love? I love a good steak cooked rare. I love my cat, and I love . . ." My sisters and I leaned forward, waiting to hear our names. "Turns," our mother said. "I love Turns."

The teacher killed some time accusing the Yugoslavian girl of **masterminding** a program of genocide, and I jotted frantic notes in the margins of my pad. While I can honestly say that I love leafing through medical textbooks devoted to severe **dermatological** conditions, the hobby is beyond the reach of my French vocabulary, and acting it out would only have invited controversy.

15   When called upon, I delivered an effortless list of things that I detest: blood sausage, intestinal pates, brain pudding. I'd learned these words the hard way. Having given it some thought, I then declared my love for IBM typewriters, the French word for *bruise*, and my electric floor waxer. It was a short list, but still I managed to mispronounce *IBM* and assign the wrong gender to both the floor waxer and the typewriter. The teacher's reaction led me to believe that these mistakes were capital crimes in the country of France.

"Were you always this *palicmkrexis?*" she asked. "Even a *fiuscrzsa ticiwelmun* knows that a typewriter is feminine."

I absorbed as much of her abuse as I could understand, thinking—but not saying—that I find it ridiculous to assign a gender to an inanimate object incapable of disrobing and making an occasional fool of itself. Why refer to crack pipe or Good Sir Dishrag when these things could never live up to all that their sex implied?

The teacher proceeded to **belittle** everyone from German Eva, who hated laziness, to Japanese Yukari, who loved paintbrushes and soap. Italian, Thai, Dutch, Korean, and Chinese—we all left class foolishly believing that the worst was over. She'd shaken us up a little, but surely that was just an act designed to weed out the deadweight. We didn't know it then, but the coming months would teach us what it was like to spend time in the presence of a wild animal, something completely unpredictable. Her temperament was not based on a series of good and bad days but, rather, good and bad moments. We soon learned to dodge chalk and protect our heads and stomachs whenever she approached us with a question. She hadn't yet punched anyone, but it seemed wise to protect ourselves against the inevitable.

Though we were forbidden to speak anything but French, the teacher would occasionally use us to practice any of her five fluent languages.

20   "I hate you," she said to me one afternoon. Her English was flawless. "I really, really hate you." Call me sensitive, but I couldn't help but take it personally.

After being singled out as a lazy *kfdtinvfm,* I took to spending four hours a night on my homework, putting in even more time whenever we were assigned an essay. I suppose I could have gotten by with less, but I was determined to create some sort of identity for myself: David the hard worker, David the cut-up. We'd have one of those "complete this sentence" exercises, and I'd fool with the thing for hours, invariably settling on something like "A quick run around the lake? I'd love to! Just give me a moment while I strap on my wooden leg." The teacher, through word and action, conveyed the message that if this was my idea of an identity, she wanted nothing to do with it.

My fear and discomfort crept beyond the borders of the classroom and accompanied me out onto the wide boulevards. Stopping for a coffee, asking directions, depositing money in my bank account: these things were out of the question, as they involved having to speak. Before beginning school, there'd been no shutting me up, but now I was convinced that everything I said was wrong. When the phone rang, I ignored it. If someone asked me a question, I pretended to be deaf. I knew my fear was getting the best of me when I started wondering why they don't sell cuts of meat in vending machines.

My only comfort was the knowledge that I was not alone. Huddled in the hallways and making the most of our pathetic French, my fellow students and I engaged in the sort of conversation commonly overheard in refugee camps.

"Sometime me cry alone at night."

25   "That be common for I, also, but be more strong, you. Much work and someday you talk pretty. People start love you soon. Maybe tomorrow, okay."

Unlike the French class I had taken in New York, here there was no sense of competition. When the teacher poked a shy Korean in the eyelid with a freshly sharpened pencil, we took no comfort in the fact that, unlike Hyeyoon Cho, we all knew the irregular past tense of the verb *to defeat*. In all fairness, the teacher hadn't meant to stab the girl, but neither did she spend much time apologizing, saying only, "Well, you should have been *vkkdyo* more *kdeynfulh.*"

Over time it became impossible to believe that any of us would ever improve. Fall arrived and it rained every day, meaning we would now be scolded for the water dripping from our coats and umbrellas. It was mid-October when the teacher singled me out, saying, "Every day spent with you is like having a **cesarean section.**" And it struck me that, for the first time since arriving in France, I could understand every word that someone was saying.

Understanding doesn't mean that you can suddenly speak the language. Far from it. It's a small step, nothing more, yet its rewards are intoxicating and deceptive. The teacher continued her **diatribe** and I settled back, bathing in the subtle beauty of each new curse and insult.

"You exhaust me with your foolishness and reward my efforts with nothing but pain, do you understand me?"

30   The world opened up, and it was with great joy that I responded, "I know the thing that you speak exact now. Talk me more, you, *plus*, please, *plus*."

Understanding the Reading

1. List the people and activities that Sedaris describes in some detail.
2. What effect does the French teacher have on her students? On Sedaris in particular?
3. What is Sedaris's attitude toward his classmates?
4. What is the one bright spot for Sedaris?
5. How does this French class compare to the one he took in New York?

Understanding the Structure, Style, and Tone

1. Is the essay strictly chronological, or does Sedaris offer some flashbacks? Point out a place in the essay where Sedaris flashes back to an earlier time.
2. How does the use of dialogue—direct speech of the teacher and students—enhance the essay?
3. What effect do the nonsense words such as *kfdtinvfm* have on the reader?
4. What is the significance of the title?
5. How does Sedaris come across in this essay? How would you describe his personality?

Making a Personal Connection

1. Write about an experience in a classroom that made you uncomfortable; then describe how you were able to cope with the experience.
2. Tell a story when someone in authority made your life and possibly others' lives miserable.

Illustration

Sex, Lies, and Conversation: Why Is It So Hard for Men and Women to Talk to Each Other? by Deborah Tannen

LET's warm up!

Think about how you communicate with a member of the opposite sex. What patterns of conversation have you noticed and what challenges have you encountered?

Deborah Tannen, a professor of linguistics at Georgetown University, researches and writes about the differences and difficulties men and women have communicating with each other. Born in Brooklyn, New York, in 1945, Tannen has written several books, including *That's Not What I Meant!* (1986), *The Argument Culture* (1998), and *You're Wearing THAT?* (2006). The following essay was published in 1990 in the *Washington Post*.

Increasing Your Vocabulary

■ **Concur:** to agree	■ **Hierarchical:** a pecking order or ranked series
■ **Crystallize:** to become clear	■ **Paradox:** a contradiction
■ **Wreak:** to get revenge on	■ **Sociolinguistic:** related to society and language
■ **Misalignment:** not matching up	■ **Cross-cultural:** a combination of several cultures
■ **Analogous:** comparable to	■ **Align:** to take one side of an issue
■ **Intrusion:** an undesired entrance or presence	■ **Resurgent:** rising up again

1   I was addressing a small gathering in a suburban Virginia living room—a women's group that had invited men to join them. Throughout the evening, one man had been particularly talkative, frequently offering ideas and anecdotes, while his wife sat silently beside him on the couch. Toward the end of the evening, I commented that women frequently complain that their husbands don't talk to them. This man quickly **concurred.** He gestured toward his wife and said, "She's the talker in our family." The room burst into laughter; the man looked puzzled and hurt. "It's true," he explained. "When I come home from work I have nothing to say. If she didn't keep the conversation going, we'd spend the whole evening in silence."

This episode **crystallizes** the irony that although American men tend to talk more than women in public situations, they often talk less at home. And this pattern is **wreaking** havoc with marriage.

The pattern was observed by political scientist Andrew Hacker in the late '70s. Sociologist Catherine Kohler Riessman reports in her new book *Divorce Talk* that most of the women she interviewed—but only a few of the men—gave lack of communication as the reason for their divorces. Given the current divorce rate of nearly 50 percent, that amounts to millions of cases in the United States every year—a virtual epidemic of failed conversation.

In my own research, complaints from women about their husbands most often focused not on tangible inequities such as having given up the chance for a career to accompany a husband to his or doing far more than their share of daily life-support work like cleaning, cooking, social arrangements, and errands. Instead, they focused on communication: "He doesn't listen to me," "He doesn't talk to me." I found, as Hacker observed years before, that most wives want their husbands to be, first and foremost, conversational partners but few husbands share this expectation of their wives.

5   In short, the image that best represents the current crisis is the stereotypical cartoon scene of a man sitting at the breakfast table with a newspaper held up in front of his face while a woman glares at the back of it, wanting to talk.

Linguistic Battle of the Sexes

How can women and men have such different impressions of communication in marriage? Why the widespread imbalance in their interests and expectations?

In the April issue of *American Psychologist,* Stanford University's Eleanor Maccoby reports the results of her own and others' research showing that children's development is most influenced by the social structure of peer interactions. Boys and girls tend to play with children of their own gender, and their sex-separate groups have different organizational structures and interactive norms.

I believe these systematic differences in childhood socialization make talk between women and men like cross-cultural communication, heir to all the attraction and pitfalls of that enticing but difficult enterprise. My research on men's and women's conversations uncovered patterns similar to those described for children's groups.

For women, as for girls, intimacy is the fabric of relationships, and talk is the thread from which it is woven. Little girls create and maintain friendships by exchanging secrets; similarly, women regard conversation as the cornerstone of friendship. So a woman expects her husband to be a new and improved version of a best friend. What is important is not the individual subjects that are discussed but the sense of closeness, of a life shared, that emerges when people tell their thoughts, feelings, and impressions.

10   Bonds between boys can be as intense as girls', but they are based less on talking, more on doing things together. Since they don't assume talk is the cement that binds a relationship, men don't know what kind of talk women want, and they don't miss it when it isn't there.

Boys' groups are larger, more inclusive, and more hierarchical, so boys must struggle to avoid the subordinate position in the group. This may play a role in women's complaints that men don't listen to them. Some men really don't like to listen, because being the listener makes them feel one-down, like a child listening to adults or an employee to a boss.

But often when women tell men, "You aren't listening," and the men protest, "I am," the men are right. The impression of not listening results from **misalignments** in the mechanics of conversation. The misalignment begins as soon as a man and a woman take physical positions. This became clear when I studied videotapes made by psychologist Bruce Dorval of children and adults talking to their same-sex best friends. I found that at every age, the girls and women faced each other directly, their eyes anchored on each other's faces. At every age, the boys and men sat at angles to each other and looked elsewhere in the room, periodically glancing at each other. They were obviously attuned to each other, often mirroring each other's movements. But the tendency of men to face away can give women the impression they aren't listening even when they are. A young woman in college was frustrated: Whenever she told her boyfriend she wanted to talk to him, he would lie down on the floor, close his eyes, and put his arm over his face. This signaled to her, "He's taking a nap." But he insisted he was listening extra hard. Normally, he looks around the room, so he is easily distracted. Lying down and covering his eyes helped him concentrate on what she was saying.

Analogous to the physical alignment that women and men take in conversation is their topical alignment. The girls in my study tended to talk at length about one topic, but the boys tended to jump from topic to topic. The second-grade girls exchanged stories about people they knew. The second-grade boys teased, told jokes, noticed things in the room, and talked about finding games to play. The sixth-grade girls talked about problems with a mutual friend. The sixth-grade boys talked about 55 different topics, none of which extended over more than a few turns.

Listening to Body Language

Switching topics is another habit that gives women the impression men aren't listening, especially if they switch to a topic about themselves. But the evidence of the 10th-grade boys in my study indicates otherwise. The 10th-grade boys sprawled across their chairs with bodies parallel and eyes straight ahead, rarely looking at each other. They looked as if they were riding in a car, staring out the windshield. But they were talking about their feelings. One boy was upset because a girl had told him he had a drinking problem, and the other was feeling alienated from all his friends.

15   Now, when a girl told a friend about a problem, the friend responded by asking probing questions and expressing agreement and understanding. But the boys dismissed each other's problems. Todd assured Richard that his drinking was "no big problem" because "sometimes you're funny when you're off your butt." And when Todd said he felt left out, Richard responded, "Why should you? You know more people than me."

Women perceive such responses as belittling and unsupportive. But the boys seemed satisfied with them. Whereas women reassure each other by implying, "You shouldn't feel bad because I've had similar experiences," men do so by implying, "You shouldn't feel bad because your problems aren't so bad."

There are even simpler reasons for women's impression that men don't listen. Linguist Lynette Hirschman found that women make more listener-noise, such as "mhm," "uhuh," and "yeah," to show "I'm with you." Men, she found, more often give silent attention. Women who expect a stream of listener-noise interpret silent attention as no attention at all.

Women's conversational habits are as frustrating to men as men's are is to women. Men who expect silent attention interpret a stream of listener-noise as overreaction or impatience. Also, when women talk to each other in a close, comfortable setting, they often overlap, finish each other's sentences, and anticipate what the other is about to say. This practice, which I call "participatory listenership," is often perceived by men as interruption, **intrusion,** and lack of attention.

A parallel difference caused a man to complain about his wife, "She just wants to talk about her own point of view. If I show her another view, she gets mad at me." When most women talk to each other, they assume a conversationalist's job is to express agreement and support. But many men see their conversational duty as pointing out the other side of an argument. This is heard as disloyalty by women, and refusal to offer the requisite support. It is not that women don't want to see other points of view, but that they prefer them phrased as suggestions and inquiries rather than as direct challenges.

20   In his book *Fighting for Life,* Walter Ong points out that men use "agonistic," or warlike, oppositional formats to do almost anything; thus discussion becomes debate, and conversation a competitive sport. In contrast, women see conversation as a ritual means of establishing rapport. If Jane tells a problem and June says she has a similar one, they walk away feeling closer to each other. But this attempt at establishing rapport can backfire when used with men. Men take too literally women's ritual "troubles talk," just as women mistake men's ritual challenges for real attack.

The Sounds of Silence

These differences begin to clarify why women and men have such different expectations about communication in marriage. For women, talk creates intimacy. Marriage is an orgy of closeness: you can tell your feelings and thoughts and still be loved. Their greatest fear is being pushed away. But men live in a **hierarchical** world, where talk maintains independence and status. They are on guard to protect themselves from being put down and pushed around.

This explains the **paradox** of the talkative man who said of his silent wife, "She's the talker." In the public setting of a guest lecture, he felt challenged to show his intelligence and display his understanding of the lecture. But at home, where he has nothing to prove and no one to defend against, he is free to remain silent. For his wife, being home means she is free from the worry that something she says might offend someone, or spark disagreement, or appear to be showing off; at home she is free to talk.

The communication problems that endanger marriage can't be fixed by mechanical engineering. They require a new conceptual framework about the role of talk in human rela-tionships. Many of the psychological explanations that have become second nature may not be helpful, because they tend to blame either women (for not being assertive enough) or men (for not being in touch with their feelings). A **sociolinguistic** approach by which male–female conversation is seen as **cross-cultural** communication allows us to understand the problem and forge solutions without blaming either party.

Once the problem is understood, improvement comes naturally, as it did to the young woman and her boyfriend who seemed to go to sleep when she wanted to talk. Previously, she had accused him of not listening, and he had refused to change his behavior, since that would be admitting fault. But then she learned about and explained to him the differences in women's and men's habitual ways of **aligning** themselves in conversation. The next time she told him she wanted to talk, he began, as usual, by lying down and covering his eyes. When the familiar nega-tive reaction bubbled up, she reassured herself that he really was listening. But then he sat up and looked at her. Thrilled, she asked why. He said, "You like me to look at you when we talk, so I'll try to do it." Once he saw their differences as cross-cultural rather than right and wrong, he independently altered his behavior.

25   Women who feel abandoned and deprived when their husbands won't listen to or report daily news may be happy to discover their husbands trying to adapt once they understand the place of small talk in women's relationships. But if their husbands don't adapt, the women may still be comforted that for men, this is not a failure of intimacy. Accepting the difference, the wives may look to their friends or family for that kind of talk. And husbands who can't provide it shouldn't feel their wives have made unreasonable demands. Some couples will still decide to divorce, but at least their decisions will be based on realistic expectations.

In these times of **resurgent** ethnic conflicts, the world desperately needs cross-cultural understanding. Like charity, successful cross-cultural communication should begin at home.

REVIEW   28-3

Understanding the Reading

1. Summarize the main ways in which men and women communicate differently, according to Tannen.

2. For each of Tannen's three main headings, give specific examples that she uses to illustrate her points.

3. What does the title of the essay add to its impact?

4. What strategies can men and women use to improve their communication?

Understanding the Structure, Style, and Tone

1. Tannen has three main headings for her essay. What was her logic in ordering them in the way they appear?

2. For each of her main headings, she provides several examples. Which examples are her strongest, most convincing ones?

3. Reread Tannen's last two paragraphs. How hopeful is she about increased understanding between husbands and wives? What was her purpose in writing this essay?

Making a Personal Connection

1. Remember a conversation that you have had recently with a member of the opposite sex. Which patterns fit with Tannen's examples and which ones do not?

2. Think of a couple whom you know well—your parents, your grandparents, close family friends, a college couple—and describe how they typically inter-act. Who talks the most? Who is more demanding? What conflicts have you observed?

Process

The Crummy First Draft by Anne Lamott

Anne Lamott, a writer of both fiction and nonfiction who lives in northern California, writes about parenting (*Operating Instructions*, 1993), dysfunctional families (*Hard Laughter*, 1980), and writing and life (*Bird by Bird*, 1994). As a recovering alcohol and drug user, Lamott has used her own experiences to inspire others to make a new start.

LET's warm up!

Envision the first draft of some of the papers that you have written. What do your first drafts usually look like and how do you write them?

Increasing Your Vocabulary

■ **Rapturous:** incredibly thrilled and happy	■ **Discretion:** caution, care
■ **Umbrage:** offense, insult	■ **Hurtle:** to rush forward with great speed
■ **Overwrought:** overly excited	■ **Ravenous:** extremely hungry
■ **Stupefying:** astonishing, amazing	

¹   For me and most of the other writers I know, writing is not **rapturous.** In fact, the only way I can get anything written at all is to write really, really crummy first drafts.

The first draft is the child's draft, where you let it all pour out and then let it romp all over the place, knowing that no one is going to see it and that you can shape it later. You just let this child-like part of you channel whatever voices and visions come through and onto the page. If one of the characters wants to say "Well, so what, Mr. Poopy Pants?" you let her. No one is going to see it. If the kid wants to get into really sentimental, weepy, emotional territory, you let him. Just get it all down on paper, because there may be something great in those six crazy pages that you would never have gotten to by more rational, grownup means. There may be something in the very last line of the very last paragraph on page six that you just love, that is so beautiful or wild that you now know what you're supposed to be writing about, more or less, or in what direction you might go—but there was no way to get to this without first getting through the first five and a half pages.

I used to write food reviews for *California* magazine before it folded. (My writing food reviews had nothing to do with the magazine folding, although every single review did cause a couple of canceled subscriptions. Some readers took **umbrage** at my comparing mounds of vegetable puree with various ex-presidents' brains.) These reviews always took two days to write. First I'd go to a restaurant several times with a few opinionated, articulate friends in tow. I'd sit there writing down everything anyone said that was at all interesting or funny. Then on the following Monday I'd sit down at my desk with my notes and try to write the review. Even after I'd been doing this for years, panic would set in. I'd try to write a lead, but instead I'd write a couple of dreadful sentences, xx them out, try again, xx everything out, and then feel despair and worry settle on my chest like an x-ray apron. It's over, I'd think, calmly. I'm not going to be able to get the magic to work this time. I'm ruined. I'm through. I'm toast. Maybe, I'd think, I can get my old job back as a clerk-typist. But probably not. I'd get up and study my teeth in the mirror for a while. Then I'd stop, remember to breathe, make a few phone calls, hit the kitchen, and chow down. Eventually I'd go back and sit down at my desk, and sigh for the next ten minutes. Finally I would pick up my one-inch picture frame, stare into it as if for the answer, and every time the answer would come: all I had to do was to write a really crummy first draft of, say, the opening paragraph. And no one was going to see it.

So I'd start writing without reining myself in. It was almost just typing, just making my fingers move. And the writing would be *terrible*. I'd write a lead paragraph that was a whole page, even though the entire review could only be three pages long, and then I'd start writing up descriptions of the food, one dish at a time, bird by bird, and the critics would be sitting on my shoulders, commenting like cartoon characters. They'd be pretending to snore, or rolling their eyes at my **overwrought** descriptions, no matter how hard I tried to tone those descriptions down, no matter how conscious I was of what a friend said to me gently in my early days of restaurant reviewing. "Annie," she said, "it is just a piece of *chicken*. It is just a bit of *cake*."

⁵   But because by then I had been writing for so long, I would eventually let myself trust the process—sort of, more or less. I'd write a first draft that was maybe twice as long as it should be, with a self-indulgent and boring beginning, **stupefying** descriptions of the meal, lots of quotes from my black-humored friends that made them sound more like the Manson girls than food lovers, and no ending to speak of. The whole thing would be so long and incoherent and hideous that for the rest of the day I'd obsess about getting creamed by a car before I could write a decent second draft. I'd worry that people would read what I'd written and believe that the accident had really been a suicide, that I had panicked because my talent was waning and my mind was shot.

The next day, though, I'd sit down, go through it all with a colored pen, take out everything I possibly could, find a new lead somewhere on the second page, figure out a kicky place to end it, and then write a second draft. It always turned out fine, sometimes even funny and weird and helpful. I'd go over it one more time and mail it in.

Then, a month later, when it was time for another review, the whole process would start again, complete with the fears that people would find my first draft before I could rewrite it.

Almost all good writing begins with terrible first efforts. You need to start somewhere. Start by getting something—anything—down on paper. A friend of mine says that the first draft is the down draft—you just get it down. The second draft is the up draft—you fix it up. You try to say what you have to say more accurately. And the third draft is the dental draft, where you check every tooth, to see if it's loose or cramped or decayed, or even, God help us, healthy.

What I've learned to do when I sit down to work on a crummy first draft is to quiet the voices in my head. First there's the vinegar-lipped Reader Lady, who says primly, "Well, *that's* not very interesting, is it?" And there's the emaciated German male who writes these Orwellian memos detailing your thought crimes. And there are your parents, agonizing over your lack of loyalty and discretion; and there's William Burroughs, dozing off or shooting up because he finds you as bold and articulate as a houseplant; and so on. And there are also the dogs: let's not forget the dogs, the dogs in their pen who will surely **hurtle** and snarl their way out if you ever *stop* writing, because writing is, for some of us, the latch that keeps the door of the pen closed, keeps those crazy, **ravenous** dogs contained. . . .

10   Close your eyes and get quiet for a minute, until the chatter starts up. Then isolate one of the voices and imagine the person speaking as a mouse. Pick it up by the tail and drop it into a mason jar. Then isolate another voice, pick it up by the tail, drop it in the jar. And so on. Drop in any high-maintenance parental units, drop in any contractors, lawyers, colleagues, children, anyone who is whining in your head. Then put the lid on, and watch all these mouse people clawing at the glass, jabbering away, trying to make you feel crummy because you won't do what they want—won't give them more money, won't be more successful, won't see them more often. Then imagine that there is a volume-control button on the bottle. Turn it all the way up for a minute, and listen to the stream of angry, neglected, guilt-mongering voices. Then turn it all the way down and watch the frantic mice lunge at the glass, trying to get to you. Leave it down, and get back to your crummy first draft.

A writer friend of mine suggests opening the jar and shooting them all in the head. But I think he's a little angry, and I'm sure nothing like this would ever occur to you.

REVIEW 28-4

Understanding the Reading

1. Summarize how Lamott writes a first draft.

2. What is Lamott's thesis or main point?

3. Who is Lamott's audience for this essay?

4. What does Lamott mean by her image of the mouse in the jar in the second to the last paragraph?

Understanding the Structure, Style, and Tone

1. How does Lamott organize her essay, explaining the process of writing the first draft?

2. Where does the essay shift between *I* and *you*? Why does Lamott shift point of view like this?

3. What is the tone of the last two sentences?

Making a Personal Connection

1. What effect do Lamott's ideas have on you as a writer? How might you change your writing approaches based on her advice?

2. Describe your process for writing your first drafts. How does it compare to the way Lamott approaches her writing?

Cause and Effect

The Tipping Point by Malcolm Gladwell

LET's **warm up!**

Think about the types of crimes that are most prevalent in your community. What are the main causes of these crimes? What effects do they have on your community?

Malcolm Gladwell was born in England in 1963 and earned a B.A. in history at the University of Toronto. He has been a staff writer for the *New Yorker* magazine since 1996. He makes sophisticated research in the social sciences and sciences understandable to the general reader. In 2005, *Time* magazine recognized him as one of the "100 Most Influential People." The following is a chapter from his book *The Tipping Point: How Little Things Can Make a Big Difference* (2000).

Increasing Your Vocabulary

■ **Spawn:** to give birth to
■ **Stagnant:** not moving or changing
■ **Waning:** approaching an end, gradually declining
■ **Impetus:** an impulse or force
■ **Solvent:** something that can make another substance dissolve
■ **Reclaim:** to save from being discarded

■ **Unambiguous:** understandable, clear, straightforward
■ **Quixotic:** changeable
■ **Exacerbate:** to make worse
■ **Charismatic:** a special ability of leadership and inspiration for others
■ **Retrofit:** to install new parts on an original structure
■ **Infraction:** breaking of the rules

1   During the 1990s violent crime declined across the United States for a number of fairly straightforward reasons. The illegal trade in crack cocaine, which had **spawned** a great deal of violence among gangs and drug dealers, began to decline. The economy's dramatic recovery meant that many people who might have been lured into crime got legitimate jobs

instead, and the general aging of the population meant that there were fewer people in the age range—males between eighteen and twenty-four—that is responsible for the majority of all violence. The question of why crime declined in New York City, however, is a little more complicated. In the period when the New York epidemic tipped down, the city's economy hadn't improved. It was still **stagnant.** In fact, the city's poorest neighborhoods had just been hit hard by the welfare cuts of the early 1990s. The **waning** of the crack cocaine epidemic in New York was clearly a factor, but then again, it had been in steady decline well before crime dipped. As for the aging of the population, because of heavy immigration to New York in the 1980s, the city was getting younger in the 1990s, not older. In any case, all of these trends are long-term changes that one would expect to have gradual effects. In New York the decline was anything but gradual. Something else clearly played a role in reversing New York's crime epidemic.

The most intriguing candidate for that "something else" is called the Broken Windows theory. Broken Windows was the brainchild of the criminologists James Q. Wilson and George Kelling. Wilson and Kelling argued that crime is the inevitable result of disorder. If a window is broken and left unrepaired, people walking by will conclude that no one cares and no one is in charge. Soon, more windows will be broken, and the sense of anarchy will spread from the building to the street on which it faces, sending a signal that anything goes. In a city, relatively minor problems like graffiti, public disorder, and aggressive panhandling, they write, are all the equivalent of broken windows, invitations to more serious crimes:

Muggers and robbers, whether opportunistic or professional, believe they reduce their chances of being caught or even identified if they operate on streets where potential victims are already intimidated by prevailing conditions. If the neighborhood cannot keep a bothersome panhandler from annoying passersby, the thief may reason, it is even less likely to call the police to identify a potential mugger or to interfere if the mugging actually takes place.

This is an epidemic theory of crime. It says that crime is contagious—just as a fashion trend is contagious—that it can start with a broken window and spread to an entire community. The Tipping Point in this epidemic, though, isn't a particular kind of person—a Connector like Lois Weisberg or a Maven like Mark Alpert. It's something physical like graffiti. The **impetus** to engage in a certain kind of behavior is not coming from a certain kind of person but from a feature of the environment.

5　In the mid-1980s Kelling was hired by the New York Transit Authority as a consultant, and he urged them to put the Broken Windows theory into practice. They obliged, bringing in a new subway director by the name of David Gunn to oversee a multibillion-dollar rebuilding of the subway system. Many subway advocates, at the time, told Gunn not to worry about graffiti, to focus on the larger questions of crime and subway reliability, and it seemed like reasonable advice. Worrying about graffiti at a time when the entire system was close to collapse seems as pointless as scrubbing the decks of the *Titanic* as it headed toward the icebergs. But Gunn insisted. "The graffiti was symbolic of the collapse of the system," he says. "When you looked at the process of rebuilding the organization and morale, you had to win the battle against graffiti. Without winning that battle, all the management reforms and physical changes just weren't going to happen. We were about to put out new trains that were worth about ten million bucks apiece, and unless we did something to protect them, we knew just what would happen. They would last one day and then they would be vandalized."

Gunn drew up a new management structure and a precise set of goals and timetables aimed at cleaning the system line by line, train by train. He started with the number seven train that connects Queens to midtown Manhattan, and began experimenting with new techniques to clean off the paint. On stainless-steel cars, **solvents** were used. On the painted cars, the graffiti was simply painted over. Gunn made it a rule that there should be no retreat, that once a car was **"reclaimed"** it should never be allowed to be vandalized again. "We were religious about it," Gunn said. At the end of the number one line in the Bronx, where the trains stop before turning around and going back to Manhattan, Gunn set up a cleaning station. If a car came in with graffiti, the graffiti had to be removed during the changeover, or the car was removed from service. "Dirty" cars, which hadn't yet been cleansed of graffiti, were never to be mixed with "clean" cars. The idea was to send an **unambiguous** message to the vandals themselves.

"We had a yard up in Harlem on One hundred thirty-fifth Street where the trains would lay up over night," Gunn said. "The kids would come the first night and paint the side of the train white. Then they would come the next night, after it was dry, and draw the outline. Then they would come the third night and color it in. It was a three-day job. We knew the kids would be working on one of the dirty trains, and what we would do is wait for them to finish their mural. Then we'd walk over with rollers and paint it over. The kids would be in tears, but we'd just be going up and down, up and down. It was a message to them. If you want to spend three nights of your time vandalizing a train, fine. But its never going to see the light of day."

Gunn's graffiti cleanup took from 1984 to 1990. At that point, the Transit Authority hired William Bratton to head the transit police, and the second stage of the reclamation of the subway system began. Bratton was, like Gunn, a disciple of Broken Windows. He describes Kelling, in fact, as his intellectual mentor, and so his first step as police chief was as seemingly **quixotic** as Gunn's. With felonies—serious crimes—on the subway system at an all-time high, Bratton decided to crack down on fare-beating. Why? Because he believed that, like graffiti, fare-beating could be a signal, a small expression of disorder that invited much more serious crimes. An estimated 170,000 people a day were entering the system, by one route or another, without paying a token. Some were kids, who simply jumped over the turnstiles. Others would lean backward on the turnstiles and force their way through. And once one or two or three people began cheating the system, other people—who might never otherwise have considered evading the law—would join in, reasoning that if some people weren't going to pay, they shouldn't either, and the problem would snowball. The problem was **exacerbated** by the fact fare-beating was not easy to fight. Because there was only $1.25 at stake, the transit police didn't feel it was worth their time to pursue it, particularly when there were plenty of more serious crimes happening down on the platform and in the trains.

Bratton is a colorful, **charismatic** man, a born leader, and he quickly made his presence felt. His wife stayed behind in Boston, so he was free to work long hours, and he would roam the city on the subway at night, getting a sense of what the problems were and how best to fight them. First, he picked stations where fare-beating was the biggest problem, and put as many as ten policemen in plainclothes at the turnstiles. The team would nab fare-beaters one by one, handcuff them, and leave them standing, in a daisy chain, on the platform until they had a "full catch." The idea was to signal, as publicly as possible, that the transit police were now serious about cracking down on fare-beaters. Previously, police officers had been wary of pursuing fare-beaters because the arrest, the trip to the station house, the filling out of necessary forms, and the waiting for those forms to be processed took an entire day—all for a crime that usually merited no more than a slap on the wrist. Bratton retrofitted a city bus and turned it into a rolling station house, with its own fax machines, phones, holding pen, and fingerprinting facilities. Soon the turnaround time on an arrest was down to an hour. Bratton also insisted that a check be run on all those arrested. Sure enough, one out of seven arrestees had an outstanding warrant for a previous crime, and one out of twenty was carrying a weapon of some sort. Suddenly it wasn't hard to convince police officers that tackling fare-beating made sense. "For the cops it was a bonanza," Bratton writes. "Every arrest was like opening a box of Cracker Jack. What kind of toy am I going to get? Got a gun? Got a knife? Got a warrant? Do we have a murderer here? . . . After a while the bad guys wised up and began to leave their weapons home and pay their fares." Under Bratton, the number of ejections from subway stations—for drunkenness, or improper behavior—tripled within his first few months in office. Arrests for misdemeanors, for the kind of minor offenses that had gone unnoticed in the past, went up fivefold between 1990 and 1994. Bratton turned the transit police into an organization focused on the smallest **infractions,** on the details of life underground.

10   After the election of Rudolph Giuliani as mayor of New York in 1994, Bratton was appointed head of the New York City Police Department, and he applied the same strategies to the city at large. He instructed his officers to crack down on quality-of-life crimes: on the "squeegee men" who came up to drivers at New York City intersections and demanded money for washing car windows, for example, and on all the other above-ground equivalents of turnstile-jumping and graffiti. "Previous police administrations had been handcuffed by restrictions," Bratton says. "We took the handcuffs off. We stepped up enforcement of the laws against public drunkenness and public urination and arrested repeat violators, including those who threw empty bottles on the street or were involved in even relatively minor damage to property. . . . If you peed in the street, you were going to jail." When crime began to fall in the city—as quickly and dramatically as it had in the subways—Bratton and Giuliani pointed to the same cause. Minor, seemingly insignificant quality-of-life crimes, they said, were Tipping Points for violent crime.

REVIEW   28-5

Understanding the Reading

1. Does the essay begin with a cause or an effect? Explain.

2. What measures did the new subway director, David Gunn, take to clean up the subways?

3. What measures did William Bratton of the transit police take to keep people from not paying their subway fares?

4. What were the effects of these measures and why did they work?

5. Explain the significance of the title.

Understanding the Structure, Style, and Tone

1. Does the essay focus more on causes or on effects? Explain.

2. List the main or necessary cause and any contributory causes.

3. What effect does the comparison of cleaning graffiti and scrubbing the deck of the *Titanic* (paragraph 5) have on the reader?

4. What is the overall tone of this essay?

Making a Personal Connection

1. Envision your community and specific neighborhoods that you are familiar with. How would this same approach work on the worst crimes that your community faces?

2. Write about another situation in which something seemingly minor has had a major effect on the outcome.

Comparison and Contrast

Aria: A Memoir of a Bilingual Childhood by Richard Rodriguez

LET's warm up!

How do you react when you encounter someone who doesn't speak English well or has a heavy accent that makes him or her difficult to understand? What are your first reactions, and how do you attempt to communicate with the nonnative speaker of English?

Richard Rodriguez, born the son of Mexican immigrants in 1944, spoke mainly Spanish until he started school. As he increasingly became a part of American culture, he experienced the contrast with his life at home with family. He received a Ph.D. in English Renaissance literature from the University of California, Berkeley. His books include *Hunger of Memory, a Memoir* (1982) and *Days of Obligation: An Argument with My Mexican Father* (1993). Some of his more controversial topics are arguments against bilingual education and affirmative action. The following passage is from *Hunger of Memory*.

Increasing Your Vocabulary

■ **Bilingual:** speaking two languages	■ **Feign:** to pretend
■ **Trivialize:** to make light of, devalue	■ **Cloister:** to seclude, hide
■ **Counterpoint:** a contrasting idea or element	■ **Lacquer:** to cover with a glossy surface coating
■ **Polysyllabic:** having more than one syllable	
■ **Falsetto:** a male voice singing at a higher pitch than its normal range	

1   I remember to start with that day in Sacramento—a California now nearly thirty years past—when I first entered a classroom, able to understand some fifty stray English words.

The third of four children, I had been preceded to a neighborhood Roman Catholic school by an older brother and sister. But neither of them had revealed very much about their classroom experiences. Each afternoon they returned, as they left in the morning, always together, speaking in Spanish as they climbed the five steps of the porch. And their mysterious books, wrapped in shopping-bag paper, remained on the table next to the door, closed firmly behind them.

An accident of geography sent me to a school where all my classmates were white, many the children of doctors and lawyers and business executives. All my classmates certainly must have been uneasy on that first day of school—as most children are uneasy—to find themselves apart from their families in the first institution of their lives. But I was astonished.

The nun said, in a friendly but oddly impersonal voice, "Boys and girls, this is Richard Rodriguez." (I *heard* her sound out: *Rich-heard Road-ree-guess.*) It was the first time I had heard anyone name me in English. "Richard," the nun repeated more slowly, writing my name down in her black leather book. Quickly I turned to see my mother's face dissolve in a watery blur behind the pebbled glass door.

5   Many years later there is something called **bilingual** education—a scheme proposed in the late 1960s by Hispanic American social activists, later endorsed by a congressional vote. It is a program that seeks to permit non-English-speaking children, many from lower-class homes, to use their family language as the language of school. (Such is the goal its supporters announce.) I hear them and am forced to say no: it is not possible for a child—any child—ever to use his family's language in school. Not to understand this is to misunderstand the public uses of schooling and to **trivialize** the nature of intimate life—a family's "language."

Memory teaches me what I know of these matters; the boy reminds the adult. I was a bilingual child, a certain kind—socially disadvantaged—the son of working-class parents, both Mexican immigrants.

In the early years of my boyhood, my parents coped very well in America. My father had steady work. My mother managed at home. They were nobody's victims. Optimism and ambition led them to a house (our home) many blocks from the Mexican south side of town. We lived among *gringos* and only a block from the biggest, whitest houses. It never occurred to my parents that they couldn't live wherever they chose. Nor was the Sacramento of the fifties bent on teaching them a contrary lesson. My mother and father were more annoyed than intimidated by those two or three neighbors who tried initially to make us unwelcome. ("Keep your brats away from my sidewalk!") But despite all they achieved, perhaps because they had so much to achieve, any deep feeling of ease, the confidence of "belonging" in public was withheld from them both. They regarded the people at work, the faces in crowds, as very distant from us. They were the others, *los gringos.* That term was interchangeable in their speech with another, even more telling, *los americanos. . . .*

In public, my father and mother spoke a hesitant, accented, not always grammatical English. And they would have to strain—their bodies tense—to catch the sense of what was rapidly said by *los gringos.* At home they spoke Spanish. The language of their Mexican past sounded in **counterpoint** to the English of public society. The words would come with ease. Conveyed through those sounds was the pleasing, soothing, consoling reminder of being at home.

During those years when I was first conscious of hearing, my mother and father addressed me only in Spanish; in Spanish I learned to reply. By contrast, English *(ingles),* rarely heard in the house, was the language I came to associate with *gringos.* I learned my first words of English overhearing my parents speak to strangers. At five years of age, I knew just enough English for my mother to trust me on errands to stores one block away. No more.

10   I was a listening child, careful to hear the very different sounds of Spanish and English. Wide-eyed with learning, I'd listen to sounds more than words. First, there were English *(gringo)* sounds. So many words were still unknown that when the butcher or the lady at the drugstore said something to me, exotic **polysyllabic** sounds would bloom in the midst of their sentences. Often, the speech of people in public seemed to me very loud, booming with confidence. The man behind the counter would literally ask, "What can I do for you?" But by being so firm and so clear, the sound of his voice said that he was a *gringo;* he belonged in public society.

I would also hear then the high nasal tones of middle-class American speech. The air stirred with sound. Sometimes, even now, when I have been traveling abroad for several weeks, I will hear what I heard as a boy. In hotel lobbies or airports, in Turkey or Brazil, some Americans will pass, and suddenly I will hear it again—the high sound of American voices. For a few seconds I will hear it with pleasure, for it is now the sound of my society—a reminder of home. But inevitably—already on the flight headed for home—the sound fades with repetition. I will be unable to hear it anymore.

When I was a boy, things were different. The accent of *los gringos* was never pleasing, nor was it hard to hear. Crowds at Safeway or at bus stops would be noisy with sound. And I would be forced to edge away from the chirping chatter above me.

I was unable to hear my own sounds, but I knew very well that I spoke English poorly. My words could not stretch far enough to form complete thoughts. And the words I did speak I didn't know well enough to make into distinct sounds. (Listeners would usually lower their heads, better to hear what I was trying to say.) But it was one thing for *me* to speak English with difficulty. It was more troubling for me to hear my parents speak in public: their high-whining vowels and guttural consonants; their sentences that got stuck with "eh" and "ah" sounds; the confused syntax; the hesitant rhythm of sounds so different from the way *gringos* spoke. I'd notice, moreover, that my parents' voices were softer than those of *gringos* we'd meet. . . .

There were many times like the night at a brightly lit gasoline station (a blaring white memory) when I stood uneasily, hearing my father. He was talking to a teenaged attendant. I do not recall what they were saying, but I cannot forget the sounds my father made as he spoke. At one point his words slid together to form one word—sounds as confused as the threads of blue and green oil in the puddle next to my shoes. His voice rushed through what he had left to say and, toward the end, reached **falsetto** notes appealing to his listener's understanding. I looked away to the lights of passing automobiles. I tried not to hear anymore. But I heard only too well the calm, easy tones in the attendant's reply. Shortly *afterward,* walking toward home with my father, I shivered when he put his hand on my shoulder. The very first chance that I got evaded his grasp and ran on ahead into the dark, skipping with **feigned** boyish exuberance.

15   But then there was Spanish. *Espanol:* my family's language. *Espanol:* the language that seemed to me a private language. I'd hear strangers on the radio and in the Mexican Catholic church across town speaking Spanish, but I couldn't really believe that Spanish was a public language, like English. Spanish speakers, rather, seemed related to me, for I sensed that we shared—through our language—the experience of feeling apart from *los gringos.* It was thus a ghetto Spanish that I heard and I spoke. Like those whose lives are bound by a barrio, I was reminded by Spanish of my separateness from *los otros, los gringos* in power. But more intensely than for most barrio children—because I did not live in a barrio—Spanish seemed to me the language of home. (Most days it was only at home that I'd hear it.) It became the language of joyful return.

A family member would say something to me and I would feel myself specially recognized. My parents would say something to me and I would feel embraced by the sounds of their words. Those sounds said: *I am speaking with ease in Spanish. I am addressing you in words I never use with* los gringos. *I recognize you as someone special, close, like no one outside. You belong with us. In the family.*

(Ricardo.)

At the age of five, six, well past the time when most other children no longer easily notice the difference between sounds uttered at home and words spoken in public, I had a different experience. I lived in a world magically compounded of sounds. I remained a child longer than most; I lingered too long, poised at the edge of language—often frightened by the sounds of *los gringos,* delighted by the sounds of Spanish at home. I shared with my family a language that was startlingly different from that used in the great city around us.

For me there were none of the gradations between public and private society so normal to a maturing child. Outside the house was public society; inside the house was private. Just opening or closing the screen door behind me was an important experience. I'd rarely leave home all alone or without reluctance. Walking down the sidewalk, under the canopy of tall trees, I'd warily notice the—suddenly—silent neighborhood kids who stood warily watching me. Nervously, I'd arrive at the grocery store to hear there the sounds of the *gringo*—foreign to me—reminding me that in this world so big, I was a foreigner. But then I'd return. Walking back toward our house, climbing the steps from the sidewalk, when the front door was open in summer, I'd hear voices beyond the screen door talking in Spanish. For a second or two, I'd stay, linger there, listening. Smiling, I'd hear my mother call out, saying in Spanish (words), "Is that you, Richard?" All the while her sounds would assure me: *You are home now; come closer; inside. With us.*

20   *"Si,"* I'd reply.

Once more inside the house I would resume (assume) my place in the family. The sounds would dim, grow harder to hear. Once more at home, I would grow less aware of that fact. It required, however, no more than the blurt of the doorbell to alert me to listen to sounds all over again. The house would turn instantly still while my mother went to the door. I'd hear her hard English sounds. I'd wait to hear her voice return to soft-sounding Spanish, which assured me, as surely as did the clicking tongue of the lock of the door, that the stranger was gone.

Plainly, it is not healthy to hear such sounds so often. It is not healthy to distinguish public words from private sounds so easily. I remained **cloistered** by sounds, timid and shy in public, too dependent on voices at home. And yet it needs to be emphasized: I was an extremely happy child at home. I remember many nights when my father would come back from work, and I'd hear him call out to my mother in Spanish, sounding relieved. In Spanish, he'd sound light and free notes he never could manage in English. Some nights I'd jump up just at hearing his voice. With *mis hermanos* I would come running into the room where he was with my mother. Our laughing (so deep was the pleasure!) became screaming. Like others who know pain of public alienation, we transformed the knowledge of our public separateness and made it consoling—the reminder of intimacy. Excited, we joined our voices in a celebration of sounds. *We are speaking now the way we never speak out in public. We are alone—together,* voices sounded, surrounded to tell me. Some nights, no one seemed willing to loosen the hold sound had on us. At dinner, we invented new words. (Ours sounded Spanish, but made sense only to us.) We pieced together new words by taking, say, an English verb and giving it Spanish endings. My mother's instructions at bedtime would be **lacquered** with mock-urgent tones. Or a word like *si* would become, in several notes, able to convey added measures of feeling. Tongues explored the edges of words, especially the fat vowels. And we happily sounded that military drum roll, the twirling roar of the Spanish *r.* Family language: my family's sounds. The voices of my parents and sisters and brothers. Their voices insisting: *You belong here. We are family members. Related. Special to one another. Listen!* Voices singing and sighing, rising, straining, then surging, teeming with pleasure that burst syllables into fragments of laughter. At times it seemed there was steady quiet only when, from another room, the rustling whispers of my parents faded and I moved closer to sleep.

REVIEW   28-6

Understanding the Reading

1. Summarize what Rodriguez is comparing or contrasting.

2. What are Rodriguez's main points of comparison or contrast between the two languages?

3. Who is Rodriguez's audience?

4. Both Sedaris and Rodriguez write about language. What are the similarities and differences between the ideas in the two essays?

Understanding the Structure, Style, and Tone

1. Does Rodriguez focus more on similarities or on differences?

2. List phrases that signal a shift from discussing English to discussing Spanish, or vice versa.

3. Where does Rodriguez use narrative to develop his ideas?

4. Describe the tone of the final sentences of the essay. How do you think that Rodriguez wants the reader to feel about his relationship to his native language of Spanish?

Making a Personal Connection

1. If you speak more than one language, explain the differences in their uses and social contexts.

2. In English, we often use different words and expressions with our friends and family than we would in a professional or academic environment. Think of some examples of such expressions and the effect they might have if spoken in a different situation.

Classification and Division

The Myth of the Latin Woman: I Just Met a Girl Named Maria by Judith Ortiz Cofer

Judith Ortiz Cofer, born in 1952 in Puerto Rico, moved with her family to Patterson, New Jersey, when she was two. Currently teaching English and creative writing at the University of Georgia, she writes about her identity as a Latina and an immigrant in such books as *The Line of the Sun* (1989) and *The Latin Deli: Prose and Poetry* (1993).

> ## LET's warm up!
>
> **Think about a** time when someone made an assumption about you based solely on your appearance. How did you feel and how did you react?

Increasing Your Vocabulary

- **Bodega:** a small grocery store specializing in Hispanic foodstuffs
- **Surveillance:** close observation
- **Coalesce:** to come together
- **Innuendo:** a hint
- **Chromosome:** the DNA part of the cell that determines heredity
- **Provocatively:** excitedly, intended to arouse or stir up
- **Machismo:** an exaggerated masculinity with emphasis on domination of women and aggressiveness.

- **Promenade:** a relaxed walk in public
- **Piropo:** an erotic street poem
- **Ditty:** a short song
- **Regale:** to entertain
- **Menial:** like a servant
- **Indelibly:** permanently
- **Retrospect:** looking back
- **Appraising:** judging
- **Faux pas:** a mistake
- **Omnipotent:** all powerful

1   On a bus trip to London from Oxford University, where I was earning some graduate credits one summer, a young man, obviously fresh from a pub, spotted me and as if struck by inspiration went down on his knees in the aisle. With both hands over his heart he broke into an Irish tenor's rendition of "Maria" from *West Side Story*. My politely amused fellow passengers gave his lovely voice the round of gentle applause it deserved. Though I was not quite as amused, I managed my version of an English smile: no show of teeth, no extreme contortions of the facial muscles—I was at this time of my life practicing reserve and cool. Oh, that British control, how I coveted it. But Maria had followed me to London, reminding me of a prime fact of my life: you can leave the Island, master the English language, and travel as far as you can,

but if you are a Latina, especially one like me who so obviously belongs to Rita Morenos gene pool, the Island travels with you.

This is sometimes a very good thing—it may win you that extra minute of someone's attention. But with some people, the same things can *make you* an island—not so much a tropical paradise as an Alcatraz, a place nobody wants to visit. As a Puerto Rican girl growing up in the United States and wanting like most children to "belong," I resented the stereotype that my Hispanic appearance called forth from many people I met.

Our family lived in a large urban center in New Jersey during the sixties, where life was designed as a microcosm of my parents' *casas* on the island. We spoke in Spanish, we ate Puerto Rican food bought at the **bodega,** and we practiced strict Catholicism complete with Saturday confession and Sunday mass at a church where our parents were accommodated into a one-hour Spanish mass slot, performed by a Chinese priest trained as a missionary for Latin America.

As a girl I was kept under strict **surveillance,** since virtue and modesty were, by cultural equation, the same as family honor. As a teenager I was instructed on how to behave as a proper senorita. But it was a conflicting message girls got, since the Puerto Rican mothers also encouraged their daughters to look and act like women and to dress in clothes our Anglo friends and their mothers found too "mature" for our age. It was, and is, cultural, yet I often felt humiliated when I appeared at an American friend's party wearing a dress more suitable to a semiformal than to a playroom birthday celebration. At Puerto Rican festivities, neither the music nor the colors we wore could be too loud. I still experience a vague sense of letdown when I'm invited to a "party" and it turns out to be a marathon conversation in hushed tones rather than a fiesta with salsa, laughter, and dancing—the kind of celebration I remember from my childhood.

5   I remember Career Day in our high school, when teachers told us to come dressed as if for a job interview. It quickly became obvious that to the barrio girls, "dressing up" sometimes meant wearing ornate jewelry and clothing that would be more appropriate (by mainstream standards) for the company Christmas party than as daily office attire. That morning I had agonized in front of my closet, trying to figure out what a "career girl" would wear because, essentially, except for Mario Thomas on TV, I had no models on which to base my decision. I knew how to dress for school: at the Catholic school I attended we all wore uniforms; I knew how to dress for Sunday mass, and I knew what dresses to wear for parties at my relatives' homes. Though I do not recall the precise details of my Career Day outfit, it must have been a composite of the above choices. But I remember a comment my friend (an Italian American) made in later years that **coalesced** my impressions of that day. She said that at the business school she was attending the Puerto Rican girls always stood out for wearing "everything at once." She meant, of course, too much jewelry, too many accessories. On that day at school, we were simply made the negative models by the nuns who were themselves not credible fashion experts to any of us. But it was painfully obvious to me that to the others, in their tailored skirts and silk blouses, we must have seemed "hopeless" and "vulgar." Though I now know that most adolescents feel out of step much of the time, I also know that for the Puerto Rican girls of my generation that sense was intensified. The way our teachers and classmates looked at us that day in school was just a taste of the culture clash that awaited us in the real world, where prospective employers and men on the street would often misinterpret our tight skirts and jingling bracelets as a come-on.

Mixed cultural signals have perpetuated certain stereotypes—for example, that of the Hispanic woman as the "Hot Tamale" or sexual firebrand. It is a one-dimensional view that the media have found easy to promote. In their special vocabulary, advertisers have designated "sizzling" and "smoldering" as the adjectives of choice for describing not only the foods but also the women of Latin America. From conversations in my house I recall hearing about the harassment that Puerto Rican women endured in factories where the "boss men" talked to them as if sexual **innuendo** was all they understood and, worse, often gave them the choice of submitting to advances or being fired.

It is custom, however, not **chromosomes,** that leads us to choose scarlet over pale pink. As young girls, we were influenced in our decisions about clothes and colors by the women—older sisters and mothers who had grown up on a tropical island where the natural environment was a riot of primary colors, where showing your skin was one way to keep cool as well as to look sexy. Most important of all, on the island, women perhaps felt freer to dress and move more **provocatively,** since, in most cases, they were protected by the traditions, mores, and laws of a Spanish/Catholic system of morality and **machismo** whose main rule was: *You may look at my sister, but if you touch her I will kill you.* The extended family and church structure could provide a young woman with a circle of safety in her small pueblo on the island; if a man "wronged" a girl, everyone would close in to save her family honor.

This is what I have gleaned from my discussions as an adult with older Puerto Rican women. They have told me about dressing in their best party clothes on Saturday nights and going to the town's plaza to **promenade** with their girlfriends in front of the boys they liked. The males were thus given an opportunity to admire the women and to express their admiration in the form of **piropos:** erotically charged street poems they composed on the spot. I have been subjected to a few *piropos* while visiting the Island, and they can be outrageous, although custom dictates that they must never cross into obscenity. This ritual, as I understand it, also entails a show of studied indifference on the woman's part; if she is "decent," she must not acknowledge the man's impassioned words. So I do understand how things can be lost in translation. When a Puerto Rican girl dressed in her idea of what is attractive meets a man from the mainstream culture who has been trained to react to certain types of clothing as a sexual signal, a clash is likely to take place. The line I first heard based on this aspect of the myth happened when the boy who took me to my first formal dance leaned over to plant a sloppy overeager kiss painfully on my mouth, and when I didn't respond with sufficient passion said in a resentful tone: "I thought you Latin girls were supposed to mature early"—my first instance of being thought of as a fruit or vegetable—I was supposed to *ripen,* not just grow into womanhood like other girls.

It is surprising to some of my professional friends that some people, including those who should know better, still put others "in their place." Though rarer, these incidents are still commonplace in my life. It happened to me most recently during a stay at a very classy metropolitan hotel favored by young professional couples for their weddings. Late one evening after the theater, as I walked toward my room with my new colleague (a woman with whom I was coordinating an arts program), a middle-aged man in a tuxedo, a young girl in satin and lace on his arm, stepped directly into our path. With his champagne glass extended toward me, he exclaimed, "Evita!"

10   Our way blocked, my companion and I listened as the man half-recited, half-bellowed "Don't Cry for Me, Argentina." When he finished, the young girl said; "How about a round of

applause for my daddy?" We complied, hoping this would bring the silly spectacle to a close. I was becoming aware that our little group was attracting the attention of the other guests. "Daddy" must have perceived this too, and he once more barred the way as we tried to walk past him. He began to shout-sing a **ditty** to the tune of "La Bamba"—except the lyrics were about a girl named Maria whose exploits all rhymed with her name and gonorrhea. The girl kept saying "Oh, Daddy" and looking at me with pleading eyes. She wanted me to laugh along with the others. My companion and I stood silently waiting for the man to end his offensive song. When he finished, I looked not at him but at his daughter. I advised her calmly never to ask her father what he had done in the army. Then I walked between them and to my room. My friend complimented me on my cool handling of the situation. I confessed to her that I really had wanted to push the jerk into the swimming pool. I knew that this same man—probably a corporate executive, well educated, even worldly by most standards—would not have been likely to **regale** a white woman with a dirty song in public. He would perhaps have checked his impulse by assuming that she could be somebody's wife or mother, or at least *somebody* who might take offense. But to him, I was just an Evita or a Maria: merely a character in his cartoon-populated universe.

Because of my education and my proficiency with the English language, I have acquired many mechanisms for dealing with the anger I experience. This was not true for my parents, nor is it true for the many Latin women working at **menial** jobs who must put up with stereotypes about our ethnic group, such as "They make good domestics." This is another facet of the myth of the Latin woman in the United States. Its origin is simple to deduce. Work as domestics, waitressing, and factory jobs are all that's available to women with little English and few skills. The myth of the Hispanic menial has been sustained by the same media phenomenon that made Mammy from *Gone with the Wind* America's idea of the black woman for generations: Maria, the housemaid or counter girl, is now **indelibly** etched into the national psyche. The big and the little screens have presented us with the picture of the funny Hispanic maid, mispronouncing words and cooking up a spicy storm in a shiny California kitchen.

This media-engendered image of the Latina in the United States has been documented by feminist Hispanic scholars, who claim that such portrayals are partially responsible for the denial of opportunities for upward mobility among Latinas in the professions. I have a Chicana friend working on a Ph.D. in philosophy at a major university. She says her doctor still shakes his head in puzzled amazement at all the "big words" she uses. Since I do not wear my diplomas around my neck for all to see, I too have on occasion been sent to that "kitchen," where some think I obviously belong.

One such incident that has stayed with me, though I recognize it as a minor offense, happened on the day of my first public poetry reading. It took place in Miami in a boat-restaurant where we were having lunch before the event. I was nervous and excited as I walked in with my notebook in my hand. An older woman motioned me to her table. Thinking (foolish me) that she wanted me to autograph a copy of my brand-new slender volume of verse, I went over. She ordered a cup of coffee from me, assuming that I was the waitress. Easy enough to mistake my poems for menus, I suppose. I know that it wasn't an intentional act of cruelty, yet of all the good things that happened that day, I remember that scene most clearly, because it reminded me of what I had to overcome before anyone would take me seriously. In **retrospect** I understand that my anger gave my reading fire, that I have almost always taken doubts in my abilities as a challenge—and that the result is, most times, a feeling of satisfaction at having won a convert when I see the cold, **appraising** eyes warm to my words, the body language change, the smile that indicates that I have opened some avenue for communication. That day I read to that woman and her lowered eyes told me that she was embarrassed at her little **faux pas,** and when I willed her to look up at me, it was my victory, and she graciously allowed me to punish her with my full attention. We shook hands at the end of the reading, and I never saw her again. She has probably forgotten the whole thing, but maybe not.

Yet I am one of the lucky ones. My parents made it possible for me to acquire a stronger footing in the mainstream culture by giving me the chance at an education. And books and art have saved me from the harsher forms of ethnic and racial prejudice that many of my Hispanic *companeras* have had to endure. I travel a lot around the United States, reading from my books of poetry and my novel, and the reception I most often receive is one of positive interest by people who want to know more about my culture. There are, however, thousands of Latinas without the privilege of an education or the entrée into society that I have. For them life is a struggle against the misconceptions perpetuated by the myth of the Latina as whore, domestic, or criminal. We cannot change this by legislating the way people look at us. The transformation, as I see it, has to occur at a much more individual level. My personal goal in my public life is to try to replace the old pervasive stereotypes and myths about Latinas with a much more interesting set of realities. Every time I give a reading, I hope the stories I tell, the dreams and fears I examine in my work, can achieve some universal truth which will get my audience past the particulars of my skin color, my accent, or my clothes.

15   I once wrote a poem in which I called us Latinas "God's brown daughters." This poem is really a prayer of sorts, offered upward but also, through the human-to-human channel of art, outward. It is a prayer for communication, and for respect. In it, Latin women pray "in Spanish to an Anglo God / with a Jewish heritage," and they are "fervently hoping / that if not **omnipotent, /** at least He be bilingual."

REVIEW   28-7

Understanding the Reading

1. Is this a classification or a division essay? Explain.

2. List the various incidents that Cofer describes in her essay.

3. What are the stereotypes of Hispanic women that Cofer refers to in her essay?

4. Why is the word *myth* used in the title of the essay?

5. What are the reasons for the widespread stereotyping of Latinas? What are the effects?

Understanding the Structure, Style, and Tone

1. How do the various incidents that Cofer describes contribute to the overall message of the essay?

2. What is the overarching tone of this essay?

3. How does Cofer order her examples in this essay?

4. What is the effect on the reader of Cofer's use of Spanish words throughout the essay?

5. What reaction do you think Cofer wants from the reader?

Making a Personal Connection

1. How do Cofer's experiences change your attitude toward those who are different from you ethnically or racially?

2. Think of a time when someone treated you a certain way because of your appearance. How did you feel and how did you react?

Definition

What Is Poverty? by Jo Goodwin Parker

LET's **warm up!**

Ponder what comes to your mind when you envision poverty? What are its physical and emotional effects?

Not much is known about Jo Goodwin Parker, the assumed author of this essay. George Henderson, a professor at the University of Oklahoma, received the essay from a person named Parker and included it in an anthology entitled *America's Other Children: Public Schools Outside Suburbia* published in 1971.

1   You ask me what is poverty? Listen to me. Here I am, dirty, smelly, and with no "proper" underwear on and with the stench of my rotting teeth near you. I will tell you. Listen to me. Listen without pity. I cannot use your pity. Listen with understanding. Put yourself in my dirty, worn-out, ill-fitting shoes, and hear me.

Poverty is getting up every morning from a dirt- and illness-stained mattress. The sheets have long since been used for diapers. Poverty is living in a smell that never leaves. This is a smell of urine, sour milk, and spoiling food sometimes joined with the strong smell of long-cooked onions. Onions are cheap. If you have smelled this smell, you did not know how it came. It is the smell of the outdoor privy. It is the smell of young children who cannot walk the long dark way in the night. It is the smell of the mattresses where years of "accidents" have happened. It is the smell of the milk that has gone sour because the refrigerator long has not worked, and it costs money to get it fixed. It is the smell of rotting garbage. I could bury it, but where is the shovel? Shovels cost money.

Poverty is being tired. I have always been tired. They told me at the hospital when the last baby came that I had chronic anemia caused from poor diet, a bad case of worms, and that I needed a corrective operation. I listened politely—the poor are always polite. The poor always listen. They don't say that there is no money for iron pills, or better food, or worm medicine. The idea of an operation is frightening and costs so much that, if I had dared, I would have laughed. Who takes care of my children? Recovery from an operation takes a long time. I have three children. When I left them with "Granny" the last time I had a job, I came home to find the baby covered with fly specks, and a diaper that had not been changed since I left. When the dried diaper came off, bits of my baby's flesh came with it. My other child was playing with a sharp bit of broken glass, and my oldest was playing alone at the edge of a lake. I made twenty-two dollars a week, and a good nursery school costs twenty dollars a week for three children. I quit my job.

Poverty is dirt. You say in your clean clothes coming from your clean house, "Anybody can be clean." Let me explain about housekeeping with no money. For breakfast I give my children grits with no oleo or cornbread without eggs and oleo. This does not use up many dishes. What dishes there are, I wash in cold water and with no soap. Even the cheapest soap has to be saved for the baby's diapers. Look at my hands, so cracked and red. Once I saved for two months to buy a jar of Vaseline for my hands and the baby's diaper rash. When I had saved enough, I went to buy it and the price had gone up two cents. The baby and I suffered on. I have to decide every day if I can bear to put my cracked, sore hands into the cold water and strong soap. But you ask, why not hot water? Fuel costs money. If you have a wood fire, it costs money. If you burn electricity, it costs money. Hot water is a luxury. I do not have luxuries. I know you will be surprised when I tell you how young I am. I look so much older. My back has been bent over the washtubs for so long, I cannot remember when I ever did anything else. Every night I wash every stitch my school-age child has on and just hope her clothes will be dry by morning.

5   Poverty is staying up all night on cold nights to watch the fire, knowing one spark on the newspaper covering the walls means your sleeping children die in flames. In summer poverty is watching gnats and flies devour your baby's tears when he cries. The screens are torn and you pay so little rent you know they will never be fixed. Poverty means insects in your food, in your nose, in your eyes, and crawling over you when you sleep. Poverty is hoping it never rains because diapers won't dry when it rains and soon you are using newspapers. Poverty is seeing your children forever with runny noses. Paper handkerchiefs cost money and all your rags you need for other things. Even more costly are antihistamines. Poverty is cooking without food and cleaning without soap.

Poverty is asking for help. Have you ever had to ask for help, knowing your children will suffer unless you get it? Think about asking for a loan from a relative, if this is the only way you can imagine asking for help. I will tell you how it feels. You find out where the office is that you are supposed to visit. You circle that block four or five times. Thinking of your children, you go in. Everyone is very busy. Finally, someone comes out and you tell her that you need help. That never is the person you need to see. You go see another person, and after spilling the whole shame of your poverty all over the desk between you, you find that this isn't the right office after all—you must repeat the whole process, and it never is any easier at the next place.

You have asked for help, and after all it has a cost. You are again told to wait. You are told why, but you don't really hear because of the red cloud of shame and the rising black cloud of despair.

Poverty is remembering. It is remembering quitting school in junior high because "nice" children had been so cruel about my clothes and my smell. The attendance officer came. My mother told him I was pregnant. I wasn't but she thought that I could get a job and help out.

I had jobs off and on, but never long enough to learn anything. Mostly I remember being married. I was so young then. I am still young. For a time, we had all the things you have. There was a little house in another town, with hot water and everything. Then my husband lost his job. There was unemployment insurance for a while and what few jobs I could get. Soon, all our nice things were repossessed and we moved back here. I was pregnant then. This house didn't look so bad when we first moved in. Every week it gets worse. Nothing is ever fixed. We now had no money. There were a few odd jobs for my husband, but everything went for food then, as it does now. I don't know how we lived through three years and three babies, but we did. I'll tell you something, after the last baby I destroyed my marriage. It had been a good one, but could you keep on bringing children in this dirt? Did you ever think how much it costs for any kind of birth control? I knew my husband was leaving the day he left, but there were no good-byes between us. I hope he has been able to climb out of this mess somewhere. He never could hope with us to drag him down.

That's when I asked for help. When I got it, you know how much it was? It was, and is, seventy-eight dollars a month for the four of us; that is all I ever can get. Now you know why there is no soap, no needles and thread, no hot water, no aspirin, no worm medicine, no hand cream, no shampoo. None of these things forever and ever and ever. So that you can see clearly, I pay twenty dollars a month rent, and most of the rest goes for food. For grits and cornmeal, and rice and milk and beans. I try my best to use only the minimum electricity. If I use more, there is that much less for food.

10   Poverty is looking into a black future. Your children won't play with my boys. They will turn to other boys who steal to get what they want. I can already see them behind the bars of their prison instead of behind the bars of my poverty. Or they will turn to the freedom of alcohol or drugs, and find themselves enslaved. And my daughter? At best, there is for her a life like mine.

But you say to me, there are schools. Yes, there are schools. My children have no extra books, no magazines, no extra pencils, or crayons, or paper and the most important of all, they do not have health. They have worms, they have infections, they have pinkeye all summer. They do not sleep well on the floor, or with me in my one bed. They do not suffer from hunger, my seventy-eight dollars keeps us alive, but they do suffer from malnutrition. Oh yes, I do remember what I was taught about health in school. It doesn't do much good. In some places there is a surplus commodities program. Not here. The county said it cost too much. There is a school lunch program. But I have two children who will already be damaged by the time they get to school.

But, you say to me, there are health clinics. Yes, there are health clinics and they are in the towns. I live out here eight miles from town. I can walk that far (even if it is sixteen miles both ways), but can my little children? My neighbor will take me when he goes; but he expects to get paid, *one way or another.* I bet you know my neighbor. He is that large man who spends his time at the gas station, the barbershop, and the corner store complaining about the government spending money on the immoral mothers of illegitimate children.

Poverty is an acid that drips on pride until all pride is worn away. Poverty is a chisel that chips on honor until honor is worn away. Some of you say that you would do *something* in my situation, and maybe you would, for the first week or the first month, but for year after year after year?

Even the poor can dream. A dream of a time when there is money. Money for the right kinds of food, for worm medicine, for iron pills, for toothbrushes, for hand cream, for a hammer and nails and a bit of screening, for a shovel, for a bit of paint, for some sheeting, for needles and thread. Money to pay *in money* for a trip to town. And, oh, money for hot water and money for soap. A dream of when asking for help does not eat away the last bit of pride. When the office you visit is as nice as the offices of other governmental agencies, when there are enough workers to help you quickly, when workers do not quit in defeat and despair. When you have to tell your story to only one person, and that person can send you for other help and you don't have to prove your poverty over and over and over again.

15   I have come out of my despair to tell you this. Remember I did not come from another place or another time. Others like me are all around you. Look at us with an angry heart, anger that will help you help me. Anger that will let you tell of me. The poor are always silent. Can you be silent too?

REVIEW   28-8

Understanding the Reading

1. How does Parker establish her credibility and voice in the first paragraph? How does she immediately connect to the reader?

2. List some of Parker's sensory details—sound, sight, smell, touch, taste.

3. Who is the *you* in the essay?

4. What is Parker's goal or purpose in this essay?

Understanding the Structure, Style, and Tone

1. How does Parker organize her definition? Does it follow the traditional essay structure—an introduction, a thesis, topic sentences, and a conclusion?

2. How do the repetition of the word *poverty*; the short, simple sentences; and the use of *you* contribute to the overall impact of the essay?

3. How would a more formal, more academic essay on poverty written by a sociologist differ from Parker's essay?

4. How would you describe the style of writing—formal, informal, educated, emotional?

5. Who wrote this essay—a sociologist, a poor person, a person close to the poor?

Making a Personal Connection

1. Think of a time that you have struggled financially. Explain your experience to someone who hasn't had to struggle.

2. Describe a difficult situation that you have encountered in the same direct, vivid, and intimate way that Parker does.

Argumentation

Death and Justice by Ed Koch

Ed Koch, mayor of New York City from 1978 to 1989, was born in 1924 in the Bronx to Polish immigrants. He earned a law degree from New York University in 1948 and has written several autobiographical tomes, a novel, and a book of essays. The following essay was published in the *New Republic* in April 1985.

Increasing Your Vocabulary

■ **Clemency:** mercy, kindness	■ **Sophistic:** plausible but misleading
■ **Reverence:** respect	■ **Discriminatory:** prejudiced
■ **Constituency:** a group of voters represented by a particular elected official	■ **Painstaking:** extremely careful
	■ **Sovereign:** power, rank
■ **Reprehensible:** worthy of blame	■ **Ambivalent:** not sure of
■ **Flagrant:** obvious	■ **Seminal:** original, beginning
■ **Implacable:** unable to change	■ **Paramount:** most important

1   Last December a man named Robert Lee Willie, who had been convicted of raping and murdering an 18-year-old woman, was executed in the Louisiana state prison. In a statement issued several minutes before his death, Mr. Willie said: "Killing people is wrong. . . . It makes no difference whether it's citizens, countries, or governments. Killing is wrong." Two weeks later in South Carolina, an admitted killer named Joseph Carl Shaw was put to death for murdering two teenagers. In an appeal to the governor for **clemency,** Mr. Shaw wrote: "Killing is wrong when I did it. Killing is wrong when you do it. I hope you have the courage and moral strength to stop the killing."

It is a curiosity of modern life that we find ourselves being lectured on morality by cold-blooded killers. Mr. Willie previously had been convicted of aggravated rape, aggravated kidnapping, and the murders of a Louisiana deputy and a man from Missouri. Mr. Shaw committed another murder a week before the two for which he was executed, and admitted mutilating the body of the 14-year-old girl he killed. I can't help wondering what prompted these murderers to speak out against killing as they entered the death-house door. Did their newfound **reverence** for life stem from the realization that they were about to lose their own?

Life is indeed precious, and I believe the death penalty helps to affirm this fact. Had the death penalty been a real possibility in the minds of these murderers, they might well have stayed their hand. They might have shown moral awareness before their victims died, and not after. Consider the tragic death of Rosa Velez, who happened to be home when a man named Luis Vera burglarized her apartment in Brooklyn. "Yeah, I shot her," Vera admitted. "She knew me, and I knew I wouldn't go to the chair."

During my 22 years in public service, I have heard the pros and cons of capital punishment expressed with special intensity. As a district leader, councilman, congressman, and mayor,

I have represented **constituencies** generally thought of as liberal. Because I support the death penalty for heinous crimes of murder, I have sometimes been the subject of emotional and outraged attacks by voters who find my position **reprehensible** or worse. I have listened to their ideas. I have weighed their objections carefully. I still support the death penalty. The reasons I maintained my position can be best understood by examining the arguments most frequently heard in opposition.

5   1. *The death penalty is "barbaric."* Sometimes opponents of capital punishment horrify with tales of lingering death on the gallows, of faulty electric chairs, or of agony in the gas chamber. Partly in response to such protests, several states such as North Carolina and Texas switched to execution by lethal injection. The condemned person is put to death painlessly, without ropes, voltage, bullets, or gas. Did this answer the objections of death penalty opponents? Of course not. On June 22, 1984, the *New York Times* published an editorial that sarcastically attacked the new "hygienic" method of death by injection and stated that "execution can never be made humane through science." So it's not the method that really troubles opponents. It's the death itself they consider barbaric.

Admittedly, capital punishment is not a pleasant topic. However, one does not have to like the death penalty in order to support it any more than one must like radical surgery, radiation, or chemotherapy in order to find necessary these attempts at curing cancer. Ultimately we may learn how to cure cancer with a simple pill. Unfortunately, that day has not yet arrived. Today we are faced with the choice of letting the cancer spread or trying to cure it with the methods available, methods that one day will almost certainly be considered barbaric. But to give up and do nothing would be far more barbaric and would certainly delay the discovery of an eventual cure. The analogy between cancer and murder is imperfect, because murder is not the "disease" we are trying to cure. The disease is injustice. We may not like the death penalty, but it must be available to punish crimes of cold-blooded murder, cases in which any other form of punishment would be inadequate and, therefore, unjust. If we create a society in which injustice is not tolerated, incidents of murder—the most **flagrant** form of injustice—will diminish.

2. *No other major democracy uses the death penalty.* No other major democracy— in fact, few other countries of any description—is plagued by a murder rate such as that in the United States. Fewer and fewer Americans can remember the days when unlocked doors were the norm and murder was a rare and terrible offense. In America the murder rate climbed 122 percent between 1963 and 1980. During that same period, the murder rate in New York City increased by almost 400 percent, and the statistics are even worse in many other cities. A study at M.I.T. showed that based on 1970 homicide rates a person who lived in a large American city ran a greater risk of being murdered than an American soldier in World War II ran of being killed in combat. It is not surprising that the laws of each country differ according to differing conditions and traditions. If other countries had our murder problem, the cry for capital punishment would be just as loud as it is here. And I daresay that any other major democracy where 75 percent of the people supported the death penalty would soon enact it into law.

3. *An innocent person might be executed by mistake.* Consider the work of Adam Bedau, one of the most **implacable** foes of capital punishment in this country. According to Mr. Bedau, it is "false sentimentality to argue that the death penalty should be abolished because of the

abstract possibility that an innocent person might be executed." He cites a study of the 7,000 executions in this country from 1893 to 1971 and concludes that the record fails to show that such cases occur. The main point, however, is this: If government functioned only when the possibility of error didn't exist, government wouldn't function at all. Human life deserves special protection, and one of the best ways to guarantee that protection is to assure that convicted murderers do not kill again. Only the death penalty can accomplish this end. In a recent case in New Jersey, a man named Richard Biegenwald was freed from prison after serving 18 years for murder; since his release he has been convicted of committing four murders. A prisoner named Lemuel Smith, who, while serving four life sentences for murder (plus two life sentences for kidnapping and robbery) in New York's Green Haven Prison, lured a woman corrections officer into the chaplain's office and strangled her. He then mutilated and dismembered her body. An additional life sentence for Smith is meaningless. Because New York has no death penalty statute, Smith has effectively been given a license to kill.

But the problem of multiple murder is not confined to the nation's penitentiaries. In 1981, 91 police officers were killed in the line of duty in this country. Seven percent of those arrested in the cases that have been solved had a previous arrest for murder. In New York City in 1976 and 1977, 85 persons arrested for homicide had a previous arrest for murder. Six of these individuals had two previous arrests for murder, and one had four previous murder arrests. During those two years, the New York police were arresting for murder persons with a previous arrest for murder on the average of one every 8.5 days. This is not surprising when we learn that in 1975, for example, the median time served in Massachusetts for homicide was less than two-and-a-half years. In 1976 a study sponsored by the Twentieth Century Fund found that the average time served in the United States for first-degree murder is ten years. The median time served may be considerably lower.

10   4. *Capital punishment cheapens the value of human life.* On the contrary, it can be easily demonstrated that the death penalty strengthens the value of human life. If the penalty for rape were lowered, clearly it would signal a lessened regard for the victims' suffering, humiliation, and personal integrity. It would cheapen their horrible experience and expose them to an increased danger of recurrence. When we lower the penalty for murder, it signals a lessened regard for the value of the victim's life. Some critics of capital punishment, such as columnist Jimmy Breslin, have suggested that a life sentence is actually a harsher penalty for murder than death. This is **sophistic** nonsense. A few killers may decide not to appeal a death sentence, but the overwhelming majority make every effort to stay alive. It is by exacting the highest penalty for the taking of human life that we affirm the highest value of human life.

5. *The death penalty is applied in a **discriminatory** manner.* This factor no longer seems to be the problem it once was. The appeals process for a condemned prisoner is lengthy and **painstaking.** Every effort is made to see that the verdict and sentence were fairly arrived at. However, assertions of discrimination are not an argument for ending the death penalty but for extending it. It is not justice to exclude everyone from the penalty of the law if a few are found to be so favored. Justice requires that the law be applied equally to all.

6. *Thou shalt not kill.* The Bible is our greatest source of moral inspiration. Opponents of the death penalty frequently cite the sixth of the Ten Commandments in an attempt to prove that

capital punishment is divinely proscribed. In the original Hebrew, however, the sixth command-ment reads, "Thou shalt not commit murder," and the Torah specifies capital punishment for a variety of offenses. The biblical viewpoint has been upheld by philosophers throughout history. The greatest thinkers of the 19th century—Kant, Locke, Hobbes, Rousseau, Montesquieu, and Mill—agreed that natural law properly authorizes the **sovereign** to take life in order to vindicate justice. Only Jeremy Bentham was **ambivalent.** Washington, Jefferson, and Franklin endorsed it. Abraham Lincoln authorized executions for deserters in wartime. Alexis de Tocqueville, who expressed profound respect for American institutions, believed that the death penalty was indis-pensable to the support of social order. The United States Constitution, widely admired as one of the **seminal** achievements in the history of humanity, condemns cruel and inhuman punishment but does not condemn capital punishment.

7. *The death penalty is state-sanctioned murder.* This is the defense with which Messrs. Willie and Shaw hoped to soften the resolve of those who sentenced them to death. By say-ing in effect, "You're no better than I am," the murderer seeks to bring his accusers down to his own level. It is also a popular argument among opponents of capital punishment, but a transparently false one. Simply put, the state has rights that the private individual does not. In a democracy, those rights are given to the state by the electorate. The execution of a lawfully condemned killer is no more an act of murder than is legal imprisonment an act of kidnapping. If an individual forces a neighbor to pay him money under threat of punish-ment, it's called extortion. If the state does it, its called taxation. Rights and responsibilities surrendered by the individual are what give the state its power to govern. This contract is the foundation of civilization itself.

Everyone wants his or her rights, and will defend them jealously. Not everyone, however, wants responsibilities, especially the painful responsibilities that come with law enforcement. Twenty-one years ago a woman named Kitty Genovese was assaulted and murdered on a street in New York. Dozens of neighbors heard her cries for help but did nothing to assist her. They didn't even call the police. In such a climate, the criminal understandably grows bolder. In the presence of moral cowardice, he lectures us on our supposed failings and tries to equate his crimes with our quest for justice.

15   The death of anyone—even a convicted killer—diminishes us all. But we are diminished even more by a justice system that fails to function. It is an illusion to let ourselves believe that doing away with capital punishment removes the murderer's deed from our conscience. The rights of society are **paramount.** When we protect guilty lives, we give up innocent lives in exchange. When opponents of capital punishment say to the state: "I will not let you kill in my name," they are also saying to murderers: "You can kill in your own name as long as I have an excuse for not getting involved."

It is hard to imagine anything worse than being murdered while neighbors do nothing. But something worse exists. When those same neighbors shrink back from justly punishing the murderer, the victim dies twice.

REVIEW   28-9

Understanding the Reading

1. What is Koch's position on capital punishment?

2. Review the types of appeals that Koch uses and give examples of each: emotional, ethical, and logical.

3. Which of Koch's counterarguments are the strongest? The weakest? Support your answers.

Understanding the Structure, Style, and Tone

1. How does Koch organize his argument?

2. What technique does Koch use to immediately grab the reader's interest in the beginning of the essay?

3. What logic does Koch use to order his points?

4. What analogies does Koch use and how believable are they?

5. How would you describe Koch's tone in this essay? Is he angry, dismayed, adamant, calm, rational, belligerent?

Making a Personal Connection

1. After reading Koch's argument in favor of capital punishment, how have your views changed and what particular points were most effective?

2. Write an essay arguing against capital punishment, using the same structure that Koch uses to support it.

Answers to Grammar Checkup and Select Exercises

GRAMMAR CHECKUP 2-1

Sentence revisions will vary.

1. F
2. F
3. F
4. F

5. S
6. F
7. S
8. F

GRAMMAR CHECKUP 3-1

          Shortly after my husband was injured, I ~~realize~~ realized just how drastically things ~~are~~ were going to change. Going places and doing things used to be spontaneous, not detrimental. Before the pain began, life ~~is~~ was life. We really didn't appreciate how fun the smallest outings ~~are~~ were. Today, grocery shopping requires a detailed short-length plan. If it's the park that we're going to, we ~~had~~ have to enjoy every minute because we'll be at home for the next few weeks doing what we call "recovery days." It is no longer how it used to be. Work is no longer an option, so forget about those worry-free days when bills were paid and we actually ~~have~~ had a savings account. Now, it's on me to pick up the slack and ~~supported~~ support my family. What a struggle that has been! For years, I didn't work outside the home while

needed
I was raising my children. When I ~~need~~ to go back into the workforce, I had
little experience under my belt, and I had to work two jobs to bring home almost
the amount of income he was earning. That meant less time with the kids.

GRAMMAR CHECKUP   4-1

1. After Paolo turned in his project, he decided that he needed a vacation.
2. Correct
3. Correct
4. Whether you're talking about hamburgers or pizza, fast food is one of the fastest growing industries.
5. While the audience booed and yelled for a refund, the actors made their getaway through the rear exit.
6. Grazing peacefully on the new grass, the cattle faced in a single direction.
7. If you follow instructions carefully, you will be able to install the new software.
8. Correct

GRAMMAR CHECKUP   5-1

Sentence revisions will vary.

1. CS
2. FS
3. FS
4. CS
5. FS

GRAMMAR CHECKUP 6-1

Sentence revisions will vary.

1. S
2. S
3. S
4. S

5. C
6. C
7. S

GRAMMAR CHECKUP 7-1

1. Everybody on the beach lost his or her towel when the wind whipped up.
2. Each of the boys had packed his camping gear correctly.
3. Sometimes law students must forget about their spring break.
4. Not everyone gets his or her exercise in the same way.
5. New students should never miss their first class.
6. No one has a (or his or her) raincoat!
7. People shouldn't tell lies to their boss even when they are at fault.
8. The staff and customers in the store looked up from their work when the famous actor walked in.
9. You shouldn't lose your temper the way you did yesterday.
10. Somebody left a (or his or her) briefcase on the afternoon train.

GRAMMAR CHECKUP 8-1

1. Online courses require students and instructors to exercise a great deal of discipline and motivation to ensure that <u>they</u> keep up with their responsibilities.

Revision: <u>to ensure that they both keep up</u>

2. Students in on-campus classes have an easier time keeping to an assignment schedule since they get used to a specific class time and place. <u>This</u> is not so easy for online students, who can choose to log on to a course at their convenience.

Revision: <u>Keeping to a schedule is not so easy</u>

3. The student senate president recently announced that <u>their</u> funds cannot be used for parking tickets.

Revision: <u>announced that senate funds cannot be used</u>

4. You can write either a 2-page review of the film or two 1-page research papers on the film's origins. <u>It</u> is due by the end of the month.

Revision: <u>Your assignment is due</u>

GRAMMAR CHECKUP 8-2

1. he
2. me
3. they

4. I
5. her

GRAMMAR CHECKUP 9-1

1. Several cartons of milk are sitting out on the counter.
2. None of the students in any of the classes wants to go on the field trip.
3. Every one of the patients has caught pneumonia.
4. In our book club, neither the Johnson girls nor Sondra wants to read *War and Peace*.
5. Each of the runners needs water at the halfway point.

GRAMMAR CHECKUP 10-1

1. The <u>parents</u> objections took the form of a massive sit-in in the school parking lot.
   <u>parents'</u>
2. <u>Its</u> a bird! <u>Its</u> a plane! <u>Its</u> Superman! <u>It's</u>
3. The plane took off from <u>it's</u> home base in New Mexico. <u>its</u>
4. The <u>cars</u> headlight needs to be replaced before dusk. <u>car's</u>
5. They <u>dont</u> have the foggiest idea what to do about <u>Marys'</u> low algebra grade.
   <u>don't; Mary's</u>

GRAMMAR CHECKUP 11-1

1. No change

2. That teacher, waving her arms wildly, needs to take a break.

3. The red package, which has been sitting in the corner for days, is too late to worry about.

4. No change

5. A pack of dogs, yelping and racing up the street, is causing a lot of commotion in the neighborhood.

CHAPTER 15, PAGE 453

Fragments in the paragraph on page 453, sentences 5–10:

5. Fragment

6. Sentence

7. Fragment

8. Fragment

9. Sentence

10. Sentence

CHAPTER 24, PRACTICE THE CONTEXT

These are the answers to the Practice the Context sentences.

1. ____A lot____ of the graphs and charts illustrate ways our legislators plan to ____allot____ the tax revenue.

2. When we found out that all the employees ____except____ union employees were willing to ____accept____ the new contract, we were angry.

3. I will bluntly ____advise____ him to keep his meddling ____advice____ to himself.

4. The new vaccine is able to ____effect____ a cure with only one side ____effect____ that will not ____affect____ most people's lifestyles.

5. I was ____all ready____ to call my dentist when I remembered I had ____already____ canceled my appointment.

6. I knew it would be ____all right____ with Mike, but it wasn't ____all right____ with his wife.

7. We wanted to divide the pizza ____between____ the two of us, but we decided to join the other group and divide it ____among____ the four of us.

8. When a large ____amount____ of lumber was returned to the store, the manager had a large ____number____ of questions.

9. ____Our____ manager wants us to pick up the cans that ____are____ on the shelf.

10. Rushing to ___insure___ his motorcycle, Larry double-checked to ___assure___ himself that his documents were in order since he needed proof of insurance to ___ensure___ his entry in tonight's bike race.

11. ___Besides___ that stack of boxes, you'll also need to move those barrels ___beside___ the exit sign.

12. All of a sudden, Jeff decides to ___brake___ in front of Starbucks and take an early ___break___ although this would ___break___ his routine.

13. I hate when they ___breathe___ next to me; their ___breath___ smells like an ashtray.

14. My wife and I decided to ___buy___ the old house ___by___ the creek.

15. Since we were touring the nation's ___capital___, we decided to visit the ___Capitol___ building to hear the debate.

16. Yesterday, Gina ___chose___ to stay at home, whereas today she may ___choose___ to wander the city streets.

17. The archeologist can ___cite___ several instances in which an ancient ___site___ has been plundered for the ___sight___ of buried treasures.

18. We will create stylish ___clothes___ made from the finest choice of ___cloths___ for tailoring.

19. People would often ___compliment___ our teamwork and would praise how our personalities ___complement___ each other.

20. We accepted the ___criteria___ she established to evaluate our performance except one ___criterion___, which we felt was unfair.

21. Dora couldn't understand why the people she trusted most would ___desert___ her. Feeling as if she were alone in a vast ___desert___, her only comfort was to nibble on her chocolate ___dessert___.

22. Although it was ___due___ this week, he did not want to ___do___ the project just yet.

23. Since the site of the cabin is much ___farther___ in the hills than we anticipated, we had to stop and ___further___ study the road map to avoid getting lost.

24. The ___less___ you exercise, the ___fewer___ calories you will burn.

25. We had a choice of two topics to research: legalized gambling or global warming. Since I'm a science major with a strong interest in ecological issues, I chose the ___latter___; however, my roommate, who had just returned from Las Vegas, chose the ___former___.

26. When he finally arrived ___here___, she was so excited to ___hear___ that she won the music award.

27. We ___heard___ the ___herd___ of cattle in the distance.

28. He attempted to cover the ___hole___ in his shirt as he got on the stage to address the ___whole___ student body.

29. From his accent, she ___inferred___ that he was from Boston; however, she was bothered when he ___implied___ that Boston was the center of culture in the United States.

30. The agency has always provided all _____its_____ members the opportunity to voice their concern, but _____it's_____ been slow in making any significant changes.

31. Richard _____knew_____ from the start the _____new_____ strategy would not increase sales.

32. I'll _____lie_____ here until they _____lay_____ the packages where they belong.

33. Yesterday's protest, _____led_____ by a tall man waving a _____lead_____ pipe, must be addressed promptly or it may _____lead_____ to unforeseeable problems.

34. Since all the pages in your report are _____loose_____, you just might _____lose_____ part of your report.

35. Everyone's _____morale_____ will increase if we make sure that all employees adhere to a strict _____moral_____ code.

36. In the _____past_____, I _____passed_____ all special training programs mandated by my company.

37. To maintain the _____peace_____ among the quarreling siblings, I gave each some sound _____piece_____ of advice.

38. The _____principal_____ addressed the students during assembly and stated that the _____principal_____ quality of a person is how he or she embraces honesty as the most important _____principle_____.

39. What the panel understood wasn't _____quite_____ what he meant, so he was _____quiet_____ for _____quite_____ a while and then explained.

40. I found it _____really_____ offensive that he wouldn't discuss the _____real_____ issues and resorted to complete fabrications.

41. He made the _____right_____ decision to _____write_____ a scandalous short story recounting his _____rite_____ of passage into manhood.

42. It seems as if every time the price of gas _____rises_____ businesses _____raise_____ the price of food.

43. He had to _____sit_____ and wait for his interview, so he _____set_____ his jacket aside and opened a book.

44. My schedule this semester is tighter _____than_____ ever, and _____then_____ I have to run to work.

45. _____There_____ is a place over _____there_____ where people go to enjoy _____their_____ favorite sports if _____they're_____ willing to spend the money.

46. We all thought we were _____through_____, but the guide told us we still had to go _____through_____ the fields. Therefore, we _____threw_____ all unnecessary supplies away to lighten our load.

47. If you want gas under _____two_____ dollars, head _____to_____ the next town _____two_____ miles south, or you can go _____to_____ the next state, _____too_____.

48. _____Whether_____ we drive or take a plane depends on tonight's _____weather_____ forecast.

49. ___We're___ really sorry you ___were___ unable to find ___where___ ___we're___ located.

50. He stormed into the kitchen and accusingly asked, "___Whose___ wine glass is this, and ___who's___ been using my shaver?"

51. ___You're___ asking me for ___your___ iPod, but you forget that ___you're___ the one who told me to leave it by ___your___ car.

INDEX